Health, Migration and Return

A HANDBOOK FOR A MULTIDISCIPLINARY APPROACH

Health, Migration and Return

A HANDBOOK FOR A MULTIDISCIPLINARY APPROACH

edited by

Peter J. van Krieken

T•M•C•Asser Press
The Hague

Published by T.M.C. ASSER PRESS,
P.O.Box 16163, 2500 BD The Hague, The Netherlands

Sold and distributed in North, Central and South America
by Kluwer Law International,
675 Massachusetts Avenue, Cambridge, MA 02139, U.S.A.

In all other countries, sold and distributed
by Kluwer Law International, Distribution Centre,
P.O.Box 322, 3300 AH Dordrecht, The Netherlands

to be cited as:
P.J. van Krieken (ed.), *Health, Migration and Return*
A Handbook for a Multidisciplinary Approach (The Hague, 2001)

ISBN 90-6704-128-9

PREFACE

The North is being increasingly confronted with a new phenomenon of migration: the so-called 'health tourism' of irregular migrants. One can already recognize a tendency among would-be migrants who either overstay their visas, or arrive under the pretext of being asylum-seekers, to come to the North with the intention of receiving medical treatment, in particular complicated surgery or other expensive forms of treatment, which they cannot get in their countries of origin, certainly not free of charge. Moreover, many others use 'illness' as a pretext or a reason for not being returned, or to obtain leave of stay.

In this respect one needs to take into account that public health services in most Western European and North American countries are already overloaded as a consequence of modern medical developments, but also in view of the general increase in the percentage of old people among the population. In many countries there are long waiting lists for non-urgent operations and contributions to health systems have to be constantly increased in order to cover the extensive costs of modern medical treatment.

The countries concerned are in a dilemma. Even if they understand from a humanitarian point of view the need for medical treatment requested by irregular migrants or for example rejectees, they are under legal and moral pressure to give priority to and to respect the interests and rights of those persons who contribute directly or indirectly to the national health service. The situation is even more complicated in respect of diseases which require permanent treatment such as kidney dialysis or medication for AIDS. The aliens concerned, however, may consider a return to their countries of origin to be inhuman and incompatible with their right to life, if they cannot receive such treatment at home.

The health protection and medical treatment of irregular migrants (including rejectees) is no doubt a very complex issue touching upon legal, medical, ethical, social, financial and humanitarian aspects, which as an issue has hitherto been neglected and which requires a multi- and interdisciplinary approach. The seminar organized in Noordwijkerhout in September 2000, and of which this Handbook is the direct result, was a first, but important step in this direction. This Handbook is, therefore, particularly welcome as it could and should trigger a wider debate on this important issue.

Winter 2001 DR. WILLIBALD PAHR

ACKNOWLEDGEMENTS

This Handbook is the outcome of a fairly long and complicated process which resulted in an expert meeting in which representatives from IOM, ICMH, WHO, ECtHR, Academia, the Executive as well as the medical and legal professions participated, all of whom à titre personnel, in order to launch a multidisciplinary debate on the difficult and sensitive issue of health and return.

The September 2000 Noordwijkerhout meeting was organized by the T.M.C. Asser Institute in close co-operation with the Netherlands IND, the Netherlands Chapter of the Society for International Development – as part of consultative sessions within their international and multidisciplinary project on the future of asylum and migration – and the Röling Foundation. All these organizations deserve proper thanks.

This Handbook is the direct result of the above expert meeting and is meant to provide the necessary material for what promises to be a lengthy debate. Lengthy, as it concerns efforts to cross bridges, to cover gaps, and to ensure communication between disciplines which are not used to meeting, not to mention debating, as they, from time to time, speak completely different languages. Lengthy also, because it involves emotions, ethics and difficult choices.

The Handbook, therefore, is a tool in an important and precious process, and the editor is thankful to the IND for having made the funds available for its publication. Thanks are also due to the excellent and expeditious English language editor Peter Morris, to Charles O. Pannenborg, Jacques de Milliano and Frans Bouwen who all gave invaluable advise, to Willibald Pahr, who once again proved to be an excellent chair and sparring partner, as well as to Ms Sabrina van Miltenburg who greatly assisted in the difficult process of creating a solid structure for this Handbook. Moreover, all the other participants and authors involved are owed thanks for their various contributions.

This Handbook is dedicated to Diederik, Katrien and Sebastiaan who, it is hoped, will not need to roam this world in search of adequate health services. After all, it is about the fish and not about the water. And then again, it may be about the water and not about the fish.

TABLE OF CONTENTS

INTRODUCTION

Peter J. van Krieken

> if services have to be provided to all,
> then not all services can be provided[1]

GOOD CASES MAKE BAD LAW

This Handbook is about the search for norms. Norms which are needed to solve often intrinsic problems. Of course, when confronted with an emotional, individualized drama, we all tend to look and act the Samaritan, and try and find the ideal solution. If an individual is in need we try to assist, but we often forget that good cases make bad law. And exceptions, particularly in a world of eager lawyers, often do make the law. So the question remains what to do in cases where we know we can help one individual, but would be forced to withdraw if that one individual would be followed by hundreds or thousands of others: charity has its limits, singular acts may have multiple consequences.

The main issue to be addressed in the context of this Handbook is in how far communities which have reached a certain level of economic and social development are obliged to share the fruits of that development with members of a different community.

The issue boils down to the question in how far solidarity amounts to egalitarianism, or, in other words, whether the better off are obliged to share, and/ or whether this sharing is without limits, without borders. This issue of 'sharing' has ethical and economic aspects, as it includes elements of (re-)allocation, mechanisms of correction and inklings of correctness. Moreover, the differences between solidarity and charity also need to be emphasized as the latter is a one-way affair, whereas the former includes mutuality, an almost contractual relationship.

Since their inception, virtually all societies have agreed on mechanisms to draw limits to the freedom of man to act according to his very own will: issues like life (thou shall not kill), property (thou shall not steal) and health (washing hands, eating habits, and, maybe, even circumcision) were already subject to rules and regulations of individuals or groups living together in a community. These rules and regulations, although very sympathetic and considerate, were not

[1] WHO Report 2000, p. xiv.

P.J. van Krieken (Ed.), Health, Migration and Return

necessarily based on humanitarianism, but rather on utilitarian, pragmatic needs, mainly based on survival instincts. In order to be effective, and to avoid the legitimacy of the imposed rules, such 'laws' were normally not agreed upon by men, but rather adopted, accepted as 'divine law'.

Ever since, societies have continued to draw lines and to find balances, ensuring survival and workable relationships. 'Law' in fact is nothing more and nothing less than the result of millennium-long efforts to redress what became to be conceived as 'ills', to help the balance shift towards favouring the weak, the poor, the less lucky. This idea can be translated into economic competition, behaviour in traffic, and so on. Law, in short, is a correction mechanism.

One of the corrections, which may be needed to be introduced, relates to the differences in health care, to the inequalities in, on the one hand, providing and, on the other, assuring access to care and cure. It is indeed fully justified to try and address the issue of why in certain regions individuals have a life expectancy of merely 45 years, whereas in others this amounts to over 80. Indeed, in a world that becomes more and more interrelated, we have agreed to a common working towards the improvement of the state of individuals and communities 'through international assistance and co-operation, especially economic and technical.'[2] Yet, whatever the efforts, a truly egalitarian world will and should never be accomplished as it would deny everything for which human beings are unique. There are differences between brothers and sisters, between families, between groups in a community, between communities and, indeed, between countries. It would amount to nothing other than flippancy to deny such differences.

The question nevertheless needs to be answered what to do with the problem of a member from a less fortunate community seeking individual assistance in a more fortunate community. And indeed the world community has agreed that if such an individual were to face persecution were he to be returned to his country of origin, asylum should be granted.

The concept of asylum, however, has been restricted to only very few characteristics. The persecution concerned should be related to race, religion, nationality (i.e. ethnic group), membership of a particular social group or political opinion.[3] This indeed means that – coupled with the very fact that there is as such no right to migration – seeking assistance, support and/or protection for reasons not related to the ones enumerated above, shall not necessarily result in access to other communities and thereby access to the services normally offered in such a community.

The above betrays a human rights approach, and most observers tend to base their contemplation on the issue at stake in this Handbook on indeed that angle. However, as will be shown, on the basis of human rights alone, no solutions can

---

[2] International Covenant on Economic, Social and Cultural Rights, 1966, Art. 2.1.

[3] See e.g. Universal Declaration of Human Rights (1948), Art. 14.1; Convention Relating to the Status of Refugees (1951), Artt. 1A2 and 33.1.

be found to what is basically a very complex issue, with inroads into various disciplines. A broader approach is needed.

MEMBERS V. NON-MEMBERS?

The above discussions of course deal with developments within societies, among the members of those societies concerned. This becomes the more apparent when modern society is compared with a 'mutual insurance system' which indeed could be considered part and parcel of the post-WWII welfare system. Calculations and budgets, education plans and the planning of fte are all based on a more or less closed system, in which the population of the society concerned are both the decision makers and the potential beneficiaries.

With the surge of migratory movements it becomes obvious that new challenges deserve new answers: are the newcomers automatically included in the 'mutual insurance system', have they immediately become co-decision makers, and are they to be considered fellow beneficiaries, and if so, under which conditions? In those cases the health system as a whole needs to provide additional services and needs to be prepared to do so, both financially and relative to manpower.

In the case of temporary migration (business, students, temporary labour), the financial aspects may be dealt with by the newcomers insuring themselves locally, or through their existing insurances based in the country of origin.

In the case of refugees and others in need of protection (e.g. victims of an ongoing war) the situation may be different. The stakes differ as well for the prospects for temporariness and the financial resources. It may after all concern new, permanent members of the society to which they fled. Most societies either call in help from the outside (e.g. NGOs, like MSF, in the case of developing countries), or allocate additional funds to cater for the medical needs of the newcomers. However, in general the obligations and responsibilities towards refugees have been fairly well defined and indicate that this category should have access on a similar footing as the inhabitants of the country of asylum.

It becomes slightly more complicated in the case of asylum seekers, i.e. persons whose access to the society has not yet been decided upon. It is generally believed that this category should enjoy access to health services, at least to emergency treatment, PHC, MCH et. al.

The stakes rise and the debate becomes more blurred when it concerns 'rejectees', i.e. the category of persons whose application has been rejected upon due process of law. And finally, the web threatens to become intangible, when those 'rejectees' (or, for that matter, newly arrived persons) apply for a residence permit **solely** on health grounds, on the differences between health services in the country of origin and the country where residence is being sought.

The latter group (rejectees) is of some concern. Societies hesitate to take a stand: feelings of sympathy and humanitarianism come into conflict with economic ground rules and the principles of the 'mutual insurance' system. Can access to someone else's system be enforced. And what would a de facto open door policy mean? This is the one topic on which a variance of reactions can and should be expected, reactions which are often dictated by the discipline or intellectual background of the person reacting: the philosopher vs. the politician, the legal expert vs. the economist?

UTILITARIAN V. HUMANITARIAN?

Most nephrologists keep a sharp eye on the issue of kidney transplantation as well as on the availability of dialysis. In some countries patients with renal problems are not necessarily referred to dialysis (not to mention: transplantation) if they have reached the age of, say, 60. In other countries the link between diabetes and renal problems is not sufficiently emphasised, whereby neglecting diabetes may have tremendous consequences. In yet other countries the availability of dialysis is limited because of financial constraints: dialysis after all costs roughly E 50,000 per year per patient, which means that shortages may be possible, again, depending on expectations, concerning referrals and available funds. The issue becomes even more apparent in the case of newly arrived refugees, asylum seekers or rejectees desperately in need of transplantations or dialysis: how is society to react?

An initial reaction tends to be humanitarian, often based on emotion, or emotion translated into moralistic stands or e.g. human rights law. Another one could be utilitarian, whereby results can be reached which need not differ from action based on a humanitarian approach. When it comes to health, this can be illustrated as follows: to ensure health to all, or at least to as many persons as is feasible, may be looked upon from a rights angle, but at the same time, investment in health pays off, as productivity will not be hindered by sick leave, thereby ensuring both a greater economic output, and a greater number of consumers who do not need to use their money for health services.

THE TEACUP STORY

As the story goes, the falling of, say, a teacup from the table on to the floor, with a thousand small pieces of crockery spread all over, normally results in a variety of reactions. It may be shock or sheer pleasure, anger or disinterest. Moreover, the scientist will be interested in the speed of the cup falling, and the chemical composition resulting in the thousand small pieces; the businessman will be interested in selling new cups (and a vacuum cleaner at the same time!), the lawyer focuses on litigation, damages and the possibility of suing the offender. Someone with a theological background may wonder what the meaning of the fall might have been, and whether this incident had been predestined.

A variety of reactions, as a result of a variety of angles, a variety of disciplines. The same would appear to be true in the case of the difficult question in how far would-be migrants should be admitted or rather turned away. The question becomes more complicated when the would-be migrant turns out to be suffering from an illness. The question whether someone could or should be returned to the country of origin whilst fully aware of the fact that the person is sick and that the health services in the country of origin are significantly below the ones in the country where residence is being sought is hence a difficult one, and deserves to be dealt with in a multidisciplinary manner.

It would appear that the issue has various dimensions, various angles from which to approach the issue: ethics, medicine, theories of justice, economics and legal norms. The following examples relating to society's approach and attitude towards health in general may bring the issue somewhat to light:

– Most societies have, when it comes to the allocation of the national budget, 'fights' as to whether to spend funds on education, infrastructure or e.g. health.

– Within the health budget the allocation (or: rationing) of funds will by itself generate intensive debate on how to spend the funds available. A classical dilemma may be found in the use of health-educational funds (10 barefoot physicians or rather one cardio-vascular specialist) or the health-related utility funds (one sophisticated operation theatre or rather 10 primary health care units).

– Also in developed countries there is often the following heated debate: should the money go to cancerresearch or rather to even more bypasses or, maybe, plastic surgery. Moreover, many deliberations deal with 'national health services' and the issue of insurance and the non-insured.

– The decisions as to which drugs/medicines are to be part of the insurance system are hotly contested, sometimes ending up in the courts.

This in fact shows that the debate as to who is entitled to enjoy the health services that are made available to the population at large is of great relevance.

STRUCTURE

The Structure of this Handbook is hence as follows:

1) Attention needs to be paid to the issue of the right to health. Are there differences between civil, political and social rights? What does the right to health contain, what does it mean, and how should it be interpreted? Does it have a cross-border impact, and what legal texts are available? In this Chapter One the full text of the General Comment on this topic as issued by the Committee under the Covenant on Economic, Social and Cultural Rights has, of course, been fully included.

2) The General Comment on health refers to the WHO Essential Drugs List. That would mean that the medical profession and health economists should be considered of relevance to the discussion on health and return. And that is why Chapter Two deals with health per se, and the standard-setting in this realm in particular. The WHO report 2000 has been scrutinized, and is believed to be of use for all the disciplines involved, a survey of the various diseases has been provided, as well as the relevant opinion of Jeffrey Sachs, the Harvard-based uttermost expert and visionary in this field. The Essential Drugs List has of course been included, together with an expert opinion on the relevance of this list. Finally, an old hand has given some insight into the 'inclusion' issues in daily practice in the Third World: it proves that each and every society, each and every community, in view of the very fact that more is possible on the technical level than financially having to draw a line, has to make decisions as to what services can be feasibly provided. It is hoped that acronyms like DALE and QALY will become familiar in non-health economics as well. Only very few appreciate that also in developed countries there is a limit to the medical services which can be made available, as recent debates on the availability of anti-cholesterol drugs have shown: drugs which have a tremendous positive impact, but which are simply considered to be far too costly.

3) The Third Chapter deals with probably the most important question of this Handbook: when and how is a society obliged to say 'yes' to an application submitted by a relative outsider, and when could or should a community say 'no' in spite of the emotional aspects involved. This aspect is probably crucial to the debate at stake, and it is hence remarkable that the experts, some from academia, others from 'the field', appear to agree on the possibilities in this very field. In fact, and this has been duly reproduced in the 'Noordwijkerhout First Steps', a community may indeed say 'no' to a request for social services submitted by someone who is neither a member of that community nor has financially contributed to the insurance system involved.

4) Chapter Four takes us back to the Human Rights debate, this time on the right to migration (quod non), the obligation to return if an application for whatever residence permit has been rejected upon due process of law, the status of foreigners both those lawfully residing and those unlawfully residing, as well as the need to take the health issue into the realm of the general migration debate. Legal texts have been provided from a great variety of sources, and, of course, the two relevant General Comments on this subject as issued by the Human Rights Committee, the committee under the 1966 Covenant on Civil and Political Rights have been duly included as they provide a true insight into the state of thinking on this subject.

5) Health and Migration have a variety of links and relationships, which is the subject of Chapter Five. Health can be a hindrance to migration, particularly in the case of formal migration under which certificates confirming good health are a prerequisite in order to be allowed to immigrate. This check has two aims: the

country of immigration would rather not be forced to see its new arrivals becoming a burden on the social security level, and secondly to prevent certain diseases from spreading among the population of the country of immigration. Within this realm it is of relevance to note that new findings appear to indicate that screening no longer prevents the illnesses and diseases from entering other countries: new mobility patterns underline that diseases that until recently were believed to have either been eradicated (TB) or limited to the Third World (Malaria) have now become part and parcel of GP practices.

Similarly, health conditions may prevent would-be passengers from boarding a plane. It is a recognized practice that passengers with an infectious disease are not allowed to travel. ICAO and/or IATA rules clearly confirm this practice, and it is not difficult to subscribe to its usefulness and logic.

Yet, health may be the exact reason for travelling as the search for a better cure and/or care may indulge migratory movements. Health gaps are now being considered as one of the determinants for such movements, not only within countries but increasingly cross-border.

In this respect the question needs to be asked whether indeed the health services in the country of arrival have a greater chance to cure the patient than services, albeit on a different level, in the country of origin. It is argued that in a great many cases, in particular where it concerns Post Traumatic Stress Disorders or Syndromes, cure may be more readily brought about in the country of origin as the home environment, the presence of peers, being among persons who have had similar traumatic experiences, and also because of the availability of traditional healing practices may be of paramount importance (apart from language and other cultural aspects).

Finally, this chapter also deals with the impact of population mobility on health in general terms, as well with the health aspects of return in the immigration context, aspects which are central to the debate.

6) With the above in mind: the WHO norms, the ethics involved, the various relationships between health and migration, as well as the human rights debates on the right to health and the right to migration, it is a logical next step to focus on legal practice. Chapter Six deals *in extenso* with the case law of the Strasbourg-based European Court of Human Rights. In no less than seven cases (both the Court and the Commission) health aspects have played a role. Introductions to the relevance of Strasbourg case law have been provided and due attention has been paid to the cases themselves, of great importance to all involved in this debate, as it clearly shows that the legal profession (in this case the Strasbourg judges) appears to have embarked on drawing lines, on setting landmarks which are principled, realistic and pragmatic.

Yet, as is shown in the final chapter, the actual practice on the ground does not yet fully use the parameters as provided by the Strasbourg institutions. Most executive bodies, most decision makers use yardsticks which are not necessarily in conformity with would be logic as regards to what not only Strasbourg indicates, but also with what the other disciplines would indicate (the medical profession, the health economists, the experts on ethics).

Hence the need for information gathering, the exchange of information, the creation of data-banks, but above all the need for looking over the fences surrounding one's own discipline.

SCYLLA AND CHARIBDIS

The Russian composer Dmitri Smirnov, born in 1948 in Minsk (now Belarus), and living in St. Albans near London, recently completed his 'Between Scylla and Charibdis' . He explains that for him these Monsters represent Morality, Politics, Philosophy and 'other dangers in our lives'.

The question, of course, needs to be asked in how far morality, politics and philosophy may be considered 'dangers in our lives': these fields of thoughts and study can after all assist us in tackling difficult questions, dilemmas or paradoxes, similarly as multidisciplinary approaches may have added value. However, it may at the same time be obvious that the mere invitation of these Scyllas and Charibdes may create unwanted complications: the philosopher may wholeheartedly disagree with the politician or the moralist, the legal expert may not wish to know what an economist might submit on a certain subject, and the surgeon turns around once the philosopher starts to speak.

Yet, in order to find solutions to the intrinsically difficult issue of health, migration and return, a unilateral approach, based on legal principles or, say, health economics alone, is bound to fail. Only a combined effort may yield some results, and this indeed involves a multidisciplinary, holistic approach. The Noordwijkerhout expert meeting was proof of such a starting point. This Handbook is not meant to provide definitive answers, nor does it claim to be complete. Its only aim is to trigger debate, and to provide the material on which such a debate could, or maybe should, be based.

MULTIDISCIPLINARY EXPERT MEETING

'The Noordwijkerhout First Steps'

1) There is a relationship between health and international population mobility (migration); it requires particular attention, study and analysis.
Such analysis has to take into account the necessity of a comprehensive migration policy including not only all different forms of migration (regular and irregular as well as refugee flows), but also the health element.

2) It is ethically defensible to give priority on health matters to members of one's own community. This could be argued from a communitarian ethical perspective (as opposed to the universal/liberal perspective),
and from a consequences-oriented approach (as opposed to the ethics of principles). Of relevance is also the impact of proximity.

3) Most national health systems are not based as such on ('real') solidarity but rather on common proper interests, resulting in a mutual insurance model, i.e. a closed system.
Attention should be paid to the shape of the present system that already now appears to be overloaded (e.g. waiting lists). Therefore this system may absorb a few irregular (non-funded) cases but not too many.

4) There is a difference between solidarity and charity. The latter makes recipients dependent and includes the notion of providing handouts to those who in principle have no right to it. Solidarity indicates that there is an element of sharing and reciprocity and contains notions of duty, responsibility and rights/real claims.
Charity for an individual may result in the breakdown of solidarity for an entire group.
The state needs to take its political responsibility seriously so that the General Practitioner can exercise his/her own responsibility, thereby avoiding existing tensions in this field.

5) Global responsibilities towards attaining social and economic rights exist and deserve to be emphasized. As to the issue of adequate health care, it could be submitted that it is acceptable to focus on improving general health conditions in a third country at the cost of denying care/cure to a third country national.

P.J. van Krieken (Ed.), Health, Migration and Return

In view of the limited means available there is a need for a balance between public and individual interests. This could be linked to communitarian ethics, consequence ethics and the argument of cost effectiveness.
Moreover, in certain countries expensive individual cure/care interventions are budgeted development expenses. As such these funds are unwisely spent from a development point of view as they cure/care (for) an individual but do not contribute to development.

6) All societies are free to decide what health services should or, as the case may be, are being made available and at what cost, albeit within the parameters set by e.g. the ICESCR, General Comment no. 14 in particular.
Obligations, if any, do not prevent differences between various health systems.
Health needs are contextually determined.
This includes responsibility for making choices on national drugs lists, treatment protocols and other medical services, e.g. on the basis of cost effectiveness (cost/benefit analysis).

7) There is a need to emphasize that even in so-called affluent societies there are limits to the level of health services available.

8) International norms (PHC, basic health services, essential drugs list) can be determined with regard to a country's obligation/responsibility. Intention, good allocation of resources, and progress within given means are some of the criteria involved, as well as (a) access, (b) selection, (c) affordability, (d) sustainable financing, and (e) delivery systems.
There are no absolute standards of health care services.

9) Migrants, in particular forced migrants (refugees, IDPs, etc.), are particularly vulnerable to mental illnesses (e.g. PTSD and PTSS). These diseases can be more effectively prevented and treated in their region/country of origin.

10) The indivisibility of first and of second generation human rights deserves to be stressed. However, there are differences e.g. the supervision mechanisms.
It is not to be excluded that in due time a Special Rapporteur on the right to health will be appointed under the auspices of the (UN) Commission on Human Rights.

11) Provisions of the European Convention on Human Rights (ECHR), in particular article 3 and to some extent articles 2, 8 and 14 are of relevance for the protection of health for migrants. The Court's Jurisdiction (e.g. D v. UK) and the Commission Decisions on Admissibility (Karara v. Finland and SCC v. Sweden) are equally relevant.

12) The ICESCR Art. 12 in conjunction with General Comment no. 14 can be considered the main determinants in the context of health and migration. The General Comment has laid down minimum obligations and refers to [systematic] violations (which may have an - in particular political – cross-border impact). The 'State' referred to in para. 39 of this GC is the State of origin, and not the State of destination (which also follows from the Human Rights Committee's General Comment 27 on freedom of movement).

13) Finally, it has to be noted that there are special regulations concerning the protection of health for certain categories of migrants such as refugees or foreign workers and that first aid in cases of emergency should not be refused.

CHAPTER 1
HUMAN RIGHTS AND HEALTH

An initial reaction on the issue of health, migration and return is to refer to the human rights regime on this issue. And indeed, throughout this Handbook, human rights play a dominant role. This Chapter 1 covers the debate on first v. second generation human rights, the extent and implications of the right to health, if any, and the meaning and usefulness of General Comments in general, and the one on the right to the highest attainable level of health in particular. Other Chapters cover the right to migration (Ch. 4) and the impact of the European Convention on Human Rights and of the case law of the European Human Rights Court in Strasbourg (Ch. 6).

This Chapter is divided in three parts: Feitsma introduces the relevant themes in the rights debate, part two contains a survey of the various articles dealing with health in a great many international instruments, and part three contains the GC on health in toto with a short introduction by, again, Feitsma. Most legal experts will consider the material contained in this Chapter part and parcel of their 'system', and the Chapter is hence above all meant for the medical profession, the experts in ethics, the health economists and the decision makers in general.

THE HUMAN RIGHTS DEBATE: HEALTH

Johan Feitsma

In the context of this Handbook, it could be submitted that the human rights debate concerned focuses on the following areas:

- *alleged differences and/or the relationship between so-called first and second generation rights*
- *the meaning and contents of a right to health*
- *the relevance of General Comments in general and of the one on health in particular.*

Various relevant legal texts have been included in Chapter 1.2 and the ICESCR Committee's General Comment on the Right to Health itself ('the right to the highest attainable standard of health') has been included in full in Chapter 1.3.

It should, of course, be recalled that issues relating to migration, asylum and rights enjoyed by non-citizens should also be considered to fall within the realm of this discussion, but this Chapter limits itself to the right to health proper, whereas in Chapter 4 attention will be paid to migration-related issues.

1. FIRST AND SECOND GENERATION: INDIVISIBILITY

It may be recalled that the 1948 Universal Declaration on Human Rights contains articles on civil and political rights as well as on social and economic rights. Efforts to 'translate' this Declaration – which after all is to be considered 'soft' law – into a binding Convention not only took a relatively long time but also focused on the issue of elaborating all these rights in just one instrument. After a while, by acceding to the unavoidable, an agreement was reached to codify these rights in two different instruments, one dealing exclusively with civil and political rights, the other with economic, social and cultural rights.

The fact that two instruments emerged also had an impact on the implementation, supervision, reporting and monitoring mechanisms. Moreover, some states preferred to accede to the civil and political rights instrument only, whereas others moved in the opposite direction. This resulted in two different structures, two

P.J. van Krieken (Ed.), Health, Migration and Return

different schools, two different approaches. Since the 1990s, however, a trend can be seen to merge the two, and to declare the human rights institution indivisible.

VAN KRIEKEN argues in the RWI report 31 (Lund 2000)[1]*:*

The second half of the twentieth century has witnessed a most remarkable development where it concerns the awareness of human values, and in particular human rights. This comes as no surprise, in view of the devastating Second World War (WWII), during which atrocities had been committed on a scale which was up until that time considered more or less unthinkable. On the basis of an increased emphasis on human rights, the relationship between the individual and the society where he/she lives changed. This was in particular true where it concernes the relationship between the governer and the governed, but also covers the relationship between individual and religion, gender, and the role of women and children in the family and in society as a whole. (...)

From a legal, rather than a philosophical point of view, the human rights instruments of 1948 and 1966 are of greatest relevance. On the one hand, because the Universal Declaration on Human Rights of 1948 contains rights which belong to both first and second generation rights, *and* because it contains some references to duties and obligations. On the other hand, it should be submitted that subsequent discussions and negotiations drew a dividing line between these generations of rights, resulting in one instrument for each of the generations: The first generation (or: classical) rights have been laid down in the International Covenant on Civil and Political Rights, whereas the second generation have been codified in the International Covenant on Social, Economic and Cultural Rights, thus acknowledging that there exists a difference, and sometimes (perceived) tension between these generations.[2]

---

[1] Health Gaps and Migratory Movements, Raoul Wallenberg Institute of Human Rights and Humanitarian Law, Lund 2000, pp 5-8. The editor was forced to delete some, if not most of the footnotes due to a lack of space.

[2] The almost perfect example can be found in the one-child policy as promoted for a long time by the PRC. It could be argued that every family is entitled to decide on the size of the family, but on the other hand, the size of the family has an impact on the well-being of society as a whole. Long- and short-term aspects play a role, as well as the issue of responsibilities vs rights.The discussions on the PRC one-child policy appear to lack the responsibility and duty element. Emphasis was put on the infringement of individual rights. It is quite obvious that any policy influencing the number of children to be born, contains an element of manipulation. It is herewith submitted, however, that some conditions need to be met in order to allow the community to embark on the road towards increased health, improved education, and, where needed, economic growth. In that context a one-child policy may be fully justified. Thereby tension might exist between civil and political rights on the one hand, and economic and social ones on the other. The challenge has to be found in working towards a balanced approach. Such an approach may in my opinion involve the pursuance of a sometimes harsh demographic or reproductive health policy.

The difference between the two can best be expressed as follows:

1) First generation rights which may not be infringed. The state, the society, the community has to refrain, to abstain from interfering. Individual deeds, actions and words need to be respected. It concerns individual rights like freedom of expression, freedom of religion, freedom of association, freedom of movement, truly classical civil and political rights.

2) Second generation rights concern issues which cannot be easily brought about by the individual. His/her civil and political rights fall short of realizing the conditions to assure work, education, health care, the social, economic and cultural rights. The individual being unable to work towards these goals, needs the assistance, the activities and organization of the community, the state. Second generation rights therefore concern the active involvement of the state, by setting up proper education systems, health care and insurance schemes, Keynesian and/or Schumpeterian economic models, and so on. It concerns, above all, the fulfilment of rights.[3]

In the context of this study, it is of relevance to question in what respect rights are limited by the mere fact that all human beings enjoy the same human rights, and that rights can hence be absolute. But by this fact alone, rights are nevertheless limited in their enjoyment as duties and responsibilties also come to the fore. The question as to the responsibility of one individual towards another in his/her enjoyment of rights needs to be addressed. Moreover, is a person responsible for the well-being of a fellow human being? Is a community responsible for the well-being of all the members of that community? Is a community responsible for the well-being of members of another community? And are human rights, if any, linked to connecting obligations and/or responsibilities?

In fact, the duty and responsibility aspects almost became lost in the last quarter of the 20th century. Efforts to draw attention to the issue of responsibilities, e.g. by the well-respected Inter State Council, with a membership of ex-presidents and ex-prime ministers from all over the world, met most unfortunately with disapproval from various, mainly academic circles, and were not seriously considered at the 1998 GA session's 3rd Committee. It should, however, be obvious that health as a concept is directly linked to issues like population growth, reproductive health, food patterns, lifestyles, education in general, training of adequate medical staff, and the allocation of sufficient funds to the health sector of any (national and international) budget. In other words, apart from the fact that

[3] In between 'respect', a first generation character and 'fulfilment', a second generation feature, one might add 'protection' which entails elements of both first and second generation (non-)activities. Toebes refers to Eide and Coomans in setting up a matrix covering these elements. It concerns a tripartite typology of state obligations, with due reference to health care and the underlying preconditions for health on the one hand, and the social dimension and freedom on the other (Toebes, The Rights to Health as a Human Right in International Law, Antwerp, Groningen, Oxford,.1999, p. 314/5).

there is no absolute right to health, it is worth focusing on the realm of health in the context of (individual) responsibilities, obligations and duties.

PAHR, however, submitted at the September 2000 Expert Meeting that a distinction between so-called first and second generation rights might create confusion: (...) The denomination of civil and political rights as first and social, economic and cultural as second generation human rights gives the impression of first and secondary importance. And indeed, in the political discussion particularly from conservative and neo-liberal groups this argument is very often used in order to refuse social, economic and cultural rights the same degree of protection as civil and political rights. (...) At least since the Teheran Human Rights Conference of 1968, the equality and equal significance of these two sets of human rights is internationally recognized. Accordingly, it is to a high degree generally accepted that the full social, economic and cultural development of all human beings is of equal importance as the safeguarding of their personal and political freedom. Pope John Paul II in a continuation of the principles already expressed in the famous Encyclica Rerum Novarum (1991) and Quadragesimo Anno (1931) when addressing the General Assembly of the UN on 2 October 1979 expressed this idea with the following words: "All these human rights taken together are in keeping with the substance of the dignity of the human being, understood in his entirety and not reduced to one dimension only."

In fact, the equality of civil and political rights, on the one side, and social, economic and cultural rights, on the other, already finds its expression in the famous claim of the French Revolution in 1789 for freedom, equality and brotherhood. Freedom and equality are realized by the civil and political rights. Brotherhood, or to use the more modern term solidarity, finds its expression in the social, economic and cultural rights. However, the distinction developed in the legal theory between these two sets of rights have also only relative importance. The first and most popular of these theories defines civil and political rights as personal rights which exclude interference by public authorities (status negativus). Social, economic and cultural rights constitute, on the other hand, obligations of the public sector to take specific actions (status positivus) or in other words they are individual rights for public services.

The contradiction is not in any case applicable. In particular, a number of traditional civil and political rights require positive action on the part of the state as well. There can be no effective protection of the right to live without persecution and punishment or any attacks on the physical integrity of persons. The right to a fair trial requires an appropriate judicial system established by the state. The prohibition of inhuman treatment obliges the public sector to guarantee at least emergency medical care. And just to mention a final example: the right to equality is today interpreted as taking such actions which are necessary to guarantee and establish equality, such as legislation to ensure equal wages for men and women.

Another distinction which has been emphasized by some lawyers is that civil and political rights are immediately actionable while social, economic and cultural rights require previous action by the state for their realization. Also this distinction is artificial and only of relative importance. Also civil and political rights, if violated by a legal provision, may not be claimed directly but the action will be directed against the legal provision which is inconsistent with a certain civil and political right which is alleged to be violated. On the other hand, when alleging the violation of social, economic and cultural rights the court or tribunal called upon to decide on such an application will have to examine the legal situation in order to discover whether it guarantees the standard required by the social, economic and cultural rights.

It is certainly true that social, economic and cultural rights may be secured in a different way and with different methods in the different countries according to their traditions. This is no doubt the case in respect of the national health system. But all have to provide the necessary standard which is consistent with the human right for the protection of health.

Not only social, economic and cultural rights may be implemented in different countries in different ways. This is also true with regard to civil and political rights. Freedom of the press, protection of privacy, freedom of movement and in particular fair legal procedures are guaranteed in quite different ways, just to mention some examples. [The distinctions should be considered as artificial ones, and presumed differences should be avoided as] such differences are very often used to protect these two sets of rights in a different way and to give less or even no protection for social, economic and cultural rights.

[In conclusion it could be submitted] that in the 19th century freedom was given priority in human rights movements, in the 20th century it was equality and in the new 21st century it is solidarity. Also social, economic and cultural rights should be given the attention they deserve.

FLINTERMAN, finally, submitted the following reflections
There is no doubt that economic, social and cultural rights are human rights. This was already recognized in the Universal Declaration of Human Rights (1948) which became the cornerstone of the international human rights structure which has been erected during the course of the past fifty years. The Universal Declaration is based on a holistic view of human rights: civil and political rights (the so-called classical rights) and economic, social and cultural rights, including the right to health, which were seen as fundamental aspects of the notion of human dignity. Later on, this holistic view was coined as the indivisibility of all human rights. Yet, due to, inter alia, different ideological views between East and West the concept of the indivisibility of all human rights was lost out of sight: economic, social and cultural rights were mainly considered, at best, as non-enforceable guiding principles for government action whereas civil and political rights

were seen as real rights to be enforced, if necessary, by court action. It was only after the end of the Cold War that the concept of the indivisibility of all human rights was once again rediscovered and re-affirmed, inter alia, in the Vienna Declaration and Programme of Action adopted by the Second United Nations World Conference on Human Rights (Vienna, 1993).

The perceived distinction between civil and political rights and economic, social and cultural rights has had a profound impact on the development of international human rights law since 1948. A prime example is the International Covenant on Economic, Social and Cultural Rights (ICESCR, 1966) which includes the right to health. This Covenant provides for a State reporting procedure as the only supervisory procedure by which the independent supervisory body, the Committee on Economic, Social and Cultural Rights (ESCR Committee), can monitor the implementation by States parties of their obligations under the Covenant. This is in stark contrast with the International Covenant on Civil and Political Rights (ICCPR, 1966) which also provides, apart from the State reporting procedure, for an individual and state complaint procedure. The individual complaint procedure is particularly important, since it enables the Human Rights Committee, the supervisory body under the ICCPR, to examine and decide upon individual allegations of violations of human rights, albeit in a non-binding way.

The ICESCR was initially very much hampered by the only existing supervisory procedure, the State reporting obligation. States parties were often late in submitting their reports or failed to do so at all. Quite often State reports were lacking in quality. Fortunately, the ESCR Committee, which is composed of 18 independent experts, has to a large extent gradually overcome these obstacles. It is noteworthy that currently, a draft Optional Protocol is pending at the UN Commission of Human Rights which will create an individual complaints procedure under the ICESCR. More importantly from a practical point of view, however, is the fact that the ESCR Committee has followed its counterpart, the Human Rights Committee under the ICCPR, in adopting General Comments. In these General Comments the ESCR Committee quite often provides very detailed and, in any case, authoritative interpretations of the obligations of States parties (currently 145 in total) under the ICESCR.

It can thus be concluded that the indivisibility stands, but that the impact of so-called first and second rights may differ, depending on definitions, enforcebility, monitoring methods and individual communications. Moreover, the characterized difference (abstain v. intervention), although gradually shifting in meaning, would still hold, in particular where it concerns some cross-border effects.

2. RIGHT TO HEALTH

As to the right to health the discussion would appear to focus to some extent on a matter of linguistics or rather semantics. Literary speaking, a right to health is as artificial as a right to happiness or a right to life beyond the statistical average of 75 years or so. Or, in the words of Kass: "It no more makes sense to claim a right to health than a right to wisdom or courage".[4]

By analyzing existing literature, the main discussion now boils down to defining the right to health as a) a right to health per se, b) a right to health care, c) a right to adequate health care, or d) a right containing two parts, health care and elements concerning the underlying preconditions for health (including a healthy environment, safe drinking water and adequate sanitation, occupational health and health-related information). All authors, however, would appear to agree that it is important to demarcate limits to the right to health and not to allow it to include everything that might involve health. Moreover, there is agreement that a right to health should be separated from e.g. the prohibition of torture and other inhuman or degrading treatment. This could also be true for the right to adequate housing. Some overlap may occur with other rights, which is logical in view of the human rights framework in general. An interesting submission would be that the right to health may overlap with the right to life on the issue of the prevention of infant mortality.

In the context of this Handbook, reference should be made to DEN EXTER, who, also on behalf of HERMANS at the September 2000 Meeting efficiently and eloquently dealt with this very issue, VAN KRIEKEN who in the above mentioned RWI report appears to be quite critical, and finally TOEBES who completed her Ph.D. on this very subject and whose 1999 contribution to the Human Rights Quarterly has been included more or less in toto, as it basically summarizes her Ph.D. thesis.

The relationship between health and human rights is in medical circles conceived to be three-fold:

1) *public health practice can burden or benefit human rights;*
2) *human rights violations adversely affect health; and*
3) *the promotion and protection of health is inextricably linked to promotion and protection of human rights.*[5]

[4] Kass, Regarding the End of Medicine and the Pursuit of Health, The Public Interest (40) 1975, (cited in Toebes 1999, op.cit. p.17).

[5] See the international quarterly journal Health and Human Rights (of which the late Jonathan Mann was its first editor), e.g. vol. 1 (1994) 7-23, vol. 2 no.1 (1995) 1-5, 134; vol. 2 no.3 (1996), pp. 113-120. In 1994 Zielinski published a special on the principles and ethics in this field (Health and Humanitarian Concerns – Nijhoff Law specials vol.5, 1994). Reference should also be made to a recent Inaugural Oration (Sidel, Leiden, November 1998) on Medicine and Human Rights, in which access to basic services and medical care occupies a central position.

The connection between health and human rights is above all illustrated by research risks, violent conflicts, military activities, freedom from war-related torture, and war-related rape and genocide, weapons of mass desrtuction, etc., in short, elements of international humanitarian law, rather than of international human rights.

In a recent publication on International Law and Infectious Diseases (Fidler, Oxford, 1999), however, it was stated that infectious diseases pose a global threat, and that international law might play a more important role in infectious disease control. It focuses, in short, on the globalization of public health.

Finally, reference should be made to Marmot (ed.), Social Determinants of Health (Oxford 1999), which aims to provide an overview of the social and economic factors which are seen as the most powerful determinants of population health in modern societies. This book claims to provide the scientific justification for isolating different aspects of social and economic life as primary determinants of health.

In the context of this Handbook, however, the focus will be on the right to health per se, and that in a human rights setting.

DEN EXTER/HERMANS

The right to health care focusing on Europe[6]

Introduction

This paper analyses the right to health care. Various expressions of this right may be distinguished. These include both individual rights and social rights which could be based upon international treaties and constitutional rights. They may be found in national health legislation and, in some cases, in case law.

Analysis of the right to health care, particularly in an international legal setting, reveal new developments relevant to the nature and scope of the right to health care. Therefore, this paper examines the legal basis of the right to health care; which forms of expression of this right may be distinguished both in the international and national legal setting? The general outline of the most important legal documents provides a framework to analyze whether or not such a right to health care can be held legally enforceable. Therefore, consideration will be given to which mechanisms the legal sources provide citizens in several selected countries to realise their legal entitlements to health care benefits. Apart from the legal instruments, the question of how the courts in these countries have interpreted the right to health care will be addressed, where applicable. Despite differences in legal structure between the selected countries, where they seem to con-

[6] The original contribution, entitled ‘The Right to Health Care in several European Countries’ contained a great many details on specific European countries but had to be edited for this Handbook due to a lack of space. Many footnotes have not been included for the same reason.

verge is on setting limitations on the right to health care. The courts have formulated conditions drawn from the acceptance that this right has to be judged within the context of limited resources. These findings could also be of use for Central and Eastern European countries facing limited resources and claims to health care entitlements.

The right to health care

Since its formal recognition as an international human right, the right to health (care) has been the issue of a lively debate. In the legal literature, an important issue concerned the subject of study: a right to health or health care? Both notions have been advocated. The controversy is not only a semantic issue; it is relevant since it defines the scope of the field of study. In the right to health approach, the concept of health has been interpreted, according to a definition given by the WHO, viz, a 'state of complete physical, mental and social well being'. This is a broad and vague phrase, defined by various determinants such as the nature and level of health care facilities, environmental and living conditions. In such a multi-dimensional setting perfect health is a rather utilistic and illusory concept since it implies that the government will guarantee 'good' health which is practically impossible. Moreover, it is difficult to define and realise as a legal right.

Instead, other legal scholars consider the right to health care as the field of research. In this conception, underlying this article, the right to health is interpreted as a right to access to health care services and facilities, whether or not physically available.

Formally recognized as a human right, the right to health care has been traditionally classified as a 'social' right, similar to the right to social security and labour. Social rights do not formally establish legal claims. Contrary to individual and political rights, social rights have a programmatic or positive character and are not intended to protect the individual but are subjective rights in a given community. Their guarantee lies in the (minimum indispensable) standards and provisions which states are bound to take.

The dichotomy between individual and social rights and subsequent obligations has been accepted for many years. However, the modern international legal literature and recent rulings of (quasi-) judicial authorities, have differentiated these opinions. The strict dualism has ever increasingly been considered as part and parcel of a continuum of rights and possible correlated obligations. These two categories of rights complement each other and are interdependent. Social rights must therefore aim at safeguarding individual rights and individual rights are to be considered in relation to the individual's participation in society. Effectuating individual entitlements of basic rights require active intervention, while social rights must aim at safeguarding individual rights. Hence the 'water-tight' division between individual and social rights has rather faded in the current socio-economic environment. Concomitantly or inherent to such a diffusion of the nature of rights, the legal status of social rights – generally considered weak –

is changing. Their interdependent and complementary characters have increased, first and foremost due to international treaties and conventions.

The right to health care in international law

Various expressions of the right to health care may be distinguished. These include both individual rights and social rights which could be based upon international treaties and declarations.

In the Universal Declaration of Human Rights (1948), Article 22 can be considered as the 'umbrella article on social rights': *'Everyone, as a member of society, has the right to social security and is entitled to the realisation, through national effort and international co-operation, and in accordance with the organisation and resources of each State, of the economic, social and cultural rights indispensable for his dignity and the development of his personality'.* There are only two limitations which may be valid: national resources and organizational methods, as available in each territory. The Declaration is without any concomitant legal obligations. However, the principles of the Declaration have been implemented in several conventions and treaties, which together form the international framework for the right to health care.

A key health care provision can be found in Article 12(1) of the International Covenant on Economic Social and Cultural Rights (ICESCR): "*the highest attainable standard of physical and mental health*" as referred to in Article 25 of the Universal Declaration of Human Rights. Although Article 12 does not define health, section 2 conceptualises the measures that should be undertaken by member states in order to achieve *'the full realisation of this right'*. As such, the commission on human rights that helped to prepare the draft relied on the definition of the WHO Constitution: "a state of complete physical, mental and social well-being and not merely the absence of disease or infirmity". Although the general formulation includes a certain responsibility of the state regarding the allocation, finance and provision of health care services, the health care claim is generally interpreted as a judicially non-enforceable entitlement to health care. Therefore, the noble aspirations of universal access to health care must be interpreted within the context of the treaty, which means: a basic level of health care, interpreted in accordance with the formulation, ratio and implementation of legal norms and economic capacities of a given society. In fact, the domestic economic capacities and the unenforceability of these international treaty provisions temper the actual meaning of the right to health care and thus access to health care services.

European health care rights

At the European level, the right to health care has been confirmed by the European Social Charter (Article 11), the regional counterpart of the ICESCR. The Charter is a creature of the Council of Europe and considered as the 'social counterpart' of the European Convention on Human Rights. According to Article 11(1) of the Charter, the right to protection of health imposes on Contracting Parties appropriate measures designed *inter alia*: 'to remove as far as possible the causes of ill-health'. In the opinion of the Committee of Independent Experts, a state can be taken to comply with this very wide and general undertaking if it provides evidence of the existence of an adequate medical and health system which has the following elements: adequate and generally available public health arrangements that provide proper medical care for the whole community and ensure the prevention and diagnosis of disease; special measures to protect the health of mothers, children and the elderly; general measures aimed at 'the prevention of air and water pollution, protection from radioactive substances, noise abatement, food control, environmental hygiene [sic] and the control of alcoholism and drugs' – all of which should be funded primarily by the state. The crux of this provision concerns the phrase 'as far as possible' that expresses the conditionally determined nature of a health care right. The level of 'adequate' medical care is primarily determined by the domestic technical, financial and geographical capabilities which obviously differ by country. Besides, given the enumeration of topics, adequate medical care is also restricted to community health-affairs like prevention, protection and promotion of public health. According to this article, individual claims concerning the delivery of health care services are not justified.

By Article 12, the right to social security, Contracting Parties undertake measures 'to establish or maintain a system of social security' (section 1). This provision it is not without meaning to health care since it refers to the International Labour Organization (ILO) Conventions and the European Code of Social Security.[7] Both treaties encompass minimum norms of provided medical care services to the categories of persons entitled. As concerns the ILO Conventions these provisions are binding on Member States who ratified these conventions. Simultaneously several constraints may be justified since an absolute right would be unaffordable due to demographic changes. Possible constraints are: excluding the application of this right to certain categories of persons, the type of beneficiary care, and quality periods of time. Such limitations have been enumerated by the different benefit packages of social/health insurance legislation.

Since both the ILO Conventions and the European Code encompass a substantial part of the population, indeed the majority of the population, the right to health care has been concretised by insurance and benefit package.

Finally, in Article 13 (1), the Charter proclaims separately the right to social and medical assistance, which require governments 'to ensure that any person who is without adequate resources and who is unable to secure such resources (...), be granted (...), in case of sickness, the care necessitated by his condition'. The meaning of "assistance" includes a definition that refers to the national com-

[7] ILO C102 Social Security (Minimum Standards) Convention, 1952; C130 Medical Care and Sickness Benefits Convention 1969; European Code of Social Security (revised), Rome 1990, ETS No. 139. However, this revised Code has not yet entered into force.

petencies concerning the scope and extend of assistance.[8] The commitment does not require states to provide a comprehensive health service, as it covers only the treatment of illness, not health promotion, and extends only to those unable to purchase care privately.

Convention on Human Rights and Biomedicine

The Biomedicine Convention was developed to protect human rights with regard to the application of biology and medicine.[9] It includes various patient' rights such as informed consent, privacy, etc. Article 3 of the Convention guarantees the right to equitable access to health care. '[P]arties taking into account health needs and available resources, shall take the appropriate measures ... to provide ... equitable access to health care of appropriate quality.' Such an interpretation imposes an obligation on States to use their best endeavours to reach it. According to the draft Comments, the aim is to ensure equitable access to health care in accordance with a person's medical needs. 'Health care' means the medical services – diagnostic, preventive, therapeutic and rehabilitative – designed to maintain or improve a person's state of health or alleviate a person's suffering. Furthermore, equitable access to health care means first and foremost the absence of unjustified discrimination. Although not synonymous with absolute equality, equitable access implies effectively obtaining a degree of care.[10] The Parties to the Convention are required to take appropriate steps to achieve this aim as far as the available resources permit. It enables the health authorities to define the nature and scope of available resources, appropriateness of necessary measures, and appropriateness of care without crystallizing individual claims. However, due to being only recently approved, the exact long-term (legal) impact is at present rather unclear. It is however not excluded that the Human Rights Court (Strasbourg) will include the Biomedicine Convention in interpreting the European Convention on Human Rights since this convention does not include an explicit health care right. Linking both conventions by the Court would definitely strengthen the legal status of the Biomedicine Convention.

Treaty of the European Community

Although from an economic perspective the influence of the European Community on health care is increasing (e.g., the production/distribution of pharmaceuticals, medical devices, and (para)medical professions), with respect to access to

[8] Article 13(4) refers to the European Convention on Social and Medical Assistance (1953) and the protocol thereto ETS No. 14. According to Article 2 "assistance" means in relation to each Contracting Party 'all assistance granted under the laws and regulations in force [...]'. Such a description restricts any claim towards those facilities granted by national laws and regulations.

[9] Officially the Convention for the protection of human rights and dignity of the human being with regard to the application of biology and medicine. Council of Europe, ETS No. 164, 1997.

[10] Comments on the provisions of the Convention, draft Convention, 1994, Article 4, no. 45.

health care, however, Community interference is still quite modest. The most direct common grounds with access to health care concern the organization, finance and provision of health care which has been explicitly excluded from Community intervention (Article 152(5) TEC). This exclusion emanates from the 'subsidiarity' principle, enshrined in Article 5 (ex 3b EC), reading: 'Community action in the field of public health shall fully respect the responsibility of the member States for the organisation and delivery of health services and medical care'. As a consequence, the Treaty considerably limits the jurisdiction of the Community with regard to health, to issues such as health prevention.

Nonetheless, the public health article (Article 152 TEC) meant a modest landmark in the predominant economic tradition of the Union. Special emphasis was put on certain areas such as measures in the veterinary and phytosanitary fields of public health importance. These are already the basis of a substantial body of Community legislation with major health implications. Since the latest amendment (Treaty of Amsterdam) such proposals fall within the public health context. Moreover, Article 152 includes measures in relation to the quality and safety organs and substances of human origin and blood and blood derivates. The scope and potential of this new provision has not yet been fully explored. However, given the importance for health protection of ensuring a safe blood supply, and the rapidly growing need for human organs and substances of human origin, the potential, taking into account national provisions on the donation of medical use of organs and blood, is considerable.[11]

The public health provision furthermore entitles the Community to take actions with a direct bearing on health protection. These include 'incentives designed to protect and improve human health, excluding any harmonisation of the laws and regulations of the Member States'.[12] This has served as a basis for the current set of eight public health programmes and for the decision on a network on the epidemiological surveillance and control of communicable diseases, and they also form the basis of the new programme.[13] In 1997, the Council adopted

---

[11] Communication from the Commission to the Council, the European Parliament, the Economic and Social Committee and the Committee of the regions on the health strategy of the European Community, Brussels 16.5.2000 COM(2000) 285 final.

[12] Art. 152(4)(c).

[13] Actions under the 1993 Public Health Framework include, inter alia: the programme of Community action on health promotion, information, education and training, the action plan to combat cancer, the programme of Community action on the prevention of AIDS and certain other communicable diseases, the programme of Community action on the prevention of drug dependence, the programme of Community action on health monitoring, the programme of Community action on injury prevention, the programme of Community action on rare diseases, and the programme on pollution-related diseases. Other activities are: a strategy on tobacco consumption, a directive on the approximation of the laws, regulations and administrative provisions of the Member States relating to the advertising and sponsorship of tobacco products; a report on smoking prevention, and a proposal for a directive on tobacco products, a strategy on blood safety and self-sufficiency and the Council Recommendation on the suitability of blood and plasma donors and the screening of donated blood;

the programme for health, and three additional endorsed programmes for (un)intentional accidents and injuries, pollution-related diseases and rare diseases programmes). Although legislative harmonisation at EU level is excluded, participation in European health programmes is likely to produce a certain degree of convergence among national health policies. 'Incentives measures' as included in the European Community's programmes to promote common objectives and practices by participating these programmes and to incorporate them in national policies.[14]

Notwithstanding the exclusive competences of national authorities regarding the organization and delivery of health services, both fields are affected by policy decisions taken at European level and provisions of EC law designed to realise the internal market (e.g., free movement and competition principles). The internal market provisions' impact on the health sector is, however, incomplete and differs by provision. To achieve a more coherent and effective approach to health issues across all different policy areas, the Commission proposed the new public health strategy setting out the Community's broad health strategy.[15] The actions under the public health framework emphasise a proper link with health-related initiatives in other policy areas such as free movement articles, consumer protection, environment, agriculture.

Bilateral treaties

Bilateral arrangements between most European countries regulate access to health care provided by social health insurance schemes. These schemes operate on the same principle, the territorial limitations of national health insurance. Those bilateral arrangements have been made for insured persons who are staying either permanently or temporarily in another country to receive medical care under the social health insurance system operating in the country concerned. So, the meaning of the right to health care has been formulated in terms of health care entitlements under national health insurance law. The bilateral arrangements are often part of a social security convention covering all social insurance schemes. Since the European Union social security regulations most bilateral treaties among EU member states that apply social security have lost their significance.[16] However, they are

---

Commission reports on health status in the Community and on the integration of health protection requirements in Community policies; Commission staff working papers on the epidemiology and surveillance of Creutzfeldt-Jakob disease and other transmissible spongiform encephalopathies; a Community network for the epidemiological surveillance and control of communicable diseases in the Community, and a Council Recommendation on the limitation of exposure of the general public to electromagnetic fields.

[14] E.g., anti-tobacco campaigns, improvement in nutrition, promotion of screening policies, training provision, information exchange and services, research and measures to promote the safety of blood.

[15] COM(2000) 285 final p.5.

[16] E.g., Regulation 1408/71 on the coordination of social security schemes.

still relevant to those persons who are covered by bilateral treaties but not the EU Regulations. This is quite a large group as the EU Regulations apply only to the employed and their families.

Conclusion

Based on the described legal documents, it can be concluded that at an international level, the right to health care has been entrenched as a fundamental human right, embedded in various treaties and conventions and ratified by member states. Characterised as a social right it was meant as a 'programmatic' right, it expressed the sincere intentions of member states to realise this right. Nonetheless, there is considerable confusion about the content and the legal status of the concept health care. Therefore, a more detailed analysis of the meaning of the right to health care is necessary.

VAN KRIEKEN

As has been stated elsewhere in this Handbook, not a great deal can be done to ensure the health conditions of an individual. This, however, may be a costly affair, and should be seen in the context of health as a 'commodity', whereby the best levels of care and cure may be purchased on the free health market which is increasingly emerging. At the other end, if one were to embark on health to all, only very few services can be made available, or: if services are to be provided to all, then not all services could be provided. It is hence of paramount importance to delineate the impact of a right to health. VAN KRIEKEN appears to be somewhat cynical (or rather: pragmatic), however, always stressing the need for a balance between what should be done and what can be done.

VAN KRIEKEN

The Importance of Adjectives[17]

An increased use of the term 'right to health' can be noticed. If this concept were to be taken literally, this would appear to be wrong. We all become sick, we all fade away, we all pass away in due time. An absolute right to health would therefore be a contradictio in terminis, a non-enforceable fantasy. It might, therefore, be more correct to embark on terminology like a 'right to health care' or a 'right to health services'. By the use of such terminology, 'rights' might indeed be realized, substantiated or materialized. Care or service, after all, means that primary health care will be provided, and that health problems will be addressed, will be looked into, although without indicating that these problems will also be solved. And it should be stressed: *it concerns care, rather than cure.*

[17] This contribution is based on Van Krieken's *Health Gaps and Migratory Movements*, RWI, Lund 2000, pp. 2-3 and 15-20.

However, it might be preferable to add an adjective to avoid any misconception of health care, and to speak of a right to *adequate* health care, in order to be more precise as to what we are looking for. But at the same time, the adjective 'adequate' again creates a problem: is it meant to be adequate in the sense of 'in accordance with the situation and the possibilities', or is it rather supposed to mean that a solution to the (health) problems at stake should be found? It is herewith submitted that it indeed concerns the care, the attention we pay to the patient, not necessarily the result, the outcome of the treatment as such. We indeed often find ourselves in a situation where certain illnesses cannot be properly treated, but where health personnel, of whichever level, do their best to be of service. Hereinafter the word adequate is therefore meant to refer to the intentions, the care per se, not the outcome. In other words, of relevance is that which is possible within the realm of the providers of the care. It would concern the progressive realization of the maximum of the available resources. But no unrealistic expectations as to any recovery should be raised. If only the best would be good enough, all patients would express the wish to be treated by Nobel Prize winners in the most sophisticated hospitals with the best catering and in the most healthy surroundings, rather than knocking at the doors of the Black Lion Hospital in Addis Ababa or any other urban or rural health centre or hospital. The concept 'adequate' reflects the commitment to do the most with the available tools and within the available means. (...)

[The human rights system] entails three generations, with a substantial difference between them. The right to health as such does not exist.

Where it concerns the first generation it can be argued that society or the State cannot prevent anyone from seeking health care, from striving for improved health. This principle could be linked to the right to liberty and security, liberty of movement, the right to own property, and the right to decide how to spend funds earned and/or accumulated. The Universal Declaration, however, formulated the health aspect in a fairly ambiguous manner, indicating that the community, the state, would face some obligations in this respect. It was agreed that

> "everyone has the right to a standard of living adequate for the health and well-being of himself and his family, including food, clothing, housing and medical care and necessary social services, and the right to security in the event of unemployment, sickness, disability, widowhood, old age or other lack of livelihood in circumstances beyond his control."[18]

[18] Universal Declaration on Human Rights, 10 December 1948, Art. 25.1. Para. 2 of this article adds: "Motherhood and childhood are entitled to special care and assistance. All children, whether born in or out of wedlock, shall enjoy the same social protection." In this context emphasis should be put on the interpretation of the term 'beyond his control', as this phrase contains a quintessential aspect of the discussion concerned.

Quite logically, this principle was not elaborated in the 1966 Covenant on Civil and Political Rights (ICCPR), but rather in its pendant, the Covenant on Economic, Social and Cultural Rights (CESCR), in which a description has been given of what a State should undertake in ensuring the well-being of its subjects. The States recognize the right of everyone to social security, including social insurance (Art. 9).

The above quoted UDHR's Art. 25 on the standard of living including medical care has been split up in an article on standard of living focusing on adequate food, clothing and housing (Art. 11), and a special one on health (Art. 12). The latter article is worth being quoted in full:

1) The States Parties (...) recognize the right of everyone to the enjoyment of the highest attainable standard of physical and mental health.
2) The steps to be taken by the States Parties to the present Covenant to achieve the full realization of this right shall include those necessary for:
   a) the provision for the reduction of the stillbirth-rate and of infant mortality and for the healthy development of the child;
   b) the improvement of all aspects of environmental and industrial hygiene;
   c) the prevention, treatment and control of epidemic, endemic, occupational and other diseases;
   d) the creation of conditions which would ensure to all medical service and medical attention in the event of sickness.[19]

Whilst analyzing this article, three aspects immediately come across as being of great interest:

- the enjoyment of the highest *attainable* standard;
- the steps shall include: prevention, treatment and control; and
- the creation of conditions which *would* assure to all medical *service* and medical *attention* in the event of sickness.

By using the term 'attainable' it is admitted that no standard is absolute. Standards are evolving and also the Charter of the United Nations refers to 'progressive development of international law'. The obligations of the State towards its subjects may – if not: should – therefore evolve with time as well. It is herewith submitted that the State, the authorities, are obliged to continuously look into possibilities to improve existing systems and schedules. Every programme should contain an element of progress. The acknowledgement that it concerns a progressive development is also reinforced by the language used in para. 2: it concerns steps to be taken to achieve the full realization of the right as defined in para. 1. Once again, it concerns an ongoing process and it means that if

[19] Toebes' 1999 dissertation provides an excellent overview of the textes préparatoires, the various drafts, proposals, amendments and discussions of both the UDHR's art.25 and the CESCR's Art.12 (pp. 36-52).

a country has as yet not succeeded in creating the conditions which would ensure to all in real need access to medical service and attention, it is not to be blamed. The yardstick is to be found in the efforts to reach that point. Critical is whether progress is being made, or whether public funds are instead being used e.g. to primarily subsidize the tertiary care needs of the top income quindile.

With regard to children, it is, of course, no surprise that the 1989 Convention on the Rights of the Child (ratified by all countries of this world, but for Somalia and the USA), contains an elaborate article in which the right of the child to the enjoyment of the highest attainable standard of health has been reconfirmed. States have committed themselves to pursue full implementation of this right, and in this respect international cooperation with a view to achieving progressively the full realisation of this right shall be promoted and encouraged. The 1966 texts have not been significantly upgraded, but for references to the environment, education and family planning.

Similarly, the 1979 UN Convention on the Elimination of All Forms of Discrimination Against Women (CEDAW) contains an article on health which can not be considered surprising or innovative, except perhaps for the family planning aspect. Art.12 reads:

States shall take all appropriate measures to eliminate discrimination against women in the field of health care, in order to ensure (...) access to health care services, including those related to family planning (...). States Parties shall ensure to women appropriate services in connection with pregnancy, confinement and the post-natal period, granting free services where necessary, as well as adequate nutrition during pregnancy and lactation.

With the above instruments in mind, it is then of interest to find out which actor effectively deals with the health issue. It was, for example, submitted that health is an individual matter which does not allow the state to intervene. The integrity of the body is one of the main principles of human rights law. So is the right to life, as expressed in Art. 6 of the ICCPR, and the prohibition of torture, as laid down in its Art. 7. And indeed, these issues can be linked to the health concerns, as practised by the Human Rights Committee, which covers first generation rights, in country reports as well as in General Comments. In that context the Committee has dealt with issues such as mortality rates, life expectancy, the impact of environmental pollution and nuclear tests, inhuman treatment, torture, and even domestic violence. However, no pertinent conclusions can be drawn.

As it would appear more logical to deal with health under the second generation and hence in the context of the CESCR, attention needs to be paid to CESCR actors, as well as international organizations like WHO and UNICEF. The CESCR is the context in which monitoring, reporting and supervision may take place. WHO and UNICEF are among the main actors which may assist towards the gradual implementation of the rights embedded in the CESCR. The World Bank also plays an active role in this field, and is thereby setting benchmarks which should be considered to relate to the CESCR.

The way the CESCR originally addressed the issue concerned left a lot to be desired, although it was probably the best one could strive for at the time of drafting. As we saw, an obligation had been laid down to take steps to the maximum of the available sources to realize a progressively acceptable and accessible system under which the health concerns can be properly addressed. Health was not defined, but at the time WHO used a definition which gives some clues:

'a state of physical, mental and social well-being, and not merely the absence of disease or infirmity.' 'Health' is to be maintained and achieved not only through the provision of health care services, but also through the dissemination of information, social services and the co-operation on the part of the public.'

The cooperation aspect needs to be underlined, as it would affirm that health is also, or in practive maybe first and foremost, a responsibility embedded with the individual, and within the family (obligations to cater to the well-being of the children, the sick and the elderly). We, as indicated above, therefore separate three levels of responsibility: the individual, the nuclear family, and the community (represented by the state and, maybe, sometimes by the international community, e.g. following or during a war or in the aftermath of non-man-made disasters). Simply put, at the end of the day it boils down to the responsibility, accessibility, affordability and quality of health care.

WHO, in its mission statements, puts major emphasis on equity. Its objective is the attainment by all peoples of the highest possible level of health. At its first World Health Assembly in 1948, it listed its top priorities in the following order: malaria, MCH, TB, STDs, nutrition and environmental sanitation. Fifty years later, these are still the main challenges. New challenges include ageing, mental health, injuries, violence and environmental interdependence. Hence the health sector development is at the core of WHO's work.

UNICEF, which originally dealt with children, has over the last decades proven to be very effective where it concerns the promotion of primary health care (PHC). Whether it concerns the provision of basic drugs, the attention paid to clean water, health education, or widespread immunization programmes, it far outclassed WHO. Only now, with Brundtland in charge of WHO, can this organization try and prove that it is as effective as originally planned. (...)

TOEBES

In her book review of Birgit TOEBES' dissertation, Alicia Ely Amin concludes that "...although Toebes' book will undoubtedly not be the last word on the right to health in international law, it is welcome as an essential first step in bringing the dialogue to a pragmatic level. Ultimately, the connections between health and human rights are so multivalent, and the notion of a right to health, itself, is so much more encompassing than what can be reflected in legal practice, that clarifying the content and significance of the human right to health will surely require going beyond the case law and reporting practices that exist. However, I share

Toebes' desire for pragmatism; as radical as the utopian promise of the full realization of a true right to health may be, beneath most revolutionary breakthroughs in human rights can be found incremental changes in normative definition, institutional effectiveness, and procedural efficiency. To paraphrase a comment that Philip Alston, former Chairman of the ESC Committee, shared with me years ago, human rights – including the right to health – enter the arena of public concern and enforcement like an elephant walking backwards: once the doors of sovereignty are opened to the small and unimposing tail, it is only a matter of time before the elephant is inside...''[20]

As indicated above, Toebes' contribution to the HRQ summarizes her views on the right to health in a superb manner:[21]

BIRGIT TOEBES

Towards an Improved Understanding of the International Human Right to Health

Introduction

In the context of international human rights, economic, social, and cultural rights are generally distinguished from civil and political rights. Although it is often asserted that both sets of rights are interdependent, interrelated, and of equal importance, in practice, Western states and NGOs, in particular, have tended to treat economic, social, and cultural rights as if they were less important than civil and political rights. Civil and political rights, for example, are frequently invoked in national judicial proceedings, and several complaint mechanisms are designed to protect these rights at the international level. In contrast, economic, social, and cultural rights are often considered nonjusticiable and are regarded as general directives for states rather than rights.

Another serious obstacle to the implementation of economic, social, and cultural rights is their lack of conceptual clarity. An economic and social right that is characterized by particular vagueness is the international human right to health. It is by no means clear precisely what individuals are entitled to under the right to health, nor is it clear what the resulting obligations are on the part of states. Given these difficulties, this article seeks to further clarify the scope and implications of the right to health in order to contribute to an improved implementation of this specific right. This article will address some definitional problems when it comes to the right to health, as well as its international codification and current implementation practice. Finally, this article will outline the scope of the right to health and the ensuing state obligations.

---

[20] Human Rights Quarterly 21.4 (1999) p. 1128.

[21] Human Rights Quarterly 21.3 (1999) 661-679. Here again, the editor regrets that he has been forced, due to space constraints, to drop the many excellent footnotes.

The Problem of Definition

When it comes to health as a human right, there is an initial problem with regard to its definition. Specifically, there is confusion and disagreement over what is the most appropriate term to use to address health as a human right. Due to this disagreement, different terms are used by various authors. The terms that most commonly appear in human rights and health law literature are: the "right to health," the "right to healthcare" or to "medical care," and to a lesser extent, the "right to health protection."

It has been argued that the term "right to health" is awkward because it suggests that people have a right to something that cannot be guaranteed, namely perfect health or to be healthy. It has also been noted that health is a highly subjective matter, varying from person to person and from country to country. It is argued, therefore, that the terms "right to healthcare" or "right to health protection" are more realistic.

At the international level, however, the term "right to health" is most commonly used. This term best matches the international human rights treaty provisions that formulate health as a human right. These provisions not only proclaim a right to healthcare but also a right to other health services such as environmental health protection and occupational health services. The term "healthcare" would accordingly not cover this broader understanding of health as a human right. Thus, in practice the term "right to health" is generally used as a shorthand expression for the more elaborate treaty texts. Using such shorthand expressions is rather common in human rights discourse; terms such as the rights to life, privacy, a fair trial, and housing have all obtained a very specific practical connotation, as has the right to health.

International Codification of the Right to Health

The right to health is firmly embedded in a considerable number of international human rights instruments. The right to health as laid down in the preamble to the Constitution of the World Health Organization (WHO) constitutes the point of departure on which most of the provisions in these instruments are based. The preamble formulates the "highest attainable standard of health" as a fundamental right of everyone and defines health as a "state of complete physical, mental and social well-being and not merely the absence of disease or infirmity." In the same vein, most treaty provisions stipulate a right to the highest attainable standard of (physical and mental) health and include a number of government obligations as well. These government undertakings usually include commitments regarding healthcare and also mention a number of underlying preconditions for health, such as occupational health, environmental health, clean drinking water, and adequate sanitation.

In addition to specific treaty provisions addressing the right to health, there are a number of general treaty provisions that stipulate that there is a universal right to health. The most well-known and influential of these provisions is Article 12 of the International Covenant on Economic, Social and Cultural Rights (ICESCR). In addition to Article 12 of the ICESCR, there are a number of other treaty provisions that stipulate a right to health for particular vulnerable groups, such as women, children, racial minorities, prisoners, migrant workers, and indigenous populations.

The documents produced during several UN World Conferences, including the Vienna Declaration, the Programme of Action of the Cairo Conference, and the Beijing Declaration and Programme of Action, have also elaborated on the meaning and scope of the international human right to health, and of international health issues generally. In fact, during the Fourth World Conference on Women, considerable attention was paid to a number of aspects relating to the health of women.

Finally, a great number of national constitutions include a right to health (care) or stipulate states' duties with regard to the health of their people. Some of these provisions existed before the international human right to health was formulated.

Implementation Practice of the Right to Health

In view of the above, it becomes clear that the problem with the right to health is not so much a lack of codification but rather an absence of a consistent implementation practice through reporting procedures and before judicial and quasi-judicial bodies, as well as a lack of conceptual clarity. These problems are interrelated: a lack of understanding of the meaning and scope of a right makes it difficult to implement, and the absence of a frequent practice of implementation in turn hampers the possibility of obtaining a greater understanding of its meaning and scope.

Reporting Procedures

International treaty monitoring bodies do not have a very clear understanding of how they should implement the right to health. Under the heading of the "right to health," these bodies deal with a great number of health-related issues in a somewhat haphazard fashion. The treaty monitoring body of the ICESCR, the Committee on Economic, Social and Cultural Rights ("the Committee"), for example, addresses the following broad range of topics within the framework of the right to health: the national health policies adopted, issues related to healthcare, issues related to environmental health, accessibility of clean drinking water and adequate sanitation, availability of health-related information, occupational health, and the accessibility of health services for various vulnerable groups. One may divide the aggregate of these issues into four larger parts: (1) general issues, (2) healthcare, (3) underlying preconditions for health, and (4) vulnerable groups and health-specific subjects. In spite of the somewhat inconsistent attitude of the Committee with regard to these four topics, one can draw important insights from an analysis of the ICESCR reporting procedure.

General Issues

Included within the category of general issues is the overall requirement that state parties make certain commitments in the area of public health. First, state parties are required to devote a sufficient percentage of their GNP to health. If, for example, military spending is high as compared to health expenditure, the Committee assumes that the country concerned should have spent its budget otherwise. Second, this health commitment entails an obligation to adopt a national health policy, including the adoption of the Primary Health Care strategy (PHC) of WHO. Also, state parties have to ensure that no disparities exist between the standard of health services offered in the private and public sectors. The Committee opines that, although the right to health may be satisfied through whatever mix of public and private sector services is appropriate in the national context, state parties are responsible for the equality of access to healthcare services, whether privately or publicly provided. Plans to privatize and decentralize healthcare services do not in any way relieve state parties of their obligation to use all available means to promote adequate access to healthcare services, particularly for the poorer segments of the population. The health legislation adopted by states is discussed; however, the type of legislation state parties must adopt is not further spelled out by the Committee.

Healthcare

As far as the provision of healthcare services is concerned, a distinction between availability, accessibility, affordability, and quality of healthcare services proves useful in order to scrutinize the Committee's approach. With regard to the *availability* of healthcare services, the Committee assesses the aggregate of hospital beds and the population per nurse and per doctor. In order to guarantee the availability of healthcare facilities, the Committee notes that state parties should encourage health personnel to stay and practice in the country. Regarding the *accessibility* of healthcare services, the Committee focuses on the most vulnerable groups, who are generally minority and indigenous populations, women, children, the elderly, disabled persons, and persons with HIV/AIDS. In addition, the Committee expresses its concern about the accessibility of healthcare facilities in remote, rural areas. State parties are to make efforts to institute rural health subcenters and to stimulate doctors and nurses to set up practice in rural areas. An important aspect of the accessibility of healthcare facilities is the *affordability* of the available services. State parties are to ensure that healthcare services are affordable for the economically underprivileged in general and for the elderly and low-income women in particular. As part of the affordability requirement, state parties must make sure that privatization does not constitute a threat to the affordability of healthcare services. Finally, state parties must ensure that the available healthcare services are of good *quality*. This requires that doctors and nurses are skilled and that equipment and drugs are adequate.

Underlying Preconditions for Health

When it comes to the underlying preconditions for health there is some overlap with other rights. In particular, there is overlap with those rights contained in Article 11 of the ICESCR: food, housing, and clothing. Of these, the most explicitly health related are food-related issues. Additional preconditions for health that are not covered by other rights but are discussed within the framework of Article 12 are access to safe water and the provision of adequate sanitary facilities, environmental hygiene, occupational hygiene, and health education. State parties have to make sure that their population has sufficient access to safe water and adequate sanitation. In particular, they have to ensure that people living in remote, rural areas have sufficient access to these facilities.

The Committee is also interested in environmental policies. However, it seeks to address environmental issues only in as far as they affect, or may affect, human health. For example, state parties have to take safety measures for protection against radioactive radiation. The area of occupational health requires the implementation and monitoring of health and safety measures in the workplace. Finally, health education requires that measures be taken to provide education concerning prevailing health problems, as well as the measures that are necessary for preventing and controlling them.

Vulnerable Groups and Health-Specific Subjects

With regard to vulnerable groups and health-specific subjects, multiple topics have emerged in the reporting procedure. When the inhabitants of remote, rural areas are concerned, state parties must ensure that there is not an imbalance between rural and urban areas when it comes to access to health services. With regard to indigenous populations, state parties are required to both guarantee respect for the cultural identity of those populations (for example, their use of traditional medicine) and to improve their health status. State parties are also required to improve poor sanitary and hygiene conditions prevailing in penal institutions. With respect to women, state parties are expected to combat maternal mortality, to provide medical assistance to low-income women, and to combat "traditional practices," including female circumcision. Moreover, state parties are to reduce infant mortality and to ensure that the rising costs of healthcare do not disadvantage the elderly.

Other important issues include the policies and practices concerning abortion. The Committee has found that the circumstances under which such practices take place are more relevant under Article 12 of the ICESCR than the legal status of abortion. Nevertheless, the legal status of abortion is an issue under discussion because the prohibition of abortion may lead to illegal and unsafe abortions. Still another area of concern for the Committee is HIV/AIDS. State parties are urged to take measures to reduce the spread of HIV/AIDS, to set up information campaigns, to adopt laws to prevent discrimination against HIV-positive persons, and to endeavor to avoid measures that discriminate against people with HIV/AIDS.

These measures are in response to some states' adoption of coercive measures, including transit restrictions to minimize the risk of the spread of AIDS, mandatory testing, and control of prostitution. Regarding drug abuse, state parties are to remain vigilant on the question of human rights violations and the means used to punish abuses. It has been observed that the drug problem cannot be solved solely by resorting to repressive measures without recognizing other serious problems, such as extreme poverty or inequality. For example, drug addicts should not necessarily be regarded as delinquents but rather as victims or patients. Finally, state parties are to take measures to combat alcoholism and to discourage minors from having access to alcoholic beverages and tobacco products.

In a more general sense, it seems that Committee members disapprove of coercive policies relating to the health of the population. Forcing people to undergo certain treatment, such as psychiatric treatment, treatment for drug addiction, HIV/AIDS testing, or forcing indigenous populations to abandon traditional healing, is generally rejected by the Committee, which emphasizes the adverse effects that such policies may have. Committee members have expressed concern that these practices give rise to violations of economic, social, and cultural rights, as well as violations of civil and political rights. In this regard, it is noteworthy to observe that some of the issues addressed by the Committee within the framework of the right to health overlap with civil and political rights.

Justiciability of the Right to Health

At the United Nations, as well as the regional and national levels, very few examples exist where courts have reviewed the right to health; however, there are some sources of inspiration for judicial review of the right to health. At the UN level there are no specific complaint procedures in force to make health rights and other economic, social, and cultural rights justiciable. Given this fact, some attempts have been made to introduce health issues in other international procedures. For example, within the context of the 1235 procedure of the UN Sub-Commission, issues related to environmental health have been brought up; however, no decision has been made. In addition, WHO requested an Advisory Opinion from the International Court of Justice concerning the right to health and the legality of the use of nuclear weapons, but this was to no avail. A final example is the World Bank, which recently introduced a special Inspection Panel before which health issues, among other things, may be addressed. Although there is perhaps a slight tendency towards attention for health issues within UN bodies, the situation is altogether not very promising.

At the regional level the situation is somewhat more encouraging. For example, the development of complaint procedures for economic, social, and cultural rights has proceeded somewhat further at the regional levels than at the United Nations. In principle, the right to health as contained in the African Charter is susceptible to invocation before and review by the African Commission, although this procedure has not often been used. The Organization of American

States has adopted a limited complaints procedure, however it has yet to come into force. However, given the limited scope of the Inter-American Protocol of San Salvador, the right to health would not be susceptible to judicial review. Nevertheless, it is possible to submit complaints to the Inter-American Commission on Human Rights (IACHR) on the basis of the right to health as provided for in the American Declaration. This, in fact, was tried in the case of the Yanomani Indians, where the IACHR declared that the right to health in Article XI of the American Declaration was violated. The Government of Brazil was held to have failed to protect the Yanomani against the exploitation of the rainforest and the detrimental health effects that could be caused. Finally, with the adoption of a complaint procedure under the European Social Charter (ESC) of the Council of Europe, the right to protection of health in the ESC will become susceptible to (quasi-) judicial review. This procedure will, however, only allow specific organizations to submit complaints, not individuals.

Inspiration for the justiciability of the right to health can be derived from the national level. In some countries either the constitutional or the international right to health has been given effect before domestic courts. Whereas some of these cases involve a right to certain healthcare facilities, others concern a right to environmental health. With regard to healthcare, a 1992 Colombian case that concerned the terminal illness of an AIDS patient is worth mentioning. In that case the Colombian Supreme Court ruled that the state was required, by the right to health in Article 13 of the Colombian constitution, to provide special protection when the lack of economic resources "prevents a person from decreasing the suffering, discrimination, and social risk involved in being afflicted by a terminal, transmissible, and incurable illness." To this end, the Court decided that the hospital was required to provide the AIDS patient the necessary services. With regard to environmental health, the well-known 1993 Philippine *Minors Oposa* case is significant. In that case the Philippine Supreme Court ruled that the state should stop providing logging licences in order to protect the health of present and future generations. The decision was based on Article II of the Declaration of Principles and State Policies of the 1987 Philippine constitution, which sets forth the rights to health and ecology.

Finally, one may derive inspiration from the justiciability of civil and political rights. On some occasions, civil and political rights have offered protections similar to that of the right to health. Again, such protections may concern access to a certain healthcare facility or protection against environmental health threats. A case indirectly involving a right to access to healthcare services has been brought before the Human Rights Committee (HRC). This body has adopted the practice of considering Article 26 ICCPR (nondiscrimination) as an autonomous provision that may include the prohibition of discriminatory actions with relation to social rights. In *Hendrika S. Vos* v. *the Netherlands*, the HRC considered whether the denial of a disability benefit constituted a violation of Article 26 of the ICCPR. Although the HRC held that there was no violation of the nondiscrimination clause in Article 26, the fact that the HRC tested the denial of the sickness benefit against Article 26 shows its willingness to read social rights into the nondiscrimination clause. Also worth mentioning is a decision by the Indian Supreme Court where the Court ruled that on the basis of the right to life contained in the Indian constitution, the claimant had a right to the available emergency medical treatment. It explained that:

> [p]roviding adequate medical facilities for the people is an essential part of the obligations undertaken by the Government in a welfare State. ... Article 21 imposes an obligation on the State to safeguard the right to life of every person. Preservation of human life is thus of paramount importance. ... Failure on the part of a Government hospital to provide timely medical treatment to a person in need of such treatment results in a violation of his right to life guaranteed under Article 21.

Regarding environmental health, a case in point is *López Ostra* v. *Spain*, which concerned the nuisance caused by a waste treatment plant and its effects on the applicant's daughter's health in the town of Lorca, Spain. The Spanish court opined that "severe environmental pollution may affect individuals' well-being and prevent them from enjoying their homes in such a way as to effect their private and family life adversely. . . ." It concluded that the municipality of Lorca had failed to take steps to respect the applicant's right to respect for her home and for her private life under Article 8 of the European Convention on Human Rights and that Article 8 had accordingly been violated.

The Creation of Conceptual Clarity with Regard to the Right to Health

In Search of its Scope and Core Content

On the basis of the above findings, one can clarify further the meaning of the right to health and delineate its scope and core content. Whereas the scope constitutes the general content of the right to health, the core content consists of those elements that a state has to guarantee under any circumstances, irrespective of its available resources.

Regarding the scope, it is important to recognize the broad character of the right to health and not recognize a right to "healthcare" only. The right to health can be said to embrace two larger parts: (1) elements related to "healthcare," and (2) elements concerning the "underlying preconditions for health" (these may include a healthy environment, safe drinking water and adequate sanitation, occupational health, and health-related information). Simultaneously, it is important to demarcate limits on the right to health and not allow it to include everything that might involve health. For example, with a few minor exceptions, the right to health does not include a prohibition against torture or inhuman and degrading treatment, nor does it include protection against arbitrary killing or medical or scientific experimentation. The right to health also does not include regular education at schools nor a right to adequate housing. It offers protection against environmental pollution only if there are clear health risks, and it is related to the right to work only if it concerns the safeguarding of industrial hygiene and the prevention, treatment, and control of occupational diseases. On the other hand, it is important to recognize that there is a certain overlap with several civil and political as well as other economic, social, and cultural rights, in that on some occasions the right to health may offer protection similar to that of other rights. For example, the right to health may overlap with other human rights where it concerns prevention of infant mortality (right to life), the safeguarding of adequate prison conditions, measures to combat "traditional practices" (prohibition of torture and inhuman and degrading treatment), and access to healthy foodstuffs (right to food).

Secondly, there is a trend among scholars and activists towards delineating a certain core in the right to health. This so-called core content consists of a set of elements that states have to guarantee immediately, irrespective of their available resources. The core content stands in contrast to some elements of the right to health that are to be realized "progressively." This core content includes those elements without which the right loses its significance; it refers to those elements that encompass the essence of the right. For the definition of the core content of the right to health, one may derive inspiration from the Primary Health Care strategy (PHC) of WHO. The core content of the right to health accordingly consists of a number of basic health services. Irrespective of their available resources, states are to provide access to: maternal and child healthcare (including family planning), immunization against the major infectious diseases, appropriate treatment for common diseases and injuries, essential drugs, and an adequate supply of safe water and basic sanitation. In addition, they should ensure freedom from serious environmental health threats.

Finally, in addition to the scope and core content, a number of guiding principles constitute the framework of the right to health. States should safeguard the availability, equality, accessibility (financial, geographic, and cultural), and quality of the above mentioned health services.

Obligations Resulting from the Right to Health

For further clarification of the normative content of the right to health, it is helpful to approach it from the angle of (state) obligations. A useful concept in this regard is the tripartite typology of duties, which assumes that obligations to respect, protect, and fulfill can be derived from each human right. An analysis of the right to health on the basis of this typology demonstrates that the right to health not only gives rise to positive obligations to protect and to fulfill but also embraces negative obligations to respect. Obligations to respect the right to health include, for example, the obligation to respect equal access to health services and to refrain from health-harming activities, as in the sphere of environmental health. The fact that an economic and social right embraces negative obligations underlines the interdependence and interrelatedness of civil and political rights with economic, social, and cultural rights. In effect, both sets of rights –

civil and political, and economic, social, and cultural – require state abstention.

Conclusion

It will take a long time for economic, social, and cultural rights to obtain the same status and impact as civil and political rights. States will continue to fear the financial commitments of guaranteeing such rights. A conceptual clarification of the separate economic, social, and cultural rights may nevertheless contribute to their recognition and implementation. In addition, this clarification reveals that economic, social, and cultural rights, equal to civil and political rights, may require state abstention, a commitment that requires no financial resources on the part of states. Simultaneously, the fact that civil and political rights may embrace positive obligations underlines the interdependence and interrelatedness of both sets of rights. If positive obligations are derived from civil and political rights, why not recognize similar obligations with regard to economic, social, and cultural rights?

As to the right to health, it has become clear that it concerns a broad right that is difficult to pinpoint. Therefore, the adoption of a General Comment on the right to health in Article 12 of the ICESCR is of the utmost importance. It is also important that reliable indicators be developed to measure states' progress in the field of health and that states, UN Specialized Agencies, and NGOs make efforts and cooperate in this regard. For the further development of the justiciability of the right to health, one may keep in mind that justiciability is a fluid concept, which implies that it may further develop in the future. Frequent application of the right to health may further enhance its justiciability.

3. GENERAL COMMENTS

As to the scope and nature of violations of economic and social rights, regard should of course be had to the 1997 Maastricht Guidelines on Violations of Economic, Social and Cultural Rights as well as the various publications on this issue by Scott Leckie.

The issue of 'violations' is not a mere academic one. In order to ascertain whether an asylum seeker is indeed in need of protection, a well-founded fear of being persecuted needs to be established, and hereto a recongized violation of a relevant civil or political right would greatly assist. In general, refugee law relies heavily on exactly such violations, although this link is neither automatic nor exhaustive. For the sake of establishing criteria towards granting residence-cum-treatment to the potential beneficiary, it would be of relevance to seek objective criteria, difficult as that may be. Of course, case-law is the most relevant one, and due attention should therefore be paid to Chapter 6 on Strasbourg. But the judiciary is also looking for criteria, and the interpretation of human rights is hence of the utmost importance. One of the key elements towards understanding human rights and a useful tool for the interpretation are General Comments. Hereinunder attention shall be paid to that fairly recent phenomenon. As far as the context is concerned reference is made to VAN KRIEKEN's Health Gaps and Migratory Movements:

Some relevance in the search for the interpretation of the universality concept in the context of social and economic rights, can be found in the dicta of the newly set up Human Rights Committee for overseeing the implementation of the 1966 Covenant on Social, Economic and Cultural Rights.

It is herewith recalled that the International Covenant on Civil and Political Rights (ICCPR) contains in Art. 28 ff a structure for the establishment and operation of a Human Rights Committee. This highly effective independent Committee, consisting of eighteen independent members, nationals of Member States and serving in their personal capacity, oversees the implementation of the ICCPR. As indicated above, this Committee has to some extent embarked on some of the aspects related to health, but in a most ambiguous manner indeed.

In comparison to the ICCPR, the CESCR provides for limited means of monitoring State compliance with the obligations laid down in the Covenant. This in itself is no easy task, as the Covenant sets goals, and long-term efforts, in fact continuing efforts. Economic, social and cultural rights were/are to be realized progressively, in contrast to the civil and political rights which were considered to have been put into immediate effect. The CESCR has been endowed with the compulsary periodic State reporting procedures (Arts. 16, 17).[22] This reporting system was felt to be as effective as the Covenant was believed to become. Unlike the ICCPR no Committee had originally been set up. This omission was redressed in 1985 by setting up a Committee on Economic, Social and Cultural Rights.[23] This supervisory body has been and still is faced with problems also common to reporting procedures in other human rights instruments, but has as an additional challenge the difficulty to set norms and to measure the obligations to progressively realize the various rights involved.

The Committee has to assist ECOSOC in monitoring compliance with the Covenant in a progressive and creative manner. It could thus be argued that the Committee is still in the process of defining the relevant yardsticks and benchmarks, not to mention the sticks and carrots, needed to indulge states in progressively realizing rights and obligations. One of the more effective methods may indeed be found in the adoption of so-called General Comments, copied after the

[22] Reports on the implementation were to be submitted to ECOSOC (Art.16 ff), which, nevertheless, was no guarantee for efficiency or effectiveness. The 1503 procedure, however, gave the ICCPR Human Rights Committee the possibility to address some of the issues, through the back door, as it were. But that possibility has not resulted in any tangible outcome.

[23] ECOSOC Res. 1985/17.

ICCPR Human Rights Committee. Thereby a prescriptive description of the norms can be provided.

As far as the country reports are concerned, the CESCR Committee hitherto appears to embark on a fairly conservative road. It stipulated in a country report quite clearly that States parties are responsible for the equality of access to health services, whether publicly or privately provided. States may in this light have problems in dismissing their responsibilities with regard to the provision of health care facilities by handing over these tasks to private providers,[24] but it is herewith submitted that these balances are bound to change. The equality of access can only refer to the agreed minimum norms of health care and health services. The extra services above these agreed minimum levels may always be bought on the private market, or by simply paying higher insurance fees.

Through the General Comments, the Committee can share the experience gained through the examination of States' reports, it can draw attention to insufficiencies, and it can stimulate the activities of all concerned in achieving progressively and effectively the full realization of the rights recognized in the Covenant.[25] Hitherto, the ESCR Committee has published relatively few general comments. These comments are nevertheless of great importance as they indicate the direction in which the implementation and interpretation of the Covenant is to move.

In its third General Comment (1990) the Committee indicated that "...any suggestion that the provisions [of the Covenant] are inherently non-self-executing would seem difficult to sustain..." Some aspects of the Covenant "...would seem to be capable of immediate application by judicial and other organs in many legal systems..."[26] Health, in whichever context, would not appear to be included, but the Commitee did stress that even in times of severe resource constraints, States parties have the duty to protect the vulnerable members of society.[27]

In its fifth General Comment [28], the Committee refers to the UN Principles for Older Persons[29], in which it inter alia has been stated that "...older persons should have access to adequate food, water, shelter, clothing and health care through the provision of income, family and community support and self-help..."

The Committee then continues to state:

---

[24] See Boerefijn & Toebes, op.cit. on p.31

[25] E/1997/22, paras. 48-51. Efforts are now being undertaken to embark on an individual complaints procedure, like the procedure set out in the Optional Protocol to the ICCPR (adopted and opened for signature, ratification and accession by GA Res. 2200 A (XXI), 16 December 1966). It remains to be seen whether this in the short run would provide the additional value needed for the furtherance of successful implementation, as individual complaints tend to generate a lot of work, and may force the Committee to embark on sensitive issues, which may temporarily frustrate rather than enhance the functioning of the Committee.

[26] Examples: Arts. 3, 7.a.i, 8, 10.3, 13.3, 13.4, 15.3.

> With a view to the realization of the right of elderly persons to the enjoyment of a satisfactory standard of physical and mental health, in accordance with article 12, paragraph 1, of the Covenant, States parties should take account of the content of recommendations 1 to 17 of the [1982] Vienna International Plan of Action on Ageing which focuses entirely on providing guidelines on health policy to preserve the health of the elderly and take a comprehensive view, ranging from prevention and rehabilitation to the care of the terminally ill. Clearly the growing number of chronic, degenerative diseases and the high hospitalization costs they involve can not be dealt with only by curative treatment. In this regard, States parties should bear in mind that maintaining health into old age requires investments during the entire life span, basically through the adoption of healthy lifestyles (food, exercise, elimination of tobacco and alcohol, etc.). Prevention, through regular checks suited to the needs of the elderly, plays a decisive role, as does rehabilitation, by maintaining the functional capacities of elderly persons, with a resulting decrease in the cost of investments in health care and social services.

In another General Comment,[30] the Committee covers the issue of persons with disabilities. The Covenant does not refer explicitly to persons with disabilities (this term being preferred to the term 'disabled persons'), but as the Covenant applies fully to all members of society, persons with disabilities are clearly entitled to the full range of rights recognized in the Covenant. Meanwhile the international community has affirmed its commitment in a number of relevant instruments.[31]

In this General Comment, the Committee indicates that the challenge of improving the situation of persons with disabilities is of direct relevance to every State party to the Covenant. The Committee continues by stating: "*... while the means chosen to promote the full realization of the economic, social and cultural rights of this group will inevitably differ significantly from one country to another, there is no country in which a major policy and programme effort is not required...*" The obligation of the various States can be defined to 'promote progressive realization of the relevant rights to the maximum of their available resources.' Abstaining from measures which might have a negative impact on the

[27] It is of interest to note that the USA, which indeed shows problems in accepting the authority of treaties cum treatybodies, displays a rather different picture. Practice differs from state to state, from the Oregon (or NY) health insurance systems to the South Carolina (or Texas) ones, the latter being totally unregulated private market systems.

[28] December 1995, adopted at the Committee's 13th session.

[29] GA Res. 46/91, December 1991.

[30] No. 5, December 1994.

[31] World Programme of Action concerning Disabled Persons, GA Res. 37/52, 3 December 1982; Guidelines for the establishment and development of national Coordinating Committees on Disablity or Similar Bodies, A/C.3/46/4, annex 1, 1990; see also ECOSOC resolution 1991/8; GA Res. 46/96 of 16 December 1991; Principles for the Protection of Persons with Mental Illness and for the Improvement of Mental Health Care, 1991; Standard Rules on the Equalization of Opportunities for Persons with Disabilities, 1993, etc.

persons concerned is not enough: "... *the obligation ... is to take positive action to reduce structural disadvantages and to give appropriate preferential treatment...*" The Committee repeats its submission made earlier in General Comment no. 3 that the duty of States parties to protect the vulnerable members of their societies "assumes greater rather than less importance in times of severe resource constraints..."

It is worth being pointed out that the right to health care, not to mention the right to health, is as such non-justiciable. This means that this right is difficult, if not impossible to invoke, and that it is not susceptible to third-party adjudication. Individual complaints to the CESCR Committee will fall on deaf ears, on procedural and legal grounds. As we saw above, the CESCR Committee can, however, criticize States in so-called Concluding Observations. But individual complaints will not be dealt with. There is, however, a possibility based on what came to be known as the 1235 procedure, as it was agreed upon in ECOSOC's 1235th Resolution (1967), setting out the framework for a complaints procedure with the Commission on Human Rights and its Sub-Commission. 'Interventions' can be entertained (written and oral complaints) which are subsequently discussed publicly during the (Sub-)Commission's yearly sessions. No such complaint cum discussion can result in a binding decision, but resolutions with a reference to a particular situation may thereupon be adopted.[32]

It should be underlined that, as yet, there are no specific complaint procedures at the UN level, but for the 1235 procedure. The WHO and the GA have, therefore, tried to put the issue of health to the ICJ in the context of the legality of the use of nuclear arms and its impact on health and environmental issues.[33] The World Bank introduced in 1993 a panel which, whilst looking into the operations of the Bank, may address health issues as well.[34] The UN as a whole, however, lacks the political clout as well as the means to embark on this issue in a comprehensive manner. It is therefore obvious that the CESCR Committee deserves the necessary assistance from its member states to be able to put the issue on the agenda in the most effective manner possible.[35]

Health is first and foremost a responsibility of each and every individual and his immediate family. In a great many aspects, however, the community, the state, will have to take action, both on the preventive and care level, as well as on

---

[32] Toebes op.cit. refers to two cases regarding environmental health in Guatamala and Ecuador, pp. 172-174.

[33] WHO approached the ICJ in 1993; the GA asked for an Advisory Opinion in 1994; Toebes op.cit. pp. 174-178.

[34] Toebes op.cit. mentions two cases (Nepal and Argentina/Paraguay) at which health issues came to the fore (pp. 178-181).

[35] On the regional level (Europe, Latin America, Africa) it can be concluded that the development of complaints procedures for second generation rights has proceeded somewhat further than the UN level, but not to the extent that one may dream of major breakthroughs (except, maybe, for the Inter-American system); Toebes, op.cit. pp. 182-188.

the cure level. Prevention and care are within the realm of most societies, poor as they may be. Cure is often a luxury, which can not easily be ascertained. Hence, in spite of efforts to put emphasis on equity, there is and there will be a gap in health care, within countries, between countries, and between continents.

Human rights touches on the issue of health care. There is, however, no right to health, but at most a right to adequate health care. States, however, may be found not to live up to their obligations. The CESCR Committee should be considered the foremost authority to point at shortcomings. Moreover, the international community has obligations as well. They too could and should be held responsible if they do not live up to what has been stated in Art. 2 of the CESCR in which mention was made of international assistance and cooperation. Yet, in spite of all the efforts, both national and international, communities may be lacking the minimum care they deserve. This lack may have a cross-border impact, in that care may be sought outside of the community, the country. The underlying principle, however, is to be seen in the need to exhaust local remedies. Moreover, it concerns communities, not just individuals.

DEN EXTER & HERMANS, at the September 2000 Expert Meeting also focused on international developments concerning the right to health care in the context of the CESCR Committee, and stated:
Since the ratification of the ICESCR, the nature and scope of its discerned rights have been the subject of debate. Restricted to the right to health care, several developments have reinforced its (judicial) basis. The latest event that may revalue the right to health care concerns the reinforcement of the so-called 'Limburg Principles' by the 'Maastricht Guidelines on Violations of Economic, Social and Cultural Rights' (1997). These guidelines elaborate the commitments of states participant to the ICESCR. A revival to these principles is the increasing importance of the Committee of Economic, Social and Cultural Rights (subsequently referred to as the Committee). This Committee is concerned with observing compliance with the Covenant by participant states and has now been in operation for ten years (1987-1997). During this decade, the Committee has developed into a quasi-judicial institution that gives an authoritative interpretation of the states' commitments emanating from the Covenant. Besides its main task of studying participant states' reports and reporting on them itself, the Committee has formulated several 'general comments' which attempt to interpret treaty provisions which are rather generally defined, and which may support participant states in understanding the meaning of the ICESCR during its implementation. One of these 'General Comments' concerns the nature of the treaty obligations of participant states according to Article 2(1) of the Covenant.[36] According to the Commit-

[36] General comment no. 3 (1990), The nature of States Parties obligations (art. 2, para. 1 of the Covenant), in: UN Doc. E/1991/23, Annex III. The main phrases of this paragraph read: Each State

tee, the main obligation in Article 2(1) is to take steps 'with a view to progressively achieving the full realisation of the rights recognized' in the Covenant. While the Committee acknowledges the constraints resulting from limited available resources, it also imposes various obligations which are of immediate effect. 'Any suggestion that the provisions indicated are inherently non-self-executing would seem to be difficult to sustain', whereas the concept of progressive realisation constitutes a recognition of the fact that full realisation of an economic, social and cultural right will generally not be achieved in a short period of time. It is a necessary flexibility device, reflecting the realities and difficulties of the real world but which, simultaneously, imposes an obligation to move as expeditiously and effectively as possible towards the full realisation of the rights in question. The flexibility and freedom in the domestic implementation of the obligations allow national governments a margin of appreciation. Nonetheless, policy freedom has been restricted by 'minimum core obligations' which a country should meet. What these minimum essential needs are, needs to be specified by the individual rights separately. By means of a General Comment on the right to the highest attainable standard of health, the Committee has interpreted the 'core obligations on health'. These criteria have been formulated in terms of obligations to respect, protect and fulfil (which incorporates an obligation to promote and to ensure) and provide guidance in defining the actions to be taken by States. It gives generic examples of measures arising from the broad definition of the right in Article 12(1), thereby illustrating the content of that right. Moreover, these examples enable one to review state parties' compliance with the Covenant.

For instance, the obligation to respect requires states to abstain from interfering directly or indirectly with the enjoyment of the recognised right. Specific legal obligations under the obligation to respect are refraining from denying or limiting equal access for all persons, including prisoners or detainees, minorities, asylum seekers and illegal immigrants to preventive, curative and palliative health services. Furthermore, obligations to respect include a State's obligation to refrain from, inter alia, prohibiting healing practices and medicines and marketing unsafe pharmaceuticals. In addition, States should also refrain from unlawfully polluting the environment. The obligation to protect requires states to take measures that prevent third parties from interfering with Article 12 guarantees. This includes, for instance, the duties of States to adopt legislation ensuring equal access to health care and health-related services provided by third parties; to ensure that the privatisation of the health sector does not constitute a threat to the availability, accessibility, acceptability and quality of health facilities, goods and

---

party to the present Covenant undertakes to take steps [...] to a maximum of its available resources, with a view to achieving progressively the full realisation of the rights recognised in the present Covenant by all appropriate means, particularly including the adoption of legislative measures.

The editor regrets to add that, once again, all the other footnotes had to be deleted for reasons of available space.

services; and to ensure that health practitioners meet appropriate standards of education, skills and ethical codes of conduct. The obligation to *promote* includes an obligation of conduct to promote public health, and the adaptation and implementation of a detailed plan of action to reduce maternal mortality. States are also required to adopt measures against environmental and occupational health hazards and against any other threat as demonstrated by epidemiological data. For this purpose they should formulate and implement national policy aimed at reducing and eliminating pollution. Finally, the obligation to *ensure* includes an obligation of result, e.g., to provide the minimum core obligations: essential preventive and primary health care facilities to those in need. Both types of obligations (to promote and to ensure) differ in legal consequences, and therefore in their binding character for national governments. The margin of discretion enable governments to enjoy a certain freedom in selecting and implementing necessary policy measures. However, universal minimum standards related to the content of these measures put the freedom into perspective.

As concerns the obligation to ensure, depriving a significant number of individuals (in this case refugees or illegal immigrants) of, for instance, essential basic health care facilities, constitutes *prima facie* a violation of the right to health care and may have immediate effect (obligation *erga omnes*). Or, in case a state cannot fulfil its obligation to provide its population with food or elementary health care on its own, then that initiates an internationally accepted obligation, an obligation that should be responded to by a legal obligation ('*opinio iuris sive necessitatis*'). This conviction of a responsive legal and moral obligation may be assumed as an *erga omnes* obligation. Needless to say, the obligation to ensure basic primary care does not necessarily imply that the government itself is *actually* responsible for the provision of health care services. Non-governmental public institutions are frequently involved in providing such services and sometimes they are even more appropriate for this task. However, this should not relieve a government from its obligation to guarantee a minimum of care in case of deficiencies in the market.

Here it is concluded that the ICESCR right to health care can be considered as a candidate right *erga omnes*, including binding obligations to respect, protect and to ensure the minimum core content such as to refrain from interfering with the enjoyment of health care, to protect equal access, and to ensure basic prevention and primary health care facilities to those in need. These obligations impose an obligation of result and may have immediate effect whereas an obligation to promote (e.g. public health) implies a conduct obligation and allows governments a broad margin of discretion in implementing necessary policy measures. In order to attribute its failure to meet these minimum core obligations due to the lack of resources, a state must demonstrate that every effort has been made to use all resources that are at its disposal in an effort to satisfy, as a matter of priority, those minimum obligations.

FLINTERMAN in his September 2000 reflections submitted:
A most relevant example of a General Comment as issued by the ESCR Committee is the one on the right to the highest attainable standard of health, General Comment no. 14, adopted in 2000. In this General Comment the ESCR Committee spells out in minute detail the obligations of States parties to implement the right to the highest attainable standard of mental and physical health as provided for in Article 12 ICESCR. A close inspection of this comment reveals that this right has been given a wide scope by the ESCR Committee. The right to health, as is the case with all other economic, social and cultural rights and civil and political rights, is of primary significance in the relationship between the state and its citizens and other persons lawfully residing in its territory. The General Comment does not expressly address the question of whether illegal, undocumented aliens or migrants are also entitled to the right to health.[37] Under general international (human rights) law States have a discretion to determine the legal status of aliens. Once the status of the alien has been legalized or regularized (e.g. the recognition of the alien as a refugee), the alien is entitled to all human rights except that the State in certain areas may impose restrictions, e.g. in the field of the right to vote and to be elected.

A person who is not lawfully residing in a particular country, cannot claim the full scope of the protection of the right to health vis-à-vis the government of that State. That does not mean that such a person is without any protection in the field of the right to health. There may be concrete situations in which persons suffering from physical or mental illness who have no valid residence title, will be entitled to continued residence (a temporary residence permit) where sending such a person back to his own country would amount to inhuman or degrading treatment in light of the quality of the health services in that country.

The right to health is of particular importance in a world which is characterized by large population movements (migration). The debate on the question of who is entitled to the right to health, and especially the right to health care, also has relevance from the perspective of all other economic, social and cultural rights. It is obvious that the gap between the "North" and many countries in the "South" not only exists in the field of health but also in many other areas of economic and social rights, such as the right to work and the right to housing. The recognition by the world community that all human rights are indivisible and that economic, social and cultural rights shall be treated on an equal footing with civil and political rights, could have a far-reaching impact on the refugees, aliens, asylum and migration policies of States around the world.

[37] Ed.: Flinterman expressly underlined that paragrpah 39 of GC 14 on respecting the enjoyment of the right to to health in other countries refers to the right to leave one's country (which is not complemented by a right to enter another one) and does not refer to an obligation to extend health services to an alien once the latter has crossed the border.

LEGAL TEXTS: HEALTH[1]

Constitution of the World Health Organisation, July 1946, *entry into force* 1948

– The enjoyment of the highest attainable standard of health is one of the fundamental rights of every human being without distinction of race, religion, political belief, economic or social condition.
– The extension to all peoples of the benefits of medical, psychological and related knowledge is essential to the fullest attainment of health.

American Declaration of the Rights and Duties of Man, Bogotá, Colombia, 1948

Article XI – Right to the preservation of health and to well-being.
Every person has the right to the preservation of his health through sanitary and social measures relating to food, clothing, housing and medical care, to the extent permitted by public and community resources.

Universal Declaration of Human Rights, 10 December 1948

Article 25
(1) Everyone has the right to a standard of living adequate for the health and well-being of himself and of his family, including food, clothing, housing and medical care and necessary social services, and the right to security in the event of unemployment, sickness, disability, widowhood, old age or other lack of livelihood in circumstances beyond his control.
(2) Motherhood and childhood are entitled to special care and assistance. All children, whether born in or out of wedlock, shall enjoy the same social protection.

European Convention on Social and Medical Assistance and Protocol Thereto, Paris, 11 December 1953

Article 6a
A Contracting Party in whose territory a national of another Contracting Party is lawfully resident shall not repatriate that national on the sole ground that he is in need of assistance.

[1] Please note that it concerns Declarations, Resolutions, Constitutions, Covenants and Conventions, all with a different legal impact (soft, hard, binding, not-binding). Moreover, not all of them have entered into force.

Article 7

a. The provisions of Article 6.a notwithstanding, a Contracting Party may repatriate a national of another Contracting Party resident in its territory on the sole ground mentioned in Article 6.a if the following conditions are fulfilled:

i. the person concerned has not been continuously resident in the territory of that Contracting Party for at least five years if he entered it before attaining the age of 55 years, or for at least ten years if he entered it after attaining that age;

ii. he is in a fit state of health to be transported; and

iii. has no close ties in the territory in which he is resident.

b. The Contracting Parties agree not to have recourse to repatriation except in the greatest moderation and then only where there is no objection on humanitarian grounds.

c. In the same spirit, the Contracting Parties agree that, if they repatriate an assisted person, facilities should be offered to the spouse and children, if any, to accompany the person concerned.

European Social Charter, Turin, 18 October 1961, *entry into force* 26 February 1965

Part I

11. Everyone has the right to benefit from any measures enabling him to enjoy the highest possible standard of health attainable.

13. Anyone without adequate resources has the right to social and medical assistance.

Article 11 – The right to protection of health

With a view to ensuring the effective exercise of the right to protection of health, the Contracting Parties undertake, either directly or in co-operation with public or private organisations, to take appropriate measures designed *inter alia:*

1) to remove as far as possible the causes of ill-health;

2) to provide advisory and educational facilities for the promotion of health and the encouragement of individual responsibility in matters of health;

3) to prevent as far as possible epidemic, endemic and other diseases.

Article 13 – The right to social and medical assistance

With a view to ensuring the effective exercise of the right to social and medical assistance, the Contracting Parties undertake:

1. to ensure that any person who is without adequate resources and who is unable to secure such resources either by his own efforts or from other sources, in particular by benefits under a social security scheme, be granted adequate assistance, and, in case of sickness, the care necessitated by his condition;

2. to ensure that persons receiving such assistance shall not, for that reason, suffer from a diminution of their political or social rights;

3. to provide that everyone may receive by appropriate public or private services such advice and personal help as may be required to prevent, to remove, or to alleviate personal or family want;

4. to apply the provisions referred to in paragraphs 1, 2 and 3 of this article on an equal footing with their nationals to nationals of other Contracting Parties lawfully within their territories, in accordance with their obligations under the European Convention on Social and Medical Assistance, signed at Paris on 11th December 1953.

International Convention on the Elimination of All Forms of Discrimination, 21 December 1965, *entry into force* 4 January 1969

Article 5

In compliance with the fundamental obligations laid down in article 2 of this Convention, States Parties undertake to prohibit and to eliminate racial discrimination in all its forms and to guarantee the right of everyone, without distinction as to race, colour, or national or ethnic origin, to equality before the law, notably in the enjoyment of the following rights:

(e) Economic, social and cultural rights, in particular:

(iv) The right to public health, medical care, social security and social services;

(vi) The right to equal participation in cultural activities;

International Covenant on Economic, Social and Cultural Rights, 1966, *entry into force* 3 January 1976

Article 7

The States Parties to the present Covenant recognize the right of everyone to the enjoyment of just and favourable conditions of work which ensure, in particular:

(b) Safe and healthy working conditions;

Article 12

1. The States Parties to the present Covenant recognize the right of everyone to the enjoyment of the highest attainable standard of physical and mental health.

2. The steps to be taken by the States Parties to the present Covenant to achieve the full realization of this right shall include those necessary for:

(a) The provision for the reduction of the stillbirth-rate and of infant mortality and for the healthy development of the child;

(b) The improvement of all aspects of environmental and industrial hygiene;

(c) The prevention, treatment and control of epidemic, endemic, occupational and other diseases;

(d) The creation of conditions which would assure to all medical service and medical attention in the event of sickness.

Convention on the Elimination of All Forms of Discrimination against Women, 18 December 1979, *entry into force* 3 September 1981

Article 12

1. States Parties shall take all appropriate measures to eliminate discrimination against women in the field of health care in order to ensure, on a basis of equality of men and women, access to health care services, including those related to family planning.

2. Notwithstanding the provisions of paragraph I of this article, States Parties shall ensure to women appropriate services in connection with pregnancy, confinement and the post-natal period, granting free services where necessary, as well as adequate nutrition during pregnancy and lactation.

Article 14

2. States Parties shall take all appropriate measures to eliminate discrimination against women in rural areas in order to ensure, on a basis of equality of men and women, that they participate in and benefit from rural development and, in particular, shall ensure to such women the right:

(b) To have access to adequate health care facilities, including information, counselling and services in family planning;

African [Banjul] Charter on Human and Peoples' Rights, adopted June 27 1981, *entry into force* 21 October 1986

Article 16

1. Every individual shall have the right to enjoy the best attainable state of physical and mental health. 2. States parties to the present Charter shall take the necessary measures to protect the health of their people and to ensure that they receive medical attention when they are sick.

Declaration on the Human Rights of Individuals Who are not Nationals of the Country in Which They Live (GA Resolution A/RES/40/144), 13 December 1985

Article 8

1. Aliens lawfully residing in the territory of a State shall also enjoy, in accordance with the national laws, the following rights, subject to their obligations under article 4:

(a) The right to safe and healthy working conditions, to fair wages and equal remuneration for work of equal value without distinction of any kind, in particular, women being guaranteed conditions of work not inferior to those enjoyed by men, with equal pay for equal work;

(b) The right to join trade unions and other organizations or associations of their choice and to participate in their activities. No restrictions may be placed on the exercise of this right other than those prescribed by law and which are necessary, in a democratic society, in the interests of national security or public order or for the protection of the rights and freedoms of others;

(c) The right to health protection, medical care, social security, social services, education, rest and leisure, provided that they fulfil the requirements under the relevant regulations for participation and that undue strain is not placed on the resources of the State.

2. With a view to protecting the rights of aliens carrying on lawful paid activities in the country in which they are present, such rights may be specified by the Governments concerned in multilateral or bilateral conventions.

Additional Protocol to the American Convention on Human Rights (1969) in the Area of Economic, Social and Cultural Rights "Protocol of San Salvador" 1988

Article 10 – Right to Health

1. Everyone shall have the right to health, understood to mean the enjoyment of the highest level of physical, mental and social well-being.

2. In order to ensure the exercise of the right to health, the States Parties agree to recognize health as a public good and, particularly, to adopt the following measures to ensure that right:

a. Primary health care, that is, essential health care made available to all individuals and families in the community;
b. Extension of the benefits of health services to all individuals subject to the State's jurisdiction;
c. Universal immunization against the principal infectious diseases;
d. Prevention and treatment of endemic, occupational and other diseases;
e. Education of the population on the prevention and treatment of health problems, and
f. Satisfaction of the health needs of the highest risk groups and of those whose poverty makes them the most vulnerable.

Convention on the Rights of the Child, 20 November 1989, *entry into force* 2 September 1990

Article 24
1. States Parties recognize the right of the child to the enjoyment of the highest attainable standard of health and to facilities for the treatment of illness and rehabilitation of health. States Parties shall strive to ensure that no child is deprived of his or her right of access to such health care services.
2. States Parties shall pursue full implementation of this right and, in particular, shall take appropriate measures:
(a) To diminish infant and child mortality;
(b) To ensure the provision of necessary medical assistance and health care to all children with emphasis on the development of primary health care;
(c) To combat disease and malnutrition, including within the framework of primary health care, through, inter alia, the application of readily available technology and through the provision of adequate nutritious foods and clean drinking-water, taking into consideration the dangers and risks of environmental pollution;
(d) To ensure appropriate pre-natal and post-natal health care for mothers;
(e) To ensure that all segments of society, in particular parents and children, are informed, have access to education and are supported in the use of basic knowledge of child health and nutrition, the advantages of breastfeeding, hygiene and environmental sanitation and the prevention of accidents;
(f) To develop preventive health care, guidance for parents and family planning education and services.
3. States Parties shall take all effective and appropriate measures with a view to abolishing traditional practices prejudicial to the health of children.
4. States Parties undertake to promote and encourage international co-operation with a view to achieving progressively the full realization of the right recognized in the present article. In this regard, particular account shall be taken of the needs of developing countries.

International Convention on the Protection of the Rights of All Migrant Workers and Members of Their Families (GA Resolution A/RES/45/158), 18 December 1990 (not yet in force; 16 ratifications as per 1 January 2001)

Article 28
Migrant workers and members of their families shall have the right to receive any medical

care that is urgently required for the preservation of their life or the avoidance of irreparable harm to their health on the basis of equality of treatment with nationals of the State concerned. Such emergency medical care shall not be refused them by reason of any irregularity with regard to stay or employment.

African Charter on the Rights and Welfare of the Child, adopted 1990, *entry into force* 1999

Article xiii – Handicapped Children

1. Every child who is mentally or physically disabled shall have the right to special measures of protection in keeping ' with his physical and moral needs and under conditions which ensure his dignity, promote his self-reliance and active participation in the community.

2. States Parties to the present Charter shall ensure, subject to available resources, to a disabled child and to those responsible for his care, of assistance for which application is made and which is appropriate to the child's condition and in particular shall ensure that the disabled child has effective access to training, preparation for employment and recreation opportunities in a manner conducive to the child achieving the fullest possible social integration, individual development and his cultural and moral development.

The States Parties to the present Charter shall use their available resources with a view to achieving progressively the full convenience of the mentally and physically disabled person to movement and access to public highway, buildings and other places to which the disabled may legitimately want to, have access to.

Article xiv – Health and Health Services

1. Every child shall have the right to enjoy the best attainable state of physical, mental and spiritual health.

2. States Parties to the present Charter[2] shall undertake to pursue the full implementation of this right and in particular shall take measures:

(a) to reduce infant and child mortality rate;

(b) to ensure the provision of necessary medical assistance and health care to all children with emphasis on the development of primary health care;

(c) to ensure the provision of adequate nutrition and safe drinking water;

(d) to combat disease and malnutrition within the framework of primary health care through the application of appropriate technology;

(e) to ensure appropriate health care for expectant and nursing mothers;

(f) to develop preventive earth care and family life education and provision of service;

(g) to integrate basic health service Programmes in national development plans;

(h) to ensure that all sectors of the society, in particular, parents, children, community leaders and community workers are informed and supported in the use of basic knowledge of child health and. nutrition, the advantages of breastfeeding, hygiene. and environmental sanitation and the prevention of domestic and other accidents;

to ensure the meaningful participation of non-governmental organizations, local communities and the beneficiary population in the planning and management of basic

---

[2] Ed.: These states are: Angola, Benin, Burkina Faso, Cameroon, Cape Verde, Lesotho, Malawi, Mali, Mauritius, Mozambique, Niger, Senegal, Seychelles, Togo, Uganda and Zimbabwe.

service programme for children; to support through technical and financial means, the mobilization of local community resources in the development of primary health care for children.

Charter of Fundamental Rights of the European Union, December 2000[3]

Article 35 – Health care
Everyone has the right of access to preventive health care and the right to benefit from medical treatment under the conditions established by national laws and practices. A high level of human health protection shall be ensured in the definition and implementation of all Union policies and activities.

[3] As yet: soft law

GENERAL COMMENT – THE RIGHT TO HEALTH

In view of the comments submitted in Chapter 1.1 it is paramount to carefully study the GENERAL COMMENT ON THE RIGHT TO HEALTH (the right to the highest attainable standard of health).[1] *This General Comment should basically speak for itself, and should be able remove any doubts as to the contents, meaning and impact of this 'right'. In the spring of 2000 the Committee under the CESCR agreed on a text which should indeed be seen as an excellent codification of what would appear to be possible and agreeable at the turn of the century.*

The text focuses on the highest attainable standard of health. It indicates in the first paragraph that the right to health includes certain components which are legally enforceable, but as it then refers to the principle of non-discrimination, it should be concluded that such a conclusion is fairly obvious, and has nothing to do with the right per se, but everything with the right to equal treatment and to the right not to be discriminated against. The 'enforceability' of the right to health per se, would thus appear to be rather limited.

The Comment pays due attention to aspects like availability, accessibility, acceptability and quality. It, is immediately added, however that the precise nature of the facilities, goods and services will vary according to numerous factors, including the country's developmental level, thereby recognizing that it does not concern an absolute level. Of interest is that due reference has been made to WHO's essential drugs list.

As to affordability it has been stated that payment for health services has to be based on the principle of equity ensuring that these services, whether privately or publicly provided, are affordable to all, including socially disadvantaged groups, and it is added that equity demands that poorer households should not be disproportionately burdened with health expenses as compared to richer households. It should hence be submitted that payment for health services is to be considered a normal feature, which indeed may mean that certain services will remain out of reach for certain groups of society, depending on the concept of disproportionality.

The legal obligations of states, of course, feature as well. Progressive realization is the key term, and is interpreted to mean that states have a specific and continuing obligation to move as expeditiously and effectively as possible towards the full realization of the CESCR's Article 12. Attention is paid to the concepts of respect, protect and fulfil, as indicated above in Toebes' contribution. The essential role of international co-operation should be recognized, and states are urged to comply with their commitment to take joint and separate action to achieve the full realization of the right to health. Also in times of emergencies, states should assist each other to the maximum of their capacities.

---

[1] COMMITTEE ON ECONOMIC, SOCIAL AND CULTURAL RIGHTS, Twenty-second session, Geneva, 25 April-12 May 2000; Agenda item 3: The right to the highest attainable standard of health: 11 August 2000. E/C.12/2000/4, CESCR General comment 14. (General Comments)

It is also submitted in the text that while only states are parties to the Covenant and thus ultimately accountable for complying with it, all members of society have responsibilities regarding the realization of this right to health. And that includes the individuals, the professionals, the NGOs, the families, the private business sector, the families, all. This would appear to underline the opinion that irresponsible behaviour may have an impact concerning automatic access to health services.

Of the utmost importance for the debate contained in this Handbook, is the question in how far this right would have a cross-border impact. It can be read that states have to respect the enjoyment of the right to health in other countries and should facilitate access to essential health facilities, goods and services in other countries, wherever possible and provide the necessary aid when required. Prima facie one might wonder whether this should be interpreted as a right to seek and enjoy health services abroad. This issue was, of course, discussed at the September 2000 expert meeting, but all participants came to the conclusion, based on the submissions by Professor Flinterman (see also elsewhere in this Chapter) that the paragraph concerned may amount to a right to seek these services abroad, i.e. the right to leave one's country (and to return, as per the GC on migration, see Chapter ...) but does not include the right to enjoy the services in a country which is not his own. If these services are made available, or if these services are for sale (health as a 'commodity'), then the alien may enjoy and/or purchase those services. A right to the enjoyment of health services outside one's country has thus definitively not been agreed upon.

The right to the highest attainable standard of health (article 12 of the International Covenant on Economic, Social and Cultural Rights); Committee on Economic, Social and Cultural Rights, Geneva 2000.

1. Health is a fundamental human right indispensable for the exercise of other human rights. Every human being is entitled to the enjoyment of the highest attainable standard of health conducive to living a life in dignity. The realization of the right to health may be pursued through numerous, complementary approaches, such as the formulation of health policies, or the implementation of health programmes developed by the World Health Organization (WHO), or the adoption of specific legal instruments. Moreover, the right to health includes certain components which are legally enforceable.[2]

2. The human right to health is recognized in numerous international instruments. Article 25.1 of the Universal Declaration of Human Rights affirms: "Everyone has the right to a standard of living adequate for the health of himself and of his family, including food, clothing, housing and medical care and necessary social services". The International Covenant on Economic, Social and Cultural Rights provides the most comprehensive article on the right to health in international human rights law. In accordance with article 12.1 of the Covenant, States parties recognize "the right of everyone to the enjoyment of the highest attainable standard of physical and mental health", while article 12.2 enumerates, by way of illustration, a number of "steps to be taken by the States parties ... to achieve the

---

[2] For example, the principle of non-discrimination in relation to health facilities, goods and services is legally enforceable in numerous national jurisdictions.

full realization of this right". Additionally, the right to health is recognized, *inter alia*, in article 5 (e) (iv) of the International Convention on the Elimination of All Forms of Racial Discrimination of 1965, in articles 11.1 (f) and 12 of the Convention on the Elimination of All Forms of Discrimination against Women of 1979 and in article 24 of the Convention on the Rights of the Child of 1989. Several regional human rights instruments also recognize the right to health, such as the European Social Charter of 1961 as revised (art. 11), the African Charter on Human and Peoples' Rights of 1981 (art. 16) and the Additional Protocol to the American Convention on Human Rights in the Area of Economic, Social and Cultural Rights of 1988 (art. 10). Similarly, the right to health has been proclaimed by the Commission on Human Rights,[3] as well as in the Vienna Declaration and Programme of Action of 1993 and other international instruments.[4]

3. The right to health is closely related to and dependent upon the realization of other human rights, as contained in the International Bill of Rights, including the rights to food, housing, work, education, human dignity, life, non-discrimination, equality, the prohibition against torture, privacy, access to information, and the freedoms of association, assembly and movement. These and other rights and freedoms address integral components of the right to health.

4. In drafting article 12 of the Covenant, the Third Committee of the United Nations General Assembly did not adopt the definition of health contained in the preamble to the Constitution of WHO, which conceptualizes health as "a state of complete physical, mental and social well-being and not merely the absence of disease or infirmity". However, the reference in article 12.1 of the Covenant to "the highest attainable standard of physical and mental health" is not confined to the right to health care. On the contrary, the drafting history and the express wording of article 12.2 acknowledge that the right to health embraces a wide range of socio-economic factors that promote conditions in which people can lead a healthy life, and extends to the underlying determinants of health, such as food and nutrition, housing, access to safe and potable water and adequate sanitation, safe and healthy working conditions, and a healthy environment.

5. The Committee is aware that, for millions of people throughout the world, the full enjoyment of the right to health still remains a distant goal. Moreover, in many cases, especially for those living in poverty, this goal is becoming increasingly remote. The Committee recognizes the formidable structural and other obstacles resulting from international and other factors beyond the control of States that impede the full realization of article 12 in many States parties.

6. With a view to assisting States parties' implementation of the Covenant and the fulfilment of their reporting obligations, this General Comment focuses on the normative

[3] In its resolution 1989/11.

[4] The Principles for the Protection of Persons with Mental Illness and for the Improvement of Mental Health Care adopted by the United Nations General Assembly in 1991 (resolution 46/119) and the Committee's General Comment No. 5 on persons with disabilities apply to persons with mental illness; the Programme of Action of the International Conference on Population and Development held at Cairo in 1994, as well as the Declaration and Programme for Action of the Fourth World Conference on Women held in Beijing in 1995 contain definitions of reproductive health and women's health, respectively.

content of article 12 (Part I), States parties' obligations (Part II), violations (Part III) and implementation at the national level (Part IV), while the obligations of actors other than States parties are addressed in Part V. The General Comment is based on the Committee's experience in examining States parties' reports over many years.

I. NORMATIVE CONTENT OF ARTICLE 12

7. Article 12.1 provides a definition of the right to health, while article 12.2 enumerates illustrative, non-exhaustive examples of States parties' obligations.

8. The right to health is not to be understood as a right to be *healthy*. The right to health contains both freedoms and entitlements. The freedoms include the right to control one's health and body, including sexual and reproductive freedom, and the right to be free from interference, such as the right to be free from torture, non-consensual medical treatment and experimentation. By contrast, the entitlements include the right to a system of health protection which provides equality of opportunity for people to enjoy the highest attainable level of health.

9. The notion of "the highest attainable standard of health" in article 12.1 takes into account both the individual's biological and socio-economic preconditions and a State's available resources. There are a number of aspects which cannot be addressed solely within the relationship between States and individuals; in particular, good health cannot be ensured by a State, nor can States provide protection against every possible cause of human ill health. Thus, genetic factors, individual susceptibility to ill health and the adoption of unhealthy or risky lifestyles may play an important role with respect to an individual's health. Consequently, the right to health must be understood as a right to the enjoyment of a variety of facilities, goods, services and conditions necessary for the realization of the highest attainable standard of health.

10. Since the adoption of the two International Covenants in 1966 the world health situation has changed dramatically and the notion of health has undergone substantial changes and has also widened in scope. More determinants of health are being taken into consideration, such as resource distribution and gender differences. A wider definition of health also takes into account such socially-related concerns as violence and armed conflict.[5] Moreover, formerly unknown diseases, such as Human Immunodeficiency Virus and Acquired Immunodeficiency Syndrome (HIV/AIDS), and others that have become more widespread, such as cancer, as well as the rapid growth of the world population, have created new obstacles for the realization of the right to health which need to be taken into account when interpreting article 12.

[5] Common article 3 of the Geneva Conventions for the protection of war victims (1949); Additional Protocol I (1977) relating to the Protection of Victims of International Armed Conflicts, art. 75 (2) (a); Additional Protocol II (1977) relating to the Protection of Victims of Non-International Armed Conflicts, art. 4 (a).

11. The Committee interprets the right to health, as defined in article 12.1, as an inclusive right extending not only to timely and appropriate health care but also to the underlying determinants of health, such as access to safe and potable water and adequate sanitation, an adequate supply of safe food, nutrition and housing, healthy occupational and environmental conditions, and access to health-related education and information, including on sexual and reproductive health. A further important aspect is the participation of the population in all health-related decision-making at the community, national and international levels.

12. The right to health in all its forms and at all levels contains the following interrelated and essential elements, the precise application of which will depend on the conditions prevailing in a particular State party:
(a) *Availability.* Functioning public health and health-care facilities, goods and services, as well as programmes, have to be available in sufficient quantity within the State party. The precise nature of the facilities, goods and services will vary depending on numerous factors, including the State party's developmental level. They will include, however, the underlying determinants of health, such as safe and potable drinking water and adequate sanitation facilities, hospitals, clinics and other health-related buildings, trained medical and professional personnel receiving domestically competitive salaries, and essential drugs, as defined by the WHO Action Programme on Essential Drugs.[6]
(b) *Accessibility.* Health facilities, goods and services[7] have to be accessible to everyone without discrimination, within the jurisdiction of the State party. Accessibility has four overlapping dimensions:
– Non-discrimination: health facilities, goods and services must be accessible to all, especially the most vulnerable or marginalized sections of the population, in law and in fact, without discrimination on any of the prohibited grounds.[8]
– Physical accessibility: health facilities, goods and services must be within safe physical reach for all sections of the population, especially vulnerable or marginalized groups, such as ethnic minorities and indigenous populations, women, children, adolescents, older persons, persons with disabilities and persons with HIV/AIDS. Accessibility also implies that medical services and underlying determinants of health, such as safe and potable water and adequate sanitation facilities, are within safe physical reach, including in rural areas. Accessibility further includes adequate access to buildings for persons with disabilities.
– Economic accessibility (affordability): health facilities, goods and services must be affordable for all. Payment for health-care services, as well as services related to the underlying determinants of health, has to be based on the principle of equity, ensuring that these services, whether privately or publicly provided, are affordable for all, including socially disadvantaged groups. Equity demands that poorer households should not be disproportionately burdened with health expenses as compared to richer households.

---

[6] See WHO Model List of Essential Drugs, revised December 1999, WHO Drug Information, vol. 13, No. 4, 1999.

[7] Unless expressly provided otherwise, any reference in this General Comment to health facilities, goods and services includes the underlying determinants of health outlined in paras. 11 and 12 (a) of this General Comment.

[8] See paras. 18 and 19 of this General Comment.

– Information accessibility: accessibility includes the right to seek, receive and impart information and ideas[9] concerning health issues. However, accessibility of information should not impair the right to have personal health data treated with confidentiality.
(c) *Acceptability.* All health facilities, goods and services must be respectful of medical ethics and culturally appropriate, i.e. respectful of the culture of individuals, minorities, peoples and communities, sensitive to gender and life-cycle requirements, as well as being designed to respect confidentiality and improve the health status of those concerned.
(d) *Quality.* As well as being culturally acceptable, health facilities, goods and services must also be scientifically and medically appropriate and of good quality. This requires, *inter alia*, skilled medical personnel, scientifically approved and unexpired drugs and hospital equipment, safe and potable water, and adequate sanitation.

13. The non-exhaustive catalogue of examples in article 12.2 provides guidance in defining the action to be taken by States. It gives specific generic examples of measures arising from the broad definition of the right to health contained in article 12.1, thereby illustrating the content of that right, as exemplified in the following paragraphs.[10]

Article 12.2 (a). The right to maternal, child and reproductive health

14. "The provision for the reduction of the stillbirth rate and of infant mortality and for the healthy development of the child" (art. 12.2 (a))[11] may be understood as requiring measures to improve child and maternal health, sexual and reproductive health services, including access to family planning, pre- and post-natal care, [12] emergency obstetric services and access to information, as well as to resources necessary to act on that information.[13]

---

[9] See article 19.2 of the International Covenant on Civil and Political Rights. This General Comment gives particular emphasis to access to information because of the special importance of this issue in relation to health.

[10] In the literature and practice concerning the right to health, three levels of health care are frequently referred to: *primary health care* typically deals with common and relatively minor illnesses and is provided by health professionals and/or generally trained doctors working within the community at relatively low cost; *secondary health care* is provided in centres, usually hospitals, and typically deals with relatively common minor or serious illnesses that cannot be managed at community level, using specialty-trained health professionals and doctors, special equipment and sometimes in-patient care at comparatively higher cost; *tertiary health care* is provided in relatively few centres, typically deals with small numbers of minor or serious illnesses requiring specialty-trained health professionals and doctors and special equipment, and is often relatively expensive. Since forms of primary, secondary and tertiary health care frequently overlap and often interact, the use of this typology does not always provide sufficient distinguishing criteria to be helpful for assessing which levels of health care States parties must provide, and is therefore of limited assistance in relation to the normative understanding of article 12.

[11] According to WHO, the stillbirth rate is no longer commonly used, infant and under-five mortality rates being measured instead.

[12] *Prenatal* denotes existing or occurring before birth; *perinatal* refers to the period shortly before and after birth (in medical statistics the period begins with the completion of 28 weeks of gestation and is variously defined as ending one to four weeks after birth); *neonatal*, by contrast, covers the period pertaining to the first four weeks after birth; while *post-natal* denotes occurrence after birth. In this General Comment, the more generic terms pre- and post-natal are exclusively employed.

[13] Reproductive health means that women and men have the freedom to decide if and when to reproduce and the right to be informed and to have access to safe, effective, affordable and acceptable methods of family planning of their choice as well as the right of access to appropriate health-care services that will, for example, enable women to go safely through pregnancy and childbirth.

Article 12.2 (b). The right to healthy natural and workplace environments

15. "The improvement of all aspects of environmental and industrial hygiene" (art. 12.2 (b)) comprises, *inter alia*, preventive measures in respect of occupational accidents and diseases; the requirement to ensure an adequate supply of safe and potable water and basic sanitation; the prevention and reduction of the population's exposure to harmful substances such as radiation and harmful chemicals or other detrimental environmental conditions that directly or indirectly impact upon human health.[14] Furthermore, industrial hygiene refers to the minimization, so far as is reasonably practicable, of the causes of health hazards inherent in the working environment.[15] Article 12.2 (b) also embraces adequate housing and safe and hygienic working conditions, an adequate supply of food and proper nutrition, and discourages the abuse of alcohol, and the use of tobacco, drugs and other harmful substances.

Article 12.2 (c). The right to prevention, treatment and control of diseases

16. "The prevention, treatment and control of epidemic, endemic, occupational and other diseases" (art. 12.2 (c)) requires the establishment of prevention and education programmes for behaviour-related health concerns such as sexually transmitted diseases, in particular HIV/AIDS, and those adversely affecting sexual and reproductive health, and the promotion of social determinants of good health, such as environmental safety, education, economic development and gender equity. The right to treatment includes the creation of a system of urgent medical care in cases of accidents, epidemics and similar health hazards, and the provision of disaster relief and humanitarian assistance in emergency situations. The control of diseases refers to States' individual and joint efforts to, *inter alia*, make available relevant technologies, using and improving epidemiological surveillance and data collection on a disaggregated basis, the implementation or enhancement of immunization programmes and other strategies of infectious disease control.

Article 12.2 (d). The right to health facilities, goods and services[16]

17. "The creation of conditions which would assure to all medical service and medical attention in the event of sickness" (art. 12.2 (d)), both physical and mental, includes the provision of equal and timely access to basic preventive, curative, rehabilitative health services and health education; regular screening programmes; appropriate treatment of prevalent diseases, illnesses, injuries and disabilities, preferably at community level; the provision of essential drugs; and appropriate mental health treatment and care. A further important aspect is the improvement and furtherance of participation of the population in

---

[14] The Committee takes note, in this regard, of Principle 1 of the Stockholm Declaration of 1972 which states: "Man has the fundamental right to freedom, equality and adequate conditions of life, in an environment of a quality that permits a life of dignity and well-being", as well as of recent developments in international law, including General Assembly resolution 45/94 on the need to ensure a healthy environment for the well-being of individuals; Principle 1 of the Rio Declaration; and regional human rights instruments such as article 10 of the San Salvador Protocol to the American Convention on Human Rights.

[15] ILO Convention No. 155, art. 4.2.

[16] See para. 12 (b) and note 8 above.

the provision of preventive and curative health services, such as the organization of the health sector, the insurance system and, in particular, participation in political decisions relating to the right to health taken at both the community and national levels.

Article 12. Special topics of broad application

Non-discrimination and equal treatment

18. By virtue of article 2.2 and article 3, the Covenant proscribes any discrimination in access to health care and underlying determinants of health, as well as to means and entitlements for their procurement, on the grounds of race, colour, sex, language, religion, political or other opinion, national or social origin, property, birth, physical or mental disability, health status (including HIV/AIDS), sexual orientation and civil, political, social or other status, which has the intention or effect of nullifying or impairing the equal enjoyment or exercise of the right to health. The Committee stresses that many measures, such as most strategies and programmes designed to eliminate health-related discrimination, can be pursued with minimum resource implications through the adoption, modification or abrogation of legislation or the dissemination of information. The Committee recalls General Comment No. 3, paragraph 12, which states that even in times of severe resource constraints, the vulnerable members of society must be protected by the adoption of relatively low-cost targeted programmes.

19. With respect to the right to health, equality of access to health care and health services has to be emphasized. States have a special obligation to provide those who do not have sufficient means with the necessary health insurance and health-care facilities, and to prevent any discrimination on internationally prohibited grounds in the provision of health care and health services, especially with respect to the core obligations of the right to health.[17] Inappropriate health resource allocation can lead to discrimination that may not be overt. For example, investments should not disproportionately favour expensive curative health services which are often accessible only to a small, privileged fraction of the population, rather than primary and preventive health care benefiting a far larger part of the population.

Gender perspective

20. The Committee recommends that States integrate a gender perspective in their health-related policies, planning, programmes and research in order to promote better health for both women and men. A gender-based approach recognizes that biological and socio-cultural factors play a significant role in influencing the health of men and women. The disaggregation of health and socio-economic data according to sex is essential for identifying and remedying inequalities in health.

---

[17] For the core obligations, see paras. 43 and 44 of the present General Comments.

Women and the right to health

21. To eliminate discrimination against women, there is a need to develop and implement a comprehensive national strategy for promoting women's right to health throughout their life span. Such a strategy should include interventions aimed at the prevention and treatment of diseases affecting women, as well as policies to provide access to a full range of high quality and affordable health care, including sexual and reproductive services. A major goal should be reducing women's health risks, particularly lowering rates of maternal mortality and protecting women from domestic violence. The realization of women's right to health requires the removal of all barriers interfering with access to health services, education and information, including in the area of sexual and reproductive health. It is also important to undertake preventive, promotive and remedial action to shield women from the impact of harmful traditional cultural practices and norms that deny them their full reproductive rights.

Children and adolescents

22. Article 12.2 (a) outlines the need to take measures to reduce infant mortality and promote the healthy development of infants and children. Subsequent international human rights instruments recognize that children and adolescents have the right to the enjoyment of the highest standard of health and access to facilities for the treatment of illness.[18]

The Convention on the Rights of the Child directs States to ensure access to essential health services for the child and his or her family, including pre- and post-natal care for mothers. The Convention links these goals with ensuring access to child-friendly information about preventive and health-promoting behaviour and support to families and communities in implementing these practices. Implementation of the principle of non-discrimination requires that girls, as well as boys, have equal access to adequate nutrition, safe environments, and physical as well as mental health services. There is a need to adopt effective and appropriate measures to abolish harmful traditional practices affecting the health of children, particularly girls, including early marriage, female genital mutilation, preferential feeding and care of male children.[19] Children with disabilities should be given the opportunity to enjoy a fulfilling and decent life and to participate within their community.

23. States parties should provide a safe and supportive environment for adolescents, that ensures the opportunity to participate in decisions affecting their health, to build life-skills, to acquire appropriate information, to receive counselling and to negotiate the health-behaviour choices they make. The realization of the right to health of adolescents is dependent on the development of youth-friendly health care, which respects confidentiality and privacy and includes appropriate sexual and reproductive health services.

24. In all policies and programmes aimed at guaranteeing the right to health of children and adolescents their best interests shall be a primary consideration.

[18] Article 24.1 of the Convention on the Rights of the Child.

[19] See World Health Assembly resolution WHA47.10, 1994, entitled "Maternal and child health and family planning: traditional practices harmful to the health of women and children".

Older persons

25. With regard to the realization of the right to health of older persons, the Committee, in accordance with paragraphs 34 and 35 of General Comment No. 6 (1995), reaffirms the importance of an integrated approach, combining elements of preventive, curative and rehabilitative health treatment. Such measures should be based on periodical check-ups for both sexes; physical as well as psychological rehabilitative measures aimed at maintaining the functionality and autonomy of older persons; and attention and care for chronically and terminally ill persons, sparing them avoidable pain and enabling them to die with dignity.

Persons with disabilities

26. The Committee reaffirms paragraph 34 of its General Comment No. 5, which addresses the issue of persons with disabilities in the context of the right to physical and mental health. Moreover, the Committee stresses the need to ensure that not only the public health sector but also private providers of health services and facilities comply with the principle of non-discrimination in relation to persons with disabilities.

Indigenous peoples

27. In the light of emerging international law and practice and the recent measures taken by States in relation to indigenous peoples, [20] the Committee deems it useful to identify elements that would help to define indigenous peoples' right to health in order better to enable States with indigenous peoples to implement the provisions contained in article 12 of the Covenant. The Committee considers that indigenous peoples have the right to specific measures to improve their access to health services and care. These health services should be culturally appropriate, taking into account traditional preventive care, healing practices and medicines. States should provide resources for indigenous peoples to design, deliver and control such services so that they may enjoy the highest attainable standard of physical and mental health. The vital medicinal plants, animals and minerals necessary to the full enjoyment of health of indigenous peoples should also be protected. The Committee notes that, in indigenous communities, the health of the individual is often linked to the health of the society as a whole and has a collective dimension. In this respect, the Committee considers that development-related activities that lead to the displacement of

---

[20] Recent emerging international norms relevant to indigenous peoples include the ILO Convention No. 169 concerning Indigenous and Tribal Peoples in Independent Countries (1989); articles 29 (c) and (d) and 30 of the Convention on the Rights of the Child (1989); article 8 (j) of the Convention on Biological Diversity (1992), recommending that States respect, preserve and maintain knowledge, innovation and practices of indigenous communities; Agenda 21 of the United Nations Conference on Environment and Development (1992), in particular chapter 26; and Part I, paragraph 20, of the Vienna Declaration and Programme of Action (1993), stating that States should take concerted positive steps to ensure respect for all human rights of indigenous people, on the basis of non-discrimination. See also the preamble and article 3 of the United Nations Framework Convention on Climate Change (1992); and article 10 (2) (e) of the United Nations Convention to Combat Desertification in Countries Experiencing Serious Drought and/or Desertification, Particularly in Africa (1994). During recent years an increasing number of States have changed their constitutions and introduced legislation recognizing specific rights of indigenous peoples.

indigenous peoples against their will from their traditional territories and environment, denying them their sources of nutrition and breaking their symbiotic relationship with their lands, has a deleterious effect on their health.

Limitations

28. Issues of public health are sometimes used by States as grounds for limiting the exercise of other fundamental rights. The Committee wishes to emphasize that the Covenant's limitation clause, article 4, is primarily intended to protect the rights of individuals rather than to permit the imposition of limitations by States. Consequently a State party which, for example, restricts the movement of, or incarcerates, persons with transmissible diseases such as HIV/AIDS, refuses to allow doctors to treat persons believed to be opposed to a government, or fails to provide immunization against the community's major infectious diseases, on grounds such as national security or the preservation of public order, has the burden of justifying such serious measures in relation to each of the elements identified in article 4. Such restrictions must be in accordance with the law, including international human rights standards, compatible with the nature of the rights protected by the Covenant, in the interest of legitimate aims pursued, and strictly necessary for the promotion of the general welfare in a democratic society.

29. In line with article 5.1, such limitations must be proportional, i.e. the least restrictive alternative must be adopted where several types of limitations are available. Even where such limitations on grounds of protecting public health are basically permitted, they should be of limited duration and subject to review.

II. STATES PARTIES' OBLIGATIONS

General legal obligations

30. While the Covenant provides for progressive realization and acknowledges the constraints due to the limits of available resources, it also imposes on States parties various obligations which are of immediate effect. States parties have immediate obligations in relation to the right to health, such as the guarantee that the right will be exercised without discrimination of any kind (art. 2.2) and the obligation to take steps (art. 2.1) towards the full realization of article 12. Such steps must be deliberate, concrete and targeted towards the full realization of the right to health.[21]

31. The progressive realization of the right to health over a period of time should not be interpreted as depriving States parties' obligations of all meaningful content. Rather, progressive realization means that States parties have a specific and continuing obligation to move as expeditiously and effectively as possible towards the full realization of article 12.[22]

---

[21] See General Comment No. 13, para. 43.
[22] See General Comment No. 3, para. 9; General Comment No. 13, para. 44.

32. As with all other rights in the Covenant, there is a strong presumption that retrogressive measures taken in relation to the right to health are not permissible. If any deliberately retrogressive measures are taken, the State party has the burden of proving that they have been introduced after the most careful consideration of all alternatives and that they are duly justified by reference to the totality of the rights provided for in the Covenant in the context of the full use of the State party's maximum available resources.[23]

33. The right to health, like all human rights, imposes three types or levels of obligations on States parties: the obligations to *respect*, *protect* and *fulfil*. In turn, the obligation to fulfil contains obligations to facilitate, provide and promote.[24] The obligation to *respect* requires States to refrain from interfering directly or indirectly with the enjoyment of the right to health. The obligation to *protect* requires States to take measures that prevent third parties from interfering with article 12 guarantees. Finally, the obligation to *fulfil* requires States to adopt appropriate legislative, administrative, budgetary, judicial, promotional and other measures towards the full realization of the right to health.

Specific legal obligations

34. In particular, States are under the obligation to *respect* the right to health by, *inter alia*, refraining from denying or limiting equal access for all persons, including prisoners or detainees, minorities, asylum seekers and illegal immigrants, to preventive, curative and palliative health services; abstaining from enforcing discriminatory practices as a State policy; and abstaining from imposing discriminatory practices relating to women's health status and needs. Furthermore, obligations to respect include a State's obligation to refrain from prohibiting or impeding traditional preventive care, healing practices and medicines, from marketing unsafe drugs and from applying coercive medical treatments, unless on an exceptional basis for the treatment of mental illness or the prevention and control of communicable diseases. Such exceptional cases should be subject to specific and restrictive conditions, respecting best practices and applicable international standards, including the Principles for the Protection of Persons with Mental Illness and the Improvement of Mental Health Care.[25]

In addition, States should refrain from limiting access to contraceptives and other means of maintaining sexual and reproductive health, from censoring, withholding or intentionally misrepresenting health-related information, including sexual education and information, as well as from preventing people's participation in health-related matters. States should also refrain from unlawfully polluting air, water and soil, e.g. through industrial waste from State-owned facilities, from using or testing nuclear, biological or chemical weapons if such testing results in the release of substances harmful to human health, and from limiting access to health services as a punitive measure, e.g. during armed conflicts in violation of international humanitarian law.

---

[23] See General Comment No. 3, para. 9; General Comment No. 13, para. 45.

[24] According to General Comments Nos. 12 and 13, the obligation to fulfil incorporates an obligation to *facilitate* and an obligation to *provide*. In the present General Comment, the obligation to fulfil also incorporates an obligation to *promote* because of the critical importance of health promotion in the work of WHO and elsewhere.

[25] General Assembly resolution 46/119 (1991).

35. Obligations to *protect* include, *inter alia*, the duties of States to adopt legislation or to take other measures ensuring equal access to health care and health-related services provided by third parties; to ensure that privatization of the health sector does not constitute a threat to the availability, accessibility, acceptability and quality of health facilities, goods and services; to control the marketing of medical equipment and medicines by third parties; and to ensure that medical practitioners and other health professionals meet appropriate standards of education, skill and ethical codes of conduct. States are also obliged to ensure that harmful social or traditional practices do not interfere with access to pre- and post-natal care and family-planning; to prevent third parties from coercing women to undergo traditional practices, e.g. female genital mutilation; and to take measures to protect all vulnerable or marginalized groups of society, in particular women, children, adolescents and older persons, in the light of gender-based expressions of violence. States should also ensure that third parties do not limit people's access to health-related information and services.

36. The obligation to *fulfil* requires States parties, *inter alia*, to give sufficient recognition to the right to health in the national political and legal systems, preferably by way of legislative implementation, and to adopt a national health policy with a detailed plan for realizing the right to health. States must ensure provision of health care, including immunization programmes against the major infectious diseases, and ensure equal access for all to the underlying determinants of health, such as nutritiously safe food and potable drinking water, basic sanitation and adequate housing and living conditions. Public health infrastructures should provide for sexual and reproductive health services, including safe motherhood, particularly in rural areas. States have to ensure the appropriate training of doctors and other medical personnel, the provision of a sufficient number of hospitals, clinics and other health-related facilities, and the promotion and support of the establishment of institutions providing counselling and mental health services, with due regard to equitable distribution throughout the country. Further obligations include the provision of a public, private or mixed health insurance system which is affordable for all, the promotion of medical research and health education, as well as information campaigns, in particular with respect to HIV/AIDS, sexual and reproductive health, traditional practices, domestic violence, the abuse of alcohol and the use of cigarettes, drugs and other harmful substances. States are also required to adopt measures against environmental and occupational health hazards and against any other threat as demonstrated by epidemiological data. For this purpose they should formulate and implement national policies aimed at reducing and eliminating pollution of air, water and soil, including pollution by heavy metals such as lead from gasoline. Furthermore, States parties are required to formulate, implement and periodically review a coherent national policy to minimize the risk of occupational accidents and diseases, as well as to provide a coherent national policy on occupational safety and health services.[26]

[26] Elements of such a policy are the identification, determination, authorization and control of dangerous materials, equipment, substances, agents and work processes; the provision of health information to workers and the provision, if needed, of adequate protective clothing and equipment; the enforcement of laws and regulations through adequate inspection; the requirement of notification of occupational accidents and diseases, the conduct of inquiries into serious accidents and diseases, and the production of annual statistics; the protection of workers and their representatives from disciplinary measures for actions properly taken by them in conformity with such a policy; and the provision of occupational health services with es-

37. The obligation to *fulfil (facilitate)* requires States *inter alia* to take positive measures that enable and assist individuals and communities to enjoy the right to health. States parties are also obliged to *fulfil (provide)* a specific right contained in the Covenant when individuals or a group are unable, for reasons beyond their control, to realize that right themselves by the means at their disposal. The obligation to *fulfil (promote)* the right to health requires States to undertake actions that create, maintain and restore the health of the population. Such obligations include: (i) fostering recognition of factors favouring positive health results, e.g. research and provision of information; (ii) ensuring that health services are culturally appropriate and that health care staff are trained to recognize and respond to the specific needs of vulnerable or marginalized groups; (iii) ensuring that the State meets its obligations in the dissemination of appropriate information relating to healthy lifestyles and nutrition, harmful traditional practices and the availability of services; (iv) supporting people in making informed choices about their health.

International obligations

38. In its General Comment No. 3, the Committee drew attention to the obligation of all States parties to take steps, individually and through international assistance and cooperation, especially economic and technical, towards the full realization of the rights recognized in the Covenant, such as the right to health. In the spirit of article 56 of the Charter of the United Nations, the specific provisions of the Covenant (articles 12, 2(1), 22 and 23) and the Alma-Ata Declaration on primary health care, States parties should recognize the essential role of international cooperation and comply with their commitment to take joint and separate action to achieve the full realization of the right to health. In this regard, States parties are referred to the Alma-Ata Declaration which proclaims that the existing gross inequality in the health status of the people, particularly between developed and developing countries, as well as within countries, is politically, socially and economically unacceptable and is, therefore, of common concern to all countries.[27]

39. To comply with their international obligations in relation to article 12, States parties have to respect the enjoyment of the right to health in other countries, and to prevent third parties from violating the right in other countries, if they are able to influence these third parties by way of legal or political means, in accordance with the Charter of the United Nations and applicable international law. Depending on the availability of resources, States should facilitate access to essential health facilities, goods and services in other countries, wherever possible and provide the necessary aid when required.[28] States parties should ensure that the right to health is given due attention in international agreements and, to that end, should consider the development of further legal instruments. In relation to the conclusion of other international agreements, States parties should take steps to ensure that these instruments do not adversely impact upon the right to health. Similarly,

sentially preventive functions. See ILO Occupational Safety and Health Convention, 1981 (No. 155) and Occupational Health Services Convention, 1985 (No. 161).

[27] Article II, Alma-Ata Declaration, Report of the International Conference on Primary Health Care, Alma-Ata, 6-12 September 1978, in: World Health Organization, "Health for All" Series, No. 1, WHO, Geneva, 1978.

[28] See para. 45 of this General Comment.

States parties have an obligation to ensure that their actions as members of international organizations take due account of the right to health. Accordingly, States parties which are members of international financial institutions, notably the International Monetary Fund, the World Bank, and regional development banks, should pay greater attention to the protection of the right to health in influencing the lending policies, credit agreements and international measures of these institutions.

40. States parties have a joint and individual responsibility, in accordance with the Charter of the United Nations and relevant resolutions of the United Nations General Assembly and of the World Health Assembly, to cooperate in providing disaster relief and humanitarian assistance in times of emergency, including assistance to refugees and internally displaced persons. Each State should contribute to this task to the maximum of its capacities. Priority in the provision of international medical aid, distribution and management of resources, such as safe and potable water, food and medical supplies, and financial aid should be given to the most vulnerable or marginalized groups of the population. Moreover, given that some diseases are easily transmissible beyond the frontiers of a State, the international community has a collective responsibility to address this problem. The economically developed States parties have a special responsibility and interest to assist the poorer developing States in this regard.

41. States parties should refrain at all times from imposing embargoes or similar measures restricting the supply of another State with adequate medicines and medical equipment. Restrictions on such goods should never be used as an instrument of political and economic pressure. In this regard, the Committee recalls its position, stated in General Comment No. 8, on the relationship between economic sanctions and respect for economic, social and cultural rights.

42. While only States are parties to the Covenant and thus ultimately accountable for compliance with it, all members of society – individuals, including health professionals, families, local communities, intergovernmental and non-governmental organizations, civil society organizations, as well as the private business sector – have responsibilities regarding the realization of the right to health. State parties should therefore provide an environment which facilitates the discharge of these responsibilities.

Core obligations

43. In General Comment No. 3, the Committee confirms that States parties have a core obligation to ensure the satisfaction of, at the very least, minimum essential levels of each of the rights enunciated in the Covenant, including essential primary health care. Read in conjunction with more contemporary instruments, such as the Programme of Action of the International Conference on Population and Development,[29] the Alma-Ata Declaration provides compelling guidance on the core obligations arising from article 12. Accord-

---

[29] *Report of the International Conference on Population and Development, Cairo, 5-13 September 1994* (United Nations publication, Sales No. E.95.XIII.18), chap. I, resolution 1, annex, chaps. VII and VIII.

ingly, in the Committee's view, these core obligations include at least the following obligations:
(a) To ensure the right of access to health facilities, goods and services on a non-discriminatory basis, especially for vulnerable or marginalized groups;
(b) To ensure access to the minimum essential food which is nutritionally adequate and safe, to ensure freedom from hunger to everyone;
(c) To ensure access to basic shelter, housing and sanitation, and an adequate supply of safe and potable water;
(d) To provide essential drugs, as from time to time defined under the WHO Action Programme on Essential Drugs;
(e) To ensure equitable distribution of all health facilities, goods and services;
(f) To adopt and implement a national public health strategy and plan of action, on the basis of epidemiological evidence, addressing the health concerns of the whole population; the strategy and plan of action shall be devised, and periodically reviewed, on the basis of a participatory and transparent process; they shall include methods, such as right to health indicators and benchmarks, by which progress can be closely monitored; the process by which the strategy and plan of action are devised, as well as their content, shall give particular attention to all vulnerable or marginalized groups.

44. The Committee also confirms that the following are obligations of comparable priority:
(a) To ensure reproductive, maternal (pre-natal as well as post-natal) and child health care;
(b) To provide immunization against the major infectious diseases occurring in the community;
(c) To take measures to prevent, treat and control epidemic and endemic diseases;
(d) To provide education and access to information concerning the main health problems in the community, including methods of preventing and controlling them;
(e) To provide appropriate training for health personnel, including education on health and human rights.

45. For the avoidance of any doubt, the Committee wishes to emphasize that it is particularly incumbent on States parties and other actors in a position to assist, to provide "international assistance and cooperation, especially economic and technical"[30] which enable developing countries to fulfil their core and other obligations indicated in paragraphs 43 and 44 above.

III. VIOLATIONS

46. When the normative content of article 12 (Part I) is applied to the obligations of States parties (Part II), a dynamic process is set in motion which facilitates identification of violations of the right to health. The following paragraphs provide illustrations of violations of article 12.

---

[30] Covenant, art. 2.1.

47. In determining which actions or omissions amount to a violation of the right to health, it is important to distinguish the inability from the unwillingness of a State party to comply with its obligations under article 12. This follows from article 12.1, which speaks of the highest attainable standard of health, as well as from article 2.1 of the Covenant, which obliges each State party to take the necessary steps to the maximum of its available resources. A State which is unwilling to use the maximum of its available resources for the realization of the right to health is in violation of its obligations under article 12. If resource constraints render it impossible for a State to comply fully with its Covenant obligations, it has the burden of justifying that every effort has nevertheless been made to use all available resources at its disposal in order to satisfy, as a matter of priority, the obligations outlined above. It should be stressed, however, that a State party cannot, under any circumstances whatsoever, justify its non-compliance with the core obligations set out in paragraph 43 above, which are non-derogable.

48. Violations of the right to health can occur through the direct action of States or other entities insufficiently regulated by States. The adoption of any retrogressive measures incompatible with the core obligations under the right to health, outlined in paragraph 43 above, constitutes a violation of the right to health. Violations through *acts of commission* include the formal repeal or suspension of legislation necessary for the continued enjoyment of the right to health or the adoption of legislation or policies which are manifestly incompatible with pre-existing domestic or international legal obligations in relation to the right to health.

49. Violations of the right to health can also occur through the omission or failure of States to take necessary measures arising from legal obligations. Violations through *acts of omission* include the failure to take appropriate steps towards the full realization of everyone's right to the enjoyment of the highest attainable standard of physical and mental health, the failure to have a national policy on occupational safety and health as well as occupational health services, and the failure to enforce relevant laws.

Violations of the obligation to respect

50. Violations of the obligation to respect are those State actions, policies or laws that contravene the standards set out in article 12 of the Covenant and are likely to result in bodily harm, unnecessary morbidity and preventable mortality. Examples include the denial of access to health facilities, goods and services to particular individuals or groups as a result of de jure or de facto discrimination; the deliberate withholding or misrepresentation of information vital to health protection or treatment; the suspension of legislation or the adoption of laws or policies that interfere with the enjoyment of any of the components of the right to health; and the failure of the State to take into account its legal obligations regarding the right to health when entering into bilateral or multilateral agreements with other States, international organizations and other entities, such as multinational corporations.

Violations of the obligation to protect

51. Violations of the obligation to protect follow from the failure of a State to take all necessary measures to safeguard persons within their jurisdiction from infringements of the right to health by third parties. This category includes such omissions as the failure to regulate the activities of individuals, groups or corporations so as to prevent them from violating the right to health of others; the failure to protect consumers and workers from practices detrimental to health, e.g. by employers and manufacturers of medicines or food; the failure to discourage production, marketing and consumption of tobacco, narcotics and other harmful substances; the failure to protect women against violence or to prosecute perpetrators; the failure to discourage the continued observance of harmful traditional medical or cultural practices; and the failure to enact or enforce laws to prevent the pollution of water, air and soil by extractive and manufacturing industries.

Violations of the obligation to fulfil

52. Violations of the obligation to fulfil occur through the failure of States parties to take all necessary steps to ensure the realization of the right to health. Examples include the failure to adopt or implement a national health policy designed to ensure the right to health for everyone; insufficient expenditure or misallocation of public resources which results in the non-enjoyment of the right to health by individuals or groups, particularly the vulnerable or marginalized; the failure to monitor the realization of the right to health at the national level, for example by identifying right to health indicators and benchmarks; the failure to take measures to reduce the inequitable distribution of health facilities, goods and services; the failure to adopt a gender-sensitive approach to health; and the failure to reduce infant and maternal mortality rates.

IV. IMPLEMENTATION AT THE NATIONAL LEVEL

Framework legislation

53. The most appropriate feasible measures to implement the right to health will vary significantly from one State to another. Every State has a margin of discretion in assessing which measures are most suitable to meet its specific circumstances. The Covenant, however, clearly imposes a duty on each State to take whatever steps are necessary to ensure that everyone has access to health facilities, goods and services so that they can enjoy, as soon as possible, the highest attainable standard of physical and mental health. This requires the adoption of a national strategy to ensure to all the enjoyment of the right to health, based on human rights principles which define the objectives of that strategy, and the formulation of policies and corresponding right to health indicators and benchmarks. The national health strategy should also identify the resources available to attain defined objectives, as well as the most cost-effective way of using those resources.

54. The formulation and implementation of national health strategies and plans of action should respect, *inter alia*, the principles of non-discrimination and people's participation. In particular, the right of individuals and groups to participate in decision-making pro-

cesses, which may affect their development, must be an integral component of any policy, programme or strategy developed to discharge governmental obligations under article 12. Promoting health must involve effective community action in setting priorities, making decisions, planning, implementing and evaluating strategies to achieve better health. Effective provision of health services can only be assured if people's participation is secured by States.

55. The national health strategy and plan of action should also be based on the principles of accountability, transparency and independence of the judiciary, since good governance is essential to the effective implementation of all human rights, including the realization of the right to health. In order to create a favourable climate for the realization of the right, States parties should take appropriate steps to ensure that the private business sector and civil society are aware of, and consider the importance of, the right to health in pursuing their activities.

56. States should consider adopting a framework law to operationalize their right to health national strategy. The framework law should establish national mechanisms for monitoring the implementation of national health strategies and plans of action. It should include provisions on the targets to be achieved and the time-frame for their achievement; the means by which right to health benchmarks could be achieved; the intended collaboration with civil society, including health experts, the private sector and international organizations; institutional responsibility for the implementation of the right to health national strategy and plan of action; and possible recourse procedures. In monitoring progress towards the realization of the right to health, States parties should identify the factors and difficulties affecting implementation of their obligations.

Right to health indicators and benchmarks

57. National health strategies should identify appropriate right to health indicators and benchmarks. The indicators should be designed to monitor, at the national and international levels, the State party's obligations under article 12. States may obtain guidance on appropriate right to health indicators, which should address different aspects of the right to health, from the ongoing work of WHO and the United Nations Children's Fund (UNICEF) in this field. Right to health indicators require disaggregation on the prohibited grounds of discrimination.

58. Having identified appropriate right to health indicators, States parties are invited to set appropriate national benchmarks in relation to each indicator. During the periodic reporting procedure the Committee will engage in a process of scoping with the State party. Scoping involves the joint consideration by the State party and the Committee of the indicators and national benchmarks which will then provide the targets to be achieved during the next reporting period. In the following five years, the State party will use these national benchmarks to help monitor its implementation of article 12. Thereafter, in the subsequent reporting process, the State party and the Committee will consider whether or not the benchmarks have been achieved, and the reasons for any difficulties that may have been encountered.

Remedies and accountability

59. Any person or group victim of a violation of the right to health should have access to effective judicial or other appropriate remedies at both national and international levels.[31] All victims of such violations should be entitled to adequate reparation, which may take the form of restitution, compensation, satisfaction or guarantees of non-repetition. National ombudsmen, human rights commissions, consumer forums, patients' rights associations or similar institutions should address violations of the right to health.

60. The incorporation in the domestic legal order of international instruments recognizing the right to health can significantly enhance the scope and effectiveness of remedial measures and should be encouraged in all cases. [32] Incorporation enables courts to adjudicate violations of the right to health, or at least its core obligations, by direct reference to the Covenant.

61. Judges and members of the legal profession should be encouraged by States parties to pay greater attention to violations of the right to health in the exercise of their functions.

62. States parties should respect, protect, facilitate and promote the work of human rights advocates and other members of civil society with a view to assisting vulnerable or marginalized groups in the realization of their right to health.

V. OBLIGATIONS OF ACTORS OTHER THAN STATES PARTIES

63. The role of the United Nations agencies and programmes, and in particular the key function assigned to WHO in realizing the right to health at the international, regional and country levels, is of particular importance, as is the function of UNICEF in relation to the right to health of children. When formulating and implementing their right to health national strategies, States parties should avail themselves of technical assistance and cooperation of WHO. Further, when preparing their reports, States parties should utilize the extensive information and advisory services of WHO with regard to data collection, disaggregation, and the development of right to health indicators and benchmarks.

64. Moreover, coordinated efforts for the realization of the right to health should be maintained to enhance the interaction among all the actors concerned, including the various components of civil society. In conformity with articles 22 and 23 of the Covenant, WHO, The International Labour Organization, the United Nations Development Programme, UNICEF, the United Nations Population Fund, the World Bank, regional development banks, the International Monetary Fund, the World Trade Organization and other relevant bodies within the United Nations system, should cooperate effectively with

[31] Regardless of whether groups as such can seek remedies as distinct holders of rights, States parties are bound by both the collective and individual dimensions of article 12. Collective rights are critical in the field of health; modern public health policy relies heavily on prevention and promotion which are approaches directed primarily to groups.

[32] See General Comment No. 2, para. 9.

States parties, building on their respective expertise, in relation to the implementation of the right to health at the national level, with due respect to their individual mandates. In particular, the international financial institutions, notably the World Bank and the International Monetary Fund, should pay greater attention to the protection of the right to health in their lending policies, credit agreements and structural adjustment programmes. When examining the reports of States parties and their ability to meet the obligations under article 12, the Committee will consider the effects of the assistance provided by all other actors. The adoption of a human rights-based approach by United Nations specialized agencies, programmes and bodies will greatly facilitate implementation of the right to health. In the course of its examination of States parties' reports, the Committee will also consider the role of health professional associations and other non-governmental organizations in relation to the States' obligations under article 12.

65. The role of WHO, the Office of the United Nations High Commissioner for Refugees, the International Committee of the Red Cross/Red Crescent and UNICEF, as well as non governmental organizations and national medical associations, is of particular importance in relation to disaster relief and humanitarian assistance in times of emergencies, including assistance to refugees and internally displaced persons. Priority in the provision of international medical aid, distribution and management of resources, such as safe and potable water, food and medical supplies, and financial aid should be given to the most vulnerable or marginalized groups of the population.

CHAPTER 2
HEALTH

Health is a subject everyone has an opinion on. That does not necessarily mean that everyone has a notion of what 'health' is really about, or of the discussions in the 'health-world'. The ins and outs of various diseases are worth being studied as well as the use and usefulness of the WHO essential drugs list (Hogerzeil). Norm- and standard-setting by WHO (van Miltenburg) has to be taken into account whenever legal experts embark on the setting criteria, defining of policy and above all regulating the implementation of the various rules and laws.

Inclusion and exclusion are daily features. Views from the field are indispensable (Mercenier) in order to appreciate the intrinsic difficulty of having to make choices, whereas Sachs gives insight into the global alternatives and the complex world of the medical and pharmaceutical industries.

2.1

INTERNATIONAL NORMS: A SURVEY OF WHO's STANDARD-SETTING[1]

Sabrina van Miltenburg

INTRODUCTION

For the benefit of the discussion in this Handbook, it is worth a while looking at the standard-setting as developed by the World Health Organisation (WHO). In this respect the most recent WHO report (2000) might serve as an ideal guide. However, before entering into the details as set out by WHO it is of relevance to note that, for example, the International Bank for Reconstruction and Development (IBRD, also known as the World Bank) would appear to have embarked on a venue in which development per se is the ultimate goal, but in which the ways to attain that goal may differ from country to country. It could for instance be argued that in view of the correlation between female literacy and the Under 5 Mortality Rate (U5MR) it might be more economic to invest in girls' education than in short-term Primary Health Care (PHC). Similarly, investment in the infrastructure may enable the country concerned to generate the funds with which education and/or PHC may be financed, meaning that priority may have to be given to economic development before embarking on the important issues of health and sanitation. Moreover, the IBRD did not fully exclude that health should also not be the sole responsibility of governments, but was also part and parcel of the privatisation process. In general, it can be submitted that the IBRD does not necessarily put 'health' on top of its agenda, although this conclusion cannot be drawn on the basis of the IBRD ('world development') 2000 report alone, as this report tends to focus on certain themes, health extensively having been dealt with in the 1993 report.[2]

[1] The content of this contribution is based on the World Health Report 2000 of the World Health Organisation. Relevant texts have been combined with corresponding parts throughout the report. Due to a lack of space the original footnotes of the report had to be omitted.

[2] Also note that in November 2000 the IBRD released a series of reports on Wealth Disparities in Health Status in 44 developing countries.

P.J. van Krieken (Ed.), Health, Migration and Return

Remarkably, some of the prominent members of the IBRD think-tank, e.g. Philip Musgrove, Alex Preker and Dean Jamison were lured by the present WHO Director, Ms Gro Harlem Brundtland, to come to Geneva to prepare the WHO 2000 report. It should be recalled that the WHO reports during the 1980s were rather strict where it concerns imposing norms on the governments of the developing world, whereas the reports of the 1990s were far more flexible and tended to go in a direction which would appear to be more in line with the policy developed by the IBRD, i.e. allowing some laissez-faire. It was therefore quite interesting to note that in spite of, or, maybe thanks to, the active participation of former IBRD staff in the WHO 2000 report, the WHO may be considered to have entered an era which is more in line with the message of the 1980s reports, including the emphasis on governmental responsibilities in this realm, albeit translated into late 1990s language (i.e. giving due emphasis to the private sector). The report is aptly entitled Health Systems: Improving Performance.

This first world health report published in the new millennium is quite sensational in making a new start through new approaches to different themes. The report contains a most useful overview in which not only a general outline of the content is given, but which also defines the objectives of the report. To give a clear view of the aims and the findings of the report, a large part of the overview can be found hereinunder. In addition, the statements made by WHO's DG in her interesting preface have been incorporated.

What makes for a good health system? What makes a health system fair? And how do we know whether a health system is performing as well as it could? These questions are the subject of public debate in most countries around the world.

Naturally, answers will depend on the perspective of the respondent. A minister of health defending the budget in parliament; a minister of finance attempting to balance multiple claims on the public purse; a harassed hospital superintendent under pressure to find more beds; a health centre doctor or nurse who has just run out of antibiotics; a news editor looking for a story; a mother seeking treatment for her sick two-year old child; a pressure group lobbying for better services – all will have their views. We in the World Health Organisation need to help all involved to reach a balanced judgement.

Whatever standard we apply, it is evident that health systems in some countries perform well, while others perform poorly. This is not due just to differences in income or expenditure: we know that performance can vary markedly, even in countries with very similar levels of health spending. The way health systems are designed, managed and financed affects peoples' lives and livelihoods. The difference between a well-performing health system and one that is failing can be measured in death, disability, impoverishment, humiliation and despair. (...)

The report breaks new ground in the way that it helps us understand the goals of health systems. Clearly, their defining purpose is to improve and protect health – but they have other intrinsic goals. These are concerned with fairness in the way people pay for health care, and with how systems respond to peoples' expectations with regard to how they are treated. Where health and responsiveness are concerned, achieving a high average level is not good enough: the goals of a health system must also include reducing inequalities, in ways that improve the situation of the worst-off. In this report attainment in relation to these goals provides the basis for measuring the performance of health systems.

In this report, health systems are defined as comprising all the organisations, institutions and resources that are devoted to producing health actions. A health action is defined as any effort, whether in personal health care, public health services or through intersectoral initiatives, whose primary purpose is to improve health.

But while improving health is clearly the main objective of a health system, it is not the only one. The objective of good health itself is really twofold: the best attainable average level – goodness – and the smallest feasible differences among individuals and groups – fairness. Goodness means a health system responding well to what people expect of it; fairness means it responds equally well to everyone, without discrimination. In The world health report 2000 devoted entirely to health systems, the World Health Organisation expands its traditional concern for people's physical and mental well-being to emphasise these other elements of goodness and fairness.

To an unprecedented degree, it takes account of the roles people have as providers and consumers of health services, as financial contributors to health systems, as workers within them, and as citizens engaged in the responsible management, or stewardship, of them. And it looks at how well or how badly systems address inequalities, how they respond to people's expectations, and how much or how little they respect people's dignity, rights and freedoms.

The world health report 2000 also breaks new ground in presenting for the first time an index of national health systems' performance in trying to achieve three overall goals: good health, responsiveness to the expectations of the population, and fairness of financial contribution. (...)

Policy-makers need to know why health systems perform in certain ways and what they can do to improve the situation. All health systems carry out the functions of providing or delivering personal and non-personal health services; generating the necessary human and physical resources to make that possible; raising and pooling the revenues used to purchase services; and acting as the overall stewards of the resources, powers and expectations entrusted to them.

Comparing the way these functions are actually carried out provides a basis for understanding performance variations over time and among countries. (...)

"Improving performance" are (...) the key words and the raison d'être of this report. The overall mission of WHO is the attainment by all people of the highest possible level of health, with special emphasis on closing the gaps within and among countries. The Organisation's ability to fulfil this mission depends greatly on the effectiveness of health systems in Member States – and strengthening those systems is one of WHO's four strategic directions. It connects very well with the other three: reducing the excess mortality of poor and marginalized populations; dealing effectively with the leading risk factors; and placing health at the centre of the broader development agenda.

Combating disease epidemics, striving to reduce infant mortality, and fighting for safer pregnancy are all WHO priorities. But the Organisation will have very little impact in these and other battlegrounds unless it is equally concerned to strengthen the health systems through which the ammunition of life-saving and life-enhancing interventions are delivered to the front line.

This report asserts that the differing degrees of efficiency with which health systems organise and finance themselves, and react to the needs of their populations, explain much of the widening gap in death rates between the rich and poor, in countries and between countries, around the world. Even among countries with similar income levels, there are unacceptably large variations in health outcomes. The report finds that inequalities in life expectancy persist, and are strongly associated with socio-economic class, even in countries that enjoy an average of quite good health. Furthermore the gap between rich and poor widens when life expectancy is divided into years in good health and years of disability. In effect, the poor not only have shorter lives than the non-poor, a bigger part of their lifetime is surrendered to disability.

In short, how health systems – and the estimated 35 million or more people they employ world-wide – perform makes a profound difference to the quality and value, as well as the length of the lives of the billions of people they serve."

CHANGING APPROACHES TO CHANGING SYSTEMS

As the report is entirely dedicated to health systems, the editors duly describe the general history of health systems all over the world. From community-based care to nationally organised health care services in all countries that equally have to deal with limits and shortages of means. Quite logically, the authors have reached the conclusion that, in the light of WHO's "Health for All" strategy, health care services cannot be provided without qualitative and quantitative limits. This has to be acknowledged and a choice has to be made on how to interpret the strategy. Consequently, the authors of the report thereby state that ***"If services are to be provided for all, then not all services can be provided."***

This report's review of the evolution of modern health systems, and their various stages of reform, leaves little doubt that in general they have already contributed enormously to better health for most of the global population during the 20th century.

Today, health systems in all countries, rich and poor, play a bigger and more influential role in people's lives than ever before. Health systems of some sort have existed for as long as people have tried to protect their health and treat diseases. Traditional practices, often integrated with spiritual counselling and providing both preventive and curative care, have existed for thousands of years and often coexist today with modern medicine.

But 100 years ago, organised health systems in the modern sense barely existed. Few people alive then would ever visit a hospital. Most were born into large families and faced an infancy and childhood threatened by a host of potentially fatal diseases – measles, smallpox, malaria and poliomyelitis among them. Infant and child mortality rates were very high, as were maternal mortality rates. Life expectancy was short – even half a century ago it was a mere 48 years at birth. Birth itself invariably occurred at home, rarely with a physician present. (...)

Health systems have undergone overlapping generations of reforms in the past 100 years, including the founding of national health care systems and the extension of social insurance schemes. Later came the promotion of primary health care as a route to achieving affordable universal coverage – the goal of health for all. Despite its many virtues, a criticism of this route has been that it gave too little attention to people's demand for health care, and instead concentrated almost exclusively on their perceived needs Systems have foundered when these two concepts did not match, because then the supply of services offered could not possibly align with both.

In the past decade or so there has been a gradual shift of vision towards what WHO calls the "universalism". Rather than all possible care for everyone, or only the simplest and most basic care for the poor, this means delivery to all of high-quality essential care, defined mostly by criteria of effectiveness, cost and social acceptability. It implies explicit choice of priorities among interventions, respecting the ethical principle that it may be necessary and efficient to ration services, but that it is inadmissible to exclude whole groups of the population.

This shift has been partly due to the profound political and economic changes of the last 20 years or so. These include the transformation from centrally planned to market-oriented economies, reduced state intervention in national economies, fewer government controls, and more decentralization.[3]

Ideologically, this has meant greater emphasis on individual choice and responsibility. Politically, it has meant limiting promises and expectations about what governments should do. But at the same time people's expectations of health systems are greater than ever before. Almost every day another new drug or treatment, or a further advance in medicine and health technology, is announced. This pace of progress is matched only by the rate at which the population seeks its share of the benefits.

---

[3] An interesting text on health care in former socialist countries can be found in the section on Health and Migration elsewhere in this Handbook.

The result is increasing demands and pressures on health systems, including both their public and private sectors, in all countries, rich or poor. Clearly, limits exist on what governments can finance and on what services they can deliver. This report means to stimulate public policies that acknowledge the constraints governments face. If services are to be provided for all, then not all services can be provided.

BEARING RESPONSIBILITY

As stated above, inequalities and gaps between rich and poor continue to exist. It is impossible to expect developing countries to reach the level of development of the Western countries in a short period of time. Should these countries even serve as their model? In fact, the situation of the developed world is everything but soul-saving or perfect. When WHO asks if the rich and healthy can subsidize the poor and sick, the question of who can be defined as rich and healthy and who as poor and sick, immediately rises. Inequalities exist within countries as well and there is always room for improvement everywhere.[4] *While both developing and developed countries are striving for better services and a better overall situation, the level of development increases in parallel. Inequalities are inevitable and factual. The focus should not be on fighting these inequalities but rather on stimulating countries to independently improve their systems. WHO takes a stand on the responsibility for improving a national health system's performance. More than once it is stated in the report that this responsibility in principle lies with governments. Of the health system functions mentioned at the beginning of this outline, according to the authors of the Report stewardship is the most important one. In the final chapter of the Report it is stated that* The health of the people must always be a national priority: government responsibility for it is continuous and permanent. (...) Stewardship is the last of the four health systems functions examined in this report, and it is arguably the most important. It ranks above and differs from the others – service delivery, input production, and financing – for

[4] Various articles on dissatisfying medical situations, inequalities and gaps within developed countries have been published quite recently, e.g. "*Internationaal vergelijkend onderzoek wijst op terreinverlies: 'Gezondheidszorg Nederland achterop'*" NRC Handelsblad (31 August 2000) ; "*Les inégalités sociales face à la santé en France: un état des lieux.*" Le Monde (12 September 2000) ; "*La desigualdad daña la salud de los españoles*" El Pais (14 November 2000) ; "*11,500 lives lost every year because of the health gap*" Independent (26 September 2000). In addition, the World Health Report 2000 states that "within all systems there are many highly skilled, dedicated people working at all levels to improve the health of their communities. As the new century begins, health systems have the power and the potential to achieve further extraordinary improvements. (...) This report finds that many countries are falling far short of their potential, and most are making inadequate efforts in terms of responsiveness and fairness of financial contribution. There are serious shortcomings in the performance of one or more functions in virtually all countries."

one outstanding reason: the ultimate responsibility for the overall performance of a country's health system must always lie with government. Stewardship not only influences the other functions, it makes possible the attainment of each health system goal: improving health, responding to the legitimate expectations of the population, and fairness of contribution. (...)Today in most countries the role of the state in relation to health is changing. People's expectations of health systems are greater than ever before, yet limits exist on what governments can finance and on what services they can deliver. Governments cannot stand still in the face of rising demands. They face complex dilemmas in deciding in which direction to move: they cannot do everything.

The Report sets out to explain why stewardship often fails and how to approach this problem in order to minimise it. Short-sightedness and an attitude of ignorance on the part of Ministries of Health are explicitly mentioned in this respect. They are accused of short-term vision, lack of interest in individuals and private (non-governmental) actors in the field of health (and beyond), too strong a focus on legislation and of refraining from sanctioning the violation and/or evasion of regulations. It is then stated that The notion of stewardship over all health actors and actions deserves renewed emphasis. Much conceptual and practical discussion is needed to improve the definition and measurement of how well stewardship is actually implemented in different settings. But several basic tasks can already be identified: formulating health policy – defining the vision and direction; exerting influence – approaches to regulation; collecting and using intelligence.

An explicit health policy achieves several things: it defines a vision for the future which in turn helps establish benchmarks for the short and medium term. (...) The tasks of formulating and implementing health policy clearly fall to the health ministry. Some countries appear to have issued no national health policy statement in the last decade; in others, policy exists in the form of documents which gather dust and are never translated into action. Too often, health policy and strategic planning have envisaged unrealistic expansion of the publicly funded health care system, sometimes well in excess of national economic growth. Eventually, the policy and planning document is seen as infeasible and is ignored.

The ultimate responsibility for the overall performance of a country's health system lies with government, which in turn should involve all sectors of society in its stewardship. The careful and responsible management of the well being of the population is the very essence of good government. For every country it means establishing the best and fairest health system possible with available resources. The health of the people is always a national priority: government responsibility for it is continuous and permanent. Ministries of health must therefore take on a large part of the stewardship of health systems.

Health policy and strategies need to cover the private provision of services and private financing, as well as state funding and activities. Only in this way can health systems as a whole be oriented towards achieving goals that are in the public interest. Stewardship encompasses the tasks of defining the vision and direction of health policy, exerting influence through regulation and advocacy, and collecting and using information. At the international level, stewardship means mobilising the collective action of countries to generate global public goods such as research, while fostering a shared vision towards more equitable development across and within countries. It also means providing an evidence base to assist countries' efforts to improve the performance of their health systems. (...)

A policy framework should recognise all three health system goals and identify strategies to improve the attainment of each. But not all countries have explicit policies on the overall goodness and fairness of the health system. Public statements about the desired balance among health outcomes, system responsiveness and fairness in financial contribution are yet to be made in many countries. Policy should address the way in which the system's key functions are to be improved.

This report finds that, within governments, many health ministries are seriously shortsighted, focusing on the public sector and often disregarding the – frequently much larger – private provision of care. At worst, governments are capable of turning a blind eye to a 'black market' in health, where widespread corruption, bribery, 'moonlighting' and other illegal practices have flourished for years and are difficult to tackle successfully. Their vision does not extend far enough to help construct a healthier future.

Moreover, some health ministries are prone to losing sight completely of their most important target: the population at large. Patients and consumers may only come into view when rising public dissatisfaction forces them to the ministry's attention.

Many health ministries condone the evasion of regulations that they themselves have created or are supposed to implement in the public interest. Rules rarely enforced are invitations to abuse. A widespread example is the condoning of public employees charging illicit fees from patients and pocketing the proceeds, a practice known euphemistically as 'informal charging'. Such corruption deters poor people from using services they need, making health financing even more unfair, and it distorts overall health priorities.

Many countries have already taken steps to safeguard the rights of patients (...). Even without legislation, the notion of patients' rights and providers' obligations can be promoted and given substance by active stewardship. Where particular practices and procedures are widely practised and known to be harmful, the ministry as a steward has a clear responsibility to combat these with public information. Pharmaceutical sales by unregistered sellers, the dangers of excessive antibiotic prescription and of non-compliance with recommended dosages should all be objects of public stewardship, with active support from information campaigns targeted at different actors – patients, the providers in question, and local health authorities.

[*In a textbox entitled "Towards good stewardship – the case of pharmaceuticals" it is illustrated*] how for one key input – pharmaceuticals – actions at different levels are needed:

Most curative and many preventive health actions depend on medicines. However, medicines also involve powerful economic interests. In poor countries over 50% of household expenditure on health is spent on medicines: within government health budgets pharmaceuticals are usually the second largest item after wages. In industrialized countries drug costs are increasing by 8–12% per year, much faster than consumer prices. Many stakeholders are concerned with pharmaceuticals: manufacturers (both research-based and generic), consumer groups, professional associations, service providers of all types, donor agencies, and different departments of government.

The health system must make essential drugs available and affordable to all who need them, ensure that drugs are of good quality, and that they are used in a therapeutically sound and cost-effective way. The following are the core roles of central government to achieve these objectives:

– ensuring the quality of medicines through effective regulation including systems for market approval, quality assurance, licensing of professionals and inspection of facilities;

– ensuring the affordability and ad-equate financing of essential drugs for the poor and disadvantaged;

– procuring essential drugs for public sector providers, or establishing central tendering with prime vendor or delivery contracts for regional and lower levels;

– developing and supporting a national programme to promote rational and cost-effective drug use by health workers and the public;

– co-ordinating the activities of all stakeholders through the development, implementation and monitoring of a national policy.

Good stewardship at the international level includes supporting governments in fulfilling these core roles. External support may also be useful in the following areas:

– nongovernmental organizations, professional and consumer networks, religious bodies, universities, and private providers need information support and management training;

– national pharmaceuticals manufacturers need training, support and supervision in good manufacturing
practice;

– regulations, training programmes and financial incentives are needed to encourage rational drugs use in the private sector.

The international community must ensure that the overwhelming health problems of the world's poorest countries feature on the agenda of drug manufacturers; mechanisms such as the Global Alliance on Vaccine Initiatives[5] and the Medicines for Malaria Venture are intended to do this.

In the technically and politically complex field of pharmaceuticals, external agencies may need guidance on the best types of support to give developing countries. For example, guidelines for good drug donation practice are available to maximize the value of donated pharmaceuticals.

REGULATION AND THE PRIVATE SECTOR

Under government stewardship the private sector should and could make a positive contribution to the improvement of health systems and their performance.

---

[5] *The report provides due attention to this concept in a textbox on p. 83 entitled* "The Global Alliance for Vaccines and Immunization (GAVI)": Every year, nearly three million children die from diseases that could be prevented with currently available vaccines, yet nearly 30 million of the 130 million children born every year are not receiving vaccinations of any kind. The great majority of unreached children – 25 million – live in countries that have less than US$ 1000 per capita GNP.

The Global Alliance for Vaccines and Immunization (GAVI) is a coalition of public and private interests that was formed in 1999 to ensure that every child is protected against vaccine-prevent-able diseases. GAVI partners include national governments, the Bill and Melinda Gates Children's Vaccine Program, the International Federation of Pharmaceutical Manufacturers Associations (IFPMA), research and technical health institutions, the Rockefeller Foundation, UNICEF, the World Bank Group, and WHO. GAVI is seeking to close the growing gap of vaccine availability between industrialized and developing countries. Beyond the six basic vaccines of the Expanded Programme on Immunization (against poliomyelitis, diphtheria, whooping cough, tetanus, measles and tuberculosis), newer vaccines, such as those for hepatitis B, Haemophilus influenzae type b (Hib), and yellow fever are now widely used in industrialized countries. A major priority is to see that all countries of the world achieve at least 80% immunization coverage by 2005. Based on current assumptions of vaccine de-livery costs it is estimated that an additional $226 million annually are needed to reach this level of cover-age in the poorest countries with the traditional EPI vaccines; to cover the same number of children with the newer vaccines, according to the guidelines adopted at GAVI's first board meeting, would require an additional $352 million.

At the second meeting of the GAVI board, held during the World Economic Forum in Davos in February 2000, the GAVI partners discussed policies for attaining the 80% immunization objective and announced a multimillion-dollar global fund for children's vaccines. Governments, businesses, private philanthropists, and international organizations are working together to manage these resources so as to provide the protection of immunisation to children in all countries, under the campaign title of "The Children's Challenge". Members of GAVI argue that protecting the world's children against preventable diseases is not only a moral imperative but an essential cornerstone of a healthy, stable global society. All countries with incomes of less than $1000 per capita GNP (74 countries worldwide, with the majority in Africa) have been invited to express their interest in collaborating with GAVI in this campaign. Nearly 50 countries, from all WHO regions, have already provided details of their immunization activities and needs. Resources from the fund will primarily be used to purchase vaccines for hepatitis B, Haemophilus influenzae type b (Hib), and yellow fever, and safe injection materials. It is envisaged that GAVI partners at the country level will collaborate with national governments to help close the gaps identified in the country proposals other than those directly related to the provision of vaccines. By placing more of the responsibility for providing the necessary information and commitment on the countries themselves, the GAVI partners are hoping that resulting efforts will be more country-driven and therefore more sustainable.

This regulation is apparently a difficult task for many governments, but fortunately it can be seen that in several countries at least efforts have been made to develop a successful framework for stewardship. This conclusion has been drawn by the authors and can be found in several parts of the report.

The ultimate responsibility for the overall performance of a country's health system lies with government, which in turn should involve all sectors of society in its stewardship. The private sector has the potential to play a positive role in improving the performance of the health system. But for this to happen, governments must fulfil the core public function of stewardship. Proper incentives and adequate information are two powerful tools to improve performance. Stricter oversight and regulation of private sector providers and insurers must be placed high on national policy agendas.

Contrary to what might be expected, the share of private health financing tends to be larger in countries where income levels are lower. But poorer countries seldom have clear lines of policy towards the private sector. They thus have major steps to take in recognising and communicating with the different groups of private providers, the better to influence and regulate them.

Where particular practices and procedures are known to be harmful, the health ministry has a clear responsibility to combat them with public information and legal measures.

To move towards higher quality care, more and better information is commonly required on existing provision, on the interventions offered and on major constraints on service implementation. Local and national risk factors need to be understood. Information on numbers and types of providers is a basic – and often incompletely fulfilled – requirement. An understanding of provider market structure and utilisation patterns is also needed, so that policy-makers know why this array of provision exists, as well as where it is growing.

An explicit, public process of priority setting should be undertaken to identify the contents of a benefit package which should be available to all, and which should reflect local disease priorities and cost effectiveness, among other criteria. Supporting mechanisms – clinical protocols, registration, training, licensing and accreditation processes – need to be brought up to date and used. There is a need for a regulatory strategy, which distinguishes between the components of the private sector and includes the promotion of self-regulation.

Consumers need to be better informed about what is good and bad for their health, why not all of their expectations can be met, and that they have rights which all providers should respect. Aligning organisational structures and incentives with the overall objectives of policy is a task for stewardship, not just for service providers.

Monitoring is needed to assess behavioural change associated with decentralising authority over resources and services, and the effects of different types of contractual relationships with public and private providers. Striking a balance between tight control and the independence needed to motivate providers is a delicate task, for which local solutions must be found. Experimentation and adaptation will be necessary in most settings. A supporting process for exchanging information will be necessary to create a 'virtual network' from a large set of semiautonomous providers.

Regulation is a widely recognized responsibility of health ministries and, in some countries, of social security agencies. (...)In keeping with the policy-making and intelligence tasks, regulation has to encompass all health actions and actors, and not just those of the health ministry or the public sector. While the public health care system is often replete with regulations, few countries (with either high or low income) have developed adequate strategies to regulate the private financing and provision of health services. (...) South Africa has recently changed earlier regulations governing medical schemes to reduce risk selection and increase risk pooling.[6] (...) Recent reforms in the Netherlands demonstrate the difficult balancing act between stronger regulation to protect consumers and increase equity, and looser rules to allow more competition.[7]

---

[6] *How this has worked in practice is described on p. 126 of the report*: The government which came to power in 1994 after South Africa's first democratic elections found itself with a health sector which mirrored the inequalities existing in the wider society. A long-established and well-developed private health care industry accounted for 61% of health care financial re-sources, while providing for the needs of only the affluent 20% of the population. The vast majority of the population had to rely upon poorly distributed, underfunded and fragmented public services. Cost escalation in the private sector typically exceeded inflation during most of the late 1980s and 1990s. The private sector responded to this by limiting benefits, increasing co-payments and accelerating the exclusion of high-risk members from cover, thereby heightening the problem of in-equality.

The new government's response to these challenges was to enact new legislation for medical schemes to offer a minimum benefits package and increased risk pooling. The fundamental principles and objectives at the core of the Act are as follows.

- Community rating. For a given product or option, the only grounds on which premiums may be varied are family size and income. Risk or age rating are prohibited.
- Guaranteed access. No one who can afford the community rated premium may be excluded on grounds of age or health status.
- Increased risk pooling. Caps on the permissible contributions and accumulations through individual medical savings accounts will ensure that a greater proportion of contributions flows into the common risk pool.
- Promoting lifetime coverage. Community rating and guaranteed access will be combined with premium penalties for those who choose only to take out cover later in life, to provide powerful incentives for affordable lifetime membership.
- Prescribed minimum benefits. Every medical scheme must guarantee to cover in full the cost of treating a specified list of conditions and procedures in public facilities, thus greatly decreasing the impact of 'dumping' patients onto the state. (...)

One important group will benefit immediately: HIV-positive members of medical schemes now have access to subsidized care, including drugs for opportunistic infections, whereas previously they were excluded or their entitlement was limited to very low benefit levels.

[7] *On p. 128 of the report it is stated that* The Netherlands' new health insurance system, authorized in 1990, for the first time required all private insurers to provide a comprehensive uniform benefits package. But it promoted competition by giving individuals a subsidy to help them buy compulsory health insurance from competing insurers. Insurers receive risk-adjusted per capita payments

MEASURABLE HEALTH

The health report devotes an entire chapter to the performance of health systems and how to measure this performance. This is important information, enabling those involved in health policy to compare, analyse and evaluate the performance of the health system in their own country. The final objective is then for them to reach conclusions and to adequately react thereto.

To assess a health system, one must measure five things: the overall level of health; the distribution of health in the population; the overall level of responsiveness; the distribution of responsiveness; and the distribution of financial contribution. (...) To assess overall population health and thus to judge how well the objective of good health is being achieved, WHO has chosen to use disability-adjusted life expectancy (DALE), which has the advantage of being directly comparable to life expectancy estimated from mortality alone and is readily compared across populations.

The box hereunder pays due attention to the DALE and DALY principles. These indexes, together with the QALY index (=qualified adjusted life years) are also valid for and used in the developed world as a standard to place limits on care and cure, often in the range of $35,000 per DALY/QALY.[8]

Summary measures of population health
No measure is perfect for the purpose of summing up the health of a population; each way of estimating it violates one or another desirable criterion. The two principal approaches are the burden of disease, which measures losses of good health compared to a long life free of disability, and some measure of life expectancy, adjusted to take account of time lived with a disability. Both ways of summarizing health use the same information about mortality and disability, and both are related to a survivorship curve, such as the bold line between the areas labelled Disability and Mortality in the figure.
The area labelled Mortality represents losses due to death, compared to a high standard of life expectancy: the burden of disease corresponds to all of that area plus a fraction of the area corresponding to time lived with disability. The fraction depends on the disability weights assigned to various states between death and perfect health. Life expectancy without any adjustment corresponds to the areas labelled Survival free of disability and Disability together, the whole area under the survivorship curve. Disability-adjusted life expectancy (DALE) then corresponds to the area for survival plus part of that for disability.
DALE is estimated from three kinds of information: the fraction of the population surviving to each age,

by the government and a separate flat rate premium from each insured person. The more efficient the insurer, the lower the premium paid by the insured. Insurers were also allowed to negotiate lower fees than officially approved provider fees, which was previously prohibited. As a result, private health insurers entered the market for the first time since 1941, and both insurers and providers became involved in quality improvement efforts, which became the focus for competition among insurers rather than competition only on price. But the new system made the goal of reducing health-related inequalities more difficult, as better-off individuals can prepay for more inclusive benefit packages.

[8] This indeed means that services (read: cure) are not provided if this would cost more that the agreed amount per DALY. This is the case with e.g. expensive cholesterol-reducing drugs for heart patients. Although available, with a known positive impact, they will not be reimbursed as they are considered too costly.

calculated from birth and death rates; the prevalence of each type of disability at each age; and the weight as-signed to each type of disability, which may or may not vary with age.
Survival at each age is adjusted downward by the sum of all the disability effects, each of which is the product of a weight and the complement of a prevalence (the share of the population not suffering that disability). These adjusted survival shares are then divided by the initial population, before any mortality occurred, to give the average number of equivalent healthy life years that a new born member of the population could expect to live.
One important difference between the burden of disease estimation using disability-adjusted life years (DALYs) and that of DALE is that the former do, but the latter do not, distinguish the contribution of each disease to the overall result. DALE has the advantage that it does not require as many choices of parameters for the calculation, and it is directly comparable to the more familiar notion of life expectancy without adjustment.

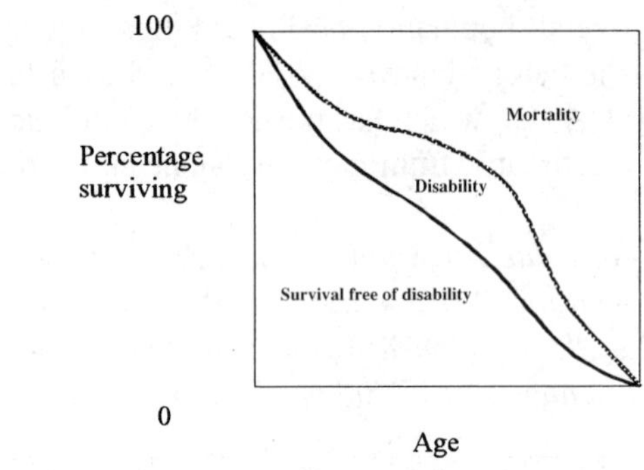

If policy-makers are to act on measures of performance, they need a clear understanding of the key functions that health systems have to undertake. The report defines four key functions: providing services; generating the human and physical resources that make service delivery possible; raising and pooling the resources used to pay for health care; and, most critically, the function of stewardship – setting and enforcing the rules of the game and providing strategic direction for all the different actors involved. (...)

To date, our knowledge about health systems has been hampered by the weakness of routine information systems and insufficient attention to research. This report has thus required a major effort to assemble data, collect new information, and carry out the required analysis and synthesis. It has also drawn on the views of a large number of respondents, within and outside WHO, concerning the interpretation of data and the relative importance of different goals.

The material in this report cannot provide definitive answers to every question about health systems performance. It does though bring together the best available evidence to date. It demonstrates that, despite the complexity of the topic and the limitations of the data, it is possible to get a reasonable approximation of the current situation, in a way that provides an exciting agenda for future work.

I hope that the report will contribute to work on how to assess and improve health systems. Performance assessment allows policy-makers, health providers and the population at large to see themselves in terms of the social arrangements they have constructed to improve health. It invites reflection on the forces that shape performance and the actions that can improve it.

Health outcomes have often been assessed in relation to inputs such as the number of doctors or hospital beds per unit of population. This approach indicates what these inputs actually produce, but it tells little about the health system's potential – what it could do if it used the same level of financial resources to produce and deploy different numbers and combinations of professionals, buildings, equipment and consumables. In these comparisons, the right measure of resources is money, since that is used to buy all the real inputs.

To assess relative performance requires a scale, one end of which establishes an upper limit or 'frontier', corresponding to the most that could be expected of a health system. This frontier – derived using information from many countries but with a specific value for each country – represents the level of attainment which a health system might achieve, but which no country surpasses. At the other extreme, a lower boundary needs to be defined for the least that could be demanded of the health system. With this scale it is possible to see how much of this potential has been realized. In other words, comparing actual attainment with potential shows how far from its own frontier of maximal performance is each country's health system.[9] (...)The overall indicator of attainment, like the five specific

---

[9] *Textbox 2.5 on p. 41 of the report explains how these upper and lower limits are determined:* "WHO's estimates of the upper and lower bounds of health system performance differ in two important ways from most analyses of what health systems actually achieve. The first is that a 'frontier' is meaningful only if no country can lie beyond it, although at least one must lie on it. The frontier or upper limit is therefore estimated by a statistical technique, which allows for errors in one direction only, minimising the distances between the frontier and the calculated performance values. (The lower bound is estimated by the conventional technique of allowing errors in either direction.) The second is that the object is not to explain what each country or health system has attained, so much as to form an estimate of what should be possible. The degree of explanation could be increased by introducing many more variables. If tropical countries show systematically lower achievement in health, because of the effects of many diseases concentrated near the equator, a variable indicating tropical location would raise the explanatory or predictive power. Similarly, if outcomes are worse with respect to equality in ethnically diverse countries, a variable reflecting that heterogeneity would explain the outcomes observed.

The difficulty with the attempt to explain as much as possible is that it leads to a different frontier, according to every additional variable. There would be one for tropical countries and another for colder climates; one for ethnically mixed countries and another for those with more uniform populations; and so on. If performance were measured relative to the frontier for each type of country, almost every health system might look about equally efficient in the use of resources, because less would be expected of some than of others. Every additional explanation would be the equivalent of a reason for not doing better. This is particularly true of explanations related to individual diseases: AIDS and malaria are major causes of health loss in many sub-Saharan African countries, but to include their effects in the estimation of the frontier means judging those countries only according to how well they control all other diseases, as though nothing could be done about AIDS and malaria. This is the reason for estimating the frontier according to nothing but expenditure and human capital, which is a general measure of society's capacity for many kinds of performance, including performance of the health system.

→

achievements which compose it, is an absolute measure. It says how well a country has done in reaching the different goals, but it says nothing about how that outcome compares to what might have been achieved with the resources available in the country. It is *achievement relative to resources* that is the critical measure of a health system's performance.

Thus if Sweden enjoys better health than Uganda – life expectancy is almost exactly twice as long – that is in large part because it spends exactly 35 times as much per capita on its health system. But Pakistan spends almost precisely the same amount per person as Uganda, out of an income per person that is close to Uganda's, and yet it has a life expectancy almost 25 years higher.

For WHO, The world health report 2000 is a milestone in a long-term process. The measurement of health systems performance will be a regular feature of all World health reports from now on – using improved and updated information and methods as they are developed.

FINANCING

An important issue related to health systems is its financing. With respect to the different aspects of this particular complex matter the report provides some important explanations, supported by relevant examples.[10]

The measures of attainment draw on data referring to the past several years, to make the estimates more robust and less susceptible to anomalous values in any one year. The measures of expenditure and human capital are similarly constructed from more than one year's data. Nonetheless, both the outcomes and the factors that determine potential performance are meant to describe the current situation of countries. They do not take into account how past decisions and use of resources may have limited what a system can actually achieve today – which could also be a reason for poor performance – nor do they say how quickly a poorly performing system might be expected to improve and come closer to the frontier.

This way of estimating what is feasible bypasses two particularly complex issues, which are well illustrated by control of tobacco-related mortality and disability. One is that many actions taken by health systems produce results only after a number of years, so that resources used today are not closely related to outcomes today. If a health system somehow persuaded all smokers to quit and no one to take up the habit, it would be many years before there was no more tobacco-induced disease burden. The other is that no health system could reasonably be expected to bring smoking prevalence down to zero any time soon, no matter how hard it tried. Determining how to evaluate progress rather than only a health system's current performance is one of many challenges for future effort."

[10] The International Labour Organisation and International Social Security Association co-published "Modelling in health Care Finance: A compendium of quantitative techniques for health care financing. Quantitative Methods in Social Protection Series" (Cichon et.al. Geneva, 2000), which provides useful information on the basics of modelling and would assist health care professionals in grasping its uses in the policy-making process. This guidebook offers the quantitative and analytic tools needed for sound resource allocation and financial governance of health systems. In addition, it creates synergies and bridges gaps between quantitative health economics, health financing and actuarial science, while presenting methods for improving the efficiency, and lowering the costs, of current health systems.

The purpose of health financing is to make funding available, as well as to set the right financial incentives for providers, to ensure that all individuals have access to effective public health and personal health care. This means reducing or eliminating the possibility that an individual will be unable to pay for such care, or will be impoverished as a result of trying to do so. (...) To ensure that individuals have access to health services, three interrelated functions of health system financing are crucial: revenue collection, pooling of resources, and purchasing of interventions.

Revenue collection is the process by which the health system receives money from households and organizations or companies, as well as from donors.[11] (...)

Pooling is the accumulation and management of revenues in such a way as to ensure that the risk of having to pay for health care is borne by all the members of the pool and not by each contributor individually. Pooling is traditionally known as the 'insurance function' within the health system, whether the insurance is explicit (people knowingly subscribe to a scheme) or implicit (as with tax revenues). (...) Pooling is the main way to spread risks among participants [and] by itself allows for equalization of contributions among members of the pool regardless of their financial risk associated with service utilization. [*The table herunder*] shows four country examples of different arrangements for spreading risk and subsidizing the poor.

Purchasing is the process by which pooled funds are paid to providers in order to deliver a specified or unspecified set of health interventions.

[11] *The following text on donor contributions can be found on p. 96 of the report*: Donor contributions, as a source of revenue for the health system, are of key importance for some developing countries. The absolute amounts of such aid have been large in recent years in Angola, Bangladesh, Ecuador, India, Indonesia, Mozambique, Papua New Guinea, the United Republic of Tanzania and several eastern European countries, but in the larger countries aid is usually only a small share of total health spending or even of government expenditure. In contrast, several countries, particularly in Africa, depend on donors for a large share of total expenditure on health. The fraction can be as high as 40% (Uganda in 1993) or even 84% (Gambia in 1994) and exceeds 20% in 1996 or 1997 in Eritrea, Kenya, The Lao People's Democratic Republic and Mali. Bolivia, Nicaragua, the United Republic of Tanzania and Zimbabwe have obtained 10% to 20% of their resources for health from donors in one or more recent years. Most aid comes in the form of projects, which are separately developed and negotiated between each donor and the national authorities. Although by no means unsuccessful, international co-operation through projects can lead to fragmentation and duplication of effort, particularly when many donors are involved, each focusing on their own geographical or programme priorities. Such an approach forces national authorities to devote significant amounts of time and effort to dealing with donors' priorities and procedures, rather than concentrating on strategic steward-ship and health programme implementation. Donors and governments are increasingly seeing the need to move away from a project approach towards wider programme support to long-term strategic development that is integrated into he budgetary process of the country. In this respect, sector-wide approaches have been effective in countries such as Bangladesh, Ghana and Pakistan.

Country	System	Spreading Risk	Subsidizing the poor
Colombia	- Multiple pools: multiple competing social security organizations, municipal health systems and Ministry of Health	- Intra-pool via non-risk-related contribution and inter-pool via a central risk equalization fund. Mandated minimum benefit package for all members of all pools.	- Intra-pool and inter-pool: salary-related contribution plus explicit subsidy paid to the insurer for the poor to join social security; supply side subsidy via the Ministry of health and municipal systems.
Netherlands	- Multiple pools: predominantly private competing social insurance organizations	- Intra-pool via non-risk-related contribution and inter-pool via a central risk equalization fund.	- Via risk equalization fund, excluding the rich.
Republic of Korea	- Two main pools: national health insurance and the Ministry of Health. - National Health insurance , however, only covers 30% of total health expenditures of any member.	- Intra-pool via non-risk-related contribution. - Explicit single benefit package for all members.	- Salary-related plus supply side subsidy via the Ministry of Health and national health insurance from Ministry of Finance allocations
Zambia	Single predominant formal pool: Ministry of Health/Central Board of health	Intra-pool, implicit single benefit package for all in the Ministry of Health System and at state level. Financed via general taxes.	Intra-pool via general taxation. Supply side subsidy via the Ministry of Health

(...) In countries where external assistance forms an important part of the health system's resources, an important expansion of this approach to policy-making and implementation is represented by sector-wide approaches (SWAPs). The essence of SWAPs is that, under government leadership, a partnership of funding agencies agrees to work together in support of a clear set of policy directions, often sharing many of the implementation procedures, such as supervision, monitoring, reporting, accounting, and purchasing.[12]

---

[12] *Box 6.3 of the report summarises the development of SWAPs*: "A sector-wide approach (SWAP) is a method of working that brings together governments, donors, and other stakeholders within any sector. It is characterized by a set of operating principles rather than a specific package of policies or activities. The approach involves movement over time under government leadership towards: broadening policy dialogue; developing a single sector policy (that addresses private and public sector issues) and a common, realistic expenditure programme; common monitoring arrangements; and more co-ordinated procedures for funding and procurement. Being engaged in a SWAP implies commitment to this direction of change, rather than the comprehensive attainment of all these different elements from the start. It implies changes to the ways in which both governments and donor agencies operate, and in their required staff skills and systems.

This approach has begun to take root primarily in some of the most highly aid-dependent countries. It has been driven by both government and donor concerns about the results of historical approaches to development assistance, which have often involved a combination of 'social sector-blind' macroeconomic adjustment policies and 'sector-fragmenting' projects. Many of the countries

FINDING A BETTER BALANCE

The report says serious imbalances exist in many countries in terms of human and physical resources, technology and pharmaceuticals. Many countries have too few qualified health personnel, others have too many. Health system staff in many low-income nations are inadequately trained, poorly-paid and work in obsolete facilities with chronic shortages of equipment. One result is a 'brain drain' of talented but demoralised professionals who either go abroad or move into private practice. Here again, the poor are most affected.

Overall, governments have too little information on financial flows and the generation of human and material resources. To rectify this, national health accounts (NHAs) should be much more widely calculated and used. They provide the essential information needed to monitor the ratio of capital to recurrent expenditure, or of any one input to the total, and to observe trends. NHAs capture foreign as well as domestic, public as well as private in-puts and usefully assemble data on physical quantities – such as the numbers of nurses, medical equipment, district hospitals – as well as their costs.

NHAs in some form now exist for most countries, but they are still often rudimentary and are not yet widely used as tools of stewardship. NHA data allow the ministry of health to think critically about input purchases by all fundholders in the health system.

The concept of strategic purchasing, discussed in this report, does not only apply to the purchase of health care services: it applies equally to the purchase of health system inputs. Where inputs such as trained personnel, diagnostic equipment and vehicles are purchased directly with public funds, the ministry of health has a direct responsibility to ensure that value for money is obtained – not only in terms of good prices, but also in ensuring that effective use is made of the items purchased.

Where health system inputs are purchased by other agencies (such as private insurers, providers, households or other public agencies) the ministry's stewardship role consists of using its regulatory and persuasive influence to ensure that these purchases improve, rather than worsen, the efficiency of the input mix.

The central ministry may have to decide on major capital decisions, such as tertiary hospitals or medical schools. But regional and district health authorities should be entrusted with the larger number of lower-level purchasing decisions, using guidelines, criteria and procedures promoted by central government.

Ensuring a healthy balance between capital and recurrent spending in the health system requires analysis of trends in both public and private spending and a consideration of both domestic and foreign funds. A clear policy framework,

---

are in Africa, for example, Burkina Faso, Ethiopia, Ghana, Mali, Mozambique, Senegal, Uganda, the United Republic of Tanzania, and Zambia. The other cluster of countries discussing or actively engaging in a SWAP is in Asia: Bangladesh, Cambodia, and Vietnam are examples."

incentives, regulation and public information need to be brought to bear on important capital decisions in the entire system to counter ad hoc decisions and political influence.

In terms of human resources, similar combinations of strategy have had some success in tackling the geographical imbalances common within countries. In general, the content of training needs to be reassessed in relation to workers' actual job content, and overall supply often needs to be adjusted to meet employment opportunities.

In some countries where the social return to medical training is negative, educational institutions are being considered for privatisation or closure. Certainly, public subsidies for training institutions often need to be reconsidered in the light of strategic purchasing. Rebalancing the intake levels of different training facilities is often possible without closure, and might free resources, which could be used to retrain in scarcer skills those health workers who are clearly surplus to requirements.

Major equipment purchases are an easy way for the health system to waste resources, when they are underused, yield little health gain, and use up staff time and recurrent budget. They are also difficult to control. All countries need access to information on technology assessment, though they do not necessarily need to produce this themselves. The stewardship role lies in ensuring that criteria for technology purchase in the public sector (which all countries need) are adhered to, and that the private sector does not receive incentives or public subsidy for its technology purchases unless these further the aim of national policy.

Providers frequently mobilise public support or subscriptions for technology purchase, and stewardship has to ensure that consumers understand why technology purchases have to be rationed like other services. Identifying the opportunity cost of additional technology in terms of other needed services may help to present the case to the public. (...)

Providing health care efficiently requires financial resources to be properly balanced among the many inputs used to deliver health services. (...) In practice, imbalances between investment and recurrent expenditures and among the different categories of inputs are frequent, and create barriers to satisfactory performance. (...)

Human resources, the different kinds of clinical and non-clinical staff who make each individual and public health intervention happen, are the most important of the health system's inputs. The performance of health care systems depends ultimately on the knowledge, skills and motivation of the people responsible for delivering services. (...) a health care system must balance investments in human capital to cover future needs as well as present demands. Some of the most critical and complex input problems relate to human resources.[13]

---

[13] Examples of problems concerning human resources and how to deal with imbalances among health care providers are given on pp. 78-79. →

For very different reasons, both developed and less developed countries record imbalances between the available inputs. (...)[*In comparing*] resource profiles for four high income countries: Denmark, Sweden, the United Kingdom, and the United States [*with those*] for Egypt, Mexico, South Africa and Thailand, four middle income countries [*which*] spend substantially less on all types of health care resources than the group of high income countries, [*it is found that*] there are considerable contrasts in the mix of resources and these differences do not seem

---

Substitution among human resources
A large number of countries face an overall shortage of physicians. Other countries that are following a long-term strategy to shift resources to primary care find that they have too many specialists and too few general practitioners. Many are dealing with the problems by substituting among various health caregivers.
– *Reorientation of specialist physicians*. While limiting admissions to specialist training and changing internship programmes is a long-term strategy to balance the professional distribution of physicians, the reorientation of specialists into family practice is a short-run substitution strategy being used, for example, in central and eastern Europe.
– *Substitution for other health professionals*. The training of a physician may cost three times more than that of a nurse. As a result, training of more nurses as well as other health professionals may be a cost-effective substitute for physicians. In Botswana, training of more nurse practitioners and pharmacists has offset the lack of physicians in some areas.
– *Introduction of new cadres*. Ensuring a closer match between skills and function may demand the creation of new cadres. In Nepal, an educational programme allowed health assistants and other health workers in rural areas to train for higher professional postings.

Human resources problems in service delivery
Numerical imbalances. A recent study of human resources in 18 low and middle income countries, one or more in each of the WHO regions, indicates that most countries experience varying degrees of shortages in qualified health personnel. In sub-Saharan Africa in particular, the limited training capacity and low pay for qualified health workers causes severe problems in service delivery. Elsewhere, for example in Egypt, over-supply is a problem. Generally, shortages and oversupply are defined relative to countries in the same region and at similar levels of development. Oversupply, thus, may be absolute, as is the case for specialist physicians in any countries of eastern Europe and central Asia, or relative to geographical location.

Training and skill mix imbalances. Health care workers are often unqualified for the tasks they perform because of a shortage of training opportunities, as in many African countries, or a mismatch between available skills and the needs and priorities of the health care system, as in eastern Europe and central Asia. The number of physicians and other health personnel with a certain type of training or qualification, however, tells only part of the story. Neither formal training nor professional affiliation necessarily equates with skill in dealing with specific problems.

Distribution imbalances. Almost all countries have some urban/rural imbalances among their human re-sources and face problems in meeting the needs of specific groups such as poor or handicapped people or ethnic minorities. It is almost universally true that providers tend to concentrate in urban areas. In Cambodia, 85% of the population live in rural areas, but only 13% of the government health workers work there. In Angola, 65% live in rural areas, but 85% of health professionals work in urban areas. In Nepal, only 20% of rural physician posts are filled, compared to 96% in urban areas.

Failure of past public policy approaches. Although progress as been made in recent years to develop national policies and plans for human resources for health, they are not fully implemented in most countries. Moreover, very few countries monitor and evaluate the progress and impact of policy implementation.

to be due primarily to differences in income or prices. (...)Whatever a country's income level, there exist efficient ways to allocate health system inputs that will allow the health system to function at its best.The efficient mix will vary over time and across countries, depending on relative prices among inputs, country specific health needs and social priorities."

PROTECTING THE POOR

In the world's poorest countries, most people, particularly the poor, have to pay for health care from their own pockets at the very time they are sick and most in need of it. They are less likely to be members of job-based prepayment schemes, and have less access than better-off groups to subsidised services.

This report presents convincing evidence that prepayment is the best form of revenue collection, while out-of-pocket payment tends to be quite regressive and often impedes access to care. In poor countries, the poor often suffer twice – all of them have to pay an unfair share through taxes or insurance schemes, whether or not they use health services, and some of them have also to pay an even more unfair contribution from their pockets. Evidence from many health systems shows that prepayment through insurance schemes leads to greater financing fairness. The main challenge in revenue collection is to expand prepayment, in which public financing or mandatory insurance will play a central role. In the case of revenue pooling, creating as wide a pool as possible is critical to spreading financial risk for health care, and thus reducing individual risk and the spectre of impoverishment from health expenditures.

Insurance systems entail integration of resources from individual contributors or sources both to pool and to share risks across the population. Achieving greater fairness in financing is only achievable through risk pooling – that is, those who are healthy subsidise those who are sick, and those who are rich subsidise those who are poor. Strategies need to be designed for expansion of risk pooling so that progress can be made in such subsidies.

Raising the level of public finance for health is the most obvious route to increased prepayment. But the poorest countries raise less, in public revenue, as a percentage of national income than middle and upper income countries. Where there is no feasible organisational arrangement to boost prepayment levels, both donors and governments should explore ways of building enabling mechanisms for the development or consolidation of very large pools. Insurance schemes designed to expand membership among the poor would, moreover, be an attractive way to channel external assistance in health, alongside government revenue.

Many countries have employment-based schemes which increase benefits for their privileged membership – mainly employees in the formal sector of the economy – rather than widen them for a larger pool. Low-income countries could encourage different forms of prepayment – job-based, community-based, or provider-based – as part of a preparatory process of consolidating small pools into larger ones. Governments need to promote community rating (i.e. each member of the community pays the same premium), a common benefit package and portability of benefits among insurance schemes, and public funds should pay for the inclusion of poor people in such schemes.

In middle income countries the policy route to fair prepaid systems is through strengthening the often substantial mandatory, income-based and risk-based insurance schemes, again ensuring increased public funding to include the poor. Although most industrialised countries already have very high levels of prepayment, some of these strategies are also relevant to them.

To ensure that prepaid finance obtains the best possible value for money, strategic purchasing needs to replace much of the traditional machinery linking budget holders to service providers. Budget holders will no longer be passive financial intermediaries. Strategic purchasing means ensuring a coherent set of incentives for providers, whether public or private, to encourage them to offer priority interventions efficiently. Selective contracting and the use of several payment mechanisms are needed to set incentives for better responsiveness and improved health outcomes.

WHO's major goal, set in 1978 in Alma Ata, is for all people to attain a level of health that would permit them to lead a socially and economically productive life. This "Health for All" strategy does not imply the end of diseases or ill-health. This would simply be impossible. What it does mean is that essential health care is accessible to everyone. Unfortunately, this goal has not (yet) been achieved. There is still an income-related health gap and in its Report WHO claims that this gap is even widening. According to the report there is hope. It states that the means to accelerate the sharing by the poor in benefits that result from economic progress, indeed exist. As mentioned earlier, the focus should be on a country's own potential and the best way to profit from this. The boxes hereunder illustrate how this can work in practice.[14]

Health knowledge, not income, explains historical change in urban–rural health differences
In the first half of the 19th century, life expectancy was much shorter in London and Paris, respectively, than in the rural areas of England and Wales or of France; a similar difference prevailed between the urban and rural areas of Sweden in the first decades of the 20th century. Large cities were unhealthy because unclean personal habits did more to spread disease when people were crowded together and because garbage and even excrement were accumulated, drawing flies and rodents and contaminating the air and water. Pollution was worsened by burning soft coal and by discharges from factories.
Crowding and poverty produce many of the same problems in the large cities of poor countries today, which typically have more polluted air and water than urban areas in richer countries. Vehicular exhaust, unknown a century ago, is already a major health threat in such areas as Delhi and Mexico City. Rapid growth has made it hard to expand such services as piped water, sewerage facilities and garbage collection fast enough to keep pace. In slum areas, even if safe water is available, many households have no access to sanitary waste disposal, and much garbage is simply dumped or burned in the open. Nonetheless the health consequences are not so severe as in European cities 150 years ago. On one

[14] WHO World Health Report 2000 pp. 5 and 10.

hand, increased knowledge of how diseases are caused and transmitted has led to valiant efforts to reduce contamination, control disease vectors and educate the population to take better care of their health.

On the other hand, even very poor urban dwellers now have better access to effective personal health care than much of the rural population, adding to the inducements to migrate to the city. Slum residents in Lima, for example, are as likely to immunize their children and to take them for medical care when sick as residents of better-off neighbourhoods, and much more likely to do so than people living in Peru's mountainous interior. Both the public health and the personal care interventions have contributed to reversing the urban–rural differences in health status; better health among urban populations is due more to the application of improved knowledge than to higher incomes in cities.

Poverty, ill-health and cost-effectiveness

The series of global estimates of the burden of disease do not distinguish between rich and poor, but an approximate breakdown can be derived by ranking countries by per capita income, aggregating from the lowest and highest incomes to form groups each constituting 20% of the world's population, and studying the distribution of deaths in each group, by age, cause and sex. These estimates show that in 1990, 70% of all deaths and fully 92% of deaths from communicable diseases in the poorest quintile were "excess" compared to the mortality that would have occurred at the death rates of the richest quintile. The figures for total losses of disability-adjusted life years (DALYs) were similar, with a larger contribution from non-communicable diseases. The large difference between the effects of communicable and noncommunicable diseases reflects the concentration of deaths and DALYs lost to communicable diseases among the global poor: about 60% of all ill-health for the poor versus 8–11 % among the richest quintile. This is strongly associated with differences in the age distribution of deaths: just over half of all deaths among the poor occur before 15 years of age, compared to only 4% among the rich. The difference between the poor and the rich is large even in a typical high-mortality African country, and much greater in a typical lower-mortality Latin American country, where deaths at early ages have almost been eliminated among the wealthy.

There are relatively cost-effective interventions available against the diseases that account for most of these rich–poor differences, and particularly to combat deaths and health losses among young children. Interventions costing an estimated $100 or less per DALY saved could deal with 8 or 9 of the 10 leading causes of ill-health under the age of 5 years, and 6 to 8 of the 10 main causes between the ages of 5 and 14 years. All of these are either communicable diseases or forms of malnutrition. Death and disability from these causes is projected to decline rapidly by 2020, roughly equalizing the health damage from communicable and non-communicable diseases among the poor. If the projected rate of de-cline of communicable disease damage could be doubled, the global rich would gain only 0.4 years of life expectancy, but the global poor would gain an additional 4.1 years, narrowing the difference between the two groups from 18.4 to 13.7 years. Doubling the pace of reduction of non-communicable disease damage, in contrast, would preferentially benefit the well-off as well as costing considerably more. The association between poverty and cost-effectiveness is only partial, and probably transitory, but in today's epidemiological and economic conditions it is quite strong.

INSURANCES

One optional aspect of health systems is formed by health insurances. It is often assumed that this is an integral part of health systems and the presence and possibilities of insurances are taken for granted. However, the fact remains that in many countries the possibility of prepaying for health care – and sometimes even cure – only exists on a small scale or simply does not exist at all. The availability of this service is not related to income, good health system performance or a good mix of resource inputs. In a highly developed country, such as the US[15] *for example, health insurance is not a matter of course. In most of Europe, on the other hand, being insured (either privately or through the NHS) is something that goes without saying.*[16] *However, the extent, costs and contents of the services provided form the subject of ongoing discussions, which are included in this chapter in order to stress the point that insurance systems a) are not automatic, b) do not cover all citizens of the North and c) are not part and parcel of Human Rights systems.*

During the 20th century, there have been three overlapping generations of health system reforms. They have been prompted not only by perceived failures in health but also by a quest for greater efficiency, fairness and responsiveness to the expectations of the people that extension to middle income nations of social insurance systems, mostly in the 1940s and 1950s in richer countries and somewhat later in poorer countries. By the late 1960s,many of the systems founded a decade or two earlier were under great stress. Costs were rising, especially as the volume and intensity of hospital-based care increased in developed and developing countries alike. Among systems that were nominally universal in coverage, health services still were used more heavily by the better-off, and efforts to reach the poor were often incomplete. Too many people continued to depend on their own resources to pay for health, and could often get only ineffective or poor quality care.

These problems were apparent, and increasingly acute, in poorer countries. Colonial powers in Africa and Asia, and governments in Latin America, had established health services that for the most part excluded indigenous populations. (...) Charitable missions and public health programmes were relied on to provide some care for the majority, much as in parts of Europe. (...)

Health facilities and clinics had been built, but primarily in urban areas. In most developing countries, major urban hospitals received around two-thirds of all government health budgets, despite serving just 10% to 20% of the population. Studies of what hospitals actually did revealed that half or more of all inpatient spending went towards treating conditions that could often have been managed by ambulatory care, such as diarrhoea, malaria, tuberculosis and acute respiratory infections.

There was, therefore, a need for radical change that would make systems more cost-efficient, equitable, and accessible. A second generation of reforms thus saw the promotion of primary health care as a route to achieving affordable universal coverage. This approach reflected experience with disease control projects in the

---

[15] In the USA the problematic situation concerning health insurance forms the subject of on-going discussions. One example can be found in an article entitled "Critical Conditions, American health care is the best in the world – if you can get it" *The Economist*, September 30th 2000.

[16] In fact, the Erasmus University in Rotterdam (the Netherlands) entertains a special chair in 'Health Insurances'.

1940s in countries such as South Africa, the Islamic Republic of Iran, and former Yugoslavia. It also built on the successes and experiments of China, Cuba, Guatemala, Indonesia, Niger, the United Republic of Tanzania, and Maharashtra State in India. Some of these countries, and others such as Costa Rica and Sri Lanka, achieved very good health outcomes at relatively little cost, adding 15 to 20 years to life expectancy at birth in a span of just two decades. In each case, there was a very strong commitment to assuring a minimum level for all of health services, food and education, along with an adequate supply of safe water and basic sanitation. These were the key elements, along with an emphasis on public health measures relative to clinical care, prevention relative to cure, essential drugs, and education of the public by community health workers. By adopting primary health care as the strategy for achieving the goal of "Health for All" at the Joint WHO/UNICEF International Conference on Primary Health Care held at Alma-Ata, USSR (now Almaty, Kazakhstan) in 1978, WHO reinvigorated efforts to bring basic health care to people everywhere.

The term "primary" quickly acquired a variety of connotations, some of them technical (referring to the first contact with the health system, or the first level of care, or simple treatments that could be delivered by relatively untrained providers, or interventions acting on primary causes of disease) and some political (depending on multisectoral action or community involvement). The multiplicity of meanings and their often contradictory implications for policy help explain why there is no one model of primary care, and why it has been difficult to follow the successful examples of the countries or states that provided the first evidence that a substantial improvement in health could be achieved at affordable cost. There was a substantial effort in many countries to train and use community health workers who could deliver basic, cost-effective services in simple rural facilities to populations that previously had little or no access to modern care. In India, for example, such workers were trained and placed in over 100 000 health posts, intended to serve nearly two-thirds of the population. (...)

The approach emphasized in the primary health care movement can be criticized for giving too little attention to people's demand for health care, which is greatly influenced by perceived quality and responsiveness, and instead concentrating almost exclusively on their presumed needs. Systems fail when these two concepts do not match, because then the supply of services offered cannot possibly align with both. The inadequate attention to demand is reflected in the complete omission of private finance and provision of care from the Alma-Ata Declaration, except insofar as community participation is construed to include small-scale private financing.

Poverty is one reason why needs may not be expressed in demand, and that can be resolved by offering care at low enough cost, not only in money but also in time and non-medical expenses. But there are many other reasons for mismatches between what people need and what they want, and simply providing medical facilities and offering services may do nothing to resolve them. In general, both the first-generation and second-generation reforms have been quite supply-oriented. Concern with demand is more characteristic of changes in the third generation currently under way in many countries, which include such reforms as trying to make "money follow the patient" and shifting away from simply giving providers budgets, which in turn are often determined by supposed needs. (...)

The ideas of responding more to demand, trying harder to assure access for the poor, and emphasizing financing, including subsidies, rather than just provision within the public sector, are embodied in many of the current third-generation reforms. These efforts are more difficult to characterize than earlier reforms, because they arise for a greater variety of reasons and include more experimentation in approach. In part, they reflect the profound political and economic changes that have been taking place in the world. By the late 1980s, the transformation from communist to market-oriented economies was under way in China, central Europe, and the former Soviet Union. Heavy-handed state intervention in the economy was becoming discredited everywhere, leading to widespread divestiture of state enterprises, promotion of more competition both internally and externally, reduction in government regulation and control, and in general, much more reliance on market mechanisms. Ideologically, this meant greater emphasis on individual choice and responsibility. Politically, it meant limiting promises and expectations about what governments should do, particularly via general revenues, to conform better to their actual financial and organizational capacities.

Health systems have not been immune from these large-scale changes. One consequence has been a greatly increased interest in explicit insurance mechanisms, including privately financed insurance. Reforms including such changes have occurred in several Asian countries, universal health insurance being introduced to different degrees in the Republic of Korea, Malaysia, Singapore and China (Province of Taiwan). Reforms to consolidate, extend or merge insurance coverage for greater risk-sharing have also occurred in Argentina, Chile, Colombia and Mexico, and a mixture of insurance and out-of-pocket health care has replaced much of the public system throughout the former communist countries. In developed countries, which already had essentially universal coverage, usually less drastic changes have taken place in how health care is financed. But there have been substantial changes in who determines how resources are used, and in the arrangements by which funds are pooled and paid to providers. General practitioners and primary care physicians, as 'gatekeepers' to the health system, have sometimes been made accountable "not only for their patients' health but also for the wider resource implications of any treatments prescribed. In some countries this role has been formalised through establishing 'budget holding' for general practitioners and primary care physicians, for example, through general practice 'fund holding' in the UK, Health Maintenance Organizations in the USA, and Independent Practice Associations in New Zealand". And in the United States, there has been a great shift of power from providers to insurers, who now largely control the access of doctors and patients to one another.

ORGANISING THE SYSTEM

In order to reach the highest attainable level of health, health services should be organised efficiently. But how is the provision of services to be organised and which services should be provided? In the Report it is stated that health systems are often insufficiently organised and fail to function properly with the result that health services are not fairly provided and distributed. It is often unjustly assumed that this is due to a lack of resources or too little government spending. The fact remains that even when all required resources are available, such as finances,(trained) personnel and equipment, it is actually organisational failures that result in health systems' poor performance.

To require the health system to obtain the greatest possible level of health from the resources devoted to it, is to ask that it be as cost-effective as it can be. This is the basis for emphasizing those interventions that give the most value for money, and giving less priority to those that, much as they may help individuals, contribute little per dollar spent to the improvement of the population's health. It is the implicit basis of the measure of performance with respect to disability-adjusted life expectancy (...). So far as the level of health is concerned, the allocative efficiency of the health system could be enhanced by moving resources from cost-ineffective interventions to cost-effective ones. The potential gains from doing this are sometimes enormous, because the existing pattern of interventions includes some which cost a great deal and produce few additional years of life.

[*The following table*] provides examples of interventions that, if implemented well, can substantially reduce the burden of disease, especially among the poor, and do so at a reasonable cost relative to results.

Examples of interventions	**Main contents of interventions**
Treatment of tuberculosis	Directly observed treatment schedule (DOTS): administration of standardized short-course chemotherapy to all confirmed sputum smear positive cases of TB under supervision in the initial (2–3 months) phase
Maternal health and safe motherhood interventions	Family planning, prenatal and delivery care, clean and safe delivery by trained birth attendant, postpartum care, and essential obstetric care for high risk pregnancies and complications
Family planning	Information and education; availability and correct use of contraceptives
School health interventions	Health education and nutrition interventions, including anti-helminthic treatment, micronutrient supplementation and school meals
Integrated management of childhood illness	Case management of acute respiratory infections, diarrhoea, malaria, measles and malnutrition; immunization, feeding/breastfeeding counselling, micronutrient and iron supplementation, anti-helminthic treatment

HIV/AIDS prevention	Targeted information for sex workers, mass education awareness, counselling, screening, mass treatment for sexually transmitted diseases, safe blood supply
Treatment of sexually transmitted diseases	Case management using syndrome diagnosis and standard treatment algorithm
Immunization (EPI Plus)	BCG at birth; OPV at birth, 6, 10, 14 weeks; DPT at 6, 10, 14 weeks; HepB at birth, 6 and 9 months (optional); measles at 9 months; TT for women of child-bearing age
Malaria	Case management (early assessment and prompt treatment) and selected preventive measures (e.g. impregnated bed nets)
Tobacco control	Tobacco tax, information, nicotine replacement, legal action
Noncommunicable diseases and injuries	Selected early screening and secondary prevention

Finally, in their concluding remarks the authors refer to the Report's main goal; improving performance. The most relevant conclusions, which apply in high as well as low and middle-income countries, are the following:

Even though we are at an early stage in understanding a complex set of interactions, some important conclusions are clear.

– Ultimate responsibility for the performance of a country's health system lies with government. The careful and responsible management of the well being of the population – stewardship – is the very essence of good government. The health of people is always a national priority: government responsibility for it is continuous and permanent.

– Dollar for dollar spent on health, many countries are falling short of their performance potential. The result is a large number of preventable deaths and lives stunted by disability. The impact of this failure is born disproportionately by the poor.

– Health systems are not just concerned with improving people's health but with protecting them against the financial costs of illness. The challenge facing governments in low-income countries is to reduce the regressive burden of out-of-pocket payment for health by expanding prepayment schemes, which spread financial risk and reduce the spectre of catastrophic health care expenditures.

– Within governments, many health ministries focus on the public sector often disregarding the – frequently much larger – private finance and provision of care. A growing challenge is for governments to harness the energies of the private and voluntary sectors in achieving better levels of health systems performance, while offsetting the failures of private markets.

– Stewardship is ultimately concerned with oversight of the entire system, avoiding myopia, tunnel vision and the turning of a blind eye to a system's failings. This report is meant to make that task easier by bringing new evidence into sharp focus.

– In order to move towards higher quality care, a better information base on existing provision is commonly required. Local and national risk factors need to be

understood. Information on numbers and types of providers is a basic – and often incompletely fulfilled – requirement.
– An explicit, public process of priority setting should be undertaken to identify the contents of a benefit package which should be available to all, including those in private schemes, and which should reflect local disease priorities and cost-effectiveness, among other criteria. Rationing should take the form of excluding certain interventions from the benefit package, not leaving out any people.
– In all settings, very high levels of fairly distributed prepayment, and strategic purchasing of health interventions are desirable. (...)To ensure that prepaid finance obtains the best possible value for money, strategic purchasing needs to replace much of the traditional machinery linking budget holders to service providers. Budget holders will no longer be passive financial intermediaries. Strategic purchasing means ensuring a coherent set of incentives for providers, whether public or private, to encourage them to offer priority interventions efficiently.
– The findings reported here (...) show that while much achievement – particularly for the level of health and some aspects of responsiveness – depends greatly on how much a system spends, it is possible to achieve considerable health equality, respect for persons, and financial fairness even at low resource levels.

CONCLUSION

Every country in the world has its own specific health system with its own particular structure. How this structure is developed depends on a great many country-specific (e.g. demographic, cultural, disease-related, financial and environmental) factors. This would mean that each system is to be assessed seperately in order to reach a fair conclusion as to its performance. It also means that it is impossible to compare countries and systems in order to rank these or to formulate advice for better performance, based on comparative studies alone. One system, applied in one country, does not necessarily have the same results, either positive or negative, when applied in another country. A system that performs well in France could be disastrous in Albania, and obviously vice versa.

A conclusion could and should be drawn that decision makers in the North, before embarking on health-related residence cases, should first increase their knowledge and understanding of health systems in their own countries; health systems in the Third World; and the global and universal norms. The WHO World Health Report 2000 thereby makes a superb start: norm-setting is indeed a complicated exercise.

DISEASES

WHO has produced a great many factsheets, most of which contain basic general information on specific illnesses and possible care and cures.[1] *These factsheets can serve as an important tool to determine the seriousness of diseases and possibilities for cures.*

With regard to the subject of this Reader; the relation between health and migration, the problems faced as a result of this relation and possible guidelines and solutions to the problems, it is important to provide some basic background information on those diseases that are most common in this respect. Therefore, it is considered useful to incorporate the most relevant factsheets.

HIV, TB AND MALARIA – THREE MAJOR INFECTIOUS DISEASES THREATS[2]
Background for the G8 discussions

The Problem
Infectious diseases are the leading killer of young people in developing countries:
- Infectious diseases are responsible for almost half of mortality in developing countries. These deaths occur primarily among the poorest people because they do not have access to the drugs and commodities necessary for prevention or cure. Approximately half of infectious disease mortality can be attributed to just three diseases – HIV, TB and malaria. These three diseases cause over 300 million illnesses and more than 5 million deaths each year.
- None of these diseases has an effective vaccine to prevent infection in children and adults.

New information shows that their economic and social burden is staggering:
- In addition to suffering and death, these diseases penalize poor communities, as they perpetuate poverty through work loss, school drop-out, decreased financial investment and increased social instability – creating sizeable social and economic costs.
- For example, Africa's GDP would be up to $100 billion greater if malaria had been eliminated years ago.
- A nation can expect a decline in GDP of 1% per year when more than 20% of the adult population is infected with HIV.
- Increasingly, infectious diseases are moving across borders. Over half of TB cases in some wealthy countries are among foreign-born populations. Over 12,000 cases of malaria were reported among European travellers last year.

---

[1] A complete list of the available factsheets can be found at http://www.who.int/inf-fs/en/index.html .
[2] *(WHO/Bg/01) Bg/01.*

Infectious diseases are a matter of national security:

- Sustainable development is feasible if countries can tame the infectious diseases that disempower their people. If these diseases continue unchecked, they damage the social fabric; diminish agricultural and industrial production; undermine political, social and economic stability; and contribute to regional and global insecurity.

We have affordable and highly effective solutions available now:

- Each of these three diseases can be prevented or treated for between $.05 and $10.
- Many low income countries have shown that, by using available tools both widely and wisely, TB deaths can be reduced five-fold, HIV infection rates can also be reduced by 80% and malaria death rates can be halved.
- But, when a country has a healthcare budget of less than, for example, $50 per capita, the costs of the tools needed to fight TB, malaria and HIV are prohibitive. Many of the world's poor people live in countries with very low budgets for health care.

Action

We need concerted action to use existing tools more effectively – i.e., both widely and wisely

We need a new mechanism to take proven interventions to scale. This mechanism would achieve internationally agreed targets to cut TB and malaria mortality by 50%, and HIV infection by 25%. It would lead to concerted action that:

- Enhances access to effective health care within the homes of those who are vulnerable to infection. Greater impact could be achieved through mass education, making mosquito nets widely available, ensuring access to condoms, and enabling people to use other essential health commodities.
- Uses novel methods to ensure quality of health services whether provided through the private, NGO or public sectors: the use of a range of delivery organisations will increase the potential to getting to all those in need:
- Offers an integration of five primary functions — advocacy for health action, financing of health care, procurement of essential commodities, delivery of services and monitoring results – for a seamless, efficient pipeline. This would lead to global catalysis of standardised and effective services, that are properly co-ordinated, and provided in an efficient manner – without duplication of effort.
- Ensures that when funds are allocated, preference is given to groups well able to deliver effective services, backed up by rigorous surveillance and monitoring routines to document the health gains that result from financial investments.

And there needs to be more development assistance

- The total spent on HIV prevention in sub-Saharan Africa (excluding South Africa) last year was $165 million from all sources. Current estimates now suggest that sums in the order of $ 2.5 billion are needed for prevention alone. Add the costs of care, and the figure rises dramatically.
- In malaria a similar picture: it is estimated that $1 billion a year is required to make a real difference. But the pay-off could be as much as $3-12 billion a year in terms of a boost to the combined GDP of countries in sub-Saharan Africa.
- In the case of TB, $1 billion spent on drugs could mean that 70% of new cases could be treated, resulting in a 50% reduction in mortality over the next 5 years.

The World Health Organization (WHO) is proposing a new framework for concerted action – a massive effort to tackle the infectious diseases which sustain poverty

- Within developing nations, new mechanisms are coming into place to stimulate effective action against infectious diseases through public services, and supplemented where necessary through private channels:
- financial support will reward the achievement of better health outcomes;
- management systems will be accountable to national governments, in ways that are responsive to the interests of people and give communities more control;
- focused partnerships will bring together public, private and voluntary organisations to provide services of consistent quality;
- social marketing will get subsidised goods to those who need them through private channels;
- service quality will be sustained through tightly managed franchises;
- such innovation, increasingly supported by Heads of State of developing countries, and their governments, will increase access to effective technologies;
- countries will be able to achieve the health outcomes they have desired for all their people.
- At a global level, WHO has established incentives to stimulate research and development into new technologies – particularly vaccines and cost-effective drugs. WHO is working for international regulatory and legal systems which balance the need to protect intellectual property and the need to ensure more equitable access to essential medicines. WHO will transform the ways in which the UN agencies work with governments, establishing new high performance efforts that get effective interventions directly to poor people.
- WHO will take advantage of means commonly used by the private sector for economies of scale in the procurement and distribution of key health care commodities and services.
- WHO is changing its tactics in the battle against communicable disease. Working with Heads of State and their governments, WHO is concentrating on getting essential goods and services directly to those in need. Working with those who can provide resources, WHO is offering mechanisms that link the funds invested directly to the results achieved. Working with those who market products, deliver services and monitor achievement, WHO is rewarding excellence.
- WHO will ensure that the international system is well able to handle additional financial commitments, service innovative partnerships, and sustain efficient ways of working. The reward is clear – better health is key – not just to reducing peoples' poverty and increasing national prosperity, but also to global stability and, for everyone, greater peace of mind.

DIABETES MELLITUS[3]

Recently compiled data show that between 120 and 140 million people suffer from

[3] WHO Fact Sheet No. 138, Reviewed November 1999 and see also The Economist, November 11th 2000, in which it is stated that tyhe number of diebetes sufferors worldwide is expected to double in the next two decades.

diabetes mellitus worldwide, and that this number may well double by the year 2025. Much of this increase will occur in developing countries and will be due to population ageing , unhealthy diets, obesity and a sedentary lifestyle.

By 2025, while most people with diabetes in developed countries will be aged 65 years or more, in developing countries most will be in the 45-64 year age range and affected in their most productive years

Diabetes mellitus is a chronic disease caused by inherited and/or acquired deficiency in production of insulin by the pancreas, or by ineffectiveness of the insulin produced. Such a deficiency results in increased concentrations of glucose in blood which in turn leads to damage of many of the body's systems, especially the blood vessels and nerves.

There are two principal forms of diabetes: Type 1, formerly known as insulin-dependent, and Type 2, formerly named non-insulin dependent. In Type 1 diabetes, the pancreas fails to produce the insulin which is essential for survival. This form develops most frequently in children and adolescents, but is being increasingly noted later in life.

Type 2 diabetes is much more common and accounts for about 90-95% of all diabetes cases worldwide. This form of diabetes occurs almost entirely in adults and results from the body's inability to respond properly to the action of insulin produced by the pancreas.

Diabetes mellitus is a hereditary disease. Certain genetic markers are known to increase the risk of developing insulin-dependent diabetes. Such markers have not been described for non-insulin dependent diabetes, though this form is strongly familial.

Symptoms: The symptoms of diabetes may be pronounced or subdued. In Type 1 diabetes, the classic symptoms are excessive secretion of urine (polyuria), thirst (polydipsia), weight loss and a feeling of lassitude. These symptoms may be less marked in Type 2 diabetes. In this form, it can also happen that no early symptoms appear and the disease is only diagnosed several years after its onset, when complications are already present.

Diagnosis: Diabetes may be diagnosed on the basis of a fasting blood glucose value, or the blood suger level taken two hours after a 75g challenge of glucose taken orally.

Insulin: It was discovered by Frederick Banting and Charles Best in 1921 in Canada. This discovery revolutionized treatment of diabetes and prevention of its complications. It transformed Type 1 diabetes from a fatal to a treatable disease. Oral hypoglycaemic agents, diet and physical exercise are other important components of treatment.

People with Type 1 diabetes are usually totally dependent on insulin injections. Such people require daily administration of insulin. For them insulin is a lifesaving medication. The majority of people suffering from diabetes have the non-insulin-dependent form. However, up to 30% of them may use insulin injections some, or all, of the time to control their condition.

Insulin is a costly medication and is unavailable or unaffordable in many poor countries, despite being listed by WHO as an essential drug.

The price of insulin (without syringes and necessary equipment for monitoring blood glucose levels) varies widely from country to country, ranging from less than US$3 to US$22 a vial. The mean cost of a vial of insulin is lowest in the Middle East (US$2.70) and Southeast Asia (US$2.80) with Africa (US$9.20) and South and Central America (US$12.20) in the middle range. However, in many African countries the cost of a vial of insulin may be the equivalent of a month's salary.

Complications: Recent research provides clear evidence of the potential for adequate treatment to delay or even prevent the long term complications of diabetes, which include blindness, kidney failure, heart attacks and even gangrene and amputation of the limbs.

DIABETIC RETINOPATHY is the leading cause of blindness and visual disability in adults in economically developed societies. Findings, consistent from study to study, make it possible to suggest that, after 15 years of diabetes, approximately 2% of people become blind while about 10% develop severe visual handicap.

Diabetes mellitus is associated with damage to the small blood vessels in the retina, resulting in loss of vision.

Loss of vision due to certain types of glaucoma and cataract may also be more common in people with diabetes than in those without the disease.

Loss of vision and blindness in persons with diabetes can be prevented by early detection and treatment of vision-threatening retinopathy: regular eye examinations and timely intervention with laser treatment, or through surgery in cases of advanced retinopathy. A recent study has demonstrated that good metabolic control can also delay the onset and progression of diabetic retinopathy.

There is evidence that, even in developed countries, a large proportion of those in need is not receiving such care due to lack of public and professional awareness. In developing countries, in many of which diabetes is now common, such care is inaccessible to the majority of the population.

Diabetes is a leading cause of RENAL FAILURE, but its frequency varies between populations and is also related to the severity and duration of the disease. Several measures to slow down the progress of renal damage have been identified. They include control of hyperglycaemia, control of hypertension and restriction of dietary protein. Screening and early detection of diabetic kidney disease are an important means of prevention.

HEART DISEASE accounts for 75 % of all deaths among people with diabetes in industrialized countries. Risk factors for heart disease in people with diabetes include cigarette smoking, hypertension, hypercholesterolaemia and obesity. Diabetes negates the protection from heart disease which pre-menopausal women, without diabetes, experience. Recognition and management of these conditions may delay or prevent heart disease in people with diabetes.

DIABETIC NEUROPATHY is probably the most common complication of diabetes. Studies suggest that 50%, or more, of people with diabetes are affected to some degree. Major risk factors of this condition are the level and duration of hyperglycaemia. Neuropathy can lead to sensory loss and damage to the limbs. It is also a major cause of impotence in diabetic men. This fact is often under-recognized. Foot care is an important means of reducing the impact of diabetic neuropathy.

DIABETIC FOOT DISEASE ULCERATION FREQUENTLY LEADING TO AMPUTATION is one of the most costly complications of diabetes, especially in communities with inadequate footwear. It is a result of both vascular and neurological disease processes. Diabetes is the commonest cause of non-traumatic amputation of the lower limb, which may be prevented by regular inspection and good care of the foot.

Diabetes in pregnancy may give rise to several adverse outcomes, including congenital malformations, increased birth weight and an elevated risk of prenatal mortality. Strict metabolic control may reduce these risks to the level of those of non-diabetic expectant mothers.

THE COSTS OF DIABETES[4]

As the number of people with diabetes grows worldwide, the disease takes an ever-increasing proportion of national health care budgets. And, without primary prevention, the diabetes epidemic will continue to grow. Even worse, diabetes is projected to become one of the world's main disablers and killers within the next twenty-five years. Immediate action is needed to stem the tide of diabetes and to introduce cost-effective care and profitable treatment strategies to reverse this process.

According to WHO, only prevention through education and a healthy lifestyle, as well as action taken early in the course of diabetes, are realistically cost-effective, and may improve drastically patients' quality of life. This is especially the case because, once diabetes complications develop, the majority of low-income countries do not have the necessary resources to treat patients. In this case, the only outcome for individuals with diabetes is a painful and distressing life and early death.

Diabetes: the size of the problem

A diabetes epidemic is underway. An estimated 30 million people worldwide had diabetes in 1985. By 1995, this number had shot up to 135 million. Now, WHO predicts a rise to an alarming 300 million by 2025. This situation is increasingly outstretching the health-care resources devoted to diabetes.

For WHO and the International Diabetes Federation, sponsors of World Diabetes Day, this two-fold increase can and must be prevented with the right measures. Without effective preventive measures, the diabetes epidemic will continue to grow.

What are the costs of diabetes?

Because of its chronic nature, the severity of its complications and the means required to control them, diabetes is a costly disease, not only for the affected individual and his/her family, but also for the health authorities. WHO estimates that, for a low-income Indian family with an adult with diabetes, 25% of income will be devoted to diabetes care. For the USA, the corresponding figure is 10%. WHO also estimates that the total health care costs of a person with diabetes in the USA are three times those for people without the condition. It is calculated, for example, that the cost of treating a person with diabetes over a period of three years in the USA comes to around US$ 10,500.

The costs of diabetes affect everyone, everywhere, but they are not only a financial problem. Intangible costs also have great impact on the lives of patients and their families and are the most difficult to quantify.

Direct costs:

Direct costs to individuals and their families include medical care, drugs, insulin and other supplies. Patients may also have to bear other personal costs, such as increased payments for health, life and automobile insurance. Last, but not least, in many cases there is also a potential loss of earnings.

Direct costs to the healthcare sector include hospital services, physician services, lab tests and the daily management of diabetes – which includes availability of products such

[4] Fact Sheet No. 236, November 1999.

as insulin, syringes, oral hypoglycaemic agents and blood-testing equipment. Costs range from relatively low-cost items, such as primary-care consultations and hospital outpatient episodes, to very high-cost items, such as long hospital inpatient stays for the treatment of complications.

Direct costs to society

A number of diabetes patients may not be able to continue working or work as effectively as they could before the onset of their condition. Sickness absence, disability, premature retirement or premature mortality can cause loss of productivity.

Intangible costs

Pain, inconvenience and anxiety are intangible costs, which are just as heavy. Individuals' quality of life is affected as a whole and life expectancy can be significantly reduced. Some activities may have to be foregone in favour of treatment, discrimination may be experienced in the workplace, obtaining jobs may be more difficult, and professional life may be shortened because of complications leading to early disability and even death. Personal relationships, leisure and mobility can also be negatively influenced. And, diabetes treatment can be time-consuming, inconvenient and uncomfortable.

Diabetes complications:

Diabetes is a life-long condition, which requires careful control if the individual is to live a full and normal life. In the long-term, the disease may lead to complications such as blindness, kidney failure and limb amputation, as well as to heart disease and stroke.

The truth is that most of the direct costs of diabetes result from its complications. And, if the predicted increase in the number of persons with complications takes place, the implications for the health services will be grave.

Research has shown that hospital admission is the major cost factor for the health-care sector. The solution is to be found in promoting increased awareness of diabetes and improved self-care for those living with the condition. In this way, the need for hospital stays could be reduced significantly, thus enabling scant resources to be dedicated to other aspects of diabetes care.

The prevention of diabetes:

In diabetes, effective prevention means more cost-effective healthcare. This may be prevention of the onset of diabetes itself (primary prevention) or the prevention of its immediate and longer-term consequences (secondary prevention).

Primary prevention protects susceptible individuals from developing diabetes. It has an impact by reducing both the need for diabetes care and the need to treat diabetic complications. A reliable example of this measure is a study undertaken among a susceptible population in China. Lifestyle modifications (appropriate diet and increased physical activity and a consequent reduction of weight), supported by a continuous education programme, were used to achieve *a reduction of at least one third* in the progression to diabetes over a six-year period.

This type of measure is easy and low-cost and can be used in even the poorest regions of the world and when resources are limited.

Secondary prevention includes early detection, prevention and treatment. Appropriate action taken at the right time is beneficial in terms of quality of life, and is very cost-effective, especially if it can prevent hospital admission.

Secondary prevention measures:

- The monitoring of high blood pressure and raised blood lipids, as well as the control of blood glucose levels, can substantially reduce the risk of developing complications and slow their progression in all types of diabetes.
- Another finance-saving strategy is the prevention of foot ulceration and amputation. Effective foot-care reduces both the frequency and length of hospital stays and the incidence of amputation in diabetes patients by as much as 50%.
- Screening and early treatment for retinopathy is also very cost-effective, given the devastating direct, indirect and intangible costs of blindness.
- Screening for protein in urine is another valid preventive measure to prevent or slow down the inevitable progression to kidney failure. Furthermore, there is evidence that screening for traces of protein is cost saving, as it allows even earlier intervention in the natural course of kidney disease.

MALARIA[5]

Malaria is by far the world's most important tropical parasitic disease, and kills more people than any other communicable disease except tuberculosis. In many developing countries, and in Africa especially, malaria exacts an enormous toll in lives, in medical costs, and in days of labour lost. The causative agents in humans are four species of Plasmodium protozoa (single-celled parasites) – P.falciparum, P.vivax, P.ovale and P.malariae. Of these, P.falciparum accounts for the majority of infections and is the most lethal. Malaria is a curable disease if promptly diagnosed and adequately treated.

Prevalence

The geographical area affected by malaria has shrunk considerably over the past 50 years, but control is becoming more difficult and gains are being eroded. Increased risk of the disease is linked with changes in land use linked to activities like road building, mining, logging and agricultural and irrigation projects, particularly in "frontier" areas like the Amazon and in South-East Asia. Other causes of its spread include global climatic change, disintegration of health services, armed conflicts and mass movements of refugees. The emergence of multi-drug resistant strains of parasite is also exacerbating the situation. Via the explosion of easy international travel, imported cases of malaria are now more frequently registered in developed countries. Malaria is re-emerging in areas where it was previously under control or eradicated e.g., in the Central Asian Republics of Tajikistan and Azerbaijan, and in Korea.

The current global picture:

- Malaria is a public health problem today in more than 90 countries, inhabited by a total of some 2 400 million people – 40% of the world's population.

[5] WHO Fact Sheet No 94, Revised October 1998.

- Worldwide prevalence of the disease is estimated to be in the order of 300-500 million clinical cases each year.
- More than 90% of all malaria cases are in sub-Saharan Africa.
- Mortality due to malaria is estimated to be over 1 million deaths each year. The vast majority of deaths occur among young children in Africa, especially in remote rural areas with poor access to health services.
- Other high-risk groups are women during pregnancy, and non-immune travellers, refugees, displaced persons and labourers entering endemic areas.
- Malaria epidemics related to political upheavals, economic difficulties and environmental problems also contribute in the most dramatic way to death tolls and human suffering.
- Malaria is endemic in a total of 101 countries and territories: 45 countries in WHO's African Region, 21 in WHO's Americas Region, 4 in WHO's European region, 14 in WHO's Eastern Mediterranean Region, 8 in WHO's South-East Asia Region, and 9 in WHO's Western Pacific Region.

Symptoms

Symptoms of malaria include fever, shivering, pain in the joints, headache, repeated vomiting, generalized convulsions and coma. Severe anaemia (exacerbated by malaria) is often the attributable cause of death in areas with intense malaria transmission. If not treated, the disease, particularly that caused by P. falciparum, progresses to severe malaria. Severe malaria is associated with death.

Transmission

Malaria is transmitted by Anopheline mosquitoes, the number and type of which determine the extent of transmission in a given area. Transmission of malaria is affected by climate and geography, and often coincides with the rainy season.

Communities Affected

More than any other disease, malaria hits the poor. Malaria endemic countries are some of the world's poorest. Costs to countries include costs for control and lost workdays – estimated to be 1-5% of GPD in Africa. For the individual, costs include the price of treatment and prevention, and lost income.

Rural communities are particularly affected. In rural areas, the rainy season is often a time of intense agricultural activity, when poor families earn most of their annual income. Malaria can make these families even poorer. In children, malaria leads to chronic school absenteeism and there can be impairment of learning ability.

Urban malaria is increasing due to unplanned development around large cities, particularly in Africa and South Asia.

Malaria and Children

Malaria kills one child every 30 seconds. This preventable disease has reached epidemic proportions in many regions of the world, and continues to spread unchecked.

In absolute numbers, malaria kills 3 000 children per day under five years of age. It is a death toll that far exceeds the mortality rate from AIDS.

African children under five years of age are chronic victims of malaria, suffering an average of six bouts a year. Fatally-afflicted children often die less than 72 hours after developing symptoms. In those children who survive, malaria also drains vital nutrients from children, impairing their physical and intellectual development. Malarial sickness is also one of the principal reasons for poor school attendance.

Yet protection of children can often be easy. Randomised control trials conducted in the Gambia, Ghana, Kenya and Burkina Faso, for example, show that about 30 per cent of child deaths could be avoided if children slept under bednets regularly treated with recommended insecticides such as pyrethroids. Unlike early insecticides such as DDT, pyrethroids are derived from a naturally occurring substance, PYRETHRUM, which is found in chrysanthemums and will remain effective for 6 to 12 months.

Malaria is also particularly dangerous during pregnancy. It causes severe anaemia, and is a major factor contributing to maternal deaths in malaria endemic regions. Pregnant mothers who have malaria and are HIV-positive are more likely to pass on their HIV status to their unborn child.

UNICEF recognises that malaria is one of the five major causes of under-five child mortality. The agency has made the disease a top priority, supporting malaria control programmes in 32 countries, 27 of which are in Africa.

Economic Costs

The estimated costs of malaria, in terms of strains on the health systems and economic activity lost, are enormous. In affected countries, as many as 3 in 10 hospital beds are occupied by victims of malaria. In Africa, where malaria reaches a peak at harvest time and hits young adults especially hard, a single bout of the disease costs an estimated equivalent of 10 working days.

Research indicates that affected families clear only 40 per cent of land for crops compared with healthy families. Knowledge about malaria is markedly low among affected populations. In one recent survey in Ghana, for example, half the respondents did not know that mosquitoes transmit malaria.

The direct and indirect costs of malaria in sub-Saharan Africa exceed $2 billion, according to 1997 estimates.

According to UNICEF, the average cost for each nation in Africa to implement malaria control programmes is estimated to be at least $300,000 a year. This amounts to about six US cents ($.06) per person for a country of 5 million people.

Malaria's reach is spreading

In malaria endemic parts of the world, a change in risk of malaria can be the unintended result of economic activity or agricultural policy that changes the use of land (e.g. creation of dams, irrigation schemes, commercial tree cropping and deforestation).

"Global warming" and other climatic events such as "El Niño" also play their role in increasing risk of disease. The disease has now spread to highland areas of Africa, for example, while El Niño events have an impact on malaria because the associated weather disturbances influence vector breeding sites, and hence transmission of the disease. Many areas have experienced dramatic increases in the incidence of malaria during extreme weather events correlated to El Niño. Moreover, outbreaks may not only be larger, but more severe, as populations affected may not have high levels of immunity. Quantitative leaps in malaria incidence coincident with ENSO (El Niño/Southern Oscillation) events have been recorded around the world: in Bolivia, Columbia, Ecuador, Peru and Venezuela in South America, in Rwanda in Africa, and in Pakistan and Sri Lanka in Asia.

In today's international world, the phenomenon of "airport malaria", or the importing of malaria by international travellers, is becoming commonplace. The United Kingdom, for example, registered 2364 cases of malaria in 1997, all of them imported by travellers. 'Weekend malaria', which happens when city dwellers in Africa return to their rural settings, is becoming an increasing problem.

Prevention and cure

Prevention of malaria encompasses a variety of measures that may protect against infection or against the development of disease in infected individuals. Measures that protect against infection are directed against the mosquito vector. These can be personal (individual or household) protection measures e.g., protective clothing, repellents, bednets, or community/population protection measures e.g., use of insecticides or environmental management to control transmission. Measures which protect against disease but not against infection include chemoprophylaxis.

In spite of drug resistance, malaria is a curable disease, not an inevitable burden. Although there is only a limited number of drugs, if these are used properly and targeted to those at greatest risk, malaria disease and deaths can be reduced, as has been shown in many countries.

Disease management through early diagnosis and prompt treatment is fundamental to malaria control. It is a basic right of affected populations and needs to be available wherever malaria occurs. Children and pregnant women, on whom malaria has its greatest impact in most parts of the world, are especially important.

In many countries, most cases of malaria are diagnosed and treated in the home or by private sector practitioners, often incompletely and with irrational regimens. This speeds up the spread of parasite resistance to antimalarial drugs, which poses another problem – a dramatic rise in the cost of treating uncomplicated malaria (which has been seen in some parts of the world).

Whereas formerly malaria control depended on insecticide spraying, now the selective use of protection methods, including vector control, is proving cost-effective and more sustainable. So, whereas house-spraying is now restricted to specific high-risk and epidemic-prone areas, increasing use is being made of insecticide-treated bednets.

Malaria control is everybody's business and everyone should contribute to it, including community members and people working in education, environment, water supply, sanitation, and community development. It must be an integral part of national health development and community action for control must be sustained and supported by intersectoral collaboration at all levels and by monitoring, training and evaluation, and operational and basic research.

Efforts to Combat Malaria

Global Malaria Control Strategy

Malaria has been a priority for WHO since its founding in 1948. Control activities are coordinated by WHO's Programme on Communicable Diseases (CDS). The four basic technical elements of WHO's Global Malaria Control Strategy are:

1. Provision of early diagnosis and prompt treatment for the disease;
2. Planning and implementation of selective and sustainable preventive measures, including vector control;

3. Early detection for the prevention or containment of epidemics; and,
4. Strengthening of local research capacities to promote regular assessment of countries' malaria situations, in particular the ecological, social and economic determinants of the disease.

Roll Back Malaria

What has been achieved to date is both a political commitment to malaria control and a progressive strengthening of national and local capacities for assessing malaria situations and selecting appropriate measures aimed at reducing or preventing the disease. National plans of action have also been developed in more than 80% of malaria endemic countries.

Recognizing the widespread political desire that had been building since the Amsterdam Summit of 1992 when the Global Malaria Control Strategy was adopted, Dr Gro Harlem Brundtland, Director-General of World Health Organization, declared upon taking office in July 1998 that there should be a deeper commitment to win the fight against malaria. This was going to require not only the commitment of the health sector, but also other governmental sectors, the private sector where activities may directly or indirectly affect the malaria situation, nongovernmental organizations, and affected communities themselves. Greater financial resources and a higher visibility for malaria campaigns would be necessary. It was thus that, through the offices of WHO, four UN-System agencies (UNDP, UNICEF, WHO and the World Bank) launched Roll Back Malaria on 30 October 1998 (see WHO Press Release and WHO Fact Sheet (No 203) on the subject for more details on the project; http://www.who.int/inf).

International Efforts

The Multilateral Initiative on Malaria (MIM) was launched in Dakar in January 1997 when a number of institutions (from both public and private sectors) joined forces to promote malaria research in Africa. The UNDP/World Bank/WHO Special Programme on Tropical Diseases (WHO/TDR) has joined the initiative, establishing a Task Force to address the needs of endemic countries and to fund activities related to strengthening research capacities in malaria; a budget of about US$3 million a year has been raised, with contributions from several institutions to support research /capacity building projects and training. The Task Force has mobilised around 40 countries and 161 partners for submitting proposals for review. Fifteen partnership projects involving 20 African and 5 European countries and the USA have been funded.

Recent advances in research and development

Field Applications

Significant progress has been made in research on, and development of, new tools for use in malaria control activities.

Insecticide treated bednets and curtains have emerged in recent years as a promising tool although their use in Africa is limited. Results from multi-centre randomized, controlled field trials in Africa supported by (TDR) suggest that in certain epidemiological situations, overall childhood mortality can be lowered by 15 to 35% through the use of insecticide-impregnated bednets. Further research is required to enhance the effectiveness of bednets or curtains in operational settings and to ensure their use in a sustainable manner.

Due to the considerable overlap in signs and symptoms of several childhood diseases, a single diagnosis for a sick child is often inappropriate. WHO and UNICEF have responded to this challenge by developing an approach referred to as the "Integrated Management of Childhood Illness". Evidence from surveys of health worker performance and of management of illness in the home suggests that improvements are likely to reduce childhood mortality significantly.

Despite the simple technology and relatively low direct costs, microscope diagnosis is still expensive, requiring an adequate infrastructure to purchase and maintain supplies and equipment, to train health workers and to ensure proper quality assurance of the service. The results of recent evaluations of standardized antigen detection tests including 'dipsticks' suggest that they have potential for use in the management of malaria disease, if accuracy can be assured and the test made affordable for those in need.

New user-friendly packaging of anti-malarials separates the dose to be taken at each time point, and provides simple non-medical information to patients. It can result in 20% more malaria sufferers following their treatment through until they are cured, and this greater compliance in turn means less possibility of drug resistance developing.

Rectal artesunate is being developed because patients in malaria endemic countries, who are commonly at high risk of death from malaria, often cannot get to health services. So an existing drug is being reformulated for a new indication: emergency treatment to cover a patient on the way to hospital. If regulatory approval is justified, the suppositories will be used for treating severely ill patients who cannot take drugs by mouth and who cannot rapidly access safe injectable treatment.

Drug and Vaccine Development

A limited number of drugs for treatment of malaria are available today. Because of worsening problems of drug resistance in many parts of the world, adequate treatment of malaria is becoming increasingly difficult. Although some new drugs have appeared in the last 20 years (e.g., mefloquine, halofantrine, artemisinin derivatives, malarone, atovaquone + proguanil, co-artemether), new (especially inexpensive and affordable) drugs and more practical formulations of existing drugs/compounds are badly needed.

In Africa, with increasing levels of chloroquine resistance and fears of toxicity and decreased efficacy for sulfadoxine/pyrimithamine, there is an urgent need for an affordable, effective and safe alternative to chloroquine. In the short-term, amodiaquine is being reconsidered as a first or second line drug in areas of chloroquine resistance. There are also studies on the combination of the short half-life antifolates, chloroproguanil and dapsone, and on pyronaridine, a Chinese synthetic compound. Both are in development by WHO/TDR.

Artemisinin derivatives presently show no cross-resistance with known antimalarials and as such are important for treating severe malaria in areas of multidrug resistance; however, they require long treatment courses and when used alone, recrudescence may occur. TDR has conducted randomised multicentre trials with intramuscular artemether and is currently developing arteether for severe/complicated disease.

Drug combinations for multidrug resistant malaria are being developed by the private sector: atovaquone+proguanil (now registered) and artemether+ benflumetol (yet to be registered).

MMV, the new Medicines for Malaria Venture, is a public/private sector initiative to develop anti-malarials and make them available in poor countries. Support for this venture is being solicited from foundations and other public sources as well as the pharmaceutical industry – it could amount to a $30 million a year programme.

In the last decade, considerable progress has been made in the search for a malaria vaccine. An effective vaccine would constitute a powerful addition to malaria control. More than a dozen candidate vaccines are currently in development, some of them in clinical trial. The hope is that an effective vaccine will be available within the next 7-15 years.

Vaccines for malaria are being developed at global level; clinical trials are ongoing in USA, Colombia, Switzerland, Australia, Papua New Guinea, Gambia and Tanzania. The three main types of vaccine being developed are:

– "Anti-sporozoite" vaccines, designed to prevent infection.
– "Anti-asexual blood stage" vaccines, designed to reduce severe and complicated manifestations of the disease. Such vaccines could lower morbidity and mortality among children under five years of age in Africa, the main risk group, and their development is given priority by WHO. Several such vaccine candidates are currently undergoing clinical and field testing.
– "Transmission-blocking" vaccines, designed to arrest the development of the parasite in the mosquito, thereby reducing or eliminating transmission of the disease.

A cost effective vaccine must be capable of being incorporated into appropriate health delivery programmes, and to provide sufficient duration of immunity. At present, it is difficult to predict when such a vaccine will become available.

Mapping of the malaria genome is being carried out by a consortium of partners, including United States National Institute of Health, the US Department of Defense, Burroughs-Wellcome Fund and the Wellcome Trust. Knowledge of the genome will open the door to more rational ways of discovering new vaccines and drugs.

Another initiative is seeking ways to inhibit the parasite's travelling from the gut of the mosquito to the saliva, where it becomes infective to man.

ROLL BACK MALARIA[6]

Upon taking office in July 1998, the World Health Organization's (WHO) new Director-General, Dr Gro Harlem Brundtland, decided that malaria was to be one of WHO's top priorities. It was evident that malaria was both a top political priority among African leaders and that it was still a major health scourge in many parts of the world, in Africa above all.

There are an estimated 300-500 million cases of malaria per year. The majority of these occur in Africa, while the vast majority of the estimated 1 million annual deaths from the disease occur among children, and mainly among poor African children. Malaria is above all a disease of the poor, impacting at least three times more greatly on the poor than any other disease. Although malaria had been a priority of WHO since its inception in 1948, malaria control efforts, Dr Brundtland found, had often suffered from a lack of financial resources and uneven implementation. She thus resolved, upon taking office, to find a means of focussing the world's attention and support on renewed and redoubled efforts to beat this scourge of the young and the poor: Roll Back Malaria.

---

[6] Fact Sheet No 203, October 1998.

RBM's objectives

Roll Back Malaria (RBM) is as an opportunity not only finally to beat a devastating disease, but also to develop endemic countries' health systems and build new means of tackling global health concerns. Thus, the goals of RBM will include:

- Support to endemic countries in developing their national health systems as a major strategy for controlling malaria;
- Efforts to develop the broader health sector (i.e., all providers of health care to the community – the public sector health system, civil society and non-governmental organisations, private health providers [including drug vendors and traditional healers] and others);
- Encouraging the needed human and financial investments, national and international, for health system development.

RBM's implementation at country level will provide an indicator of the effectiveness of these health systems, while the programme will also serve as a model for WHO in developing both other global health and development initiatives and new methods of controlling infectious diseases.

RBM: a new approach to malaria control

WHO will establish a functioning partnership with a range of organizations at global, regional and country levels, which results in development of a sustained capacity to address malaria (and other priority health problems). WHO's partners in RBM will include malaria endemic countries, other UN organisations (on 30 October 1998, the United Nations Development Programme, UNICEF, the World Bank and the World Health Organization announced that the four agencies were launching RBM jointly and that they would cooperate in all aspects of its activities, see press release WHO/77), bilateral development agencies, development banks, non-governmental organisations and the private sector.

WHO's role in the global partnership will be to:

- Provide strategic direction and catalyse actions;
- Provide an RBM secretariat of approximately eight to 10 people at its Geneva headquarters;
- Work to build and sustain country and global partnerships;
- Arrange the provision of technical endorsement, directly, or through approved resource networks, for both a collective strategy and for individual partners' actions;
- Ensure that all aspects of progress of RBM are monitored;
- Provide global accountability for RBM;
- Broker technical assistance and finance on behalf of those who need it;
- Undertake responsible advocacy for the RBM approach to reducing malaria-related suffering.

The role of UN partner agencies

UNICEF will:

- provide support to intensified malaria control efforts via its country programmes.
- work with Government & NGO partners to: give special attention to reducing the terrible toll of malaria on young children and pregnant women; further strengthen support for community-based and local action to improve health and nutrition; focus on making insecticide treated mosquito nets available to all families that need them and

on ensuring that every child with malaria has access to early and effective treatment; mobilize leaders (community, district and national) to make effective malaria control a priority.
- at international level, raise additional funds for country activities, and focus support on 10 of the most severely-affected countries in the next two years.
- take lead responsibility for developing an impregnated bednet resource network.

UNDP has committed to the following actions, as malaria has important implications for health and poverty. Effective responses will require broad-based support across sectors and the involvement of a range of development partners. At country level, UNDP will:
- Create capacity for integration of malaria-related action into national poverty eradication policies, strategies and programmes.
- Strengthen, through Sustainable Human Development activities, the balance of action among state, private sector, civil society and communities themselves, to ensure that people have access to basic social services and productive assets.
- Work through the UN Resident Coordinator system to encourage collaborative programming in support of intersectoral action and resource mobilization.

At regional/sub-regional levels, UNDP will:
- Support links between Sub-regional Resource Facilities (SURFs), providing technical referral services to country offices and the Roll Back Malaria resource support networks;
- Collaborate with WHO Regional Offices to strengthen capacity of relevant regional inter-governmental organizations (ISO) in support of Roll Back Malaria.

At global level, UNDP is:
- Providing continuing support for the UNDP/World Bank/WHO Special Programme for Research & Training in Tropical Diseases (TDR), which has as a major focus the development of drugs and tools for malaria control and adapting research in local settings.

The World Bank Group strongly supports the Roll Back Malaria global partnership. Malaria has a major impact on social and economic development. Consequently, the Bank has committed to:
- Increasing World Bank investments in malaria control and research;
- Facilitating resource mobilization to support RBM;
- Enhancing a more effective involvement of Departments of Finance, Economics, Infrastructure, Agriculture and others to become full partners in reducing malaria as a break on economic growth;
- Exploring innovative finance mechanisms to deliver support;
- Supporting research on the economic aspects of malaria;
- Helping establish private-public partnerships with industry on new malaria products.

Together with Roll Back Malaria partners, the Bank will actively pursue these activities through its country programmes and research agendas. Malaria must be reduced as a negative factor on macro-economic growth.

RBM's first focus: Africa

The Roll Back Malaria campaign will focus first on Africa. It is aimed at:
- upgrading health delivery systems at both the local and national levels in malarious countries;
- intensifying use of bednetting (nets coated with insecticide) to prevent night-time biting by malaria-carrying mosquitoes;

- mapping of malaria regions and of medical facilities to better direct health resources;
- developing new drugs for victims already infected with malaria;
- coordinating the development and testing of new malaria drugs and vaccines;
- developing methods to address malaria in emergencies, (eg., refugee and post-war situations).

At country level, RBM will work towards development of sustained capacity to address malaria (and other priority health problems) that is adapted to local realities, and delivering measurable and properly validated results. RBM will support the building of coalitions for action at regional and country level, and assist with development of clear, evidence based action plans at country and regional levels. RBM will develop a systematic approach to monitor progress and results, and broker financial and technical inputs into countries.

RBM will support Resource Networks which will facilitate the implementation of RBM in endemic countries by providing support in specialised areas, e.g.:

- Needs assessment and intervention at district level;
- Sector-wide approaches and financing;
- Quality and supply of anti-malarials at the local level;
- Implementation of bed net programmes, including supply of nets and insecticides;
- Improving quality of care at the home;
- Geographic mapping of malaria and health care;
- Prevention and control of epidemics;
- Monitoring of drug and insecticide resistance;
- Malaria control in war-torn zones.

Most victims of malaria die simply because they do not have access to health care close to their home, or their cases are not recognized as malaria by health care professionals. In addition, life saving drugs are often not available. In Africa, RBM will create a network of teams to go into villages and analyze treatment and prevention practices at the household and community level, the availability and quality of health care by the public and private sector, and potential local partners. RBM will provide technical and financial support for each analysis through this network at the district level.

In African districts with stable, high transmission malaria, RBM will simultaneously seek to significantly improve early diagnosis and appropriate treatment of malaria-related fevers in children, early treatment/prevention in pregnant women, and personal protection for children and pregnant mothers through the use of insecticide impregnated bednets (IIBNs). In many districts, this will require reinforcement of the local public and private health sector, focusing on activities at the community level. RBM will also attempt to upgrade the training of health care providers to ensure quality care after the campaign ends.

RBM will set up a resource network throughout Africa to forecast malaria epidemics and their prevention. The network will link surveillance information from countries and regional surveillance systems and establish the means of routine and rapid analysis of this information for forecasting and early detection of epidemics. Regional, sub-regional or country strategies for epidemic preparedness and emergency action will be formulated. The resource network will also be used to track the quality and supply of drugs used to treat malaria.

Geographic mapping of malaria and health care

For countries participating in RBM, national malaria information will be integrated with regional information to produce a comprehensive national malaria control map, as part of the international mapping of the disease. The information will allow a better estimation of the burden of malaria and the population at risk, and hence a better assessment for RBM. It will also provide more reliable and area-specific information for national and international advocacy for malaria control. Where RBM operations have started, information on the availability and quality of health services and the results of monitoring and evaluation will be added to the data base.

The road forward

RBM will be in a "roll-out" phase until the end of 1999. By that date, RBM will have:

- Supported countries in Africa to develop implementation plans for high transmission, stable malaria, that meet the overall objectives of RBM;
- Advanced plans for other malaria situations, i.e., epidemic malaria and malaria in other regions of the world.

The general objective of RBM will be to significantly reduce the global burden of malaria through interventions adapted to local needs and by reinforcement of the health sector. Goals are to be set by countries based on situation analyses and assessment of feasibility, and could include: malaria morbidity and mortality goals; financial goals (e.g., significant increase in resources available for community level activities in health care); accessibility goals (e.g., Percentage of population with access to early and adequate treatment); coverage goals (e.g., Proportion of the targeted population with insecticide treated bed nets); health sector reform goals (e.g., New partnerships with private sector health care providers); goals of policy change (eg., Significant changes in policy favouring evidence-based strategy development).

Performance indicators will also be used to assess the RBM Project: WHO's link with external partners e.g., capacity of WHO to support the global partnership. WHO's impact on country level operations. WHO's in-house working arrangements.

RBM team

Roll Back Malaria will be run with a central team of eight to 10 people headquartered in WHO in Geneva. The team will be led by Dr David Nabarro, who until his appointment as RBM project manager was Chief Health Advisor and Strategic Director of the United Kingdom Department for International Development.

TUBERCULOSIS[7]

Tuberculosis kills 2 million people each year. The global epidemic is growing and becoming more dangerous. The breakdown in health services, the spread of HIV/AIDS and the emergence of multidrug-resistant TB are contributing to the worsening impact of this disease.

[7] WHO Fact Sheet No 104, Revised April 2000.

In 1993, the World Health Organization (WHO) took an unprecedented step and declared tuberculosis a global emergency, so great was the concern about the modern TB epidemic.

It is estimated that between 2000 and 2020, nearly one billion people will be newly infected, 200 million people will get sick, and 35 million will die from TB – if control is not further strengthened.

Infection and Transmission

TB is a contagious disease. Like the common cold, it spreads through the air. Only people who are sick with pulmonary TB are infectious. When infectious people cough, sneeze, talk or spit, they propel TB germs, known as bacilli, into the air. A person needs only to inhale a small number of these to be infected.

Left untreated, each person with active TB will infect on average between 10 and 15 people every year. But people infected with TB will not necessarily get sick with the disease. The immune system 'walls off' the TB bacilli which, protected by a thick waxy coat, can lie dormant for years. When someone's immune system is weakened, the chances of getting sick are greater.

- Someone in the world is newly infected with TB every second.
- Nearly one percent of the world's population is newly infected with TB each year.
- Overall, one-third of the world's population is currently infected with the TB bacillus.
- 5–10 percent of people who are infected with TB become sick or infectious at some time during their life.

Global and Regional Incidence

Each year, more people are dying of TB. New outbreaks have occurred in Eastern Europe, where TB deaths are increasing after almost 40 years of steady decline. In terms of numbers of cases, the biggest burden of TB is in south-east Asia.

- TB kills about 2 million people each year.
- Around 8 million people become sick with TB each year.
- Over 1.5 million TB cases per year occur in sub-Saharan Africa. This number is rising rapidly as a result of the HIV/AIDS epidemic.
- Nearly 3 million TB cases per year occur in south-east Asia.
- Over a quarter of a million TB cases per year occur in Eastern Europe.

Factors Contributing to the Rise in TB

– **HIV is accelerating the spread of TB**

HIV and TB form a lethal combination, each speeding the other's progress. HIV weakens the immune system. Someone who is HIV-positive and infected with TB is many times more likely to become sick with TB than someone infected with TB who is HIV-negative. TB is a leading cause of death among people who are HIV-positive. It accounts for about 15% of AIDS deaths worldwide. In Africa, HIV is the single most important factor determining the increased incidence of TB in the last ten years.

– **Poorly managed TB programmes are threatening to make TB incurable**

Until 50 years ago, there were no drugs to cure TB. Now, strains that are resistant to a single drug have been documented in every country surveyed and, what is more, strains of

TB resistant to all major anti-TB drugs have emerged. Drug-resistant TB is caused by inconsistent or partial treatment, when patients do not take all their drugs regularly for the required period because they start to feel better, doctors and health workers prescribe the wrong treatment regimens or the drug supply is unreliable. A particularly dangerous form of drug-resistant TB is multidrug-resistant TB (MDR-TB), which is defined as the disease due to TB bacilli resistant to at least isoniazid and rifampicin – the two most powerful anti-TB drugs. MDR-TB is rising at alarming rates in some countries, especially in the former Soviet Union, and threatens global TB control efforts.

From a public health perspective, poorly supervised or incomplete treatment of TB is worse than no treatment at all. When people fail to complete standard treatment regimens, or are given the wrong treatment regimen, they may remain infectious. The bacilli in their lungs may develop resistance to anti-TB drugs. People they infect will have the same drug-resistant strain. While drug-resistant TB is treatable, it requires extensive chemotherapy (up to two years of treatment) that is often prohibitively expensive (often more than 100 times more expensive than treatment of drug-susceptible TB), and is also more toxic to patients.

WHO and its international partners are have formed the DOTS-Plus Working Group, which is attempting to determine the best possible strategy to manage MDR-TB. One of the goals of DOTS-Plus is to increase access to expensive second-line anti-TB drugs for WHO-approved TB control programmes in low and middle income countries.

– **Movement of people is helping the spread of TB**

Global trade and the number of people travelling in aeroplanes have increased dramatically over the last forty years. In many industrialized countries, at least one-half of TB cases are among foreign-born people. In the US, nearly 40% of TB cases are among foreign-born people.

The number of refugees and displaced people in the world is also increasing. Untreated TB spreads quickly in crowded refugee camps and shelters. It is difficult to treat mobile populations, as treatment takes at least six months. As many as 50 percent of the world's refugees may be infected with TB. As they move, they may spread TB.

Other displaced people such as homeless people in industrialized countries are at risk. In 1995, approximately 30 percent of San Francisco's homeless population and 25 percent of London's homeless were reported to be infected with TB. These figures compare to overall prevalences of 7 percent in the United States and 13 percent in the United Kingdom. The prevalence of infection in prisons can be even higher.

Effective TB Control

The WHO-recommended treatment strategy for detection and cure of TB is DOTS. DOTS combines five elements: political commitment, microscopy services, drug supplies, surveillance and monitoring systems and use of highly efficacious regimes with direct observation of treatment.

Once patients with infectious TB (bacilli visible in a sputum smear) have been identified using microscopy services, health and community workers and trained volunteers observe and record patients swallowing the full course of the correct dosage of anti-TB medicines (treatment lasts six to eight months). The most common anti-TB drugs are isoniazid, rifampicin, pyrazinamide, streptomycin and ethambutol.

Sputum smear testing is repeated after two months, to check progress, and again at the end of treatment. A recording and reporting system documents patients' progress throughout, and the final outcome of treatment.

- DOTS produces cure rates of up to 95 percent even in the poorest countries.
- DOTS prevents new infections by curing infectious patients.
- DOTS prevents the development of MDR-TB by ensuring the full course of treatment is followed.
- A six-month supply of drugs for DOTS costs US $11 per patient in some parts of the world. The World Bank has ranked the DOTS strategy as one of the "most cost-effective of all health interventions."

Since DOTS was introduced on a global scale, millions of infectious patients have received effective DOTS treatment. In half of China, cure rates among new cases are 96 percent. In Peru, widespread use of DOTS for more than five years has led to the successful treatment of 91 percent of cases.

By the end of 1998, all 22 of the high burden countries which bear 80% of the estimated incident cases had adopted DOTS. 43 percent of the global population had access to DOTS, double the fraction reported in 1995. In the same year, 21 percent of estimated TB patients received treatment under DOTS, also double the fraction reported in 1995.

WHO targets are to detect 70 percent of new infectious TB cases and to cure 85 percent of those detected. Six countries had achieved these targets in 1998. Governments, non-governmental organizations and civil society must continue to act to improve TB control if we are to reach these targets worldwide.

MENTAL HEALTH[8]

Since the inception in 1946 of the World Health Organization (WHO), its Member States have always considered **mental well-being** as an integral part of the general definition of health. In the Preamble to the WHO Constitution, health has been defined as "a state of complete physical, **mental** and social well-being and not merely the absence of disease or infirmity".

Mental health is a complex phenomenon which is determined by multiple social, environmental, biological and psychological factors and depends in part on the successful implementation of public health efforts to control neuropsychiatric disorders such as **depression, anxiety disorders, schizophrenia, dementia and epilepsy**.

Today, as many as **1500 million people worldwide** are estimated to be suffering at any given time from some kind of neuropsychiatric disorder, including mental, behavioural and substance abuse disorders. A third of them may be affected by more than one neuropsychiatric ailment. Three-quarters of those affected live in developing countries.

Mental illness accounts for a significant proportion of disability due to disease and imposes a heavy burden in terms of human suffering, stigmatization of the mentally ill and their families, and direct and indirect costs.

[8] WHO Fact Sheet No. 130, August 1996.

The major types of psychiatric and neurological disorders, generally perceived as public health problems, include:

MOOD (AFFECTIVE) DISORDERS which affect around **340 million people worldwide** at any given time. They are characterized by a change in mood, which a person cannot control, to depression or elation. Such disorders typically take the form of either **bipolar affective disorders** or **unipolar depressive disorders**.

- In bipolar affective disorders, the patient goes through repeated episodes of elation and overactivity (**mania**) and lowered mood and decreased energy (**depression**).
- **Mania** can be accompanied by delusions and hallucinations (disembodied voices or visions), uncontrollable excitement, incessant talking, decreased sleep, and loss of normal social inhibitions.
- **Depression** has the same clinical characteristics as those found in **unipolar depressive disease**: unaccountable sadness, diminished pleasure in daily life, weight change, disturbed sleep patterns, fatigue, feelings of worthlessness and self-blame, as well as diminished ability to concentrate and indecisiveness. Chronic depression, or dysthymia, is characterized by the persistence of such symptoms over several years.
- Depression is estimated to be present in 10% of all those seeking care at primary health care facilities worldwide.
- In the United States alone, depression costs some US$44 billion annually, which is about the same as the costs resulting from heart disease. It represents some 30% of the total estimated annual cost of US$148 billion for all mental illness.
- The worst consequence of depression is suicide. Together with alcohol and drug abuse and psychosis, depression is implicated in at least **60% of suicides**, which in 1990 accounted for **1,6%** of the world's deaths.
- Depression is estimated to rank fifth in illness burden among women, and seventh among men in developing countries.

ANXIETY DISORDERS are estimated to affect some **400 million** people at any point in time. They are characterized by symptoms of anxiety and avoidance behaviour and include **panic disorder, phobias, obsessive-compulsive disorder,** and **post-traumatic stress disorder**.

- **Panic disorder** is marked by unpredictable episodes of intense fear or discontent, which can last for minutes or hours, and include shortness of breath, dizziness, palpitations, tremor, sweating, and often a fear of dying or "going crazy".
- **Phobias** are characterized by a persistent and uncontrollable fear of certain situations (for example, where physical escape would be difficult, embarrassment or humiliation possible, etc.) or of a particular stimulus (such as dogs, snakes, insects, blood, etc.).
- **Obsessive-compulsive disorder** is distinguished by intrusive, distressing, and senseless thoughts and by repetitive illogical behaviour to ward off misfortune, such as unnecessary and uncontrolled washing of hands.
- **Post-traumatic stress disorder (PTSD)** manifests itself after a catastrophic or unusual experience and persists long after the event and, in certain cases, interferes with an individual's functioning. Typical symptoms include flashbacks and dreams of the traumatic event, insomnia, numbness, detachment from other people, and an avoidance of activities and situations that can reawaken painful memories.
- **PTSD** is common among victims of man-made and natural disasters, military activities (for both soldiers and civilians), violence, ethnic cleansing and genocide, torture and repression, as well as among refugees.

SCHIZOPHRENIA includes a group of severe psychiatric disorders that usually start in late adolescence or early adult life and often become chronic and disabling. These disorders place a heavy burden on the patient's family and relatives, both in terms of the direct and indirect costs involved and the social stigma associated with the illness, sometimes over generations. Such stigma often leads to isolation and neglect.

- **There is an estimated 45 million people with schizophrenia in the world, more than 33 million of them in the developing countries.**
- In acute schizophrenia the clinical signs and symptoms are more pronounced and may include delusions (false beliefs), hallucinations, jumbled and incoherent thoughts, a mood out of keeping with thoughts, and lack of awareness of being ill.
- Epidemiological studies in Europe and North America have shown schizophrenia to be more prevalent in low-income populations. Individuals from lower income groups, whose values, socioeconomic background, education and culture are different from those of the professionals who treat them, are more readily diagnosed as schizophrenic.
- To date, research has provided little evidence for understanding the social origins of schizophrenia. But it does provide strong support for the hypothesis that social and cultural factors affect the course and prognosis of the disease.
- People affected with schizophrenia who live in developing countries seem to be more responsive to treatment than those in developed countries. A WHO follow-up study of people, diagnosed as suffering from schizophrenia in nine countries, suggested that two years after the first treated episode of the disease, **58%** were reported to have recovered in Nigeria, 50% in India, and only **8%** in Denmark.
- The cost of schizophrenia to society is enormous. In the United States, for example, the direct cost of treatment of schizophrenia has been estimated to be close to 0.5% of the gross national product.

DEMENTIA is a brain syndrome usually of a chronic or progressive nature, which is manifested by a decline of memory, comprehension, learning capacity, language and judgement, as well as of the ability to think and to calculate. This syndrome occurs in Alzheimer's disease (AD dementia), in some but not all cases of cerebrovascular disease, and in other conditions affecting the brain, such as Pick disease, Creutzfeldt-Jacob disease and Parkinson disease.

- **Worldwide, around 22 million people suffer from dementia.**
- Global incidence rates for dementia of all types have been estimated to be less than 1% per annum, with the risk of the age-specific AD and vascular dementia rising steeply above the age of 60 years.
- AD and vascular dementia far outnumber other cases of dementia and are the two principal kinds of dementia in the elderly (senile dementia). The senile dementias have assumed great importance in public health because more people today live into the age of high risk.
- The number of people suffering from senile dementia in Africa, Asia and Latin America may exceed **80 million in 2025**.
- Because of the increasing number of road-accidents and strokes, which can cause brain damage, presenile dementia is a major problem in many countries.
- There is an association between a past history of heavy drinking and the onset of dementia or depression in later life.

EPILEPSY is a neurological disorder which is characterized by totally uncontrollable fits that occur repeatedly, sometimes more than once a day. They start suddenly, are accompanied by convulsions and stop abruptly with or without loss of consciousness.

- Epilepsy is estimated to affect approximately **one in every 130 people worldwide.** In all, there are more than **40 million** people of all ages and social conditions who are affected by epilepsy with **2 million new cases each year. Eighty per cent of those affected live in developing countries.**
- People affected with epilepsy are highly stigmatized. One of the reasons is that in many countries, epilepsy is erroneously perceived as an infectious disease. The affected people and their families are shunned to the point of isolation.
- **More than 80% of newly-diagnosed patients with epilepsy can be successfully treated** today with anti-epilepsy drugs and lead normal lives. In many cases adequate treatment can be provided at an average cost of **US$5 per patient per year**. Unfortunately, half of those affected are treated improperly or not at all.
- Some infections and brain injuries are among the major causes of epilepsy. Epilepsy may be caused by genetic factors and infectious diseases in the prenatal period, by birth asphyxia and brain injury during labour, and, in the post-natal period, by febrile convulsions, infectious (e.g meningitis, encephalitis) and parasitic (e.g. malaria, schistosomiasis) diseases and brain damage caused by alcohol, trauma or toxic substances (e.g. lead, pesticides).
- Prevention of epilepsy is possible through prenatal care, safe delivery, control of fever in children, reduction of brain injury, control of infectious and parasitic diseases, and genetic counselling.

Current research provides strong evidence that **mental disorders are of biopsychosocial origin**.

- There is a strong interrelationship between some tropical disease and neuropsychiatric disorders and impairments. Infestations of cysticercosis (tapeworm), for example, may result in brain lesions leading to epileptic seizures.
- The quality of a person's social environment influences both his or her vulnerability to mental illness and the course of that illness. Poverty, overcrowded living conditions, job insecurity, marital problems, man-made and natural disasters, ethnic violence and violence against women, children and the aged, wars – all of these influence negatively the mental health of the world's populations.
- Demographic factors such as population ageing and urbanization accentuate the public health and social magnitude of mental illness.
- Substance abuse – harmful use of alcohol, illicit drugs and other psychoactive substances – aggravates all other forms of mental illness and has also been proved to have a major negative impact on public health in general.

MENTAL HEALTH AND PRIMARY HEALTH CARE[9]

The World Health Organization (WHO) emphasizes primary health care as a vital means to achieve its goal of health for all by the year 2000. Likewise, WHO advocates that

[9] Fact Sheet No 129, Revised November 1997.

mental health care should be decentralized and integrated into primary health care, with the necessary tasks carried out as far as possible by general health workers rather than by specialists in mental health*. *Attention to mental health is essential if primary health care is to be effective.*

This means not only the diagnosis and treatment of mental disorders: mental health care is part of those activities subsumed under the treatment of "common diseases", and as such is an essential element of primary health care. Health promotion must of necessity include concern for psychological well-being and the quality of mental and emotional health.

Scope of mental health in primary health care

Mental health as a component of primary health care comprises two distinct areas which are often confused. The first emphasizes the practical relevance of psychosocial and behavioural science skills in general health care. These skills are vital to improving general health care facilities, promoting mental and emotional health, and thereby enhancing the quality of life. They have rarely been included as tasks of health care workers, and this needs to change.

The second area concerns control of mental and neurological diseases. This area is generally better understood by health professionals, and has often been regarded as too highly specialized for general health workers. However, research suggests that general health personnel are also capable of managing many mental and neurological disorders, both in terms of prevention as well as diagnosis and treatment. Mental illness does not always need specialized treatment, and even severe mental illness can be managed outside the hospital; equipping primary health care workers to deal with these problems avoids wastage of effort and cost. *Responsibility for mental health is not an extra burden for primary health care services; on the contrary, it increases their effectiveness.*

Involving the community

As stated in the Declaration of Alma Ata (1978), health care systems must involve the community at every level of planning and development in order to provide appropriate treatment for the sick and to promote positive health. Communities must cease to be merely passive recipients of health care and assume responsibility for their own health and well-being. Perhaps in no area is this principle more relevant than mental health, where professionals have often been distant from the communities they serve because of the physical seclusion of mental health care facilities and socio-economic class distinctions between care providers and clients.

There must be constant dialogue between mental health workers and key groups capable of expressing fundamental community concerns and attitudes. For example, traditional healers are a rich source of information on community values, fears, ideas and needs, and on accepted methods of handling many problems at all levels. The assessment process should seek to answer at least three basic questions:

- What does the community see as its mental health, psychosocial and emotional problems?
- Which members of the community are considered to be emotionally vulnerable, or at risk of psychosocial or other mental breakdowns?
- What does the community believe needs to be done about such problems, either through community intervention or by the health worker or other workers?

Mental health and human rights

Several UN documents consecrate the basic human rights of persons with mental disorders. These include the UN's Universal Declaration of Human Rights (1948); the International Covenant on Economic, Social and Cultural Rights (1976), which recognizes the right of all to enjoyment of the highest attainable standard of physical and mental health; and Principles of Persons with Mental Illness and the Improvement of Mental Health Care ("UN Principles"), adopted by the UN General Assembly in December 1991.

In order to promote adherence to the standards and guarantees put forth in these documents, WHO has published Ten Basic Principles of Mental Health Care Law, which provides key reference principles and implementation guidelines with the least influence possible from given cultures or legal traditions. The document was drawn from a comparative analysis of mental health laws in 60 jurisdictions at the federal, state and provincial levels, comprising 45 countries with mental health laws and others which operate with informal systems. WHO is also in the process of publishing additional guidelines for assessing and implementing adherence to the UN Principles.

Mental health, man-made disasters and population displacements

It is estimated that more than 26 million people are affected by massive population movements. More than 13 million are refugees. Others include persons granted temporary protection and those allowed to stay in another country on humanitarian grounds. But while many refugees and displaced persons suffer physically, far more suffer psychological harm, and there is now growing concern about addressing this aspect of their trauma, and this can be done using a primary health care approach.

Probably the best example of this new focus is in former Yugoslavia, where WHO played a leadership role in coordinating and providing technical assistance to a large-scale interagency effort, one involving nearly 200 projects, which assisted tens of thousands of refugees and displaced persons with psychosocial trauma counselling. As part of this effort, WHO established six "regional models" for mental health in Bosnia and Herzegovina, Croatia and the Federal Republic of Yugoslavia (Serbia and Montenegro), conducted a series of training courses in post-traumatic stress therapy for local health care professionals, and made an assessment of changes in the epidemiology of mental health problems under war conditions. A new WHO project is underway in Rwanda to provide a mental health component into the various regional general health services.

Together with the United Nations High Commissioner for Refugees (UNHCR), WHO has prepared special guidelines for relief aid personnel, community workers, primary health care practitioners, primary school teachers and others who provide support to refugees and displaced persons who have fled war or disaster. Entitled Mental Health and Refugees, it is written in simple language for people who have no special training in psychology or mental health.

STRENGTHENING COMMUNITY MENTAL HEALTH SERVICES AND PRIMARY CARE[10]

Community mental health services and primary care

During the past 20 years there have been radical changes in psychiatric care in Europe as a result of "deinstitutionalisation" of psychiatric patients. That is to say, those previously kept in large public mental hospitals were now discharged and reintegrated into the community where they received treatment and care. It had become clear that these institutions caused long-term damage to individuals' health and ability to function in society.

Deinstitutionalisation means (1) avoiding mental hospital admissions through the provision of community treatment alternatives, (2) the release into the community of all institutionalised patients who have been given adequate preparation for such a change, and (3) the establishment and maintenance of community support systems for non-institutionalised people.

Whilst the deinstitutionalisation process is much more advanced in Western Europe than in Eastern Europe, the issue of strengthening community mental health services is relevant for all European countries.

There is broad scientific support for the belief that an approach to treatment and care based on deinstitutionalisation and its replacement by community treatment and care leads to better results in respect to (1) global symptoms of mental illness, (2) psycho-social adjustment, (3) admission and readmission rates to mental hospitals, (4) length of hospital stay, (5) employment and (6) reduced burden for the family.

Clinical trials have shown that the important elements of an effective response to mental health and neurological problems are psychological and social intervention (independent living skills, training in social skills, vocational training, social support networks, family intervention) and pharmacotherapy (neuroleptics, lithium, antidepressants and anxiolytics).

For most disorders it is essential that pharmacotherapy be used in combination with other specific psychological and social interventions.

The efficacy of these treatments will be reduced substantially if they are not delivered within the context of a comprehensive and coordinated delivery service.

Requirements of a comprehensive community mental health service include:

- crisis intervention
- beds for acute episodes of severe and acute illness in general hospitals
- long-stay accommodation with a 24-hour staff in home-like units, for people with enduring mental illness who need regular supervision of medication and daily monitoring of their mental state but who do not require the continuous presence of medical staff
- day care programmes
- concerted outreach efforts
- supported housing
- home services

---

[10] Fact Sheet No 219, April 1999.

- occupational rehabilitation programmes
- patient and family support services
- multidisciplinary health care teams.

Requirements of primary health care are (1) an adequately trained staff to assess, diagnose and manage mental problems, (2) availability of essential drugs for the treatment of mental disorders, (3) establishment of effective links with more specialist care, including well developed criteria for referral, methods of shared care, adequate information systems and communication, and (4) creation of appropriate links with other community and social services.

WHO is supporting the creation of a number of demonstration projects in 14 countries to strengthen community mental health services and primary health care. The major themes include (1) increasing the awareness of the community and educating it about mental health, (2) deinstitutionalisation, (3) reorganisation of mental health services, (4) creation of community mental health services and outreach programs, (5) training of primary care providers, (6) training of psychiatrists, and (7) psycho-social rehabilitation.

2.3

THE WHO MODEL LIST OF ESSENTIAL DRUGS AS A STANDARD OF CARE?

Hans Hogerzeil

ACCESS TO ESSENTIAL MEDICINES IN DEVELOPING COUNTRIES

The problem of access to essential drugs

No health care is possible without essential drugs. The total number of people who have access to essential drugs has grown from ±2.1 billion in 1977 to an estimated 3.8 billion in 1999. Yet, about one-third of the world's population lack regular access to essential drugs; in the poorest parts of Africa and Asia over 50% still lack access to drugs. In public services, drug costs are the second largest part of health care costs (after salaries); in developing countries, they are also the highest proportion of out-of-pocket health care costs. In many developed countries over 70% of pharmaceuticals are publicly funded through public health services or social security. However, in developing and transitional economies 50% to 90% of drugs are paid for by patients themselves.

New challenges

In many developing countries health sector reform is leading to insufficient public funding for essential drugs. New essential drugs are often very expensive. For example, new essential drugs for tuberculosis, HIV/AIDS, bacterial infections and malaria are 50-200 times as expensive as the established drugs (most of which are available as generic products) which are no longer effective due to increasing antimicrobial resistance. New global trade agreements, such as the World Trade Organisation and TRIPS (Trade Related Intellectual Property Rights)[1] expand and

[1] Ed.: The UNDP Human Development Report 2000 explains: "The agreement on Trade-Related Aspects of Intellectual Property Rights, or TRIPS, is one of the pillars of the Uruguay Round agreements, and also one of the most contentious. It tightens intellectual property rights protection for the creator. It introduces an enforceable global standard by linking intellectual property rights with trade, making them binding and enforceable through the World Trade Organization processes." TRIPS therefore also covers patents on drugs.

P.J. van Krieken (Ed.), Health, Migration and Return

extend patent protection for new drugs and will make them more expensive in developing countries.

Access to essential drugs depends on four factors:
1. Rational selection – Identifying the most cost-effective treatment based on local disease patterns, drug efficacy, drug safety, drug quality and cost, leading to treatment guidelines for health workers and to lists of essential drugs to guide drug procurement in the public sector, and reimbursement.

2. Affordable prices – For all essential drugs: reduce import duties, taxes, and distribution margins; for off-patent essential drugs: increased competition through price information, generic tendering and generic substitution; pooled procurement and price negotiations; for newer patented essential drugs: price information, therapeutic substitution, equity pricing, and TRIPS safeguards such as parallel import and compulsory licensing;

3. Sustainable financing – The preferred options are general government revenues and social health insurance, which allow for risk-pooling and cross-subsidising between rich and poor, leading to greater equity and solidarity. In the short-term, households need to be assisted in obtaining the best value for their out-of-pocket payments. Temporary solutions are user fees which should be used with caution, and drug donations, development loans and endowment funds for the eradication and control of specific communicable diseases, on the basis of good governance or as part of debtrelief.

4. Reliable health and supply systems – Reliable drug supply systems and health facilities with trained staff and diagnostic equipment, are all needed to ensure safe and effective treatment, and to reduce risks and waste linked to irrational drug use. Innovative public-private approaches are being pursued to ensure the timely availability of drug supplies of ensured quality in the health care system.

THE WHO MODEL LIST OF ESSENTIAL DRUGS

Essential drugs are those drugs that satisfy the health care needs of the majority of the population, at a price they and the community can afford; they should therefore be available at all times and in adequate amounts, and in appropriate dosage forms.

The selection of essential drugs is a two-step process

In most countries the selection of essential drugs is a two-step process. First, market approval of a pharmaceutical product is usually granted on the basis of efficacy, safety and quality, and rarely on the basis of a comparison with other products already on the market, or cost. This regulatory decision defines the availability of the drug in the private sector. In addition, most public drug procurement schemes have mechanisms to limit procurement or reimbursement to certain drugs. For these decisions an evaluation is necessary, based on a comparison between various drug products and on considerations of "value for money". This is the second step.

What is the WHO Model List of Essential Drugs?

The WHO Model List of Essential Drugs serves as a model for the second step in the selection process. Every two years since 1977 it has been updated by the WHO Expert Committee on Essential Drugs, consisting of experienced scientists and clinicians from all regions of the world. The last revision took place in December 1999. The current Model List contains 306 active ingredients and is divided into a main list and a complementary list. There is a separate category of "reserve antimicrobials", which are useful for a wide range of infections but cannot be recommended for unrestricted use.

The WHO list is a model for national and institutional essential drugs lists. By the end of 1999 a total of 146 member states had an official national list of essential drugs, of which 115 had been updated in the last five years. None of these lists is the same as the WHO list. Many national lists are linked to national standard treatment guidelines used for training and supervision, and serve as a guide for drug supplies in the public sector, drug benefits within reimbursement schemes, drug donations, and local production. In other words, the list of essential drugs indicates, from a public health point of view, the priorities for all aspects of the pharmaceutical system.

Common questions regarding the WHO Model List of Essential Drugs:

– Is the WHO Model List binding on national governments?
For two reasons the inclusion of a new drug on the WHO list is not a regulatory decision and is not binding on national governments. First, because the list is not a global standard but only a model list; national and institutional bodies are recommended to develop their own list following the model process. Secondly, the list is intended to reflect public health relevance (the second step in the selection process) and not market approval.

– Is the WHO Model List a restrictive list?
The WHO Model List and national essential drugs lists are not intended to guide market approval and to restrict the entry of drugs into the private sector (this is done by the national regulatory process). A list of essential drugs is a positive list, mainly intended to define priority drugs for public procurement and reimbursement, and for the training of health personnel.

– Are drugs excluded from the WHO Model List solely because of their cost?
Besides clinical efficacy and safety, the total cost and relative cost-effectiveness are major criteria in the selection of essential drugs. The list is intended as a guide for

national decisions on public sector procurement and reimbursement, indicating "value for money" in view of competing health care demands.

CAN THE WHO MODEL LIST BE USED AS A STANDARD FOR THE HEALTH CARE SYSTEM?

Three observations are relevant in this regard.

1. The WHO Model List of Essential Drugs is what it says: a model. Most developing countries have developed their own national list of essential drugs. This national list is used to define the range of drugs which are available in governmental health facilities, either free of charge or against nominal payment.
2. Because of economic developments and health sector reform, public funding in many developing or transitional countries has become insufficient to ensure free health care and free provision of essential drugs. As health insurance coverage is also very limited, 70-90% of all health care costs (most of that being drug costs) are paid out-of-pocket.
3. In most countries, and especially in urban areas, most essential drugs are available on the private market; often even without prescription.

Access to health care is not the same as access to *free* health care. The most essential health care facilities are usually available in urban areas in most developing countries; but they are rarely free of charge. Not the WHO Model List but the national list of essential drugs may give an impression of the standard of health care in the public sector. However, a much better yardstick for the quality of health care in a given country is the newly developed WHO health care index[2], as published in the World Health Report 2000, which is based on a weighted judgement of factors such as the level and distribution of health care, fair financing, and responsiveness.

---

[2] Ed.: In the statistical annex of its World Health Report 2000 WHO estimates, among other things, overall health system attainment and overall health system performance. The top five countries of health system attainment are Japan, Switzerland, Norway, Sweden and Luxembourg. The bottom five in the list are Liberia, Niger, Somalia, the Central African Republic and Sierra Leone. WHO attributes the best overall health system performance to France, Italy, San Marino, Andorra and Malta, while ranking Nigeria, the Democratic Republic of the Congo, the Central African Republic, Myanmar and Sierra Leone last on the list.

2.2

WHO ESSENTIAL DRUGS LIST

In its General Comment on the right to the highest attainable standard of health the Committee on Economic, Social and Cultural Rights mentions the availability of essential drugs as one of the integral parts of the right to health. The definition of essential drugs has been determined on the basis of WHO's Action Programme on Essential Drugs. Obviously, WHO's essential drugs list can be considered as an internationally accepted guideline. The provision of essential drugs may differ from country to country, based on specific demands related to specific illnesses. In 1998 WHO produced a Factsheet[1] *on the concept of the WHO Model List of Essential Drugs and in particular on the tenth report, which was published in 1997, containing improvements and updated information. In this factsheet it is stated that* "Over the last 20 years the WHO Model List has proven to be an invaluable tool for saving lives and improving health through more rational use of drugs, wider access to drugs, and improved drug quality. (...) The WHO Model List of Essential Drugs is considered to be as an informational and educational tool for professionals and consumers. Since concern about health care costs is now a priority even in developed countries, the Model List is of greater importance than ever as an aid to developing treatment guidelines, national formularies, consumer drug information, and other measures to improve drug use. The List also serves as the basis for WHO model drug information, a new model formulary, and basic drug quality tests. The List should be seen in the context of national drug policies which address not only drug use, but also procurement and supply strategies, drug financing, drug donations, and research priorities. (...) The following selection criteria are being used for inclusion of drugs on the list: Sound and adequate data of efficacy and safety from clinical studies; evidence of performance under different health care settings; availability in a form in which quality, including adequate bioavailability, can be assured; stability under the anticipated conditions of storage and use; total cost and relative cost-effectiveness of the treatment; and preference for single compounds. Where drugs appear to be similar in the above respects, comparative pharmacokinetic properties and the availability of facilities for manufacture or storage are used as secondary criteria. The procedures for updating the list are currently under review and may be revised in the future."

It is of paramount importance to note and emphasize that the international community also agreed on an Emergency Health Kit. Such a Kit could also serve as a norm in the decision-making process concerning the issue at stake in this Handbook and has been referred to in the above mentioned Factsheet on Essential Drugs.

"About 250 of the 306 active substances on the 1999 Model List are included in WHO standard treatment guidelines; 55 are included in the interagency New Emergency Health Kit. All drugs on the Model List are included in the WHO Model Formulary, and are a priority for inclusion in the International Pharmacopoea and Basic Tests."

---

[1] WHO Factsheet No. 198 (1998).

The Tenth WHO Essential Drugs List (WHO Model List, revised December 1999) has become an indispensable part of this Handbook and has thus been incorporated.

Essential Drugs[2]

Section 1: Anaesthetics

1.1 GENERAL ANAESTHETICS AND OXYGEN

ether, anaesthetic (1c) (2)	inhalation
halothane (2)	inhalation
ketamine (2)	injection, 50 mg (as hydro-chloride)/ ml in 10-ml vial
nitrous oxide (2)	inhalation
oxygen	inhalation (medicinal gas)
¤[3] thiopental (2)	powder for injection, 0.5 g, 1.0 g (sodium salt) in ampoule

---

[2] Ed.: As to antiretroviral (ARV) drugs WHO states that: "Zidovudine and nevirapine to prevent Mother-to-Child-Transmission are included on the current list. However, ARVs for the treatment of HIV/ AIDS were not included because there was insufficient evidence that they can be used safely and effectively in resource-poor health care situations. Their inclusion was neither proposed nor supported by UNAIDS or the WHO/HSI department at the last meeting. The issue will be considered again at the next revision in autumn 2001.

ARVs are not the only drugs needed for the prevention and treatment of HIV/AIDS. An analysis of all guidelines for the prevention and treatment of HIV/AIDS published by UNAIDS and WHO shows that a total of 117 drugs are being recommended. Of these, 75 are already on the WHO Model List of Essential Drugs." (source: WHO Factsheet, op.cit.)

[3] Ed.: ¤: This symbol indicates that it concerns an example of a therapeutic group. Various drugs can serve as alternatives

When the strength of a drug is specified in terms of a selected salt or ester, this is mentioned in brackets; when it refers to the active moiety, the name of the salt or ester in vrackets is preceded by the word "as". Many drugs included in the list are preceded by a box (¤) to indicate that they represent an example of a therapeutic group and that various drugs could serve as alternatives. It is imperative that this is understood when drugs are selected at national level, since choice is then influenced by the comparative cost and availability of equivalent products. Examples of acceptable substitutions include:

- Hydrochlorothiazide: any other thiazide-type diuretic currently in broad clinical use.
- Hydralazine: any other peripheral vasodilator having an antihypertensive effect.
- Senna: any stimulant laxative (either synthetic or of plant origin).
- Sulfadiazine: any other short-acting, systemically active sulfonamide unlikely to cause crystalluria.

Numbers in parentheses following drug names indicate:

(1) Drugs subject to international control under: (a) the Single Convention on Narcotic Drugs (1961); (b) the Convention on Psychotropic Substances (1971); or (c) the United Nations Convention against Illicit Traffic in Narcotic Drugs and Psychotropic Substances (1988).
(2) Specific expertise, diagnostic precision, individualization of dosage or special equipment required for proper use.
(3) Greater potency or efficacy.
(4) In renal insufficiency, contraindicated or dosage adjustments necessary.
(5) To improve compliance.
(6) Special pharmacokinetic properties.
(7) Adverse effects diminish benefit/risk ratio.
(8) Limited indications or narrow spectrum of activity.
(9) For epidural anaesthesia.
(10) Sustained-release preparations are available. A proposal to include such a product in a national list of essential drugs should be supported by adequate documentation.
(11) Monitoring of therapeutic concentrations in plasma can improve safety and efficacy.

Letters in parentheses following the drug names indicate the reasons for the inclusion of complementary drugs:

(A) When drugs in the main list cannot be made available.
(B) When drugs in the main list are known to be ineffective or inappropriate for a given individual.
(C) For use in rare disorders or in exceptional circumstances.
(D) Reserve antimicrobials to be used only when there is significant resistance to other drugs on the list.
Drugs are listed in alphabetical order.

1.2 LOCAL ANAESTHETICS

¤ bupivacaine (2, 9)	injection, 0.25%, 0.5% (hydrochloride) in vial injection for spinal anaesthesia, 0.5% (hydrochloride) in 4-ml ampoule to be mixed with 7.5% glucose solution
¤ lidocaine	injection, 1%, 2% (hydrochloride) in vial injection, 1%, 2% (hydrochloride) + epinephrine 1:200 000 in vial injection for spinal anaesthesia, 5% (hydrochloride) in 2-ml ampoule to be mixed with 7.5% glucose solution topical forms, 2–4% (hydrochloride) dental cartridge, 2% (hydrochloride) + epinephrine 1:80 000
Complementary drug	
ephedrine (C) (For use in spinal anaesthesia during delivery to prevent hypotension)	injection, 30 mg (hydrochloride)/ml in) 1-ml ampoule

1.3 PREOPERATIVE MEDICATION & SEDATION FOR SHORT-TERM PROCEDURES

atropine	injection, 1 mg (sulfate) in 1-ml ampoule
chloral hydrate	syrup, 200 mg/5 ml
¤ diazepam (1b)	injection, 5 mg/ml in 2-ml ampoule tablet, 5 mg
¤ morphine (1a)	injection, 10 mg (sulfate or hydrochloride) in 1-ml ampoule
¤ promethazine	elixir or syrup, 5 mg (hydrochloride)/5 ml

Section 2: Analgesics, Antipyretics, Nonsteroidal Anti-Inflammatory Drugs (NSAIDs), Drugs Used to Treat Gout and Disease-Modifying Agents used in Rheumatic Disorders (DMARDs)

2.1 NON-OPIOID ANALGESICS & NSAIDs

acetylsalicylic acid	tablet, 100–500 mg suppository, 50–150 mg
¤ ibuprofen	tablet, 200 mg, 400 mg
paracetamol	tablet, 100–500 mg suppository, 100 mg syrup, 125 mg/5 ml

2.2 OPIOID ANALGESICS

¤ codeine (1a)	tablet, 30 mg (phosphate)
¤ morphine (1a)	injection, 10 mg (sulfate or hydrochloride) in 1-ml ampoule oral solution, 10 mg (hydrochloride or sulfate))/5 ml tablet, 10 mg (sulfate)
Complementary drug	
¤ pethidine (A) (1a, 4)	injection, 50 mg (hydrochloride) in 1-ml ampoule tablet, 50 mg, 100 mg (hydrochloride)

2.3 DRUGS USED TO TREAT GOUT

allopurinol (4)	tablet, 100 mg
colchicine (7)	tablet, 500 µg

2.4 DISEASE-MODIFYING AGENTS USED IN RHEUMATIC DISORDERS

azathioprine (2)	tablet, 50 mg
chloroquine (2)	tablet, 100 mg, 150 mg (as phosphate or sulfate)
cyclophosphamide (2)	tablet, 25 mg
methotrexate (2)	tablet, 2.5 mg (as sodium salt)
penicillamine (2)	capsule or tablet, 250 mg
sulfasalazine (2)	tablet, 500 mg

Section 3: Antiallergics and Drugs Used in Anaphylaxis

¤ chlorphenamine	tablet, 4 mg (hydrogen maleate) injection, 10 mg (hydrogen maleate) in 1-ml ampoule
¤ dexamethasone	tablet, 500 µg, 4 mg injection, 4 mg dexamethasone phosphate (as disodium salt) in 1-ml ampoule
epinephrine	injection, 1 mg (as hydro-chloride or hydrogen tartrate) in 1-ml ampoule
hydrocortisone	powder for injection, 100 mg (as sodium succinate) in vial
¤ prednisolone	tablet, 5 mg

Section 4: Antidotes and Other Substances Used in Poisonings

4.1 NON-SPECIFIC

¤ charcoal, activated	powder
ipecacuanha	syrup, containing 0.14% ipecacuanha alkaloids calculated as emetine

4.2 SPECIFIC

acetylcysteine	injection, 200 mg/ml in 10-ml vial
atropine	injection, 1 mg (sulfate) in 1-ml ampoule
calcium gluconate (2, 8)	injection, 100 mg/ml in 10-ml ampoule
deferoxamine	powder for injection, 500 mg (mesilate) in vial
dimercaprol (2)	injection in oil, 50 mg/ml in 2-ml ampoule
¤ DL-methionine	tablet, 250 mg
methylthioninium chloride (methylene blue)	injection, 10 mg/ml in 10-ml ampoule
naloxone	injection, 400 µg (hydrochloride) in 1-ml ampoule
penicillamine (2)	capsule or tablet, 250 mg
potassium ferric hexacyano-ferrate(II) 2H2O (Prussian blue)	powder for oral administration
sodium calcium edetate (2)	injection, 200 mg/ml in 5-ml ampoule
sodium nitrite	injection, 30 mg/ml in 10-ml ampoule
sodium thiosulfate	injection, 250 mg/ml in 50-ml ampoule

Section 5: Anticonvulsants/ Antiepileptics

carbamazepine (10, 11)	scored tablet, 100 mg, 200 mg
¤ diazepam (1b)	injection, 5 mg/ml in 2-ml ampoule (intravenous or rectal)
ethosuximide	capsule, 250 mg syrup, 250 mg/5 ml
magnesium sulfate	injection, 500 mg/ml in 2-ml ampoule and 10-ml ampoule
phenobarbital (1b, 11)	tablet, 15–100 mg elixir, 15 mg/5 ml
phenytoin (7, 11)	capsule or tablet, 25 mg, 50 mg, 100 mg (sodium salt) injection, 50 mg (sodium salt)/ml in 5-ml vial
valproic acid (7, 11)	enteric coated tablet, 200 mg, 500 mg (sodium salt)

Complementary drug

¤ clonazepam (B) (1b)	scored tablet, 500 μg

Section 6: Anti-infective Drugs

6.1 ANTHELMINTHICS

6.1.1 INTESTINAL ANTHELMINTHICS

albendazole	chewable tablet, 400 mg
levamisole	tablet, 50 mg, 150 mg (as hydrochloride)
¤ mebendazole	chewable tablet, 100 mg, 500 mg
niclosamide	chewable tablet, 500 mg
praziquantel	ablet, 150 mg, 600 mg
pyrantel	chewable tablet, 250 mg (as embonate) oral suspension, 50 mg (as embonate)/ml

6.1.2 ANTIFILARIALS

diethylcarbamazine	tablet, 50 mg, 100 mg (dihydrogen citrate)
ivermectin	scored tablet, 3 mg, 6 mg

Complementary drug

suramin sodium (B) (2, 7)	powder for injection, 1 g in vial

6.1.3 ANTISCHISTOSOMALS AND OTHER ANTITREMATODE DRUGS

praziquantel	tablet, 600 mg
triclabendazole	tablet, 250 mg

Complementary drug

oxamniquine (C) (8)	capsule, 250 mg syrup, 250 mg/5 ml

6.2 ANTIBACTERIALS

6.2.1 BETA LACTAM DRUGS

¤ amoxicillin	capsule or tablet, 250 mg, 500 mg (anhydrous) powder for oral suspension, 125 mg (anhydrous)/5 ml
ampicillin	powder for injection, 500 mg, 1 g (as sodium salt) in vial
benzathine benzylpenicillin	powder for injection, 1.44 g benzylpenicillin (= 2.4 million IU) in 5-ml vial
benzylpenicillin	powder for injection, 600 mg (= 1 million IU), 3 g (= 5 million IU) (sodium or potassium salt) in vial

¤ cloxacillin	capsule, 500 mg, 1 g (as sodium salt) powder for oral solution, 125 mg (as sodium salt)/5 ml powder for injection, 500 mg (as sodium salt) in vial
phenoxymethylpenicillin	tablet, 250 mg (as potassium salt) powder for oral suspension, 250 mg (as potassium salt)/ 5 ml
procaine benzylpenicillin	powder for injection, 1 g (= 1 million IU), 3 g (= 3 million IU) in vial
Restricted indications	
¤ amoxicillin + ¤ clavulanic acid (D)	tablet, 500 mg + 125 mg
ceftazidime (D)	powder for injection, 250 mg (as pentahydrate) in vial
¤ ceftriaxone (D)	powder for injection, 250 mg (as sodium salt) in vial
imipenem + cilastatin (D)	powder for injection, 250 mg (as monohydrate) + 250 mg, (as sodium salt) 500 mg (as monohydrate) + 500 mg in vial (as sodium salt)
6.2.2 OTHER ANTIBACTERIALS	
¤ chloramphenicol (7)	capsule, 250 mg oral suspension, 150 mg (as palmitate)/5 ml powder for injection, 1 g (sodium succinate) in vial
¤ ciprofloxacin	tablet, 250 mg (as hydrochloride)
¤ doxycycline (5, 6)	capsule or tablet, 100 mg (hydrochloride)
¤ erythromycin	capsule or tablet, 250 mg (as stearate or ethyl succinate) powder for oral suspension, 125 mg (as stearate or ethyl succinate) powder for injection, 500 mg (as lactobionate) in vial
¤ gentamicin (2, 4, 7, 11)	injection, 10 mg, 40 mg (as sulfate)/ml in 2-ml vial
¤ metronidazole	tablet, 200–500 mg injection, 500 mg in 100-ml vial suppository, 500 mg, 1 g oral suspension, 200 mg (as benzoate)/5 ml
nalidixic acid (8)	tablet, 250 mg, 500 mg
nitrofurantoin (4, 8)	tablet, 100 mg
spectinomycin (8)	powder for injection, 2 g (as hydrochloride) in vial
¤ sulfadiazine (4)	tablet, 500 mg injection, 250 mg (sodium salt) in 4-ml ampoule
¤ sulfamethoxazole + trimethoprim (4)	tablet, 100 mg + 20 mg, 400 mg + 80 mg oral suspension, 200 mg + 40 mg/5 ml injection, 80 mg + 16 mg/ml in 5-ml and 10-ml ampoule
trimethoprim (8)	tablet, 100 mg, 200 mg injection, 20 mg/ml in 5-ml ampoule
Complementary drugs	
chloramphenicol (C)	oily suspension for injection, 0.5 g (as sodium succinate)/ ml in 2-ml ampoule
clindamycin (B) (8)	capsule, 150 mg injection, 150 mg (as phosphate)/ml

Restricted indications

vancomycin (D)	powder for injection 250 mg (as hydrochloride) in vial

6.2.3 ANTILEPROSY DRUGS

clofazimine	capsule, 50 mg, 100 mg
dapsone	tablet, 25 mg, 50 mg, 100 mg
rifampicin	capsule or tablet, 150 mg, 300 mg

6.2.4 ANTITUBERCULOSIS DRUGS

ethambutol (4)	tablet, 100–400 mg (hydrochloride)
isoniazid	tablet, 100–300 mg
isoniazid + ethambutol (5)	tablet, 150 mg + 400 mg
pyrazinamide	tablet, 400 mg
rifampicin	capsule or tablet, 150 mg, 300 mg
rifampicin + isoniazid (5)	tablet, 60 mg + 30 mg, 150 mg + 75 mg, 300 mg + 150 mg tablet, 60 mg + 60 mg, 150 mg + 150 mg (for intermittent use 3 times weekly)
rifampicin + isoniazid + pyrazinamide (5)	tablet, 60 mg + 30 mg + 150 mg, 150 mg + 75 mg + 400 mg tablet, 150 mg + 150 mg + 500 mg (for intermittent use 3 times weekly)
rifampicin + isoniazid + pyrazinamide + ethambutol	tablet,150 mg + 75 mg + 400 mg + 275 mg
streptomycin (4)	powder for injection, 1 g (as sulfate) in vial

Complementary drug

thioacetazone + isoniazid (A)	tablet, 50 mg + 100 mg, (5, 7) 150 mg + 300 mg

---

Additional reserve antituberculosis drugs for the treatmentof drug-resistant tuberculosis should be used in specialized centres only with WHO-recommended TB control strategy, DOTS, and treatment programmes.

6.3 ANTIFUNGAL DRUGS

amphotericin B (4)	powder for injection, 50 mg in vial
¤ fluconazole	capsule, 50 mg injection, 2 mg/ml in vial oral suspension, 50 mg/5-ml
griseofulvin (7)	capsule or tablet, 125 mg, 250 mg
nystatin	tablet, 100 000, 500 000 IU lozenge, 100 000 IU pessary, 100 000 IU

Complementary drugs

flucytosine (B) (4, 8)	capsule, 250 mg infusion, 2.5 g in 250 ml
potassium iodide (A)	saturated solution

6.4 ANTIVIRAL DRUGS

6.4.1 ANTIHERPES DRUGS

aciclovir (8)	tablet, 200 mg powder for injection, 250 mg (as sodium salt) in vial

6.4.2 ANTIRETROVIRAL DRUGS

Adequate resources and specialist oversight are a prerequisite for the introduction of this class of drugs.

nevirapine (8)	tablet, 200 mg oral solution, 50 mg/5 ml
zidovudine (8)	capsule, 100 mg, 250 mg injection, 10 mg/ml in 20-ml vial oral solution, 50 mg/5 ml

---

Drugs for treatment of HIV/AIDS include nucleoside reverse transcriptase inhibitors (NRTIs), non-nucleoside reverse transcriptase inhibitors (NNRTIs) and protease inhibitors (PIs). Zidovudine and nevirapine have been shown to reduce or prevent mother-to-child transmission of HIV infection. **This is the only indication for which they are included here**. Single drug use with zidovudine, except in pregnancy, is now regarded as obsolete because of the development of resistance. Triple therapy is beyond the budgets of most national drug programmes and therefore HIV/AIDS treatment policies must be decided at country or institutional level.

6.5 ANTIPROTOZOAL DRUGS

6.5.1 ANTIAMOEBIC AND ANTIGIARDIASIS DRUGS

¤ diloxanide	tablet, 500 mg (furoate)
¤ metronidazole	tablet, 200–500 mg injection, 500 mg in 100-ml vial oral suspension, 200 mg (as benzoate)/5 ml

6.5.2 ANTILEISHMANIASIS DRUGS

¤ meglumine antimoniate	injection, 30%, equivalent to approx. 8.5% antimony, in 5-ml ampoule
pentamidine (5)	powder for injection, 200 mg, 300 mg (isetionate) in vial

Complementary drug

amphotericin B (B) (4)	powder for injection, 50 mg in vial

6.5.3 ANTIMALARIAL DRUGS

(a) FOR CURATIVE TREATMENT

¤ chloroquine	tablet, 100 mg, 150 mg (as phosphate or sulfate) syrup, 50 mg (as phosphate or sulfate)/5 ml injection, 40 mg (as hydro-chloride, phosphate or sulfate)/ ml in 5-ml ampoule
primaquine	tablet, 7.5 mg, 15 mg (as diphosphate)
¤ quinine	tablet, 300 mg (as bisulfate or sulfate) injection, 300 mg (as dihydrochloride)/ml in 2-ml ampoule

Complementary drugs

¤ doxycycline (B) (for use only in combination with quinine)	capsule or tablet 100 mg (hydrochloride)
mefloquine (B)	tablet, 250 mg (as hydrochloride)
¤ sulfadoxine + pyrimethamine (B)	tablet, 500 mg + 25 mg

Restricted indications

artemether (D)	injection, 80 mg/ml in 1-ml ampoule
artesunate (D)	tablet, 50 mg

(b) FOR PROPHYLAXIS

chloroquine	tablet, 150 mg (as phosphate or sulfate) syrup, 50 mg (as phosphate or sulfate)/5 ml
doxycycline	capsule or tablet, 100 mg (hydrochloride)
mefloquine	tablet, 250 mg (as hydrochloride)
proguanil (for use only in combination with chloroquine)	tablet, 100 mg (hydrochloride)

6.5.4 ANTIPNEUMOCYSTOSIS AND ANTITOXOPLASMOSIS DRUGS

pentamidine (2)	tablet, 200 mg, 300 mg
pyrimethamine	tablet, 25 mg
sulfamethoxazole + trimethoprim	injection, 80 mg + 16 mg/ml in 5-ml and 10-ml ampoule

6.5.5 ANTITRYPANOSOMAL DRUGS

(a) AFRICAN TRYPANOSOMIASIS

melarsoprol (2)	injection, 3.6% solution
pentamidine (2)	powder for injection, 200 mg, 300 mg (isetionate) in vial
suramin sodium	powder for injection, 1 g in vial

Complementary drug

eflornithine (C)	injection, 200 mg (hydro-chloride)/ ml in 100-ml bottles

(b) AMERICAN TRYPANOSOMIASIS

benznidazole (7)	tablet, 100 mg
nifurtimox (2, 8)	tablet, 30 mg, 120 mg, 250 mg

6.6 INSECT REPELLENTS

diethyltoluamide	topical solution, 50%, 75%

Section 7: Antimigraine Drugs

7.1 FOR TREATMENT OF ACUTE ATTACK

acetylsalicylic acid	tablet, 300–500 mg
ergotamine (1c) (7)	tablet, 1 mg (tartrate)
paracetamol	tablet, 300–500 mg

7.2 FOR PROPHYLAXIS

¤ propranolol	tablet, 20 mg, 40 mg (hydrochloride)

Section 8: Antineoplastic and Immunosuppressive Drugs and Drugs Used in Palliative Care

8.1 IMMUNOSUPPRESSIVE DRUGS

Adequate resources and specialist oversight are a prerequisite for the introduction of this class of drugs.

¤ azathioprine (2)	tablet, 50 mg
	powder for injection, 100 mg (as sodium salt) in vial
¤ ciclosporin (2)	capsule, 25 mg
(for organ transplantation)	concentrate for injection, 50 mg/ml in 1-ml ampoule

8.2 CYTOTOXIC DRUGS

Adequate resources and specialist oversight are a prerequisite for the introduction of this class of drugs.

asparaginase (2)	powder for injection, 10 000 IU in vial
bleomycin (2)	powder for injection, 15 mg (as sulfate) in vial
calcium folinate (2)	tablet, 15 mg
	injection, 3 mg/ml in 10-ml ampoule
chlorambucil (2)	tablet, 2 mg
chlormethine (2)	powder for injection, 10 mg (hydrochloride) in vial
cisplatin (2)	powder for injection, 10 mg, 50 mg in vial
cyclophosphamide (2)	tablet, 25 mg
	powder for injection, 500 mg in vial
cytarabine (2)	powder for injection, 100 mg in vial
dacarbazine (2)	powder for injection, 100 mg in vial
daunorubicin (2)	powder for injection, 50 mg (as hydrochloride) in vial
dactinomycin (2)	powder for injection 500 µg in vial
¤ doxorubicin (2)	powder for injection, 10 mg, 50 mg (hydrochloride) in vial
etoposide (2)	capsule, 100 mg
	injection, 20 mg/ml in 5-ml ampoule
fluorouracil (2)	injection, 50 mg/ml in 5-ml ampoule
levamisole (2)	tablet, 50 mg (as hydrochloride)
mercaptopurine (2)	tablet, 50 mg
methotrexate (2)	tablet, 2.5 mg (as sodium salt)
	powder for injection, 50 mg (as sodium salt) in vial
procarbazine	capsule, 50 mg (as hydrochloride)
vinblastine (2)	powder for injection, 10 mg (sulfate) in vial
vincristine (2)	powder for injection, 1 mg, 5 mg (sulfate) in vial

8.3 HORMONES AND ANTIHORMONES

¤ prednisolone	tablet, 5 mg
	powder for injection, 20 mg, 25 mg (as sodium phosphate or sodium succinate) in vial
tamoxifen	tablet, 10 mg, 20 mg (as citrate)

8.4 DRUGS USED IN PALLIATIVE CARE

The WHO Expert Committee on Essential Drugs recommended that all the drugs mentioned in the WHO publi-cation Cancer Pain Relief: with a Guide to Opioid Availability, 2nd edition, be considered essential. The drugs are included in the relevant sections of the model list according to their therapeutic use, e.g. analgesics.

Section 9: Antiparkinsonism Drugs

¤ biperiden	tablet, 2 mg (hydrochloride) injection, 5 mg (lactate) in 1-ml ampoule
levodopa + ¤ carbidopa (5, 6)	tablet, 100 mg + 10 mg, 250 mg + 25 mg

Section 10: Drugs affecting the Blood

10.1 ANTIANAEMIA DRUGS

ferrous salt	tablet, equivalent to 60 mg iron oral solution, equivalent to 25 mg iron (as sulfate)/ml
ferrous salt + folic acid (nutritional supplement for use during pregnancy)	tablet, equivalent 60 mg iron + 400 μg folic acid
folic acid (2)	tablet, 1 mg, 5 mg injection, 1 mg (as sodium salt) in 1-ml ampoule
hydroxocobalamin (2)	injection, 1 mg in 1-ml ampoule

Complementary drug

¤ iron dextran (B) (5)	injection, equivalent to 50 mg iron/ ml in 2-ml ampoule

10.2 DRUGS AFFECTING COAGULATION

desmopressin (8)	injection, 4 μg (acetate)/ml in 1-ml ampoule nasal spray, 10 μg (acetate)/ metered dose
heparin sodium	injection, 1000 IU/ml, 5000 IU/ml, 20 000 IU/ml in 1-ml ampoule
phytomenadione	injection, 10 mg/ml in 5-ml ampoule tablet, 10 mg
protamine sulfate	injection, 10 mg/ml in 5-ml ampoule
¤ warfarin (2, 6)	tablet, 1 mg, 2 mg and 5 mg (sodium salt)

Section 11: Blood Products and Plasma Substitutes

11.1 PLASMA SUBSTITUTES

¤ dextran 70	injectable solution, 6%
¤ polygeline	injectable solution, 3.5%

11.2 PLASMA FRACTIONS FOR SPECIFIC USE 1

Complementary drugs

¤ factor VIII concentrate (C) (2, 8)	dried
¤ factor IX complex (coagulation factors II, VII, IX, X) concentrate (C) (2, 8)	dried

Section 12: Cardiovascular Drugs

12.1 ANTIANGINAL DRUGS

¤ atenolol	tablet, 50 mg, 100 mg
glyceryl trinitrate	tablet (sublingual), 500 μg
¤ isosorbide dinitrate	tablet (sublingual), 5 mg
¤ verapamil (10)	tablet, 40 mg, 80 mg (hydrochloride)

12.2 ANTIARRHYTHMIC DRUGS

¤ atenolol	tablet, 50 mg, 100 mg
digoxin (4, 11)	tablet, 62.5 μg, 250 μg oral solution, 50 μg/ml injection, 250 μg/ml in 2-ml ampoule
lidocaine	injection, 20 mg (hydrochloride)/ml in 5-ml ampoule
verapamil (8, 10)	tablet, 40 mg, 80 mg (hydrochloride) injection, 2.5 mg (hydrochloride)/ml in 2-ml ampoule

Complementary drugs

epinephrine (C)	injection, 1 mg (as hydrochloride)/ml
isoprenaline (C)	injection, 20 μg (hydrochloride)/ml
¤ procainamide (B)	tablet, 250 mg, 500 mg (hydrochloride) injection, 100 mg (hydrochloride)/ml in 10-ml ampoule
¤ quinidine (A) (7)	tablet, 200 mg (sulfate)

12.3 ANTIHYPERTENSIVE DRUGS

¤ atenolol	tablet, 50 mg, 100 mg
¤ captopril	scored tablet, 25 mg
¤ hydralazine	tablet, 25 mg, 50 mg (hydrochloride) powder for injection, 20 mg (hydrochloride) in ampoule
¤ hydrochlorothiazide	scored tablet, 25 mg
methyldopa (7)	tablet, 250 mg
¤ nifedipine (10)	sustained-release formulations tablet, 10 mg
¤ reserpine	tablet, 100 μg, 250 μg injection, 1 mg in 1-ml ampoule

Complementary drugs

prazosin	tablet, 500 μg, 1 mg (mesilate)
¤ sodium nitroprusside (C) (2, 8)	powder for infusion, 50 mg in ampoule

12.4 DRUGS USED IN HEART FAILURE

¤ captopril	scored tablet, 25 mg
digoxin (4, 11)	tablet, 62.5 μg, 250 μg oral solution, 50 mg/ml injection, 250 μg/ml in 2-ml ampoule
dopamine	injection, 40 mg (hydrochloride)/ml in 5-ml vial
¤ hydrochlorothiazide	tablet, 25 mg, 50 mg

12.5 ANTITHROMBOTIC DRUGS

acetylsalicylic	acid tablet, 100 mg

Complementary drug

streptokinase (C)	powder for injection, 100 000 IU, 750 000 IU in vial

12.6 LIPID-LOWERING AGENTS

The WHO Expert Committee on Essential Drugs recognzes the value of lipid-lowering drugs in treating patients with hyperlipidaemia. Beta-hydroxy-beta-methylglutaryl-coenzyme A (HMG CoA) reductase inhibitors, often referred to as "statins", are potent and effective lipidlowering drugs with a good tolerability profile. Several of these drugs have been shown to reduce the incidence of fatal and non-fatal myocardial infarction, stroke and mortality (all causes), as well as the need for coronary by-pass surgery. All remain very costly but may be costeffective for secondary prevention of cardiovascular disease as well as for primary prevention in some very high-risk patients. Since no single drug has been shown to be significantly more effective or less expensive than others in the group, none is included in the model list; the choice of drug for use in patients at highest risk should be decided at national level.

Section 13: Dermatological Drugs (topical)

13.1 ANTIFUNGAL DRUGS

benzoic acid + salicylic	acid ointment or cream, 6% + 3%
¤ miconazole	ointment or cream, 2% (nitrate)
sodium thiosulfate	solution, 15%

Complementary drug

selenium sulfide (C)	detergent-based suspension, 2%

13.2 ANTI-INFECTIVE DRUGS

¤ methylrosanilinium chloride	aqueous solution, 0.5%
(gentian violet)	tincture, 0.5%
neomycin +	ointment, 5 mg
¤ bacitracin (7)	neomycin sulfate + 500 IU bacitracin zinc/g
potassium permanganate	aqueous solution, 1:10 000
silver sulfadiazine	cream, 1%, in 500-g container

13.3 ANTI-INFLAMMATORY AND ANTIPRURITIC DRUGS

¤ betamethasone (3)	ointment or cream, 0.1% (as valerate)
¤ calamine lotion	lotion
¤ hydrocortisone	ointment or cream, 1% (acetate)

13.4 ASTRINGENT DRUGS

aluminium diacetate	solution, 13% for dilution

13.5 DRUGS AFFECTING SKIN DIFFERENTIATION AND PROLIFERATION

benzoyl peroxide	lotion or cream, 5%
coal tar	solution, 5%
dithranol	ointment, 0.1–2%
fluorouracil	ointment, 5%
¤ podophyllum resin (7)	solution, 10–25%
salicylic	acid solution 5%
urea	ointment or cream, 10%

13.6 SCABICIDES AND PEDICULICIDES

¤ benzyl benzoate	lotion, 25%
permethrin	cream, 5%
	lotion, 1%

13.7 ULTRAVIOLET-BLOCKING AGENTS

Complementary drugs

topical sun protection agent with activity against UVA and UVB (C)	cream, lotion or gel

Section 14: Diagnostic Agents

14.1 OPHTHALMIC DRUGS

fluorescein	eye drops, 1% (sodium salt)
¤ tropicamide	eye drops, 0.5%

14.2 RADIOCONTRAST MEDIA

¤ amidotrizoate	injection, 140–420 mg iodine (as sodium or meglumine salt)/ml in 20-ml ampoule
barium sulfate	aqueous suspension
¤ iohexol	injection, 140–350 mg iodine/ml in 5-ml, 10-ml and 20-ml ampoule
¤ iopanoic	acid tablet, 500 mg
¤ propyliodone (For administration only into the bronchial tree).	oily suspension, 500–600 mg/ml in 20-ml ampoule

Complementary drug

¤ meglumine iotroxate (C)	solution, 5 – 8 g iodine in 100–250 ml

Section 15: Disinfectants and Antiseptics

15.1 ANTISEPTICS

¤ chlorhexidine	solution, 5% (digluconate) for dilution
¤ ethanol	solution, 70% (denatured)
¤ polyvidone iodine	solution, 10%

15.2 DISINFECTANTS

¤ chlorine base compound	powder (0.1% availablem chlorine) for solution
¤ chloroxylenol	solution, 4.8%
glutaral	solution, 2%

Section 16: Diuretics

¤ amiloride (4, 7, 8)	tablet, 5 mg (hydrochloride)
¤ furosemide	tablet, 40 mg
	injection, 10 mg/ml in 2-ml ampoule
¤ hydrochlorothiazide	tablet, 25 mg, 50 mg
spironolactone (8)	tablet, 25 mg

Complementary drug

¤ mannitol (C)	injectable solution, 10%, 20%

Section 17: Gastrointestinal Drugs

17.1 ANTACIDS AND OTHER ANTIULCER DRUGS

aluminium hydroxide	tablet, 500 mg oral suspension, 320 mg/5 ml
¤ cimetidine	tablet, 200 mg injection, 200 mg in 2-ml ampoule
magnesium hydroxide	oral suspension, equivalent to 550 mg magnesium oxide/10 ml

17.2 ANTIEMETIC DRUGS

metoclopramide	tablet, 10 mg (hydrochloride) injection, 5 mg (hydrochloride)/ml in 2-ml ampoule
¤ promethazine	tablet, 10 mg, 25 mg (hydrochloride) elixir or syrup, 5 mg (hydrochloride)/5 ml injection, 25 mg (hydrochloride)/ml in 2-ml ampoule

17.3 ANTIHAEMORRHOIDAL DRUGS

¤ local anaesthetic, astringent and anti-inflammatory drug	ointment or suppository

17.4 ANTI-INFLAMMATORY DRUGS

hydrocortisone	suppository, 25 mg (acetate) ¤ retention enema
¤ sulfasalazine (2)	tablet, 500 mg suppository, 500 mg retention enema

17.5 ANTISPASMODIC DRUGS

¤ atropine	tablet, 0.6 mg (sulfate) injection, 1 mg (sulfate) in 1-ml ampoule

17.6 LAXATIVES

¤ senna	tablet, 7.5 mg (sennosides) (or traditional dosage forms)

17.7 DRUGS USED IN DIARRHOEA

17.7.1 ORAL REHYDRATION

oral rehydration salts (for glucose–electrolyte solution)	powder, 27.9 g/l

Components	g/l
sodium chloride	3.5
trisodium citrate dihydrate 2	2.9
potassium chloride	1.5
glucose	20.0

17.7.2 ANTIDIARRHOEAL (SYMPTOMATIC) DRUGS

¤ codeine (1a)	tablet, 30 mg (phosphate)

Section 18: Hormones, other Endo-crine Drugs and Contraceptives

18.1 ADRENAL HORMONES AND SYNTHETIC SUBSTITUTES

¤ dexamethasone	tablet, 500 µg, 4 mg injection, 4 mg dexamethasone phosphate (as disodium salt) in 1-ml ampoule
hydrocortisone	powder for injection, 100 mg (as sodium succinate) in vial
¤ prednisolone	tablet, 1 mg, 5 mg

Complementary drug

fludrocortisone (C)	tablet, 100 µg (acetate)

18.2 ANDROGENS

Complementary drug

testosterone (C) (2)	injection, 200 mg (enantate) in 1-ml ampoule

18.3 CONTRACEPTIVES

18.3.1 HORMONAL CONTRACEPTIVES

¤ ethinylestradiol + ¤ levonorgestrel	tablet, 30 µg + 150 µg,
¤ ethinylestradiol + ¤ levonorgestrel	tablet, 50 µg+ 250 µg (pack of four)
¤ ethinylestradiol + ¤ norethisterone	tablet, 35 µg + 1.0 mg
levonorgestrel	tablet, 0.75 mg (pack of two)

Complementary drugs

¤ levonorgestrel (B)	tablet, 30 µg
medroxyprogesterone acetate (B) (7, 8)	depot injection, 150 mg in 1-ml vial
norethisterone enantate (B) (7, 8)	oily solution, 200 mg/ml in1-ml ampoule

18.3.2 INTRAUTERINE DEVICES

copper-containing device

18.3.3 BARRIER METHODS

condoms with or without spermicide (nonoxinol)

diaphragms with spermicide (nonoxinol)

18.4 ESTROGENS

¤ ethinylestradiol	tablet, 10 µg, 50 µg

18.5 INSULINS AND OTHER ANTIDIABETIC AGENTS

¤ glibenclamide	tablet, 2.5 mg, 5 mg
insulin injection (soluble)	injection, 40 IU/ml in 10-ml vial, 100 IU/ml in 10-ml vial
intermediate-acting insulin	injection, 40 IU/ml in 10-ml vial, 100 IU/ml in 10-ml vial (as compound insulin zinc suspension or isophane insulin)

metformin	tablet, 500 m (hydrochloride)
18.6 OVULATION INDUCERS	
¤ clomifene (2, 8)	tablet, 50 mg (citrate)
18.7 PROGESTOGENS	
norethisterone	tablet, 5 mg
Complementary drug	
medroxyprogesterone acetate (B)	tablet, 5 mg
18.8 THYROID HORMONES AND ANTITHYROID DRUGS	
levothyroxine	tablet, 50 µg, 100 µg (sodium salt)
potassium iodide	tablet, 60 mg
¤ propylthiouracil	tablet, 50 mg

Section 19: Immunologicals

19.1 DIAGNOSTIC AGENTS

tuberculin,3 purified protein derivative (PPD)	injection

19.2 SERA AND IMMUNOGLOBULINS 4

anti-D immunoglobulin (human)	injection, 250 µg in single-dose vial
¤ antitetanus immunoglobulin (human)	injection, 500 IU in vial
antivenom serum	injection
diphtheria antitoxin	injection, 10 000 IU, 20 000 IU in vial
immunoglobulin, human normal (2)	injection (intramuscular)
immunoglobulin, human normal (2, 8)	injection (intravenous)
¤ rabies immunoglobulin	injection, 150 IU/ml

19.3 VACCINES 5

19.3.1 FOR UNIVERSAL IMMUNIZATION

BCG
diphtheria
pertussis
tetanus
hepatitis B
measles
poliomyelitis

19.3.2 FOR SPECIFIC GROUPS OF INDIVIDUALS

influenza
meningitis
mumps
rabies
rubella

typhoid
yellow fever

Section 20: Muscle Relaxants (peripherally acting) and Cholinesterase Inhibitors

¤ alcuronium chloride (2)	injection, 5 mg/ml in 2-ml ampoule
¤ neostigmine	tablet, 15 mg (bromide) injection, 500 µg, 2.5 mg (metilsulfate) in 1-ml ampoule
pyridostigmine bromide (2, 8)	tablet, 60 mg injection, 1 mg in 1-ml ampoule
suxamethonium chloride (2)	injection, 50 mg/ml in 2-ml ampoule powder for injection
Complementary drug	
vecuronium bromide (C)	powder for injection, 10 mg in vial

Section 21: Ophthalmological Preparations

21.1 ANTI-INFECTIVE AGENTS

¤ gentamicin	solution (eye drops), 0.3% (as sulfate)
¤ idoxuridine	solution (eye drops), 0.1% eye ointment, 0.2%
silver nitrate	solution (eye drops), 1%
¤ tetracycline	eye ointment, 1% (hydrochloride)

21.2 ANTI-INFLAMMATORY AGENTS

¤ prednisolone	solution (eye drops), 0.5% (sodium phosphate)

21.3 LOCAL ANAESTHETICS

¤ tetracaine	solution (eye drops), 0.5% (hydrochloride)

21.4 MIOTICS AND ANTIGLAUCOMA DRUGS

acetazolamide	tablet, 250 mg
¤ pilocarpine	solution (eye drops), 2%, 4% (hydrochloride or nitrate)
¤ timolol	solution (eye drops), 0.25%, 0.5% (as maleate)

21.5 MYDRIATICS

atropine	solution (eye drops), 0.1%, 0.5%, 1% (sulfate)
Complementary drug	
epinephrine (A)	solution (eye drops), 2% (as hydrochloride)

Section 22: Oxytocics and Antioxytocics

22.1 OXYTOCICS

¤ ergometrine (1c)	tablet, 200 µg (hydrogen maleate) injection, 200 µg (hydrogen maleate) in 1-ml ampoule
oxytocin	injection, 10 IU in 1-ml ampoule

22.2 ANTIOXYTOCICS

¤ salbutamol (2)	tablet, 4 mg (as sulfate) injection, 50 μg (as sulfate)/ml in 5-ml ampoule

Section 23: Peritoneal Dialysis Solution

intraperitoneal dialysis solution (of appropriate composition)	parenteral solution

Section 24: Psychotherapeutic Drugs

24.1 DRUGS USED IN PSYCHOTIC DISORDERS

¤ chlorpromazine	tablet, 100 mg (hydrochloride) syrup, 25 mg (hydrochloride)/5 ml injection, 25 mg (hydrochloride)/ml in 2-ml ampoule
¤ fluphenazine (5)	injection, 25 mg (decanoate or enantate) in 1-ml ampoule
¤ haloperidol	tablet, 2 mg, 5 mg injection, 5 mg in 1-ml ampoule

24.2 DRUGS USED IN MOOD DISORDERS

24.2.1 DRUGS USED IN DEPRESSIVE DISORDERS

¤ amitriptyline	tablet, 25 mg (hydrochloride)

24.2.2 DRUGS USED IN BIPOLAR DISORDERS

carbamazepine (10, 11)	scored tablet, 100 mg, 200 mg
lithium carbonate (2, 4)	capsule or tablet, 300 mg
valproic acid (7, 11)	enteric coated tablet, 200 mg, 500 mg (sodium salt)

24.3 DRUGS USED IN GENERALIZED ANXIETY AND SLEEP DISORDERS

¤ diazepam (1b)	scored tablet, 2 mg, 5 mg

24.4 DRUGS USED IN OBSESSIVE COMPULSIVE DISORDERS AND PANIC ATTACKS

clomipramine	capsules, 10 mg, 25 mg (hydrochloride)

Section 25: Drugs Acting on the Respiratory Tract

25.1 ANTIASTHMATIC DRUGS

¤ aminophylline (2)	injection, 25 mg/ml in 10-ml ampoule
¤ beclometasone	inhalation (aerosol), 50 μg, 250 μg, (dipropionate) per dose
¤ epinephrine	injection, 1 mg (as hydrochloride or hydrogen tartrate) in 1-ml ampoule
ipratropium bromide	inhalation (aerosol), 20 μg/dose
¤ salbutamol	tablet, 2 mg, 4 mg (as sulfate) inhalation (aerosol), 100 μg (as sulfate) per dose syrup, 2 mg (as sulfate)/5 ml injection, 50 μg (as sulfate)/ml in 5-ml ampoule respirator solution for use in nebulizers, 5 mg (as sulfate)/ml

theophylline (10, 11)	tablet, 100 mg, 200 mg, 300 mg
Complementary drug	
¤ cromoglicic acid (B)	inhalation (aerosol), 20 mg (sodium salt) per dose

25.2 ANTITUSSIVES

¤ dextromethorphan	oral solution, 3.5 mg (bromide)/5 ml

Section 26: Solutions correcting Water, Electro-lyte and Acid–base Disturbances

26.1 ORAL

oral rehydration salts (for glucose– for composition see section 17.7.1 electrolyte solution)

potassium chloride	powder for solution

26.2 PARENTERAL

glucose	injectable solution, 5% isotonic, 10% isotonic, 50% hypertonic
glucose with sodium chloride	injectable solution, 4% glucose, 0.18% sodium chloride (equivalent to Na + 30 mmol/l Cl – 30 mol/l)
potassium chloride (2)	11.2% solution in 20-ml ampoule, (equivalent to K + 1.5 mmol/ml, Cl – 1.5 mmol/ml)
sodium chloride	injectable solution, 0.9% isotonic (equivalent to Na + 154 mmol/l, Cl – 154 mmol/l)
sodium hydrogen carbonate	injectable solution, 1.4% isotonic (equivalent to Na + 167 mmol/l, HCO 3 – 167 mmol/l) 8.4% solution in 10-ml ampoule (equivalent to Na + 1000 mmol/l, HCO 3 – 1000 mmol/l)
¤ compound solution of sodium lactate	injectable solution

26.3 MISCELLANEOUS

water for injection 2-ml, 5-ml, 10-ml ampoules

Section 27: Vitamins and Minerals

ascorbic	acid tablet, 50 mg
¤ ergocalciferol	capsule or tablet, 1.25 mg (50 000 IU) oral solution, 250 mg/ml (10 000 IU/ml)
iodine (8)	iodized oil, 1 ml (480 mg iodine), 0.5 ml (240 mg iodine) in ampoule (oral or injectable) solution, 0.57 ml, (308 mg iodine) in dispenser bottle capsule, 200 mg
¤ nicotinamide	tablet, 50 mg
pyridoxine	tablet, 25 mg (hydrochloride)
¤ retinol	sugar-coated tablet, 10 000 IU (as palmitate) (5.5 mg) capsule, 200 000 IU (as palmitate) (110 mg) oral oily solution, 100 000 IU/ml in multidose dispenser (as palmitate)

	water-miscible injection, 100 000 IU (as palmitate) (55 mg) in 2-ml ampoule
riboflavin	tablet, 5 mg
¤ sodium fluoride	in any appropriate formulation
thiamine	tablet, 50 mg (hydrochloride)
Complementary drug	
calcium gluconate (C) (2, 8)	injection,100 mg/ml in 10-ml ampoule

2.5

SACHS, THE ECONOMIST AND HEALTH

When it comes to health-related information gathering, both for the legal expert, the layman and the medical expert, the Economist proves to be indispensable. Not only concerning economics and politics, but also on the subject of health, this London-based weekly tends to provide the necessary background and insight for being kept updated and for forming an opinion. The policy maker, the executive as well as the medical professional will appreciate the usefulness of the Economist and, indeed, in this Handbook some relevant material has been put together for this very purpose.[1] *Of course, the Economist may primarily focus on (the need to reform) the British National Health System (NHS) and the Medicaid Systems cs in the USA, but it also pays ample attention to health issues in general, as well as the impact of the burden of disease on the economy and economic development.*

The material contained in this Handbook is centred around two key pieces which were contributed to the Economist (by invitation) by Jeffrey Sachs, the Harvard-based scholar and expert, who has the insight and creativity to present innovative ideas. Sachs is Director of the Centre for International Development and Professor of International Trade at Harvard. A prolific writer, he has advised the governments of many developing and Eastern European countries.

In his contribution on 'helping the world's poorest',[2] *SACHS focuses on the need to mobilize global science and technology to address the Third World crisis of,*

---

[1] The Economist paid attention to the WHO 2000 report in its June 24th, 2000 issue; to diabetes on November 11th, 2000; it wrote on the exportation of Cuba's health system on October 28th, 2000; on getting cheap drugs to poor countries on September 30th, 2000; on the US health care system on July 22nd, 2000; on the AIDS epidemic on e.g. July 15th and December 2nd, 2000; on leprosy on December 2nd, 2000; on the health of nations on June 24th, 2000; on life expectancy on June 10th, 2000; and it elaborated on European health and its significant differences on December 10th, 1998 ("... Strong community health care and good coverage by public health programmes help to explain why Nordic countries rank so highly. Italy ranks fourth, partly because of a dramatic improvement in immunisation rates. Other Mediterranean countries, such as Greece and France, are also high on the list, thanks to good diets and lower levels of heart disease. Northern European countries fare worse, with their poor diets and lifestyles. Britain, for instance, ranks 14th and Germany 16th. But the unhealthiest countries in Europe are in the east, where diets are bad and health care is dominated by costly and inefficient hospitals. Russia is the sickest man of Europe ...").

[2] The Economist, August 14th, 1999.

inter alia, public health, which indeed is strongly linked to demographic stress as well. It is to be recalled that the total amount of development aid covers at most 33% of what the Third World loses by not being able to export its products to the First World, which, if this were to be taken into account would create win/win situations. However, financial and technical aid will be needed to improve good governance, to assist towards decreasing the public debt, and to create the structures for progress and development.

SACHS says on, for example, the science at the ecological divide:
"... In this context, it is worth noting that the inequalities of income across the globe are actually exceeded by the inequalities of scientific output and technological innovation. The chart below shows the remarkable dominance of rich countries in scientific publications and, even more notably, in patents filed in Europe and the United States.

The role of the developing world in one sense is much greater than the chart indicates. Many of the scientific and technological breakthroughs are made by poor-country scientists working in rich-country laboratories. Indian and Chinese engineers account for a significant proportion of Silicon Valley's workforce, for example. The basic point, then, holds even more strongly: global science is directed by the rich countries and for the rich-country markets, even to the extent of mobilising much of the scientific potential of the poorer countries.

The imbalance of global science reflects several forces. First, of course, science follows the market. This is especially true in an age when technological leaps require expensive scientific equipment and well-provisioned research laboratories. Second, scientific advance tends to have increasing returns to scale: adding more scientists to a community does not diminish individual marginal productivity but tends to increase it. Therein lies the origin of university science departments, regional agglomerations such as Silicon Valley and Route 128, and mega-laboratories at leading high-technology firms including Merck, Microsoft and Monsanto. And third, science requires a partnership between the public and private sectors. Free-market ideologues notwithstanding, there is scarcely one technology of significance that was not nurtured through public as well as private care.

If technologies easily crossed the ecological divide, the implications would be less dramatic than they are. Some technologies, certainly those involving the computer and other ways of managing information, do indeed cross over, and give great hopes of spurring technological capacity in the poorest countries. Others – especially in the life sciences but also in the use of energy, building techniques, new materials and the like – are prone to "ecological specificity". The result is a profound imbalance in the global production of knowledge: probably the most powerful engine of divergence in global well-being between the rich and the poor ..."

SACHS then continues to elaborate a plan of action to find a solution to counter the negative aspects of market mechanisms, whilst fully making use of that same mechanism:

"... Consider malaria. The disease kills more than 1m people a year, and perhaps as many as 2.5m. The disease is so heavily concentrated in the poorest tropical countries, and overwhelmingly in sub-Saharan Africa, that nobody even bothers to keep an accurate count of clinical cases or deaths. Those who remember that richer places such as Spain, Italy, Greece and the southern United States once harboured the disease may be misled into thinking that the problem is one of social institutions to control its transmission. In fact, the sporadic transmission of malaria in the sub-tropical regions of the rich countries was vastly easier to control than is its chronic transmission in the heart of the tropics. Tropical countries are plagued by ecological conditions that produce hundreds of infective bites per year per person. Mosquito control does not work well, if at all, in such circumstances. It is in any event expensive.

Recent advances in biotechnology, including mapping the genome of the malaria parasite, point to a possible malaria vaccine. One would think that this would be high on the agendas of both the international community and private pharmaceutical firms. It is not. A Wellcome Trust study a few years ago found that only around $80m a year was spent on malaria research, and only a small fraction of that on vaccines.

The big vaccine producers, such as Merck, Rhône-Poulenc's Pasteur-MérieuxConnaught and SmithKline Beecham, have much of the in-house science but not the bottom-line motivation. They strongly believe that there is no market in malaria. Even if they spend the hundreds of millions, or perhaps billions, of dollars to do the R&D and come up with an effective vaccine, they believe, with reason, that their product would just be grabbed by international agencies or private-sector copycats. The hijackers will argue, plausibly, that the poor deserve to have the vaccine at low prices – enough to cover production costs but not the preceding R&D expenditures.

The malaria problem reflects, in microcosm, a vast range of problems facing the HIPCs [Highly Indebted Poor Countries] in health, agriculture and environmental management. They are profound, accessible to science and utterly neglected. A hundred IMF missions or World Bank health-sector loans cannot produce a malaria vaccine. No individual country borrowing from the Fund or the World Bank will ever have the means or incentive to produce the global public good of a malaria vaccine. The root of the problem is a much more complex market failure: private investors and scientists doubt that malaria research will be rewarded financially. Creativity is needed to bridge the huge gulfs between human needs, scientific effort and market returns.

The following approach might work. Rich countries would make a firm pledge to purchase an effective malaria vaccine for Africa's 25m newborn children each year if such a vaccine is developed. They would even state, based on appropriate and clear scientific standards, that they would guarantee a minimum purchase price – say, $10 per dose – for a vaccine that meets minimum conditions of efficacy, and perhaps raise the price for a better one. The recipient countries might also be asked to pledge a part of the cost, depending on their incomes. But nothing need be spent by any government until the vaccine actually exists.

Even without a vast public-sector effort, such a pledge could galvanise the world of private-sector pharmaceutical and biotechnology firms. Malaria vaccine research would suddenly become hot. Within a few years, a breakthrough of profound benefit to the poorest countries would be likely. The costs in foreign aid would be small: a few hundred million dollars a year to tame a killer of millions of children. Such a vaccine would rank among the most effective public-health interventions conceivable. And, if science did not deliver, rich countries would end up paying nothing at all.

Malaria imposes a fearsome burden on poor countries, the AIDS epidemic an even weightier load. Two-thirds of the world's 33m individuals infected with the HIV virus are sub-Saharan Africans, according to a UN estimate in 1998, and the figure is rising. About 95% of worldwide HIV cases are in the developing world. Once again, science is stopping at the ecological divide.

Rich countries are controlling the epidemic through novel drug treatments that are too expensive, by orders of magnitude, for the poorest countries. Vaccine research, which could provide a cost-effective method of prevention, is dramatically under-funded. The vaccine research that is being done focuses on the specific viral strains prevalent in the United States and Europe, not on those which bedevil Africa and Asia. As in the case of malaria, the potential developers of vaccines consider the poor-country market to be no market at all. The same, one should note, is true for a third worldwide killer. Tuberculosis is still taking the lives of more than 2m poor people a year and, like malaria and AIDS, would probably be susceptible to a vaccine, if anyone cared to invest in the effort.

The poorer countries are not necessarily sitting still as their citizenry dies of AIDS. South Africa is on the verge of authorising the manufacture of AIDS medicines by South African pharmaceutical companies, despite patents held by American and European firms. The South African government says that, if rich-country firms will not supply the drugs to the South African market at affordable prices (ones that are high enough to meet marginal production costs but do not include the patent-generated monopoly profits that the drug companies claim as their return for R&D), then it will simply allow its own firms to manufacture the drugs, patent or no.[3] In a world in which science is a rich-country prerogative

[3] Ed.: The year 2000 witnessed many calls to action. A five-company initiative announced in May led to front-page reports that Merck, Hoffmann-La Roche, Bristol-Myers Squibb, Glaxo Welcome and Boehringer would make AIDS medicines widely available in the poorest countries at deep discounts. But by 1 January 2001 only one of the companies had disclosed actual price cuts. In March 2000, Pfizer proposed to donate Diflucan, a powerful anti-fungal agent that nearly one in ten

while the poor continue to die, the niceties of intellectual property rights are likely to prove less compelling than social realities.

There is no shortage of complexities ahead. The world needs to reconsider the question of property rights before patent rights allow rich-country multinationals in effect to own the genetic codes of the very foodstuffs on which the world depends, and even the human genome itself. The world also needs to reconsider the role of institutions such as the World Health Organisation and the Food and Agriculture Organisation. These UN bodies should play a vital role in identifying global priorities in health and agriculture, and also in mobilising private-sector R&D towards globally desired goals. There is no escape from such public-private collaboration. It is notable, for example, that Monsanto, a life-sciences multinational based in St Louis, Missouri, has a research and development budget that is more than twice the R&D budget of the entire worldwide network of public-sector tropical research institutes. Monsanto's research, of course, is overwhelmingly directed towards temperate-zone agriculture ..."

SACHS elaborates on this idea in a contribution on 'a new map of the world' which was published June 2000.[4] *Moreover, he proposes to 'rethink' aid. It is often submitted that true globalization is the result of, and will result in the free movement of goods, capital, services and people. But the simple question needs to be asked again and again whether First World Countries need Third World Tomato Pickers, or rather Third World Tomatoes (which prove to be quite tasty). Moreover, the time may have come to ask whether the Indian IT experts should move to the USA and Germany, or whether the industries should invest in Bangalore instead. In fact, by dialling a local frequent flyer number, one runs a fair chance of being connected with either Dublin or New Delhi. Moreover, the accounts of e.g. the Röling Foundation are checked in Kuala Lumpur rather than in Amsterdam where they were sent in the first place. Globalization is about moving marginal industries to countries where they have added value, rather than hiring cheap, often illegal, labour to keep those industries afloat. Globalization is about agreeing that people cannot be equated to capital, goods or services. The total of the world's development aid covers a mere 33% of the losses encountered by the Third World by not being able to export their products. The European Union spends each and every ten days the yearly UNHCR budget meant to assist 15 million refugees and displaced persons. Abolishing agricultural subsidies might*

African AIDS patients requires for survival, to donate the drug to those in need, albeit limited to patients in South Africa only. Early December 2000 an agreement had actually been signed. A US$ 1 billion offer to assist turned out to be Export-Import bank loans, at commercial interest rates, to buy American drugs at market prices. IBRD announced a US$500 million AIDS funding pool, but still regards anti-retroviral drugs as cost-ineffective, and thus in fact discouraging borrowers from buying those drugs. (Source: IHT, December 28, 2000)

[4] The Economist, June 24th, 2000

have a tremendous impact on migratory movements. It may enable a great many persons to produce at home the products they would otherwise be asked to produce in a foreign country.

When SACHS talks about rethinking aid, he submits:
"... Much of the world, perhaps 2 billion people or more, will fail to share in the benefits of global growth without a complete change in international strategy. This needs to be undertaken on several fronts:
– **Public health and population.** The burden of disease on poor countries, especially in sub-Saharan Africa, is simultaneously a humanitarian catastrophe, a daunting barrier to development, and (through its effects on population) a first-order threat to critical regions of high biodiversity. Foreign investors shun the worst-affected economies, and the burdens of ill-health block development in other ways too. Sick children often face a lifetime of diminished productivity because of interruptions in schooling together with cognitive and physical impairment.

Donor countries' efforts to control infectious disease in the poor countries are small. Worldwide support for malaria control in Africa is probably little more than $50m-75m a year, although malaria claims perhaps 2m lives annually (a million or more directly, and another million or so from diseases in which malaria is a factor). Donor efforts for AIDS control in Africa have averaged no more than a few tens of millions of dollars a year in the past decade. The disease now claims more than 2m lives a year in Africa, with around 4m new infections a year, and around 23m infected Africans overall. Donor support for immunisation has been so small that many poor countries have not even begun to introduce vaccines that have been used routinely in the rich countries for years, and which could greatly reduce death and disease in Africa at modest cost. A donation of up to $1 billion by the Gates Foundation will at last address this urgent problem.

A serious effort would start with a proper battle against these lethal infectious diseases. The Clinton administration, rightly if belatedly, has recognised AIDS in the developing world as a national-security problem for the United States, because of the potential of the disease to destabilise vast regions. Africa's leaders have recently pleaded for $1 billion a year in donor support to help them partially reverse the devastation of malaria. The UN has pleaded for another $4 billion a year to address the AIDS epidemic. A few billion more is needed to address the growing epidemic of TB, and the millions of deaths due to measles, diarrhoeal diseases and other communicable illness.

In all, these initiatives would demand perhaps $10 billion a year from the rich countries. At roughly $10 per person per year for the 1 billion citizens of the first world, the cost of saving millions of lives is paltry.
– **Connecting the marginalised regions.** In recent years NAFTA has bound Mexico into the global high-tech economy and the European Union has developed new trading arrangements with North Africa and Central Europe. These

preferential approaches have greatly helped the immediate beneficiaries, but harm more distant regions by drawing FDI and trade away. The cartelisation of global shipping makes things worse: trade routes linking marginal traders with major markets tend to be much less competitive than the high-volume routes. A new multilateral trade round, with a focus on better market access for the poorest countries, could do much to put this right.

The World Bank and IMF must adopt a new approach in helping marginalised regions to connect to the world economy. Both reject the use of special incentives to attract FDI, such as export-processing zones, tax holidays, and joint ventures between host governments and foreign investors, even though these methods have worked for others. When Costa Rica wanted to attract Intel, it gave incentives. Israel has done the same. Ireland's rapid growth was supported by low rates of corporate tax applied to foreign investments. Rich and poor countries could design co-operative schemes to bring new technologies to the marginalised regions, sharing the fiscal costs.

Information technology offers another huge opportunity, because it can overcome many of the disadvantages of distance. A landlocked region, say Mongolia, surely would have a comparative advantage in IT-based service exports (software, data transcription, telemarketing) as against export-oriented manufactures. America has a sophisticated industrial policy for the uptake of IT; so should the developing countries. Even more important, the political leadership of the developing countries should work with leaders of the IT industry to develop policies for a rapid increase in bandwidth in the poor countries.

– **Fostering technological advance**. At the core of the global divide is the vast inequality in innovation and diffusion of technology. Globalisation policy has barely scratched the surface of this central problem. World Bank lending and grants for science and technology are probably less each year than one-tenth of the R&D budget of a single large American pharmaceutical company. The World Bank devotes around $50m a year to tropical agricultural research, around $10m to tropical health research, and a little more in a scattering of other loans. Merck's R&D budget in 1999 was $2.1 billion.

The model to emulate is the Rockefeller Foundation, the pre-eminent development institution of the 20th century, which showed what grant aid targeted on knowledge could accomplish. Rockefeller funds supported the eradication of hookworm in the American South; the discovery of the Yellow Fever vaccine; the development of penicillin; the establishment of public-health schools (today's undisputed leaders in their fields) all over the world; the establishment of medical faculties in all parts of the world; the creation and funding of great research centres such as the University of Chicago, the Brookings Institution, Rockefeller University, and the National Bureau of Economic Research; the control of malaria in Brazil; the founding of the research centres that accomplished the green revolution in Asia; and more. Not one of these accomplishments was assisted by means of a high-conditionality country loan.

The Rockefeller Foundation worked mainly with universities and governments. A new strategy of technological promotion must be based on an interplay of academia, government and industry, with participation from rich and poor alike. A first step would be a promise by international high-tech firms to increase their technological co-operation with developing countries, combined with a far greater commitment by the poor countries to promote science and technology. The big drugs companies give hundreds of millions of dollars in medicines to poor countries, and under pressure they have agreed to supply anti-AIDS drugs at low cost. But they could do more.

First-world universities and scientific associations could and should help too. Many American and European universities have established overseas campuses or long-term exchange relationships, but these are typically directed towards undergraduate education rather than long-term collaborative research. Research links are under-funded. American universities receive more than $25 billion a year in philanthropic and foundation giving. They ought to devote much more of these funds to deepening their research and teaching relationships with partner institutions in developing countries.

Philanthropy is only part of the answer. Public money will also be needed. Last year Michael Kremer and I proposed to use public-sector pledges to buy new vaccines as a way to direct global research towards malaria, TB and AIDS. President Clinton adopted that approach in proposed new tax breaks for successful vaccine developers. Public funding should aim at a combination of new "push" strategies, in which R&D efforts directed at poor-country problems are explicitly subsidised, and "pull" strategies in which market incentives are enhanced by rich-country commitments to buy new technologies on behalf of the poor countries.

At the government-to-government level, the international community should make a firm commitment to promote scientific and technological capacity in the poor countries. As part of this, rich countries should exercise restraint in the use of property rights. Rich countries are unilaterally asserting rights of private ownership over human and plant genetic sequences, or basic computer codes, or chemical compounds long in use in herbal medicines. These approaches are of dubious legitimacy and will worsen global inequities. A better balance needs to be struck between incentives for innovation on one hand, and the interests of the poorest on the other ..."

In conclusion it should be submitted that any debate on whether or not to cater for the needs of those who have been able to reach the 'North' should always be seen in the wider context of global development, globalization, existing divides and the need to invest in those activities which yield the best results. It concerns long-term thinking, long-term approaches of which the short-term patient may become the victim. But growth has never occurred without pain.

THIRD WORLD REALITIES: EXAMPLES OF NON-INCLUSION

Pierre Mercenier

When it comes to drawing lines, it is quite remarkable to note that virtually all Third World health projects take it for granted that not all potential patients will have access to services on offer. Moreover, the necessary reforms are not easy to implement. Mercenier explains that the realities on the ground shall be governed by common sense in order to avoid misunderstanding, failures and/or an unavoidable breakdown

1. When "Third World Realities" are considered, the first statement to make is that a comparison between Third World situations and those of Western countries is irrelevant. The policies for the provision of health services in developed countries are, to a large extent, irrational due to the following factors:
   - A lack of efficiency: private services, in a state of monopoly, involve higher costs due to inflation as regards medical procedures, whether these involve examinations, drugs, or surgery, which are often at best useless, at worst counter productive. This being so, under the umbrella of false ethical considerations only preventing false negatives are taken into consideration, while false positives are not.[1]
   - A lack of "prise en charge": people are considered to be consumers to be satisfied rather than citizens to be educated. The systems do not create the conditions for the real 'participation' of people in the management of their own health. People are submitted to the financial and spiritual exploitation of the 'medico-industrial complex.'
   - As to both efficiency and 'prise en charge', it can be submitted that what is affordable in rich countries is not in poor ones: the price of irrationality is too high for underdeveloped economies, which are, moreover, completely dependent.

[1] T.J. Scheff, Behavioural Sciences 8: P. 97.107 (1963).

P.J. van Krieken (Ed.), Health, Migration and Return

2. Are there any alternatives? The answer is definitely 'yes'. Not wishing to disregard other experiments, I have chosen to present our experiment in the district of Kasongo (former Zaire), because it is the one I can best present as evidence. The 'zone of Kasongo' is a typical 'district', under the present international meaning, with a population of about 200.000 inhabitants, 30.000 of whom reside in the main town, the rest residing in the rural areas, with density becoming thinner depending on the distance to the main town. The latter enjoys the services of a central hospital. The experiment to develop the 'District Health System' started in 1971 and lasted until 1988, in a gradually degrading economic and political environment.
   The strategy consisted of five components:
   - The constitution of an integrated District Management Team.
   - The technical and human promotion of the health auxiliaries present in the district.
   - Supporting the hospital in playing its role as a reference centre for all the population in the district, but with an emphasis on making that role a rational one.
   - Developing first line health service coverage by health centres, each of them covering about 10,000 people, with the full participation of the people.
   - Organizing integrated care (curative, preventive and promotional) at the first level in the health centres.

   Self- financing was not an initial concern, but was gradually developed as a tool for participation: educate people to understand that resources are not unlimited and demonstrate what their own monetary contributions were intended for. Consequently, people should appreciate that health services have a cost.

   Solidarity was sought at the health centre level:
   - Solidarity between those registered (all those people residing in the area covered) was achieved by a system of flat-rate payments covering episodes of diseases (or high-risk medical conditions like pregnancy and delivery), included the costs of referral to hospital when required (the cost of delivery was included in the rate for antenatal care). Thus, the surplus payment for light episodes covered the costs of heavier episodes.
   - Solidarity between the health centre team and the people in the sense that those registered had a full health 'prise en charge' with for example, external activities such as home-visits for patients with chronic diseases (like tuberculosis) or with long-term health problems (like birth control).

   People from outside the area of solidarity were not refused services for short-term needs but could not benefit from the solidarity system: they had to pay a fee for services at the health centres and the hospital, and, for example, they did not benefit from the organised follow-up.

The system worked routinely from about 1975, and the coverage had reached about 80 % of the population by 1986. An evaluation of cost was made in 1979. The cost of the whole system was calculated to amount to 3 US$ per inhabitant per year, of which US$ 1 for first line services, and US$ 2 for additional services.

The Kasongo type of experiment was illustrative of the concretization of the approach to health systems which received international recognition at the World Health Organisation Conference at Alma Ata in 1978 entitled 'Primary Health Care', bearing the political slogan of 'Health for All in 2000'.
A Congolese (formally Zairian) doctor, who had worked in Kasongo for more than eight years, presented his doctoral thesis on the Kasongo experiment in 1988 under the title 'Health for All, it is possible'.

3. So why did the WHO, and other agencies, not succeed in achieving a gradual implementation of Primary Health Care? I will merely propose a list of factors which I encountered, each of which I believe being readily understandable:

A. General factors:

– The general situation of underdevelopment does not in itself create the necessary fertile soil for innovation by rational solutions due to corruption, uncertainty, lack of leadership, financial as well as psychological dependence upon rich countries, the image of which is often counterproductive, etc.

B. Political factors:

– The bureaucracy, of the WHO itself, but also of other institutions (for example: it took nine years between the Alma Ata and Harare Conferences to recognize that the development of Primary Health Care required a decentralisation of decision-making and to formulate the concept of the District Health System as a basis for future planning):

– The financing of vertical programmes preferably to establish a stable infrastructure;

– The neo-liberal philoophy of privatisation with the illusion of unrealistic complete self-financing;

– Resistance to real decentralisation;

– The education of medical doctors, etc.

C. Conceptual factors:

– The contradictions among experts, and an inability to bridge the gap between traditional Public Health (based on the rational top-down approach to health problems) and the provision of health care (based on the bottom-up response to people's perceived needs);

– The contradictions between the administrative approach, requiring norms and targets, and the management approach of creating a complex system with all the tensions involved (for example, the tension between top-down rationality and bottom-up sensitivity).

4. But what is the relative importance of each of these factors, and probably many others, in blocking the situation in each local, regional or national situation? This is largely theoretical. In fact, each of these factors involves a large degree of misunderstanding as regards the conceptual model, and a large degree of opposition from those who fear that they will lose a privileged position. For example, a hospital director, whose social recognition as well as material resources are based on attracting as many patients as possible, has no interest in understanding the role of the hospital in a District Health System where promoting first level health care might endanger his relative monopoly. In the same way, a co-operation agency, whether public or private, has no interest in developing a complex system while a vertical programme provides quicker and more visible results, even if they are not sustainable. The real concrete answer is to test, in each individual situation, how to overcome the encountered resistance, before tackling the new situations. This requires a flexible, but systematic, approach inspired by the methods of operational and action research.[2]

5. It is clear that the responsibility of wealthy countries pertains to the whole process, whether by means of national policies or by means of their influence within the international agencies. Consistent policies have been lacking. It is too often the case that, expecting quick and visible results from a simplistic understanding of complex situations, failures and frustrations, have resulted, which in turn have led to in pendulum policies: 'if this does not work, let's try something else'. Dilemmas are the result: is it really a case of responding to human rights requirements when we are only able to meet, with great expense, the needs of a privileged few, because we have failed to provide elementary services to the masses? Where do 'human rights' stop and where does charity start?

---

[2] Daniel Grodos and Pierre Mercenier: A clearer methodology – Health Systems Research for more effective action. *Studies in Health Service Organisations and Policy*, 15/2000.

CHAPTER 3
ETHICS

Too often, 'experts' believe that they can reach conclusions without having regard to the underlying principles of society, mutuality, interdependency and communities in general. One needs to know how the world of ethics reacts to the issue of migration, health and return. The writings of Tholen and Weiner on the one hand and the contributions by Dupuis and Wirtz on the other are essential for any effort to see this complex issue perspective and in context. De Milliano, finally, provides a relevant observation based on experiences in the 'real world', in this case the recent Great Lake drama.

CHAPTER
ETHICS

ETHICS, SOVEREIGNTY AND MIGRATION

The 1996 special issue of the International Migration Review (IMR) on Ethics, Migration and Global Stewardship,[1] *a number of contributions focused on the political philosophy and ethics behind and beyond migration. Teresa Sullivan for instance developed a language for ethical discourse on migration and examined the extent to which choices may be made at the micro-level and at the macro-level. The concepts of cultural distance, reciprocity, the role of the individual and of the state and their interrelationships can be evaluated in perspective of choice. Indeed, ethics is about choices.*

As to morality, there are two approaches. As Carens argues in that same IMR issue, the realistic approach wants to avoid too large a gap between the 'ought' and the 'is' and focuses on what is possible, given existing realities. The idealistic approach requires to assess the current reality in the light of the highest ideals. Discussions about the ethics of migration require a full range of perspectives using both approaches.

In his recent Ph.D. on aliens policy and justice,[2] *THOLEN argues:*
(...) First of all there is the issue whether the members of a country are justified in deciding on admission of foreigners. In all modern nations this is common practice and most people approve of it, but are they right in doing so? Secondly, supposing that some kind of immigration policy is justified, do strangers that are in some sense near to the citizens have priority in entry over others? And finally: should every immigrant automatically receive full Membership status, or may (must?) the host country stipulate special conditions?

In his comprehensive theory of justice Walzer takes a stand on these issues. He doesn't doubt that existing political communities are justified in protecting their own existence. In national politics the members are free to decide on the future shape of the community, and this includes their decisions on immigration policy. However, he finds there are four guidelines relevant to the judgement in immi-

[1] IMR, Vol XXX, No.1, Spring 1996.

[2] J.H.M.M. Tholen, *Vreemdelingenbeleid en Rechtvaardigheid?* Nijmegen 1997, with a summary in the English (pp. 213-215) from which the excerpts contained in this Chapter have been taken.

gration issues: the principle of mutual aid (to help people in need), the kinship principle, a special responsibility towards fellow nationals, and the concept of 'paying ones debts' (to help those whose neediness was in some way caused by the potential host nation.) Walzer states that individuals admitted should automatically receive full membership status – supplemental naturalization requirements are out of the question.

Walzer's argument makes one wonder: does he actually offer any reasons or does he simply describe standing procedure in immigration policy? Why does he take existing nations and their focus on self determination as a starting point? In the present day, can one still take seriously a theory that ascribes such a significance to autonomous nations? Isn't Walzer here, just as Aristotle once did when he idealized the city-state, concentrating on a political entity at a time it already shows signs of dissolution?

Other writers on justice in migration, Carens for instance, do not start their evaluation from existing nations that try to protect their distinctiveness. Doing so, they say, amounts to giving privileges to some people at the expense of others. These writers think it appropriate to start from the fundamental moral stance that politics and institutional organisation should be judged on the criterion of mutual human respect. Carens finds that Walzer's conventionalist method doesn't leave enough room for moral evaluation.

Carens tries to show us that several theories that take human dignity as their starting point all lead to the same conclusion, although they may differ from each other in other ways. The individual right to free migration is the ultimate conclusion of libertarian, liberal egalitarian and utilitarian theories.

A closer look at Caren's argument does raise some questions, though. How can these theories take a plurality of political entities into account, if all people stand in the same moral relationship towards one another? And what exactly is the value and meaning of particular cultural and social groups? (Ch. 5-7.)

An insight into the meaning and value of particular communities is given by writers often referred to as the 'communitarians'. These communitarians do not present moral theories that use the concept of individual equality as a starting point of reference. Instead they focus on peoples' relationships to specific others. These are relationships which people do not choose, but which they find themselves confronted with. They are the setting within which a person's identity is formed and they are the preconditions for individual development. These relationships are valued, because of their particularity, because people can call them *mine.* The communitarians do not address the issue of admission to and exclusion from membership within these relationships. Their theoretical perspective does not even seem to allow for such an investigation. According to communitarians membership is a given. From their perspective the possibility of (moral) relationship with outsiders is excluded.

That leaves us with a peculiar duality. Theories that give priority to the equal worth of every individual cannot take the meaning and value that a particular community has for its members, into account. And theories that do, don't take into account the worth of individuals as such, therefore neither that of outsiders. From both perspectives an evaluation of acts of admission and exclusion is problematic. Isn't there then a third way, that unites the best of these two perspectives?

Several writers have tried to overcome the duality. Some have described it in terms of the relationship to a specific culture and community versus the value of an individual with the ability to exercise free will. They point out that this ambivalence can easily be dissolved by understanding cultural relationships as a product of individual choice. Others describe the duality in terms of partiality versus impartiality. They try to solve this tension by postulating that any virtue of partiality can be deduced from the obligation to be impartial. Both strategies to dissolve the duality, however, do fail. The 'solution' always seems to imply some magical disappearing act. The stalemate between the two perspectives remains. This theoretical impasse has a political counterpart: conflicting individual and collective rights.

One can lament over this *cul de sac*, but one can also look for another route. Such other route is one that does not focus on rights of individuals or collectivities. That only brings us to the impasse of competing claims: a right of free migration versus the right of self-determination of nations. On the more promising route there is no talk of rights, but of a responsibility to offer help. Walzer's theory takes this track. (...)

The question should then be asked what this responsibility to offer help stands for: does it mean to allow each and every migrant to one's country and/or community, or rather to focus on the countries of origin (micro v. macro) and to look upon this issue in the context of, for example, development aid. Moreover, it is worth studying in how far micro assistance to the immigrant hurts the interests of the country of origin (brain drain, delay of shifting industries to Third World countries) and whether short term interests counter long term ones: if true globalization is about making this world more balanced, the responsibility to offer help may result in outcomes which neither address a right to free migration nor the right of self-determination. Although this issue as such us not addressed by Weiner (he too divides the subject with on the one hand claims of outsiders and on the other principles of national sovereignty which he equates with the moral obligation of states to the best for their own citizens), it is nevertheless felt that Weiner's thought provoking survey should be part and parcel of a Handbook which is meant to stir a debate on health, migration and return, a debate in which ethics should play an important role. As WEINER states:[3]

[3] The following excerpts have been taken from Myron Weiner, Ethics, National Sovereignty and the Control of Immigration, International Migration Review, Vol. 30, Spring 1996 (no. 113), pp. 171-197; most footnotes have been deleted, which is the sole responsibility of the editor.

In a world of global inequalities, persecution, and violence, are states ethically obligated to open their borders as wide as is economically feasible and politically acceptable to their citizens? Is migration a basic human right or are the claims of outsiders superseded by the principle of national sovereignty that the moral obligation of states is to do the best for their own citizens? How should we weigh these conflicting moral claims? This article examines the debate between these two positions, focusing on the issues of open borders, migration selectivity, the capacity of sovereign states to control entry, the moral claims of refugees, the relationship between sovereignty[4] and justifiable intervention) and the role of public opinion in migration policies.

Underlying much of the debate over migration and refugee policies is the fundamental moral contradiction between the notion that emigration is widely regarded as a matter of human rights (for a liberal view on the right of emigration, see Whelan, 1981:636–653) while immigration is regarded as a matter of national sovereignty (see Sohn and Buergenthal, 1992:3). The United Nations Universal Declaration of Human Rights and the Helsinki Accords assert a universal right of emigration; yet all governments and international organizations agree that governments have the right to determine those to admit and to whom citizenship should be granted. But if people are free to leave, where are they to go? Are states then obliged to take in migrants from poor countries? Refugees in flight? Are they obliged to grant citizenship to guestworkers and to regularize the status of illegal migrants? Underlying many of these policy questions are fundamental moral issues posed, on the one hand, by the conflicting claims and rights of those who seek admission and, on, the other, by the concerns of governments and their citizens to control their borders and protect themselves against what they regard as threats to their security economic well-being, political stability; and cultural identity. Political theorists have traditionally been concerned with defining the rights and duties of citizens and of those who live within national boundaries, only recently with the claims of outsiders who seek admission, Over the centuries, political theorists have defined and expanded our conception of the rights of individuals, but they have done so within the framework of the state. As a result, in liberal democratic societies the right to move within the country has become as much of a right as freedom of speech, assembly or religion, but international law does not guarantee the right of people to move from one country to another. The question is whether the moral justification for freedom of movement within countries can and should be extended to freedom of movement among countries.

Migration and refugee policies raise moral issues because, directly or indirectly, they involve the exercise of coercion. Within countries, restrictions on the

[4] The concept of state or national sovereignty is used here not only in the familiar sense of legal or political freedom by a government from external control – though obviously bounded and contingent in numerous ways – but also in the sense of the obligations of a state to its citizens.

movement of people are decried because they are coercive. However, it is also coercion that prevents people from freely moving across international boundaries. Coercion takes place when ships carrying would-be refugees are halted at sea and sent home, guards prevent undocumented migrants from crossing a border, refugees are confined to camps or forcibly repatriated, illegal migrants are rounded up by the police, employers are fined for hiring illegal migrants, and individuals are arrested for providing sanctuary to unsuccessful refugee claimants. Whenever coercion is employed by the state to prevent people from doing what they want to without apparent harm to others – both within and outside the state a moral issue arises.

Migration policy also raises the issue of fairness. Citizenship is determined by country of birth or by the citizenship of our parents, not by choice. Consequently, one's life chances depend upon being born in a prosperous country or to parents who are citizens of a prosperous country; where there are opportunities for advancement and there is no persecution. Individuals born in a poor, autocratic country; where there are few opportunities, and where those who have particular beliefs or belong to particular ethnic or religious communities are treated badly, are truly unfortunate. The fact that one's opportunities can so strongly and permanently be constrained by the simple chance of birth seems unfair.

RESTRICTIVE ENTRY

To most citizens, however, the argument in favour of national sovereignty with respect to control over migration appears to be commonsensical. Let us consider what the consequences might be if a country had completely open borders to anyone who wished to enter. While this approach seems to take the moral high ground by avoiding coercion, it clearly jeopardizes the well-being of the host population and threatens politicide. A safe and prosperous country that declares its borders open risks being overwhelmed by a massive influx of immigrants from poor and/or violent countries. If the country then provides these immigrants with the same benefits it offers its own citizens (education for children, healthcare, unemployment benefits, etc.), its social services and welfare services may be stretched to the limit, The country's own poor may find themselves pushed aside by migrants prepared to work at lower wages. If the number of migrants is large enough, the local population may find itself outnumbered by people who speak another language, belong to. another culture, and perhaps seek to change the political system. As the number of migrants grows, the local population may become xenophobic, resulting in the growth of anti-migrant political organizations, violence, and social disorder. Poor countries might also be at risk if their borders are open. Peasants from densely populated neighbouring countries might freely enter in search of land and employment, thereby putting pressure on the local population. Refugees from civil conflict might cross the border and damage the local ecology by cutting firewood, consuming water, generating waste, and destroying grass lands. The indigenous population might become acutely afraid of domination by the intruding ethnic group, especially if the community is one with which it has a history of enmity.

Any country, rich or poor, that opened its borders might soon find other states taking advantage of its beneficent policy. A neighbouring country whose elite wanted a more homogeneous society could now readily expel its minor[ties. A government that wanted a more egalitarian society could dump its unemployed and its poor. An authoritarian regime could rid itself of its opponents; a country could empty its jails, mental institutions, and homes for the aged. In an extreme case, an overcrowded populous country could take over a hypothetically generous country simply by "transferring" a large part of its population, and an aggressive country would no longer need tanks and missiles for an invasion.

Notwithstanding these objections, some political theorists argue that liberal democratic societies ought to have open borders, or that, short of open borders, a liberal democratic country should take in as many migrants and refugees as its citizenry will allow. The primary criterion for admission, these theorists insist, should not be the needs of the host country but the plight of those who seek admission.

The Debate over Open Admissions

The philosopher John Rawls provides the starting point for theorists who take this position.[5] Rawls agues that people, not knowing anything about their own personal situation (e.g., their class, race, or ability) who could choose the kind of society in which they wanted to live from behind this "veil of ignorance," would follow self-interest and choose to live in a society in which institutions were constructed to benefit those who were the least well off (what Rawls calls "the difference principle"). Inequalities of wealth and power and income, in other words, would be acceptable only insofar as they ultimately benefited those in the society who were least well off. In this aspect, Rawls' theory stems from the assumptions of classical liberalism, with its notions of liberty, justice as fairness, and the right to equality.

For Rawls, the "original position" (starting from a "veil of ignorance") is necessary for thinking about the issues of justice within a given society but others have argued that this approach should be applied universally across different societies (...). These philosophers and legal scholars argue that, since it is purely a matter of chance whether we are born in a country that is peaceful, democratic, and prosperous or in a country that is poor, authoritarian, and torn by civil conflict, starting from the original position we would all dearly prefer to be born in

[5] J. Rawls, *A Theory of Justice*, Cambridge MA, 1971.

the peaceful, democratic, prosperous society; From a liberal egalitarian perspective there are, therefore, no grounds for limiting membership in any society to those who happen to be born there. Birthplace and parentage are, as Carens writes, "arbitrary from a moral point of view." Free migration across open borders would enable those who were born in disadvantaged countries to improve their position by moving to a place where they would have greater opportunity; If, by moving, the worse-off can thereby improve their position, Carens argues, the well-being of current citizens is irrelevant. Carens also says that it is irrelevant if open borders generate an influx of a people from another culture or if the numbers of migrants are large enough to undermine the dominance of the existing culture. The claims of locals, Carens asserts, should not be given priority over the claims of others simply by virtue of their citizenship.[6] The moral argument for free migration thus grows out of the reality that there are gross economic inequalities between states. When differences are vast, freedom of movement would enable individuals to avail themselves of opportunities to improve their income and general well-being and to increase their freedom and safety From this point of view, both notions *of jus sanguinis* and *jus soli* are fundamentally unfair, for they deny freedom of choice. Why should citizenship rights automatically be conferred on individuals who, through no act of their own, happen to be born in a particular place or to parents who are citizens of that country?

Yet, while the arguments put forth by Rawls, Carens and others make open borders and free movement seem morally clear-cut, there are contending moral considerations which suggest that open borders may generate great injustices. Michael Walzer, in his 1983 book,[7] asserts that it is also moral to develop policies which preserve a particular way of life. Walzer distinguishes between "members" and "strangers," *i.e.,* those who belong to our political community and those who do not, and he writes that "the theory of justice must allow for the territorial state, specifying the rights of its inhabitants and recognizing the collective right of admission and refusal". Countries, writes Walzer, are somewhat like clubs which can (and should) regulate admissions. We, who are members of a community define who we are, what kind of community we want to have, and whom we should admit into it. We can give membership to strangers, but we are not obliged to except under special circumstances.

---

[6] The best immigration policy from a utilitarian perspective would be the one that maximized overall economic gains. In this calculation, current citizens would enjoy no privileged position. The gains and losses of aliens would count just as much. Now the dominant view among both classical and neo-classical economics is that the free mobility of capital and labour is essential to the maximization of overall economic gains. But the free mobility of labour requires open borders. So, despite the fact that the economic costs to current citizens are morally relevant to the utilitarian framework, they would probably not be sufficient to justify restrictions. (Carens, Aliens and Citizens: The Case for Open Borders, *The Review of Politics,* 49(2), Spring 1987, p. 263).

[7] M. Walzer, *Spheres of Justice: A Defense of Pluralism and Equality*, NY 1983.

If someone is in urgent need and the risks and costs of giving aid are low, we ought to help the injured stranger not on the basis of justice but on the basis of charity But giving help – which may lead us to offer the hospitality of our home (or our country) – does not necessarily require that we admit the stranger to membership in our community.

Walzer further argues that people who belong to a community will defend their local politics and culture against strangers, and that if the state did not rake on this responsibility we would not have a world without walls but rather we would "create a thousand petty fortresses.... The distinctiveness of cultures and groups depends upon closure and, without it, cannot be conceived as a stable feature of human life, if this distinctiveness is valued, as most people seem to believe, then closure must be permitted somewhat". Walzer therefore finds value in the sovereign state not because it is exclusive, but because it provides for greater inclusiveness than would be possible if it did not exist. Building upon Walzer, then, the debate over open borders and the broader issue of whether governments have greater obligations to their own citizens than to others has grown to involve the philosophers who call themselves "communitarians." The issue is whether "community" is valued and, therefore, whether members of a community have rights and obligations toward one another that transcend those toward individuals who do not belong to the community For our purposes, "community" can be defined as coterminous with nationality; and "nationals" can be defined as citizens of a political institution known as the *state.*

Global egalitarians dismiss the idea of community as an impediment to a just world. "The socialist tradition," explains David Miller, "has been overwhelmingly hostile to nationality as a source of identity; usually regarding it merely as an artificially created impediment to the brotherhood of man."[8] Like the socialists, the globalists (and many with this view would regard themselves as socialists) place the highest value on egalitarianism. Consequently, those who subscribe to the ideals of global justice put aside notions of community and the value which a community places upon itself – which may be liberty; a sense of common identity and mutual obligation to one another.

The global egalitarian position is thus in opposition to those who want to improve the well-being of the population within their own country and who, therefore, weigh proposals for immigration against such considerations as its impact on the welfare system, employment, the delivery of educational benefits and healthcare, the environment, and inter-group relations. From this perspective, migration should be permitted only when it best serves the interests of the country and its citizens rather than serving the interests of the migrants. Many global egalitarians advocating immigration seek to avoid this drum by stressing the

[8] Miller, Community and Citizenship, in: Avineri and de-Shalit (eds), *Communitarianism and Individualism,* Oxford, 1992 on p. 87.

compatibility of migration with national well-being, for example by pointing to the contribution migrants make to economic growth, the taxes they pay in return for social benefits, and the benefits of cultural diversity. However, those who take this latter position in effect have conceded the argument that whether a country should or should not have migrants needs to be based upon an empirical consideration of costs and benefits, rather than a philosophical position in favour of global equality

For globalists, the highest moral value is distributive justice. The preservation of a nation's existence, its political order, political institutions, and cultural identity and of the well-being and interests of its citizens are subordinate to the goal of global distributive justice. Global redistribution – through open borders or foreign aid – is regarded not as a humanitarian act, but as a moral imperative. Globalists thus pay little attention to, whether the adoption of their principles in a world comprised of sovereign states would lead to an improvement or a worsening of the human condition in any specific country The adoption, for example, of a globalist position on migration by a single country puts that country at risk when other countries choose not to open their borders. A*s* we suggested earlier, migration can then become an act of aggression against the country with open borders as one country disposes of its unwanted upon another. Under such circumstances, an open door to migrants might very well do more harm than good to large numbers of people. Moreover, if a state chooses not to give preference to the well-being of its own citizens over the well-being of citizens of other countries, then, as Walzer suggests, local communities and regions within the country might protect themselves by imposing restrictions upon entry or discriminating against foreign residents, generating the very opposite result from what the globalists intend.

There are, of course, many sensible reasons why governments might welcome immigrants: they may meet labor-force needs in industry, the service sector, or agriculture; they may bring cultural diversity and cosmopolitanism to countries whose citizens would like to be less parochial; they may provide entrepreneurship and other needed skills and talents; the country may regard itself as a "home" to people with whom its citizens have historic, cultural or religious ties; and families of immigrant origin may want to bring in their relatives and other members of their ethnic community A government may also choose to open its borders to one or more neighboring countries with which it shares free trade and similar living standards. But these policies fall within the normal framework of a state's domestic and foreign policies. None implies moral obligation.

In addition, there may be ideological reasons for a country to encourage migration. For traditional immigrant countries such as the United States, Canada and Australia, there is a popular ideological presumption in favour of continued migration. Many Americans, for example, see immigration as a way of reasserting the image of America as a land of opportunity, still capable of offering success and fortune to those admitted. For Israel, the admission of Jews from anywhere in the world is essential to the Zionist conception of the state as a haven for world Jewry The costs of absorption, the availability of housing and employment, the potential social dislocations are not relevant considerations in deciding whether Jews should be admitted.

However, though there are numerous reasons a country might support and encourage immigration, many governments choose to severely limit or even close their borders to migration. The reasons given for restricting migration, as previously noted, are numerous. In some countries local inhabitants are fearful that a large influx of immigrants will overwhelm them, reducing them to a demographic minority and threatening their cultural and political dominance. Other countries fear that migration will exacerbate problems of overcrowding, poverty, unemployment, and xenophobia. And in some countries citizens have such a strong sense of an exclusive cultural identity that the incorporation into citizenship of even a small number of outsiders is unacceptable.

The moral stance that global justice can be served by a world of open borders in which individuals are free to move wherever they wish presumes a world without borders, without states, without repressive regimes, without vast differences in the health, education and welfare services offered by governing authorities, and without vast differences in incomes and employment. In the absence of these conditions the noble vision becomes a nightmare, for the consequences of opening the borders of a country in extreme situations can be the erosion of the institutions and values that liberal societies have created for themselves and which make them attractive to outsiders. In the real world of states, governments are morally responsible to their own citizens and to those who legally reside within their territory (...).

THE LIMITS AND USES OF MORAL REASONING IN PUBLIC POLICY

As with most issues of public policy, conflicts over immigration and refugee policies typically reflect group and institutional interests. Behind debates over these policies, however, often lie fundamental issues of public values and of conflicting moral considerations that are rarely made explicit. With the end of the cold war, there is emerging a greater moral and political consensus on universal human rights than ever before and a willingness to at least consider what international regimes might be created to embody and institutionalize this consensus. But there is also a widespread recognition that international population movements create major problems for states and that states have a legitimate right to limit these flows when their interests are affected. Thus, there is a need to balance state interests with moral considerations in the formulation of migration policies.

There is not – and to restate the thesis of this paper – there cannot be an international consensus on the question of whether governments should admit migrants. Indeed, if an international consensus is emerging, it is that no government is obligated to admit migrants, that migration is a matter of individual national policy that most governments need more effective control over their borders, that more forceful measures are needed to halt illegal migration and the growth of worldwide migrant smuggling, that improved procedures are needed to distinguish genuine asylum seekers and refugees suffering from persecution and violence from individuals who use these procedures to migrate, that "temporary" guestworker policies do not work Also, in formulating migration policies government should give increasing importance to whether the skills and education levels of migrants strengthen the economy, rather than to the needs of the migrants themselves. There is a consensus that refugees and asylees are in need of protection, but disagreement on who should be granted protection, how best to adjudicate asylum claims, and where and what kind of protection is desirable. There is a widespread view among the Western powers and many governments in the Third World that states cannot retreat behind the principle of national sovereignty if their mistreatment of their own citizens or their inability to maintain internal order results in massive flights. Disagreement exists, however, over what steps – if any – should be taken by the international community:

In some policy areas – mostly notably in the field of health, biogenetics, and in policies relating to the use of nuclear weapons – explicit attention has been paid to moral questions. The development of the field of applied ethics has been directed not at offering moral solutions to complex policy issues but rather at identifying the moral questions and specifying the trade-offs among alternative moral principles. Similarly, the task in the migration and refugee field is to extract the moral assumptions from the policy debates, to identify the dilemmas posed by conflicting moral principles, and to suggest how an explicit examination of moral issues can clarify policy choices. The moral issues with respect to migrants and refugees have been transformed in recent years by the emergence of a movement in support of universal human rights which transcend international boundaries so that many citizens feel they have moral obligations to those who live outside their boundaries. But citizens in liberal societies also wish to weigh these claims against the needs and claims of their own citizens.

Moral reasoning differs from other kinds of reasoning about public policies. Typically, policy decisions are based on weighing costs and benefits, evaluating effectiveness, and considering political consequences – all of which have moral implications – but this is not the same as employing moral reasoning. Efforts to apply moral reasoning often flounder in a quagmire of conundrums and moral contradictions. While these often cannot be resolved, one must at least understand what they are.

There is, first of all, the need to distinguish between personal morality and the application of moral principles to public policy. The moral choices we make as individuals need not, and often should not, be the same as the moral choices made by policymakers. A woman may have a moral objection to aborting her foetus, but that is not an argument for a public policy that bans abortions. One may be a pacifist, but that is not an argument for a public policy of disarmament. One may have a moral aversion to pornography, but that is not an argument for censorship. One may be willing to accommodate a poor immigrant in one's home, but that is not an argument for a policy to admit poor people from other countries. Personal ethics are a poor basis for public choices because they do not take into account the costs such policies impose upon others. Similarly, personal benefits from previous policies that permitted the migration of one's parents for example, are not justification for a liberal migration policy; either past or present.

It is also important to distinguish, as Max Weber did, between two kinds of ethics: the ethics of ultimate ends, which pursues an absolute ideal; and the ethics of responsibility; which requires that political leaders choose courses that are often less than ideal. Policymakers must not consider simply whether policies are in some abstract sense moral, but also whether there is a reasonable likelihood that morally desirable objectives can be achieved. The morality of an act should be judged by its probable consequences not by its intent; good intentions are not a sufficient basis for choosing moral policies since many well-intended policies have had bad results. A policy, for example, that induces people to take hazardous risks for desirable ends *(e.g.,* a policy that leads individuals to flee their country in unseaworthy boats) may have morally unsound consequences.

An apparently morally justifiable policy; moreover, can sometimes lead to costly results and imprudent actions. Policymakers may have to make the difficult judgment of whether military action to provide protection for internally displaced persons will lead to a more costly war that will inflict even greater loss of human life. Support for a persecuted ethnic minority demanding self-determination, for example, might lead to a civil war and large-scale violence. Military intervention in another country to halt persecution or stop violent conflict also, if soldiers are killed, may lead to premature withdrawal that could result in greater harm to those originally intended to receive help. Similarly, policies intended to reduce the numbers of people who fall into a particular category targeted for aid (poor, disabled, refugees, etc.) may inadvertently increase their numbers. As economists point out, we get more of what we subsidize. When, for example, governments offer entitlements to the disabled, the number of people who find ways to get themselves classified as disabled increases. The more benefits we offer asylum seekers (legal aid, free housing, medical care, food, employment), the more people are likely to seek asylum. This is not an argument against helping the disabled, the poor, single parents, asylees, refugees, etc., but a warning that the greater the entitlements the narrower the definition must be of who is qualified to receive them. Migration and refugee policies are based upon definitional distinctions as to who are beneficiaries. For each category (asylees, refugees, guestworkers, permanent migrants) there must be precise rules as to who qualifies for what benefits. Both the criteria and the entitlements must be dear and the logic behind them morally defensible as well as administratively practical; poorly defined criteria combined with generous entitlements are an invitation to abuse.

Moral reasoning also requires that we distinguish between unjust policies and injustices in the implementation of policies. While juries and judges may render unfair verdicts, it does not necessarily follow that the laws upon which these verdicts are based are unjust. Similarly, those who review asylum cases may unjustly send someone back home to cruel treatment or even death, but the criteria for granting asylum may be reasonable. Incorrect judgements are often a regrettable effect of just policies and can be addressed by improved adjudication procedures and better trained personnel. Advocates of open borders who use instances of unjust decisions as arguments for admitting all who claim asylum are, therefore, just as misguided as advocates of total exclusion who point to abuses by asylum claimants as grounds to admit no one. Abuses either by those who administer laws or by those who are its beneficiaries should not be grounds for adopting policies or procedures that are less just.

Confusion over the morality of policies, as distinct from the morality of implementation, often stems from uneven application of the rules. Policies, and their implementation, should not be arbitrary; they should be reasonably consistent and they should be seen as based upon principles that people recognize as being fair. Just as individuals should not be arbitrarily arrested for a crime or arbitrarily freed, so. individuals should not be arbitrarily admitted into a country or arbitrarily rejected. Much of the unease over migration and refugee policies is the result of inconsistent, often arbitrary; acts by policymakers or by those who administer policies. For example, individuals are sometimes granted asylum if they come from one authoritarian state, but not from another. Individuals in identical circumstances were treated automatically by the United States as refugees, for example, if they came from Cuba, but as economic migrants if they came from Haiti. A consular official may arbitrarily give an entry visa to one person but not to another, or may grant asylum to one claimant while denying it to another. Policies that are inconsistent, arbitrary or patently unfair generate cynicism and become a legitimate basis for public outrage.

Not all the difficulties of applying moral reasoning to public policy are generated by confusion over what aspects of policy – outcomes, implementation, or the policy itself – must be just. Incorporating morality in public policy Often entails making difficult choices among divergent values. It is morally attractive to treat all human beings equally without regard to their nationality; but is a military commander morally wrong to adopt a military strategy intended to minimize deaths among his own troops at the cost of increasing deaths among his enemies, including their *civilians?* Is it morally wrong for a government to be concerned with the effect of the size arid composition of a migrant or refugee influx upon the well-being of its own population, or to give preference to immigrants with whom its own citizens have ties of kinship and culture? These judgements often offend those who would apply universalistic criteria, but one ought not to render morally meaningless their basis in the ties of affection that bind families, communities, and citizens. Issues of moral choice are particularly complex when we try to decide which strangers require our help and how we balance our own needs and self-interests against those of strangers and even enemies. These difficult moral choices arise because resources are always limited and because one person's gain often entails someone else's loss.

Finally, the incorporation of moral reasoning into public policies requires that we recognize that we cannot resolve debates over migration with reference to principles of absolute justice. The issues are difficult to resolve in large part because there are conflicting claims, conflicting values, and conflicting rights. No principles of absolute justice can help us decide how many migrants should be admitted, whether preferences for admission should be given to people with skills and high levels of education or to the unskilled, whether preferences should be given to the spouses, parents and minor children of citizens but not to their siblings, whether or not a country should admit guestworkers, whether refugee status should be granted to anyone whose human rights are violated or only to those who are persecuted or are threatened with violence, and what kinds of controls are appropriate for dealing with illegal migrants. The moral questions posed by each of these issues cannot be resolved without consideration of the impact of one policy upon another and upon the effects of policy decisions upon the larger society If immigration is not a basic human right – and it cannot be as long as there are states – then each country must weigh conflicting claims and consider the consequences of alternative policies for their own citizens. It is important that we not conflate issues of public interest, public values, and fundamental human rights. Migration and refugee issues cannot simply be reduced to moral questions, but neither, as we have suggested throughout this essay, are they solely questions of national sovereignty in which moral judgements play no role.

3.2

THE ETHICS AND PRINCIPLES OF HEALTH CARE PROVISIONS

Heleen Dupuis

THE (MORAL) BASIS FOR HEALTH CARE PROVISIONS

In many Western societies the Constitution places an obligation on society, more specifically on the government, to provide goods and benefits to its citizens, among which are the health care services. In the Dutch Constitution, for instance, Article 22 states that the government must take measures for the improvement of public health. Many consider this article to be the self-evident basis of a general 'right to health care' on the part of the citizens. However, the interpretation of this article is unclear. If the article were to be interpreted in a strict sense, it would only mean that the rights of the citizens would be limited to measures for the improvement of public health. Its meaning would also entail that there is no such thing as a right to health care in general. This is in fact the case. Strictly speaking, the system of health care, as we know it in the Netherlands, is indeed not based on rights, but on reciprocity and mutuality, which means that citizens pay for their health care insurance, and are therefore given access to health care provisions as defined by the conditions of their insurance. But most Dutch people still believe in a right to health care, merely because they are simply unable to believe that something so important is not a right as such.

And there is no doubt that this right is generally considered to be something more than a moral right: it is also considered as a legal right, which is – again - in reality not the case, because health care in the Netherlands is only provided on the basis of medical insurance.

SOLIDARITY AND RECIPROCITY

In the Netherlands there is also the belief that solidarity is the basis of our health care system.

Solidarity is a moral virtue. In the case of health care its meaning is, above all, that there is a general concern in society for those citizens with increased health

P.J. van Krieken (Ed.), Health, Migration and Return

risks and fewer opportunities in life. In the Netherlands this means in practice that people with poor health and little money have access to the entire arsenal of health care. But there is no doubt that our health care system is only an expression of a certain measure of solidarity in as far as the insurance premiums which people pay are related to their incomes: those who earn less, pay less for their health care.

At the same time, reciprocity and mutuality are equally important. This means that people contribute by paying insurance premiums, on the basis of a "well-understood self-interest".

So there is a certain tension between solidarity and reciprocity. On the one hand, the belief is that our health care system is based on solidarity, while, on the other, the arrangements concerning health care provisions demonstrate something different: the costs of health care are for the large part paid for by the citizens themselves, in the form of premiums for health care insurance, whether public or private, obligatory or by free choice. This fact has some very important implications for the problems concerning the rights of immigrants to our health care provisions.

HEALTH CARE AS A CLOSED SYSTEM

The consequence of this is that claims for health care services by others, namely those who do not pay for their health care insurance, are basically not valid. They should have no access to health care provisions, because the system has been organised around the specific rights of the citizens to all kinds of health care, but – again - these rights depend entirely on the payment of medical insurance. As a consequence, someone who does not belong to the groups who participate, whether by means of an obligatory social health insurance fund, or private insurance, has no access to those services. There are some minor exceptions, namely some prevention programmes initiated and paid for by the state, and some very basic provisions for (emergency) care.

In every other respect we have a closed system of health care provisions. It would require a very special and strong justification to infringe this system, because every infringement from outside jeopardises the care for the insiders, especially in the case of very complicated and expensive medical treatment. The idea that wealthy countries such as many EU countries could easily cope with claims for health care from persons other than their own citizens is erroneous. Even in wealthy countries the distribution of health care services is a continuous problem, leading to many interventions and all kinds of endeavours to limit expenditure and to focus on a just and wise distribution of health care provisions.

RIGHTS TO HEALTH CARE: A BASIC HUMAN RIGHT?

Much has been written about first and second generation human rights, especially concerning the implied obligations for governments and public authorities. The general opinion is that in the case of first generation human rights the government should remain passive, whereas it should take an active role in the case of second generation rights. The question remains, however, whether the proclamation of the second generation of human rights is more than a recommendation for each specific government to do as much as is possible to organize a workable and effective health care for its own citizens. But in actual fact it does not constitute a strong right to health care, neither for the citizens of that specific state, nor for others. If we suppose that some countries simply do not have the necessary means to provide for adequate health care, or do not want to invest the necessary funds for this purpose, does this mean that their citizens should have free access to other countries' health care systems? Is there an overriding moral duty for the more wealthy countries to feel responsible for the so-called health gaps and to act accordingly?

A DIFFERENT LINE OF ARGUMENTATION

I would like to venture a different line of argumentation and to focus on something other than a right for everyone with a health gap to have access to every health care system. What I would like to do is to point to the fact that health care, and certainly 'high-tech' health care, as we have in the Western countries, is only a minor determinant of health and life expectation. Very basic medical and mostly non-medical provisions are much more important for people's health status, as has been superbly demonstrated, among others, by Thomas McKeown. Indeed, fresh water, adequate nutrition, birth spacing, safe sex, and other important life-style determinants (such as not smoking) and, above all, primary education are the real keys to a better, healthier and longer life. A right to health care without these provisions would even be entirely meaningless.

In the Western countries we are becoming increasingly aware of the fact that it is not cure that is so important in health care, but rather that prevention and care are of paramount importance.

Bone-marrow transplantation, heart surgery, many cancer therapies and even AIDS therapies are not essential for, nor do they make up the core, of health care. On the contrary, we should be very critical in this respect, because of their doubtful cost-benefit ratios. If such a thing as a right to health care would exist, such therapies would certainly not be a part thereof.

MOTIVES OF MERCY

All this sounds very hard-hearted, and one may wonder whether this is all an ethicist has to say in a debate on immigration and health care. Real life is not as easy as simply saying there is no right to health care, neither for the citizens in the countries with a very well-developed health care system, nor for those outside those countries. Every one of us can imagine situations where it is almost impossible to manage. Imagine a physician in a large hospital who is confronted with a very ill but illegal person. What should he do? Basically, the answer should be nothing other than to relieve some of the worst problems and to send the man or woman back to where he/she came from. The physician in question has no right to use our health care system for those other than the persons entitled to it. And he should certainly not help such a person secretly and at the expense of the hospital. But if as a society we feel responsible and if we want to do something for very ill but illegal people in our countries, that is for the worst cases, those who for reasons of common humanity cannot be left without care, then we should set a specific budget aside for this purpose, so that it becomes visible how much expenditure is needed. Such practice should never remain under the carpet. This would not be fair on those who pay their insurance premiums. But if society would indeed decide to set some funds aside for (illegal) immigrants, then a quota will be needed, in order not to create a too attractive situation for all kinds of people with health deficiencies. It is regrettable that such a strict position should be adopted, but there is unfortunately no other possibility.

OTHER OPTIONS

Suppose we have sufficient motives to do something positive to improve the health of citizens from Third World countries, then one thing is certain: offering AIDS medication, cancer therapies or hemodialysis to a few immigrants within our borders would be unwise and unfair to their fellow citizens. It would be much fairer and just to use the money needed for such therapies to start primary health care projects in these Third World countries – which would be of great significance for relieving suffering. This would be a better way to spend money than to provide access to our costly therapies for only a few foreign citizens.

CONCLUSIONS

There are also quite a few arguments against providing access to our health care system to 'health immigrants'.

The first is that fairness towards our own citizens who pay for their health care insurance compels us not to give access to others.

The second is that it is also not effective to do so because the sort of medical care that is requested by those immigrants is not really important and would only provide temporary relief to a very few people at a high cost.

The third is that it is also unfair to spend so much money on one person whereas many more of the fellow citizens in the home countries are in need of the most basic medical care, which could be paid for at a similar cost.

The fourth argument is that if we would like to help people from Third World countries, we should indeed start primary health care projects at home, which will certainly have much more significance for the lives and well-being of those persons concerned.

3.3

HEALTH CARE AND MIGRATION: SOME ETHICAL REMARKS

Raoul Wirtz

The problem of health care and migration is an extremely complex one. It revolves around concepts that are notoriously difficult to define such as justice, fairness and solidarity. It involves boundaries that are difficult to delineate; such as national boundaries, qualifications for citizenship and admittance to the highly complex system of Western medical (health) care systems. The problem is augmented by responsibilities that are disreputably interwoven, namely those of physicians, health care managers, quasi-governmental organizations and Ministries, to name but a few of the stakeholders.

Another cause of this complexity in the debate is the prominence of (conflicting) values. The problem of health care and immigration is a highly ethical problem. Facts and values are frequently not clearly distinguished, norms and ethical principles have very different meanings for different stakeholders and emotions frequently play an important role in the debate. Clearing the ethical field appears to be an important preliminary step towards a proper view of the problem of health care and immigration. This contribution is an attempt to sort out some of the ethical difficulties. I will be forced to conclude, however, that the problem of health and migration neatly parallels some fundamental divisions in ethical theory, which cannot be resolved easily in any general way.

PRINCIPLE OR CONSEQUENCE?

A well-known distinction made in ethical theory is the distinction between consequence-oriented reasoning and principle-oriented reasoning. Very briefly stated, principle-oriented reasoning justifies actions on the basis of a shared understanding of the importance of one or more ethical principles whereas consequence-oriented reasoning justifies actions on the basis of the desired ethical outcomes of the action. A conflict between principle-oriented and consequence-oriented reasoning is easily detected in the topic of health and migration. The central ethical

P.J. van Krieken (Ed.), Health, Migration and Return

principle relating to a physician (and probably also institutions such as hospitals and Municipal Health centres) is to provide due care (within the limits of medical possibilities and consent) to any patient, regardless of his or her background, race, nationality etc. The rationale behind this principle is consensus concerning the value of trust in the medical field. We believe that everybody should be able to receive medical care. This value is supported by another important ethical principle for any professional, including a medical professional, namely the principle of confidentiality. A criminal with a gun-shot wound seeking help from a general practitioner is protected from state prosecution by this principle of confidentiality. A physician reporting an illegal immigrant to the IND would be in breach of the principle of confidentiality. Refusing to treat a sick patient on the ground of his or her (suspected) illegal status would be a breach of the principle of due care.

On the other hand, the consequences, of all physicians abiding by these principles constitute a growing concern, which is shared by many. This is the basic concern that an unlimited growth in the demand for (Western) health care will (or already does) clog the health system and will thus jeopardize adequate health care for all. Without answering the question whether this fear is justified by the current or expected rate of immigration or health care 'tourism', one can well see that this would be an ethically undesirable outcome in the sense that less people will be able to obtain health care. With the shift in moral reasoning, from principle to consequence, we have also moved the ethical perspective. We have moved from *a* physician having to decide whether to treat *a* patient, led by the principle of due care, to 'society' at large having to decide who will receive what health care and on what grounds. This shift, epitomized by Hardin as 'the tragedy of the commons', entails the consideration that every single, ethically defensible, action by every individual physician has a doubtful ethical consequence for all. On this level, a new ethical principle should be introduced, namely the principle of fairness. This principle pertains to the question of how, on what grounds or arguments, benefits and burdens should be divided in society at large. It is to this principle that I will now turn.

LIBERALISM OR COMMUNITARIANISM?

The principle of fairness has been a central principle in political philosophy since *A Theory of Justice* by John Rawls was published in 1972. The two fundamental principles relating to justice as fairness developed by Rawls are:

Each person has an equal claim to a completely adequate scheme of equal basic rights and liberties, a scheme which is compatible with the same scheme which applies to all; and within this scheme equal political liberties, and only those liberties, are to be guaranteed their fair value.

Social and economic inequalities must satisfy two conditions: first, they must relate to positions and offices open to all under conditions of fair equality of opportunity; and second, they are of the greatest benefit to the least advantaged members of society.[1]

Whosoever is prepared to position him/herself behind the 'veil of ignorance', abstracted from 'contingencies' such as personal talents, race, religious beliefs and character traits, will be led towards the principles of justice by using his or her own reasoning. This 'starting point' of the discussion, behind the veil of ignorance, which Rawls calls the 'original position', has been subject to an elaborate body of criticism. The body of criticism is in fact so vast that it has led to a schism in political philosophy known as the liberalism versus communitarianism debate. One of the central points of criticism from the communitarian point of view is the possibility and the desirability to 'abstract' from such fundamental 'contingencies' as talents, traits, race and religion. In fact, some of the communitarians, argue that these 'contingencies' constitute the greater part of one's personality from which no reasonable individual would or could abstract him or herself. Any political philosophy, they argue, should take these 'contingencies' and the specifics of one's community as a starting point for any discussion concerning fairness.

What contribution can the liberal or communitarian perspective make to the ethical problems of migration and health care?[2] Roughly speaking, a liberal perspective can easily accommodate international justice but would have to face the problem of justifying limits to solidarity, whereas a communitarian perspective could easily justify limits to international inclusion but would have to face the problem of finding reasons for solidarity. Communitarians have, as Trappenburg puts it, a bad reputation concerning matters of international justice.[3] The reason for this is that although a specific community isaccepted as it is, it is nevertheless defined at the expense of other communities, the defining criterion being the 'otherness' of other communities vis-á-vis one's own. Without being specific as to what amounts to a community (e.g. a municipality, a subculture, a country, a region, a continent) communitarians do not have great difficulties in drawing the boundaries of a community. From a communitarian perspective, one could argue that political and health care institutions are part of the specific and historically evolved idiosyncrasy of a community, and should in principle be limited to members of the community sharing the history and 'culture' of that community. Emphasizing the 'otherness' of other communities does however raise the following question: 'Why bother about other communities at all?'. The moral grounds for sharing benefits such as those resulting from a developed health care system are

[1] J. Rawls, *Political Liberalism*, Colombia, University Press NY, 1993, pp. 5-6.

[2] The liberal perspective is discussed by Rawls in his book entitled *The Law of Peoples,* Harvard University Press, Cambridge, Mass. London, 1999.

[3] M. Trappenburg, *De dokter en de illegaal. Een verhandeling over de morele achtergronden van de Koppelingswet en over sociale rechtvaardigheid in internationaal perspectief.* Preadvies NVBe, 1997, p. 43.

limited to charity or 'doing good', very noble but at the same time not very compelling moral principles. The ad hoc and non-committing character of the moral principle of doing good is an insufficient moral ground for an internationally-oriented redistribution of health care benefits.

The liberal starting point is universal in its nature. A minimum degree of 'shared background' is taken as a prerequisite for any theory of justice, but, as Rawls puts it, the difficult task is this:

> "we must find some point of view, removed from and not distorted by the particular features and circumstances of the all-encompassing background framework, from which a fair agreement between persons regarded as free and equal can be reached"[4].

Abstracting from any specific personal trait means that the theories of justice apply to every human being qua human being, or, more specifically, to the world population at large. Ideally, principles relating to a fair distribution of health care benefits should include every world citizen. This ideal not only has obvious practical problems. It also raises a moral question, namely the question of compliance. The prominent feature in the liberal perspective is reason. Not only does (universal) reason constitute the essential defining trait of the human being qua human being, but reason is also the compelling force by which to persuade people to comply with a fair scheme of dividing (health care) benefits. But does this most general trait of humankind have sufficient compelling force to drive people towards a global fair distribution of health care benefits? Thomas Hobbes, the 17th century political philosopher, used this ruse of reason to compel human passions. But he was of the opinion that this ruse could only enchant for a very short time, only just sufficient enough to install a Leviathan, a forceful government institution, which would thereafter have sufficient power to compel and control its citizens. This indicated Hobbes' doubts concerning the durability of the compelling force of reason. The universal trait of reason and the universal logic of a good reason have a very limited compelling force.

MORAL RULE OR MORAL IDEAL?

In their 'Bioethics: A return to fundamentals' Gert, Culver and Clouser make a distinction between moral rules and moral ideals.

> "In contrast with the moral rules, which prohibit doing those kinds of actions which cause people to suffer some harm or increase the risk of their suffering some harm, the moral ideals encourage one to do those kinds of actions which lessen the amount of

[4] Rawls, 1993, op.cit. p. 23.

harm suffered (including providing goods for those who are deprived) or decrease the risk of people suffering harm."[5]

The difference between moral rules and moral ideals, according to Gert & co., is that only moral rules have the possibility of being impartially obeyed all of the time. In contrast to a breach of a moral rule, a breach of a moral ideal cannot be punished.

International solidarity concerning a just distribution of health care benefits, in this view, is a moral ideal, not a moral rule. The distinction made by Gert & co. is practical: "No one can impartially follow moral ideals all of the time; indeed, it is humanly impossible to follow moral ideals all of the time, impartially or not, because everyone needs to sleep sometimes."[6] Does this practical argumentation free us from a moral obligation to justly distribute health care benefits? The answer to this question is yes, in view of the fact that by any comparison the demand for health care provisions internationally exceeds the supply. On the other hand, the answer is also no, in view of the fact that a current state of affairs is not a valid moral argument for not changing this state of affairs. We could, so to speak, always sleep in turns.[7] How strong is the moral ideal of international solidarity?

RATIONALITY OR SOLIDARITY?

From the communitairian criticism an insight is gained that the presumed 'shared background' plays a much more important role in persuading people to embark on a fair distribution of (health care) benefits than liberal thinkers acknowledge. What do people share when they have a 'shared background'? This could be a range of factors, including humanity, race, destiny, citizenship, institutions and risks. Most contemporary health care systems are based on the latter elements of a shared background, namely shared citizenship, institutions and, importantly, shared risks. [8] It is not kinship or companionship, but solidarity, insurance and economic market principles which constitute the compelling force in these health care systems. All of which presuppose a certain degree of reciprocity, or, in one way or another, a certain degree of interdependency. This reciprocity is grounded in a more or less prolonged physical proximity.

Physical proximity plays an influential role in the foundations of the moral principle of solidarity. It enables what the Dutch Choices in Healthcare Commit-

---

[5] B. Gert, C.M. Culver, K.D. Clouser, *Bioethics: A Return to Fundamentals.* Oxford University Press, New York, Oxford, 1997, p. 41.

[6] Ibid. p. 42.

[7] E.g. a global egalitarian principle, as discussed in Rawls, 1999, op. cit. p. 118.

[8] Compare A. de Swaan, *Zorg en Staat. Welzijn, onderwijs en gezondheidszorg in Europa en de Verenigde Staten in de nieuwe tijd*, Amsterdam, Bert Bakker, 1989.

tee (Commissie Keuzes in de zorg) called an awareness of togetherness, the founding constituent of solidarity.[9] Physical proximity grounds rationality in mutual involvement, and provides compelling force for the moral principle of solidarity. Proximity, on a more instrumental basis, also enables a necessary means of control, making free-riding more difficult. In the Dutch case, the principle of solidarity in the health care insurance system primarily implies that every citizen pays for health insurance, but citizens who earn more pay more, and secondly that health risks are collectively paid for. A free-rider is someone who earns a great deal but nevertheless manages to pay a low insurance contribution or someone whose way of life involves health risks that are disproportionate to his insurance contribution. Within national boundaries, this kind of free-riding constitutes a problem in itself. In an international context, it could not be contained at all. Not being able to verify whether those on a low income do really benefit from the higher contributions of those on a high income because free riding cannot be controlled, would certainly put an end to the principle of solidarity. And the health risks of those in developing countries are in general disproportionately high compared to Western citizens.

The question that arises is 'what are the limits of physical proximity?' How is proximity institutionalized? What is its range? An illegal resident in the waiting-room of a general practitioner is physically present. If the general practitioner diagnoses that treatment is necessary, he has a moral obligation to help this illegal patient as indicated earlier. Nevertheless, his illegal status excludes him from any (collective) insurance scheme. The concept of citizenship institutionalizes physical proximity. With this, the boundaries of shared background, in terms of shared health risks and shared burdens, are drawn. With the growing mobility of growing numbers of people, however, the concept of citizenship is changing rapidly. There is a growing need to be able to differentiate between the possibility of access to different social institutions in society, for different people. This need is the most obvious in the case of health care and education. Should resident illegal immigrants *as a rule* be given necessary medical care and education? Should they be given a limited and temporary form of citizenship? Is temporary'or 'partial' citizenship at all possible? Twenty years ago, these options would have been seen as exceptions to the general rule of lifelong 'full' citizenship. How feasible and how desirable is 'tailor-made citizenship'? Different types of citizenship would enable us to differentiate between various forms of proximity and to institutionalize these forms. The clear disadvantage of differentiated citizenship would not only be the practical complexity of the system, but also the emergence of a group of 'second class' citizens and hence of an institutionalized social division of citi-

---

[9] An advisory commission advising the Dutch Government on a fair health care distribution in 1990 (Commissie keuzen in de zorg) used the following definition of solidarity: 'the awareness of togetherness and the willingness to bear the resulting responsibilities'.

zens.[10] This would be the opposite of the fundamental ideal of a universal solidarity on the basis of a shared humanity.

One of the reasons for the shifting definition of the concept of citizenship is migration. Another reason is the fact that national boundaries are becoming more and more transparent due to the process of globalization. In this process, citizenship plays the paradoxical role of defining one's nationality. In the national context citizenship is weakened and *de facto* differentiated; in the international context it defines one's nationality. The growing transparency of national boundaries parallels a process of growing interdependency. Globalization leads to a factual, as opposed to a moral, reciprocity. Nevertheless, this reciprocity still has a long way to go in order to constitute a global 'shared background'.

CONCLUDING REMARKS

How strong are the moral grounds for an international (re)distribution of health care benefits? Should *all* the residents of a nation, including non-citizens and illegal residents, benefit to an equal degree? Every individual physician has the moral duty to treat *any* person who turns up his waiting-room (provided that medical treatment is necessary and consent is given). The principles of due care and confidentiality conflict with the resulting consequences of (possible) changes to Western health care systems. On a community level, the question of fair distribution of health care benefits arises. From a communitairian perspective, limiting benefits to the community is defensible, international (re)distribution needs to be justified. From a liberal perspective international (re)distribution is defensible and a limit to this (re)distribution needs to be justified. This debate revolves around a different assessment of the importance of a 'shared background'. In the national distribution of health care the concept of solidarity plays a crucial role. Reciprocity and physical proximity are features of a 'shared background' and are fundamental to solidarity. Both are problematic grounds for international solidarity, although due to the process of globalization reciprocity on an international scale is *de facto* becoming stronger.

[10] Cf. H. van Gunsteren, *Eigentijds burgerschap*. WRR Publicatie. Den Haag, Sdu Uitgeverij, 1992, p. 72.

COMPASSION, SOLIDARITY AND ITS LIMITS: A MORAL DILEMMA

Jacques de Milliano

At the edge of ethics and the real world, there might be a need for some food for thought, and the following observations based on personal experiences might therefore contribute to the debate, the red line through this Handbook.

Solidarity with the suffering individual (or population) who is in need or danger is considered to be a cornerstone of our modern societies. When somewhere in the world there is a famine or an epidemic of meningitis, measles and/or cholera, the images of misery reach our living-rooms within 24 hours and aid workers will reach the area within 48 hours. Money is collected, medicines and food are brought in and assistance can commence.

The logos and mission statements of the international actors tell us that they are neutral, impartial and independent. Their primary drive to act is human misery. A dense network of humanitarian actors has developed since WWII: intergovernmental organisations such as UNHCR and UNICEF, WHO, WFP and others with specific mandates in the field of combating/preventing disease, protecting specific groups like women, children and refugees. International non-governmental organisations are strengthening those mandates; they are the active channels through which citizens express their solidarity with populations in need. In general I am convinced that this international response mechanism to human suffering has contributed to making this world a slightly better place to live in.

On the other hand, the realities on the ground have proved that humanitarian actions, in some specific cases, have had substantial negative side-effects concerning the fate of populations they are supposed to improve: the equation that human need is equal to an instant humanitarian action deserves to be reconsidered.

THE GOMA EXAMPLE

As an example, the Great Lake refugee crisis, 1994–1996, might be illustrative of this intrinsic problem. Over one million Hutu refugees crossed the border be-

P.J. van Krieken (Ed.), Health, Migration and Return

tween Rwanda and Zaire in July 1994. A cholera epidemic and other infectious diseases, like shigella and dysentery, gave rise to a large-scale humanitarian catastrophe. A large-scale humanitarian operation was set up to provide food, clean water and medicines. So far, so good. But at the same time humanitarian action substantially contributed to restoring the power structure: the power held by the very same Interhamwee leaders who had been responsible during the preceding months for the genocide of moderate Hutus and the Tutsis.

An analysis by Medecines Sans Frontières (MSF, in which I personally played an active role) at the time was that the humanitarian action itself bore a high degree of responsibility for restoring the grip of the Hutu leaders on the Hutu population, leaders whose objective was, in their own words "to complete the genocide".

So, humanitarian aid became a substantial tool for the leaders to use in order to make the people dependent on them for their survival: the Hutu leaders did de facto control the distribution of food and medicines by a sophisticated mechanism for including and excluding members of the population.

Moreover, the trade in humanitarian goods enabled the Hutu leaders to pay for rearmaments purposes: a BBC documentary at that time explained in detail how aircraft bringing in food from Oostende (Belgium), Heathrow and Eastern Europe also carried weapons and ammunition.

So, well-intended international humanitarian action, which focused on reducing the immediate suffering of the civilian population, in reality contributed to restoring the power of a genocidal leadership combined with the further destabilisation of the whole region. Today a major part of the destabilisation inherent in the Great Lakes region – Uganda, Rwanda and Congo – has its origins in a well-intended but badly managed international humanitarian response. (Other examples can be found in the Sierra Leone crisis, the Liberia crisis, etc, even to the extent that warlords deliberately create famine among the local population because they know that humanitarian aid by the international community will be given 'unconditionally'.)

Could this have been prevented? Was the necessary information available? The answer is yes, the information was available, but making humanitarian assistance conditional was not considered to be politically correct.

Three months after the arrival of one million refugees in Goma, MSF compiled a report – 'breaking the cycle (of impunity)' – where all those facts were laid bare. This was to be of no avail, however, as no reactions were forthcoming. So we faced a moral dilemma: the long-term negative impact of humanitarian assistance on the well-being of the population was outweighting the short-term positive impact on human suffering. Should we have asked the doctors to stop treating the patients in the hospital tents because of the overall negative impact of their work on the population? It sounded like a theoretical question, but it was not. It was a moral dilemma splitting the whole organisation. After setting a deadline for our presence and after writing a second report ('deadlock in the refugee crisis') MSF decided to withdraw its medical teams. It no longer wanted to contribute towards feeding 'the monster', the genocidal power-system.

We all know the aftermath. An endless chain of humanitarian and political catastrophes in the area. In 1998 I spent two 2 months in Congo on behalf of MSF, and indeed I could notice that the Interhamwee had been armed by Kabila to fight the neighbouring Tutsi regimes. In fact, 24 factions are currently fighting each other these days.

So, the bare question in the Goma example is this: can one ask a doctor to stop treating patients because the actions of all the doctors together contribute to strengthening the power of those responsible for the genocide which in the end will result in even more violence. Or, to put the question in a positive sense: can one design one's humanitarian actions in such a way that one can find an optimum solution in dealing with the individual suffering and the well-being of the home society.

Such questions can be addressed as follows:

1. Well-intended humanitarian action contributes in highlighting the humanitarian dimension of a crisis, but it often also hides the broader and more complex political crisis. So, the complexity of a vast political crisis in a local society can be reduced to a simple image of disease, famine, medicine and food aid.
2. International solidarity with a population in need, if reduced to the mere notion of compassion, can do more harm than good.
3. The lesson I have learned is that genuine solidarity should take into account the benefits for the individuals we support or protect, and the systemic effects of our humanitarian actions/activities on their societies at home.

GOMA, HEALTH AND MIGRATION

What is the meaning of all this as far as the debate on health, migration and return is concerned? First of all, it is not a plea to stop humanitarian aid for those who are in need. It is rather a plea to look more carefully at the systemic impact of our humanitarian action on the well-being of the home society, the society which the immigrants have left behind.

The dramatic death in 1999 of the two boys from Guinea Conakry – frozen to death in the landing gear of a Sabena aircraft – and their last letter clearly demonstrated the heart of the issue when they wrote: "we are fleeing disease, poverty, lack of work ... we have no future... our families have no future..." And so they were looking for a new future elsewhere. These boys are for me the symbol that genuine solidarity consists of supporting the home societies by creating the necessary conditions so that their home societies can develop. This amounts to investing in medical care, schooling, infrastructure, and so on.

In my opinion an undesirable result of well-intended solidarity would be that we continue to invest huge amounts of money in care for individuals from the

Third World here in Europe in stead of taking care of their home societies. Our main effort should be directed towards creating the necessary conditions to stimulate developments at the local level; developments which result in people remaining in their home societies. From the public health point of view this approach makes sense. The central question is which place (here or there) and in which aspects (prevention in the form of, for example, immunization and/or curative care, TB, malaria, HIV) should we invest money in health care so as to provide an optimum contribution to the health and thus the well-being of the population.

The same public health questions are on a daily basis emerging in developed countries as well: do we invest in more heart or kidney transplants or in the prevention of hart disease through cholesterol reducing medication. Where do we spend the Euro's in order to have a maximum impact on the health of the population.

So spending money on cardiac surgery for Third World patients in Europe means that 1000 fewer children will be vaccinated. In Dutch society there is a kind of consensus that in introducing new technologies or a new medication a saved life may cost around $ 15,000 a year. It sounds crude, but it is a reality. So, what is the price we are willing to pay to save an individual life. And should figures also be applied to immigration flows.

The assumption in this approach is that – when discussing migration and health – if we consider people to be part of a broader society at home; that we also take responsibility for the well-being of these societies. That is what development aid is all about; and we, therefore, need to find a balance between the responsibility to deal with short-term individual suffering and the responsibility to cater in a constructive way for thelong-term urgent needs of the societies of the countries of origin.

BENCHMARKS, YARDSTICKS

As to finding such a balance, it can be remarked that also in humanitarian assistance benchmarks are used, implicitly or explicitey as to which intervention is the most cost-effective in order to have an impact on the health of the population as a whole. So, in a refugee camp one focuses on the 10 major diseases which can be cured or prevented at a reasonable price; if the price for a pateint with an 11th disease is too high it will not be considered because it will be at the cost of curing, maybe, 10 other patients.

It is therefore – with the above in mind – herewith submitted

- humanitarian action including medical care should be more than an emotional response to individual suffering;
- we have to include the public health dimension from the point of view that individuals are part of a home society;

- this is also true in the case if the individual is outside his/her home society;
- we have to look at the impact of our humanitarian actions beyond the medical field: do we strengthen the home society or do we undermine it by our actions; for example, are we unintentionally focusing our care on an elite which have no intention of participating in the development of their society?
- compassion has its limits there where it clashes with genuine broader solidarity with the home society.

This may be considered to be food for thought which may be of relevance in this debate. I trust that the undoubtedly ongoing debate will use, highlight and elaborate some of the issues raised in this contribution.

CHAPTER 4
HUMAN RIGHTS, MIGRATION AND RETURN

This Chapter should be looked upon as a continuation of the debate which was entered into in Chapter 1, the human rights debate. This Chapter, introduced by Feitsma, tries to tackle the issue of the right to migration, the status of rejectees (van Krieken) and the issue of return (Grimmer and Palinsky). Relevant legal texts on migration and return have been duly included as well as the General Comments concerned. Bouwen, in his contribution, submits that the migration discussion should include the health issue, and should refrain from focusing on labour- and asylum-related migration only.

4.1

THE HUMAN RIGHTS DEBATE: MIGRATION AND RETURN

Johan Feitsma

In the above Chapter on 'ethics' due attention has been paid to the topic of migration, in particular to the ethical and moral approach to the phenomenon of migration. Some experts argue that migration is to be accepted as a fact of life, and should, maybe, even be promoted in view of globalization and the greying of many societies, whereas others submit that societies are fully entitled to decide who is and who is not to become a member of that society.

If 'law' is the codification of the will of the general public, if 'law' contains elements of idealism (de lege lata v. de lege ferenda) it should then be emphasized that a right to migration has not been agreed upon. It is recalled that the right to migration contains a right to e-migrate, not to im-migrate. Of course, the case of the asylum seekers and/or refugees is different. The asylum seeker has the right to seek asylum, which contains access to the procedure, and in most cases access to the territory, whereas the right to enjoy asylum of course goes hand in hand with access to the territory (and the entitlement to a travel document, in order to leave that territory).

The main UN documents keep fairly silent on this issue: the 1985 GA Declaration on the Human Rights of Individuals Who are not Nationals of the Country in Which They Live focuses on the rights of those (lawfully) residing in a foreign country and does not touch on the issue of migration as such. The same is true for the 1990 Convention on the Rights of Migrant Workers and Their Families, which however touches on the issue of undocumented aliens, normally an euphemism for illegal entrants. Yet, the latter Convention has been ratified by a mere 16 countries only, and although it may enter into force during the course of 2001/2002 (as only 20 ratifications are needed) the limited 'enthusiasm', particularly on the part of receiving countries, is a clear indication of the impact of this Convention

If the right to migration has as yet not been recognized – and this is not due to happen in the foreseeable future – then the issue of return should be taken into consideration as well. If an application for e.g. asylum or a residence permit fails, return is the only feasible alternative. Countries of origin are obliged to take their citizens back, and the obligation to cooperate with the State from

P.J. van Krieken (Ed.), Health, Migration and Return

which the individual needs to return home has now also been reconfirmed as a principle of international law. This issue is of the utmost importance as across the board only 20% of all applications meet with success, which indeed means that an overwhelming majority of would-be migrants or asylum seekers have to return home. In fact, it is generally forgotten that also refugee law contains a cessation clause, that protection is more often than not of a temporary nature and that labour migration might, therefore, be limited in time. Hence, the logical link between migration on the one hand and return on the other.

As Bouwen submits, the migration debate is only about to start, and indeed, it is recalled that the Brussels' Commissioner responsible for asylum and migration, António Vitorino, did launch a year-long debate on those issues late November 2000 which should result in some conclusions at the Brussels December 2001 European Council Summit. Bouwen proposes to include the health issue in the general migration debate, as it is bound to become an important topic which goes over and above migration proper and which may have an impact which should force us to rethink migration itself and international co-operation.

Van Krieken focuses on the status of aliens in general and rejectees (those whose application for asylum or another residence permit has been rejected upon due process of law) in particular. He emphasizes that a society by rejecting an application in fact submits that there is another society (read: country of origin) in which the rejectee can enjoy the rights, services, responsibilities and duties as agreed upon in that very society. Too often, he submits, receiving countries only focus on the relationship between the rejectee and the society of the receiving country, whereas saying 'no' to an applicant implies saying 'yes' to the relationship between the applicant/rejectee and his/her country of origin.

Grimmer and Palinsky, finally, deal with the challenging issue of return: is return a responsibility with and for the country which rejected the application or rather a responsibility on the part of the individual applicant/rejectee and/or the country of origin. The outcome of that question may indeed have an impact on the question in how far health services should be made available to rejectees, and/or whether illness is a reason to delay return, or to grant a residence status after all.

In order to provide the necessary background, legal texts have been included on the subject of migration and return (Chapter 4.2) and in Chapter 4.3 due attention has been paid to the General Comments as provided by the Human Rights Committee on Art. 12 of the International Covenant on Civil and Political Rights (ICCPR, 1966). These GCs appear to confirm that, at least in the legal arena, consensus falls far short of recognizing a right to immigration.

MIGRATION AND HEALTH: NO ESCAPE!

Frans Bouwen

1. THE CHALLENGE

"Global is not universal!", Professor Ninan Koshy from Trivandrum, India, recently shouted in the midst of a special Seminar on 'non refugee related migration'.[1] For people from the South as well as the North of this globe he stressed the importance of certain values, norms, standards and instruments remaining non-negotiable and universal. How right he was and is, because in Northern terms we do live with the concept of 'globalisation', but this process of 'globalisation' for millions does not equate with the existing understanding and interpretation of 'universality'. Indeed, after the Second World War the world did *not* introduce a 'global' declaration on human rights, but a *Universal* Declaration on Human Rights; the international community did *not* work towards several 'global' Conventions, Protocols, Treaties and Charters, but wanted to agree upon those by *universal* consensus; and last, but certainly not least, the continuing need for worldwide health care is a true *universal* demand rather than only one minor aspect of 'globalisation'. For the people and masses of the South, but also in fact for the people with their masses from the North, apart from a particular process beyond certain established forms of control, 'globalisation' is increasingly a mere product of a Northern industrialised way of thinking and acting; it blows over the globe, affecting it positively as well as negatively.

It already causes international and internal disparities. As Peter Stalker, consultant to the International Labour Organisation (ILO) correctly put it: 'Globalization may in the end not flatten international disparities but merely re-sort countries into new categories of rich and poor',[2] including a heightening of internal disparities. Referring to the world of refugees, asylum seekers and migrants – cumulatively some 150 million persons recognised as such[3] – also the Secretary-

[1] The Society for International Development – Netherlands' Chapter – within the framework of a three-year Project on the theme 'the Future of Asylum and Migration' focused at one of its four seminars on 'non refugee related migration' (29 September 2000, the Peace Palace, The Hague). The SID NL keeps to the Chatham House rules, but Prof. Koshy, one of the 35 international participants, agreed to this quotation being made public. Prof. Ninan Koshy is Professor of International Relations and English Literature, and was the former Director of the Commission of the Churches on International Affairs of the World Council of Churches, Geneva, CH.

[2] Peter Stalker, *Workers Without Frontiers*, ILO, Geneva, CH, 2000. p.140.

[3] Sources: UNHCR 1999, World Bank 1999, and the *World Migration Report* 2000, IOM/UN, Geneva, 2000.

General of the United Nations, Kofi Annan, on October 2, 2000, in his address to the UNHCR Executive Committee stated to the High Commissioner and the audience: "you have become part of 'a containment strategy', by which this world's more fortunate and powerful countries seek to keep the problems of the poorer world at arms's length. How else can one explain the disparity between relatively generous funding for relief efforts in countries close to the frontiers of the prosperous world, and the much more parsimonious effort made for those who suffer in remoter parts of Asia or Africa? And how else can one explain the contrast between the generosity which poor countries are expected to show, when hundreds of thousands of refugees pour across their frontiers, and the precautions taken to ensure that as few asylum seekers as possible ever reach the shores of rich countries?"

Most unfortunately these negative and even threatening aspects are too often ignored, neglected or interpreted differently during the process of globalisation itself. This causes negative attitudes on the part of the 'agents of globalisation', human beings themselves, which do not link the positive aspects of globalisation to the need to retain the non-negotiability of fundamental and universal norms and values.

In particular, the world of those on the move is *the* example of how difficult and complex it has become to bridge the 'universal' with the 'global' as described above. It is no longer an academic discourse or subject which can be dealt with within one particular discipline. All disciplines must come together in a multidisciplinary and interdisciplinary way. Therefore, from a multidisciplinary and interdisciplinary perspective there is an urgent need to analyse the issue, and to look for innovative ways to respond to the most urgent practical needs. This is a major *challenge* which can no longer be avoided and which will remain within the setting of world priorities for the next decades to come. Here the health dimension in relation to all forms of migration is a most crucial one for immediate consideration by the various disciplines.

BUT, before becoming involved with this, first of all the various disciplines which in one way or another do have to occupy themselves with the issue, forcibly or not, must come to understand about whom and about what they are speaking about when referring to 'those on the move'.

2. THE CONFUSION

Who are or what is actually on the move? In daily practice there exists a real confusion concerning the basic terms and concepts when describing the phenomenon of those on the move. Refugees are confused with non-refugee related migrants, internally displaced persons are wrongly called asylum seekers, illegal migrants are equated with rejected asylum seekers, protection of refugees is being discussed within the framework of priorities concerning humanitarian assistance, and often the whole package of human rights as well as the health dimensions of immediate relevance to those in need of protection are being shelved for reasons of legal practice or different political interests. Of course, a vocabulary or rather terminology has evolved during the course of the last century, but it has not been accepted by all and therefore cannot be called definitive, let alone 'universal'.

In political terms during many Parliamentary debates the discourse shows no careful use of basic terms and concepts related to asylum seekers, refugees and migrants. One's own national political and party political interests often prevail over the search for true implementation efforts of existing international refugee law. A way out of the confusion finds somewhat too solid ground in only discussing methods for halting to the increasing numbers arriving at external borders.

Nevertheless, the confusion continues to exist, and both rightly but more often wrongly, it gives rise to an understanding of the terms asylum, refugee and migration issues as danger, threat and pressure. Hence, ad hoc measures hitherto form a response, but do not offer any durable and sustainable solution, and hence there is no *universal* response looming on the horizon of a globalizing world.

At the same time the issue of 'those on the move' will increase, particularly from an international and interregional perspective. It cannot be stopped, and if there are no legal means offered to the persons concerned, even more illegal means will be made available, and furthermore, this illegal route will inevitably be followed.

Therefore it is of the utmost importance that all those who are dealing with asylum and migration in one way or another acknowledge, first of all, their own confusion concerning this matter, secondly, to develop an attitude of courage to approach the issue step by step by *inter alia* coming to terms with the relevance of concepts and, thirdly to start an innovative interdisciplinary and multidisciplinary common exercise to face the future challenges, with their political consequences.

3. BASIC TERMS AND CONCEPTS

In order to ultimately arrive at a common acceptance of basic terms and concepts as a first step towards a universal response to the issue we are discussing, we may thankfully refer to parts of Gilbert Jaeger's 'Basic Terms and Concepts.'[4] Jaeger has occupied from 1959 onwards several directorial positions in the UNHCR. In the 1970s he was Director of Assistance, and later Director of Protection. Under his leadership a small team produced the famous UNHCR Handbook on the determination of refugee status (1979), and for over half a century he has helped

[4] Gilbert Jaeger, *Basic Terms and Concepts*, Brussels, 2000.

and supported governmental and non-governmental circles in finding a common language and interpretation of the terms and concepts referred to.

3.a **Persons**

Refugee

The word *refugee* applies particularly to persons seeking refuge from religious, political or other forms of persecution, but in general also to persons who flee from any danger or trouble, including runaways and fugitives from justice.

The term *refugee* which we normally refer to has been defined in Article 1 of the *1951 Convention relating to the status of refugees* (particularly in Section A (2)) and has been amended and completed by Article I of the *1967 Protocol relating to the status of refugees.*

A wider definition of the term refugee has been adopted in Article I of the *OAU Convention governing the specific aspects of refugee problems in Africa* of 10 September 1969, and inspired by the OAU Convention. Such a wider definition has also been recommended for Central America, Mexico and Panama by the *Cartagena Declaration on Refugees* adopted by the Cartagena Colloquium at Cartagena de Indias on 22 November 1984:

> " ... the definition or concept of a refugee to be recommended for use in the region is one which, in addition to containing the elements of the 1951 Convention and the 1967 Protocol, includes among refugees persons who have fled their country because their lives, safety or freedom have been threatened by generalized violence, foreign aggression, internal conflicts, massive violation of human rights or other circumstances which have seriously disturbed public order."

Asylum seeker

The term refers to an alien who requests asylum because he/she believes that he/she is a refugee. Official international definitions are given in Article 1 of the *Convention determining the State responsible for examining applications for asylum lodged in one of the Member States of the European Communities* of 15 June 1990 (Dublin Convention). This article defines the *applicant for asylum* and the *application for asylum.*

Asylee

The term *asilado* has been used in Latin American treaties from the 19th and 20th centuries but also in the municipal law of other countries, e.g. Spain or France (*asilé*).

The *asylee* is an alien to whom asylum has been granted. This may be territorial, political or diplomatic asylum, very often not related to the Convention & Protocol.

Rejectee
The term 'rejectee' refers to a person whose asylum application has been rejected by due process of law.

Migrant
The term *migrant* applies to "a person who migrates" i.e. "who leaves one's country to settle in another" as the shorter Oxford English Dictionary puts it. Within the meaning of the *International Convention on the protection of the rights of all migrant workers and members of their families* adopted by the UN General Assembly on 18 December 1990 specific reference is made to *migrant workers*:

> "The term 'migrant worker' refers to a person who is to be engaged, is engaged or has been engaged in a remunerated activity in a State of which he or she is not a national." (Art. 2.1)

Displaced person
This term refers to both internally displaced persons and to externally displaced persons. According to early definitions (1940s, 1950s) it concerns

> "... a person who, as a result of the actions of the authorities of the regimes has been deported from, or has been obliged to leave his country of nationality or of former habitual residence, such as persons who were compelled to undertake forced labour or who were deported for racial, religious or political reasons ..."

Internally displaced persons are persons in 'a refugee-like situation' who have not left the territory of the State of their nationality or habitual residence.

Repatriant
This term refers to a former refugee who has returned to the country of her/his nationality or former habitual residence.

Returnee
A *returnee* is a person who has returned to the country of her/his nationality or former habitual residence. In refugee literature, resolutions etc., the term normally refers to persons who were not considered refugees *stricto sensu* when they were residing in the country from which they have returned.

3.b **Concepts**

Protection
Protection is a particularly complex concept. It is immediately derived from the verb to protect: to defend or guard from injury or danger, to keep safe, to take care of, to extend patronage to (*Shorter Oxford English Dictionary*). All these meanings apply to the protection of refugees.

The first aspect of the *protection of persons* is "the *internal, legal protection* which every national may claim from his State of nationality under its municipal law". Under present human rights principles and treaties, internal legal protection is (or should be) afforded by the State to all persons legally living on its territory, including asylum seekers and refugees.

Where refugees are concerned the type of protection normally referred to is *international protection.* The UNHCR has in recent years developed *new protection strategies* essentially based on *prevention*, on *protection in the country of origin*. This protection through prevention is aimed at:

- stabilising the people in the country of potential departure;
- averting the necessity of fleeing;
- implementing the right to remain;
- implementing the various human rights;
- implementing especially the rights of national or ethno-religious minorities;
- promoting appropriate legal instruments and institutions of protection;
- implementing the principles of the responsibility of the State towards its own citizens and to other States.

These preventive protection strategies, however, cannot always be put into practice as they normally require the consensus of the government directly concerned.

Temporary protection

Temporary protection is the admission on the territory of a State of a group or category of aliens not on account of international treaty provisions but because they require international protection upon leaving the State of their nationality or habitual residence, and the granting of a status to these aliens concerning civil, economic, social and cultural rights enabling them to lead a normal life, during their temporary stay.

Temporary protection is an ancient modality for admitting aliens. In recent years it has been applied in the 1980s to refugees and displaced persons from Indo-China (*boat people*) and between 1992 and 1997 to refugees and displaced persons from the former Yugoslavia.

The time may now be ripe to embark upon a process which should result in the adoption of a Protocol to the 1951 Refugee Convention focusing on the status of persons in need of temporary protection, in particular the victims of internal and external aggression, i.e. war.

Admission

The first tangible act of protecting a refugee or rather an asylum seeker is her/his *admission to the territory* of the State where she/he seeks refuge. The next act of protection is her/his *admission to the procedure,* i.e. to the *asylum procedure* or the procedure for the *determination of refugees status*.

Non-admission, removal

The negative aspects of admission are the *refusal*, the *non-admission* of the asylum seeker *at the border* or, if she/he has already entered the territory, the various methods of return eventually amounting to *forcible removal*:

– *refoulement* within the meaning of Art. 33 of the 1951 Convention;
– *expulsion* within the meaning of Arts. 32 or 33 of the 1951 Convention;
– *deportation, forcible repatriation*, which are forms of *expulsion* within the terminology of some States.

Asylum procedure, determination procedure

Treaties relating to refugees cannot be applied without identifying the persons who are refugees. Hence the *procedure for the determination of refugees status.* The determination procedure normally implements *municipal law* provisions and has, therefore, specific aspects in each State, sometimes at variance with international refugee law.

Other Contracting States resort to an *ad hoc determination* of refugee status when the need arises. In situations of a mass influx the authorities have resorted to *collective determination* of refugee status which is often a *prima facie determination.*

In practically all countries the consequence of a positive determination of refugee status is the *grant of durable asylum* to the asylum seeker. (During the determination procedure the asylum seeker is in a situation of *provisional or temporary asylum.*) Furthermore, asylum rather than refugee status is considered in many countries to be the real issue. For these reasons the determination procedure is very often referred to as the *asylum procedure.*

Under the International Refugee Organisation (IRO) the determination procedure was called the *eligibility procedure.* There were eligibility officers, eligibility tribunals, etc. The term *eligibility* was gradually abandoned and replaced by the much clearer *determination of refugee status.*

Migration

"To leave one's country to settle in another" is a fundamental aspect of mankind's history. In the early part of the 20th century sociologists and jurists made a clear distinction between *migration* motivated by economic and social factors and *refugee movements* motivated by a lack of State protection and an infringement of human rights. In contrast, in recent years the trend has been to consider all population movements in terms of migration aspects. Hence the concept of *forced migration* which is often used to designate refugee movements.

A majority of migration movements belong to the category of *illegal migration* as the immigrants do not comply with the relevant municipal law regulations, particularly those relating to entry visas.

Irregular migration refers to *irregular movements of refugees and asylum seekers who have already found protection in a particular country.* The Executive Committee of the UNHCR in 1989 adopted Conclusion No. 58 (XL) on this problem.

Burden-sharing, responsibility-sharing

For reasons of geographic propinquity, but also for other reasons as well, asylum seekers generally flee to a limited number of (neighbouring) countries. These countries request the assistance of other countries by invoking the principles of *international solidarity* and of *burden-sharing*. For a number of years NGOs have been tending to use the expression *responsibility-sharing*.

In actual practice, *burden-sharing* is difficult to attain. A European *Council Resolution of 25 September 1995 on burden-sharing with regard to the admission and residence of displaced persons on a temporary basis* and a European *Council Decision of 4 March 1996 on an alert and emergency procedure for burden-sharing with regard to the admission and residence of displaced persons on a temporary basis* have so far not had any practical effects.

4. 'UNRAVELLING THE CONTEXTS'

If one could in principle agree on the basic terms and concepts as elaborated in the above paragraph, one could then carefully look into the context itself.

In terms of asylum, refugee and migration it is the context that plays the major role. Not so much the causes, but the contexts determine different impacts on a worldwide scale: demographic, geopolitical, transnational, social, health, economic, and religious.[5] In this respect, governments have settled contractual obligations based on Conventions, Protocols, Treaties and Charters, which yield consequences, but nowadays due to ongoing globalizing processes these contexts rapidly vary. They give rise to different models of interaction whereby clear, transparent and universal answers have not yet been provided by any one actor.

It is indeed the context which counts, but the context is no longer completely in the hands of existing governments alone. Contexts, so to say, after common agreement on basic terms and concepts, need to be 'unravelled'. It is thereby essential to start making distinctions between the existing refugee and migration regimes. The causes are often quite clear, although complex, and they can still be found and formulated within basic terms and concepts. What is at stake is that the contexts, as said, vary, and require new responses which must include additional and different actors in society. The health sector, the corporate sector, the financial world, the labour markets, the media, the commitment by non-governmental organisations, and even bona fide agents of trafficking: all, hopefully positively, will be bound to play a new, complementary and 'compatible' role in influencing the contexts in which (actually, only with good governance by governments) the

[5] See e.g. Van Krieken (Ed.), *The Asylum Acquis Handbook*, The Hague 2000, p. 82.

refugee, asylum and migration issue will have to take place. Without this, serious protection and even management gaps will occur and daily practices will deteriorate.

That context is first of all the world. The world subject to globalisation will face new forms of disparities resulting in a tremendous increase in the gap between the poor and the rich. Persons, in particular young adults, currently living in poor areas will not wait to see improvement coming. Instead they will organise themselves cross-nationally, cross-culturally, cross-socially and cross-economically to find new a life in the rich areas. In the absence of a universal world migration policy some will even try to become 'club-class migrants' – particularly in the IT world – , but the bulk of those will instead belong to the huge mass of all sorts of migrants. They are not refugees! The political, economic, financial, social, and health sectors of any society will have to deal with this development and cannot escape from it. Existing procedures, reception, integration, return and development programmes, all originating from the recent past, will eventually not be able to fully respond to this trend by merely improving existing national legal and social instruments. By including partners of the South, the North may look for ways and means to bear full responsibility in facing this particular context as it is and as it stands, from within a true global perspective, and no longer from within a (sub-)regional interest only. The North will gain much more by co-operating with the South at an equal global partnership level.

The full and wide dimensions of tomorrow's migration issues are here at stake, including the health dimension. For example, as one medical doctor from Uganda indicated recently, what would be the response of the world if in a few years' time the ebola virus would be able to adapt itself, and what if that virus will be able to transport itself via the bronchia? What would be the consequences for general public health care, if this most deadly virus would travel together with migrants, be they legal or illegal, from the South to the North, and from the South to the South? Already there is the example of forms of open TB which do now appear in parts of the world where for years it was judged to be free of it. The context of the world stage with regard to the full and wide dimensions of tomorrow's migration issues do demand innovative and urgent responses, taking into account interdisciplinary and multidisciplinary knowledge. The health dimension is an integral part of this.

Within this context the health sector may well help by *starting* to set up a universal world migration policy to deal with those most urgent issues at stake. Nowadays, a universal migration policy does not in fact exist. Also there are no clear signs from the traditional asylum and migration sectors – mainly governments, inter- and non-governmental organisations – of wanting to create such a universal migration policy. Here the health sector with other partners including the traditional ones may start playing a *catalysing role*. Like a general practitioner who refers patients to specialists *after* first having carried out examination and deciding on policy/treatment, so the health sector may well operate and function to work towards a universal response to asylum and migration from a multidisciplinary perspective.

The peculiar present day and future migration issues, however, must not affect the legitimacy of people who exercise the human right to 'seek and enjoy' asylum because they are indeed in need of protection. That is a different matter, and during the 'unravelling' exercise they should continue to be treated within the spirit of the most liberal interpretation of the *1951 Convention relating to the status of refugees* and the *1967 Protocol relating to the status of refugees*. Here at a worldwide level one may consider, again from an interdisciplinary and multidisciplinary perspective, whether the time is ripe after the fall of the Berlin Wall and given the process of globalisation to opt for a new additional Protocol. This Protocol could focus on the changes which have taken place while still allowing the spirit of the *1951 Convention relating to the status of refugees*.

If upon the initiative of the health sector such an 'unravelling' exercise could be put into motion, it will also contribute to a new awareness concerning the issue among the general public, which means the following: national and international politicians will eventually have to follow; it will furthermore be a real and needed attack against mala fide traffickers who currently profit from the absence of a universal migration policy. It may also provide room for reaching the conclusion that asylum seekers, refugees and migrants are human entities who do exist on their own; they demand different interrelated treatment and response. Legal experts and politicians have so far not taken such an initiative, but this may start from an unexpected but well-known corner: the international health sector. In fact, the health issue may be considered to be one of the most striking illustrations of the need to attain a comprehensive migration policy, whilst fully living up to the commitments under the system of universal human rights.

The context is the world stage, and this context is split up into countries, states, areas, regions, even cities, groups and gender, the context is also the issue of asylum, refugee and migration itself and, finally, the context is us as human actors; 'unravelling' ourselves in a new interdisciplinary and multidisciplinary way may open up new ways for setting a world scene which will be able to deal with the asylum, refugee and migration issue as one of the earth's most burdesome tasks the responsibility for which we must exercise and act together at the universal level.

5. ACTING TOGETHER BY LINKING THE MATTER IN QUESTION

If 'step by step with migration' one is able and willing to see the challenge concerning asylum and migration, if one is able and willing to come to terms with the concepts, and if one is able and willing to 'unravel' the contexts – thereby making use of the health sector as a motivating power, as a trigger for in-depth *discussions* and for developing new visions – then as actors we must not be afraid to act within the framework of sophisticated experiments. Any interdisciplinary and multidisciplinary exercise concerning this theme is by definition an experiment. It should be open and accessible to sincere criticism, and must not be seen beforehand as a threat to existing and established instruments and offices on asylum and migration.

In order to fully entertain the global vs universal approach (meaning that no globalization should be allowed if this would be contrary to the need to uphold the universal human rights system), we may wish to appreciate that the health realities urge us to rethink the migration concept as a whole. That should be done whilst fully being aware of the need to link the various disciplines involved, not only from a Northern point of view, but also with due regard to the African and Asian views.

Health should indeed be considered an exemplary illustration of the dynamics and challenges involved. The voice of the health discipline needs to be heard world-wide, particularly also with regard to migrants, asylum seekers and refugees. A true interdisciplinary and multidisciplinary approach is needed to provide answers to the health and migration challenge. There is no longer any possible escape from this theme. The Expert Meeting on 'Health and Migration' (September 14th and 15th, 2000, at Noordwijkerhout, the Netherlands) was an important and encouraging step towards linking concepts which were hitherto believed to be too far apart to be connected.

THE LEGAL STATUS OF REJECTEES

Peter van Krieken

HUMAN RIGHTS AND NON-NATIONALS[6]

The international aspects of the human rights regime are primarily to be found in the commitment of countries towards other countries as to the treatment of their subjects. These commitments have been laid down in international treaties, in an international context. Moreover, the countries concerned, the States Parties, have, through monitoring mechanisms, including the various independent committees,

---

[6] To a great extent based on Chapter 4 of my Health Gaps and Migratory Movements, Lund 2000.

given up some of their 'domestic jurisdiction.'[7] Human rights themselves, however, describe above all the relationships between the individual subjects and their authorities.

It is hence submitted that it is not automatically correct to state that all human rights befall all those present on the territory of the country concerned. It is in particular of relevance to focus on the legal status and position of non-subjects in their host society, those residing illegally in particular. From the outset it is herewith submitted that someone who has submitted an application which has been rejected upon due process of law, is supposed to leave the territory of the country concerned, and should hence be considered an illegal, someone who is no longer lawfully present. The term 'rejectee' thus refers to and falls under the generic 'persons unlawfully residing'.

As to aliens in general, most fortunately the human rights regime is not necessarily limited to the citizens (or: nationals) of the State concerned. In fact, many of the rights listed in the International Bill of Human Rights cover subjects as well as aliens, legally residing foreigners, as well as illegally residing foreigners, in the same way as it covers civil servants, university professors and prisoners alike.

There are some differences, though, between the first and second generation rights, as codified in 1966. Moreover, under some articles aliens are excluded from enjoying some specific rights:
– the civil and political rights cover "... all individuals within its territory and subject to its jurisdiction ..." (Art. 2.1). Article 25 is a logical exception, indicating that to vote and to be elected is limited to 'every citizen.' Interestingly, this article also contains a para. 3, in which it has been laid down that "every citizen shall have the right and the opportunity to have access, on general terms of equality, to public service in the country." There is no need to underline the fact that public service is not meant to mean services such as health, education and social security, but rather employment as a public (or: civil) servant.[8]

Concerning the second generation rights, it has been laid down that the economic, social and cultural rights will be exercised "... without discrimination of any kind as to race, colour ... national or social origin, birth or other status ..." (Art. 2.2). This text remains silent on the non-nationals vs nationals issue, as national origin would rather refer to minority groups. Whether or not non-nationals are entitled to enjoy the rights concerned, becomes, however, clear from Art. 2.3: "developing countries may determine to what extent they would guarantee the

[7] In fact one of the main accomplishments of the last 50 years or so, is the increasingly limited meaning of domestic jurisdiction (art.2.7 of the UN Charter), originally limited by Chapter 5 of the Charter, but now mainly by human rights mechanisms.

[8] See on the various proposed texts: Bossuyt's *Guide to the Travaux Préparatoires of the ICCPR*, Dordrecht et al. 1987, at pp. 471-478. It is worth pointing out in this respect that gradually non-nationals are given the possibility to participate in elections, on the one hand European Elections, on the other local elections.

economic rights (...) to non-nationals." This indeed indicates that the rights in these instruments in principle cover nationals and non-nationals alike. The question then needs to be answered whether the non-nationals are assumed to be legally, or lawfully staying in the country concerned, and/or whether illegally residing non-nationals would also benefit under the Covenants.

Art. 12 of the CCPR indicates that everyone *lawfully* within the territory shall have the right to liberty of movement and freedom to choose his residence, thereby implying that those not lawfully residing, i.e. without a permit or title, do not enjoy these very rights. It is, however, recalled that in an early draft mention was made of the requirement of the State 'to promote and protect the health of its nationals.' An objection to that wording was raised by the UNHCR, as limiting the provision of health to nationals would possibly deprive refugees of the possibility to secure medical care. A reference to nationals was hence dropped.[9]

Art. 13 is even more explicit: "... an alien lawfully in the territory (...) may be expelled therefrom only in pursuance of a decision reached in accordance with law ..." This implies that aliens *not* lawfully in the territory can be expelled more easily, which would indicate the deprivation of certain rights he/she may rightly or wrongly have enjoyed. The question thus remains whether the alien, not lawfully residing in the territory, but who has not been expelled is entitled to enjoy the various freedoms, rights and social security as listed in the Covenants. Although the answer to this question would appear to be quite obvious, it takes today's Western European democracies a great deal of discussion and political manoeuvering to reach the obvious:

- primary education (which is/should be compulsory and available free to all) shall be provided to everyone, irrespective of legal status
- urgent, life-saving treatment shall be available to all, irrespective of status
- access to the administration and/or the courts to apply for a residence status should be available to all, again irrespective of legal status.[10]

THE 1985 GA DECLARATION ON NON-NATIONALS

The issue at stake continues to remain in spite of what has been stated above in a rather blurred fashion. This was reflected for example by the action which the General Assembly took by passing a resolution on this issue, probably in order to

[9] Toebes (1999) pp. 42/43; it should be noted, though, that the 1951 Convention relative to the Status of Refugees contains a provision under which the health aspects can be considered to have been dealt with: art. 20 states that 'The Contracting States shall accord to refugees lawfully staying in their territory the same treatment with respect to public relief and assistance as is accorded to their nationals.'

[10] Yet, in certain cases the result of the application will have to be awaited outside the country for which the permit has been requested.

try and codify certain principles. But by doing so, it not only created some clear-cut views, it also confused certain issues.

By the Resolution concerned (40/144, 13 December 1985), a Declaration had been adopted with the correct, yet remarkable title: 'Declaration on the Human Rights of Individuals Who are not Nationals of the Country in which They Live' (sic). It concerns a GA resolution, and hence soft law. Yet, it is worth quoting some of the relevant articles, as it was confirmed that with improving communications and the development of peaceful and friendly relations among countries, individuals increasingly live in countries of which they are not nationals, and as it was thus recognized that the protection of human rights and fundamental freedoms provided for in international instruments should also be ensured for individuals who are not nationals of the country in which they live.[11]

After providing a definition of the term alien in Art. 1 ('any individual who is not a national of the State in which he or she is present'), Art. 2.1 of the Declaration is immediately striking when stressing that:

> 'Nothing in this Declaration shall be interpreted as legitimizing the illegal entry into and presence in a State of any alien, nor shall any provision be interpreted as restricting the right of any State to promulgate laws and regulations concerning the entry of aliens and the terms and conditions of their stay or to establish differences between nationals and aliens. However, such laws and regulations shall not be incompatible with the international legal obligations of that State, including those in the field of human rights.'

Art. 4 of the Declaration confirms that aliens shall observe the laws of the State in which they reside or are present and regard with respect the customs and traditions of the people of that State. In Arts. 5 and 6 some of the first generation rights have been listed. Art. 7 confirms the principle that an alien lawfully in the territory may be expelled only in pursuance of a decision reached in accordance with law. Again, no mention is made of those residing illegally.

In Art. 8 social and economic rights have been touched upon (safe and healthy working conditions, fair wages, equal renumeration), but also the right to join trade unions. On the issue of health the following can be read (Art. 8.1):

> 'Aliens lawfully residing in the territory of a State shall also enjoy, in accordance with the national laws, the following rights, subject to their obligations under Article 4 (...): the right to health protection, medical care, social security, social services, education, rest and leisure, provided that they fulfil the requirements under the relevant regulations for participation and that undue strain is not placed on the resources of the State.'

[11] GA Res. 40/144, preambule, parapraphs 5 and 6. The use of the word 'should' deserves to be emphasized as it would appear to indicate that the protection of human rights had hitherto not been ensured.

The Declaration concerned would appear to confirm a fairly restrictive reading of the 1966 Covenants where it concerns the extension of rights to non-nationals. The exceptions being declared possible, the virtual exclusion of illegals would appear to confirm that the present state of human rights focuses on citizens, and, rightly, tries to be accommodating to non-nationals, as long as they are lawfully present.

THE EXHAUSTION OF LOCAL REMEDIES

It is fully appreciated that there are significant differences between the various States. On no account could a claim be addressed which would be based on the non-relationship between the State and a non-subject.[12] It is therefore quite logical to request the complainant to seek redress for any ills within his/her own community. This principle is called the exhaustion of local (or: domestic) remedies.

As human rights primarily deal with the relationship between the individual and his/her own community, a principle which has been reflected in the asylum principle, where redress can be sought elsewhere in the case of persecution, in case there are no internal flight alternatives, it follows that all assumed rights should be enjoyed in principle in the country of origin, the community of which the individual is a member. Only if the local community is violating the individual's rights or neglecting the obligations to such an extent that the situation amounts to persecution, without internal alternatives being available, may remedies be sought elsewhere. This is also valid for issues like employment, health, and cultural rights.

We then have to look into refugee law, to decide when exactly a lack of adequate health care would amount to persecution. And indeed, if the patient would be denied access to health care, or would be denied available treatment *because* of his race, religion, ethnic origin, political opinion or particular social group as per the 1951 Refugee Convention, persecution in accordance with the refugee definition could be established. In those cases, if indeed no internal alternatives are available, protection deserves to be extended, and hence health services should be provided as per the national rules and regulations.[13] According to the

---

[12] As we saw above, the whole system is based on the inter-state network, meaning that States may address the non-compliance of other States, and/or may await the result of the Committee reporting system, or of individual communications/complaints, in as far as applicable.

[13] There is no need to underline the very fact that breaches of health, e.g. by torturing or other inhuman or degrading treatment, inflicted because of reasons of race, religion, social or ethnic backgrounds or political opinion, may per se amount to persecution. Moreover, a serious risk to be exposed to torture results in *de facto* asylum as per the 1984 Convention Against Torture. This, however, is not the subject of this study. See e.g., my Torture or Asylum, *Israel Yearbook of Human Rights*, 1985, pp. 143-161.

1951 Refugee Convention, Art. 24, the social security (including legal provisions in respect of employment injury, occupational diseases, maternity, sickness and disability) to be accorded should be the same as is accorded to nationals. However, (Art. 24.1.b.i and ii):

> There may be appropriate arrangements for the maintenance of acquired rights and rights in the course of acquisition;
> National laws or regulations of the country of residence may prescribe special arrangements concerning benefits which are payable wholly out of public funds (...).

In practice, in the EU countries, refugees, upon having acquired the legal status as such, are indeed generally treated in the same way as is accorded to nationals.

THE NON-REFUGEES

In general, where it concerns legally residing aliens, efforts need to be made to clarify the status (students, tourists, migrant workers) and the rights and responsibilities involved. It is up to the individual relationship whether or not access to health services should be made available. The tourist or student should in principle have health insurance before entering the country, or, alternatively, a local insurance contract should be entered into before an application for (temporary) residence would meet with success. In the case of migrant workers, the obligations for taking care of the migrants could be placed with the individuals, the employers, the state of origin, or the state of residence through access to the health system in general (and indeed by paying the taxes and premiums involved), or by signing up with appropriate insurance schemes in either the country of (temporary) residence or the country of origin, as long as the alien if sufficiently covered.

Many if not most of the asylum seekers enter the country of potential asylum illegally. Although the 1951 Refugee Convention contains a specific reference to this issue, in which it has been stated that illegal entry should not be considered an offence or misdemeanour, as long as the refugees/asylum seekers come directly from the country of persecution and submit their application without delay,[14] hardly any use is made of this proviso. Most of those who illegally enter the country of destination, in practice legalize their stay by officially applying for asylum. Thereby, their status has become 'legal', and (some) health services are provided. In some countries a collective insurance for all asylum seekers has been

[14] Article 31.1 reads as follows: "The Contracting States shall not impose penalties, on account of their illegal entry or presence, on refugees who, *directly* from a territory where their life or freedom was threatened in the sense of Article 1, enter or are present in their territory without authorization, provided they present themselves *without delay* to the authorities and show good cause for their illegal entry or presence." [emphasis added]

arranged, in others specific services are being made available. The levels of service, however, differ widely.[15] By declaring the applicant to be a refugee, health services should be made available as per the above mentioned principles.

Those who do not apply for asylum, or whose application has been rejected and who have been requested to leave the territory of the country concerned, could, or rather, should be considered to reside illegally, and should hence be called 'illegals'.

With regard to illegally residing aliens, in particular the ones who claim that they are in need of treatment because their country of origin cannot cater for the needs concerned, it should be underlined that compliance with the CESCR obligations differs from country to country. The term 'progressive realization of the relevant rights to the maximum of the available resources' is the relevant terminology. It could be argued that the human rights network has developed to such an extent that in the case of an obvious breach of the obligations accepted under the CESCR such a breach might have an impact on the relationship between the victim and the authorities of another country. However, before any such claim could be properly addressed, the claimant should prove that his country is actively breaching the Covenant, and that no alternative remedies can be sought which includes the exhaustion of local remedies. Moreover, the international community must have indicated that the fellow State party is indeed in breach of its Treaty obligations, and the international community, either on a bilateral basis, but preferably through unequivocal reports submitted by the Committee, must have undertaken efforts to redress the ills, and/or have been negligent as to its responsibilities under the CESCR's Art. 2.

It is hence herewith submitted that the impact of the international bill of human rights on health-related claims to obtain a residence permit in countries where the standard of health provisions is significantly better than in the country of origin is nil, but for certain, fully certified cases, particularly when as we have seen above, the patient is denied access to existing health services and/or denied care and cure, if available, for reasons of his race, religion, ethnic or particular social group or political opinion.

The services to be provided to the non-refugees are thus limited to the most obvious ones, the cases in which life is in immediate danger and/or where the lack of immediate treatment would without any doubt result in a life-threatening situation (accidents, acute appendicitis, heart failure). But even this submission would appear to lack a firm legal basis embedded in international law.

[15] In the Netherlands as in many other European countries, the asylum seeker receives access to all kinds of assistance virtually immediately (except, sometimes, for the so-called Dublin claimants). In France, however, only the asylum seekers who have legally entered the country have access to those services, thereby excluding all the asylum seekers who are unable to prove that they either entered legally, or reside legally.

CONSEQUENCES OF NON-RETURN[16]

Some countries have reached a stage under which the non-return would allow the illegally residing alien to virtually legalize his/her stay. The idea goes that if the authorities of the country where asylum has been sought do not actively return or deport the rejectee, the latter would be allowed to stay, and moreover would be allowed to enjoy the various services on offer (social security, education, education grants, access to hospitals, etc.). This line of thinking denies some of the basic principles at stake, namely that the rejectee who has also received an order to leave the territory of the country where he had sought asylum, is obliged to leave the territory concerned. The obligation lies with the individual, the alien, not with the authorities concerned. Non-compliance with this principle should never result in any obligation of the guest-community to extend social and/or economic benefits. Again, the only exception being an immediate danger to life.[17]

---

[16] See also the contribution by Grimmer and Palinksy elsewhere in this Chapter.

[17] The anomaly which has been created during the last couple of years as to the relationship between the rejectee and the authorities of the country where a residence permit has been sought is to some extent mind-boggling. Some lobbies appear to claim that if an application for residence has been rejected, the authorities have the obligation to ensure that the rejectee leaves the territory concerned. If the authorities would not take the appropriate action, so the misconception goes, the rejectee may be considered to be allowed to continue his/her stay in that country, and the stay may hence be considered legal. The anomaly in this construction ought to be obvious, but it is apparently necessary to underline the principles at stake:
– asylum seekers are entitled to apply for asylum (except for e.g. war criminals, UDHR, Art. 14.2);
– (potential) migrants are entitled to apply for a residence permit (although in some cases the application will be rejected outright, without having been dealt with on its merits);
– sometimes applications will have to be submitted outside the country one wishes to reside in;
– if applications are submitted in the country where one whishes to reside, the underlying principle is that, if indeed the applicant arrived there on his/her own initiative, and by his/her own means (with or without the help of an agent) – which almost always is the case (exceptions being formal or informal resettlement cases) – the individual is and remains responsible for his/her departure, if indeed the authorities indicate that the individual should depart from the territory concerned.

No obligation whatsoever rests with the authorities of the country concerned, but for the relationship between the authorities and the inhabitants of that country. The latter relationship may indeed result in the obligatory efforts in order to prevent the rejectee from unduly prolonging his/her stay in the country concerned. Any lack of action in this respect has an impact on the relationship between the authorities and the subjects of the country concerned, but not on the relationship between the authorities and the rejectee. In all cases the latter is obliged to make efforts to depart, if requested to do so. In case he/she lacks the funds and/or papers, problems can be discussed with the authorities. There is no need to deny that authorities are in general quite forthcoming when confronted with these kinds of requests.

At any rate, it should be underlined that Art. 13 of the ICCPR indicates that the expulsion of aliens lawfully in the territory shall take place only in pursuance of a decision reached in accordance with the law. It may a fortiori be submitted that aliens unlawfully in the territory do not therefore necessarily enjoy these same guarantees. Yet, and rightly so, it is now accepted in most Northern and Western countries, that the one residing illegally, can also only be expelled in pursuance of decisions reached in accordance with the law. State practice, therefore, has fortunately developed beyond the minimum guarantees of this 1966 Covenant.

SERVICES ELSEWHERE

What is at stake here, is that 'rejectees' – often at a very late stage – claim that they are in need of medical treatment and that they hence deserve a (temporary) residence permit. Elsewhere in this Handbook attention will be paid to state practice (Chapter 6), but it is already here submitted that in some social welfare states, the borderline between legal and illegal residence became blurred. The request to be allowed to undergo treatment turns many, if not most 'illegals' quite 'illogically' into 'legal' residents, because of the simple fact that their request is being dealt with, and because the applicants are allowed to remain in that country, pending the outcome of the request. Whilst in the waiting room, some level of services will be conferred on the claimants. Thus many persons, although not allowed to stay in those countries, nevertheless find ways to benefit from many of the services normally limited to subjects or foreigners residing legally: education, health and sometimes unemployment benefits.[18]

Such a reaction does not appear to be logical. It denies the very fact that rejectees by definition have a community, a society where they can enjoy the services as per what that society or community has agreed upon. By the mere membership of another society (i.e. the country of origin) the enjoyment of services in accordance with the standards set in that country is assured. Rejectees do not need to have the best of both worlds. It is too often forgotten that second generation human rights have a very limited cross-border impact, if at all, and that by focusing on the relationship between the applicant and the country of residence, one forgets that there is already a human rights relevant relationship, namely the one between that applicant and his/her country of origin.

The latter relationship ought to dominate the discussions concerning the status of rejectees.

[18] Where it concerns the truly 'illegals', this of course shows a lack of interaction between the various governmental agencies. In some countries, where a more strict ID-system has been introduced, the chances of such 'oversights' are less. Access to services of course do not necessarily turn an illegal stay into a legal one, and cuts may, if not should, occur any time. Arguments that the applicants have paid taxes are of no relevance. Some of the taxes are paid across the board (e.g. VAT), some others are paid whilst working (income tax, social premiums). The payment of these premiums may account for access to social services, but have in principle no impact on the legality of the stay. Authorities are free to request the incumbent to leave the country and to cut any services which the person concerned enjoyed. In some cases, some of the 'social security taxes' may be reimbursed (contributions to pension funds, for example).

RETURN, PRINCIPLES AND PROBLEMS

Kirk Grimmer and Erik Palinsky

INTRODUCTION

Over the past two decades, there have been many opinions on the issue of the return of rejected asylum seekers (rejectees).[19] These opinions vary due to the different interpretations of the obligations of states based on international law. This survey is based on three articles[20] that contain the two following opinions.

First, there is the idea that the returning state should share the burden of responsibility for returning rejected asylum seekers to their country of origin. Gregor Noll states that under international obligations the "return of rejectees might be faced with constraints emerging from human rights law ... and promotes voluntary return because enforcement practices entail a considerable risk of human rights violations."

Second, there is the opinion of Peter van Krieken that return is first and foremost the responsibility of the rejectee and the "prohibition on forcible return is no longer linked to the non-refoulement principle, but to the ordinary laws and regulations governing residence, expulsion and extradition of foreigners."

While discussing the above two opinions, the present authors will discuss the subjects of rejectees and returnees and the practices of voluntary repatriation, readmission agreements and expulsion in accordance with the individuals concerned, the countries of origin and the countries of asylum.

---

[19] We use the term 'rejectee' to describe the asylum seeker whose application has been rejected upon due process of law. (In general, please note that we have tried to limit the footnotes to the absolute minimum).

[20] The articles which we took as the basis for this contribution are: Peter van Krieken, Repatriation of Refugees Under International Law, *Netherlands Yearbook of International Law*, 1982, pp. 93 –123; Gregor Noll, Rejected Asylum Seekers: The Problem of Return, *UNHCR Working Paper* no. 4, Geneva, May 1999, pp. 1–38 (which to some extent was based on his The Non-Admission and Return of Protection Seekers in Germany, *International Journal of Refugee Law (IJRL)*, Vol. 9, 1997, pp. 415-452); and Peter van Krieken, Return and Responsibility, *International Migration*, Quarterly Review, Vol. 38, no. 4, 2000, pp. 23–39. Noll and Van Krieken appear to have covered all the various aspects of the discussion concerned. However, mention should also be made of: Johan Feitsma, Repatriation Law and Refugees, *Netherlands Quarterly of Human Rights (NQHR)*, 1989, Vol. 7(3) pp. 294-307; Kai Hailbronner, *Rückübernahme eigener und fremder Staatsangehöriger*, Heidelberg, 1996; and, albeit somewhat outdated, Göran Melander, *Refugees in Orbit*, IUEF, Geneva, 1976. On UNHCR's official views, see *Voluntary Repatriation, International Protection*, Geneva 1996. Of relevance are also: James C. Hathaway, The Meaning of Repatriation, *IJRL* 1997 9(4) and the 1997 study by a WG on Refugees (European University Institute 97/12) on *Repatriation, Legal and Policy Issues concerning Refugees from the Former Yugoslavia.*

This survey should begin by pointing out certain documents of international law that specify the relationships between the countries of origin towards their rejected nationals and the countries of asylum. The purpose of this is to point out the actors on the international stage and their degree of involvement in dealing with this controversial issue. The second part of the survey will try to assist the reader in understanding the development of these instruments of international law in relation to historical events that have had a major influence on the rising number of global migrants. During the 1990s, the number of migrants rose exponentially, creating utilitarian and regional approaches towards migration and its control in general. Therefore, the third section juxtaposes the two current positions based on the writings of Van Krieken and Noll and the implications of each interpretation. Finally, the conclusion will attempt to draw together some suggestions on how to deal with this growing problem.

INSTRUMENTS OF INTERNATIONAL LAW

Dealing with the problems of migration and return, mention should be made of the concept of 'triptych' that defines the right to migration in the 1948 Universal Declaration of Human Rights. These three articles (13, 14 and 15) are related to each other and should not be studied in isolation. Article 13.1 refers to the internal issue of each state in accordance with the 'right to freedom of movement and residence.' Globalists, however, normally refer to global migration by emphasizing para. 2 of that same article, which states that, "everyone has the right to leave any country, including his own, and to return to his country." Yet, we are here confronted with an incomplete feature: a right to leave is not matched by any right to enter a country not one's own. Based on these lines, we can deduce that there is no right to immigration. Also the text of the 1966 Covenant on Civil and Political Rights, which followed the 1948 UDHR, does not contain any support for such a right. In order to solidify these facts, we can note General Comment no.15, 1986 by the Human Rights Committee that "the Covenant does not recognize the right of aliens to enter or reside in the territory of a State party. It is in principle a matter for the State to decide who it will admit to its territory." General Comment no. 27, 1999, confirms this principle (para. 4): "... The question whether an alien is 'lawfully' within the territory of a State is a matter governed by domestic law, which may subject the entry of an alien to the territory of a State to restrictions, provided they are in compliance with the State's international obligations. In that connection the Committee has held that an alien who entered the State illegally ...", which would appear to underline the limits to a presumed right of immigration, if it exists at all.

Article 14 addresses a specific migratory group, these are the refugees. It says that "everyone has the right to seek and to enjoy in other countries asylum from persecution," and can thus be looked upon as the exception to the principle that there is no right to immigration: if the latter were to exist, then there would be no specific need to spell out the right to seek asylum The 'right to enjoy' is an entitlement only if the country of asylum actually grants asylum. This acceptance by the county of asylum is based on the person's "well-founded fear of being persecuted for reasons of race, religion, nationality, membership of a particular social group or political opinion" as laid down in the 1951 Refugee Convention, Article 1A2. As per Article 33 of the 1951 Convention and Article 3 of both the 1950 European Convention on Human Right (ECHR) and the 1984 Convention Against Torture (CAT), such a person cannot be returned to his country of origin.[21]

Article 15 could be closely related to Article 13 since it deals with a right to nationality and it can be seen as a membership card providing re-entry to the country of origin as well as access to the services being provided in that country.

Even though individual rights are mentioned in the UDHR and the ICCPR as well as in the other conventions mentioned above, it must be realized that treaties are signed between countries and the authorities of these countries commit themselves to act according to certain principles, to abstain from certain actions (first generation human rights) or to actively involve themselves by taking certain measures (second generation). The obligations are undertaken vis-à-vis other members states, not towards the subjects themselves. "The State acts as an 'agent,' a caretaker ... is not a purpose in itself. It has been created to be of service."[22] While signing these treaties, states create instruments to implement them and these are international organizations. Therefore, it could be concluded that international organizations and states are the only ones obliged to act under these international law obligations.[23] However, individuals have been successful in claiming their rights, for example through an international court or special complaint procedures (1235, 1503-procedure, 1st Protocol to the International Covenant on Civil and Political Rights (ICCPR). However, these complaints usually refer to the authorities' lack of will in carrying out these obligations towards their own nationals, those residing on their territory and falling under their jurisdiction. Since their establishment, the interpretations of the above conventions, articles and additional documents, in relation to return, have been changing over the past decades on the basis of historical development and the different kinds of migratory movements which reached their peak after the Cold War during the time of globalization.

[21] This is normally referred to as the non-refoulement principle, but whereas Art. 33 of the 1951 Refugee Convention is combined with residence and other rights (as contained in that Convention), Art. 3 of both the 1950 ECHR and 1984 CAT, only point towards non-return and do not oblige the state parties to grant residence rights.

[22] See e.g. Van Krieken, Disintegration and Statelessness, *NQHR* 1/1994, pp. 23-33 on 24.

[23] Article 35 of the 1951 Refugee Convention stating that 'the Contracting States undertake to cooperate with the Office of the United Nations High Commissioner for Refugees,' created for the purpose of this convention, can provide a specific example.

DEVELOPMENTS IN HUMANITARIAN AND HUMAN RIGHTS ISSUES

The foundation of humanitarian and human rights laws under international obligations, as we know them today, took place in the early 1950s at the beginning of the Cold War. "Clearly, what western governments had in mind when UNHCR was created and the UN Refugee Convention was drawn up were refugees fleeing communist regimes."[24]

The first major case that the UNHCR had to deal with was the exodus of Hungarian refugees fleeing the 1956 Soviet invasion of Hungary.[25] The UNHCR's representatives tried to ensure that all repatriation requests were made on a fully voluntary basis and it was generally agreed that the repatriation issue was a matter between the two countries involved, Hungary and Austria. Such a UNHCR involvement and the superior role of the states in the question of non-voluntary return refers to Article 1 of the Statute of the Office of the UNHCR, "... [UNHCR] acting under the authority of the General Assembly, shall assume the function of providing international protection, under the auspices of the United Nations to refugees who fall within the scope of the present statute and of seeking permanent solutions for the problem of refugees by assisting governments and, subject to the approval of the governments concerned, private organizations to facilitate the voluntary repatriation of such refugees ,or their assimilation within new national communities ..."

During the 1960s and 1970s, the decolonization process around the globe moved the focus away from Europe and widened the scope of the refugee definition in the 1951 Refugee Convention because new independence and civil wars had created refugees fleeing not just a fear of persecution but war and violence related to this process as well. Even though the 1951 Convention had to be supplemented to by a new Protocol, which covered these refugees, the position of the state with regard to non-voluntary return remained unchanged. It was at this time that the ICCPR entered into force and the position of the state grew stronger in relation to migration and return. Article 12.3 stated, 'the above mentioned rights [reflecting those in Article 13 of the UDHR] shall not be subject to any restrictions except those which are provided by law, are necessary to protect national security, public order (*ordre public*), public health or morals, or the rights and freedoms of others, and are consistent with the other rights recognized in the present Covenant.'

"Improved communications, easier access to air transport and growing numbers of people seeking better economic and social opportunities" and the growing restrictions by industrialized countries created a situation that "some would-be

[24] UNHCR, *The State of the World's Refugees: Fifty Years of Humanitarian Action*, Oxford University Press, Oxford, 2000, pp. 5 (hereinafter referred to as *UNHCR 2000*)

[25] Of around 200,000 refugees (*UNHCR 2000*), some 18,000 returned home, many of them assisted by the UNHCR, many independently (see Van Krieken, 1982).

migrants turned to the asylum channel"[26] during the 1980s and continued into the 1990s. This situation invoked "debate about the states' obligations towards people who travel half-way around the world to seek asylum, when they might have found an alternative closer to home."[27]

Currently, of the above estimated 150 million 'travellers', probably about 25 percent belong to the humanitarian group and no less than 3 to 4 million illegals residing in both the US and the European Union are due to human trafficking and non-compliance with return obligations on the part of rejectees (the question of forced return and expulsion has been discussed by the above two authors – Peter van Krieken and Gregor Noll).

RETURN, RESPONSIBILITY AND COOPERATION

a) **Return**

The Memorandum of Understanding between the United Nations High Commissioner for Refugees (UNHCR) and the International Organization for Migration (IOM) (May 1997) paragraph 29, defines rejected asylum seekers as "people who, after due consideration of their claims to asylum in fair procedures, are found not to qualify for authorized stay in a country concerned." While addressing 'fair procedures', UNHCR and IOM expect states to comply with the international obligations of Article 14 of the UDHR, Article 1A2 of the 1951 Refugee Convention and Article 3 of both the 1984 Convention Against Torture and the 1950 European Convention on Human Rights. Assuming that industrialized democracies are the Parties to these instruments and fully respect them, these organizations should not have any objections to the decisions taken to determine an individual's refugee status in the countries of the North.

However, even though taking into account democratic institutions, procedures and states[28], Gregor Noll still invokes a so-called dichotomy between migratory control and international refugee protection. According to this author, "if negative decisions in asylum procedures are not implemented, it is said, the credibility of the whole asylum system is called into question." In other words, democracies breach obligations under international law merely to achieve credibility for their asylum systems, to implement migratory control and certain diversity for its own populations. However, if such cases occur, in many cases the individual also has the possibility to approach an international Commission or Court, such as the one

---

[26] E.g. *UNHCR 2000*, p.156.

[27] E.g. *UNHCR 2000*, p.157.

[28] Noll, in his above article, clearly states that "if the **electorate** is in favor of a restrictive approach vis-à-vis aliens at large, it may appear attractive for politicians to implement return policies strictly."

in Strasbourg, claiming that a return home would expose him/her to treatment forbidden under, for example, Article 3 ECHR. So there is always a possibility to double-check such decisions. In sum, this means that there are a number of legal procedures agreed upon under international law obligations, which could be used by asylum seekers to present their case. However, once an international Commission or Court reaches a negative decision, the asylum seeker becomes an alien within the territory of the country where he/she has sought refuge and, as mentioned above, he/she falls automatically under national jurisdiction. It also means that the former refugee loses refugee protection benefits. Such a situation might lead to continued, although illegal residence, which may appear a better option than return. And it has to be realized that because of today's already high number of illegal residents in industrialized countries, if the authorities have a responsibility at all, it is a responsibility towards their own community to ensure that no (read, not too many illegal) persons continue to reside there. To fulfil this obligation towards their own nationals, states also make use of non-voluntary return and expulsion. In various cases, the practice of (preventive) detention has been used for this purpose. As Noll rightly states, "detention must not only be based on law and decided in a proper procedure, but is limited to serve a narrowly circumscribed purpose." Such a 'narrowly cirumscribed purpose' is to be found in Article 5(1)(f) of the 1950 ECHR, stating "the lawful arrest or detention of a person to prevent his effecting an unauthorized entry into the country or of a person against whom action is being taken with a view to deportation or extradition." And what needs to be added is that this kind of detention and deportation itself has to be implemented with respect for the human rights, safety and dignity of the person.

While addressing basic human rights, both authors, Noll and Van Krieken have devoted attention to Article 4 of the 4th Protocol of the ECHR, which forbids mass expulsion. Both authors basically agree that not all expulsions involving greater numbers of returning rejected asylum seekers constitute mass expulsions, as long as all cases have been individually screened, including concerning the due process of law. Therefore, no further comment is required.

However, the main goal of these authorities is to promote voluntary return. With regard to Noll, "to promote voluntary return, states have used incentives (for example, benefits in the country of origin) as well as sanctions (withdrawal of benefits in the country where asylum was sought)." According to this author, these kinds of 'sanctions' place a question mark against the voluntary and non-voluntary return of rejectees. However, it has to be pointed out that former asylum seekers cannot enjoy refugee protection, once after a fair procedure they are found not to qualify for refugee status. On the other hand, the rejectee cannot also enjoy benefits which are available to nationals of a particular country, since he/she entered another state territory at his/her own free will, exposing him/herself to another community, which has further no obligations towards him/her. Therefore, the only possibility for such a person, based on international law followed by domestic law, is to return. However, a rejectee who is confronted with insurmountable problems created by the authorities of the country of origin might be considered to be allowed access to some support (i.e. access to the social welfare system) while awaiting the outcome of the various procedures.

With regard to incentives supporting voluntary return, Gregor Noll is strongly in favour of financial assistance not only to the individual, but also to the community he/she is coming from to avoid a 'pull' factor. An example is the Swiss Government initiative, when "individual return assistance transmutes into a rudimentary form of community development, intended to improve living conditions that might otherwise lead to renewed migration pressures and/or attempts." Such an initiative may, however, have the opposite result. Worse, by embarking on such an approach, precious time may be lost, as negotiations will linger on, expectations will be raised, and the suggestion created that without such a programme no return should be undertaken or promoted. Representatives of other communities from the country of origin might try to enter the country providing such assistance in order to obtain these kinds of benefits for their community in the country of origin as well. Therefore, any assistance should be seen as something additional, never a starting point. This indeed means that if discussions do not yield the desired results, return should be implemented as if nothing had happened in the first place. Otherwise, the returning country would become the victim of its own 'reaching out'.

While discussing problems of return, there is a need to mention a responsibility on the part of the actors involved. Until now, only the practices of returning states have been discussed; however, these practices were invoked in order to face the denial of responsibilities by the countries of origin and the individuals themselves.

b) **Responsibility**

Bearing in mind the section on Instruments of International Law, as well as General Comments of the Committee on Human Rights, it is clear that the following statement by Gregor Noll on duty to admit is nothing more than a mere misinterpretation of an international obligation. He claims that "The right of a state to remove non-citizens from its territory has been extrapolated to produce a duty to receive by the country of origin. If the same line of argument, which views a duty as correlative to a right, were applied in the field of human rights, the right to leave would produce a duty to admit. In order for the former to be effective, one has to construct the latter."

However, according to Van Krieken, "by submitting an application for asylum, the individual recognizes the existence of human rights, and subscribes to that system as a whole. In this respect, it has to be emphasized that there are no rights without duties, as indicated in the UDHR [Article 29]." Therefore, once rejected, a former asylum seeker has a duty to return to his own country, and this country has a duty to readmit its own national.[29] Both authors discussed in this survey equally share such a point of view.

c) **International Cooperation**

However, the majority of asylum seekers are not in possession of travel documents or ID cards, because of losing or destroying them. Considering this situation, the return of rejectees and the screening of asylum seekers become difficult. In accordance with this situation, the Commission of the European Communities' Proposal for a Council Directive, Provisional Version of 21 September 2000, on Article 28.1(a), dealing with an applicant's submission of insufficient information to determine fully his/her identity or nationality, stated: "... In these cases the application can be dismissed as manifestly unfounded if, in addition, there are serious reasons for considering that he has in bad faith destroyed or disposed of an identity or travel document that would otherwise help determine his identity or nationality."

Another aspect of the problem is the unwillingness of a country of origin to readmit its nationals by prolonging the procedures for issuing travel documents. Such unwillingness can be based on the undesirability to accept certain groups as elements of its population and economy. "Expatriates may provide considerable net transfers to the country of origin" (Noll, 1999). The issue of readmission is repeated on a number of occasions, and Van Krieken provided some examples in his article on Return and Responsibility.

– The General Assembly has underlined state responsibility as it relates to countries of origin, including facilitating the return of their nationals who are not refugees.[30]

– The Cairo Declaration, following the 1994 Cairo Conference on Population and Development. This document, the result of a major UN conference attended by the representatives of virtually all countries, refers in chapter X (10.20) to the responsibilities concerned: '... Governments of countries of origin of undocumented migrants and persons whose asylum claims have been rejected have the responsibility to accept the return and reintegration of those persons, and should not penalize such persons on their return ...'

– Second, UNHCR's ExCom Conclusions have been referring to this issue since the mid-1990s. At the 48th session of the Executive Committee the following text was supported:

---

[29] The above mentioned General Comment no. 27 (1999) focuses also on the right to (re-)enter one's own country in para's 19-21.

[30] GA Res 45/150 of 14 December 1990, para 9; GA Res 46/106 of 16 december 1991, para 10; GA Res 47/105 of 16 december 1992, para. 10. Reference could also be made to the 1990 Convention on on the Protection of All Migrant Workers and Members of Their Families (thus far 16 ratifications only) which promotes measures regarding the orderly return of migrants to their country of origin.

> '... Executive Committee (...) reaffirms the right of all persons to return to their countries, and the responsibility of States to facilitate the return and reintegration of their nationals ...'[31]

Both instruments would indeed appear to underline the responsibilities and duties at stake. However, economic development assistance represented by readmission agreements between the country of return and the country of origin proved to be the most successful tool in order to achieve the acceptance of readmission responsibility. Noll remarks that such agreements might be an adequate solution and "an effective tool to overcome bilateral difficulties, to reaffirm the obligation to readmit, to regulate the timing and number of returns, and to specify procedural rules." However, it is paramount to realize, as Van Krieken points out, that "in spite of the usefulness of such instruments, it is important to emphasize that readmission agreements are no *conditio sine qua non*." What this actually means is that readmission agreements extend beyond international law obligations. If such a readmission agreement has been signed merely because the country of origin was not willing to cooperate concerning the readmission of its own citizens, directly or indirectly, this kind of agreement can be seen as blackmail.[32]

In this kind of difficult international environment, concerning problems of return, states begin to look towards international organizations for support and influence. As has already been mentioned in the section on Development in Humanitarian and Human Rights Issues, the UNHCR was created to supervise voluntary repatriation. According to Article 1 of the IOM Constitution, one of its purposes and functions is "to provide services ... for voluntary return migration, including voluntary return." Since both organizations were created during the time of the Cold War, the full right to deal with non-voluntary return has been given to states. However, at the end of 1990s the situation has changed. In May 1997 both organizations signed the already mentioned Memorandum of Understanding concerning rejected asylum seekers. Concerning this group, IOM and UNHCR take the view that "the return and readmission of such persons should only be considered when the asylum seeker has exhausted all possibilities to be allowed to stay." Members of the UNHCR's Executive Committee, addressing international cooperation, went even further by stating in their 1998 conclusion that:

---

[31] ExCom, General Conclusion no. 81 (1997); worth mentioning is also the ExCom Standing Committee document EC/46/SC/CRP.36 of 28 May, 19996, which exclusively focuses on 'return of persons not in need of international protection'. Although this document falls short of clearly addressing the responsibility of countries of origin, it underlines the general principles and indicates that UNHCR "is willing to support States in their efforts to return categories categories of rejected asylum-seekers".

[32] See for an interesting view on this issue: Abell N. Albuquerque, The Compatibility of Readmission Agreements with the 1951 Convention relating to the Status of Refugees, *IJRL* Vol. 11, 1999, pp. 60-83.

> "... The Executive Committee (...) recommends to States that strategies for facilitating the return, in safety and dignity, of persons not in need of international protection be examined within a framework of international cooperation; and encourages UNHCR to continue, in cooperation with other appropriate international organizations, to look into ways in which the return process of individuals, determined through fair and effective procedures not to be in need of international protection, can be facilitated ..."[33]

International cooperation will also have a positive outcome at the regional level. In Europe, under the Treaty of Amsterdam, the Community objectives in the area of immigration policy also include the repatriation of persons illegally resident in a Member State (Article 63 (3) of the (consolidated) Treaty establishing the European Community). During 1999 – 2004, asylum and migration policies, security and social cohesion will be completely transferred from the Third to the First Pillar, which will unite and ease practices across the region securing the application of human rights and obligations under the 1951 Refugee Convention.

Moreover, the recent (December 2000) 'Palermo Convention' on international crime with its various Protocols on inter alia the prevention, suppression and punishment of trafficking persons (which includes an article on 'repatriation of victims of trafficking in persons'). Another protocol addresses the smuggling of migrants by land sea and air which also clearly underlines the principles elaborated in this contribution.[34]

---

[33] The 1997 ExCom also dealt with this issue, albeit from a slightly different angle, and the conclusion has been criticized by e.g. Michael Barutciski (Involuntray repatriation when Refugee Protection is no Longer Necessary: Moving Forward after the 48th Session of the Executive Committee, *IJRL* Vol 10/1998 pp. 236-255.

[34] The relevant Articles of these Protocols are as follows:

(A) Protocol to Prevent, Suppress and Punish Trafficking Persons, Especially Women and Children:

Article 7: Status of victims of trafficking in persons in receiving States

1. In addition to taking measures pursuant to article 6 of this Protocol, each State Party shall consider adopting legislative or other appropriate measures that permit victims of trafficking in persons to remain in its territory, temporarily or permanently, in appropriate cases.

2. In implementing the provision contained in par. 1 of this article, each State Party shall give appropriate consideration to humanitarian and compassionate factors.

Article 8: Repatriation of victims of trafficking in persons

1. The State Party of which a victim of trafficking in persons is a national or in which the person had the right of permanent residence at the time of entry into the territory of the receiving State Party shall facilitate and accept, with due regard for the safety of that person, the return of that person without undue or unreasonable delay.

2. When a State Party returns a victim of trafficking in persons to a State Party of which that person is a national or in which he or she had, at the time of entry into the territory of the receiving State Party, the right of permanent residence, such return shall be with due regard for the safety of that person and for the status of any legal proceedings related to the fact that the person is a victim of trafficking and shall preferably be voluntary.

3. At the request of a receiving State Party, a requested State Party shall, without undue or unreasonable delay, verify whether a person who is a victim of trafficking in persons is its national or had the right or permanent residence in its territory at the time of entry into the territory of the receiving State Party. →

In the end, levels of cooperation could be characterized according to the following concept by Van Krieken:

– Return should be implemented in safety and dignity;
– Returnees should cooperate and their personal responsibility should be stressed;
– Countries of origin should appreciate their own responsibility in this respect;
– Countries of origin should appreciate any gesture, not as a *conditio sine qua non*, but as something extra, something additional;
– At the PR level all concerned should be made aware of the above principles;

IOM [and UNHCR] involvement should be sought; and such involvement should not necessarily be limited to voluntary return.

---

4. In order to facilitate the return of a victim of trafficking in persons who is without proper documentation, the State Party of which that person is a national or in which he or she had the right of permanent residence at the time of entry into the territory of the receiving State Party shall agree to issue, at the request of the receiving State Party, such travel documents or other authorization as may be necessary to enable the person to travel to and re-enter its territory.
5. This article shall be without prejudice to any right afforded to victims of trafficking in persons by any domestic law of the receiving State Party.
6. This article shall be without prejudice to any applicable bilateral or multilateral agreement or arrangement that governs, in whole or in part, the return of victims of trafficking in persons.
(B) Protocol against the Smuggling of Migrants by Land, Sea and Air
Article 18: Return of smuggled migrants
1. Each State Party agrees to facilitate and accept, without undue or unreasonable delay, the return of a person who has been the object of conduct set forth in article 6 of this Protocol and who is its national or who has the right of permanent residence in its territory at the time of return.
2. Each State Party shall consider the possibility of facilitating and accepting the return of a person who has been the object of conduct set forth in article 6 of this Protocol and who had the right of permanent residence in its territory at the time of entry into the receiving State in accordance with its domestic law.
3. At the request of the receiving State Party, a requested State Party shall, without undue or unreasonable delay, verify whether a person who has been the object of conduct set forth in article 6 of this Protocol is its national or has the right of permanent residence in its territory.
4. In order to facilitate the return of a person who has been the object of conduct set forth in article 6 of this Protocol and is without proper documentation, the State Party of which that person is a national or in which he or she has the right of permanent residence shall agree to issue, at the request of the receiving State Party, such travel documents or other authorization as may be necessary to enable the person to travel to and re-enter its territory.
5. Each State Party involved with the return of a person who has been the object of conduct set forth in article 6 of this Protocol shall take all appropriate measures to carry out the return in an orderly manner and with due regard for the safety and dignity of the person.
6. States Parties may cooperate with relevant international organizations in the implementation of this article.
7. This article shall be without prejudice to any right afforded to persons who have been the object of conduct set forth in article 6 of this Protocol by any domestic law of the receiving State Party.
8. This article shall not affect the obligations entered into under any other applicable treaty, bilateral or multilateral, or any other applicable operational agreement or arrangement that governs, in whole or in part, the return of persons who have been the object of conduct set forth in article 6 of this Protocol.

CONCLUSION

It has to be concluded that considering the above statements within the context of this paper, voluntary return has to be induced since individuals only possess a right to leave their own country, not a right to enter a country which is not their own. Where it concerns 'push and pull' factors, a successful instrument will probably limit alternatives and enable rejectees to draw the acceptable conclusion that return, in safety and dignity, is the only viable 'way out'. To achieve such an outcome, active cooperation between international and regional actors is already required for screening an asylum seeker concerning the situation in the country of origin and the possibility of his/her return, once rejected. Readmission agreements might serve as a successful solution to the present difficulties involved with return. However, they should be seen as a gesture, not as a duty. Automatic assistance and non-expulsion policies only create further 'pull' factors and increase the problem of return. Global economic development policy might be the best solution to relieve the pressure on migratory movements towards the North. However, as indicated elsewhere in this Handbook, differences between North and South will always exist and the twain shall never meet.[35] This should indeed result in continued and increased awareness concerning 'push and pull' factors as well as 'carrot and stick' policies.

[35] See e.g. Richard Kapuscinski on Africa and related issues in his recent book 'Ebony' (1999).

LEGAL TEXTS: MIGRATION AND RETURN[1]

American Declaration of the Rights and Duties of Man, Bogotá, Colombia, 1948

Article VIII – Right to residence and movement
Every person has the right to fix his residence within the territory of the state of which he is a national, to move about freely within such territory, and not to leave it except by his own will.

Universal Declaration of Human Rights, 10 December 1948

Article 13
(1) Everyone has the right to freedom of movement and residence within the borders of each state.
(2) Everyone has the right to leave any country, including his own, and to return to his country.

Protocol No. 4 to the ECHR, 16 November 1963, in force

Article 2 – Freedom of movement
(1) Everyone lawfully within the territory of a State shall, within that territory, have the right to liberty of movement and freedom to choose his residence.
(2) Everyone shall be free to leave any country, including his own (...)

Article 3 – Prohibition of expulsion of nationals
(2) No one shall be deprived of the right to enter the territory of the state of which he is a national.

International Convention on the Elimination of All Forms of Discrimination, 21 December 1965, *entry into force* 4 January 1969

Article 5
In compliance with the fundamental obligations laid down in article 2 of this Convention, States Parties undertake to prohibit and to eliminate racial discrimination in all its forms and to guarantee the right of everyone, without distinction as to race, colour, or national or ethnic origin, to equality before the law, notably in the enjoyment of the following rights:

---

[1] Please note that it concerns Declarations, Resolutions, Constitutions, Covenants and Conventions, all with a different legal impact (soft, hard, binding, not-binding). Moreover, not all of them have entered into force. It should also be emphasized that this survey focuses on migration only, and excludes asylum and asylum-related legal texts.

(d) Other civil rights, in particular:
(i) The right to freedom of movement and residence within the border of the State;
(ii) The right to leave any country, including one's own, and to return to one's country;

International Covenant on Civil and Political Rights, 16 December 1966, *entry into force* 23 March 1976

Article 12
1. Everyone lawfully within the territory of a State shall, within that territory, have the right to liberty of movement and freedom to choose his residence.
2. Everyone shall be free to leave any country, including his own.
3. The above-mentioned rights shall not be subject to any restrictions except those which are provided by law, are necessary to protect national security, public order (ordre public), public health or morals or the rights and freedoms of others, and are consistent with the other rights recognized in the present Covenant.
4. No one shall be arbitrarily deprived of the right to enter his own country.

American Convention on Human Rights, Costa Rica, 22 November 1969, *entry into force* 18 July 1978

Article 22. Freedom of Movement and Residence
1. Every person lawfully in the territory of a State Party has the right to move about in it, and to reside in it subject to the provisions of the law.
2. Every person has the right lo leave any country freely, including his own.
3. The exercise of the foregoing rights may be restricted only pursuant to a law to the extent necessary in a democratic society to prevent crime or to protect national security, public safety, public order, public morals, public health, or the rights or freedoms of others.
4. The exercise of the rights recognized in paragraph 1 may also be restricted by law in designated zones for reasons of public interest.
5. No one can be expelled from the territory of the state of which he is a national or be deprived of the right to enter it.
6. An alien lawfully in the territory of a State Party to this Convention may be expelled from it only pursuant to a decision reached in accordance with law.
7. Every person has the right to seek and be granted asylum in a foreign territory, in accordance with the legislation of the state and international conventions, in the event he is being pursued for political offenses or related common crimes.
8. In no case may an alien be deported or returned to a country, regardless of whether or not it is his country of origin, if in that country his right to life or personal freedom is in danger of being violated because of his race, nationality, religion, social status, or political opinions.
9. The collective expulsion of aliens is prohibited.

African [Banjul] Charter on Human and Peoples' Rights, adopted June 27, 1981, *entry into force* 21 October 1986

Article 12

1. Every individual shall have the right to freedom of movement and residence within the borders of a State provided he abides by the law.
2. Every individual shall have the right to leave any country including his own, and to return to his country. This right may only be subject to restrictions, provided for by law for the protection of national security, law and order, public health or morality.
3. Every individual shall have the right, when persecuted, to seek and obtain asylum in other countries in accordance with laws of those countries and international conventions.
4. A non-national legally admitted in a territory of a State Party to the present Charter, may only be expelled from it by virtue of a decision taken in accordance with the law.
5. The mass expulsion of non-nationals shall be prohibited. Mass expulsion shall be that which is aimed at national, racial, ethnic or religious groups.

Declaration on the Human Rights of Individuals Who are not Nationals of the Country in Which They Live (GA Resolution A/RES/40/144), 13 December 1985

Article 1

For the purposes of this Declaration, the term "alien" shall apply, with due regard to qualifications made in subsequent articles, to any individual who is not a national of the State in which he or she is present.

Article 4

Aliens shall observe the laws of the State in which they reside or are present and regard with respect the customs and traditions of the people of that State.

Article 5

2. Subject to such restrictions as are prescribed by law and which are necessary in a democratic society to protect national security, public safety, public order, public health or morals or the rights and freedoms of others, and which are consistent with the other rights recognized in the relevant international instruments and those set forth in this Declaration, aliens shall enjoy the following rights:

(a) The right to leave the country; (...)

3. Subject to the provisions referred to in paragraph 2, aliens lawfully in the territory of a State shall enjoy the right to liberty of movement and freedom to choose their residence within the borders of the State.
4. Subject to national legislation and due authorization, the spouse and minor or dependent children of an alien lawfully residing in the territory of a State shall be admitted to accompany, join and stay with the alien.

International Convention on the Protection of the Rights of All Migrant Workers and Members of Their Families (GA Resolution A/RES/45/158), 18 December 1990 (not yet in force; 16 ratifications as per 1 January 2001)

Article 8

1. Migrant workers and members of their families shall be free to leave any State,

including their State of origin. This right shall not be subject to any restrictions except those that are provided by law, are necessary to protect national security, public order (ordre public), public health or morals or the rights and freedoms of others and are consistent with the other rights recognized in the present part of the Convention.
2. Migrant workers and members of their families shall have the right at any time to enter and remain in their State of origin.

Article 39
1.Migrant workers and members of their families shall have the right to liberty of movement in the territory of the State of employment and freedom to choose their residence there.

Charter of the Fundamental Rights of the European Union, December 2000 (soft law)

Article 45 – Freedom of movement and of residence
1. Every citizen of the Union has the right to move and reside freely within the territory of the Member States.
2. Freedom of movement and residence may be granted, in accordance with the Treaty establishing the European Community, to nationals of third countries legally resident in the territory of a Member State.

Return Related Texts

On the issue of return, the following texts may be considered of relevance:

– Protocol No. 4 to the ECHR, 16 November 1963 (in force)
Article 4 – Prohibition of collective expulsion of aliens
Collective expulsion of aliens is prohibited

– The International Convention on the Protection of the Rights of All Migrant Workers and Members of Their
Families (not in force)
Article 67
1. States Parties concerned shall co-operate as appropriate in the adoption of measures regarding the orderly return of migrant workers and members of their families to the State of origin when they decide to return or their authorization of residence or employment expires or when they are in the State of employment in an irregular situation.
2. Concerning migrant workers and members of their families in a regular situation, States Parties concerned shall co-operate as appropriate, on terms agreed upon by those States, with a view to promoting adequate economic conditions for their resettlement and to facilitating their durable social and cultural reintegration in the State of origin.
Article 68
1. States Parties, including States of transit, shall collaborate with a view to preventing and eliminating illegal or clandestine movements and employment of migrant workers in

an irregular situation. The measures to be taken to this end within the jurisdiction of each State concerned shall include:
(a) Appropriate measures against the dissemination of misleading information relating to emigration and immigration;
(b) Measures to detect and eradicate illegal or clandestine movements of migrant workers and members of their families and to impose effective sanctions on persons, groups or entities which organize, operate or assist in organizing or operating such movements;
(c) Measures to impose effective sanctions on persons, groups or entities which use violence, threats or intimidation against migrant workers or members of their families in an irregular situation.
2. States of employment shall take all adequate and effective measures to eliminate employment in their territory of migrant workers in an irregular situation, including, whenever appropriate, sanctions on employers of such workers. The rights of migrant workers vis-a-vis their employer arising from employment shall not be impaired by these measures.

– The General Assembly has underlined state responsibility as it relates to countries of origin, including facilitating the return of their nationals who are not refugees.[2]

– The Cairo Declaration, a result of the 1994 Cairo (UN) Conference on Population and Development, refers in chapter X (10.20) to the responsibilities concerned:
'... Governments of countries of origin of undocumented migrants and persons whose asylum claims have been rejected have the responsibility to accept the return and reintegration of those persons, and should not penalize such persons on their return ...'

– UNHCR's ExCom Conclusions have been referring to this issue since the mid-1990s. At the 48th session of the Executive Committee the following text was supported:
'... Executive Committee (...) reaffirms the right of all persons to return to their countries, and the responsibility of States to facilitate the return and reintegration of their nationals ...'[3]

– UNHCR's Executive Committee, addressing international cooperation, went even further by stating in their 1998 Conclusion that:
"...The Executive Committee (...) recommends to States that strategies for facilitating the return, in safety and dignity, of persons not in need of international protection be examined within a framework of international cooperation; and encourages UNHCR to continue, in cooperation with other appropriate international organizations, to look into

---

[2] GA Res 45/150 of 14 December 1990, para 9; GA Res 46/106 of 16 December 1991, para 10; GA Res 47/105 of 16 December 1992, para. 10. Reference could also be made to the 1990 Convention on on the Protection of All Migrant Workers and Members of Their Families (thus far 16 ratifications only) which promotes measures regarding the orderly return of migrants to their country of origin.

[3] ExCom, General Conclusion no. 81 (1997); worth mentioning is also the ExCom Standing Committee document EC/46/SC/CRP.36 of 28 May, 19996, which exclusively focuses on 'return of persons not in need of international protection'. Although this document falls short of clearly addressing the responsibility of countries of origin, it underlines the general principles and indicates that UNHCR "is willing to support States in their efforts to return categories categories of rejected asylum-seekers".

ways in which the return process of individuals, determined through fair and effective procedures not to be in need of international protection, can be facilitated..."

- Article 63 (3) of the (consolidated) Treaty establishing the European Community: 'The Council [shall adopt]measures on immigration policy [also within the area of] illegal immigration and illegal residence, including repatriation of illegal residents'

- Charter of Fundamental Rights of the European Union, December 2000[4]
Article 34 – Social security and social assistance
(...) 2. Everyone residing and moving legally within the European Union is entitled to social security benefits and social advantages in accordance with Community law and national laws and practices (...)
Article 45 – Freedom of movement and of residence
1. Every citizen of the Union has the right to move and reside freely within the territory of the Member States.
2. Freedom of movement and residence may be granted, in accordance with the Treaty establishing the European Community, to nationals of third countries legally resident in the territory of a Member State.

– Moreover, the recent (December 2000) 'Palermo Convention' on international crime is of relevance, as well as its various Protocols on inter alia the prevention, suppression and punishment of trafficking persons (which includes an article on 'repatriation of victims of trafficking in persons'). The Protocol which addresses the smuggling of migrants by land sea and air also underlines the principles re return.
The relevant Articles of these Protocols are as follows:
(A) Protocol to Prevent, Suppress and Punish Trafficking Persons, Especially Women and Children:
Article 7: Status of victims of trafficking in persons in receiving States
1. In addition to taking measures pursuant to article 6 of this Protocol, each State Party shall consider adopting legislative or other appropriate measures that permit victims of trafficking in persons to remain in its territory, temporarily or permanently, in appropriate cases.
2. In implementing the provision contained in par. 1 of this article, each State Party shall give appropriate consideration to humanitarian and compassionate factors.
Article 8: Repatriation of victims of trafficking in persons
1. The State Party of which a victim of trafficking in persons is a national or in which the person had the right of permanent residence at the time of entry into the territory of the receiving State Party shall facilitate and accept, with due regard for the safety of that person, the return of that person without undue or unreasonable delay.
2. When a State Party returns a victim of trafficking in persons to a State Party of which that person is a national or in which he or she had, at the time of entry into the territory of the receiving State Party, the right of permanent residence, such return shall be with due regard for the safety of that person and for the status of any legal proceedings related to the fact that the person is a victim of trafficking and shall preferably be voluntary.

[4] As yet: soft law

3. At the request of a receiving State Party, a requested State Party shall, without undue or unreasonable delay, verify whether a person who is a victim of trafficking in persons is its national or had the right or permanent residence in its territory at the time of entry into the territory of the receiving State Party.
4. In order to facilitate the return of a victim of trafficking in persons who is without proper documentation, the State Party of which that person is a national or in which he or she had the right of permanent residence at the time of entry into the territory of the receiving State Party shall agree to issue, at the request of the receiving State Party, such travel documents or other authorization as may be necessary to enable the person to travel to and re-enter its territory.
5. This article shall be without prejudice to any right afforded to victims of trafficking in persons by any domestic law of the receiving State Party.
6. This article shall be without prejudice to any applicable bilateral or multilateral agreement or arrangement that governs, in whole or in part, the return of victims of trafficking in persons.
(B) Protocol against the Smuggling of Migrants by Land, Sea and Air
Article 18: Return of smuggled migrants
1. Each State Party agrees to facilitate and accept, without undue or unreasonable delay, the return of a person who has been the object of conduct set forth in article 6 of this Protocol and who is its national or who has the right of permanent residence in its territory at the time of return.
2. Each State Party shall consider the possibility of facilitating and accepting the return of a person who has been the object of conduct set forth in article 6 of this Protocol and who had the right of permanent residence in its territory at the time of entry into the receiving State in accordance with its domestic law.
3. At the request of the receiving State Party, a requested State Party shall, without undue or unreasonable delay, verify whether a person who has been the object of conduct set forth in article 6 of this Protocol is its national or has the right of permanent residence in its territory.
4. In order to facilitate the return of a person who has been the object of conduct set forth in article 6 of this Protocol and is without proper documentation, the State Party of which that person is a national or in which he or she has the right of permanent residence shall agree to issue, at the request of the receiving State Party, such travel documents or other authorization as may be necessary to enable the person to travel to and re-enter its territory.
5. Each State Party involved with the return of a person who has been the object of conduct set forth in article 6 of this Protocol shall take all appropriate measures to carry out the return in an orderly manner and with due regard for the safety and dignity of the person.
6. States Parties may cooperate with relevant international organizations in the implementation of this article.
7. This article shall be without prejudice to any right afforded to persons who have been the object of conduct set forth in article 6 of this Protocol by any domestic law of the receiving State Party.
8. This article shall not affect the obligations entered into under any other applicable treaty, bilateral or multilateral, or any other applicable operational agreement or arrangement that governs, in whole or in part, the return of persons who have been the object of conduct set forth in article 6 of this Protocol.

4.3

GENERAL COMMENTS ON MIGRATION

It is not always sufficiently realized that the main impact of Human Rights Conventions lies neither in the agreement or the text, nor in the signature or ratification. The value of the human rights instruments has to be sought in the implementation on the one hand, and the supervision of such implementation and the monitoring as such on the other. It was quite revolutionary when in 1951 sovereign States agreed to cooperate with the UNHCR in the latter's duty of supervising the application of the provisions of the 1951 Refugee Convention.[1] *It was similarly important that the 1966 ICCPR contained the agreement to set up an independent body, the Human Rights Committee, in order to deal with reports, communications and the like. Of particular relevance is the possibility to 'transmit general comments'. States Parties may then submit to the Committee observations on those comments.*[2]

General Comments have since become an important tool for the purpose of interpretating of the human rights instruments concerned, as well as for the 'progressive development of international law', as 'law' is believed to be non-static.

In the context of the Chapter on the right to migration and the status of aliens in countries not their own, the two General Comments concerned deserve to be included in full.

The first one (No. 15 from 1986) focuses on the position of aliens under the ICCPR. Paragraphs 5 and 6 thereof appear to be the most relevant in the context of this handbook: the ICCPR does not recognize the right of aliens to enter or reside in the territory of a State party, but for some specific exceptions. It is in principle a matter for each State to decide who it will admit to its territory. Consent for entry may be given subject to conditions relating to e.g. movement, residence and employment. However, once aliens are allowed to enter the territory they are entitled to the right set out in the ICCPR.

The second GC (No. 27, 1999) focuses on the freedom of movement, that is above all in the country of which one is a citizen, but also in a foreign country, in case one is lawfully within the territory of that country. The question whether an alien is 'lawfully' within the territory of a State is a matter governed by domestic law, as is underlined in parapraph 4 of this GC.

The GCs concerned appear to confirm the fairly restrictive reality on the (legal) ground, and should hence also be seen in the context of the ethics debate on migration in general, above in Chapter 3, as well as in the context of the return issue.

For the sake of clarity, ICCPR's Art. 12 is once again cited:

> 1) Everyone lawfully within the territory of a State shall, within that territory, have the right to liberty of movement and freedom to choose his residence.
> 2) Everyone shall be free to leave any country, including his own.

---

[1] Convention relating to the Status of Refugees, 1951, Art. 35.1.

[2] ICCPR, 1966, Art. 40.

3) The above-mentioned rights shall not be subject to any restrictions except those which are provided by law, are necessary to protect national security, public order (ordre public), public health or morals or the rights and freedoms of others, and are consistent with the other rights recognized in the present Covenant.

4) No one shall be arbitrarily deprived of the right to enter his own country.

GENERAL COMMENT 15: THE POSITION OF ALIENS UNDER THE COVENANT, 1986[3]

1. Reports from States parties have often failed to take into account that each State party must ensure the rights in the Covenant to "all individuals within its territory and subject to its jurisdiction" (art. 2, para. 1). In general, the rights set forth in the Covenant apply to everyone, irrespective of reciprocity, and irrespective of his or her nationality or statelessness.

2. Thus, the general rule is that each one of the rights of the Covenant must be guaranteed without discrimination between citizens and aliens. Aliens receive the benefit of the general requirement of non-discrimination in respect of the rights guaranteed in the Covenant, as provided for in article 2 thereof. This guarantee applies to aliens and citizens alike. Exceptionally, some of the rights recognized in the Covenant are expressly applicable only to citizens (art. 25), while article 13 applies only to aliens. However, the Committee's experience in examining reports shows that in a number of countries other rights that aliens should enjoy under the Covenant are denied to them or are subject to limitations that cannot always be justified under the Covenant.

3. A few constitutions provide for equality of aliens with citizens. Some constitutions adopted more recently carefully distinguish fundamental rights that apply to all and those granted to citizens only, and deal with each in detail. In many States, however, the constitutions are drafted in terms of citizens only when granting relevant rights. Legislation and case law may also play an important part in providing for the rights of aliens. The Committee has been informed that in some States fundamental rights, though not guaranteed to aliens by the Constitution or other legislation, will also be extended to them as required by the Covenant. In certain cases, however, there has clearly been a failure to implement Covenant rights without discrimination in respect of aliens.

4. The Committee considers that in their reports States parties should give attention to the position of aliens, both under their law and in actual practice. The Covenant gives aliens all the protection regarding rights guaranteed therein, and its requirements should be observed by States parties in their legislation and in practice as appropriate. The position of aliens would thus be considerably improved. States parties should ensure that the provisions of the Covenant and the rights under it are made known to aliens within their jurisdiction.

5. The Covenant does not recognize the right of aliens to enter or reside in the territory of a State party. It is in principle a matter for the State to decide who it will admit to its

---

[3] The position of aliens under the Covenant, (Twenty-seventh session, 1986) 11 April 1986.

territory. However, in certain circumstances an alien may enjoy the protection of the Covenant even in relation to entry or residence, for example, when considerations of non-discrimination, prohibition of inhuman treatment and respect for family life arise.

6. Consent for entry may be given subject to conditions relating, for example, to movement, residence and employment. A State may also impose general conditions upon an alien who is in transit. However, once aliens are allowed to enter the territory of a State party they are entitled to the rights set out in the Covenant.

7. Aliens thus have an inherent right to life, protected by law, and may not be arbitrarily deprived of life. They must not be subjected to torture or to cruel, inhuman or degrading treatment or punishment; nor may they be held in slavery or servitude. Aliens have the full right to liberty and security of the person. If lawfully deprived of their liberty, they shall be treated with humanity and with respect for the inherent dignity of their person. Aliens may not be imprisoned for failure to fulfil a contractual obligation. They have the right to liberty of movement and free choice of residence; they shall be free to leave the country. Aliens shall be equal before the courts and tribunals, and shall be entitled to a fair and public hearing by a competent, independent and impartial tribunal established by law in the determination of any criminal charge or of rights and obligations in a suit at law. Aliens shall not be subjected to retrospective penal legislation, and are entitled to recognition before the law. They may not be subjected to arbitrary or unlawful interference with their privacy, family, home or correspondence. They have the right to freedom of thought, conscience and religion, and the right to hold opinions and to express them. Aliens receive the benefit of the right of peaceful assembly and of freedom of association. They may marry when at marriageable age. Their children are entitled to those measures of protection required by their status as minors. In those cases where aliens constitute a minority within the meaning of article 27, they shall not be denied the right, in community with other members of their group, to enjoy their own culture, to profess and practise their own religion and to use their own language. Aliens are entitled to equal protection by the law. There shall be no discrimination between aliens and citizens in the application of these rights. These rights of aliens may be qualified only by such limitations as may be lawfully imposed under the Covenant.

8. Once an alien is lawfully within a territory, his freedom of movement within the territory and his right to leave that territory may only be restricted in accordance with article 12, paragraph 3. Differences in treatment in this regard between aliens and nationals, or between different categories of aliens, need to be justified under article 12, paragraph 3. Since such restrictions must, *inter alia*, be consistent with the other rights recognized in the Covenant, a State party cannot, by restraining an alien or deporting him to a third country, arbitrarily prevent his return to his own country (art. 12, para. 4).

9. Many reports have given insufficient information on matters relevant to article 13. That article is applicable to all procedures aimed at the obligatory departure of an alien, whether described in national law as expulsion or otherwise. If such procedures entail arrest, the safeguards of the Covenant relating to deprivation of liberty (arts. 9 and 10) may also be applicable. If the arrest is for the particular purpose of extradition, other provisions of national and international law may apply. Normally an alien who is expelled must be allowed to leave for any country that agrees to take him. The particular rights of

article 13 only protect those aliens who are lawfully in the territory of a State party. This means that national law concerning the requirements for entry and stay must be taken into account in determining the scope of that protection, and that illegal entrants and aliens who have stayed longer than the law or their permits allow, in particular, are not covered by its provisions. However, if the legality of an alien's entry or stay is in dispute, any decision on this point leading to his expulsion or deportation ought to be taken in accordance with article 13. It is for the competent authorities of the State party, in good faith and in the exercise of their powers, to apply and interpret the domestic law, observing, however, such requirements under the Covenant as equality before the law (art. 26).

10. Article 13 directly regulates only the procedure and not the substantive grounds for expulsion. However, by allowing only those carried out "in pursuance of a decision reached in accordance with law", its purpose is clearly to prevent arbitrary expulsions. On the other hand, it entitles each alien to a decision in his own case and, hence, article 13 would not be satisfied with laws or decisions providing for collective or mass expulsions. This understanding, in the opinion of the Committee, is confirmed by further provisions concerning the right to submit reasons against expulsion and to have the decision reviewed by and to be represented before the competent authority or someone designated by it. An alien must be given full facilities for pursuing his remedy against expulsion so that this right will in all the circumstances of his case be an effective one. The principles of article 13 relating to appeal against expulsion and the entitlement to review by a competent authority may only be departed from when "compelling reasons of national security" so require. Discrimination may not be made between different categories of aliens in the application of article 13.

GENERAL COMMENT 27, FREEDOM OF MOVEMENT (1999)[4]

1. Liberty of movement is an indispensable condition for the free development of a person. It interacts with several other rights enshrined in the Covenant, as is often shown in the Committee's practice in considering reports from States parties and communications from individuals. Moreover, the Committee in its general comment No. 15 ("The position of aliens under the Covenant", 1986) referred to the special link between articles 12 and 13.[5]

2. The permissible limitations which may be imposed on the rights protected under article 12 must not nullify the principle of liberty of movement, and are governed by the requirement of necessity provided for in article 12, paragraph 3, and by the need for consistency with the other rights recognized in the Covenant.

3. States parties should provide the Committee in their reports with the relevant domestic legal rules and administrative and judicial practices relating to the rights protected by

---

[4] Freedom of movement (Art.12), 02 November 1999, CCPR/C/21/Rev.1/Add.9, CCPR General Comment 27 (67) .

[5] HRI/GEN/1/Rev.3, 15 August 1997, p. 20 (para. 8).

article 12, taking into account the issues discussed in the present general comment. They must also include information on remedies available if these rights are restricted.

Liberty of movement and freedom to choose residence (para. 1)

4. Everyone lawfully within the territory of a State enjoys, within that territory, the right to move freely and to choose his or her place of residence. In principle, citizens of a State are always lawfully within the territory of that State. The question whether an alien is "lawfully" within the territory of a State is a matter governed by domestic law, which may subject the entry of an alien to the territory of a State to restrictions, provided they are in compliance with the State's international obligations. In that connection, the Committee has held that an alien who entered the State illegally, but whose status has been regularized, must be considered to be lawfully within the territory for the purposes of article 12.[6] Once a person is lawfully within a State, any restrictions on his or her rights guaranteed by article 12, paragraphs 1 and 2, as well as any treatment different from that accorded to nationals, have to be justified under the rules provided for by article 12, paragraph 3.[7] It is, therefore, important that States parties indicate in their reports the circumstances in which they treat aliens differently from their nationals in this regard and how they justify this difference in treatment.

5. The right to move freely relates to the whole territory of a State, including all parts of federal States. According to article 12, paragraph 1, persons are entitled to move from one place to another and to establish themselves in a place of their choice. The enjoyment of this right must not be made dependent on any particular purpose or reason for the person wanting to move or to stay in a place. Any restrictions must be in conformity with paragraph 3.

6. The State party must ensure that the rights guaranteed in article 12 are protected not only from public but also from private interference. In the case of women, this obligation to protect is particularly pertinent. For example, it is incompatible with article 12, paragraph 1, that the right of a woman to move freely and to choose her residence be made subject, by law or practice, to the decision of another person, including a relative.

7. Subject to the provisions of article 12, paragraph 3, the right to reside in a place of one's choice within the territory includes protection against all forms of forced internal displacement. It also precludes preventing the entry or stay of persons in a defined part of the territory. Lawful detention, however, affects more specifically the right to personal liberty and is covered by article 9 of the Covenant. In some circumstances, articles 12 and 9 may come into play together.[8]

---

[6] Communication No. 456/1991, *Celepli v. Sweden*, para. 9.2.

[7] General comment No. 15, para. 8, in HRI/GEN/1/Rev.3, 15 August 1997, p. 20.

[8] See, for example, communication No. 138/1983, *Mpandajila v. Zaire*, para. 10; communication No. 157/1983, *Mpaka-Nsusu v. Zaire*, para. 10; communication Nos. 241/1987 and 242/1987, *Birhashwirwa/ Tshisekedi v. Zaire*, para. 13.

Freedom to leave any country, including one's own (para. 2)

8. Freedom to leave the territory of a State may not be made dependent on any specific purpose or on the period of time the individual chooses to stay outside the country. Thus travelling abroad is covered, as well as departure for permanent emigration. Likewise, the right of the individual to determine the State of destination is part of the legal guarantee. As the scope of article 12, paragraph 2, is not restricted to persons lawfully within the territory of a State, an alien being legally expelled from the country is likewise entitled to elect the State of destination, subject to the agreement of that State.[9]

9. In order to enable the individual to enjoy the rights guaranteed by article 12, paragraph 2, obligations are imposed both on the State of residence and on the State of nationality.[10] Since international travel usually requires appropriate documents, in particular a passport, the right to leave a country must include the right to obtain the necessary travel documents. The issuing of passports is normally incumbent on the State of nationality of the individual. The refusal by a State to issue a passport or prolong its validity for a national residing abroad may deprive this person of the right to leave the country of residence and to travel elsewhere.[11] It is no justification for the State to claim that its national would be able to return to its territory without a passport.

10. The practice of States often shows that legal rules and administrative measures adversely affect the right to leave, in particular, a person's own country. It is therefore of the utmost importance that States parties report on all legal and practical restrictions on the right to leave which they apply both to nationals and to foreigners, in order to enable the Committee to assess the conformity of these rules and practices with article 12, paragraph 3. States parties should also include information in their reports on measures that impose sanctions on international carriers which bring to their territory persons without required documents, where those measures affect the right to leave another country.

Restrictions (para. 3)

11. Article 12, paragraph 3, provides for exceptional circumstances in which rights under paragraphs 1 and 2 may be restricted. This provision authorizes the State to restrict these rights only to protect national security, public order (*ordre public*), public health or morals and the rights and freedoms of others. To be permissible, restrictions must be provided by law, must be necessary in a democratic society for the protection of these purposes and must be consistent with all other rights recognized in the Covenant (see para. 18 below).

12. The law itself has to establish the conditions under which the rights may be limited. State reports should therefore specify the legal norms upon which restrictions are founded. Restrictions which are not provided for in the law or are not in conformity with

[9] See general comment No. 15, para. 9, in HRI/GEN/1/Rev.3, 15 August 1997, p. 21.

[10] See communication No. 106/1981, *Montero v. Uruguay*, para. 9.4; communication No. 57/1979, *Vidal Martins v. Uruguay*, para. 7; communication No. 77/1980, *Lichtensztejn v. Uruguay*, para. 6.1.

[11] See communication No. 57/1979, *Vidal Martins v. Uruguay*, para. 9.

the requirements of article 12, paragraph 3, would violate the rights guaranteed by paragraphs 1 and 2.

13. In adopting laws providing for restrictions permitted by article 12, paragraph 3, States should always be guided by the principle that the restrictions must not impair the essence of the right (cf. art. 5, para. 1); the relation between right and restriction, between norm and exception, must not be reversed. The laws authorizing the application of restrictions should use precise criteria and may not confer unfettered discretion on those charged with their execution.

14. Article 12, paragraph 3, clearly indicates that it is not sufficient that the restrictions serve the permissible purposes; they must also be necessary to protect them. Restrictive measures must conform to the principle of proportionality; they must be appropriate to achieve their protective function; they must be the least intrusive instrument amongst those which might achieve the desired result; and they must be proportionate to the interest to be protected.

15. The principle of proportionality has to be respected not only in the law that frames the restrictions, but also by the administrative and judicial authorities in applying the law. States should ensure that any proceedings relating to the exercise or restriction of these rights are expeditious and that reasons for the application of restrictive measures are provided.

16. States have often failed to show that the application of their laws restricting the rights enshrined in article 12, paragraphs 1 and 2, are in conformity with all requirements referred to in article 12, paragraph 3. The application of restrictions in any individual case must be based on clear legal grounds and meet the test of necessity and the requirements of proportionality. These conditions would not be met, for example, if an individual were prevented from leaving a country merely on the ground that he or she is the holder of "State secrets", or if an individual were prevented from travelling internally without a specific permit. On the other hand, the conditions could be met by restrictions on access to military zones on national security grounds, or limitations on the freedom to settle in areas inhabited by indigenous or minorities communities.[12]

17. A major source of concern is the manifold legal and bureaucratic barriers unnecessarily affecting the full enjoyment of the rights of the individuals to move freely, to leave a country, including their own, and to take up residence. Regarding the right to movement within a country, the Committee has criticized provisions requiring individuals to apply for permission to change their residence or to seek the approval of the local authorities of the place of destination, as well as delays in processing such written applications. States' practice presents an even richer array of obstacles making it more difficult to leave the country, in particular for their own nationals. These rules and practices include, *inter alia*, lack of access for applicants to the competent authorities and lack of information regarding requirements; the requirement to apply for special forms

[12] See general comment No. 23, para. 7, in HRI/GEN/1/Rev.3, 15 August 1997, p. 41.

through which the proper application documents for the issuance of a passport can be obtained; the need for supportive statements from employers or family members; exact description of the travel route; issuance of passports only on payment of high fees substantially exceeding the cost of the service rendered by the administration; unreasonable delays in the issuance of travel documents; restrictions on family members travelling together; requirement of a repatriation deposit or a return ticket; requirement of an invitation from the State of destination or from people living there; harassment of applicants, for example by physical intimidation, arrest, loss of employment or expulsion of their children from school or university; refusal to issue a passport because the applicant is said to harm the good name of the country. In the light of these practices, States parties should make sure that all restrictions imposed by them are in full compliance with article 12, paragraph 3.

18. The application of the restrictions permissible under article 12, paragraph 3, needs to be consistent with the other rights guaranteed in the Covenant and with the fundamental principles of equality and non-discrimination. Thus, it would be a clear violation of the Covenant if the rights enshrined in article 12, paragraphs 1 and 2, were restricted by making distinctions of any kind, such as on the basis of race, colour, sex, language, religion, political or other opinion, national or social origin, property, birth or other status. In examining State reports, the Committee has on several occasions found that measures preventing women from moving freely or from leaving the country by requiring them to have the consent or the escort of a male person constitute a violation of article 12.

The right to enter one's own country (para. 4)

19. The right of a person to enter his or her own country recognizes the special relationship of a person to that country. The right has various facets. It implies the right to remain in one's own country. It includes not only the right to return after having left one's own country; it may also entitle a person to come to the country for the first time if he or she was born outside the country (for example, if that country is the person's State of nationality). The right to return is of the utmost importance for refugees seeking voluntary repatriation. It also implies prohibition of enforced population transfers or mass expulsions to other countries.

20. The wording of article 12, paragraph 4, does not distinguish between nationals and aliens ("no one"). Thus, the persons entitled to exercise this right can be identified only by interpreting the meaning of the phrase "his own country".[13] The scope of "his own country" is broader than the concept "country of his nationality". It is not limited to nationality in a formal sense, that is, nationality acquired at birth or by conferral; it embraces, at the very least, an individual who, because of his or her special ties to or claims in relation to a given country, cannot be considered to be a mere alien. This would be the case, for example, of nationals of a country who have there been stripped of their nationality in violation of international law, and of individuals whose country of nationality has been incorporated in or transferred to another national entity, whose nationality is being denied them. The language of article 12, paragraph 4, moreover,

[13] See communication No. 538/1993, *Stewart v. Canada.*

permits a broader interpretation that might embrace other categories of long-term residents, including but not limited to stateless persons arbitrarily deprived of the right to acquire the nationality of the country of such residence. Since other factors may in certain circumstances result in the establishment of close and enduring connections between a person and a country, States parties should include in their reports information on the rights of permanent residents to return to their country of residence.

21. In no case may a person be arbitrarily deprived of the right to enter his or her own country. The reference to the concept of arbitrariness in this context is intended to emphasize that it applies to all State action, legislative, administrative and judicial; it guarantees that even interference provided for by law should be in accordance with the provisions, aims and objectives of the Covenant and should be, in any event, reasonable in the particular circumstances. The Committee considers that there are few, if any, circumstances in which deprivation of the right to enter one's own country could be reasonable. A State party must not, by stripping a person of nationality or by expelling an individual to a third country, arbitrarily prevent this person from returning to his or her own country.

CHAPTER 5
HEALTH AND MIGRATION

Chapter 5 focuses on the many relationships between health and migration. Health has traditionally been a condition to be acceptable for immigration, but health is now increasingly becoming a reason for emigration. Moreover, the health of immigrants is affected by migratory movements themselves and by the general and personal situation in the country of arrival. Moreover, health systems in countries of arrival have to cope with new health-related challenges. Carballo puts some order in the various aspects, whereas Gushulak in his two contributions focuses on the impact of population mobility and the health aspects of return. Besseling covers migration health in general, whereas Forgács, Beaumont and den Exter/Hermans give insight in a variety of health related migration forms. Due attention has been paid to the issue whether some illnesses are a direct result of migration itself and to the question where treatment would have the best results (de Jong/TPO).

5.1

HEALTH DETERMINANTS IN MIGRANTS: THE IMPACT OF POPULATION MOBILITY ON HEALTH

Brian Gushulak

Increasing and evolving in conjunction with other general globalization factors, population mobility and migration are associated processes that influence many aspects of society. The health and well-being of migrants and other mobile populations is an important factor in a world where increasing globalization and expanding travel take place against a background of profound disparity and differences in many significant determinants of health and disease. The movement of populations between locations where there are large differences in health indicators, or where there are differences in the nature and practice of health care is a growing international issue. This movement across gaps in disease prevalence or between different patterns of health care delivery can have significant effects on the health of the migrants themselves, and can create challenges for the practice and management of health and immigration services in the community that receives them. Differences in the social and physical environment between the migrant's origin and destination affect both individual and population health. This presentation will explore those influences in an integrated manner, beginning before the migration journey and continuing into the arrival and integration phase of the migratory process.

POPULATION MOBILITY AND MIGRATION

Traditional approaches to "immigration" and "migration" are in many cases based on historical patterns of population redistribution. For nations that have historically sought out or encouraged foreign migration such as Australia, Canada and the United States, major patterns of population flow have, until rather recently, reflected (with some exceptions i.e. Asian labour migration in the 19th century) population movements between similar cultural backgrounds and health characteristics. These traditional population movements tended to reflect primarily the movement of populations from European origins.

P.J. van Krieken (Ed.), Health, Migration and Return

Several factors have significantly influenced some of the traditional patterns of movement during the past 30 years. Migrants and mobile populations have become much more diverse in response to evolving situations that encourage or discourage international population flows. Some of these new influences have affected the health and well-being of migrants and the non-mobile populations within which migrants settle or work.

> It is much more important to know what sort of a patient has a disease, than what sort of disease a patient has.[1]
>
> William Osler

THE IMPACT OF PERCEPTIONS CONCERNING HEALTH ISSUES ASSOCIATED WITH MIGRATION

From a sociological perspective, concerns about health risks posed by outsiders have always been based on the desire to protect oneself and one's own from external threats. When the threat manifests itself as a disease or malady it has been all too easy to transfer the fear to those who are believed to carry or transmit the illness. The dichotomy between the valid desire to protect the health of the public while preserving the rights and freedoms of travellers and migrants has been a continual point of consideration and discussion related to border and frontier health practices.

Many of these perceptions continue to influence national approaches to migration health, as witnessed by the preponderance of focus on infectious diseases in immigration medical screening. However, as more investigation and study take place we are observing a growing interest in the relationship between population mobility and non-infectious and chronic diseases.

THE IMPACT OF GLOBALIZATION ON MIGRATION HEALTH

During the past 15 years, the process of systematic globalization has extended into the process of population mobility. This has produced fundamental changes and created new challenges in the area of migration health. Many of these consequences have direct impact in nations and states that, historically, did not consider themselves immigration-receiving nations and did not have pre-existing immigration or migration health processes and polices in place to address some of the health aspects of large mobile populations.

[1] Dubos RJ. Mirage of Health: Utopias, Progress and Biological Change. New Brunswisk, NJ: Rutgers University Press, 1987.

Other challenges that complicate issues of "the have" resulted from the political changes that have marked the past two decades.

During the post-Second World War era of East-West political polarization, the permanent resettlement of populations of refugees was a consequence of post-disturbance/conflict displacement. Large numbers of political refugees were permanently resettled following these events, and these movements made up a significant component of refugee movements.

The so-called new world order has changed this paradigm and as we embark on a new century and millenium, there has been a marked change in the way in which displaced and some refugee populations are managed. Instead of permanent resettlement, such as was observed following the end of the conflict in South East Asia, the intent is now directed at returning as many of these populations as possible to their place of origin following the creation of a stable situation. A current example of this practice can be observed with those who were displaced by the conflict in the Former Yugoslavia. After receiving temporary asylum and safe haven in many countries, the majority of those who fled are being induced to return home.

This process of return, rather than permanent resettlement, poses a new set of health challenges to those who deal with migration health. Many of the challenges result from the fact that the migratory journey is now a two-way movement. The health of the refugee in this situation now reflects the health characteristics of his or her point of origin, the experience of health and medical care at the temporary destination and then the influence of returning to a region whose health infrastructure may now be different than it was when they left.

Additionally, another area of change resulting from our rapidly globalizing world has been the facilitation of high-speed travel. In order to improve and ease mobility it has become increasingly easier to cross boundaries and borders. As an adjunct to easier international travel, the speed of the journey has increased as well. Modern air travel has made it possible to move from almost anywhere in the world to any other destination in a matter of a couple of days or less.

This combination of high-speed travel and reduced border formality has had profound impacts on the assessment and management of health and mobile populations.

When a journey exceeded the incubation of an infectious disease it was possible to assess the health of migrating populations at the time those individuals reached the border or frontier post. Those who were ill could be referred for appropriate treatment, if that was available, or further isolated until the risk of transmission had passed. An additional advantage resulting from the presentation of illness and disease at the border was that medical specialists adept at dealing with the diseases of mobile populations could be concentrated at these centres.

In the modern world of air travel it is possible to complete long intercontinental journeys during the clinically silent, incubation period of many infectious diseases. Arriving individuals, who may be infected with a disease of international public health interest, can be clinically well. This fact has all but invalidated many of the principles and paradigms of both human quarantine and immigration medicine.

They have also produced downstream consequences for the control of some infectious diseases in nations that receive large numbers of migrants. Where it was once effective to concentrate medical expertise in rare and exotic diseases at major points of entry where ill arrivals were more likely to present themselves for evaluation, it is no longer so. Arriving migrants and travellers with unusual or rare imported diseases are now more likely to present themselves after arrival at a distance from the frontier or port of entry. In order to effectively recognize, diagnose and manage these illnesses, some of which, such as malaria, may be life-threatening, increased capacity in travel and migration medicine is now needed throughout countries and nations that receive mobile populations.

THE DEMOGRAPHY OF MOBILE POPULATIONS: MIGRANTS ARE NOT A HOMOGENOUS GROUP

It is estimated that, at the present time, annual global mobile human populations include:[2]

Permanent Migrants	1 – 2 Million
Asylum Seekers	circa 1,200,000
Refugees	11,700,000
Returned Refugees	2,500,000
Status A concern (i.e. IDPs)	6,900,000
Migrant Workers	120,000,000
Travellers	670,000,000

[2] *Source*: UNHCR Refugees by Numbers 2000. Available from URL http://www.unhcr.ch/un&ref/numbers/numb2000.pdf. See also:
Stalker P. Workers without Frontiers. The Impact of Globalization on International Migration. ILO (International Labour Organization) 2000, Geneva.
WTO (World Tourism Organization) Press Release: Tourism Growth in 1999 to Reach Pre-Crisis Levels. London November 15, 1999. Available from URL http://www.world-tourism.org/pressrel/rellist.htm.

Yet, against this diverse pattern of human mobility there is even greater diversity within the broad groups defined in the preceding table.

Immigrants and refugees, as defined under the appropriate conventions, are non-homogenous populations and vary considerably in relation to their origin, ultimate destination, social and economic backgrounds as well as health characteristics.

Populations of asylum seekers and refugee claimants also differ in terms of their national and geographic origin, the nature and method of arriving at the destination where asylum is claimed. Additionally, these populations differ in their exposure to violence and trauma depending upon the social, political and military situations that gave rise to their migratory journey.

One further component of this broad group are those who have been unsuccessful in their claim for asylum or permanent residence and who may not have returned to their place of origin. These populations may have irregular or non-official status that may influence health outcomes as a consequence of limited access to some aspects of health and social services, depending upon the jurisdiction.

A similar diversity is observed in a broad category of migrant workers, a population that can vary from actively recruited "high tech" foreign-born employees with official status at their place of employment, to illegal "low tech" workers who may have been trafficked into the nation of employment. Issues of access and the use of health care services by migrant labour populations are important aspects as some of these groups have a high risk of ill-health and injury.

These examples of diversity and non-homogeneity in migrant populations are important because, in many cases, policies and programmes designed to manage some of the issues of health in mobile populations do not sufficiently reflect the disparities in the populations they have been designed to deal with. In traditional immigration-receiving nations, programmes may have been designed to reflect patterns of population mobility and health issues that are no longer as relevant to modern cohorts of migrants. Other programmes may have been designed to deal with regular or legal migrant populations and may not be able to adequately address the needs of irregulars or illegal groups.

These imbalances between the services and care available, and the needs and nature of the populations they are designed to serve can result in an ineffective use of resources and may not adequately address current health needs. Within migration-receiving nations the diversity of new arrivals can be associated with significant differences in health characteristics between cohorts of migrants. Societies tend to classify or associate migrants as a homogenous group of new arrivals. It is not uncommon to see epidemiological studies refer to the "foreign born" as a single cohort.

As those who work with migrant communities know, this group is profoundly diverse and the geographic origin of migrants can significantly affect the health characteristics of these populations. In New Zealand, for example, it has been observed that increases in the prevalence of diabetes are related to migration. However, specific groups of migrants to that country have significantly different disease rates.[3] Thus intervention or prevention strategies directed at migrant communities should take into account population-specific factors. The diversity and breadth of migrant communities in many metropolitan areas can make this a daunting and expensive task. The level of appreciation and understanding of the diversity of health characteristics between migrants and mainstream populations, and between the migrants themselves, by health care providers and policy makers may also be limited.

RECENT EXAMPLES OF IMPORTANT INFLUENCES ON THE HEALTH OF MIGRANT AND MOBILE POPULATIONS

Some of the most significant and important factors that have recently influenced the health of migrants are:

1. Changes in the origin and composition of mobile populations
In the traditional immigration-receiving nations there have been significant shifts in the origin of mobile populations. Traditional migratory flows were towards North America and Australia from Europe. Major immigrant groups at these destinations now originate from Asia, Central and South America and Africa. A significant health issue resulting from this demographic shift, for example, has been the move to population flows from tropical and sub-tropical regions. Immigration health screening practices, designed decades past to manage health issues in European migrants, may not adequately deal with tropical diseases.[4]

2. Increasing diversity of migrant populations
Traditional migrants tended to be young families or single males moving to establish new residence or for employment. The hardships and difficulties associated with the migratory process, particularly in terms of labour migration, defined this demographic situation. Changes resulting from globalization factors, including the nature of employment and the ease and speed of travel, have allowed those patterns to evolve. Migrants now encompass more diverse groups in terms of age and gender and the movements of the very young, the elderly, and single-parent families (often headed by women) can create special challenges for those who are required to deal with migrant health.

---

[3] Simmons D. Harry T. Gatland B. Prevalence of known diabetes in different ethnic groups in inner urban South Auckland. New Zealand Medical Journal. 1999;112(1094):316-9.

[4] Paxton LA, Slutsker L, Schultz LJ, Luby SP, Meriwether R, Matson P, Sulzer AJ Imported malaria in Montagnard refugees settling in North Carolina: implications for prevention and control. Am J Trop Med Hyg. 1996;54:54-57.

One other traditional weakness in approaches to examining the health of migrants has been the difficulty in obtaining easily generalizable conclusions from the multiplicity of groups and sub-populations that comprise migrant communities.

Specific health studies are often focused on small cohorts originating from a specific time and place.[5] As refugees require mandatory medical examination in many locations and, due to the fact that the funding and support for refugee health problems is provided from specific government sources, there has been considerable study of certain diseases in cohorts of refugees.

Studies looking at other groups of migrants are less numerous.

3. Sustained and increasing global disparity in health indicators

In spite of the great advances produced by medical science during the past 50 years, the world in the year 2000 still displays marked differences in the incidence and prevalence of serious illness and disease. While the developed world has managed to adequately deal with most of the infectious disease scourges of mankind, they remain major health problems and killers in many of the areas of the world where mobile populations originate. Malaria, tuberculosis, HIV and other infectious diseases occur in much higher prevalence in regions of the world where many migrants originate.

It is not only in the incidence and prevalence of disease that disparities in health characteristics are observed. The economic situation of nations influences the level and complexity of available health care services, and there are profound differences between the orientation of the health systems. For example, medical practices in the developed world tend to have more capacity directed at preventive and supportive services, while acute treatment and patient management are major issues in the developing nations.

Once again, these differences in both the nature of diseases and ill-health and in the measures directed at delivering health care, can vary considerably between the origin of the migrant and that migrant's permanent or temporary destination. These disparities can complicate the provision and delivery of health care to mobile populations.

PREVALENCE GAPS: THE CONCEPT OF HIGH PREVALENCE TO LOW PREVALENCE MOVEMENT

We live in a world of inequity. The amount and quality of resources directed at the protection of public health varies between regions and nations as health officials attempt to deal with competing priorities. This disparity in public health

---

[5] Nelson KR, Bui H, Sarnet JH. Screening in Special Popualtions; A "Case Study" of Recent Vietnamese Immigrants. Am J Med 1997;102:435-440.

control measures is often associated with an increased prevalence of infectious diseases among poorer and rural populations.[6] Consequently, the migration and movement of people between the developing or rural world to more developed or urban areas creates a bridge across these prevalence gaps.

As a result of this bridging activity, cohorts travelling from regions where certain diseases are of high prevalence may move to destinations where the same disease is rare, or has been eliminated. This is commonly seen in the case of migrants from regions of the world with high levels of tuberculosis,[7] or in travellers moving from areas where vaccine-preventable diseases continue to circulate.[8] This disparity, which is referred to in migration health as *prevalence gap,* can pose significant challenges for those who deal with or provide public health assistance to migrants. Some of these diseases, such as tuberculosis or certain vaccine-preventable diseases, generate legally mandated public health responses in countries of destination; others, such as infections that are resistant to several antibiotics, or which are complicated, such as HIV, can be costly to treat.

The prevalence gap situation becomes more obvious when the disease or illness in question has mandated or regulated control recommendations at the low prevalence destination. In these situations, the migration or movement of individuals from areas of higher prevalence can be associated with considerable demand for medical or public health intervention in the area of low prevalence. For example, it has been recently reported that the current rise in the absolute number of newly detected pediatric HIV-1 infections in the Netherlands is predominantly due to the growing group of children born to parents who originate from HIV-endemic countries.[9]

IMPLICATIONS OF THE DIVERSITY OF HEALTH CHARACTERISTICS IN MOBILE POPULATIONS

While the size of the migrant or foreign-born population is increasing, the diversity in traditional immigration-receiving nations that accept migrants globally is increasing as well.

---

[6] WHO. Bridging the Gaps. The World Health Report 1995. Geneva. 1995.

[7] McKenna MT, McCray E Onorato I. The Epidemiology of Tuberculosis among Foreign-Born Persons in the United States. NEJM 1995;332:1071-1076.

[8] CDC. Measles – United States, 1997. MMWR 1998;47:273-276.

[9] De Kleer IM. Uiterwaal CS. Nauta N. Hirasing RA. Prakken AB. de Graeff-Meeder ER. [Increase of reported HIV-1 infections in children in The Netherlands, 1982-1997: more vertical transmission and a greater proportion of children other than Dutch children]. Article in Dutch. Nederlands Tijdschrift voor Geneeskunde. 1999;143(33):1696-700.

"Although 62% of all immigrants currently living in Canada are of European origin, 74% of immigrants who have arrived in Canada within the past 10 years are of non-European origin: approximately 53% are from Asia, 15% from Latin America, 6% from Africa and 26% from other areas of the world".[10]

As migrant communities become larger components of society, the special and specific health requirements of these mobile populations will generate particular demands on health care services, both therapeutic and preventive. The differences in the prevalence and presentation of illness and disease, coupled with the cultural and economic implications of migration, will require the development or implementation of targeted programmes and systems. Examples may already be observed in many areas in Europe, North America and Australia where cultural and linguistic factors have been shown to influence access to and the utilization of health care.

THE RELATIONSHIP BETWEEN THE PHASE OF THE MIGRATORY MOVEMENT AND THE HEALTH CONSEQUENCES OF MIGRATION

A variety of events and factors can make individuals and populations susceptible to particular health risks, and affect the specific characteristics of their individual and population health. In focusing on mobile and migrant populations, influences on health can be categorized and associated with specific stages or phases of the process of migration.

Those phases are:

1. The Pre-Migration Situation

All societies have within them differences in health and disease that result from numerous factors. Depending on the situation, migrant populations will reflect the health conditions present in general population before it became mobile. These pre-existing health characteristics can be the result of economic status, education, housing and access to health care (including preventive health measures such as immunization or education). Not all of these factors are negative and some migrant populations may arrive at their destination displaying better health characteristics than the receiving population. This situation, often described in the traditional immigration receiving nations is known as the *healthy migrant effect*. For example, in Canada it has been observed that migrants arriving from non-European regions, particularly females, have smoking rates

[10] Fowler N. Providing primary health care to immigrants and refugees: the North Hamilton experience. Can Med Asso J 1998;159:388-391.

that are lower than those for people born in Canada and immigrant populations from Europe.[11]

These factors are particularly noticeable during the immediate post-migration period and are significant in the areas of chronic or debilitating diseases.[12] This "healthy migrant" has various explanations: it has been associated with the presence of immigration medical screening, designed to reduce the migration of those with chronic disease, and has also been suggested to be due to selective factors that passively support movement and establishment by younger, healthier cohorts.

Other examples of this kind include some malignancies,[13] diseases of senescence and lifestyle.

The presence and nature of pre-existing health factors in mobile populations and migrants are an important predictor of the subsequent health impact associated with the process of migration.

2. The Migratory Journey Itself

The process of migration, independent of the reason, can have serious implications for the health of the affected populations. Depending upon the nature of the movement there may be some exposure to additional health risks during travel. Risks of these types are more commonly encountered by displaced and irregular/illegal migrants who move with less planning and resources than regular immigrants or organized labour migrants. In refugee or trafficking situations during the movement phase individuals may be deprived of basic necessities such as food, water, emergency health care, security and personal safety.

Additionally, these individuals may be exposed to unhealthy environmental factors, violence and dangerous means of transport. In many cases, some of the most vulnerable are the elderly, the very young and women.

3. The Reception Phase

The nature, level of development and capacity of the locations that receive or accommodate mobile populations can similarly affect the health of migrants in this phase of the process. Once again, there is profound diversity in the degree to which certain populations are affected. Regular, organized migrants are normally presented with fewer challenges in this regard than the irregular unorganized arrivals. These differences can be very important in the consideration of migrant

---

[11] Chen J, Ng E, Wilkins R. The health of Canada's immigrants in 1994. Health Rep 1996;7(4):33-45.

[12] Chen J. Ng E. Wilkins R. The health of Canada's immigrants in 1994-95. Health Reports. 1996;7(4):33-45, 37-50.

[13] Gordon N.H: Cancer. In: Loue S Editor. Handbook of Immigrant Health. Plenum Press. New York, 1998;389-406.

health, as policies and practices may be designed with organized migrants as the target group. The tendency for some systems to consider migrants as a homogeneous group (i.e. generally referring to asylum seekers, failed asylum seekers and convention refugees as "refugees") can complicate health care provision and planning.[14]

Diverse mobile populations may have different access to and levels of housing, nutrition, security, accesses to sanitation and health care following arrival at their permanent or transient destination. Each of these factors can support and improve the health of mobile populations, and differences in access can have immediate or long-term health outcome implications. Those migrants who have been most compromised before or during the displacement often remain the most vulnerable on arrival.

The environment into which migrants are introduced following their arrival can affect their physical and psycho-social health and well-being. Physical health can be influenced by poverty,[15] overcrowding, and poor quality accommodation, which can influence the prevalence of infectious diseases such as respiratory and gastrointestinal illnesses. The stress and pressures associated have been demonstrated to influence mental health as well, and there is evidence that state-supported housing may reduce the amount of mental illness in new arrivals.[16]

4. Return Migration

The last, and in some cases, continuing component of population mobility in the migratory context involves the permanent or temporary return of the migrants to their place of origin. In some situations this may never take place or the process return may be delayed for extended periods of time, years or even generations.

Some of the most important health concerns during this phase of migration are related to the status and availability of services at the place of return.

For refugees, the displaced and failed asylum seekers, conflict or disaster may have damaged or destroyed medical infrastructures. Social and political events may have affected access to health care, as has been recently observed in the region of the Former Yugoslavia where an integrated national health system has been fragmented, complicating access to what used to be national services such as complicated surgery, cancer treatment or transplantation. Adequate housing, heat or sanitation may not have been restored. There may be a lack of educational or employment opportunities that limit the development and reintegration of the returned population.

---

[14] Loutan L, Bierens de Haan D, Subilia L: [The health of asylum seekers: from communicable disease screening to post-traumatic disorders]. [Article in French] Bull Soc Pathol Exot 1997; 90: 233-237.

[15] Davis SK Ethnic and Socioeconomic Factors as Determinants of Health Status. JAMA280:1989.

[16] Ponizovsky A. Perl E. Does supported housing protect recent immigrants from psychological distress? International Journal of Social Psychiatry. 1997;43(2):79-86.

For regular migrants who have moved from the developing to the developed world, return migration also poses risks. Lengthy residence in areas of low prevalence may reduce herd immunity to infections that are still prevalent in the area of origin. Children born in the developed world to migrant parents from tropical origins now often return to the family's historical place of residence to visit relatives. These cohorts of migrants have an increased risk of acquiring infections yet they may not receive adequate travel medicine advice.

LONG-TERM IMPLICATIONS OF POPULATION MOBILITY IN THE DEVELOPED WORLD

1. Gaps in health care access

While there are significant exceptions such as professional migrants and the increasing global mobility of skilled workers, many migrant populations are economically deprived and remain so for some time following relocation.

This economic hardship can influence health by limiting either the access to or use of health care services, both preventive and therapeutic.

Studies in New York, for example, have demonstrated that in some populations of adolescent migrants, the duration of residence was strongly and directly associated with access to ambulatory care after adjustment for ethnicity. In this study, migrants from the Caribbean, particularly recent immigrants, have reduced access to ambulatory care.[17] In migrant-receiving nations with universal health insurance programmes, such as Canada, migrants may have similar access to health care providers and institutions but their use of some of these services is still less than that of the local population.[18] Whether this is because they are healthier, or are less likely to seek treatment for conditions where native-born populations readily resort to these services is not totally defined.

Whatever the reason, whether it is due to economic, educational or cultural factors, reduced access to health care services can have two consequences.

1. It deprives populations of the care required, affecting mortality and morbidity
2. It can support or sustain differences in health characteristics between population sub-groups.

---

[17] Sonis J. Association between duration of residence and access to ambulatory care among Caribbean immigrant adolescents. American Journal of Public Health. 1998;88(6):964-6.

[18] Wen SW. Goel V. Williams JI. Utilization of health care services by immigrants and other ethnic/cultural groups in Ontario. Ethnicity & Health. 1996; 1(1):99-109.

IMPACT OF ECONOMICS AND CULTURE

When hospital or health care service utilization patterns are studied[19] it is evident that the use of existing services by migrants varies markedly when compared to mainstream or native-born populations. Because concepts such as health, illness and disease have significant cultural components it is not surprising that the use of health care services will be strongly influenced by cultural backgrounds. Cultural influences are often observed in the recognition, acceptance and management of mental or psychosocial illnesses. In immigrant-receiving nations, ethnocultural factors play a significant role in the utilization of psychiatric services by immigrant populations.[20]

BROADER IMPACTS OF CULTURE

Culture and social factors can markedly affect the actual measurement of health determinants in migrant communities. Concepts such as disease, health, hospitals, clinics, home care and drugs are very culturally sensitive. Differences in the way they are appreciated and used can affect health. In the developed world, particularly at the health policy level, concepts such as community health and home care are joining preventive care as major health initiatives. Whether or not these policies have been formulated in a cultural context taking into account the demographics of migrant communities, which may have differing understandings concerning the nature and use of health care services, is difficult to determine.

These will be important considerations, given the growth in some areas of health care such as home care. In the United States, between 1980 and 1996, the number of patients receiving Medicare-sponsored home care grew by a factor in excess of 400%.[21] The specific cultural and ethnic implications of this aspect of care in new arrivals are not well documented.

IMPACT ON MEDICAL EDUCATION

Providers will need to be aware of the cultural, linguistic and historical approaches to health in migrant communities.[22]

---

[19] Naish J, Brown J, Denton B. Intercultural consultations: investigation of factors that deter non-English speaking women from attending their general practitioners for cervical screening. BMJ 1994;309:1126-8.

[20] Roberts N. Crockford D. Psychiatric admissions of Asian Canadians to an adolescent inpatient unit. Canadian Journal of Psychiatry. 1997;42(8):847-51.

[21] Montauk SL Home Health Care American Family Physician 1998;58:1608-1614.

[22] Carrillo EJ Green AR, Betancourt JR. Cross-Cultural Primary Care: A Patient-Based Approach. Ann Int Med 1999;130:829-834.

THE PUBLIC HEALTH IMPORTANCE OF MIGRATION HEALTH

The primary importance of modern population mobility in terms of general public health relates to the economic and health outcome benefits that will result from the earlier recognition of the different health needs of specific migrant cohorts.[23] The appreciation of those differences and the awareness that, in the current context, mobile populations represent a microcosm of global disparities in health and disease will benefit both immediate and future adequate planning for services.

A better appreciation of the implications of population mobility will hopefully affect the timing of the delivery of public health interventions for migrant communities. This will also avoid delays in the diagnosis and treatment of diseases that may be more common in migrants but less well recognized at the migrant's destination. Finally, it is now possible to diagnose and treat several illnesses and infections of public health importance during the pre-departure phase of the immigration health assessment. This activity can allow for the cost-effective management of some diseases in populations before they arrive at their destination, reducing post-arrival public health interventions, and reducing the burden placed on the newly arrived migrants in terms of the often required public health follow up.[24]

These outcomes will be both cost-effective and will improve and sustain the health of the migrant.

AREAS FOR FUTURE AND ONGOING STUDY

Moves to reduce or eliminate existing disparities will require:

A better definition of sub-populational differences in relation to preventing disease, promoting health and delivering appropriate care.

Improved collection and use of standardized data to correctly identify all high-risk populations and to monitor the effectiveness of health interventions targeting these groups.

Studies to develop a better understanding of the relationships between health status and different migration and cultural backgrounds

[23] Hernandez DJ, Charney E: Editors. From Generation to Generation. The Health and Well-Being of Children in Immigrant Families. Committee on the Health and Adjustment of Immigrant Children and Families, National Research Council and Institute of Medicine. National Academy Press. 1998, Washington.

[24] Bloland P; Colmenares J; Gartner G; Schwartz IK; Lobel H (1995) Cost and Appropriateness of Treating Plasmodium falciparum Infections in the United States. *Journal of Travel Medicine* 1,16-21.

5.2

EMERGING HEALTH CHALLENGES IN THE CONTEXT OF MIGRATION

Manuel Carballo

INTRODUCTION

Globalisation seen from the perspective of migration is not a new phenomenon. Migration has probably always been a central and necessary part of economic and social development everywhere and has required the relatively free movement of people across as well as within borders. There have always been communities and countries needing new human capital and looking outside their national borders to satisfy this need. At the same time there have probably always been situations in history when people have been forced to uproot and leave their homes and communities because of economic, social and political threats. They too have traditionally looked elsewhere, including outside their frontiers, for solutions. This dynamic interaction between countries that need "new blood" and people looking for safe havens and "new opportunities" is unlikely to change. Migration will no doubt remain a key and integral feature of development and societal change everywhere and for the same reasons that it has always done.

Migration is rarely without its problems, however. The health implications of uprooting, movement and resettlement, for example, are complex and far-reaching. While some of these implications and related challenges are beginning to be understood, the health parameters of migration have tended to be neglected even though workable solutions to the needs of migrants and refugees are feasible while at the same time respecting national capacities.

CHANGING NATURE OF MIGRATION

Two key aspects of global migration have changed in recent times and have contributed to a changing health and health care scenario. The first concerns the speed of migration; the second concerns its relative ease. Everywhere in the world, be it in developed or developing countries, the pace of population movement has grown exponentially. Within and between countries more people

P.J. van Krieken (Ed.), Health, Migration and Return

are now moving faster than has ever been possible or seen before. They are doing so by road, air and sea in ever-accelerating ways and to such an extent that in some cases the demographic and social profiles of countries are changing in its wake. The spatial scope of population movement has also grown and people are now routinely going further than was previously feasible, crossing not only geo-political and cultural frontiers but also major ecological ones as well.

The second characteristic that has changed is that improvements in transportation have come together with a global view that continues to be broadened by a combination of an internationalised media and public education that is reaching more people. As a result, the concept of migration is becoming easier to grasp at a time when it is also becoming easier to put into practice. This is creating space for a widening pattern of circular migration that is increasingly meeting the needs of market principles of supply and demand that call for human capital, as well as materials, to move to and from places of production.

The implications of this emerging scenario for health and disease are many. They range from communicable to non-communicable health problems, and include the impact migrants have on health care systems in the countries of reception. How to prevent or at worst mitigate these problems and implications is a challenge that many countries are ill-prepared to deal with because they have been seemingly caught unaware of the accelerating magnitude of migration and what it means for health.

PERSISTING PARAMETERS

Migration always meets someone's needs, and in that sense it is unlikely that the pace of migration will ever really change. For example, within countries that now constitute the European Union (EU), out-migration traditionally constituted a safety valve that permitted countries to divest themselves of "excess" people at times of impending economic and political crisis. For the New World that became a safe haven to Europeans, migration brought much needed human capital, new ideas, investment and socio-demographic strength.

Despite its positive features migration has nevertheless always presented complex health and social questions. Even when migration is planned and structured around well calculated national labour needs, the entry of new human resources into a society often prompts unforeseeable health and social problems that are difficult and costly to manage. Health and social services, together with housing and employment, for example, are sectors that are immediately challenged by the process of mass in-migration.

CHANGING CHALLENGES

Global migration is changing in a number of ways. In Europe, for instance, countries that until recently were once net exporters of human capital have now become magnets for immigrants and are beginning, albeit reluctantly, to be net importers of people now from other regions. As the principles of free movement become more established, and as EU membership expands, the potential for people to move into and within the EU will increase. Much the same is occurring elsewhere in the world too. South-to-south migration is growing rapidly, and wars and political instability are provoking more and larger refugee movement than ever before.

The challenge presented by this changing scenario is a complex one for a variety of reasons. One of those reasons is that while some countries may objectively need and benefit from "new blood", the reality is that with the exception of traditional "receiving" countries such as the USA, Canada and Australia, few others have formulated the policies and practices that can make migration orderly and productive. Another is that even where such policies have been put in place, the mounting pace and pressure of migration often overwhelms and finds loopholes in these policies and practices.

The major underlying problem, however, is that countries that are attractive to migrants are not always or necessarily those that feel they need or are likely to benefit from large in-migrations. Many countries today feel they can no longer absorb the number of people that are seeking entry. Nor are they necessarily willing or able to invest in the welfare of newcomers.

HEALTH IMPLICATIONS

Even under ideal circumstances, migration is always replete with health and social challenges for migrants. It is also pregnant with challenges for the societies they move into, be it on a temporary or permanent basis. For, no matter whether migration is so-called "voluntary" or forced, it is always a disruptive process that poses far-reaching physical and psychosocial threats to the people concerned. It requires a break with tradition, community and family, cultural value systems and accepted ways of functioning and dealing with the world. It then imposes demands on migrants to quickly develop new psychological and social survival skills at a time when they may be poorly prepared, and when receiving societies may not be in a position (or willing) to reciprocate with back-up support.

Thus while on the one hand migrants take with them health profiles that reflect their social and economic "origins", how they lived and what their health was like there, they are also at times confronted with situations that offer little opportunity to throw off that baggage. A number of examples are cited below because they reflect more so than others, the complexity of the health and migration situation facing countries and migrants.

COMMUNICABLE DISEASES

Most migrants move because of economic pressure and hence tend to come from poor socio-economic backgrounds. The health "baggage" they carry with them reflects those backgrounds, and few diseases are more typical of chronic poverty and poor social development than tuberculosis. As a result, many European countries where TB had been otherwise controlled are now seeing the epidemiology of the problem change in the wake of in-migration. In Denmark, for example, the incidence of foreign-born cases of TB has risen significantly over the past ten years. Similarly in the UK approximately 40% of all new TB cases are reported to occur in people arriving from the economically poor parts of the world such as the Indian sub-continent.[1] Others have reported similar patterns in the Netherlands; in Germany and France migrants are considered to be three and six times respectively more likely to be diagnosed with TB than non-migrants.[2]

Although the immediate conclusion often tends to be that migrants bring health problems such as TB with them, the reality is more complex and is conditioned by the fact that most migrants not only come from poor health environments, but that most of them often move into social situations that offer little protection against diseases of poverty. Thus even in the Netherlands, Austria and France surveys indicate that migrants are compelled by a variety of circumstances to live in sub-standard housing where overcrowding and poor sanitation enhance the risk of the spread of TB. (WHO, 1996). Similarly, in Italy Carchedi & Picciolini have referred to poor housing and limited access to health services as serious precursors to TB in migrant communities there.[3]

REPRODUCTIVE HEALTH

The reproductive health of women migrants presents another area of grave concern. In the UK the Office of Population Censuses and Surveys reports that babies of Asian mothers tend to have lower birth-weights than other babies, and

---

[1] Some of the references have been included in the bibliography at the very end of this Handbook.

[2] Denmark: Prinsze, F. (1997). Tuberculosis in countries of the European Union. *Infectieziektenbulletin*, 8(2), 25-27; UK: Karmi 1997; The Netherlands: De Jong and Wesenbenk; Germany: Huismann et al.; France: Glibier; all in: Huismann, Weilandt & Geiger (Eds,), *Country Reports on Migration and Health in Europe*, Bonn: Wissenschaftliches Institut der Ärzte Deutschlands e.V., 1997.

[3] The Netherlands: De Jong & Wesenbenk, France: Gliber, Spain: Gaspar, Italy: Carchedi & Picciolini all in Huisman c.s. 1997 op.cit.; for Austria: Hammer, G. (1994). Lebensbedingungen ausländischer Staatsbürger in Österreich, in: *Statitische Nachrichten*, pp. 914-926; see also: WHO, *Groups At Risk: WHO Report On the Tuberculosis Epidemic,* Geneva, 1996.

perinatal and post-neonatal mortality rates are highest among immigrants from Pakistan and the Caribbean. In Belgium the highest perinatal and infant mortality rates tend be for babies born to women from Morocco and Turkey, and a similar picture emerges from Germany where perinatal and neonatal mortality rates are higher in foreign-born groups, especially Turkish migrants, than in other communities.[4] Much the same observation has been made for immigrant groups in Spain where premature births, low birth-weight, and complications of delivery are all more common among women from sub-Saharan Africa, Central and South America than in the non-migrant population.

Here again part of the problem appears to be not only that the women and mothers concerned come from poor backgrounds, but that as migrants they continue to live and work in conditions (including family conditions) that impose continued behavioural risks to the reproductive health of women. Many of them do not benefit from health information about how to protect their sexual lives, and contraceptive knowledge and practices is generally poor. Whether they are not being "reached" by otherwise available information, or whether they are not culturally open to the new information that is available is not clear. Whatever the cause, the economic and human costs involved are heavy for both migrants and the receiving societies.

OCCUPATIONAL HEALTH

Occupational health and safety has also become an important concern in the context of migrant labour. In Europe occupational accident rates tended to be twice as high for immigrants than for "nationals", and were the cause of considerable long-term morbidity. In Germany, it was reported that occupational accidents occur more often among immigrants than they do among "nationals" even though migrants go on to make far fewer insurance claims than nationals do. Similarly, in France, over 30% of all occupational accidents resulting in permanent disabilities involved non-French workers, and in Spain migrant agricultural labourers are now known to suffer from depression, neurological disorders, heart complaints and miscarriages at a rate that is significantly in excess of those for "national" workers.[5]

Just as in the case of TB, the reasons for these elevated accident rates are many. One of the first is that migrants tend (at least initially) to move into low

[4] For Belgium, see: Muynck, for Germany, see Huismann c.s. in Huisman et al., op. cit. (1997).

[5] On occupational accidents in general: Bollini and Siem, 1995; Germany, Huismann et al.; France: Gibier; both in Huismann c.s., op. cit.; on Spain: Parron, T. et al. (1992). *Estudio de los riesgos ocasionadoes por el uso de plaguicidas en la zona del Poniente almeriense*. Ponencia presentada al "Curso sobre Inmigración y Enfermedades Transmisibles". Nerja, Malaga, and: Castelló, S.F. (1992). *Condiciones de trabajo y seguridad e higiene en los invernaderos*. Ponencia presentada al "Curso sobre Inmigracion y Enfermedades Transmisibles." Nerja, Malaga.

skilled temporary employment that employers often consider too short or too menial to justify major investments in training and supervision. This lack of training is made worse by language problems and a lack of communication between migrants and employers. Short-term (seasonal) migrant workers also often lack familiarity with the machinery they are expected to manipulate, and arrive with different cultural attitudes to safety. In the case of agricultural labour, which in southern Europe constitutes a major proportion of all migrant work, there are also problems associated with poor working conditions, especially where workers are confined to work and living spaces where exposure to pesticides and other chemicals is both chronic and excessive.

PSYCHOLOGICAL PROBLEMS

Within the overall framework of migration and health, psycho-social problems have rightly received considerable attention. In many ways they underlie many of the other health problems encountered by migrants and the services that respond to them.

Psychosomatic problems are a common problem among migrants and a major cause of morbidity and work-days lost. Moroccan immigrants in Belgium were found to be up to five times more likely to develop peptic ulcers than Belgian nationals. Stress-related ulcers are also reported to be a frequent source of illness among immigrants in Germany and the Netherlands. Symptoms such as frequent headaches, anxiety attacks, dermatitis, and sleeping disorders are frequent problems among migrants in Sweden and refugees in Spain where hypochondria and paranoia is also frequently referred to.[6]

Alcohol and drug abuse may also be a growing problem in the context of migration. In Amsterdam, it was found that half of the people using methadone bus programmes were foreign born, and 45% of detainees in youth penitentiaries in the Netherlands were children of migrants. The reasons for drug use among the children of immigrants vary considerably, but in France, it has been seen as a manifestation of social marginalization and an expression of anger/frustration at the difficulties children have with integration. A study of psychological stress and coping among Greek immigrant adolescents in Sweden tended to confirm this, and similar observations have also been reported from Germany. Carballo and Morival (1998) found family disorganisation to be a major factor, but of equal

[6] For Belgium (Muynck), Germany (Huisman et al.), Sweden (Janson) and Spain (Gaspar), see Huismann c.s, op.cit., 1997; for the Netherlands: van Wieringen, J.C.M., Leentvaar-Kuupers, A.L., Brouwer, H.J. et al. (1986). *Morbiditeitspatroon en huisartsgeneeskundig handelen bij etnische groeperingen.* Amsterdam: Universiteit van Amsterdam, Instituut voor Huisartsgeneeskunde.

importance is the fact that the children of migrants appear to be targeted by people selling drugs and who apparently recognize their vulnerability.[7]

CONCLUSION

These examples highlighted above are by no means exhaustive. The process of migration and resettlement is full of health problems and concerns. What these examples do, however, is shed light on a problem that is becoming increasingly complex, costly and technically difficult to manage. Yet at the same time, many of the health problems highlighted here, as well as others, could be prevented through more comprehensive policies and programmes that would build on current epidemiological evidence and knowledge.

Underlying the response to the health problems of migrants and migration, however, is an urgent need for regional and inter-regional agreements designed to prevent not only the risk of morbidity among migrants, but more importantly the need for people to leave their countries of origin in the numbers they are doing now. Assistance directed at enhancing the health development process in poor countries would probably contribute to social and economic development as well. In so doing, it would go far in alleviating the burden on people in those countries, and might make migration a less necessary option. It goes without saying that it would also make migration more healthy and productive if and when it did occur.

[7] See in general: Carballo and Morival (1998); for Amsterdam: de Jong, J.T.V.M. (1994). Ambulatory mental health care for migrants in the Netherlands. *Curare*, 17(1), 5-34; for France: Ait Menguellet, A. (1988), Toxicomanie et immigration maghrebine, in: *Les adolescent dit maghrebins de deuxième gènèration en France*. Congrès de Psychiatrie et de Neurologie de langue française, 86émé session. Chambery, 13-17 Juin 1988, 351-359. Paris: Masson; Yahyaoui, A. (1992). *Toxicomanie et pratique sociale*, Grenoble: La pensèè Sauvage/APPAM; Yakoub, S. (1993). Reflexions à propos de toxicomanes maghrébins incarcéres: approches juridique, socio-ethnique, ethno-clinique, *Migrations*; Bendahman, H. (1993). *Cultures, marginalité et deviance: de l'inquiétante étrangeté de l'autre à l'exclusion socialte*. Thionville: Espace Resource ; Boylan, M. (1995). Acculturation et conduites addictives chez les jeunes d'origine maghrébine. *Interventions* (48) 17-19; for Sweden: Giannopoulou, I. (1988). Patterns of alcohol and drug use and indicators of psychological distress among immigrant Greek adolescents. In: *Congrès international sur l'alcoolisme et les toxicomanies*, 35, ICAA CIPAT, Oslo, 31 Juillet – 6 Aout 1988. Vol. 2, 130-139; for Germany: Akbiyik, O. (1990). Un centre d'accueil pour toxicomanes migrants, *Bull. Liaison CNDT*, 16, 178-188.

HEALTH RELATED MOVEMENTS

In this Chapter attention will be paid to health-related movements in general. It consists of a triptych, all three parts describing different yet related issues: health-related migration in, to and from the former socialist countries (Dr. Forgács); internal health movements, with emphasis on the Third World (Beaumont, MD); and the example of cross-border health services in the EU Maastricht 'Triangle' (Hermans and Van Exter).

1. HEALTH CARE AND HEALTH-RELATED MIGRATION IN THE FORMER SOCIALIST COUNTRIES

Ivan Forgács

The former socialist economies (FSE) were characterised by strictly closed national borders. Yet, the provision of health care for citizens from other socialist countries was freely available thanks to various mutual agreements among these countries. Migration – either legal, or illegal – was practically impossible among these countries and the health care (HC) administrations were not faced with medical problems relating to migration. The so-called 'solidarity-based' health provision for a few 'more equal' citizens of friendly countries was, financially speaking, not very significant.

After the collapse of the European socialist economies the borders between the FSEs and towards the established market economies (EME) were opened and migration rapidly increased. The resulting uncontrolled migration was basically the result of three causes:

- economic, resulting from different living standards, working conditions and the different level of HC among these countries;
- political, due to the local (civil) wars within the region;
- national, due to the several border changes in the region during this century

P.J. van Krieken (Ed.), Health, Migration and Return

and the growing nationalism, as a rebound effect of the former so-called 'socialist internationalism'.

The special features of migration within the FSEs are:

- Repatriation: the returnees are citizens of a foreign (mostly Western) country, but are of FSE (ethnic) origin; they enjoy the same social health insurance conditions and natural health provision as the native citizens.
- Immigration: immigrants have foreign citizenship and nationality and they mainly emanate from the least developed countries; the reason for their immigration is an economic one and they often intend to continue their journey to Western-European countries; ill-health, or tropical diseases are common in this group.
- Family reunification or marriage with foreign citizens: the health insurance conditions can be compared with those available for returnees.
- Health care related migration: the aim is to make use of the advantages of the health care system (high-tech., better hospital conditions, or the lower cost of the health care) in the recipient country.
- Wars, disasters: this situation is especially important as many civil wars have resulted in massive refugee movements (e.g. Bosnia, Kosovo); health services are provided, often on an emergency basis due to the huge numbers involved.
- Same ethnic stock in neighbouring countries: some countries are faced with the issue of 'nationals' living in neighbouring countries and having the citizenship of those countries who seek medical services in the 'home' country (e.g. Romanian Hungarians) due to a difference in the level of services; care and cure is normally provided free of charge.
- Especially during the first five years of the political changes a large number of physicians (about 3000 doctors) repatriated to the former socialist countries, resulting in an unplanned and unforeseen increase in the number of physicians.

SPECIAL FORMS OF HEALTH MIGRATION FROM THE 'WEST' TO THE FORMER 'EAST'

Based on the purchasing parity of Western currencies, the fees for health services in the FSEs are significantly lower, than in the 'West'. A moderate health-related migration can be noticed, especially concerning those forms of health provisions where the urgency and high-tech treatment are is not essential (for example: dentistry, balneo-therapy, etc.)

Migrations from the former socialist countries to the 'West' are mainly for economic reasons. Among these economic migrants are, on the one hand, often highly educated professionals, and, on the other – a fairly recent trend – uneducated minority groups.

In the FSE countries the state owned and controlled accessible, but rather low quality, free of charge health care systems (HCS). More often than not, neither the providers nor the state as the financer had any idea concerning the cost of the services. In most FSE countries the financing system for the HCS changed in the early 1990s and a compulsory, solidarity-based (Bismarck-like) social and health insurance system was introduced without any significant changes to the real HC expenditures. The HC cost in the FSE is currently around 10-30 % of the EU average corresponding with the GDP differences of these countries. A primary problem for the FSEs is the markedly lower GDP (due to the inherited low productivity) and this consequently results in lower health expenditures. Yet, among these transient economies there are significant differences in health expenditures and in the quality of care relating in particular to high-tech treatment and the provision of pharmaceuticals. Recently this high-tech gap has been identified as one of the main reasons for the health-related migration, both from FSEs to the 'West' (very exceptional cases only) and within the FSEs, i.e. from the relatively poorer countries to the relatively wealthier ones. But because the 'richer' countries among the FSEs are still relatively poor, the increased costs health care for these migrants creates financial difficulties for the providers and for social insurance as well. This is especially the case because the services for these patients often involve the most expensive high-tech methods.

It is worth emphasizing that the main limiting factors for the HCS in FSEs are the shortage of high-tech services/equipment and the extremely expensive pharmaceuticals, whilst the wages of those involved are extremely low, about 5-10% of the EU average. Paradoxically enough, the FSEs are characterised by a high number of doctors and hospital beds, parallel with low technology and the relatively poor quality of care.

The FSEs unequivocally agreed on the urgent need for health care reform. The goals of such a reform and the obstacles to be overcome are almost the same in each country in this region. Unfortunately during the last ten years the FSEs have failed to introduce proper health care reforms.[1]

---

[1] Among the goals of such a reform are the following: to reduce the central Government's budget; to improve the quality of clinical care; to improve the responsiveness of providers to patients' needs; to attract new capital to the health sector; to improve the health status of the population at large; to decrease employment in the health sector; to improve the efficiency of health care delivery; to increase choice; to transfer resources from hospital care to primary care and health promotion.

The following obstacles have been encountered: a lack of clear agreement as to the goals in either Parliament and/or the Ministry of Health; a lack of continuity relating to leadership among health policy makers; a lack of funds for new technologies to support reform, e.g. computer information systems; a weak economy; a lack of experience with new health insurance programmes to pay for health services; a lack of experience in building and sustaining political coalitions for health policy changes; lack of relevant data for reform planning and evaluation; the fact that physicians want more income before they will support reforms; the lack of formal plans for implementing the desired reforms; impatience on the part of the general public which does not allow for phased implementation; a fear of public dissatisfaction with the reform process and the results; and, finally, un-

Various obstacles have hindered the politicians in taking the proper action and these obstacles are mainly related to the old problems: the reorientation towards a market-oriented but socially acceptable health economy is very slow. The social insurance system is unable to fulfil its solidarity function and health policy lacks the preventive strategy and community support. A policy and programme to build on the strengths of the existing system, while introducing managed changes step-by-step, is necessary.

A short-term possible solution would be for the more developed countries to assist in the training of the health management personnel in the poorer countries in order to prepare them for the introduction of a more cost effective and quality oriented HCS.[2]

The long-term solution is the development of the economy, combined with an effective health promotion policy together with a cost-benefit oriented health care management.

2. IN-COUNTRY MOVEMENTS: SIMILARITIES BETWEEN NORTH AND SOUTH

Willem Beaumont

In order to fully appreciate cross-border health-related movements, it is paramount to study so-called internal health-related movements, both in developed and developing countries. It is submitted that such movements depend on a) the availability of services, b) the quality of the services, c) financial means, and d) an awareness of the differences in services. Moreover, the quality, accessibility (e.g. drug-trials) and availability and the financing of drugs may also play a role.

A. DEVELOPED COUNTRIES

In his remarkable book on health, cancer and comebacks, the winner of two Tours de France, Lance Armstrong, describes how he, upon a preliminary diag-

willingness on the part of physicians and hospitals to change practice and management as reforms are proposed.

[2] Such training courses were for example organized and financed by the IOM for Kosovar doctors in 1999, and in 2000 at the Department of Public Health Medicine at Semmelweis University, Budapest.

nosis started to shop around for the best available treatment combined with the best opportunity to continue his profession as a cyclist. He thereby visited at least three or four hospitals, MDs and cancer experts all over the USA. He finally settled, and with hindsight rightly so, for a clinic in Indianapolis.[3]

This example shows a phenomenon which was hitherto relatively unknown in the developed world: health shopping practices. More and more patients ask for a second (or a third) opinion before submitting themselves to specific treatment, especially concerning treatment with long-term consequences. This was and is in the Western and Northern European countries looked upon with some hesitation, as it is often still considered to be a statement of no confidence in the medical doctor initially involved. In addition, it adds extra costs which are not necessarily welcomed in an insurance-driven system. The very moment when health becomes a 'commodity', a product which can, to some extent, be 'purchased', then shopping becomes a more accepted and sometimes even advisable activity.

This 'shopping' should in general be seen as a result of changes in the character of society as a whole. The traditional agricultural societies were bound to limit themselves in their search for 'health': mobility was far from being taken for granted, funds were not always available, and the social structure made it difficult to 'by-pass' a local physician, in as far as the latter was present. This changed with industrialization which involved major migratory movements, to which urbanization was intrinsically linked (both as a cause and as a result). Health services during the time of industrialization were purchased or were often based on some forms of charity (mainly church-related). A lack of funds generally hindered access, and insurance systems were not yet in place. Private organizations catered for the medical needs of the poor, however.

A following stage can be symbolized as the social welfare state, in particular from the 1950s onwards, which involved fairly generous insurance systems, under which virtually all or most of those in need of health services could find the assistance needed.[4] This fairly strict system was based on mutual trust which allowed no room for 'shopping' as referred to above: this is your GP, this is your local hospital and discontent was looked upon with disdain.

Now that we have entered the 'information and knowledge' era, it is considered normal for the patient to surf the internet in order to find the best possible treatment, which is also linked to the change in the character of the insurance system which now caters for greater flexibility, and hence health-related-movements. It could thus be submitted that such movements can be expected to increase rather than decrease.

---

[3] Lance Armstrong,/Jenkins: *It´s not about the bike; my journey back to life*, NY 2000.

[4] The heated discussions in the United States on the quality and the availability of medical care at the beginning of the Clinton administration and during the Bush-Gore presidential campaigns leave some room for thought concerning this statement. Quite a number of citizens are not able to insure themselves and remain dependant on charity. In the USA more than 10% of the total population remain uninsured.

Elsewhere in this volume, reference is made to intra-European Union cross-border movements and it is demonstrated that such movements cannot be taken for granted. A new phenomenon will be the renting out of utilities (e.g. operation theatres plus support staff) to specialists and patients from foreign countries, enabling the latter to surpass local (bureaucratic) limits on medical services.[5]

B. THE THIRD WORLD

The characteristics of health service patterns and hence health-related movements are not only related to the four elements mentioned above in the introduction, but can also be found in a) a lesser degree of urbanization, b) a different insurance system (above all based on the extended family), c) a lack of decentralization of health care, d) a very limited national health budget, and e) the significant differences in renumeration under the public health system and as a private practitioner or specialist.

In general it can be stated that in the Third World the well to do can purchase the necessary health service for themselves or for their extended family. Also people working for certain companies have a greater opportunity to receive adequate health care for them and for their family as one of the fringe benefits under their contract of employment. In the countryside, however, health provisions are rare and their quality is in many cases poor. When someone becomes ill in the countryside, they often first try local, traditional healing practices. When this proves to be ineffective, Western-based medicine is resorted to. It then depends on the financial means (and the disease) whether it is felt necessary to travel to the nearest hospital and thus to a major city. In quite a number of cases – again, depending on the funds available – travel to the 'capital' to find the necessary treatment (or to find the drugs!) is deemed advisable. Distances can be substantial, but it is often forgotten that travel in Third World countries is intensive and frequent.[6]

This need to travel is of course due to one of the major challenges involved: trained medical doctors (and nurses) are often not inclined to work in the countryside. This can be because their family want to remain in the capital, but mostly it is because of all the possibilities which the big town offers, not least the possibility of a flourishing private practice and the urge to be close to the economic and political centre.

---

[5] A Dutch insurance company is proposing to have hip operations carried out in Southern Spain by two Dutch specialists for the benefit of their also Netherlands-based clients (Haagse Courant, November 2000).

[6] Working in Ethiopia I was confronted with an unexpected phenomenon. Having prescribed a patient ampicillin without charging, I learned later by accident, that this person did not trust the free drugs and travelled 250 km to Addis Ababa to purchase, as he discovered later, exactly the same drug.

In quite a number of Third World countries hospitals outside the bigger cities are run by Churches, NGOs and/or foreign medical staff, which may somehow be seen as urging to the country concerned to set up a proper system, but is nevertheless welcomed by all (that is both the potential patients and the establishment) as a suitable solution to a cumbersome problem: who wishes to spend his/her professional career in the field ?[7]

Wealthy families often do not want to be treated in their own country, but tend to visit clinics abroad, assisted by acquaintances who know their way around. This is also often the very same group which insists on training specialists for their own country, at the cost of training a multiple number of general practitioners and paramedical staff.

C. URBANIZATION

Urbanization in the Third World is still in its infancy, in spite of the many cities with over one or even ten million inhabitants, and yet it should be appreciated that health services will inevitably focus on big cities rather than the countryside. Taking market mechanisms into account, it is not to be expected that decentralized services, i.e. outside the urban areas, will be readily made available. Moreover, the tendency that well-meaning NGOs, churches and foreigners will focus on providing health services in so-called far-away areas, adds to the above patterns. Only when a balance can be found, i.e. when it becomes attractive to set up a practice in suburbs or regional centres, will this trend be discontinued. This depends to a great extent on the financial attractiveness of agricultural activities, or agri-business in general, and on substantial increases to national health budgets.

Yet, improvements can be made by training more medical personnel. In that way, market mechanisms will prevent the automatism to seek employment in the big city: setting up a practice 'in the field' may in due time become both financially and job-satisfaction-wise a viable alternative.

D. CROSS-BORDER MOVEMENTS

In view of the above, it should come as no surprise that cross border movements, i.e. the search for the best available health services, are quite logical, and represents a phenomenon which is bound to continue, as long as countries of arrival

[7] The maintenance of hospitals, particularly the ones in far-off places is often restricted by very limited budgets. The choice, however, between investing in PHC and e.g. the construction of a luxury hospital should be an obvious one. Moreover, the correlation of e.g. female education and the U5M may indicate that education should be invested in, sometimes at the cost of short term-health services.

provide the services which are desired. Under no circumstances will a generous policy change such a pattern. On the contrary: it will increase this tendency up to the point of complete saturation, i.e. a breakdown of Western European health services based on closed insurance systems, and/or a privatization of the access to such services, a development resulting in the situation prevailing at the end of the 19th century and the beginning of the 20th century under which access to services was for a great many subjects dependent on charity, rather than solidarity. In the modern world travelling has become possible for a far bigger group, e.g. paid for by the family living in a developed country. As a tourist or 'on a family visit' they now come to visit certain specialists or to have specific treatment, which in popular terminology amounts to health tourism. That does not necessarily mean that the treatment or a similar quality is not available in their own country. In this respect the creativity can be fairly impressive. It is quite common practice in the Netherlands for one to take a visiting family member to one's general practitioner, without the latter charging for the consultation. Another common technique, certainly in the main cities, is for the patient from abroad to make use of the insurance card of a relative or a friend, not during regular working hours though, but in the evening or the weekend when there is little chance of them being confronted with the family doctor. Sometimes these practices come to light by accident, e.g. by case- and contact-finding when someone is admitted with an infectious disease. Others present themselves as asylum seekers.[8]

E. CONSEQUENCES

When a relatively small number of people are treated without being insured, the closed solidarity insurance system, together financed by the healthy and the sick, can cope, but when the numbers become larger and the treatments more expensive, the system gradually becomes stretched to its limits, as is the case in the Netherlands.[9]

---

[8] Another known technique has recently been brought to the attention of the public at large, when in a rape-murder case a suspect was traced in Turkey. This person was a suspect because he had disappeared from a centre for asylum seekers in the immediate vicinity at the time of the crime. He told his story to Dutch television. It was well known in his circles in Turkey, that when one applies for political asylum in the Netherlands (he was of Kurdish origin) that one would receive medical treatment whilst awaiting a decision on the asylum request. He needed a cardiac operation, that could be performed in Turkey, but that would be expensive, so he presented himself in the Netherlands as an asylum seeker and after recovering from his operation he simply disappeared from the centre for asylum seekers concerned and returned home (DNA investigation cleared him as a suspect).

[9] In the Netherlands we are confronted with a shortage of doctors for different reasons, one of them being a rather recent tendency on the part of doctors to work only during their official working hours. This development is in line with the general tendency in Dutch society and is greatly enhanced by the great influx of female doctors, who want to have more time for their families. Because

In acute and life-threatening situations everybody present in the Netherlands has a right to be treated. The problem therefore mainly lies with the treatment of those who are not insured, when they have chronic diseases and/or diseases requiring surgery.

The subject of the 'incorrect use of health insurance' is a quite sensitive matter because of its emotional aspects. One heartbreaking case or another will be always be highlighted in the case of argument. If the government and/or private groups create special funds for the treatment of 'health tourists', the closed insurance system based on the solidarity of the participants can survive. Otherwise it will gradually break up, always to the detriment of the weaker in society, a fact apparently not fully understood by most politicians (or perhaps they consider it politically unwise to bring it up). Court decisions on the right to treatment will have great consequences for the future of our health system, and as to whether it can survive with the same quality.

An important question in this respect is for example whether an individual enjoys the right to the quality of health care of his country of origin or that of the country of temporary residence. Imagine the cumulative financial consequences of seemingly deserving individual cases and the resulting health migration. If HIV carriers would have the right to multiple drug treatment because it is not available in the country of origin, millions of infected people from Third World countries would run up a bill of $ 20,000 for each person for each year of treatment. These drugs would in no time demolish the Western health services, financially and in terms of manpower.[10]

F. SHORT-TERM TRANSFER

Sometimes we can find in the media extreme examples of patients, often children, brought to a hospital in a Western country in order to receive the most expensive treatments and operations and often not surviving anyway. Just imagine how many children's lives could have been saved with that money in the patient's country of origin.

Working for eight years in the Horn of Africa I was confronted with the effects which plastic surgery combined with a stay over a longer period of time in a

---

they mostly only work the official hours or, as many prefer, part-time the male doctors follow suit. In The Hague one 'old style' general practitioner therefore has to be replaced by 1.3 'new style' practitioners (DHV Haaglanden, The Hague, 2000). Because of the fact that in the Netherlands medical studies have had a 'numerus fixus' and since this difference in output was not anticipated, there will be a shortage of Dutch doctors for at least a decade.

[10] In the Netherlands a growing number of illegal immigrants who are HIV-infected are already being treated with multiple drug treatment. In The Hague 37% of patients on HIV multiple drug treatment have come from Third World countries. (P. van Leeuwen, GGD Den Haag, November 2000)

Dutch hospital, had on children. They had serious problems readjusting to their own surroundings after all the attention, presents and a different lifestyle. Quite soon the policy was changed to plastic surgery in the country of origin. Many children and adults can receive the necessary medical treatment for a fraction of the total costs of one child in the Netherlands without the aforementioned side-effects.

In discussions on this subject the key issue seems to be the following: is one allowed to calculate the costs involved, or can emotion not be quantified. We all know that the money used to cure that one patient would have made a tremendous difference for the community of origin as a whole, if and when those funds could have been used for that purpose. But indeed, human nature will never find the balance between emotio and ratio.

One of the other articles included in this volume mentions the far superior treatment of mental problems, also those caused by war experiences, in or near the country of origin. Not only are the results much better, far more people can helped.[11] This is an example of a number of diseases and illnesses that can be perfectly treated by qualified medical staff in developing countries. The appearance of the hospital buildings is often more obvious to the eye than the quality of the treatment given.

G. A NEW PHENOMENON

In the paragraph above I maintained that treatment in the country of origin can be beneficial for the patient in question. The strengthening of health care in the Third World should therefore be given high priority. However, the latest trend in health services, and this is certainly so in the Netherlands, is to hire personnel from Third World countries. This is to be regretted for the following reasons:

- it lures away badly needed personnel from the very countries where such medical staff may, relatively speaking, have a greater impact than in the West (e.g. a South African nurse will work in the Netherlands probably far under his/her capacity and expertise, in other words resulting in a waste of human resources);[12]

[11] An interesting development is the request by general practitioners to be provided with expert Bosnian psychiatrists to assist in cases concerning Bosnian refugees and asylum seekers enjoying temporary protection in the Netherlands. It would indeed be more logical to work towards an early repatriation of the patient involved (if such repatriation is indeed feasible for security reasons) and to allow the patient to participate in Bosnia-based PTSD programmes.

[12] This point needs some explanation for those not accustomed with the health care systems of developing countries. Nurses in developing countries, due to the lack of more qualified medical staff, are often far more involved in curing, i.e. diagnosing illnesses and prescribing treatment than in the developed countries, – and understandably so.

– the idea that these employees would be eager to return upon having been employed for just a couple of years is contrary to what most migration experts have experienced (except for the fairly effective Swiss system where no one is allowed to work for longer than 9 months, and may only return 3 months later, i.e. they are forced to spend three months back in the country of origin);
– the dog bites tail theory becomes true: the number of third country nationals needing medical services in a country like the Netherlands is significant;[13] moreover, 'medical tourism' has become a trend (compare the differences in the access to care (not to mention: cure) between e.g. South Africa and Western Europe), and in order to provide the necessary care, additional staff will be imported, which will result in lower levels of care in the country of origin, which will in turn generate an increased search for care outside the country, etcetera, etcetera;[14]
– it neglects the relevance of markets (salaries for medical personnel should increase if there is a need for such employees);
– it tries to hide the failures in the educational and training systems whereby more emphasis should have been placed on the training of relevant experts (both physicians per se and the supporting medical staff)

If the trend were not to stop, and if indeed such an exchange of medical staff were to be looked upon as a result of globalization patterns, then it could be submitted that such practices would only be acceptable if the receiving country would ensure that e.g. for every medic hired, two or even better three medical staff would be trained and educated; i.e. the country of destination commits itself to ensuring the training (including funds plus overheads) of double or triple the number of such persons hired. Compared with the costs now being expended in order to find medical staff this could even be cheaper in the long run.

H. CONCLUSION

Knowledge concerning health migration is very limited and deserves to be intensified. All the various aspects need to be taken into account, but it should be underlined that emotion is not the best of guides. Emotion can often be a good guide in health care, but it is certainly not the only such guide. The realities of the world should be taken into consideration, not only one's ideology as to how it should be.

---

[13] Statistics show that the newly arrived have a significantly higher presence in the waiting rooms of both the general practitioner and the hospitals than the rest of the populace.

[14] A most remarkable recent development concerns the wish by many immigrants to undergo medical treatment in their country of origin. This is particularly true for the elderly and patients and the terminally ill. Under the present health insurance rules, this is difficult to accomplish, but steps are now undertaken to look into this logical yet remarkable development, which also should have an impact on the general idea re care and cure in the Third World (Volkskrant, 7 December 2000)

The price to pay for avoiding political discussions on this subject could be twofold: the breakdown of the health insurance system in the developed countries and important time and means to improve the infrastructure of the health care in developing countries being lost. Global patterns are not to be denied. Yet communities alone are responsible for the well-being of their community. It is in that context that solutions need to be found. An open health-migration policy and practice are bound to result in chaos and may well in the end result in the breakdown of, for example, the socio-democratic social welfare system. It is questionable whether one should strive for such an objective.

3. CROSS-BORDER SERVICES: THE MAASTRICHT TRIANGLE

Herbert Hermans and André den Exter

(In order to appreciate cross-border activities when it comes to the seeking for and provision of health services, it is of paramount importance to note that even within the European Union with its many agreements and its extremely high level of cooperation, such cross-border features are very rare. On behalf of the European Commission, a Cross-Border Health Care Project was undertaken in order to explore how citizens living in the 'Euregio Meuse-Rhine', the area between Aix-la-Chapelle (Aachen), Liege and Maastricht, can obtain improved access to health services in the Member States concerned: Belgium, Germany and the Netherlands. In that project, the main attention was focused on practical issues of cross-border health care. First results have shown that the new cross-border health alliances have resulted in improved possibilities for patients to have access to more health care facilities than before. In this way the creation of health care alliances could also be an example for future collaboration between the countries in Western, Central and Eastern Europe. This article also analyses the rights of patients to cross-border care in the Euregion.)[15]

[15] Based on 'Cross-border Alliances in Health Care: International Co-operation between Health Insurers and Providers in the 'Euregio Meuse-Rhine', Croatian Medical Journal, Vol 40, No. 2, June 1999, pp. 266-272; the text has been slightly adapted to this Volume and most footnotes had to be deleted for reasons of space or were alternatively included in the text.

INTRODUCTION

(...) The project [concerned] aimed at creating international co-operation between insurers and providers and to resolve impediments to the free movement of persons. In this project an alliance between hospitals and (social) health care insurers (sickness funds) has been created in order to investigate and stimulate existing and future possibilities for patients and insured persons in relation to cross-border health care. (...)

The operational programme was subdivided into several subprojects which have been undertaken by the participants in the alliance during the programme. This programme was partly based upon previous research also (partly) funded by the Interreg (I) programme of the European Union. In that earlier programme comprehensive descriptive analytical work was carried out which focused on a description of health care indicators at the national level for the three member states, a description of the national hospital financing systems, an analysis of cross-border care issues as well as the extent of care between hospitals joining the project and a comparative analysis of hospital care on the basis of patient data.

BACKGROUNDS AND CHARACTERISTICS

The 'Euregio Meuse-Rhine', is one of the 40 Euregions in the European Union,as defined by the European Community (EC). It involves parts of Belgium, Germany and the Netherlands and, moreover, three languages: Dutch, German and French. Approximately 3.7 million people live in this Euregion and its central area is quite densely populated. More specifically, it consists of parts of the Dutch province of Limburg (Middle and South Limburg); the Province of Limburg (Belgium); the Province of Liège, including the German speaking community, and the former district of the federal state Aachen ('ehemalig Regierungsbezirk Aachen' in Germany).

Convergence of health care systems could be seen as a long-term trend. Due to the growing importance of cost-containment in the member states, competition within national health care systems is also increasing. This places purchasers of care and insurers on an international scale.

CREATING THE ALLIANCE

In the last decade, developments in the health care sector of the European countries working together in the 'Euregio Meuse-Rhine' have taken place at a great pace. Cost control, increases in the scale of technological developments and specialised care dominate the health care debate.[16] Health care providers have to adapt their knowledge and skills to the changing circumstances of cross-border health care for patients and the pace of technological progress. Besides primary care providers, the organization and finance of secondary care providers will experience substantial changes in the three collaborating countries in the very near future. These, and the aforementioned changes, stimulate contractual relationships between purchasers (Dutch sickness funds, German Krankenkassen and Belgian mutualities) and providers to form new alliances (e.g., concerning agreements and contracts relating to highly specialized clinical care and the transborder use of medical equipment and personnel). Despite the existing divergences, the need for cost containment and the enhancement of the quality of care will also impel actors to co-operate with each other.

In the 'Euregio Meuse-Rhine' health care providers on the one hand, and health care insurers (sickness funds) on the other, have collaborated during the past decade.[17] This close cooperation has built the framework for the new health care alliance in the Euregion.

THE THEORETICAL PERSPECTIVE OF COUNTERVAILING POWERS

This development towards a new kind of health care alliance could be seen in the theoretical perspective of countervailing powers. John Kenneth Galbraith introduced the theory of 'countervailing power' in his 'American Capitalism', 1952. The establishment of more and more permanent groups that stand ready to pressure corporations have become the most important countervailing power to corporations in the United States. Light et al. transferred this concept into the health care sector by recognizing several parties, not merely buyers and sellers in health care. In his opinion, this concept opens the door to alliances between two or more parties. Patients and consumers have so far had hardly any voice in how health care is organized, prioritized, funded and monitored. However, patients and their agents (e.g. in some cases health insurers and in other cases health care providers) are increasingly behaving like well-informed consumers, who want to have access to the best possible and available medical care.[18] Therefore changes in the organization, rules and realization of patients' rights to cross-border care are necessary. A first change in the concept of organizing health care is the strengthen-

[16] Dreiländertreffen Foundation, Home Care for the Cancer Patient. Main points of an inventory in the Euregion Maas-Rijn. (Dreiländertreffen Foundation, Maastricht: 1995).

[17] B. Starmans, R. Leidl, G. Rhodes, "A comparative study on cross-border hospital care in the Euregio MeuseRhine, *European Journal of Public Health* (1997; 7, 3 Supplement): 33-41.

[18] D. Light, Countervailing powers. A framework for professions in transition. In: T. Johnson, G. Larkin, M. Saks editors. Health professions and the State in Europe. (London/New York: Routledge, 1995):25-41; and K. Kesteloot et al., "The reimbursement of the expenses for medical treatment received by 'transnational' patients in EU-countries". *Health Policy,* (1995;33): 43-57.

ing of the position and the influence of patients/insured persons, so that they can bring more balance into the health care system by countering the influence of health care professionals on decision-making. Basic principles and priorities for managing change are the following:

- the citizen's voice and choice should make as significant a contribution to shaping health care services as the decisions taken at other levels of economic, managerial and professional decision-making;
- the citizen's voice should be heard on issues such as the content of health care, contracting, the quality of services in the providers/patient relationship, the management of waiting lists and the handling of complaints;
- the exercise of choice and of other patients' rights, require extensive, accurate and timely information and education. This entails access to publicly verified information on health services' performance.

In addition to these principles and priorities the basic needs of patients/insured persons and a simplification of the existing rules (less bureaucracy) relating to cross-border care have been chosen as benchmarks for the creation of the cross-border health care alliance in the Euregion.

FROM CONTRACTING TO EFFECTIVE RELATIONSHIPS

The newly-formed health care alliance focuses on long-term success, moving from the mechanics of merely contracting to new relationships between purchasers, providers, governments, patients (-organizations), the insured persons and (other) health care authorities. Agreement on the new health care alliance was difficult because the participants not only had to cross real (physical) borders but also even more difficult cultural borders and had to move from (in most cases) an adversarial (contractual) approach to one based upon effective relationships. In several Western European countries, including in particular Germany and the Netherlands, the introduction of market forces was the result of the belief that choice, efficiency and quality within the health care system would be enhanced by competition between provider units for contracts from the purchasers, and the purchaser-provider relationship should ensure that providers are challenged to meet purchaser objectives, and that they employ innovative and creative approaches in this direction The necessary involvement of consumers, previously on the periphery of the contracting process adds a further dimension to the prioritization of resources.

The emphasis on effective relationships takes the focus of the mechanism of contract sophistication and places it on health gain. To reach agreements between purchasers and providers appeared to be time-consuming due to resistance among the different participating groups, and individuals in particular, in the complicated transnational health care arena. All actors in this health care arena were beginning to recognize that earlier solutions are inadequate because they do not satisfy the criteria of being effective (attaining health care policy objectives), efficient (doing so at the lowest possible cost) and equitable (i.e. sharing the burden among the members of a target group in a fair manner). New answers were needed that do satisfy these criteria. Such a shift was only possible by means of all actors together bringing their expertise into the programme. However, working together in this programme could only work under strict and limited conditions. It had to offer advantages to all parties; safeguards had to be taken for third parties, and agreements had to be made within the decision-making structure of the programme. These decisions should have binding effects on all parties. In developing the programme structure and creating the alliance, process is often as important as content. Therefore a great deal of time has been invested in creating the structure of the health care alliance.(...)

METHODOLOGY AND SUBPROJECTS

Health care is structured differently in the neighbouring countries of this Euregion. Therefore the initiators decided to join forces and work together on the improvement of the present situation concerning cross-border care. For the inventory of the current situation three important information sources have been used. First of all, information has been gathered by a literature study and completed by a study of the relevant legal sources (national and international legislation and agreements, case law and legal doctrine). The second information source for the inventory were surveys relating to the main issues of different subprojects. Questionnaires were developed and distributed among patients and insured persons at the same time that they received their authorization for cross-border health care. The third information source, and perhaps the most important in this programme, was the stimulation of the (improvement of) involvement by participating and non-participating health care practitioners, hospitals and governmental and non-governmental authorities. So far, the project has been conducted as a form of action research with a strong component for creating and strengthening health care alliances. Concrete action-research pilots have been started upon the initiative of providers for the reduction of waiting lists for patients concerning specific health care provisions like Ophthalmology and Orthopaedia. These projects have been agreed upon by both co-operating health insurers and providers. (...)

The programme was divided into several subprojects, which had to be elaborated in 2 years. The first subproject involves an inventory of the current situation of Traumatology, Ambulance Care and Emergency Care. In this project, mainly carried out by the participating hospitals, a platform of involved health care practitioners, hospitals and competent authorities was created in order to investigate and level any existing barriers to cross-border ambulance care, trauma care and emergency care.

A second subproject was introduced by transforming an existing project in the Netherlands called 'Zorg op Maat' (Tailor-made Care) into the Interreg II programme on a reciprocal basis. In the existing project 'Zorg op Maat' a registration system for the existing cross-border health care had been created by monitoring Dutch patients who received pre-authorised care in the neighbouring countries on an experimental basis in which the existing regulations (E112) were eased (by creating an E112+). (...) In the reciprocal programme not only Dutch patients were monitored but Belgian and German patients also.

The third subproject dealt with the similarities and differences in health insurance schemes of the different countries as well as co-payments with regard to the different health services patients are entitled to under this programme.

The fourth subproject included the investigation into the possibilities for cross-border health care based on the principle of reciprocity. In this subproject high care technologies should be made accessible to patients coming from the other parts of participating countries in the Euregion. For instance Oncology treatments for children in Germany, the Netherlands and Belgium at the cooperating hospitals in Aachen, Maastricht, Liège and Genk (for Belgian, German and Dutch patients), kidney-dialysis (in particular for Dutch patients) and Rehabilitation facilities (for Belgian and German patients) in Hoensbroek in the Netherlands. Further, an analysis of the differences in the regulation, financing and quality of medical devices in the three countries was undertaken. In particular, health insurers (sickness funds) are interested in purchasing medical devices in the other participating countries for their insured persons.

Finally, concrete improvements in transparency have been elaborated for instance in the case of co-payments which have to be paid by patients crossing the borders of the Euregion. In Belgium it is sometimes quiet unclear for foreigners, and even for Belgian insured perons, which co-payments have to be paid for which health care benefits. The programme has stimulated sickness funds (mutualities) to develop lists of contracted or preferred providers (practitioners/medical specialists) and which (additional) prices for co-payments of health care services can be expected for which health care benefits.

BASIC RIGHTS OF PATIENTS TO CROSS-BORDER CARE IN THE EUREGION

Strengthening the position and influence of patients/insured persons was chosen as one of the priorities for the creation of the cross-border alliance in the Euregion. The rights of patients to receive health care in the other participating countries of the Euregion are dependent upon the rights of patients as entrenched in the legislation of the three states and the recognition of these rights in international (particularly European) legislation.

The legal system of the state itself assures patients of a certain level of access to medical care. The claimed 'right to health care abroad' is regulated by a complex web of laws and regulations which govern the action of patients, health care providers, governments and 'third-party payers'. These laws and regulations, both on a national and European level, serve diverse purposes. The most important of these is to strike a balance between individual freedoms and public needs and interests.

The interpretation of these laws and regulations, which allow patients to receive treatment in other EU states, reflects the balance between the different governments' desires to both help patients and to realise individual patient rights and the general social desire to allocate and utilise resources efficiently both within and between the EU health care systems.

Within the Interreg II programme a general trend can be distinguished which seeks to reaffirm the right to treatment and care abroad, to adequate social cover (including access to foreign care) and adequate information concerning the available health services in the other member states. In other words, this implies the existence of a right to benefit from the supply of health care facilities within the whole 'Euregio Meuse-Rhine'. This right forms the basis of the rights for patients to cross-border health care in the Euregion.

Despite these established principles, it is undeniable that users' expectations in the different countries cannot be completely met. Access to care is limited by choices that have been made in the project and treatments that have been postponed by existing waiting lists (in particular in the Netherlands). This is attested by several petitions and claims made by patients, particularly in emergency cases, to receive treatment outside their country of origin.

The central position of the patient in the programme has been stressed in working papers and basic documents. In specific situations administrative procedures and covenants are still required because (until recently) health insurers and providers (in most cases) had to be authorised by governments to permit patients to be treated abroad. Multilateral and bilateral agreements were also the proper instruments for the regulation of rights in the legal social security systems.

The social dimension of the right of access to care means a right to benefit from the supply of health services. This right, based upon the administrative legislation of the different Euregion member states, forms the basis of the right of patients to cross-border health care in the Euregion. The patients are dependent upon those benefits available within the particular health care system and the entitlements deriving from public health care legislation. In the Treaty of the European Communities (EC Treaty), the free movement of goods, services, capital and persons is regulated. The law of the EC rests on the basic principles of freedom and equality, non-discrimination, proportionality and subsidiarity. They find expression in the EC Treaty's provisions on the free movement of goods and workers between member states, on the co-ordination of national social security systems and on the provision of services.

THE CRUCIAL ROLE OF THE COURT OF JUSTICE OF THE EUROPEAN COMMUNITIES

The Court of Justice of the European Communities has played an important role in this respect in realizing patients' rights and entitlements in the Euregion. It has produced a number of cases in which common rules and principles have been established that also apply to migration and cross-border care within the Euregion. Workers and the self-employed (according to the Court's rulings this also includes unemployed economically inactive persons with voluntary insurance and part-time workers) and their family members have a fairly wide coverage under EC law co-ordinated according to EC regulations. In practice, the competent institutions in the member states did not appear to be reluctant to authorise treatment in the other states of the EU. However, the Court has consistently held that the free movement of workers would be frustrated if a migrant were to lose social security benefits, including health care benefits, guaranteed under the law of a member state. The rights of patients are based upon the free movement both of persons and services. Within the context of the free movement of services (defined by Articles 59 and 60 of the EC Treaty), the case law of the Court of Justice of the European Communities in the *Luisi* and *Carbone* cases from 1984, also extended the coverage to cases where it is not the person providing the services who moves, but the person who wishes to receive the service does so by moving to the state where the provider is established. This interpretation allows tourists, recipients of medical treatment and persons on study and business travel to be covered by regulations relating to the free provision of services. (...)

RIGHTS OF PATIENTS IN THE 'EUREGIO MEUSE-RHINE'

The EU regulations mentioned above establish conditions under which an E112 cannot be refused by the competent national authorities. The participating countries in the Euregion more or less follow the EU rules.

To obtain (a reimbursement of the costs of) medical treatment in another Euregion member state the patient must, in most cases, still obtain the approval of a competent health insurer (third-party payer). In the Euregion, starting in the Netherlands, patients received an extended authorization (during the time-span of the project 'Zorg op Maat') for treatments abroad. Patients in Germany and Belgium could be referred subject to the same conditions under which the E112 forms were issued. Patients had to follow different procedures in the various Euregion member states to obtain an E112 form. Not only did the procedures vary from country to country, but the criteria to acquire authorization were also different in the participating member states. The programme focused on eliminating these differences and on improving the process of having access to health care services abroad.

When and how authorization to receive treatment in another EU member state was granted was (until recently) dependent on the coverage criteria for health insurance within the country of stay. Because of the judgements of the Court of the European Communities the free movement of goods and the freedom to provide services is not absolute and controlling health expenditure must be taken into consideration.

Within each health care system of the Euregion member states, rules have been developed to limit coverage for services under public or private insurance. These rules refer to 'screening criteria' or 'referral criteria' which are (so far) also dependent on relevant clinical indications or findings. Patients who wish to obtain services having failed to meet the relevant criteria of the insurer in their own member state, generally had to do so at their own expense. However, patients (usually through their physicians) could attempt to obtain special authorization from designated neutral physicians. In effect they pleaded 'extenuating circumstances' and requested an exemption from the rules. Similar coverage criteria were in place for in-patient acute medical, surgical or psychiatric treatment.

One can readily see that the thresholds contained in the coverage rules largely determined the number of patients who received the desired care under the health insurance of the member states. As such, these rules served to balance the patients' freedom to obtain desired services against the overall costs imposed on the beneficiaries of the health care system as a whole.

The above-mentioned procedures and criteria differed a great deal across the Euregion member states. To improve the confusing situation, a general outline of new procedures have been described in the programme. In the health care systems of the Euregion member states, a patient with a perceived health need for a particular treatment could seek the advice of a professional, generally a physician or another provider who counsels the patient. Generally, this must be done within the context of the health insurance coverage of the patient.

The next step in the process is for the provider to determine whether the patient's health insurance covers the desired procedure by reference to the criteria. If the patient's condition matches the applicable insurance rules, the procedure is covered and may be obtained within the health insurance cover. If the patient does not match these coverage rules, the patient may either forego the recommended service despite the professional's advice or may obtain the service using private funds. Alternatively, the patient and the provider may elect to appeal for coverage within the health insurance, setting forth their reasons to an ostensibly neutral third party physician on whose opinion the desired procedure should be provided. A judgement that the service should not be provided is, as a rule, not final and can be appealed against by the patient to a second-level judge or court which can either uphold or overturn the denial of coverage.

CONCLUSIONS AND FUTURE PERSPECTIVES

First results have shown that the new cross-border health alliances have resulted in improved possibilities for patients to have access to more health care facilities than before. Alliances between health insurers and providers have been approved and facilitated by the different governmental organizations which are also involved in this project.

This article has also analyzed the rights of patients to cross-border care in a Euregion. Although the EU and the EC Treaty form a narrow legal basis for the realization of patients' rights, the impacts of EC regulations and EC Court decisions are considerable, particularly because of the most recent decision in the *Decker* and *Kohll* cases of the Court of Justice of the European Communities. In the case of cross-border health care, a balance can be found between the rights and the criteria by which to allow patients, sometimes on the basis of pre-authorized medical (hospital) care in other cases on the basis of ambulatory care, to receive treatment in other Euregion countries. This could also be an example of future collaboration between the present member states of the European Union and the countries in Central and Eastern Europe.

Areas of tension can be found in the practical realization of the rights of patients to be treated in other Euregion member states. The rules of authorization were different and the interpretation of these rules also varied from state to state. A solution to these problems, which have been complicated by the recent European Court decisions, can be found in the creation of a more uniform and simple procedure. Ultimately, the main purpose of the programme is to strengthen the position and the influence of the patient so as to stimulate and to create real possibilities for cross-border health care for social insured patients not only in the 'Euregio Meuse-Rhine' but also within the future perspective of collaboration between the countries in Western, Central and Eastern Europe. Euregions could be a new and appealing platform by which to realize patients' rights. Building up the mentioned alliances could also form a practical first step in this direction.

MIGRATION HEALTH

Monique Besseling

In this contribution attention will be paid to a specific link between migration and health. Apart from the many aspects that have been dealt with elsewhere in this Handbook, this contribution focuses on the health risks related to people on the move and to mobile populations in general.

"Increasingly it is being recognized that security threats are not only external, but also internal. They cover not only military aspects but also political, social and economic concerns, such as poverty and unemployment, population explosion and environmental degradation, resurgent nationalism and social tensions, uncontrolled migration and coerced displacement, the proliferation of narcotics, crime and small arms."[1]

With the fall of the Berlin Wall and the end of the Cold War, the notion of "international security" carries a whole new meaning. The end of the Cold War has generated a chain of new and diverse population displacements, translocations and movements. It has produced essential shifts in both the course and procedure of resettling refugee populations resulting from political conflict.[2]

We are being increasingly confronted with a mobile population. "Immigrants hunt for economic opportunities in distant countries, refugees and displaced persons are forced to move across international borders while those who seek asylum use difficult or unorthodox means to gain access to foreign shores; foreign students seek educational opportunities outside of their home country; the number of tourist and short-term visitors continues to grow in both number and

---

[1] Stockholm International Peace Research Institute. "International Security and Refugee Problems After the Cold War: Assuring the Security of People: the Humanitarian Challenge of the 21st Century." *Olof Palme Memorial Lecture by Mrs. Sadako Ogata*. Stockholm, June 1995.

[2] International Organization for Migration. "Migration and Health in the Year 2000 – Whither The Future?" *Migration and Health Newsletter*. Jan. 2000: 1 (Much of what follows has been based on the International Organization for Migration [IOM] Newsletters, and, in general, due to a lack of space, footnotes have been limited to an absolute minimum).

P.J. van Krieken (Ed.), Health, Migration and Return

diversity; and migrant workers move to new employment opportunities in increasing numbers."[3] The growing scale of migratory movements poses new questions concerning health both in the country which one leaves, and at the same time in the receiving country. "Migrants are particularly vulnerable to health problems. Many migrants and refugees ... suffer from communicable diseases such as tuberculosis or hepatitis, as well as respiratory diseases associated with poor nutrition, cold, overcrowding, inadequate sanitation, water supply and housing, compounded by limited access to health care."[4]

Throughout the 20th century the world made great progress in microbiology, immunology, public health, vector control and clinical medicine which assured greater regulation of those infections that caused mass illnesses and deaths. Shortly thereafter came advances in the area of "virology, pharmacology, vaccine development and epidemiology appeared to be the harbingers of the end of the spectre of epidemic disease, exemplified by the actual elimination of Smallpox from the globe." Although the past century has shown great advances in know-how, technology and the specific characteristics of certain illnesses, infectious disease remains a threat to many segments of people in this world.

As the author L.B. Reichman puts it "the single infectious disease responsible for the largest number of deaths worldwide is tuberculosis. The irony associated with this fact does not result from the persistent threat of unknown or unusually complicated infections but rather that the largest cause of mortality is a disease that is both treatable and preventable. If humanity cannot deal effectively with infections that it understands and can treat, how will it deal with the new and emerging infectious disease threats where the armamentarium of control measures is more limited?"[5]

The International Organization for Migration states that, for numerous reasons, the epidemiology and regulation of quite a few communicable illnesses is linked to many of the same factors that influence migration. Features which support the occurrence of a high concentration of certain infectious diseases such as overcrowding, deforestation, urbanization, climate change, poverty, natural and civil disasters and the lack of access to health care, are also characteristics that encourage, maintain or nourish the migratory movements of groups of

---

[3] "People on the Move: New Thinking on Migration Health". *A Discussion Paper*. Prepared by: Global Surveillance and Field Epidemiology Health Canada and Health Policy Division Citizenship and Immigration Canada with the assistance of The Metropolis Project. Dec. 5-7, 1999: 2, hereinafter cited as *Discussion Paper*.

[4] Council of Europe, Parliamentary Assembly, Committee on Migration, Refugees and Demography. Rapporteur: Lord Ponsonby. "*Health Conditions of Migrants and Refugees in Europe*." 9 Feb. 2000, doc. 8650 (hereinafter quoted as *Ponsonby Report*).

[5] Reichman LB. "Tuberculosis elimination – What' to stop us", *Tubercle and Lung Disease*, 77:1 1996. Supplement. Report of Plenary Session. Conference on Global Health and the Annual Meeting of the International Union Against Tuberculosis and Lung Disease (IUATLID) Paris, France 2-5 October 1996, as quoted in the IOM Newsletter, op. cit., p. 1.

people. In addition, another important factor influencing migration is the increasing regional disparities the effectiveness in disease control. As a result the differences in the incidence and prevalence of infectious diseases between regions of the world and between social and economic strata of groups of individuals are significant. The relationship between infectious disease control and the mobility of people between regions of high and low prevalence has historically guided much of the interest and practice of organized quarantine and migration health activity.

Throughout this contribution the term migration health will refer to the definition given by the discussion paper entitled "People on the Move: New Thinking on Migration Health" that resulted from the 1999 symposium. "Migration health refers to the health issues, conditions and risks related to mobile populations, whether they be regular or irregular immigrants, refugees, asylum seekers, visitors, students, temporary workers, travelers, or returning nationals. Migration health affects migrants, their families and communities, the populations of their country of origin, and the destination country or countries."

Increasing migration goes hand in hand with the need for new and improved health policies to deal with the challenges of migration health. It was only ten years ago in February 1990, when the International Organization of Migration and the World Health Organization co-sponsored the Migration Medicine Seminar, which was "the first international conference on the health needs of refugees, migrant workers, and other uprooted people and long-term travelers."[6] Over the past decade, globalization and integration, in addition to technological advancement have all increased the mobility of populations. The magnitude of this movement creates greater public health risks. Migratory movements were until recently reasonably foreseeable, as the above-mentioned discussion paper (1999) describes; today, "cycles of change in immigration patterns are measured in months and years instead of decades, making it more difficult to anticipate health risks and needs and plan responses in advance. As well, greater political instability results in sudden and less predictable refugee "surges" often requiring immediate asylum, and presenting urgent health needs." ... "The past ten years have seen regional and global economic successes as well as episodes of chaos and concern. These social, financial and political events have been accompanied by parallel advances and challenges in health, science and medicine."

The dilemmas and issues raised at the Migration Medicine seminar a decade ago continue to be tackled as new issues arise. "The concept of Migration Medicine, used at the seminar in 1990, has been replaced by the more comprehensive Migration Health approach. The recognition of the importance of health as opposed to the traditional focus on medicine or disease has been one of

---

[6] International Organization for Migration. "Migration and Health in the Year 2000 – Whither The Future?" *Migration and Health Newsletter.* Jan. 2000: 1.

the major changes in the manner in which these issues are addressed in migrants and mobile populations." The diseases discussed at the 1990 seminar included tuberculosis, leprosy, STDs, hepatitis and HIV and these are all still of crucial importance today. However, the focus on specific diseases has expanded in the direction of, for example, "the relationships between health and in its broader context poverty, discrimination, vulnerability, education and access to services." Therefore the historical method of straightforward identification and management of disease in a variety of populations has stretched to incorporate efforts to better comprehend and restructure the connected social, educational and economic issues that are the eventual sources of the particular diseases.[7]

Immigration medical screening can be split into two groups, "the first group is those procedures and practices proposed to identify and manage or exclude infectious diseases of public health importance. Examples of diseases in this group include tuberculosis, sexually transmitted diseases, some viral hepatities, and some parasitic infections. The second major category of illness and disease for which screening is undertaken is less commonly practiced but is a major component of migration health programs in some nations with national health insurance programs such as Canada and Australia. In these areas, immigration medical screening is undertaken to identify illness and disease that may be costly or complicated to treat. The rationale presented by nations that screen immigrants for these diseases is that the admission of large numbers of migrants with illnesses of this type may imbalance or affect the allocation of scarce or costly medical resources." Many countries are witnessing increases in migration with the goal of health treatment or the treatment of ill-health or diseases. As a consequence the pressure on the health care system increases. "However between the 1960s and 1990s medical health screening for public health reasons assumed a reduced level of importance. Interest in the practice waned and fewer recourses were devoted to the practice."[8]

The IOM has discussed the fact that traditional medical screening is moving away from the infectious disease basis which was common in 1990. It has moved from disease detection for the purpose of denying or delaying admission to a more epidemiological and public health balanced approach of screening. The more calculated, empirical method will allow for an improved management and prevention of adverse outcomes, be they clinical or economic.

Concerns for infectious diseases in mobile populations will however remain. Tuberculosis remains the most serious infectious disease associated with immigration health. The different levels of diseases such as malaria, hepatitis C and HIV continue to ensure interest and attention in terms of their potential to

[7] International Organization for Migration. "Migration and Health in the Year 2000 – Whither The Future?" *Migration and Health Newsletter*. Jan. 2000: 1.

[8] International Organization for Migration. "Immigration Medical Screening: A Move Towards Public Health Risk Management". *Migration and Health Newsletter*. Feb. 2000: 1.

affect the health of both the migrants and the communities within which they transfer and live. The most important change, however, has been the move towards a less restrictive method of dealing with the above mentioned diseases. "In 1999 for example, the United States provided easier access to waivers for HIV positive refugees which would allow them to resettle in spite of the infection. Earlier in the decade, Canada has waived its admission restrictions for refugees suffering from illnesses which they could have been denied entry on the basis of excessive demand for health or social services."[9]

In 1998 the International Center for Migration and Health (ICMH), completed an evaluation of health and health care consequences of migration within and into the European Union. This analysis, funded by the European Commission, concluded that contagious diseases ought to remain a concern. "For example, the prevalence of immigrant related TB is increasing noticeably in many parts of the EU. One of the many issues is many countries no longer routinely offer screening and treatment to newcomers, even if they are arriving from countries with high TB profiles."[10]

The February 2000 report entitled "Health Conditions of Migrants and Refugees in Europe" prepared by the Committee on Migration, Refugees and Demography, states that even though there is little evidence that these diseases present a major threat for the receiving communities, the danger of spreading within migrant communities is a problem. "Migrants tend to move into social economic environments that continue to expose them to poverty related diseases. Thus even in countries such as the Netherlands, Austria, France, Italy, Spain and Portugal, substandard housing, overcrowding and poor sanitation are common. Because migrants also tend to remain socially excluded (at least initially) from host societies, they often fail to come into contact with, or effectively use, otherwise available health care services. This is especially marked in the case of migrants who move for short-term work, and even more so for "unofficial" migrants."[11]

In addition, maternal and child health has also become a major concern in the context of immigration, and in many EU countries pregnancy and perinatal health indicators among immigrant groups call for new attitudes and approaches to protecting the health of immigrant women and children.[12]

"In the Netherlands, the change from a country with net emigration to one with immigration has resulted in decreased literacy rates, increased mortality

---

[9] International Organization for Migration. "Migration and Health in the Year 2000 – Whither The Future?" *Migration and Health Newsletter*. Jan. 2000: 2.

[10] International Organization for Migration. "The Migrant as Traveler" *Migration and Health Newsletter* Jan. 1998: 5

[11] *Ponsonby Report*, see above n. 4.

[12] International Organization for Migration. "The Migrant as Traveler" *Migration and Health Newsletter* Jan. 1998: 5

rates for children under five years of age and decreased life expectancy for the population living in Amsterdam."[13]

Health Canada and Citizenship Immigration Canada, with the assistance of the Metropolis Project, organized a symposium in 1999 to tackle emerging trends and issues evolving from increasing mobility. The goal of the symposium was to discuss novel ideas and paradigms for migration health, to confront existing notions and restrictions or shortcomings of migration and quarantine legislation, and to look forward to new developments in the years ahead. For example, the Discussion Paper on the symposium states that in 1999 Canada admitted over 7,000 Kosovars, at first 5,000 being offered a temporary safe haven and, according to the medical screening results, the rate of infectious tuberculosis in this group was approximately 22 times the rate in the resident Canadian population.

Many countries have had to hastily deal with an inflow of refugees or asylum seekers; in Canada[14], for example, this has resulted in uneven screening and missed opportunities to offer early treatment. "In August 2000, 240 desperate refugees were airlifted to Quebec from a refugee camp in a highly malarious[15] area on the border of Kenya and Burundi. Shortly after arrival, 13 cases of acute malaria caused by three species of malaria occurred in 11 different communities. None of the refugees were screened for malaria infection."[16]

In 1997 a study entitled, *Prevalence of Hepatitis B, C, and D Markers in Sub-Saharan African Immigrants*, published by the *Journal of Clinical Gastroenteral*, 25(4) 1997, focused on the prevalence of viral hepatitis A, B and C (HAV, HBV, HCV, respectively) in different parts of the world and the association between increasing migration and population mobility with the movement of disease between areas of different prevalence. They concluded that an association could be made between migration and population mobility, and the movement of disease between areas. "The authors noted the public health importance of these diseases as many illegal or irregular migrants have no access to the National

---

[13] *Discussion Paper* (see n. 3) on p. 5.

[14] Canada is starting to increasingly acknowledge the influence of health challenges associated with migrating peoples. The Discussion Paper stated: "In Toronto, approximately 3% of the tuberculosis isolates are now multiple-drug resistant (MDR-TB) from foreign-born persons. This rate MDR-TB places the city on par with some of the world's least developed nations. The increase in irregular arrivals through illegal trafficking will exacerbate the problems. The prevalence of infectious hepatitis B in one boatload of Chinese "boat people" who arrived in 1999 was 34% compared with approximately 0.01% in the resident Canadian population."

[15] It is estimated that malaria kills one child every thirty seconds. Barbara Crossette, "UN and World Bank Unite to Wage War on Malaria", N.Y. Times, Oct. 31, 1998.

[16] "People on the Move: New Thinking on Migration Health". *A Discussion Paper*. Prepared by: Global Surveillance and Field Epidemiology Health Canada and Health Policy Division Citizenship and Immigration Canada with the assistance of The Metropolis Project. Dec. 5-7, 1999: 5.

Public Health systems and there are no specific care programs designed for this group, they elude detection and control of contagious diseases." [17]

A key development during the past ten years has been the realization that health in moving and migratory populations is no longer exclusively the concern of those who traditionally work with immigrants and refugees, namely the national quarantine services and immigration health officers. A consequence of globalization and an increasingly mobile labour force is the greater need for "health care providers, social scientists, health planners, policy makers, and medical educators"[18] to unravel and better comprehend the health care issues associated with moving masses. This need has led to a vast amount of new information, research and studies on migration health.

The proceedings of the above-mentioned 1999 symposium include new directions in the approach to migration health. It claims that a new course in migration health is needed, one with a twofold purpose, on the one hand shielding the health of the receiving population and, on the other, improving the health of the migrating population. To sustain the health of both populations, legislation, guidelines and agendas should improve the determinants of health, encourage good health and avert ill-health conditions and illnesses, and include health safety procedures explicit to migrant populations.

In numerous regions of the world there are many projects underway that involve health as related to population mobility and migration. Recognizing mutual aspects that can successfully be used in different circumstances will be a constructive and an efficient strategy. Knowledge in one situation will provide an insight into another. There are numerous areas of current interest and research in the field of migration health. "They include the relationship between access to health care services by migrant and mobile populations and health outcomes, the importance of culture and ethnicity in planning and development of population health programs; and the need to better manage the consequences of moving between locations with profound disparities in health."[19]

Few countries have produced wide-ranging guidelines on migration. "Indeed even though economic pressures on countries are leading to a greater awareness of, and sensitivity to, the process of migration, as late as 1995 only 40% of countries had actually introduced policies on the subject." In the 1970s the number of countries laying down policies to limit or reduce immigration increased and, in 1995, 33 % of the countries had followed this trend. Developed countries introduced the restrictive policies in order to limit entrance. In the

---

[17] International Organization for Migration. "Immigration and Medical Screening: A Move Towards Public Health Risk Management". *Migration and Health.* Feb. 1998: 3.

[18] International Organization for Migration "Migration and Health in the Year 2000 – Whither The Future?" *Migration and Health Newsletter.* Jan. 2000: 2.

[19] "Migration and Health in the Year 2000 – Whither The Future?" *Migration and Health Newsletter.* International Organization and Migration. 1/2000

majority of countries, "legal conditions for permanent status have become more stringent and gaining citizenship has become increasingly difficult." And looking at the health perspective, only a few countries "have seen fit to ensure migrants with the type of socially and culturally tailored services they need, and in many parts of Europe there are many migrants who are falling outside the scope of existing health and social services. [T]he data indicate that because of economic and legal reasons, the housing and occupational environment of migrants often places them at risk of communicable and non-communicable health problems."[20] "Migrants and new arrivals bring with them two important health-related characteristics to their destination, firstly they reflect the epidemiological and clinical characteristics and patterns of disease and illness relative to their place of origin. Secondly, they bring with them their cultural understanding and perspectives on health, illness and treatment." The *Discussion Paper* (see note 3) proposes some new guidelines in immigration programmes and measures, and it includes, firstly, pre-migration initiatives, secondly, health interventions at and near the time of arrival and departure, thirdly, health services and support after migration and finally, research and knowledge development.

Therefore in an environment where "more than ever, unprecedented numbers of persons are on the move around the globe; when they move, microbes, including pathogens, move with them" [21] and given "the symbiosis that is inevitably created between the health of migrants and their host populations, this is an area that calls for much greater attention than it has been given to date."[22] An enhanced understanding of the health status of migrants and moving populations will be a vital part of universal health surveillance and disease management.

A wide-ranging method of migration health entails open thinking. A move forward would involve broad "legislative, procedural and program initiatives to reduce risk and enhance health."[23] New policies and agendas[24] will move past

---

[20] *Ponsonby Report* see n. 4.

[21] International Organization for Migration Annual Report 1999. "The Origins of Migration Health Services" p. 8.

[22] *Ponsonby Report* see n. 4.

[23] *Discussion Paper* see n. 3, p. 9.

[24] Council of Europe, Parliamentary Assembly, Draft Recommendation, Committee on Migration, Refugees and Demography. Rapporteur: Lord Ponsonby. "Health Conditions of Migrants and Refugees in Europe". 9 Feb. 2000.doc. 8650.

1. The growing scope of migratory movements all over the world raises specific health questions in both sending and receiving countries.

2. Migrants are particularly vulnerable to health problems. Many migrants and refugees, in particular those moving from a poor socio-econmic environment to Europe, suffer from communicable diseases such as tuberculosis or hepatitis, as well as respiratory diseases associated with poor nutrition, cold, overcrowding, and inadequate sanitation, water supply and housing, compounded by limited access to health care. →

infectious diseases towards chronic diseases, mental health, reproductive health, and the critical determinants of health such as socio-economic conditions, discrimination and integration in the host society.

---

3. Moreover, due to their vulnerable situation and to cultural obstacles in host countries, migrants and refugees appear to be more exposed than the rest of the population to other types of health problems, such as reproductive, occupational, and mental health problems.
4. Given the inevitable interdependence between the health of migrants and their host countries' populations, this issue is of general concern and should be given high importance.
5. The Assembly considers the right to health associated with access to health care to be one of the basic universal human rights and should be equally applied to all people including migrants, refugees and displaced persons.
6. The Assembly is greatly concerned that in many European countries there are migrants who fall outside the scope of existing health and social services.
7. The Assembly also expresses serious concern that few countries have developed comprehensive health policies concerning migrants and refugees. In general migrants and refuges are not provided with health services that are socially and culturally adjusted to their needs.
8. Health care provision in the context of clandestine migration is another serious problem that requires further examination.
9. Consequently, the Assembly recommends that the Committee of Ministers:
   i. Examine national laws and policies in regard to the health of migrants and refugees with a view to developing a comprehensive, harmonized approach in all member states;
   ii. Organize exchanges of experience and information on the subject between the member states, with the participation of the appropriate governmental agencies and non-governmental organizations, including migrants' and refugees' associations;
   iii. Instruct the appropriate committee to develop, in consultation with the relevant governmental and non-governmental organizations, guidelines to be addressed to the member states on the health conditions of migrants and refugees in Europe;
   iv. Foster the standardization of health screening and the criteria of its application to migrants and refugees;
   v. Review policies for the protection of migrants in the face of occupational risks;
   vi. Foster the setting up of a European system for the systematic collection and sharing of health care statistics concerning migrants and refugees;
   vii. Encourage member states:
      a. To develop specific information programs for migrants and refugees covering their rights in the field of health care and education in prevention;
      b. To help associations of migrants and refugees to promote health education by financing the provision of educational documentation and through the training of staff recruited from migrant and refugee communities;
      c. To encourage migrants and refugees to get involved in routine national and local health care and disease prevention programs;
      d. To examine more closely the problem of cultural obstacles in the way of access to health care including the question of translation/interpretation;
      e. To establish programs designed to train health care providers to be more sensitive to the needs and backgrounds of migrants and refugees.

IN NO POSITION TO HELP ASYLUM SEEKERS[1]

Jeroen Corduwener

Asylum seekers should be cared for in their own region if at all possible. Not because they are not welcome in the Netherlands, but because Dutch society seems unable to provide them with the reception they deserve. Joop de Jong, Professor of Mental Health and Culture at the Vrije Universiteit, Amsterdam, is making desperate efforts to convince the Dutch government to adopt a different policy. "Once in the Netherlands, refugees experience more trauma than they did before."

He admits that it is a prickly subject. "Asylum seekers should avoid coming here at all costs", but it has to be said, believes Joop de Jong, Professor of Mental Health and Culture at the Vrije Universiteit, Amsterdam, and Director of the internationally renowned Transcultural Psychosocial Organisation (TPO). "Because our society is totally unequipped to receive refugees from other countries. The refugees don't understand the kind of help we offer and we have no understanding of their cultural backgrounds. The result is that these people experience more trauma in the Netherlands than they did before."

De Jong is the only professor in the Netherlands concerned with the psychological trauma of asylum seekers. "There's little to be had in the Netherlands in this field – few books and no scholarly literature. We keep going on our own expertise and experience." Over the last ten years, know-how has been gained with the TPO, an organisation with its headquarters in Amsterdam's inner city, operating in more than fifteen countries worldwide. Countries that are or have been torn apart by war: Algeria, Burundi, the Gaza Strip, Cambodia, Ethiopia, India, Kosovo ... "We work in those countries with local teams who know the local rites and customs. Our workers try to alleviate the psychosocial impact the war has had on people, mainly working in post-conflict situations where there are many displaced persons and refugees traumatised by violence."

The key-questions asked by the TPO teams are what problems does one encounter, are they different to the pre-war situation, which problems are new,

[1] This text is a translation of an article in Dutch, published in *Onze Wereld*, December 2000.

P.J. van Krieken (Ed.), Health, Migration and Return

how can the situation be improved? “Ten years ago, we started in Mozambique, where people were suffering under the violence of Renamo and Frelimo, the conflicting parties of the eighties and nineties. From then on, we developed into the most specialist NGO in this field in the world.” The World Heath Organisation (WHO) is one of the TPO’s most important principals. With his expertise, De Jong is highly critical of the way in which asylum seekers are treated and assisted in the Netherlands. “People who are on the run have lost the three central certainties in their lives. From our point of view, these certainties are the assumption that tomorrow will always be all right, that the world is a safe place and that bad things happen to someone else, never to you. These certainties are essential for human functioning and, once lost, victims find themselves in a traumatic situation.” De Jong continues: “The way in which these people are received in the Netherlands is at least as traumatic as the experiences they encountered in their own countries. There are a number of reasons for this – the extremely long waits in asylum seekers’ centres, the language barrier, the lack of assimilation opportunities and career relapses.”

A recent survey in which the TPO was involved examined the problems of Afghan refugees in the Netherlands. For the last two years, the majority of asylum seekers coming to the Netherlands originate from Afghanistan: in 1999 there were 4,400 refugees, while this number totalled some 1500 by March this year. In Drenthe, a survey was made into a group of Afghan refugees with residence status who have been living in the Netherlands for anything from three months to ten years. Almost seventy percent of those interviewed suffered from severe mental complaints due to language difficulties, unemployment or lack of retraining options (more than half of the group had successfully completed university degrees in their own country). In almost all cases, the mental problems were not related to war-related traumas. Less than half the Afghan refugees involved in the survey had received medical help in the Netherlands and if medical treatment had been offered, it had generally concentrated on dealing with external – physical – symptoms. Only seven percent had been treated for mental problems.

Each year, the Ministry of Justice spends roughly three billion guilders on aliens policy, half of which goes to asylum seekers. De Jong: “That is a huge amount of money. But there is only a fraction of that amount for social and welfare work. We’re at the end of the chain – our signals go unheeded.”

The Dutch welfare system is not equipped to help or to receive asylum seekers, says De Jong. The regional institutes for mental health care and doctors often do not know how to help foreigners because they have no knowledge of their cultural backgrounds. “Ten years ago, we and a number of experts wrote to the Ministry of Health, indicating the importance of a multicultural approach in the welfare sector. There was no response. People do not think they need to consult experts on tackling this problem. I recently received my first invitation to explain my vision at a seminar.” This congress was held in September.

In the meantime, De Jong's views have changed. "I'm not saying we shouldn't receive asylum seekers. But if we do, as a society we should be able to receive them and to give them the right kind of help. Admitting four thousand Kosovars, as we did last year, is a great gesture as far as the international community is concerned. But did anyone at the Ministry of Justice stop to think about what that meant for those people? And were there experts available to help people suffering from war traumas in their own tongue? If you don't ask questions like this, you're not acting responsibly. Then you've got to have the courage to say – sorry, we can't allow you in."

De Jong believes that there is a time bomb ticking away in Dutch society. "We're neglecting an entire group of refugees. People are kept on ice in asylum seekers centres. Husbands and wives wait for years together in a room, languishing away, not allowed to work, with nothing left to say to each other. That's the reality. You can't just go on as though this will have no impact – because we're letting large groups of people simply waste away."

De Jong does not understand why the authorities have not learnt from the experiences gained with helping survivors of the Nazi regime or Japanese prisoner of war camps. "After years and even decades, the victims are still plagued by recurrent problems. And refugees are in the same position."

De Jong blames the lack of realisation on "narrow-mindedness in The Hague." "The government takes an 'autistic' approach. Signals just aren't recognised. Nobody in The Hague wonders about what's going wrong. Then when it's too late, there are bound to be reactive measures. The problem starts with asylum policy being the responsibility of the Ministry of Justice. That ministry takes far too rigid an approach to the refugee issue, as though it was a judicial matter. The Ministry for International Development is just round the corner, but there's no dialogue or exchange of expertise. The same applies to the Ministry of Health. If the three ministries got together to discuss the problem, the policy could be restructured."

De Jong thinks it is absurd that, each year, the Dutch Ministry of Justice spends just as much on the reception of asylum seekers as the total budget of the refugee organisation of the United Nations, the UNHCR. "Give me five million guilders a year and I'll set up effective reception programmes in the countries where refugees come from. People should be received in their own region wherever possible. It's not just cheaper, but better for those involved. Then at least they'd be understood in their own culture. And then the State Secretary of Justice, Cohen, wouldn't have to be a sort of modern-day Hansje Brinker, sticking his thumb in the dyke to stop it from bursting." De Jong admits that it is an exaggeration. "But people are better off if they can stay in their own surroundings. The fact that they don't stay in their own countries right now is mainly because the regions in question just don't have the amenities. But these could be created in a European context – with conflict prevention – *early warning systems*. But mainly by spending the funds allocated to refugees in the regions they actually live in." It is the logical consequence of 'Fort Europe'. "If we pull up the drawbridge over here and implement a restrictive policy that's fine – but by doing so, we're not helping to prevent war in other parts of the world. It's Europe's expensive duty to take financial measures to ensure that refugees can be taken care of in their regions."

By way of example, De Jong refers to the enormous influx of lone under-age asylum seekers. In 1997 there were 2,600, although now double that figure are entering each year. "They should really be sent back if at all possible. Our research shows that minors recover relatively well once the war or conflict from which they were fleeing is over. But this is only possible if they are in a situation in which they feel at home – in their own family or with relatives or in their own village. In non-Western cultures, the social ties are very broad. Young people escaping to Europe never feel at home because Europe isn't their home. So they're bound to suffer more from stress and trauma." The Ministry of Justice has developed a special reception and aid model for under-age asylum seekers, but it utterly circumvents the young people's cultural backgrounds and problems.

People wanting to be admitted should be screened 'on entry' according to De Jong, to assess their education and qualities. "People potentially able to contribute to society here could be admitted. If you know a person's qualifications and ability from the outset, they can prepare themselves for a future here and we can find a place for him or her. This avoids creating a new social 'lower class' which is happening at the moment – trained physicists having to work as street cleaners." People should take responsibility for becoming part of society. "Let them explore and develop their potential and follow training courses. Maybe that should even be an admission criterion – what's your educational background. This is quite usual in America, where they select the most promising refugees. That's their quota. If you set different quotas for different categories you could also increase the Netherlands's absorption capacity."

Is this random selection? Insulted, De Jong shakes his head. "First of all, at the moment only the people with money manage to reach Europe. The paupers stay behind. That's also a form of selection. But if those people do come, you're not only creating a problem for them but for us, too, if they're unable to adjust to our way of life. And in the Netherlands our reception problem isn't one of capacity, but of creating an underclass – certain groups threaten to become marginalised through lack of education, assistance and integration. If we go on like this, we'll only create racial problems – and that's due to pure negligence."

5.6

TREATMENT SUR PLACE

In the above interview it has been indicated that, first, it is neither easy to confirm a PTSD/PTSS, nor to deny it, and second, that the chances of recovery are generally much higher if one is treated in one's own environment, that is the country and area of origin. It could even be submitted that non-treatment in the country of origin might yield better results than treatment in an alien environment. Such a submission is of the utmost importance now that many of those who claim a residence permit cum treatment in the European Union do so on the basis of a presumed PTSD/PTSS. It is hence of relevance to look into the methodology, quality and expertise of the organizations involved in treatment sur place, i.e. in the country, area or region of origin..

Awareness of the challenges involved during the 1990s and the book 'International Responses to Traumatic Stress'[1] *bears witness to this development. The chapters on provisions of psychosocial support, traumatized children, traumatized women and traumatized populations as a whole are quite revealing, not only as to the scars involved, but particularly as to the efforts to overcome the negative impact of criminal activities, violations of human rights, forced displacement, armed conflict and natural disasters on human beings. It also becomes clear that treatment sur place is feasible, possible and generally recognized as the most effective way of addressing this issue. The request for Bosnian psychiatrists to treat Bosnian women in the countries of asylum should also be seen in this context: priorities, effectiveness and, one might submit, common sense should be included in the decision-making processes. This would also be true for the assessment of the needs of child soldiers who have found their way to the North, and is similarly relevant for (other) unaccompanied minors because there is widespread consensus in child psychology and psychiatry that the family and the cultural context are the main vehicles for children to overcome massive traumatic stress.*

Many organizations, international, national and non-governmental alike, have now put this issue on their agendas. Experiences in e.g. West Africa and the Great Lake district would appear to show the positive impact of providing assistance towards healing the mental wounds.

The following text, of which Professor De Jong (the director of the Transcultural Psychosocial Organization (TPO)) is the author, would appear to illustrate the background, goals, purposes and indeed the methodology of such involvement in a clear and illustrative manner.

Millions around the world have been exposed to atrocities – starvation, torture, and the deaths of relatives. Their physical and mental suffering is enormous. Yet, most interna-

[1] Edited by Yael Danieli, Nigel Rodley and Lars Weisaeth, and with a foreword by Boutros Boutros-Ghali, UN NY, 1996.A subsequent book with a similar bearing will be published under the aegis of the UN in 2001 and will be called: Trauma in War and Peace. Prevention, Practice and Policy, edited by Bonnie Green, John Fairbank, Matt Friedman, Joop de Jong and Terry Kean. Reference should also be made to the WHO/UNHCR manual entitled Mental Health of Refugees.

tional aid organisations focus only on the physical aspects of their pain. Little attention is directed to their mental problems. Mental disorders can seriously disable people. Without fully functioning citizens, it is impossible to create a well-functioning society. The fact that the problems [often] exceed physical difficulties and include psychological pain, is slowly gaining credence. TPO has developed a programme to help large groups of traumatised people regain their emotional stability.

The programme begins with a culturally sensitive scientific assessment of the content and severity of the psycho-social problems. Intervention is then based on understanding the problems in their cultural context, and is carried out in working closely with local health workers and traditional healers.

Children are not only passive victims of violence, they can also be forced to become fighting soldiers. They become witnesses to unimaginable atrocities. Research on child refugees in Mozambique showed that 77 percent of the children had witnessed murder, moreover, 51 percent were abused or tortured. Many actually saw their parents or other family members being killed. Large number of them had their own body parts – hands, noses, ears, and even genitalia – cut off. In our own investigation among Sudanese children in North Uganda, we found that more than 90 percent of the children experienced loss of properties and lack of food, 80 percent lost a family member, and about 60 percent witnessed the death of a family member, suffered from lack of water, poor health or no medical aid. About one fourth of the children had been tortured or kidnapped. Obviously, these children develop serious mental traumas. Their complaints could last for a few days or weeks, but, unless treated, are more likely to continue for months and years. Symptoms include immature behaviours for their age such as incontinence, exaggerated dependence, nightmares, even repeated rocking motions with their bodies, and head-banging. They often refuse to eat, and have a variety of psychosomatic complaints including headaches, dizziness, and stomach-aches. Older traumatised children often are exceptionally nervous, restless, and irritated.

Adults and children alike suffer from mental malaise such as Post Traumatic Stress Syndrome (PTSS) and depressive disorder. They are fearful and easily panicked. They have nightmares and day time flashbacks of distressing images. They become depressed, apathetic and lack a prospective for their future. Violence, as a way of releasing pressure, often occurs within their families and their communities. In countries with large groups of traumatised people, such as Cambodia, Ethiopia, and Mozambique, people's reduced ability to function can seriously limit the country's development. In spite of all these problems, little attention has been paid to the mental health of refugees. A common thought is: "as long as they eat and have shelter, things will be okay". Such thinking reduces victims of war and disaster to individuals without a psyche, that is people who merely require material aid or who only experience physical problems. Moreover, the poor mental health of refugees is a threat to their quality of life and their life expectancy. Providing aid is more than providing food and shelter. Aid also is aimed toward restoring, and preventing further deterioration of the refugees' mental health. Providing only physical and material aid can bring refugees to helplessness and dependence, resulting in a loss of self-esteem which inhibits them from taking responsibility for their future. On the basis of years of experience with large groups of traumatised people from different cultures, TPO's experts have become convinced of the fact that attention to psychosocial problems is essential to empower people to continue their life and to contribute to the building of a new, more harmonious community.

Local collaborators and local culture form the base of the programme. Victims of atrocities are likely never to forget what has happened to them. However, it is possible to empower them to function again. Psychological help needs to be provided as early as possible in order to reduce the consequences of trauma, maintain self-esteem and prevent the re-traumatization of already traumatised people. Western therapeutic intervention which most commonly occurs by individual treatment, often with psychiatric medication, is not appropriate given the large numbers and the fact that [it concerns] for the most part low-income countries. In collaboration with experts from Africa, Asia, and Europe, TPO has developed an intervention programme for large numbers of traumatised people.[2] The TPO programme adapts various methods of intervention for each situation and culture, but always tries to work with the community to help them solve their own psycho-social problems. By focusing on strengthening self-confidence, creating a more fulfilling life, and developing new social networks, refugees begin to gain confidence in their future. Collaboration with other aid organisations and local organisations is always essential to allow refugees access to existing services. Group activities, such as self-help groups for torture and rape survivors, are used to reduce post traumatic stress. Vocational skills training stimulates income generating activities and assists poor communities to achieve some independence.

The programme starts with the assessment of the psycho-social problems. We have found that problems are diverse. In one [situation] the biggest problem can be recovering from rape. [In another] the largest difficulty may be working with violent or uncooperative children who act out as a result of being traumatised. In some countries, HIV-counselling is an important issue. Once the local sets of problems are defined, methods are devised to intervene, usually by combining western ideas with local and traditional ways of dealing with emotional difficulties. To be successful in the implementation of intervention strategies, a core group of local health workers, teachers, traditional healers, community leaders, etc., is trained by local and international specialists. They teach core group participants how to recognise mental illness and how to use appropriate therapeutic techniques.

Understanding and treating collective trauma is a new field. Consequently, scientific research plays a key role. One important topic of research is the identification of 'local idioms of distress', that is the local language people use to express their mental or physical problems. Another research effort attempts to understand each culture's local methods of helping traumatised people, and to find ways to work within the local system of care. Evaluation and action research is also important. This research elucidates how an intervention in one situation, might be modified to be of use in another. Evaluative research also supplies information that is needed to refine, adapt, and improve our programs. The research also contributes to the development of a multi-site human rights database.

---

[2] Ed.: TPO is just one of many organizations involved. Many NGOs, often in collaboration with UNICEF or the Red Cross are active in this field. See e.g. Dubrow, Liwski, Palacios and Gardinier: *Traumatized Children, Helping Child Victims of Violence, the contribution of NGOs*, in: Daniele op.cit. pp. 327-346. The Transcultural Psychosocial Organisation (TPO) will publish in 2001 a book with Plenum Press, to be called *Trauma, War and Violence*, edited by Joop de Jong, listing a range of organisations active in this field. Mention should also be made of the International Society for Traumatic Stress Studies and the World Federation for Mental Health (forum groups, rather than 'implementors').

The programme is based on different disciplines: public mental health, psychology, psychiatry, anthropology, psychotherapy and epidemiology.

The programme is based on the following principles:

- The psychosocial and mental health problems of refugees can be recognised and treated and it is possible to prevent aggravation of problems.
- The most effective way to implement interventions is through methods that are accepted in the local culture.
- Collaboration with communities is necessary.
- If possible, local professionals and health workers need to be employed.
- Programs should be from 5 to 6 years duration, in order to adequately train a local core group to continue the programme without, or with only sporadic assistance, from TPO.
- Knowledge- and skills training are considered as essential parts of the programme.
- Culture-specific interventions and prevention are central to the programme.
- Research is necessary for a successful programme.
- Ethnocentrism should be avoided.

The impact of an organization such as TPO should not be overlooked: the multiplier effect combined with experience, professionalism and devotion would appear to yield results which deserve to be highlighted in the debate on health, migration and return. TPO's North Uganda and Cambodia programmes undoubtedly serve as reference material for similar activities elsewhere. TPO itself is also active in Algeria, Burundi, Ethiopia, Gaza, India (Tibetans), Kosovo, Nepal, Mozambique, Namibia, DR Congo, North-Sri Lanka, and Sudan.

NORTH UGANDA

In 1994, TPO started a project to provide psycho-social help to 230,000 Sudanese refugees living in the West Nile-area. Focus groups and interviews with key people were organised to gain a deeper understanding of their problems. This resulted in a long list of problems, such as overpopulation, poor sanitation, high infant mortality, domestic violence, inadequate food rations, alcohol abuse, and criminality. Significantly, they also mentioned repeatedly how difficult it was to cope with their past traumatic experiences. A TPO anthropologist talked with local healers to understand how these problems were locally expressed and traditionally treated. Particular attention was paid to the role of rituals in helping people. This information was then used to help develop culturally appropriate interventions and training materials. Eighteen candidates with a prerequisite education were selected to participate in a Training of Trainers course in counselling and community based interventions, given by the expatriate staff. The contents of the training and training materials were based on the WHO/UNHCR book Mental Health of Refugees. Adapted modules were added to fit the northern Ugandan cultural context. After the course the participants continued to receive supervision by TPO's expatriate staff. After six months of work under TPO supervision, six of the eighteen local trainees were selected to become trainers or counsellors. After receiving additional education, they began training psychiatric nurses, medical assistants, teachers, pastoral workers, and local healers. In addition, the whole group of trainees continued to make home visits in the camps and to assess psycho-social problems. They tailored interventions to meet specific needs. Some refugees took part in counselling groups to talk about traumatic events, others were involved with self-help groups so they could learn how to give and receive support to re-build the community. Seminars were being organised to train camp leaders, their assistants and health care workers who engage in medical care or income generating activities. Even though the project mostly deals with psycho-social problems, people with severe mental illnesses also report for treatment. Health workers, therefore, are provided with a training followed by a supervision in identifying and treating severe mental illnesses. For psycho-social problems there is a special infrastructure within the project. This includes counselling rooms in all the camps. For the treatment of the severe mentally ill there is a co-operation with the existing primary health care facilities.

CAMBODIA

Prior to the civil war, the Cambodian population was exposed to carpet bombing, followed by the lengthy civil war. Three million people died, which is more than twenty percent of the country's population. Since the civil war has receded in scope, nearly 300,000 people returned from the Thai border-camps to the regions where they were born and raised. Throughout these ordeals, almost all Cambodians suffered severe trauma. However, until recently there has been no mental health care in the country. TPO believed that before appropriate aid could be provided in Cambodia, an assessment, in the context of the local cultures, had to be carried out. Accordingly, in addition to demographic information and assessing the standard Western types of psychological symptomatology, narrative interviews with people from different sections of the population were obtained, in order to understand the local idioms of distress and to know about the specific forms of help-seeking behaviour, social networks, coping styles and explanatory models. Then, an investigation was made to document the existing local health facilities in each village, district, and province. The information revealed that the traditional healers were able to focus on crises, such as marital problems or community conflicts, but did not pretend to be able to treat all the mental health problems. As was the case in Uganda, thousands of people with severe mental illness and epilepsy asked for help. On the basis of this information, teaching ideas were formulated and training materials developed. For example, TPO developed a model which provided these people with treatment and after care in the village, district or at the provincial level. Criteria were also developed to select trainees who were trained by the core group to work in the community. The core group members received eight months of training by the TPO expatriate professional staff. They also learned to work with the local healers, which helped the core group to become accepted by the community. One of the most employed intervention technique was the development of self-help groups in the villages. For many of the participants this was the first time they ever discussed their experiences. After five years of TPO involvement, the program covers two million Cambodians and is now transformed into a local sustainable Cambodian NGO.

AN OVERVIEW OF THE HEALTH ASPECTS OF RETURN IN THE IMMIGRATION CONTEXT

Brian Gushulak

The health and medical aspects involved with the return of migrants in an irregular situation and incarcerated asylum seekers are very complex issues. In spite of that complexity and the association of a variety of technical and ethical issues with the medical considerations, with the exception of anecdotal reports describing the death of restrained deportees on aircraft[1, 2] there is little published information or recommendations specifically related to medical matters associated with these practices.

I. INTRODUCTION: THE CONCEPT OF DIVERSITY IN HEALTH

Considering the medical issues associated with the return of migrants, the concerns relate to one basic issue. That is the global lack of equivalence in health care systems[3] and wide variances in disease risk or prevalence rates. Looking at the current global situation, this issue can be described in a simple overview based on the level of health care at the origin and destination of the migratory journey. In this short presentation, major impacts on health during the return migration journey will be considered in relation to global health disparity. However, as noted above, there is a paucity of published information on health outcomes related to the forced repatriation of migrants.

---

[1] Amnesty International. Report EUR 14/01/99. Belgium. Correspondence with the Government Concerning the Alleged Ill-Treatment of Detained Asylum Seekers. Available From http://www.amnesty.org/ailib/aipub/1999/EUR/41400199.htm.

[2] Roeggla G. Death of an asylum seeking Nigerian in police custody. BMJ 1999;318:1291.

[3] The WHO defines a health system as comprising all the organizations, institutions and resources that are devoted to producing health actions. A health action is defined as any effort, whether in personal health care, public health services or through intersectoral initiatives, whose primary purpose is to improve health. (WHO The World Health Report 2000, Health Systems: Improving Performance, Geneva, May 2000, p. xi).

P.J. van Krieken (Ed.), Health, Migration and Return

The awareness of the relationship between population mobility and disease has recently increased, due to the growing appreciation of the importance of disease persistence, emergence and re-emergence.[4] Whatever the cause, when disparity in the environment, events and economic status occur, population movement across these disparities or gaps, be they differences in disease distribution, socio-economic status, education levels, availability and accessibility to health care, for example, can produce a direct impact on the individual's and community health. It is important to note that the direction of health impacts may be neutral, negative or positive for the individual and the host population.[5]

The concepts of individual and population health are important considerations when issues of health are explored. Individual outcomes for a particular situation or event may differ from aggregate or population-based outcomes for the same event. An example may be the risk of serious illness such as coronary heart disease or cancer. National or population-specific rates may show a decrease or increase based on the rate of the disease as expressed against a population denominator. Yet, individuals may still acquire the diseases even in situations where the general picture may be improving.

Immigration legislation and regulation tend to be individually focused and many of the legal procedures associated with the determination of residency are centred on the individual case. Consequently, the health-related impact of movement or return on a specific individual may have more relevance than population or community-based outcomes. The following discussion will focus primarily on the health of the individual but will also comment on the wider impact that migratory movements may have on the health of the general population.

The latter concern, that of the health of the wider population, can be an important aspect in large volume return programmes such as observed in the region of the former Yugoslavia or East Timor. Following the cessation of hostilities large numbers of displaced or evacuated former residents return to locations with damaged health systems or to situations where there are insufficient health care providers. The actual impact on reconstruction/rehabilitation of large-scale returns in these post-conflict environments is currently poorly reported.

---

[4] Holmes KK. Human ecology and behavior and sexually transmitted bacterial infections. Proc Natl Acad Sci USA 1994; 91: 2448-2455.

[5] Geddes M, Parkin DM, Khlat M, Balzi D Editors. Cancer in Italian Migrant Populations. IARC Scientific Publications #123. International Agency for Research on Cancer. 1993. Lyon, France.

II. TYPES OF MOVEMENT AS DEFINED BY HEALTH SITUATIONS AT THE ORIGIN AND DESTINATION

A. Neutral Health Movements

There are two basic types of return movements that can be considered as having a neutral impact on the health of the individual undertaking the journey. Due to the neutral nature of the process there is minimal to no impact or effect on the health of the mainstream population at either the origin or the destination.

1. Individuals are returned or moved between states that have equivalent health care systems

In these situations, for the individual migrant, there is no difference between access to, or availability of health care services at the two locations. Movement or return between these two environments is neutral in terms of individual health as reflected by access to or utilization of health systems. Examples can be seen in return between Western European States.

2. Individuals are moved or returned between states that have similar disease distribution

In a manner analogous to the process described above, movements of this type occur when individuals relocate between locations that have similar risks for disease and illness. Movements between regions of Western Europe and parts of North America are examples of this type of process.

B. Movements that may have a Beneficial Impact on Health

Following the outline above, there are two types of return movements that can be considered beneficial to the individual migrant. In situations of this type, the movements generally have minimal to no adverse effects on population health (examples can be found in the limited transmission of tuberculosis from migrants to native-born Canadians or the minimal impact of Hepatitis C infection in migrants on the mainstream US population).

Over time an improvement in health is noted either through a reduction in disease and illness that were common at the migrant's origin or through better prevention and treatment of other conditions.

1. Individuals are returned or moved to a location where the health care system/ services are in an improved state or more easily accessible than they are at the initial location

In these situations, for the individual migrant, the journey can be viewed as a positive undertaking in terms of access to or utilization of health systems. The most common examples are noted in movements from the developing world to the developed world although there are several examples where there "*is far too much variation in outcomes among countries which seem to have the same resources and possibilities.*"[6]

2. Individuals are moved or returned to a location where the incidence and prevalence of disease or illness is less than observed at the migrant's origin

Movements of this type occur when individuals relocate between sites that have elevated risks for disease and illness to destinations where the disease risks are less common. Once again the most common examples of this form of movement are seen in journeys from the tropical or developing world to the developed world, where public health services have controlled or modulated disease prevalence. Poverty has clearly been demonstrated to be one of the most important factors in affecting ill health and death from both infectious diseases and non-infectious reasons and many of the health differences between global locations are related to what are called rich-poor differences.[7] Irregular migrants often attempt to bridge these rich-poor gaps and returning them across the gaps can affect their health.

C. **Movements Associated with a Negative Health Outcome**[8]

Some international journeys can result in situations where the traveller arrives at a destination where health conditions are less secure than they were at the place of origin. These negative health movements are the most problematic from an immigration and return perspective and may be disadvantageous for the individual.

---

[6] WHO The World Health Report 2000, Health Systems: Improving Performance, Geneva, May 2000, p. 3.

[7] Gwatkin DR Guillot M. The burden of disease among the world's poor: Current situaiton, future trends and implications for policy. Washington DC, Human Development Network of the World Bank, 2000.

[8] Human behavioural factors influence the distribution and prevalence of disease on a local, regional and international basis. In all of the above-noted situations, individual behaviour, personal financial status, educational and cultural factors may affect or influence the health of the individual migrant.

1. Individuals move or are returned from a location to a destination where health care services or access to health care is less developed

In movements or returns of this nature, the journey may place the individual in situations where his or her health care outcomes may be compromised. In this situation, negative impacts on individual health may also have significant negative impacts on the health of the community as a whole, due to problems related to managing the consequences of disease introduction. Examples of compromised individual health include situations where the arriving returnee requires services or treatments that are not available or accessible (chronic renal failure, complicated surgery). Examples of the impact on community health include the introduction of drug resistant infections or the arrival of vector borne diseases carried by the migrant into a site where the local health care system is poorly equipped to manage them.

2. Movement or return of individuals to locations where the prevalence of serious disease and illness is greater than at the origin of the journey

Movements or returns of this type can transport individuals to locations where the risks of disease acquisition and illnesses are more prevalent than at the origin. Examples include returns to areas of elevated infectious disease prevalence, (malaria, yellow fever, tuberculosis, etc.).

III. THE EFFECT OF RETURN ON INDIVIDUAL HEALTH OUTCOMES

Against the background of the possible influences on health that are associated with the migration and return movements, it is possible to consider individual health outcomes that may result from these processes. These outcomes also present themselves in a basic framework in which health is associated with the movement process.

In relation to individual health, outcomes affected by migration and return can be considered in the following manner.

A. **Health on Arrival**

On arrival at their destination or place of registration, prior to the determination for return, migrants will be either healthy or ill. Their status will depend on a variety of issues, including personal background, geographic origin, economic and social background and the nature and extent of the migratory journey.

B. **Health During the Phase before Return**

During the sojourn before their return journey, an individual migrant's health can be affected in four ways.

1. No change in status; the migrant remains in the same state of health as he or she displayed on arrival;
2. Improvement of those with pre-existing illness either through access to health care or secondary factors such as nutrition, prevention or support activities;
3. Acquisition of illness by those who were healthy on arrival;
4. Worsening of pre-existing conditions in those who had pre-existing illness.

C. **Health During and After Return**

As noted during the residence phase of the migration process, individual health during and after the return phase can be influenced in four ways.
1. No change in status, the migrant remains in the same state of health as he or she displayed before return.
2. Improvement of those with pre-existing illness either through access to health care or secondary factors such as nutrition, prevention or support activities following return.
3. Acquisition of illness by those who were healthy at the time of return or in whom pre-existing conditions worsened following return.

These factors are summarized in the following table.

Table I. Health Outcomes as considered by Phase of Migratory Process

	Migration Phase		
	Arrival	**Sojourn**	**Return**
Health Status	Health Outcome		
Initially Healthy	No Change Deterioration or new Disorder	No Change Deterioration or new Disorder	No Change Deterioration or new Disorder
Initially Ill	Improvement No Change Deterioration Acquisition of new Disorder	Improvement No Change Deterioration Acquisition of new Disorder	Improvement No Change Deterioration Acquisition of new Disorder

IV. ISSUES ASSOCIATED WITH HEALTH AND RETURN IMMIGRATION

When the process of return is considered from a health perspective, major issues become apparent. These include the provision of medical care during the refugee determination system, the provision of medical services during the return phase and the difficulties with appropriate services on arrival in the case of health negative movements.

A. **Medical Care During Confinement / Incarceration**

Extending medical care to individuals who are directly under the control of the state can take several forms. Commonly, it involves the provision of adequate and appropriate care and treatment to those who are incarcerated for criminal or legal offences. These services are often straightforward and appropriate as the intent is to improve or sustain the health of the individual. Issues can arise when the services or prevention activities are designed for situations that may indicate a lack of state supervisory control such as safe-sex or drug awareness programmes in prisons.

When the services involve a deleterious outcome for the detainee the problems become much more complicated. If return is portrayed as being a risk to the health of the migrant, similar issues can be raised.

There are various codes of conduct and recommendations that are supposed to guide medical staff in their behaviour towards detained individuals. The origin of some of them go back to the end of the Second World War while more modern ones have been developed during and as a result of the South African apartheid situation.

While these recommendations exist, the actual consequences to medical personnel who become involved with the issues depends on the jurisdiction, code of ethics, and code of conduct where the individual health care professional is registered or working.

In the first two situations, where adequate services can be found after the deportation journey, medical concerns are limited to those associated with the provision of care to incarcerated people. As long as the individual is incarcerated or restrained (i.e. until the end of the deportation or return journey) this is best done by medical staff directly hired, supervised and in the employ of the state. That means that the ethical issues are left to the government health care worker and his or her licensing body.

B. **Specific Issues Related to Asylum Seekers**

The delivery of appropriate health care to asylum seekers is a complicated undertaking that is further hampered by the refugee determination system itself. For a variety of reasons some legislative – some operational, some political – the majority of asylum seekers are not returned. Depending upon the jurisdiction, more than 80% of those arriving in Western European states who formally seek asylum are not returned.

However, during the determination process, which may take considerable time, their indeterminate status and local situation may negatively affect their health. In this manner, it can be postulated that a more rapid determination system with a reduction processing time could diminish some of the stress and ill-health created by the lack of a final decision.

This could be particularly important in the area of mental health. Some populations of asylum seekers are reported to have elevated rates of psychiatric and mental health conditions.

"Dr Gary Reynolds, a consultant in public health medicine in Birmingham, said that not all asylum seekers had psychiatric problems but that certainly the way they were treated added to their stress.'"[9]

Much of the concern is centred on the effects of detention and incarceration of asylum seekers. Several medical studies report serious mental and emotional effects that detention has had on asylum seekers' health.[10] In a recent study of detained asylum seekers, Dr Christina Pourgourides noted that "the responses to detention can manifest as symptoms which form constellations consistent with psychiatric diagnoses of depression, post-traumatic stress disorder, anxiety and psychosis. It should however be apparent that these symptoms can also be understood as universal manifestations of suffering and misery. This suffering and misery is generated by the practice of detention."

C. **Issues Related to Medical Care During the Return Journey**

In these situations, health service delivery is influenced, in ethical terms, by the nature of the return journey in terms of motivation.

1. Voluntary or spontaneous movements that involve the consent or non-objection of the individual are relatively straightforward even if the health care services at the destination are less comprehensive than they are at the origin

Individuals exercising their free will to return, even to a less optimal health environment, may only require assistance during travel to ensure that they are supported during the journey.

Examples of this type include current voluntary returns to Kosovo or Bosnia.

2. Forced returns or deportations are more problematic given the lack of free will or self-determination on the part of the individual

In these situations, the undertaking can be seen or portrayed as the forced imposition of an outcome that can negatively affect the health of the migrant. A number of complicated ethical and operational issues arise.

---

[9] Beecham L, Medicopolitical digest *BMJ* 1997;314:1836.

[10] Salinsky, M. Detaining Asylum Seekers. BMJ 1997;213:456.

D. Issues of Compromised medical care after return

This group is the most problematic, and in ethical terms and given the nature of modern irregular migratory movements from the developing to the developed world, the most relevant for the proposal at hand. Here, because the journey will return a sick individual to a place where the health care services are not as "good" as they were at the point of origin, the deportation or return can be seen as directly worsening the health or well-being of the returnee/deportee.

These issues can be considered from two perspectives, one from the viewpoint of community health and the second from the perspective of the returning individuals themselves.

1. Community Health Issues

a) Individual or Small Group Return

From a community perspective, the return of a single person or a small number of individuals will produce impacts on a health system in only a few specific and unusual situations. These situations will occur when the illness or disease is exotic or rare enough that special, unusual or exceptional measures would be required for management. Examples include the introduction of a serious infectious or communicable disease of potentially epidemic consequences, such as the rare viral heamorrhagic fevers (ebola virus hemorrhagic fever), antigenic shift influenza or transspecies migration of serious disease (variant CJD). In those situations exceptional and costly control measures could be required that could be extensive enough to generate health system-wide impact.

Some actual examples have been observed in non-immigration related travel situations, most recently in the return of humanitarian workers from Sierra Leone.[11] During the preparation of this paper it was not possible to identify any published reports of diseases of this nature being associated with deportation or the return of failed asylum seekers or the journeys of returning refugees.[12]

For the remainder of health conditions, and the most commonly occurring situations, the return of individuals or small groups of people will have no population-based impact on the local health care system. If care cannot be provided, the individual will become part of an existing cohort unable to access those services. If local care is available, the returned individual will access the health care delivery system according to the local situation as influenced by social and economic factors.

---

[11] Anonymous. Imported case of Lassa Fever in the Netherlands. Eurosurveillance Weekly Issue 30, July 27, 2000.

[12] The author is familiar with a single episode where an asylum seeker claimed to be a contact for a communicable disease of international public health importance at the initial arrival phase. In this situation there was no transportation of the illness.

b) Large-Scale Returns

Return programmes that involve the movement of large populations on the other hand do have the potential to create a health system impact on the receiving society. In these scenarios, the resiliency and service provision capacity of the health sector is tested by the introduction of large numbers of returnees. Situations could be anticipated where a health care system, already under severe stress, could be significantly affected by the service demands of large numbers of new arrivals. Managing the health issues of the new arrivals could be difficult in these situations and acute needs could impact on longer-term health sector planning. Examples include the return of the chronically ill to the region of the Former Yugoslavia and include medical conditions such as renal failure, cancer and congenital heart disease. Published evidence related to impacts of this type are rare.

Recent examples of return movements of this type have been undertaken in parts of the area of the Former Yugoslavia. Tens of thousands of displaced individuals have returned to Bosnia and more recently to Kosovo. Reports on significant impacts on the health sector at the community level are not noted in published medical literature at this time. Returning large numbers of sick individuals, either voluntarily or forcibly, to locations where health care services are under stress can be anticipated to retard or impact on local development.

These situations are common in post-conflict and post-crisis environments[13] and can be seen as delaying rehabilitation/reconstruction or hampering economic recovery.[14]

"As Serbia and Kosovo emerge from yet another European war, their people's health and the region's health care, scientific research, and medical education have been seriously damaged and disrupted."[15]

While there are anecdotal reports of the demands placed on the health care systems of the receiving nations, they primarily focus on the effect on returnees themselves and not the mainstream population. It is hoped that more detailed evaluation of the community health impact of large-scale return will be undertaken or reported in the near future.

2. Individual Health Issues

For the individual returnee, the direct impact on his or her health can be seen as independent from the number of returnees. The underlying individual concern will be the ability of the system to provide care.

---

[13] Mehic-Basara N; Ceric I; Lagerkvist B. Refugees, returnees and rehabilitation. Med Arh 1999;53:39-41.

[14] ECRE Position on Returns to Kosovo. June 2000. Available at http://www..ecre.org/archive/kosovoreturns.html

[15] Horton R Croatia and Bosnia: the imprints of war – I. Lancet 1999;353 :2139-2144.

The nature of that gap in care provision may however be internally or externally generated and can perceived be in that context.

If the inability to receive care is a result of national resource allocation or decisions regarding health care priorities, the adverse outcome can be seen to rest with the national health service system and the returnee risks outcomes similar to other residents in the nation. In this scenario the return process can be seen in a passive light and the return journey simply places the individual back in his or her local health care environment.

If, however, large-scale return pushes a health care sector into a situation where certain individual services are no longer available, the process of return can be seen as the reason for the lack of health care. In this situation if the health care is not available, the process of returning an individual can be viewed as supporting the reduction in health or in some cases hastening the death of the individual.

V. SUMMARY

It is clear that if the process of deportation is determined to be unjust or unethical, medical assistance provided before or during the process is viewed in a similar manner.[16]

In conclusion,

1) Depending on the nature and scale of the return process, removal can produce several legal and medical implications in the context of both individual and community health.

2) Often the logistical considerations of large-scale return do not take into account the health implications of the return and post-return process.

3) The ethical considerations of removal should involve both legal and medical considerations.

4) Quantitative studies on the relationship between migrant returns and health, at both the individual and community level, are needed.

---

[16] Doronzynski A. French doctors apologise for wartime antisemitism. *BMJ* 1997;315:1111-1116.

CHAPTER 6
LEGAL PRACTICE

This final Chapter contains to a great extent the *pièce de résistance* as it deals extensively with the one institution which hitherto has consequently tried to set criteria in the context of return and the real risk of degrading and/or inhuman treatment as a result of such return. The Strasbourg based ECHR organs (Commission and Court) have in a number of judgements given their views on this issue, views which should be considered leading in that Europe at least has a legal framework on the basis of which legally tenable conclusions can be drawn. Van Krieken focuses on the need to draw a line, de Boer-Buquicchio bases her observations on Strasbourg insights, whereas Träskelin submits views on the basis of his involvement with one of the Commission cases.

The relevant articles of the European Convention on Human Rights and Fundamental Freedoms have been included for easy reference. Ample attention has been paid to the seven cases in which 'health' has played a major role. It should assist all involved, that is including the medical profession, the economists, the ethicist and others, towards realizing that some criteria have meanwhile been developed, and that these criteria may indeed make sense.

Baker, finally, gives a useful survey of the way the various individual countries deal with health and return. He comes to the conclusion that a lack of understanding, a lack of knowledge and a lack of information yields undesirable results. He submits that closer cooperation and harmonization is badly needed to ensure acceptable solutions be found on this sensitive and complex issue.

6.1

STRASBOURG: THE SEARCH FOR CRITERIA

Whenever the 'North' is confronted with a request for residence-cum-treatment it needs to find the appropriate answer. Although such an answer should be based on input from all possible angles (economists, ethics, Third World experts, psycho-social specialists) it is the reality of today's Trias Politica that the Executive and the Judiciary will have rely on the laws promulgated by the Legislature. Those laws, of course, should be in accordance with international obligations.

The search for criteria is, therefore, above all a legal search. It has been argued that the ICESCR, and its Committee in particular could be an important indicator as to whether violations in this realm, i.e. in the country of origin, are likely to occur. The reports of that Committee are worth being scrutinized as to indications to this effect. But even then, – and this would also appear to have been recognized in the General Comment on the Right to health – it remains to be seen whether it would concern a right with a cross-border impact, particularly not if the principle or rather the condition of the exhaustion of local remedies has not been fulfilled.

As long as the legislator does not speak out in more precise terminology on this sensitive issue, regard has to be had to existing articles in the predominant international treaties, that is, whilst looking for international norms, values and regulations. And the ones that come to mind are all related to the question of how far a State would violate human rights conventions if it were to return a person suffering from an illness to his/her country of origin, without having checked whether the treatment needed is available and/or affordable.

What it boils down to is the question whether such a forced return would amount to torture or other inhuman or degrading treatment. Such treatment has been strictly and absolutely, i.e. without any exception having been declared admissible, laid down in both the European Convention on Human Rights and Fundamental Freedoms (ECHR, 1950) and the Convention Against Torture (CAT, 1984). Also in view of the possibility for the individuals concerned to approach institutions set up under those Conventions in the case of an obligation to return, the dicta of the institutions concerned (the Commission and the Court under the ECHR, the Committee under the CAT) would appear to be of paramount importance and relevance.

P.J. van Krieken (Ed.), Health, Migration and Return

Of course, it concerns negative obligations ('thou shall not forcibly return') but the non-treatment would also then be considered to amount to such degrading or inhuman treatment.

In this Chapter some authors, among whom the Deputy Registrar of the EctHR in Strasbourg and a Finnish Supreme Court Judge who had been involved in the Karara case present various views, although divergences appear to be minimal. The ECHR has been included in Chapter 6.2 and the Court and Commission cases to which references are made can be found in extenso in Chapter 6.3.

DRAWING THE LINE

Peter van Krieken[1]

European involvement with human rights has been quite intensive. Europeans are fierce champions in promoting human rights and stressing the universality of universal human rights. Originally, the European Convention on Human Rights (ECHR) was thought to have a positive impact on those member states of the Council of Europe, which were believed to lag behind in their development towards the modern post-WWII social welfare state. But quite soon it became clear that the very same ECHR could also turn against the ones, which were believed to act in full conformity with that ECHR. Not only the UK, but also the Netherlands and Sweden were confronted with dicta they might not have expected.

Moreover, some of the articles became the subject of an ever more generous interpretation. Some of these were moved from the classical field into the socio-economic one, whereby the state was forced not only to abstain, but to take positive action as well. This was for example the case with the unity of the family principle. Originally, Art. 8 was meant to ensure that the authorities would not unlawfully interfere in family life. It later became an obligation for the authorities to make sure that family life could be enjoyed, which resulted in a positive obligation to reunify families, not just of the subjects/nationals, but also the non-nationals. Only quite recently the Court in Strasbourg (ECtHR) embarked, with respect to non-nationals, on the logical line that in a great many cases family life

---

[1] *Health Gaps and Migratory Movements*, Raoul Wallenberg Institute, Report 31, Lund 200, on pp. 61-71. For editing purposes, most of the many footnotes have been deleted.

could also be enjoyed in the country of origin, whereby the positive obligation was reinterpreted, more in line with the (original) meaning of the ECHR.

The other interesting example can be found in Art. 3, the article dealing with inhuman and degrading treatment. Originally this provision was meant to ensure that the authorities would not expose their own subjects to inhuman or degrading treatment on their territory. This principle was logically extended to cover nationals about to be extradited to a non-European country[2] and somewhat later to all lawfully present on the territory. But in the course of time, it also started to cover aliens whose presence was not legal, and whose relation to the authorities of their countries of origin could result in the treatment forbidden under this European Convention. It was then generally agreed that if there were a real risk that aliens lawfully, or unlawfully present, would be exposed to such inhuman treatment upon return, the aliens concerned should indeed not be expelled or returned.[3]

Where it concerns expected maltreatment like torture, abuse, a fairly firm line of thinking has now emerged. Case law is being developed,[4] and Art. 3 has become a well-respected partner of Art. 33 of the 1951 Refugee Convention.

In the field of health, however, the argumentation appears to be somewhat muddled.

In an early ruling (Tanko, 1994), the Commission indicated that a lack of care may amount to a situation in which Art. 3 may be violated. It concerned a Ghanaian, whose application for political asylum had been rejected, and who thereupon submitted that he would face serious problems due to an eye-disease. The Commission was of the opinion that appropriate drugs could be taken home to the country of origin and that the real risk criterion had not been met.

In one of its first dicta where elements related to health came to the fore (D. v UK), the Court indicated that "aliens who have served their prison sentences and are subject to expulsion cannot in principle claim any entitlement to remain on the territory of a contracting state in order to continue to benefit from medical, social or other forms of assistance provided by that state during their stay in prison."

---

[2] Cf. re Schoering, a German whose extradition to the US was prevented as long as the death penalty, or death row, were not completely excluded, ECtHr, 7 July 1989.

[3] That, however, did not mean that a residence title/permit should be provided/issued. [Moreover] it is worth adding that Art. 3, unlike Art. 33 of the Refugee Convention, is absolute and lacks a clause under which certain categories would be exempted from protection. This is logical, as Art. 3 was originally meant to cover nationals/subjects only. [It is therefore not to be excluded that in due time proposals will be submitted to the effect that Art. 3 will be ever so slightly revised.]

[4] A number of cases have meanwhile been dealt with (Tamil, Chilean, Indian) but there is no final word on the matter. Moreover, it will be of great interest to see how the new, expanded court will deal with these cases. For a by now outdated overview, see UNHCR's EuroSeries, vol.2 no. 3, 1996, on the ECHR and the protection of asylum seekers and displaced persons.

In this case the Court nevertheless ruled that Art. 3 also applies to inhuman treatment brought about by unintentional acts and that the expulsion of a foreigner dying from AIDS to a country which lacks the appropriate means of treatment would constitute a violation of this provision.

However, the Court underlined that in arriving at its conclusion it had taken into account 'the very exceptional circumstances and the compelling humanitarian considerations at stake.' The above quoted statement on services enjoyed, therefore, would appear to be the starting point for any policy/jurisdiction development, quite logical in view of the practical consequences of any decision to the contrary.

The UK, in its reaction, underlined that

> 'the court did insist that the case had very special circumstances, i.e. the almost total absence of medical and social care in St. Kitts for this particular individual, the critical stage of his fatal illness i.e. very near to death and the care from which he would be wrenched. It was therefore concluded that the numbers of cases to which the expanded Article 3 could apply is very small.'[5]

(...)These cases had been preceded by a case in which health as such did not play the upper hand, but was of overall relevance. It concerns the Cruz-Varas case, a Chilean sent back home whilst his case was still pending in Strasbourg (1989). The Court ruled that deportation, in spite of Cruz-Varas' suffering from a PTSS and in spite of the fact that his mental health situation deteriorated upon deportation, did not amount to a breach of Art. 3.

In March 1998, the European Commission (ECHR[6]) concluded in a report on the case of the ex-Zairean who had both the AIDS virus and Kaposi Syndrome, that repatriation to the newly renamed Democratic Republic of Congo would constitute a violation of Art. 3. In its report the Commission stated that the repatriation of this ex-Zairean to a country where he would probably not be able to benefit from the necessary medical treatment and where he would have to confront an illness such as AIDS at an advanced stage, all alone, without family support, would constitute an ordeal preventing him from preserving his human dignity while his illness pursues its inevitably painful and fatal course. In the

[5] The UK stressed that in their opinion Art. 3 ECHR could be held to be limited to intentional acts of the authorities or from non-State bodies. The UK indicated that "The Court ruling in this case means that Article 3 can also apply where the source of the offending treatment arises from factors outside the control of the authorities there and even when, in itself, the treatment does not infringe Convention standards." Quite remarkably, experts indicate that St. Kitts is one of the few Carribean countries that has a medical school/faculty (Cuba and Jamaica being the other ones...).

[6] It is recalled that the procedure under the ECHR used to be two-fold: the Commission could declare the case admissible, and could thereupon indicate in its opinion that the case be dealt with by the Court. As per Protocol 11, this dual approach has been replaced by a singular one. The Court now deals with both the application, the admissibility and the judgement, albeit by different 'organs' within the Court (e.g. a Committee deals with admissibility).

Finnish case (see below) the Commission underlined that in this ex-Zairean case the infection had already reached an advanced stage necessitating repeated hospital stays and where the care facilities in the receiving country were precarious. The French decided to settle this case out of Court, and agreed to grant the ex-Zairean a residence permit.

Two months later, the Commission made public a decision on the admissibility of an application lodged by a Ugandan national who was HIV positive and was faced with repatriation from Finland where he had been sentenced to over 11 years' imprisonment. In this case repatriation was not believed to be a violation of Art. 3. This, in spite of submissions (i.e. medical opinions) that

a) interruption of the medication would result in an acceleration of the illness
b) adequate medical treatment in Uganda could not be assured (*cure*)
c) there was a lack of friends and relatives in Uganda (*care*).

The applicant himself claimed that if he were returned, he would be treated as an outcast, and would lack the means to receive proper care, whether medical or psychological.

The Commission, however, reached the conclusion that the illness had "... not yet reached such an advanced state that [...] deportation would amount to treatment proscribed by Article 3 ..." The Commission, in reaching this conclusion, took the situation and conditions in Uganda into due account.

Of relevance to this case were also that

a) the President of the Commission decided to indicate to the Finnish Government that it was desirable not to deport the applicant until the Commission had been able to examine the application,
b) the Commission granted the applicant legal aid,
c) due regard had been had to both the Court case D v UK, and the ex-Zairean/ Commission cases.

The benchmarks are therefore:

– the state of the illness (advanced stage) and
– the conditions in the country of origin (precarious care facilities).

Of the utmost importance would appear to be the inherent, implicit acknowledgement that although the illness might upon the return become more manifest, and that although interruption of the medication would result in the acceleration of the illness, return would not amount to a breach of Art. 3. This includes the assumption that the level of treatment in Uganda is well below the level of treatment in Finland. It indeed means that the emphasis lies with the possibility of treatment in general, *not* the level of treatment. It would also allow for the conclusion that the deportation of someone seriously ill, and hence most probably not capable of travelling, would also prevent a deportation order from being executed. In this respect it is once again underlined that the application was considered inadmissible, which in European human rights language means that the Commission has not considered it necessary to deal with this case in extenso. (...) [I]t is felt that, thanks to the Finnish case, the chances of a balanced approach are now more realistic.

HEALTH AND THE COURT

Maud de Boer-Buquicchio[7]

At first sight there is no link between the theme of this Handbook and the ECHR. The ECHR guarantees neither the right to enter or to remain on the territory of a state of which one is not a national nor the right to the enjoyment of good health. The first claim fails on account of the sovereign rights of States to control aliens' entry and residence, and the second because it falls within the category of social and economic rights that are in principle outside the scope of the ECHR. These are regulated at Council of Europe level primarily in the European Social Charter.[8]

Yet, as we will see below, the Court is not prevented from scrutinizing whether States, in taking decisions to remove aliens, comply with the Convention's provisons if their health is seriously affected by the measure.

An important question of principle in this respect is embodied in Article 1 of the Convention which provides that the rights and freedoms enshrined in the Convention (and its additional Protocols) are to be guaranteed by the Contracting States "to everyone within their jurisdiction". The enjoyment of the Convention rights is independent of the nationality or other status of the individual. The principle of non-discrimination is further underlined by Article 14 of the Convention which qualifies race or national origin as a non-justifiable ground for distinctive treatment. It should be added immediately, however, that the prohibition of discrimination in the ECHR has no independent or autonomous existence and that any benefit from it for the individual depends on the existence of other substantive norms in the Convention.

The restrictive immigration policy in a number of States has led to an increasing number of applications presented to the former European Commission of Human Rights, competent before the entry into force of the 11th Protocol to receive individual applications, a task currently incumbent on the European Court of Human Rights. The argument frequently invoked, and in exceptional circumstances accepted by the Commission and the Court, was that the State, by deporting an individual to a State in which the applicant has plausible fears for politically-motivated reprisals with inherent risks for his/her physical well-being, infringed Article 3 of the Convention which prohibits inhuman or degrading treatment.

---

[7] The views here expressed are solely those of the author and do not necessarily reflect the views of the Court.

[8] See e.g. Article 13: the right to social and medical assistance.

The number of cases in which this claim was upheld is relatively low for two reasons: first of all, the threshold set for finding a breach of Article 3 is particularly high and must reach a minimum level of severity.[9] Secondly, both the Commission and the Court require the production of evidence and substantiation going beyond a mere description of the generally prevailing political climate in the receiving country affecting political opponents. Applicants cannot always meet this requirement.[10]

In resisting these applications some Governments argued that by refusing entry to aliens on the territory of the State (and keeping them in transit zones at international airports) they had not even started exercising jurisdiction and were not answerable to the control organs of the Convention for that reason. Such a narrow approach was never accepted.[11] The State's responsibility can be engaged by any deportation measure – whether combined with a refusal of entry or following a stay deemed to be illegal for one reason or another – which physically affects an individual and which could lead to a situation where that individual risks treatment contrary to Article 3.

The absolute prohibition of inhuman or degrading treatment is of course not limited to situations arising out of politically motivated situations, where the proscribed forms of treatment emanate from intentionally inflicted by of the public authorities in the receiving country or from non-state bodies in that country when the authorities there are unable to afford protection. This means that considerations as to adequate health care can be relevant.

Indeed in the case of D. v the UK, which related to the proposed removal of an alien drug courier dying of Aids to his country of origin (St Kitts) where he had no accommodation, no family, moral or financial support and no access to adequate medical treatment, the Court accepted that the source of the risk could stem from factors which cannot either directly or indirectly engage the responsibility of the public authorities of that country.[12]

However, the conclusion reached by the Court in that case – that Article 3 would be violated if the deportation measure were to be implemented – was based on the specific circumstances of that case in which the applicant was at an advanced stage of a terminal and incurable illness, and had been receiving facilities which were linked to his imminent death.

In the case of B.B. v. France, which concerned a Congolese national suffering from Aids and who was subject to deportation to his country of origin where he would in all likelihood not receive appropriate medical treatment, the Court did not rule on the merits of the alleged violation as the French authorities, in the

---

[9] E.g. Vilvarajah and others, judgment of 30 .10. 91, § 107.

[10] Ibidem, § 111.

[11] See for example the separate opinion of Mr Loukaides to the Report of the Commission in the case of Vijayanathan and Pusparajah v. France.

[12] No 146/199/767/964, judgment of 02.05.97.

course of the proceedings before the Court, granted a residence order to the applicant, who, as a result, lost his status as a "victim" in terms of the Convention.[13]

The conclusion of the Court in the case of D. should be read with reference to its exceptional circumstances, as indeed the Court went to considerable lengths to point out.

It is precisely for that reason that other applications where the applicant challenged deportation measures on account of medical conditions failed. For example, in the case of Karara v. Finland the Commission rejected a claim by an applicant who challenged his proposed deportation to Uganda on account of his HIV infection as the illness had not yet reached such an advanced stage as in the case of D.

Likewise, in the case of SCC v Sweden[14] relevant considerations were the relatively recent and early diagnosis and treatment, the availability of treatment in the receiving country and the fact that relatives of the applicant lived there. This all shows, again, that the Court makes an overall assessment, taking into account all the circumstances surrounding the case.

The fact that a friendly settlement was achieved between the parties in the case of Tatete v. Switzerland,[15] in which the applicant, a citizen of Zaïre, had argued that she was entitled to remain in Switzerland after her request for asylum had been rejected on the basis of the absence of comparable treatment in her home country for her HIV-related illnesses, should not be construed either as an admission of a violation by the Swiss Government or as a finding to that effect by the Court.

It would appear that considerations of a humanitarian nature rather than a strict legalistic approach in terms of the Convention have resolved these cases in favour of the applicants.

It is however important to consider further the implications of the above quoted D. judgment. From the strictly legal point of view the finding by the Court that D's deportation to St. Kitts would amount to inhuman treatment, (a) does not automatically lead to a right to remain in the country and (b), still less does it confer a right to benefit from a social security system to which others have made contributions.

Viewed from this perspective, the above case law does not really constitute an answer to the original question: does the ECHR provide a legal framework for claims by aliens to benefit from health care facilities in the Contracting States?

---

[13] Judgment of 07.09.98. Similarly in the Commission's decision in Agyemang Badu v. France (No. 18211/91, decision of 28.06.93), where the case was communicated to the Government under Articles 3 and 8 on humanitarian grounds, and declared inadmissible when the applicant was permitted to remain in France.

[14] No 46553/99, decision of 15. 02.00.

[15] No 41874/98, judgment of 06.07.00.

Here, other normative clauses of the Convention may come into play. In the first place I would like to refer to the case of Gaygusuz v. Austria, which concerned the refusal by the Austrian authorities to grant emergency assistance to an unemployed man of Turkish nationality who had exhausted his entitlement to unemployment benefit on the ground that he did not have Austrian nationality. The Court found this decision to be in breach of Article 14 of the Convention in conjunction with Article 1 of the First Protocol.[16] The Court's finding was based in particular on the fact that the applicant had made contributions to the unemployment insurance fund. Although the above case was not directly related to health care, it is likely that similar conclusions would apply to claims to entitlement to medical care if based on contributions.

However, we can see the full scope of the problem we are here discussing when we look at the situation of individuals who have not made any contribution to any public system of public health care and where facilities would need to be provided on the basis of the principle of solidarity rather than that of mutual assistance.

As pointed out above, the degree of severity of the suffering required to engage the responsibility of the public authorities under Article 3 of the Convention is particularly high. It is for this reason also that an application in the 1980s before the Commission by a destitute woman who could not afford to pay her electricity bills, whose electricity supply had been cut off by the Belgian authorities and who argued her case on the basis of Article 3 of the Convention as the lack of heating seriously affected the well-being of her children and herself, was unsuccessful.[17]

This does not mean, however, that where that level has not been reached, individuals are left entirely in a legal vacuum and without any protection under the ECHR. The suggestion is that Article 8 of the Convention, which provides for the right to respect for private life and which is not solely concerned with imposing on States a negative obligation of non-interference but also implies positive obligations, to the extent that physical integrity is an inherent part of this guarantee,[18] could constitute a basis on which aliens who are denied a minimum of care required by their health conditions could successfully argue their case.

The structure of Article 8 is quite different from that of Article 3. Where Article 3 contains an absolute prohibition, Article 8 permits interferences (disregarding positive or negative undertakings), provided such interference pursues a legitimate aim and that the contested measure (or the absence thereof) is proportionate to the aim pursued.

In the application of this balancing exercise in a case of interference with an individual's right to respect for physical integrity, the following elements will

[16] No 39/1995/545/631, judgment of 16.09.96.

[17] No 14641/89, decision of 09.05.90.

[18] Cf. X and Y v. the Netherlands, judgment of 26.03.00, § 22.

affect the weight given to the various interests: the severity of the disease, the availability of medical care in the receiving country, on the one hand, and that of general interest such as the motives underlying the deportation order (such as illegal entry, or the existence of a criminal record), and the existence of family life, on the other.

In this respect the case of Nasri v. France constitutes an interesting precedent although the Article 8 issue in this case was one of respect for family life rather than for private life: the deportee was an Algerian deaf-mute, whose condition was aggravated by illiteracy and for whom family relations were particularly important in that they could help to prevent him from lapsing into a life of crime, the manifestation of which had triggered off the deportation order. In this case, notwithstanding the seriousness of the offence committed (gang-rape), the Court considered that the scales tipped in the applicant's favour and found that there would be a violation of Article 8 of the Convention if the decision to deport the applicant were executed.[19]

The few cases brought before the Convention's organs do not cover the full range of health care. They all concerned situations of medical treatment of illnesses and not, for example, access to birth assistance, or to care for the elderly or physically or mentally handicapped, areas in which considerations pertaining to physical integrity are equally relevant. The Court does not lay down any policy rules for Member States on how to deal with the growing problems arising out of increasing migration to the economically more developed States in the field of administration of public health care. Its jurisprudence develops on the basis of cases brought before it, in which the notion of victim is central. In all these areas the limits of permissible conduct for the authorities in this area are traced by the ECHR. The exact implications will unfold as applications are submitted to the Court.

DEPORTATION AND SERIOUS ILLNESS IN LEGAL PRAXIS

Kai Träskelin

As a representative of the Finnish Supreme Administrative Court, I would like to describe to you the legal practice that has evolved in Finland when people in deportation cases suffer from some serious illness. I will focus on cases where it

---

[19] No 18/1994/465/564, judgment of 13.07.95.

is already known during the deportation proceedings that the illness is fatal and beyond cure.

In Finnish legal praxis it has become established practice for courts to quash deportation and allow continued residence if the person is seriously ill and has lived in the country for a long time. This rule applies even if it is found that the person concerned has either entered, or resides in, the country without a valid permit. Rather than making reference to human rights instruments that prohibit inhuman treatment in general terms, however, the grounds for such practice can be found in the principles of proportionality and equity which are considered of great importance in administrative law generally and in matters concerning aliens especially.

In comparison with other European countries, the number of aliens in Finland is small, in the case both of people with residence permits and those seeking asylum. Typically, courts are only called upon to consider deportation in the case of people who – for some reason or another – have forfeited the right to continue to reside in Finland. It may be that the original personal reason for entering Finland ceases to be relevant, for example in cases where people complete their studies or their marriage breaks up soon after entry into Finland. The majority of deportation cases, however, concern people who have been convicted for repeated offences, organized crime or severe crimes for the protection of others. In such cases expulsion is based on a special reason, namely the maintenance of public order and safety.

When special circumstances barring deportation are considered, application of the principles of proportionality and equity within the framework of overall legal discretion require that the weight given to the grounds for deportation should vary in accordance with the severity of the illness from which the person suffers. The more serious the illness is, the less weight should be given to the grounds for deportation in the particular case. For instance, the state of health of the person concerned can be considered to constitute a factor relevant to the overall assessment of that person's ties with his country of residence if he has lived in the country for a long time because of studies or a marriage that has now ended. An overall assessment should be made of the individual circumstances of each case, implying that even less serious illnesses that do not constitute a bar to deportation *per se* may tip the balance against deportation in a particular case, in view of proportionality and equity.

In contrast, in cases where the person has been found guilty of serious drug-related or violent offences, the current case law regarding the application of Article 8 of the Convention for the Protection of Human Rights and Fundamental Freedoms (ECHR) dictates that an individual's right to family life must be considered to yield to the interests of public order and safety. Except in very unusual circumstances, after completing a prison sentence persons may no longer appeal in the name of inhuman treatment to the protection referred to in Article 3 of the ECHR in order to obtain medical, social or other forms of assistance from the country of residence (European Court of Human Rights 2.5 1997 D vs. the United Kingdom[20]).

Finnish legal praxis[21] takes the view that the "very unusual circumstances" just referred to could be a serious illness that requires continuous hospital care or hospital care at regular intervals. This usually means caring for people with mental health problems in cases where legal overall discretion has concluded that to be expelled from the country in the middle of periods of necessary treatment is unreasonable. No extensive praxis yet exists to indicate which illnesses should be interpreted as so serious that periods of treatment can only properly be carried out in the country of residence, for instance when opportunities for treatment in the home country of the person are non-existent or not self-evident.

In the case of serious illnesses where medical treatment cannot cure the disease but only retard its advance or postpone the terminal stage, the stage of the disease reached, the patient's general condition and capacity to cope with travelling, and opportunities for continued medical and hospital treatment in the home country have to be taken into account when deportation is being considered. Examples of such illnesses are serious cancer cases and HIV/AIDS. As yet, legal praxis in Finland applies only to HIV and AIDS patients.

Just when the European Commission of Human Rights and the European Court of Human Rights were dealing with case D v. the United Kingdom (ECtHR 2.5.1997 concerning a person from St. Kitts in an advanced stage of AIDS), in Finland we had in the Supreme Admistrative Court a case[22] concerning a citizen from former Zaire. This person was in an advanced stage of AIDS and also suffered from related Kaposi Syndrome of the lungs. She attended hospital every two weeks for cytostatic treatment. Her general condition was very poor and it was obvious that she would not be able to cope much longer as an outpatient, and would need continuous hospital care.

Consideration of this case in Finland took so long that the European Court of Human Rights had already issued its ruling on the case D v. the United Kingdom 2.5.1997. In this case, the Court took the view that, considering the health of the person concerned, deportation to St. Kitts would violate Article 3. The Court noted that the applicant was in the terminal stage of AIDS. An abrupt withdrawal of the care facilities provided in the respondent State together with the predictable lack of adequate facilities as well as of any form of moral or social

---

[20] ECtHR, D v. United Kingdom, 2.5.1997. [Editor's note: all the ECtHR and Commission cases mentioned in this contribution have been included in this Reader and notes have therefore been limited to the absolute minimum.]

[21] KHO 29.10.1993 no. 4309, KHO 9.12.1993 no. 4954, KHO 31.12.1994 no. 5602, KHO 18.3.1994 no. 1022, KHO 5.7.1994 no. 3094, KHO 29.12.1994 no. 6658, KHO 24.1.1995 no. 205, KHO 8.3.1995 no. 742, KHO 26.4.1995 no. 1865, KHO 27.3.1996 no. 910, KHO 4.9.1996 no. 2992, KHO 28.8.1996 no. 2580, KHO 4.2.1997 no. 228, KHO 9.7.1997 no. 1718 among others.

[22] KHO 19.7.1997 no. 2267, no. 4187/3/96.

support in the receiving country would hasten the applicant's death and subject him to acute mental and physical suffering. In view of those very exceptional circumstates, bearing in mind the critical stage which the applicant's fatal illness had reached and given the compelling humanitarian considerations at stake, the Court stated that the implementation of the decision to remove him to St. Kitt's would amount to inhuman treatment.

In the former Zairean case, the Finnish Supreme Administrative Court passed judgement on September 17, 1997.[23] The Court had no doubts about its final ruling. Legal praxis had already adopted the position that it was unreasonable, in a deportation situation, to cut a person off from hospital care or medical care requiring repeated treatment. The judgement drew a line on when a deportation decision could be considered to amount to inhuman treatment in violation of Article 3 of the ECHR when the disease was a decisive factor in legal overall discretion concerning the case. Finland's new Constitution Act includes a similar prohibition on inhuman treatment of any person.

The Court ruling noted not only the AIDS diagnosis but also the fact that the Zairean's general condition had deteriorated considerably and that she would soon be needing not only cytostatic treatment but also hospital care because she could no longer manage at home and there was the threat of infections. The Court also noted that the disease would advance and probably lead ultimately to a need for longer-term hospital care. The majority of the Court's members took the view that Article 3 of the ECHR on inhuman treatment had not been violated, so the judgement was justified on a basis of overall legal discretion. The Court was of the opinion that, in view of the circumstances, there were no adequate reasons for deportation, and that the terminal stage of AIDS testified to in the medical certificate and its incurable status, together with all the other considerations and circumstances affecting the case meant that deportation would have been against the Finnish national Aliens Act. Thus this case was not judged to involve the very unusual circumstances found in ECtHR case D v. the United Kingdom 2.5.1997. This was because in the Finnish case the former Zairean had parents and 3 children in her homeland, so the same end-result was reached by overall legal discretion following the principles of proportionality and equity. A minority of the Court's members argued for the decision to repeal the deportation on the grounds that the terminal illness and the fact that it would probably lead to a need for longer-term hospital care meant that deportation would have resulted in treatment violating human dignity vis-à-vis the provisions of the Finnish Constitution Act and thus also amount to a violation of Article 3 of the ECHR.

In my own view, the Finnish Supreme Administrative Court decision can be viewed as being in line with general legal praxis in Finland. The family ties in former Zaire of the Zairean seeking asylum was the main difference compared

[23] KHO 19.7.1997 no. 2267.

with what constituted 'very unusual circumstances' in the European Court of Human Rights ruling in the case of the terminal-stage AIDS patient in D v. the United Kingdom, who would have been alone and probably not given treatment in his homeland.

It was a mere six months later in the disadvantaged political situation in former Zaire when the European Commission of Human Rights issued its report dated 9.3.1998 to the European Court of Human Rights in the case of a former Zairean B.B. v. France.[24] Here, the Commission pointed out that the repatriation of this ex-Zairean in an advanced stage of AIDS to a country where he would probably not have access to the necessary medical treatment and where he would have to confront an illness such as AIDS at an advanced stage, all alone, without family support, would constitute an ordeal not allowing him to preserve his human dignity while his illness pursued its inevitably painful and fatal course. Later on, this case was settled in the European Court of Human Rights, when France decided to settle the case out of court and agreed to grant the ex-Zairean a residence permit.

The final outcomes in the Finnish and French cases not handled by the European Court of Human Rights were equally humane and reasonable, and the minor differences in detail would only have been significant in terms of formal questions concerning the principle of inhuman treatment. In both cases the applicants were permitted to stay on humanatarian grounds.

I think that even if the issue concerns a country of residence and a home country with very different standards of social and health care, when very unusual circumstances in the final stage of a disease are assessed, social ties and networks in the home country are viewed as equally important when medical help in the terminal phase can no longer improve a patient's status but only help to reduce his pain.

The only case on deportation and state of health in Finland to reach the European Commission of Human Rights concerned a Ugandan man who was HIV-positive. ECtHR 9.5.1998 Karara v. Finland. Between December 1991 and September 1992 the husband was found guilty of several rapes and was sentenced for these and for attempted murder to over 11 years in prison, as he was considered to have acted in full knowledge of being HIV-positive. As the Ugandan had been found guilty of a violent offence for which he had received a legally valid sentence, there was justification under law for his deportation.

The Supreme Administrative Court[25] had to decide whether, in view of his state of health and other matters bearing on the case, it was unreasonable or inhuman to deport the Ugandan to his home country. According to medical reports, he had been receiving treatment from July 1992 onwards because of

---

[24] B.B. v. France, Comm. report 9.3.1998, cited in ECtHR 29.5.1998, 40900/98, Karara v. Finland, p. 8.

[25] KHO 19.7.1997 no. 2267.

being HIV-positive, but he was in good physical condition and showed almost no symptoms. During the court proceedings he was receiving a combination of two drugs, but as these were ceasing to be effective the doctor judged that later in the year this treatment would have to be changed to therapy combining 3 drugs. If medication stopped or a changeover was made to a single drug unable to affect the course of the HIV infection, the care achievements gained would probably be lost within a few months. The disease would move on to a "symptomatic" stage of HIV infection, though this would not yet be the AIDS stage. An unmedicated patient would run a roughly 40 per cent risk of developing a consequential HIV disease leading to a diagnosis of AIDS over the next 3 years. On the other hand, evidence was also obtained in the court that it would be possible for HIV/AIDS patients in Uganda to obtain basic AZT treatment.

The Supreme Administrative Court found, based on the report on the Ugandan's state of health, that he would probably not get the same standard of care as he had received in Finland if he was deported to Uganda. His health would therefore possibly deteriorate and the disease would progress to the AIDS stage faster. However, taking account of the report on his state of health at the time the ruling was given, his deportation to Uganda could not be considered inhumane or degrading treatment as referred to in Article 3 of the ECHR. The Court then exercised overall legal discretion, weighing up the deportation principle on the one hand and the various factors that argued against it, and only opting for deportation when the arguments for deportation are more weighty than those against it. The Court in fact pointed out that being found guilt of repeated crimes of violence was considered to weigh more heavily than the arguments against deportation, that is, protection of family life, the man's state of health and the medical treatment needed. The claims made concerning the Ugandan's involvement in the fighting in Rwanda and that deportation would discriminate against him on the basis of race and colour were found unconvincing and had been made only for the purpose of preventing him from being deported.

The Ugandan appealed to the European Commission of Human Rights, claiming that deportation would put him at immediate risk of death because of the HIV and thus lead to treatment violating Article 3 of the ECHR. In its reply to the appeal, the Finnish Government pointed to the Ugandan Government's commitment to the large-scale UNAIDS campaign, which called for efficient monitoring of drug distribution at reduced rates and the establishment of hospital places and a new specialized hospital in June 1998 for HIV patients. Though the Ugandan due to be deported would not get as individually tailored treatment in Uganda as in Finland, this did not automatically mean that he would lack proper treatment if deported there.

The Commission compared the case to D v. United Kingdom ECtHR 2.5.1997, pointing to the very exceptional circumstances in the latter case, which concerned the terminal phase of AIDS. The Commission stressed, however, that a foreigner subject to deportation does not have the right to appeal to the need for continuous medical, social and other assistance in his country of residence, even after completing a prison sentence. The Commission also referred to its report dated 9.3.1998 on the case of B.B. v. France, in which a person with advanced AIDS required repeated periods in hospital, and where treatment facilities in the home country were uncertain.

Against this background, the Commission took the view that the Ugandan applicant's sickness had not yet reached a stage at which his deportation would have violated Article 3 of the ECHR, also taking account of conditions in Uganda. The Commission ruled that deporting the applicant to Uganda would not be a violation of Article 3.

There is a recent case from the new ECtHR concerning expulsion and a refusal of a residence permit for a Zambian national infected by HIV. The case is ECtHR 15th February 2000, S.C.C. v Sweden. The applicant, a Zambian national, was the wife of a diplomat at the Zambian embassy in Stockholm and lived in Sweden from 1990 to early 1994. She returned to Sweden later in 1994, after her husband's death in Zambia. She applied for a residence permit, alleging that her husband's relatives threatened her life and that she had been offered a job at the Zambian embassy. The immigration authorities, however, rejected her application. She lodged an appeal against this refusal, relying on the fact that she had contracted HIV and claiming that she should therefore be granted a residence permit on humanitarian grounds. The doctor she had visited several times reported that no treatment could be started unless she was given a long-term residence permit. However, the applicant's appeal and further applications were all rejected. Her doctor delivered a certificate stating that her condition had deteriorated to such an extent that treatment had been started.

The Court found the case inadmissible under Articles 2 and 3. The Court stated that complaints under Article 3 are subject to close scrutiny when the source of the risk of proscribed treatment in the receiving country stems from factors which cannot engage either directly or indirectly the responsibility of the public authorities of that country, or which, taken alone, do not in themselves infringe the standards of this Article. All the circumstances surrounding the case are to be scrupulously examined, especially the applicant's personal situation in the deporting State. However, aliens who are subject to expulsion cannot in principle claim any entitlement to remain in the territory of a contracting State in order to continue to benefit from medical, social or other forms of assistance provided by that State. Only in exceptional circumstances will the implementation of a decision to remove an alien result in a violation of Article 3 by reason of compelling humanitarian considerations. In the instant case, the applicant's medical status was diagnosed in 1995 and her anti-HIV treatment only recently started. The Swedish health authorities rightly concluded that, when assessing the humanitarian aspects of a case like this, an overall evaluation of the infected alien's state of health should be made rather than letting the HIV diagnosis in itself be decisive. According to the Swedish embassy, AIDS treatment is available in Zambia. Furthermore, the applicant's children and most of her relatives live there. Taking into consideration the conjunction of all these elements, the applicant's situation was not such that her deportation would have amounted to ill-treatment.

On the basis of the legal praxis that I have outlined, it is easy for me to agree with the interpretation of the term 'right to health' put forward in an article and a report by special advisor Van Krieken. The latter proposes the addition of the adjective 'adequate' to this phrase, to reflect the commitment to use all available means and resources to ensure that societies throughout the world do their best to improve and/or maximize their health services.[26] If the term 'right to adequate health' were used as the grounds for a judgement in considering the deportation of a sick person in legal praxis, and at the same time courts' opportunities for obtaining correct and up-to-date information about the standard of public health and social services in each country, as well as about related cultural matters, were increased, courts would be able to ensure reasonable outcomes that would also be humane in terms of the sick person. Thus we can say that the aim of increasing information, serves both the justice of court judgements and the legal protection and human treatment of deportees.

[26] Peter van Krieken, Health and Continued Residence: Reason or Pretext, *European Journal of Health Law* 7/2000 pp 29-46, on p. 30; and Peter van Krieken, *Health Gaps and Migratory Movements*, Raoul Wallenberg Institute, Report no. 31, Lund 2000, pp. 2-3.

LEGAL TEXTS: ECHR

CONVENTION FOR THE PROTECTION OF HUMAN RIGHTS AND FUNDAMENTAL FREEDOMS AS AMENDED BY PROTOCOL NO. 11[1]

The governments signatory hereto, being members of the Council of Europe,
Considering the Universal Declaration of Human Rights proclaimed by the General Assembly of the United Nations on 10th December 1948;
Considering that this Declaration aims at securing the universal and effective recognition and observance of the Rights therein declared;
Considering that the aim of the Council of Europe is the achievement of greater unity between its members and that one of the methods by which that aim is to be pursued is the maintenance and further realisation of human rights and fundamental freedoms;
Reaffirming their profound belief in those fundamental freedoms which are the foundation of justice and peace in the world and are best maintained on the one hand by an effective political democracy and on the other by a common understanding and observance of the human rights upon which they depend;
Being resolved, as the governments of European countries which are like-minded and have a common heritage of political traditions, ideals, freedom and the rule of law, to take the first steps for the collective enforcement of certain of the rights stated in the Universal Declaration,
Have agreed as follows:

Article 1 – Obligation to respect human rights
The High Contracting Parties shall secure to everyone within their jurisdiction the rights and freedoms defined in Section I of this Convention.

Section I – Rights and freedoms

Article 2 – Right to life
1. Everyone's right to life shall be protected by law. No one shall be deprived of his life intentionally save in the execution of a sentence of a court following his conviction of a crime for which this penalty is provided by law.

[1] Rome, 4 November 1950, entry into force 3 September 1953. The text of the Convention had been amended according to the provisions of Protocol No. 3 (ETS No. 45), which entered into force on 21 September 1970, of Protocol No. 5 (ETS No. 55), which entered into force on 20 December 1971 and of Protocol No. 8 (ETS No. 118), which entered into force on 1 January 1990, and comprised also the text of Protocol No. 2 (ETS No. 44) which, in accordance with Article 5, paragraph 3 thereof, had been an integral part of the Convention since its entry into force on 21 September 1970. All provisions which had been amended or added by these Protocols are replaced by Protocol No. 11 (ETS No. 155), as from the date of its entry into force on 1 November 1998. As from that date, Protocol No. 9 (ETS No. 140), which entered into force on 1 October 1994, is repealed and Protocol No. 10 (ETS No. 146) has lost its purpose.

2. Deprivation of life shall not be regarded as inflicted in contravention of this article when it results from the use of force which is no more than absolutely necessary:
   a. in defence of any person from unlawful violence;
   b. in order to effect a lawful arrest or to prevent the escape of a person lawfully detained;
   c. in action lawfully taken for the purpose of quelling a riot or insurrection.

Article 3 – Prohibition of torture
No one shall be subjected to torture or to inhuman or degrading treatment or punishment.

Article 4 – Prohibition of slavery and forced labour (...)

Article 5 – Right to liberty and security
1. Everyone has the right to liberty and security of person. No one shall be deprived of his liberty save in the following cases and in accordance with a procedure prescribed by law:
   a. the lawful detention of a person after conviction by a competent court;
   b. the lawful arrest or detention of a person for non-compliance with the lawful order of a court or in order to secure the fulfilment of any obligation prescribed by law;
   c. the lawful arrest or detention of a person effected for the purpose of bringing him before the competent legal authority on reasonable suspicion of having committed an offence or when it is reasonably considered necessary to prevent his committing an offence or fleeing after having done so;
   d. the detention of a minor by lawful order for the purpose of educational supervision or his lawful detention for the purpose of bringing him before the competent legal authority;
   e. the lawful detention of persons for the prevention of the spreading of infectious diseases, of persons of unsound mind, alcoholics or drug addicts or vagrants;
   f. the lawful arrest or detention of a person to prevent his effecting an unauthorised entry into the country or of a person against whom action is being taken with a view to deportation or extradition.
2. Everyone who is arrested shall be informed promptly, in a language which he understands, of the reasons for his arrest and of any charge against him.
3. Everyone arrested or detained in accordance with the provisions of paragraph 1.c of this article shall be brought promptly before a judge or other officer authorised by law to exercise judicial power and shall be entitled to trial within a reasonable time or to release pending trial. Release may be conditioned by guarantees to appear for trial.
4. Everyone who is deprived of his liberty by arrest or detention shall be entitled to take proceedings by which the lawfulness of his detention shall be decided speedily by a court and his release ordered if the detention is not lawful.
5. Everyone who has been the victim of arrest or detention in contravention of the provisions of this article shall have an enforceable right to compensation.

Article 6 – Right to a fair trial
1. In the determination of his civil rights and obligations or of any criminal charge against him, everyone is entitled to a fair and public hearing within a reasonable time

by an independent and impartial tribunal established by law. Judgment shall be pronounced publicly but the press and public may be excluded from all or part of the trial in the interests of morals, public order or national security in a democratic society, where the interests of juveniles or the protection of the private life of the parties so require, or to the extent strictly necessary in the opinion of the court in special circumstances where publicity would prejudice the interests of justice.

2. Everyone charged with a criminal offence shall be presumed innocent until proved guilty according to law.
3. Everyone charged with a criminal offence has the following minimum rights:
   a. to be informed promptly, in a language which he understands and in detail, of the nature and cause of the accusation against him;
   b. to have adequate time and facilities for the preparation of his defence;
   c. to defend himself in person or through legal assistance of his own choosing or, if he has not sufficient means to pay for legal assistance, to be given it free when the interests of justice so require;
   d. to examine or have examined witnesses against him and to obtain the attendance and examination of witnesses on his behalf under the same conditions as witnesses against him;
   e. to have the free assistance of an interpreter if he cannot understand or speak the language used in court.

Article 7 – No punishment without law (...)

Article 8 – Right to respect for private and family life

1. Everyone has the right to respect for his private and family life, his home and his correspondence.
2. There shall be no interference by a public authority with the exercise of this right except such as is in accordance with the law and is necessary in a democratic society in the interests of national security, public safety or the economic well-being of the country, for the prevention of disorder or crime, for the protection of health or morals, or for the protection of the rights and freedoms of others.

Article 9 – Freedom of thought, conscience and religion (...)

Article 10 – Freedom of expression (...)

Article 11 – Freedom of assembly and association (...)

Article 12 – Right to marry (...)

Article 13 – Right to an effective remedy

Everyone whose rights and freedoms as set forth in this Convention are violated shall have an effective remedy before a national authority notwithstanding that the violation has been committed by persons acting in an official capacity.

Article 14 – Prohibition of discrimination

The enjoyment of the rights and freedoms set forth in this Convention shall be secured without discrimination on any ground such as sex, race, colour, language, religion, political or other opinion, national or social origin, association with a national minority, property, birth or other status.

Article 15 – Derogation in time of emergency (...)

Article 16 – Restrictions on political activity of aliens
Nothing in Articles 10, 11 and 14 shall be regarded as preventing the High Contracting Parties from imposing restrictions on the political activity of aliens.

Article 17 – Prohibition of abuse of rights
Nothing in this Convention may be interpreted as implying for any State, group or person any right to engage in any activity or perform any act aimed at the destruction of any of the rights and freedoms set forth herein or at their limitation to a greater extent than is provided for in the Convention.

Article 18 – Limitation on use of restrictions on rights
The restrictions permitted under this Convention to the said rights and freedoms shall not be applied for any purpose other than those for which they have been prescribed.

Section II – European Court of Human Rights

Article 19 – Establishment of the Court
To ensure the observance of the engagements undertaken by the High Contracting Parties in the Convention and the Protocols thereto, there shall be set up a European Court of Human Rights, hereinafter referred to as "the Court". It shall function on a permanent basis.

Article 20 – Number of judges (...)

Article 21 – Criteria for office (...)

Article 22 – Election of judges (...)

Article 23 – Terms of office (...)

Article 24 – Dismissal (...)

Article 25 – Registry and legal secretaries (...)

Article 26 – Plenary Court (...)

Article 27 – Committees, Chambers and Grand Chamber
1. To consider cases brought before it, the Court shall sit in committees of three judges, in Chambers of seven judges and in a Grand Chamber of seventeen judges. The Court's Chambers shall set up committees for a fixed period of time.
2. There shall sit as an *ex officio* member of the Chamber and the Grand Chamber the judge elected in respect of the State Party concerned or, if there is none or if he is unable to sit, a person of its choice who shall sit in the capacity of judge.
3. The Grand Chamber shall also include the President of the Court, the Vice-Presidents,

the Presidents of the Chambers and other judges chosen in accordance with the rules of the Court. When a case is referred to the Grand Chamber under Article 43, no judge from the Chamber which rendered the judgment shall sit in the Grand Chamber, with the exception of the President of the Chamber and the judge who sat in respect of the State Party concerned.

Article 28 – Declarations of inadmissibility by committees
A committee may, by a unanimous vote, declare inadmissible or strike out of its list of cases an application submitted under Article 34 where such a decision can be taken without further examination. The decision shall be final.

Article 29 – Decisions by Chambers on admissibility and merits
1. If no decision is taken under Article 28, a Chamber shall decide on the admissibility and merits of individual applications submitted under Article 34.
2. A Chamber shall decide on the admissibility and merits of inter-State applications submitted under Article 33.
3. The decision on admissibility shall be taken separately unless the Court, in exceptional cases, decides otherwise.

Article 30 – Relinquishment of jurisdiction to the Grand Chamber (...)

Article 31 – Powers of the Grand Chamber (...)

Article 32 – Jurisdiction of the Court
1. The jurisdiction of the Court shall extend to all matters concerning the interpretation and application of the Convention and the protocols thereto which are referred to it as provided in Articles 33, 34 and 47.
2. In the event of dispute as to whether the Court has jurisdiction, the Court shall decide.

Article 33 – Inter-State cases (...)

Article 34 – Individual applications
The Court may receive applications from any person, non-governmental organisation or group of individuals claiming to be the victim of a violation by one of the High Contracting Parties of the rights set forth in the Convention or the protocols thereto. The High Contracting Parties undertake not to hinder in any way the effective exercise of this right.

Article 35 – Admissibility criteria
1. The Court may only deal with the matter after all domestic remedies have been exhausted, according to the generally recognised rules of international law, and within a period of six months from the date on which the final decision was taken.
2. The Court shall not deal with any application submitted under Article 34 that:
   a. is anonymous; or
   b. is substantially the same as a matter that has already been examined by the Court or has already been submitted to another procedure of international investigation or settlement and contains no relevant new information.
3. The Court shall declare inadmissible any individual application submitted under Article 34 which it considers incompatible with the provisions of the Convention or

the protocols thereto, manifestly ill-founded, or an abuse of the right of application.
4. The Court shall reject any application which it considers inadmissible under this Article. It may do so at any stage of the proceedings.

Article 36 – Third party intervention (...)

Article 37 – Striking out applications

1. The Court may at any stage of the proceedings decide to strike an application out of its list of cases where the circumstances lead to the conclusion that:
   a. the applicant does not intend to pursue his application; or
   b. the matter has been resolved; or
   c. for any other reason established by the Court, it is no longer justified to continue the examination of the application.

   However, the Court shall continue the examination of the application if respect for human rights as defined in the Convention and the protocols thereto so requires.
2. The Court may decide to restore an application to its list of cases if it considers that the circumstances justify such a course.

Article 38 – Examination of the case and friendly settlement proceedings (...)

Article 39 – Finding of a friendly settlement (...)

Article 40 – Public hearings and access to documents

1. Hearings shall be in public unless the Court in exceptional circumstances decides otherwise.
2. Documents deposited with the Registrar shall be accessible to the public unless the President of the Court decides otherwise.

Article 41 – Just satisfaction

If the Court finds that there has been a violation of the Convention or the protocols thereto, and if the internal law of the High Contracting Party concerned allows only partial reparation to be made, the Court shall, if necessary, afford just satisfaction to the injured party.

Article 42 – Judgments of Chambers

Judgments of Chambers shall become final in accordance with the provisions of Article 44, paragraph 2.

Article 43 – Referral to the Grand Chamber (...)

Article 44 – Final judgments (...)

Article 45 – Reasons for judgments and decisions

1. Reasons shall be given for judgments as well as for decisions declaring applications admissible or inadmissible.
2. If a judgment does not represent, in whole or in part, the unanimous opinion of the judges, any judge shall be entitled to deliver a separate opinion.

Article 46 – Binding force and execution of judgments

1. The High Contracting Parties undertake to abide by the final judgment of the Court in any case to which they are parties.
2. The final judgment of the Court shall be transmitted to the Committee of Ministers, which shall supervise its execution.

Article 47 – Advisory opinions

1. The Court may, at the request of the Committee of Ministers, give advisory opinions on legal questions concerning the interpretation of the Convention and the protocols thereto.
2. Such opinions shall not deal with any question relating to the content or scope of the rights or freedoms defined in Section I of the Convention and the protocols thereto, or with any other question which the Court or the Committee of Ministers might have to consider in consequence of any such proceedings as could be instituted in accordance with the Convention.
3. Decisions of the Committee of Ministers to request an advisory opinion of the Court shall require a majority vote of the representatives entitled to sit on the Committee.

Article 48 – Advisory jurisdiction of the Court

The Court shall decide whether a request for an advisory opinion submitted by the Committee of Ministers is within its competence as defined in Article 47.

Article 49 – Reasons for advisory opinions

1. Reasons shall be given for advisory opinions of the Court.
2. If the advisory opinion does not represent, in whole or in part, the unanimous opinion of the judges, any judge shall be entitled to deliver a separate opinion.
3. Advisory opinions of the Court shall be communicated to the Committee of Ministers.

Article 50 – Expenditure on the Court

The expenditure on the Court shall be borne by the Council of Europe.

Article 51 – Privileges and immunities of judges

Section III – Miscellaneous provisions

Article 52 – Article 59 (...)

STRASBOURG CASE LAW

THE RELEVANT CASES

It is not always easy to fully appreciate the impact of the European human rights system, as many of the decisions tend to be overlooked. It is quite natural to focus on the more sensational or surprising decisions of the Court, rather than on the Commission decisions to declare a case non-admissible. Those latter cases are, in the opinion of this editor, often at least as important as the headline cases of the Court proper.

This observation would also appear to be true in the cases dealing with residence-cum-health questions: a lot of attention has been paid to the D. (St. Kitts) v. UK case, whereas the Karara case, declared inadmissible by the Commission might be considered to have been equally important. It has thus been decided to include in this Reader all the relevant cases (although not all of them in full, for the simple reason of accessibility and space constraints). Most of the cases are now available on the internet anyway, which should enable the interested reader to surf to the indicated site.

1. Court Cases
Cruz Varas v. Sweden[1]

The Cruz Varas case became above all famous for the 10-9 vote on the question whether countries (in this case Sweden) had to agree with a Commission's request to delay a deportation pending a case with 'Strasbourg'. The Swedish Government maintained that no obligation exists under the Convention to comply with a Commission indication under Rule 36. Of interest for the issue at stake is that the subject of a Post Traumatic Stress Syndrom vs return played a role. One of the questions the Court had to deal with was whether the psycho-psychiatric aspects of the case a) had to be taken into account, and b) would have resulted in a real risk argument as per Article 3.
It was inter alia submitted:

27. A further medical opinion was produced in evidence prepared by Dr Søndergaard, a specialist in psychiatric diseases at the Karolinska Hospital. That opinion, dated 28 June 1989, stated that, from the manner in which he presented his story and his reactions while telling it, there were strong indications that he suffered from a post-traumatic stress syndrome. Dr Søndergaard found him to be considerably shaken and on the borderline of what he could tolerate.

---

[1] The case is numbered 46/1990/237/307. The first number is the case's position on the list of cases referred to the Court in the relevant year (second number). The last two numbers indicate the case's position on the list of cases referred to the Court since its creation and on the list of the corresponding originating applications to the Commission.

44. The applicants have submitted a medical report drawn up by Dr Mariano Castex (Professor of Psychiatry, University of Buenos Aires) following an examination of the first applicant in February 1990. The report includes the following statement:
"As a conclusion one may state that Mr Hector Cruz Varas suffers a serious 'post-traumatic stress disorder' instilled in him as a consequence of the torture and ill-treatment suffered in Chile in the past years. The exposure to high insecurity, and the return to his native land, has increased the pathological dimension of his sufferings, and if arrangements are not made for an adequate psychological and psychiatric treatment, he might suffer from a worsening of his mental disorder with unforeseeable consequences not only for him, but for his wife and child, the latter badly needing a father if one reads carefully the report on the child."

45. A further psychiatric report dated 9 October 1990 was drawn up by Dr Søndergaard following a detailed examination of the applicant in September 1990. The report stated that the first applicant must have experienced "a stressful event of catastrophic proportions". It concluded that he showed the "obvious stigmata of a post-traumatic stress disorder".

72. (...) The Government further contended that the evidence they have gathered since his expulsion supports their belief that he had not been politically active or a member of the FPMR or persecuted by the police. Finally the Government maintained that the medical evidence submitted by the first applicant only shows that he had at some time in the past been subjected to maltreatment. It does not show that he was tortured by the Chilean authorities or by persons for whom the Chilean Government could be held responsible.

73. The Commission, on the other hand, accepted that Mr Cruz Varas had been subjected in the past to treatment contrary to Article 3 by persons for whom the Chilean State was responsible. However, in view of the political evolution which had taken place in Chile, the Commission did not consider that there existed a real risk that he would again be exposed to such treatment.

77. The Court takes note of the medical evidence submitted by the applicants and, in particular, the evidence of Dr Jacobsson who found that the first applicant's physical injuries and demeanour while recounting his experiences were consistent with his allegations (see paragraphs 26 and 39-40 above). Having regard to Dr Jacobsson's experience in examining victims of torture, this evidence supports the view that the applicant has, at some stage in the past, been subjected to inhuman or degrading treatment. According to the Commission the only plausible explanation for this treatment is that it was carried out by persons for whom "the then Chilean regime" was responsible. There is no element in the material before the Court, however, apart from the first applicant's allegations, which provides direct evidence for this conclusion.

As to the question whether the first applicant's expulsion involved such trauma that it amounted to a breach of Article 3 it can be read:

83. It is recalled that ill-treatment must attain a minimum level of severity if it is to fall within the scope of Article 3. The assessment of this minimum is, in the nature of things, relative; it depends on all the circumstances of the case, such as the nature and context of

the treatment, the manner and method of its execution, its duration, its physical or mental effects and, in some instances, the sex, age and state of health
of the victim (...).

84. In the present case the first applicant was considered to be suffering from a post-traumatic stress disorder prior to his expulsion and his mental health appeared to deteriorate following his return to Chile (see paragraphs 27 and 44 above). However, it results from the finding in paragraph 82 that no substantial basis has been shown for his fears. Accordingly the Court does not consider that the first applicant's expulsion exceeded the threshold set by Article 3.

C. Recapitulation
86. In sum, there has been no breach of Article 3 (*with a vote of 18-1*).

D. v. UK [2]

In the case of D. v. the United Kingdom

The European Court of Human Rights, sitting, in accordance with Article 43 (art. 43) of the Convention for the Protection of Human Rights and Fundamental Freedoms ("the Convention") and the relevant provisions of Rules of Court A (2), as a Chamber composed of the following judges (...),
Having deliberated in private on 20 February and 21 April 1997,
Delivers the following judgment, which was adopted on the last-mentioned date:

PROCEDURE (...)

AS TO THE FACTS

I. Particular circumstances of the case
A. The applicant
6. The applicant was born in St Kitts and appears to have lived there most of his life. He is one of seven children. One sister and one brother moved to the United States in the 1970s and the rest of the family appears to have followed at unspecified dates. The applicant visited the United States in 1989 to try to join his family. During his stay there he was arrested on 5 September 1991 for possession of cocaine and subsequently sentenced to a three-year term of imprisonment. After one year, he was paroled for good behaviour and deported on 8 January 1993 to St Kitts.

B. The applicant's arrival in the United Kingdom and subsequent imprisonment
7. The applicant arrived at Gatwick Airport, London, on 21 January 1993 and sought leave to enter the United Kingdom for two weeks as a visitor. He was found at the airport terminal to be in possession of a substantial quantity of cocaine with a street value of about 120,000 pounds sterling (GBP). The immigration officer refused him leave to enter

[2] The case is numbered 146/1996/767/964.

on the ground that his exclusion was conducive to the public good and gave him notice that he would be removed to St Kitts within a matter of days. However, after being arrested and charged, the applicant was remanded in custody and subsequently prosecuted for being knowingly involved in the fraudulent evasion of the prohibition on the importation of controlled drugs of class A. He pleaded guilty at Croydon Crown Court on 19 April 1993 and was sentenced on 10 May 1993 to six years' imprisonment. He apparently behaved well while in H.M. Prison Wayland and was released on licence on 24 January 1996. He was placed in immigration detention pending his removal to St Kitts. Bail was granted by an adjudicator on 31 October 1996 after the Commission's report had been made public.

C. Diagnosis of AIDS

8. In August 1994, while serving his prison sentence, the applicant suffered an attack of pneumocystis carinii pneumonia ("PCP") and was diagnosed as HIV (human immunodeficiency virus)-positive and as suffering from acquired immunodeficiency syndrome (AIDS). The infection appears to have occurred some time before his arrival in the United Kingdom.

9. On 3 March 1995, the applicant was granted a period of compassionate leave to be with his mother whose air fare to the United Kingdom to visit him had been covered by charitable donations.

10. On 20 January 1996, immediately prior to his release on licence, the immigration authorities gave directions for the applicant's removal to St Kitts.

D. The applicant's request to remain in the United Kingdom

11. By letter dated 23 January 1996, the applicant's solicitors requested that the Secretary of State grant the applicant leave to remain on compassionate grounds since his removal to St Kitts would entail the loss of the medical treatment which he was currently receiving, thereby shortening his life expectancy (see paragraphs 13 and 14 below). This request was refused on 25 January 1996 by the Chief Immigration Officer. In his letter of refusal addressed to the applicant's solicitors the Chief Immigration Officer stated: "In reaching this decision full account was taken of paragraph 4 of the Immigration and Nationality Department B Division Instructions regarding AIDS and HIV-positive cases. You will be aware that paragraph 4 of this instruction which relates to persons whose applications are for leave to enter the United Kingdom states [see paragraph 27 of the judgment below] ... While we are saddened to learn of Mr D[...]'s medical circumstances we do not accept, in line with Departmental Policy, that it is right generally or in the individual circumstances of this case, to allow an AIDS sufferer to remain here exceptionally when, as here, treatment in this country is carried out at public expense, under the National Health Service. Nor would it be fair to treat AIDS sufferers any differently from others suffering medical conditions ..."

E. Judicial review proceedings

12. On 2 February 1996, the applicant applied unsuccessfully to the High Court for leave to apply for judicial review of the decision to refuse him leave to enter. On 15 February 1996, the Court of Appeal dismissed his renewed application. It found that section 3 of the Immigration Act 1971 drew a distinction between leave to enter and leave to remain.

It held that the Chief Immigration Officer had correctly treated Mr D.'s application as an application for leave to enter and was not required to take into account paragraph 5 of the Home Office guidelines which applied to applications for leave to remain (see paragraphs 27 and 28 below). As to the applicant's argument that the Home Office acted unreasonably or irrationally in not acceding to the compassionate circumstances of his plea, Sir Iain Glidewell stated in his judgment: "Nobody can but have great sympathy for this applicant in the plight in which he finds himself. If he is to return to St Kitts it seems that he will be unable to work because of his illness. His expectation of life, if the medical evidence is correct, may well be shorter than it would be if he remained under the treatment that he is receiving in the United Kingdom, and in any ways his plight will be great. On the other hand he would not be here if he had not come on a cocaine smuggling expedition in 1993; and if he had not been imprisoned he would have gone back to St Kitts, if he had ever come here at all, long before his AIDS was diagnosed. Taking account of the fact that the Court must give most anxious scrutiny to a decision which involves questions particularly of life expectancy, as this one apparently does, nevertheless I cannot find that an argument in this case that the decision of the Chief Immigration Officer was irrational is one that has any hope of success at all. Putting it the opposite way, it seems to me to be one which was well within the bounds of his discretion, and thus is not one with which the Court can properly interfere."

F. Reports on the applicant's medical condition, treatment and prognosis

13. Since August 1995, the applicant's "CD4" cell count has been below 10. He has been in the advanced stages of the illness, suffering from recurrent anaemia, bacterial chest infections, malaise, skin rashes, weight loss and periods of extreme fatigue.

14. By letter dated 15 January 1996, Dr Evans, a consultant doctor, stated: "His current treatment is AZT 250 mgs. b.d. and monthly nebulised pentamidine, he occasionally takes mystatin pastilles and skin emollients. In view of the fact that [the applicant] has now had AIDS for over 18 months and because this is a relentlessly progressive disease his prognosis is extremely poor. In my professional opinion [the applicant's] life expectancy would be substantially shortened if he were to return to St Kitts where there is no medication; it is important that he receives pentamidine treatment against PCP and that he receives prompt anti-microbial therapy for any further infections which he is likely to develop ..."

15. In a medical report provided on 13 June 1996, Professor Pinching, a professor of immunology at a London hospital, stated that the applicant had suffered severe and irreparable damage to his immune system and was extremely vulnerable to a wide range of specific infections and to the development of tumours. The applicant was reaching the end of the average durability of effectiveness of the drug therapy which he was receiving. It was stated that the applicant's prognosis was very poor and limited to eight to twelve months on present therapy. It was estimated that withdrawal of the proven effective therapies and of proper medical care would reduce that prognosis to less than half of what would be otherwise expected.

G. Medical facilities in St Kitts

16. By letter dated 20 April 1995, the High Commission for the Eastern Caribbean States informed the doctor treating the applicant in prison that the medical facilities in St Kitts did not have the capacity to provide the medical treatment that he would require. This was

in response to a faxed enquiry of the same date by Dr Hewitt, the managing medical officer at H.M. Prison Wayland. By letter of 24 October 1995, Dr Hewitt informed the Home Office of the contents of the letter from the High Commission, which had also been sent to the Parole Unit on 1 May 1995. He stated that the necessary treatment was not available in St Kitts but was widely and freely available in the United Kingdom and requested that due consideration be given to lifting the deportation order in respect of the applicant. By letter dated 1 August 1996, the High Commission for the Eastern Caribbean States confirmed that the position in St Kitts has not changed.

17. By letter dated 5 February 1996, the Antigua and Barbuda Red Cross informed the applicant's presentatives that they had consulted their officer on St Kitts who stated that there was no health care providing for drugs treatment of AIDS. Results of enquiries made by the Government of the authorities in St Kitts suggest that there are two hospitals in St Kitts which care for AIDS patients by treating them for opportunistic infections until they are well enough to be discharged, and that an increasing number of AIDS sufferers there live with relatives.

H. The applicant's family situation in St Kitts

18. The applicant has no family home or close family in St Kitts other than, according to information provided by the Government, a cousin. His mother, who currently lives in the United States, has declared that her age, bad health and lack of resources prevent her from returning to St Kitts to look after her son if he were to be returned there. She has also stated that she knew of no relatives who would be able to care for him in St Kitts.

I. The applicant's situation since the adoption of the Commission's report

19. When granted bail on 31 October 1996 (see paragraph 7 above) the applicant was released to reside in special sheltered accommodation for AIDS patients provided by a charitable organisation working with homeless persons. Accommodation, food and services are provided free of charge to the applicant. He also has the motional support and assistance of a trained volunteer provided by the Terrence Higgins Trust, the leading charity in the United Kingdom providing practical support, help, counselling and legal and other advice for persons concerned about or having AIDS or HIV infection.

20. In a medical report dated 9 December 1996 Dr J.M. Parkin, a consultant in clinical immunology treating the applicant at a London hospital, noted that he was at an advanced stage of HIV infection and was severely immunosuppressed. His prognosis was poor. The applicant was being given antiretroviral therapy with "D4T" and "3TC" to reduce the risk of opportunistic infection and was continuing to be prescribed pentamidine ebulisers to prevent a recurrence of PCP. Preventative treatment for other opportunistic infections was also foreseen. Dr Parkin noted that the lack of treatment with anti-HIV therapy and preventative measures for opportunistic disease would hasten his death if he were to be returned to St Kitts.

21. The applicant was transferred to an AIDS hospice around the middle of January 1997 for a period of respite care. At the beginning of February there was a sudden deterioration in his condition and he had to be admitted to a hospital on 7 February for examination. At the hearing before the Court on 20 February 1997, it was stated that the applicant's condition was causing concern and that the prognosis was uncertain. According to his counsel, it would appear that the applicant's life was drawing to a close much as the experts had predicted (see paragraph 15 above).

II. Relevant domestic law and practice

22. The regulation of entry into and stay in the United Kingdom is governed by Part 1 of the Immigration Act 1971. The practice to be followed in the administration of the Act for regulating entry and stay is contained in statements of the rules laid by the Secretary of State before Parliament ("the Immigration Rules").

23. Section 3 (1) provides that a person who is not a British citizen shall not enter the United Kingdom unless given leave to do so in accordance with the provisions of the Act. Leave to enter may be granted for a limited or for an indefinite period.

24. Under section 4 (1) of the Act the power to grant or refuse leave to enter is exercised by immigration officers whereas the power to grant leave to remain in the United Kingdom is exercised by the Secretary of State. These powers are exercisable by notice in writing given to the person affected.

25. A person, such as the applicant, who has been refused leave to enter but is physically in the United Kingdom pending his removal and seeks to be allowed to stay there does not fall to be treated as applying for leave to remain. Since no leave to enter had been granted to the applicant, it was right according to the judgment of Sir Iain Glidewell in R. v. Secretary of State for the Home Department, ex parte D. (Court of Appeal, 15 February 1996) for the immigration officer to treat his application as an application for leave to enter rather than for leave to remain.

A. Policy guidelines on how to proceed in cases in which persons seeking to enter or remain in the United Kingdom are suffering from AIDS or are HIV-positive

26. The Immigration and Nationality Department of the Home Office issued a policy document (BDI 3/95) on this subject in August 1995. Paragraph 2 of the guidelines specifies that the fact that a person is suffering from AIDS or is HIV-positive is not a ground for refusing leave to enter or leave to remain if the person concerned otherwise qualifies under the Immigration Rules. Equally, this fact is not in itself a sufficient ground to justify the exercise of discretion where the person concerned has not met the requirements of the Rules. The policy guidelines distinguish between applications for leave to enter and applications for leave to remain.

27. On applications for leave to enter (paragraph 4 of the guidelines), where the person is suffering from AIDS, the policy and practice is to adhere to the provisions of the Immigration Rules in the normal way. Where such a person does not qualify under the Rules, entry is refused.

28. On applications for leave to remain (paragraph 5 of the guidelines), the application should be dealt with normally on its merits under the applicable Rules. However, there is a discretion outside the Rules which can be exercised in strong compassionate circumstances. Paragraph 5.4 states that: "... there may be cases where it is apparent that there are no facilities for treatment available in the applicant's own country. Where evidence suggests that this absence of treatment significantly shortens the life expectancy of the applicant it will normally be appropriate to grant leave to remain."

B. Other relevant materials

29. Among the documentary materials submitted by the applicant, are the following.

1. International policy statements on human rights and AIDS

30. International concern about AIDS has resulted in the adoption of several international texts which have addressed, inter alia, the protection of the human rights of the victims of the disease. Thus, the United Nations Commission on Human Rights adopted a resolution on 9 March 1993 on the protection of human rights in the context of human immunodeficiency virus or acquired immunodeficiency syndrome in which it called upon "all States to ensure that their laws, policies and practices introduced in the context of AIDS respect human rights standards".

31. At a Summit of Heads of Government or Representatives of forty-two States meeting in Paris on 1 December 1994, a declaration was adopted in which the participating States solemnly declared their obligation "to act with compassion for and in solidarity with those with HIV or at risk of becoming infected, both within [their] societies and internationally".

2. Extract of the WHO report on "Health conditions in the Americas", 1994, Volume II, concerning St Kitts and Nevis

32. "Health and living conditions ... there are a number of serious environmental problems, such as inadequate disposal of solid and liquid waste – especially untreated sewage – into coastal lands and waters, resulting in coastal zone degradation, fish depletion and health problems (gastro-enteritis) ..."

33. According to this publication, there are two general hospitals in St Kitts, one with 174 beds and the other with 38. There is also a "cottage" hospital with 10 beds. There are two homes providing geriatric care.

3. "Treatment issues – a basic guide to medical treatment options for people with HIV and AIDS" produced in April 1996 by the Terrence Higgins Trust

34. This guide describes the three medical strategies available for treating HIV infection and AIDS: using anti-HIV drugs which attack HIV itself to delay or prevent damage to the immune system, treating or preventing opportunistic infections which take advantage of damage to the immune system and strengthening and restoring the immune system. Amongst the first category, several drugs can be used, including AZT (also known as Zidovudine or its tradename Retrovir). This belongs to a family of drugs called nucleoside analogues which inhibit an enzyme produced by HIV called reverse transcriptase (RT). If RT is inhibited, HIV cannot infect new cells and the build-up of virus in the body is slowed down. However, the existing drugs are only partially effective and at best can only delay the worsening of HIV-related disease rather than prevent it.

35. As regards the second category, persons whose immune systems have been significantly damaged are vulnerable to a range of infections and tumours known as opportunistic infections. These commonly include cytomegalovirus (herpes virus), Kaposi's sarcoma, anaemia, tuberculosis, toxoplasmosis and PCP. PCP is a form of pneumonia which in people infected with HIV may affect the lymph nodes, bone marrow, spleen and liver

as well as the lungs. Steps to avoid such infections include taking care with food and drink and prophylactic treatment by drugs. In the case of PCP, which was a common cause of death during the first years of the epidemic and is still one of the commonest AIDS illnesses, options include the long-term taking of antibiotics such as cotrimoxazole and the use of nebulised pentamidine which is intended to protect the lungs.

36. In relation to the third category, treatment which strengthens or restores the immune system, research has yet to produce any clear results.

PROCEEDINGS BEFORE THE COMMISSION

37. The applicant lodged his application (no. 30240/96) with the Commission on 15 February 1996. He alleged that his proposed removal to St Kitts would be in violation of Articles 2, 3 and 8 of the Convention (art. 2, art. 3, art. 8) and that he had been denied an effective remedy to challenge the removal order in breach of Article 13 (art. 13). The Commission declared the application admissible on 26 June 1996. In its report of 15 October 1996 (Article 31) (art. 31), it expressed the opinion that Article 3 (art. 3) would be violated if the applicant were to be removed to St Kitts (eleven votes to seven); that it was unnecessary to examine the complaint under Article 2 (art. 2) (unanimously); that no separate issue arose under Article 8 (art. 8) (unanimously); and that there had been no violation of Article 13 (art. 13) (thirteen votes to five). The full text of the Commission's opinion and of the two separate opinions contained in the report is reproduced as an annex to this judgment.[3]

FINAL SUBMISSIONS TO THE COURT

38. In their memorial and at the oral hearing the Government requested the Court to decide and declare that the facts disclose no breach of the applicant's rights under Articles 2, 3, 8 or 13 of the Convention (art. 2, art. 3, art. 8, art. 13). The applicant requested the Court in his memorial and at the oral hearing to find that his proposed removal from the United Kingdom would, if implemented, constitute a breach of Articles 2, 3 and 8 of the Convention (art. 2, art. 3, art. 8) and that he had no effective remedy in respect of those complaints in breach of Article 13.

AS TO THE LAW

I. ALLEGED VIOLATION OF ARTICLE 3 OF THE CONVENTION (art. 3)

39. The applicant maintained that his removal to St Kitts would expose him to inhuman and degrading treatment in breach of Article 3 of the Convention (art. 3), which provides: "No one shall be subjected to torture or to inhuman or degrading treatment or punishment."

---

[3] (Ed.: not included in the present volume).

A. Arguments of those appearing before the Court

1. The applicant

40. The applicant maintained that his removal to St Kitts would condemn him to spend his remaining days in pain and suffering in conditions of isolation, squalor and destitution. He had no close relatives or friends in St Kitts to attend to him as he approached death. He had no accommodation, no financial resources and no access to any means of social support. It was an established fact that the withdrawal of his current medical treatment would hasten his death on account of the unavailability of similar treatment in St Kitts. His already weakened immune system would not be able to resist the many opportunistic infections to which he would be exposed on account of his homelessness, lack of proper diet and the poor sanitation on the island. The hospital facilities were extremely limited and certainly not capable of arresting the development of infections provoked by the harsh physical environment in which he would be obliged to fend for himself. His death would thus not only be further accelerated, it would also come about in conditions which would be inhuman and degrading.

41. In June 1996, his life expectancy was stated to be in the region of eight to twelve months even if he continued to receive treatment in the United Kingdom. His health had declined since then. As he was now clearly weak and close to death, his removal by the respondent State at this late stage would certainly exacerbate his fate.

2. The Government

42. The Government requested the Court to find that the applicant had no valid claim under Article 3 (art. 3) in the circumstances of the case since he would not be exposed in the receiving country to any form of treatment which breached the standards of Article 3 (art. 3). His hardship and reduced life expectancy would stem from his terminal and incurable illness coupled with the deficiencies in the health and social-welfare system of a poor, developing country. He would find himself in the same situation as other AIDS victims in St Kitts. In fact he would have been returned in January 1993 to St Kitts, where he had spent most of his life, had it not been for his prosecution and conviction.

43. The Government also disputed the applicant's claim that he would be left alone and without access to treatment for his condition. They maintained that he had at least one cousin living in St Kitts and that there were hospitals caring for AIDS patients, including those suffering from opportunistic infections (see paragraph 17 above). Even if the treatment and medication fell short of that currently administered to the applicant in the United Kingdom, this in itself did not amount to a breach of Article 3 standards (art. 3).

44. Before the Court the Government observed that it was their policy not to remove a person who was unfit to travel. They gave an undertaking to the Court not to remove the applicant unless, in the light of an assessment of his medical condition after the Court gives judgment, he is fit to travel.

3. The Commission

45. The Commission concluded that the removal of the applicant to St Kitts would engage the responsibility of the respondent State under Article 3 (art. 3) even though the risk of being subjected to inhuman and degrading treatment stemmed from factors for which

the authorities in that country could not be held responsible. The risk was substantiated and real. If returned, he would be deprived of his current medical treatment and his already weakened immune system would be exposed to untreatable opportunistic infections which would reduce further his limited life expectancy and cause him severe pain and mental suffering. He would be homeless and without any form of moral, social or family support in the final stages of his deadly illness.

B. The Court's assessment

46. The Court recalls at the outset that Contracting States have the right, as a matter of well-established international law and subject to their treaty obligations including the Convention, to control the entry, residence and expulsion of aliens. It also notes the gravity of the offence which was committed by the applicant and is acutely aware of the problems confronting Contracting States in their efforts to combat the harm caused to their societies through the supply of drugs from abroad. The administration of severe sanctions to persons involved in drug trafficking, including expulsion of alien drug couriers like the applicant, is a justified response to this scourge.

47. However, in exercising their right to expel such aliens Contracting States must have regard to Article 3 of the Convention (art. 3), which enshrines one of the fundamental values of democratic societies. It is precisely for this reason that the Court has repeatedly stressed in its line of authorities involving extradition, expulsion or deportation of individuals to third countries that Article 3 (art. 3) prohibits in absolute terms torture or inhuman or degrading treatment or punishment and that its guarantees apply irrespective of the reprehensible nature of the conduct of the person in question (see, most recently, the Ahmed v. Austria judgment of 17 December 1996, Reports of Judgments and Decisions 1996-VI, p. 2206, para. 38; and the Chahal v. the United Kingdom judgment of 15 November 1996, Reports 1996-V, p. 1853, paras. 73-74).

48. The Court observes that the above principle is applicable to the applicant's removal under the Immigration Act 1971. Regardless of whether or not he ever entered the United Kingdom in the technical sense (see paragraph 25 above) it is to be noted that he has been physically present there and thus within the jurisdiction of the respondent State within the meaning of Article 1 of the Convention since 21 January 1993. It is for the respondent State therefore to secure to the applicant the rights guaranteed under Article 3 (art. 3) irrespective of the gravity of the offence which he committed.

49. It is true that this principle has so far been applied by the Court in contexts in which the risk to the individual of being subjected to any of the proscribed forms of treatment emanates from intentionally inflicted acts of the public authorities in the receiving country or from those of non-State bodies in that country when the authorities there are unable to afford him appropriate protection (see, for example, the Ahmed judgment, loc. cit., p. 2207, para. 44). Aside from these situations and given the fundamental importance of Article 3) in the Convention system, the Court must reserve to itself sufficient flexibility to address the application of that Article in other contexts which might arise. It is not therefore prevented from scrutinising an applicant's claim under Article 3 where the source of the risk of proscribed treatment in the receiving country stems from factors which cannot engage either directly or indirectly the responsibility of the public authorities of that coun-

try, or which, taken alone, do not in themselves infringe the standards of that Article. To limit the application of Article 3 in this manner would be to undermine the absolute character of its protection. In any such contexts, however, the Court must subject all the circumstances surrounding the case to a rigorous scrutiny, especially the applicant's personal situation in the expelling State.

50. Against this background the Court will determine whether there is a real risk that the applicant's removal would be contrary to the standards of Article 3 (art. 3) in view of his present medical condition. In so doing the Court will assess the risk in the light of the material before it at the time of its consideration of the case, including the most recent information on his state of health (see the Ahmed judgment, loc. cit., p. 2207, para. 43).

51. The Court notes that the applicant is in the advanced stages of a terminal and incurable illness. At the date of the hearing, it was observed that there had been a marked decline in his condition and he had to be transferred to a hospital. His condition was giving rise to concern (see paragraph 21 above). The limited quality of life he now enjoys results from the availability of sophisticated treatment and medication in the United Kingdom and the care and kindness administered by a charitable organisation. He has been counselled on how to approach death and has formed bonds with his carers (see paragraph 19 above).

52. The abrupt withdrawal of these facilities will entail the most dramatic consequences for him. It is not disputed that his removal will hasten his death. There is a serious danger that the conditions of adversity which await him in St Kitts will further reduce his already limited life expectancy and subject him to acute mental and physical suffering. Any medical treatment which he might hope to receive there could not contend with the infections which he may possibly contract on account of his lack of shelter and of a proper diet as well as exposure to the health and sanitation problems which beset the population of St Kitts (see paragraph 32 above). While he may have a cousin in St Kitts (see paragraph 18 above), no evidence has been adduced to show whether this person would be willing or in a position to attend to the needs of a terminally ill man. There is no evidence of any other form of moral or social support. Nor has it been shown whether the applicant would be guaranteed a bed in either of the hospitals on the island which, according to the Government, care for AIDS patients (see paragraph 17 above).

53. In view of these exceptional circumstances and bearing in mind the critical stage now reached in the applicant's fatal illness, the implementation of the decision to remove him to St Kitts would amount to inhuman treatment by the respondent State in violation of Article 3. The Court also notes in this respect that the respondent State has assumed responsibility for treating the applicant's condition since August 1994. He has become reliant on the medical and palliative care which he is at present receiving and is no doubt psychologically prepared for death in an environment which is both familiar and compassionate. Although it cannot be said that the conditions which would confront him in the receiving country are themselves a breach of the standards of Article 3 (art. 3), his removal would expose him to a real risk of dying under most distressing circumstances and would thus amount to inhuman treatment. Without calling into question the good faith of the undertaking given to the Court by the Government (see paragraph 44 above), it is to be noted

that the above considerations must be seen as wider in scope than the question whether or not the applicant is fit to travel back to St Kitts.

54. Against this background the Court emphasises that aliens who have served their prison sentences and are subject to expulsion cannot in principle claim any entitlement to remain in the territory of a Contracting State in order to continue to benefit from medical, social or other forms of assistance provided by the expelling State during their stay in prison. However, in the very exceptional circumstances of this case and given the compelling humanitarian considerations at stake, it must be concluded that the implementation of the decision to remove the applicant would be a violation of Article 3.

II. ALLEGED VIOLATION OF ARTICLE 2 OF THE CONVENTION (...)

55. The applicant further maintained that the implementation by the United Kingdom authorities of the decision to remove him to St Kitts would be in breach of Article 2 of the Convention [on the right to life].

56. The applicant contended that his removal to St Kitts would engage the responsibility of the respondent State under Article 2. He is terminally ill, and the medical evidence submitted to the Court (see paragraphs 14-15 and 20-21 above) confirmed that his already reduced life expectancy would be further shortened if he were to be suddenly deprived of his current medical treatment and sent back to St Kitts. There would, he argued, be a direct causal link between his expulsion and his accelerated death such as to give rise to a violation of the right to life. He submitted that Article 2 (art. 2) denoted a positive obligation to safeguard life which in the circumstances in issue required the Government not to take a measure which would further reduce his limited life expectancy.

57. The Government did not dispute the fact that the removal of the applicant to St Kitts and the consequential loss of the current medical treatment would hasten his death. However, the threat to his life expectancy stemmed not from factors for which the Government could be held responsible but from his own fatal illness in conjunction with the lack of adequate medical treatment in the receiving country. Article 2 was therefore not applicable to the circumstances in issue. In any event the substance of the applicant's complaints could not be separated from the arguments he advanced in furtherance of his allegation under Article 3 and for that reason were best dealt with under the latter provision.

58. The Commission did not find it necessary to decide whether the risk to the applicant's life expectancy created by his removal disclosed a breach of Article 2. It considered that it would be more appropriate to deal globally with this allegation when examining his related complaints under Article 3.

59. The Court for its part shares the views of the Government and the Commission that the complaints raised by the applicant under Article 2 are indissociable from the substance of his complaint under Article 3 in respect of the consequences of the impugned decision for his life, health and welfare. It notes in this respect that the applicant stated before the Court that he was content to base his case under Article 3. Having regard to its finding that the removal of the applicant to St Kitts would give rise to a violation of Article 3 (see

paragraph 54 above), the Court considers that it is not necessary to examine his complaint under Article 2.

III. ALLEGED VIOLATION OF ARTICLE 8 OF THE CONVENTION

60. The applicant also alleged that his proposed removal to St Kitts would violate his right to respect for his private life, as guaranteed by Article 8 of the Convention [on privacy and family life]. (...)

64. Having regard to its finding under Article 3 (see paragraph 54 above), the Court concludes that the applicant's complaints under Article 8 raise no separate issue.

IV. ALLEGED VIOLATION OF ARTICLE 13 OF THE CONVENTION

65. The applicant complained that he had no effective remedy in English law in respect of his complaints under Articles 2, 3 and 8 of the Convention. He contended that this gave rise to a breach of Article 13 of the Convention [on effective remedy] (...)

73. The applicant thus had available to him an effective remedy in relation to his complaints under Articles 2, 3 and 8 of the Convention. Accordingly there has been no breach of Article 13.

V. APPLICATION OF ARTICLE 50 OF THE CONVENTION

74. Article 50 of the Convention (art. 50) provides: "If the Court finds that a decision or a measure taken by a legal authority or any other authority of a High Contracting Party is completely or partially in conflict with the obligations arising from the Convention, and if the internal law of the said Party allows only partial reparation to be made for the consequences of this decision or measure, the decision of the Court shall, if necessary, afford just satisfaction to the injured party."

A. Costs and expenses (...)

FOR THESE REASONS, THE COURT UNANIMOUSLY

1. Holds that the implementation of the decision to remove the applicant to St Kitts would violate Article 3 of the Convention;
2. Holds that having regard to its conclusion under Article 3 it is not necessary to examine the applicant's complaint under Article 2 of the Convention;
3. Holds that the applicant's complaint under Article 8 of the Convention gives rise to no separate issue;
4. Holds that there has been no violation of Article 13 of the Convention;
5. Holds

(a) that the respondent State is to pay the applicant, within three months, 35,000 (thirty-five thousand) pounds sterling in respect of costs and expenses less 33,216 (thirty-three thousand two hundred and sixteen) French francs to be converted into pounds sterling at the rate applicable at the date of delivery of the present judgment;

(b) that simple interest at an annual rate of 8% shall be payable from the expiry of the above-mentioned three months until settlement.

Done in English and in French, and delivered at a public hearing in the Human Rights Building, Strasbourg, on 2 May 1997. (...)[4]

---

[4] Ed: such a dictum is then followed up by a decision of the Committee of Ministers as per the ECHR. This Committee noted that the UK had duly implemented the decision and declared the case closed:

RESOLUTION DH (98) 10, CONCERNING THE JUDGMENT OF THE EUROPEAN COURT OF HUMAN RIGHTS OF 2 MAY 1997 IN THE CASE OF D. AGAINST THE UNITED KINGDOM (Adopted by the Committee of Ministers on 18 February 1998 at the 618th meeting of the Ministers' Deputies)

The Committee of Ministers, under the terms of Article 54 of the [ECHR]

Having regard to the judgment of the European Court of Human Rights in the D. case delivered on 2 May 1997 and transmitted the same day to the Committee of Ministers;

Recalling that (...)

Whereas in its judgment of 2 May 1997 the Court unanimously: held that the implementation of the decision to remove the applicant to St. Kitts would violate Article 3 of the Convention;

– held that having regard to its conclusions under Article 3 it was not necessary to examine the applicant's complaint under Article 2 of the Convention;

– held that the applicant's complaint under Article 8 of the Convention gave rise to no separate issue;

– held that there had been no violation of Article 13 of the Convention;

– held:

(a) that the respondent State was to pay the applicant, within three months, £35 000 (thirty-five thousand pounds sterling) in respect of costs and expenses less 33 216 (thirty three thousand two hundred and sixteen) French francs to be converted into pounds sterling at the rate applicable at the date of delivery of the present judgment;

(b) that simple interest at an annual rate of 8% should be payable from the expiry of the above-mentioned three months until settlement.

Having regard to the Rules adopted by the Committee of Ministers concerning the application of Article 54 of the Convention;

aving invited the Government of the United Kingdom to inform it of the measures which had been taken in consequence of the judgment of 2 May 1997, having regard to United Kingdom's obligation under Article 53 of the Convention to abide by it;

Whereas, during the examination of the case by the Committee of Ministers, the Government of the United Kingdom gave the Committee information about the measures taken to avoid the impending violation as found in the present judgment; this information appears in the appendix to this resolution;

Having satisfied itself that on 11 August 1997, the Government of the United Kingdom paid the applicant the sum provided for in the judgment of 2 May 1997 including the default interest due, i.e. 31 680.75 pounds sterling,

Declares, after having taken note of the information supplied by the Government of United Kingdom that it has exercised its functions under Article 54 of the Convention in this case.

And in the Appendix to this Resolution it can be read:

Information provided by the Government of the United Kingdom during the examination of the D. case by the Committee of Ministers

The Government of the United Kingdom granted the applicant an indefinite leave which will permit him to remain in the country, where he will continue to receive adequate medical treatment and palliative care.

Bamba Bamba: Case of B.B. v. France [5]

The European Court of Human Rights, (...)
Having deliberated in private on 29 June and 27 August 1998,
Delivers the following judgment, which was adopted on the last-mentioned date:

PROCEDURE (...)

1. The case was referred to the Court by the European Commission of Human Rights ("the Commission") on 27 April 1998, within the three-month period laid down by Article 32 § 1 and Article 47 of the Convention. It originated in an application (no. 30930/96) against the French Republic lodged with the Commission under Article 25 by a Congolese citizen (a national of what was formerly Zaïre, hereinafter "the Democratic Republic of Congo"), Mr B.B., on 2 April 1996. The applicant asked the Court not to reveal his identity. The Commission's request referred to Articles 44 and 48 and to the declaration whereby France recognised the compulsory jurisdiction of the Court (Article 46). The object of the request was to obtain a decision as to whether the facts of the case disclosed a breach by the respondent State of its obligations under Articles 3 and 8 of the Convention. (...)

5. Meanwhile, on 7 May 1998 the Registrar had received from the Government a request that the Court order the case to be struck out of the list as the applicant could no longer argue that he was a "victim" within the meaning of Article 25 of the Convention (Rule 49 § 2), the Minister of the Interior having on 9 April 1998 made an order against the applicant requiring him to live in the Val d'Oise *département*. On 2 June 1998 the Registrar received the applicant's observations on the request for the case to be struck out. In a letter of 17 June 1998 the Secretary to the Commission communicated the Delegate's observations on that request.

6. On 18 June 1998 the Commission had produced the file on the proceedings before it, as requested by the Registrar on the instructions of the President of the Chamber.

7. On 27 August 1998 the Chamber decided to dispense with a hearing in the case, having satisfied itself that the conditions for this derogation from its usual procedure had been met (Rules 26 and 38).

AS TO THE FACTS

I. THE CIRCUMSTANCES OF THE CASE

8. Mr B.B., a national of the Democratic Republic of Congo, is currently subject to an order requiring him to reside in the Val d'Oise *département*. He is suffering from the Aids virus compounded by Kaposi's syndrome and presents signs of acute immunosuppression.

---

[5] (47/1998/950/1165).

9. The applicant was born in Kinshasa in 1954. He arrived in France in 1983 and was given leave to remain that was successively renewed until 1988, when, owing to the employment situation, he was refused a further renewal. He returned to Zaïre in December 1988, but came back to France in December 1989 because of the political situation there. Shortly afterwards, he made an application for political refugee status to the French Office for the Protection of Refugees and Stateless Persons (*OFPRA*). His application was rejected in 1993. That decision was confirmed in 1995 after his application had been reconsidered. The applicant says that his father, an opponent of the Mobutu regime, was executed in 1967 and that his four brothers are all political refugees, two in France and two in Belgium.

A. The applicant's conviction

10. On 22 January 1995 the applicant was charged with transporting, possessing, offering to supply, buying and selling drugs and immigration offences. He was arrested that day and committed to stand trial before the Bobigny Criminal Court.

11. On 8 September 1995 the Bobigny Criminal Court acquitted the applicant on the counts of transporting, offering to supply, and buying and selling drugs but found him guilty of possessing drugs and unlawfully entering and staying in France. It sentenced him to two years' imprisonment and made an order permanently excluding him from French territory.

12. From June to November 1995 the applicant was held in the national public hospital at Fresnes. A medical certificate drawn up on 30 November 1995 during that period of detention reads as follows: "I, the undersigned Dr Bouchard, certify that Mr [B.B.], who was born on 27 January 1954, is suffering from the HIV infection and acute immunosuppression. He needs an antiviral treatment that is currently available only in Europe and North America. Suspension of the order permanently excluding him from French territory would be desirable on humanitarian grounds. Medical follow-up has been organised at the Pitié Salpétrière."

13. Between November 1995 and 27 March 1996 the applicant served his sentence at Fleury-Mérogis Prison, where Dr Lemaire certified that: "Mr [B.B.] is suffering from an illness whose prognosis is currently reserved and which requires biological and clinical follow-up at very regular intervals. Treatment has been started which must under no circumstances be interrupted. Mr [B.B.] is receiving treatment and will continue to do so after his release in a specialised department of the Paris public-health service."

14. Meanwhile, on 30 January 1996 the Paris Court of Appeal had upheld the decision of the court below to acquit the applicant of some of the offences and reduced his sentence to eighteen months' imprisonment, but had upheld the permanent exclusion order.

B. The procedure for the applicant's deportation

1. The decision to expel the applicant to the Democratic Republic of Congo

15. The applicant was released on 27 March 1996. That same day the prefect of the Essonne *département* made an administrative order for the applicant's detention so that the permanent exclusion order could be enforced. He advised the applicant that he would be deported to his country of origin on a flight departing at 11 p.m. on 2 April.

16. On 28 March 1996 the judge delegated by the President of Évry *tribunal de grande instance* ordered that the applicant should remain in detention until 2 April 1996.

17. On the same day the applicant appealed against that order to the Paris Court of Appeal, which on 30 March 1996 upheld the order for the applicant's continued detention on the following grounds:
"Neither the appellant's condition nor the existence of a permanent exclusion order (section 28 *bis* of the Ordinance of 2 November 1945) constitute sufficient grounds to justify as an exceptional measure making a compulsory residence order if no passport or other proof of identity has been produced... Order upheld."

2. Compulsory residence order

18. On 1 April 1996 the applicant's representative applied for a compulsory residence order to be made, to which the Minister of the Interior acceded on 4 April, requiring the applicant to reside at a designated address in Paris.

3. Applications for the prefect's decision to be suspended and quashed

19. Mr B.B. had made several applications to the Versailles Administrative Court for a stay of execution of the prefect's decision of 27 March 1996. He had also sought an order suspending that decision or quashing it.

20. On 4 July 1996 the Versailles Administrative Court ordered that execution of the prefect's decision be suspended for three months, holding: "The documents on the case file show that Mr [B.B.]'s condition requires treatment that would not be available to him in Zaïre. It follows that the prefect made a clear error of judgment by choosing, further to the permanent exclusion order made against Mr [B.B.] by the Paris Court of Appeal on 30 January 1996, Zaïre as the country of destination..."

21. On 26 September 1996 it quashed the prefect's decision of 27 March 1996 for the following reasons:
"The documents on the case file show, firstly, that Mr [B.B.] is in the advanced stages of a serious illness causing a substantial loss of immunity whose progression can only be arrested by appropriate treatment and, secondly, that such treatment is unavailable in his country of origin to which he must be deported under the impugned decision. It follows that the prefect of the Essonne *département* made a clear error in his assessment of the consequences which the impugned decision could have on the applicant's personal situation. It follows from the foregoing that the impugned decision must be quashed. Consequently, the application for a stay of execution of that decision has become devoid of purpose."

4. Applications for rescission of the exclusion order

22. On 26 February and 12 April 1996 Mr B.B. wrote to the public prosecutor at the Paris Court of Appeal requesting that the exclusion order be rescinded owing to the seriousness of his condition. On 17 March 1997, as he had received no reply from the public prosecutor, the applicant repeated his request for the exclusion order to be rescinded. That request will be heard on 8 September 1998.

C. The applicant's immigration status since the Commission's report of 9 March 1998

23. On 9 April 1998 the Minister of the Interior made a compulsory residence order pursuant to section 28 of Ordinance no. 45-2658 of 2 November 1945, as amended (see paragraph 27 below). That order, which rescinded the compulsory residence order made on 4 April 1996 (see paragraph 18 above), provided as follows: "Having regard to the judgment of the Paris Court of Appeal of 30 January 1986 in which an order was made against Mr [B.B.], a national of the Democratic Republic of Congo, ... permanently excluding him from French territory for an offence under the drug-trafficking legislation, Having regard to the new information that has been obtained;

Considering that Mr B.B. is not currently able to leave French territory; Having regard to the compulsory residence order made against the above-named on 4 April 1996;

ORDERS

ARTICLE 1: The compulsory residence order referred to above is rescinded.

ARTICLE 2: Until he is able to comply with the order made against him, the above-named shall reside where required to by the prefect of the Val d'Oise *département.*

ARTICLE 3: In that *département* he shall report periodically to the police or gendarmerie in accordance with conditions to be laid down by decree of the prefect of the Val d'Oise *département...*"

24. On 9 April 1998 the Minister of the Interior also wrote to the prefect of the Val d'Oise *département* and to the prefect of the Paris *département* to give them instructions as to how his decision was to be enforced. His letter to the former read as follows: "Further to your fax and the telephone conversations referred to in the reference to this letter, I would inform you that, in view of Mr [B.B.]'s personal circumstances, I have today issued an order requiring him to reside in your *département*, where he is now living, instead of at his Paris home. You will find enclosed for service and enforcement an official copy of that order. Please send me a formal note to confirm that service has been effected. Would you please also provide Mr B.B. with any safe conduct that he may need to enable him to attend the Salpétrière Hospital in Paris, where he is being treated."

D. The applicant's condition since the Commission's report was adopted

25. A medical certificate dated 29 May 1998 contains the following conclusions: "I, the undersigned, doctor of medicine, certify that Mr [B.B.], who was born in Kinshasa on 27.01.54, has been receiving regular treatment in this department for infection with the HIV virus compounded by a Kaposi skin disease that is currently progressive. That disease now makes it necessary to restart chemotherapy with a combination of Adriamycin-Vincristine-Bleomycin. His HIV infection is now insufficiently arrested by antiretroviral triple therapy combining Stavudine-Lamuvidine-Indinavir, as he presents a large viral load of 100,000 copies/ml and acute immunosuppression with lymphocytes CD4 at 25/mm^3. Mr [B.B.]'s clinical, biological, immunological and virological condition therefore means that he must attend a specialised service as regularly as possible and that he be given care and treatment that is unavailable in his country of origin. Dr Valantin – Pitié-Salpétrière Hospital."

E. Situation in the Democratic Republic of Congo

26. The applicant has produced a number of medical certificates referring to the fact that it is impossible for his illness to be treated in his country of origin. In a report of 28 Janu-

ary 1997 on the situation in what was formerly Zaïre, the Commission on Human Rights of the Economic and Social Council of the United Nations noted:
"Statistics show that no progress has been made; instead, the situation has worsened for lack of appropriate policies... A study carried out by the Association for the Protection of the Local Heritage of the Bas-Fleuve reported that in this region, in addition to many epidemic illnesses ..., there is a serious ... Aids problem and a lack of effective, realistic official programmes to combat that disease..."

(...)

PROCEEDINGS BEFORE THE COMMISSION

32. Mr B.B. applied to the Commission on 2 April 1996. He relied on Article 3 of the Convention, complaining that if he was deported to what was formerly Zaïre that would amount to treatment contrary to Article 3 of the Convention as it would reduce his life expectancy because he would not receive the medical treatment his condition demanded. He also argued that his deportation would infringe his right to respect for his family life as guaranteed by Article 8 of the Convention.

33. The Commission declared the application (no. 30930/96) admissible on 8 September 1997. In its report of 9 March 1998 (Article 31), it expressed the opinion that there would be a breach of Article 3 (twenty-nine votes to two) and that no separate issue arose under Article 8. The full text of the Commission's opinion and of the separate opinion contained in the report is reproduced as an annex to this judgment [not attached].

AS TO THE LAW

34. The Government invited the Court to strike the case out of the list. They relied on two factors of which the Commission had been unaware since the relevant information had been communicated to it on the day its report had been adopted: the Versailles Administrative Court had on 26 September 1996 quashed the prefect of the Essonne *département*'s decision to enforce the order excluding the applicant from French territory (see paragraph 21 above) and a compulsory residence order had been made against the applicant on 9 April 1998 (see paragraph 23 above). Those measures meant that the applicant no longer risked being deported to the Democratic Republic of Congo and was no longer a "victim". The Government invoked Rule 49 § 2 of Rules of Court A, which provides: "When the Chamber is informed of a friendly settlement, arrangement or other fact of a kind to provide a solution of the matter, it may, after consulting, if necessary, the Parties, the Delegates of the Commission and the applicant, strike the case out of the list."

35. The applicant invited the Court to proceed with the consideration of the case. (...)

36. The Delegate of the Commission shared the Government's view that the fact that a compulsory residence order had been made on 9 April 1998 meant that the applicant was no longer a "victim", since no steps were being taken to expel him to his country of origin and he continued to receive treatment in France.

37. The Court notes that there has been no friendly settlement or arrangement in the instant case. The compulsory residence order made on 9 April 1998 was unilateral in character and issued by the French authorities after the Commission had adopted its report. It considers, however, that the order constitutes an "other fact of a kind to provide a solution of the matter".

In his initial application to the Convention institutions, the applicant's main argument was that if he was deported to what was formerly Zaïre there would be a considerable risk of his being exposed to treatment which was contrary to Article 3 of the Convention, as he would not be able to receive in his country of origin the treatment his serious medical condition required.

The Court accepts that the compulsory residence order dated 9 April 1998 (see paragraph 23 above) does not signify that there has been a change in the applicant's situation since it merely rescinds a similar measure imposed in April 1996 in order to restore it with effect in a different *département*. It appears, however, that as regards Article 3 of the Convention the measure reflects, through its continuity and duration, the French authorities' intention to allow Mr B.B. to receive the treatment his present condition requires and to guarantee him, for the time being, the right to remain in France. In that connection, it should be noted that in their memorial of 16 July 1998 the Government indicated that they "[had] not shown any intention of actually deporting Mr B.B.".

The Court sees that as tantamount to an undertaking by the French Government not to expel the applicant to his country of origin, the risk of a potential violation therefore having ceased, at least until such time as any new factors emerge justifying a fresh examination of the case.

(...)

40. Accordingly, it is appropriate to strike the case out of the list. The Court, however, reserves the power to restore it to the list if new circumstances arise justifying such a measure (...)

FOR THESE REASONS, THE COURT UNANIMUSLY:
Decides, subject to the reservation set out at paragraph 40 above, to strike the case out of the list. (...)

Tatete v. Switzerland[6]

PROCÉDURE (...)

4. Le 18 novembre 1999, la Cour a déclaré la requête recevable. Elle a également décidé, en application de l'article 39 § 1 du règlement de la Cour, de proroger jusqu'à

[6] Requête no 41874/98, 6 juillet 2000.
Ed.: The text of this judgment is available in French only. The case can to some extent be compared with the Bamba Bamba one (see above under C.1.b): Ms Tatete entered Switzerland illegally. Born 1964 in Kinshasa, she has three children, and would appear to be the daughter of an Air Zaïre director: she has lived in a number of neigbouring countries. .Ms Tatete has been hospitalized on a number of occasions: HIV+ (state C3), TB, Hepatitits, pneumonia. As in the Bamba Bamba case, the

nouvel ordre l'indication donnée au Gouvernement selon laquelle il serait souhaitable de ne pas procéder au renvoi de la requérante vers la République démocratique du Congo.

5. Après un échange de correspondance, le Gouvernement et les représentants de la partie requérante sont parvenus à un règlement amiable de l'affaire par courriers des 2 et 18 mai 2000.

EN FAIT

6. Née à Kinshasa en 1964, la requérante vécut en Côte-d'Ivoire, au Zaïre et au Cameroun, au gré des changements de postes de son père, lequel occupait des fonctions dirigeantes au sein de la compagnie d'aviation Air Zaïre. A compter de 1985, elle étudia la gestion puis le droit à l'université de Congo-Brazzaville.

7. La requérante a trois enfants, une fille née de Ja. en 1988 et deux fils nés respectivement de D. en 1992 et de Je. en 1993. Le premier enfant vit chez la soeur de la requérante, le second chez la mère de celle-ci et le troisième avec son père, Je.

8. La requérante quitta son pays le 10 février 1997. Elle arriva en Suisse, illégalement, le 17 février 1997 ; le même jour, elle y déposa une demande d'asile. Entendue les 21 février et 10 mars 1997, elle déclara qu'elle avait décidé de s'expatrier pour échapper aux pressions des services de sécurité zaïrois.

9. Le 19 mars 1997, l'Office fédéral des réfugiés rejeta la demande d'asile de la requérante, au motif que ses allégations n'étaient pas crédibles, et ordonna son renvoi de Suisse dans un délai échéant le 15 mai 1997.

10. Cette décision fut confirmée, sur recours de la requérante, par la Commission suisse de recours en matière d'asile (« la Commission de recours ») le 12 septembre 1997.

11. Le 23 septembre 1997, la requérante sollicita la réouverture de son dossier, alléguant que sa cause n'avait pas été entendue équitablement et se plaignant de ce que les autorités de son pays ne respectaient pas les principes démocratiques élémentaires d'un Etat de droit.

12. La requérante fut hospitalisée du 23 septembre au 16 octobre 1997. Le 8 octobre 1997, l'hôpital de Zofingen adressa à l'Office fédéral des réfugiés un certificat médical qui signalait que la requérante était atteinte du syndrome de l'immunodéficience acquise (sida), la maladie en étant au stade C3 selon la classification CDC, et souffrait notamment d'une pneumonie. Un report du renvoi de la requérante de deux à trois semaines était préconisé pour raisons médicales.

---

case at Strasbourg has been settled (ex Art. 39 ECHR), and Ms Tatete has been granted a temporary residence permit. The Swiss authorities, however, made it very clear that they allowed Ms Tatete to remain on humanitarian grounds only, explicitly excluding Art. 3 ECHR. It would indeed have been of some interest to find out in how far the Court would have followed the D v UK judgement, or rather the Karara and SCC dicta.

13. Le 13 octobre 1997, considérant que la requérante n'avait allégué aucun fait ou moyen de preuve nouveau, la Commission de recours déclara irrecevable sa demande du 23 septembre 1997 visant à obtenir la réouverture de son dossier.

14. La requérante fut à nouveau hospitalisée du 5 au 19 novembre 1997.

15. Le 23 décembre 1997, la requérante sollicita de l'Office fédéral des réfugiés le réexamen de sa situation. Elle alléguait qu'en raison du stade avancé de sa maladie et de la situation sanitaire difficile prévalant à Kinshasa, un retour dans son pays équivaudrait à une mise en danger concrète.

16. Le 8 janvier 1998, la requérante produisit un certificat médical de l'hôpital du canton d'Argovie. Le certificat précisait que la requérante, soignée depuis le 2 décembre 1997 dans cet établissement, était atteinte notamment d'une infection HIV au stade C3, d'une tuberculose et d'une hépatite ; qu'un traitement adapté du sida stabiliserait l'état du système immunitaire et réduirait le risque de développement de nouvelles maladies ; qu'en l'état actuel du traitement, un contrôle médical mensuel était nécessaire ; qu'une fois traitée pour la tuberculose, la requérante devrait pouvoir bénéficier d'une trithérapie contre le sida, ce qui permettrait d'améliorer le pronostic à moyen terme. Ce document concluait que le renvoi de la requérante, s'accompagnant d'un arrêt brutal de la thérapie, provoquerait des complications de sa maladie à court terme.

17. Le 12 janvier 1998, l'Office fédéral des réfugiés rejeta la demande en réexamen du 23 décembre 1997 aux motifs, d'une part, qu'à Kinshasa, où la requérante avait vécu avant son arrivée en Suisse, la tuberculose et l'hépatite pouvaient être traitées et, d'autre part, que si les soins prodigués en Suisse pouvaient retarder l'évolution du sida, cette maladie n'était pas curable et menait tôt ou tard à la mort. Il releva en outre que la requérante n'avait pas de parents en Suisse alors que dans son pays d'origine vivaient sa mère, deux soeurs et ses trois enfants, lesquels constitueraient un entourage bénéfique pour les problèmes psychiques dont elle souffrait. Enfin, l'Office fédéral des réfugiés disposa que des médicaments pourraient être remis à la requérante lors de son départ ainsi que des indications à l'intention de ses futurs médecins.

18. Le 11 février 1998, la requérante recourut contre cette décision auprès de la Commission de recours. Elle soutenait essentiellement qu'en raison de l'impossibilité d'accéder à un traitement sérieux dans son pays d'origine, son renvoi méconnaîtrait les articles 2 et 3 de la Convention.

19. Le recours fut rejeté le 6 avril 1998 par la Commission de recours pour des motifs similaires, en substance, à ceux développés par l'Office fédéral des réfugiés.

EN DROIT

20. Le 2 mai 2000, la Cour a reçu la déclaration suivante de la part du Gouvernement :
" 1. Le Gouvernement suisse, tout en étant pleinement conscient du drame humain que vit la requérante à l'instar de milliers d'autres personnes atteintes du SIDA, est d'avis que la responsabilité d'un Etat contractant qui envisage de renvoyer un non national dans son pays d'origine ne peut être engagée, sous l'angle de l'article 3 CEDH, pour la seule et

unique raison que l'intéressé pourrait bénéficier d'un meilleur traitement médical dans l'Etat d'accueil. Ainsi, tenant compte de l'ensemble des circonstances du cas d'espèce, l'exécution du renvoi de Mme Tatete dans son pays d'origine ne se heurterait pas aux exigences de l'article 3 CEDH.
2. C'est donc au regard de considérations humanitaires exclusivement que le Gouvernement suisse accorde une autorisation provisoire à Mme Tatete au sens de l'article 14a alinéa 4 de la loi fédérale sur le séjour et l'établissement des étrangers.
3. La Confédération suisse verse à la requérante, à titre gracieux, la somme de 6 000 francs suisses, à titre d'indemnité forfaitaire, toutes causes de préjudice confondues, inclus les frais et dépens encourus par la requérante en Suisse et à Strasbourg à raison des faits qui ont donné lieu à l'introduction devant la Commission européenne des droits de l'homme de la requête n 41874/98.
4. Le présent règlement amiable ne saurait en aucun cas être considéré comme un précédent.
5. Compte tenu des engagements mentionnés sous chiffres 2 et 3, la requérante et le Gouvernement suisse demandent à la Cour de rayer l'affaire du rôle conformément aux articles 39 CEDH et 62 alinéa 3 de son Règlement intérieur, le règlement amiable proposé s'inspirant du respect des droits de l'homme tels que les reconnaissent la Convention et ses Protocoles et étant de nature à fournir une solution au litige".

21. Le 22 mai 2000, la Cour a reçu la déclaration suivante des représentants de la requérante :
"(...) par égard pour les intérêts supérieurs de notre cliente, nous estimons devoir accepter l'offre modifiée déposée par la Confédération en date du 2 mai 2000".

22. La Cour prend acte du règlement amiable auquel sont parvenues les parties (article 39 de la Convention). Elle est assurée que ledit règlement s'inspire du respect des droits de l'homme tels que les reconnaissent la Convention ou ses Protocoles (articles 37 § 1 *in fine* de la Convention et 62 § 3 du règlement).

23. Partant, il échet de rayer l'affaire du rôle.

par ces motifs, la cour, À l'unanimitÉ,
Décide de rayer l'affaire du rôle (...).

2. Commission Cases
Tanko v. Finland

AS TO THE ADMISSIBILITY OF Application No. 23634/94 by Ibrahim TANKO against Finland
The European Commission of Human Rights sitting in private on 19 May 1994, the following members being present: (...)

Having regard to Article 25 of the Convention for the Protection of Human Rights and Fundamental Freedoms;
Having regard to the application introduced on 4 March 1994 by Mr. Ibrahim TANKO against Finland and registered on 8 March 1994 under file No. 23634/94;

Having regard to the report provided for in Rule 47 of the Rules of Procedure of the Commission;
the observations submitted by the respondent Government on 4 April 1994 and the observations in reply submitted by the applicant on 24 April 1994; and the additional observations submitted by the applicant on 5 May 1994 and the additional observations in reply submitted by the Government on 10 May 1994;
Having deliberated;
Decides as follows:

THE FACTS

The applicant is a citizen of Ghana born in 1957. He is a bricklayer by profession. (...).

The facts of the case, as submitted by the parties, may be summarised as follows.

Particular circumstances of the case: On 1 April 1988 the applicant was allegedly arrested and detained for two days by his employer on suspicion of having participated in a demonstration arranged by Muslims at his work place. During his detention he was allegedly assaulted. He allegedly managed to escape from detention with the help of a friend. The applicant left Ghana for Burkina Faso on 5 April 1988, leaving his family behind in Ghana. From Burkina Faso he continued on the same day to Libya. In Libya he remained until 10 April 1989, when he left for Tunisia. On 27 April 1989 he left Tunisia for Turkey, from where he went to Cyprus on 30 April 1989. On 1 May he returned to Turkey and on 6 May 1989 he went back to Cyprus. On 9 May 1989 he again returned to Turkey, from where he went to Syria. On 19 September 1989 he left Syria for Egypt, from where he went to Saudi-Arabia on 8 March 1990. In June 1990 he returned to Egypt. On 22 September 1990 he left Egypt for Finland, where he immediately requested asylum and a residence permit. This was refused by the Ministry of the Interior (sisäasiainministeriö) on 13 November 1992. The applicant appealed, referring, inter alia, to the fact that in the autumn of 1992 it had been discovered that he is suffering from glaucoma, an eye illness, which had most likely been caused by the assault to which he had allegedly been subjected during his detention in Ghana. The appeal was rejected by the Asylum Board (turvapaikka-lautakunta) on 10 February 1993 after it had obtained a negative opinion from the Ministry of the Interior. On 8 June 1993 the Ministry of the Interior ordered the applicant's expulsion. The applicant's appeal against the expulsion order was rejected by the Supreme Administrative Court (korkein hallinto-oikeus) on 11 February 1994.

In a report of 24 August 1993 submitted by ophthalmologist A.V. the following is stated in regard to the applicant's illness: (translation from Finnish) "[The applicant's illness] requires regular ophthalmological controls and probably an operation in the near future. The operation might have to be carried out at very short notice. It requires at least the resources of a university hospital and could not successfully be carried out in [Ghana]. [If the applicant is not operated on], the suppression of [his] illness will require continuous medication. If the medication is interrupted [due to] its uncertain availability in [Ghana], ... [the applicant] might lose his eyesight. [H]e might suffer severe pain and his eye might have to be removed. [An eye removal could only be carried out] by a hospital specialised in ophthalmology. ..."

In a further medical report of 22 February 1994 A.V. stated that a sudden increase of the pressure in the applicant's eye might render him blind and necessitate an operation. A.V. further confirmed that the applicant was awaiting examination at the University Hospital of Helsinki in order to have his need for an operation determined.

On 31 March 1994 the Ministry of the Interior decided to postpone the enforcement of the applicant's expulsion order until a possible operation has taken place and his necessary follow-up treatment has been concluded.

A medical report of 27 April 1994, submitted by ophthalmologist P.P. of the Helsinki University Hospital in regard to the applicant's disease, concludes as follows: (translation from Finnish)

" ... [The applicant] suffers from a secondary glaucoma in his left eye. ... The eye pressure is normal with [his] current medication. [There is] no need for an operation or laser treatment. The applicant [should] continue his [present] medication. ... [As from now on he should] undergo an ophthalmological examination twice a year and later possibly once a year. ..."

In a further medical report of 5 May 1994 P.P. confirmed that the applicant's illness could for the time being be treated with eye drops twice a day and that an operation was therefore not required. No prediction as to possible further treatment needed by the applicant could be made at present. An ophthalmological examination was recommended in about six months.

In the light of the medical reports of 27 April and 5 May 1994 the Ministry of the Interior on 9 May 1994 revoked its decision of 31 March 1994 and considered that the applicant's expulsion could be carried out.

Relevant domestic law (...)

COMPLAINTS

1. The applicant complains that the enforcement of his expulsion would subject him to a risk of losing his eyesight in view of the inadequate facilities for treating him and possibly operating on him in Ghana. He invokes Article 3 of the Convention.
2. On 9 March 1994 the applicant supplemented his application by complaining that his return to Ghana would also constitute a lack of respect for his physical integrity and thereby for his private life, as guaranteed by Article 8 of the Convention.
3. In his observations of 9 March 1994 the applicant also invoked Article 14 of the Convention in conjunction with the above-mentioned provisions, given that his return to Ghana would interrupt his care merely on the basis that he is no longer lawfully resident in Finland.

PROCEEDINGS BEFORE THE COMMISSION

The application was introduced on 4 March 1994 and registered on 8 March 1994. On 7 March 1994 the Commission decided, pursuant to Rule 36 of the Commission's Rules of Procedure, that it was desirable in the interests of the parties and the proper conduct of the proceedings not to return the applicant to Ghana until the Commission had had an opportunity to examine the application. The Commission further decided, pursuant to Rule 48 para. 2 (b), to bring the application to the notice of the respondent Government and to invite them to submit written observations on its admissibility and merits with reference to Articles 3 and 8 of the Convention.

The Government's observations were submitted on 4 April 1994. On 15 April 1994 the Commission prolonged its indication under Rule 36 until 20 May 1994. The applicant's comments on the Government's observations were submitted on 24 April 1994. Additional observations were submitted by the applicant on 5 May 1994 and by the Government on 10 May 1994.

THE LAW

The applicant complains that the enforcement of his expulsion would subject him to a risk of losing his eyesight in view of the inadequate facilities for treating him and operating on him in Ghana. He invokes Article 3 of the Convention (...).

The Government consider that this complaint is manifestly ill-founded. No substantial grounds have been shown for believing that the applicant, due to the current state of his illness and his allegedly insufficient possibilities of obtaining adequate care in Ghana, would face a real risk of being subjected to treatment contrary to Article 3 (Art. 3), should he be returned to that country. The applicant's assertion that the care facilities in Ghana are insufficient is only corroborated by the statement of ophthalmologist A.V. dated 24 August 1993. His opinion, however, cannot in this respect be regarded as authoritative.

The applicant considers that he has shown that his present treatment and regular ophthalmological examinations are necessary and that an interruption of this care would lead to severe pain and possibly to the loss of his eyesight. Ghana is a poor developing country and the applicant has no financial means of his own. The effects of his expulsion would therefore be serious and irrevocable and subject him to inhuman treatment. Should an operation be considered necessary, it is uncertain when this could take place in Finland and how long his recuperation would last. Both his individual situation at that stage and the general situation in Ghana at that time would be uncertain.

The Commission recalls that Contracting States have the right to control the entry, residence and expulsion of aliens. The right to political asylum is not protected in either the Convention or its Protocols (Eur. Court H.R., Vilvarajah and Others judgment of 30 October 1991, Series A no. 215, p. 34, para. 102). However, expulsion by a Contracting State of an asylum seeker may give rise to an issue under Article 3 (Art. 3) of the Convention, and hence engage the responsibility of that State under the Convention, where substantial grounds have been shown for believing that the person concerned would face a real risk of being subjected to torture or to inhuman or degrading treatment or punishment in the country to which he is to be expelled (ibid., p. 34, para. 103). A mere possibility of ill-treatment is not in itself sufficient to give rise to a breach of Article 3 (Art. 3) (ibid., p. 37, para. 111). The Commission does not exclude that a lack of proper care in a case where someone is suffering from a serious illness could in certain circumstances amount to treatment contrary to Article 3 (Art. 3).

In the present case the Commission observes, however, that the most recent expert opinions concerning the applicant's disease conclude that for the time being he is not in need of an operation, but that he should continue to receive his present medication. On the evidence before it concerning both his individual situation and the general situation in Ghana, the Commission does not find it established that the applicant could not obtain this medication in that country or bring it with him when returned there. The Commission also notes that the applicant's family is residing in Ghana. For the above reasons, there are no substantial grounds for believing that he would be exposed to a real risk of being subjected to treatment contrary to Article 3 (Art. 3) of the Convention, if expelled to that country in his present state of health.

It follows that this aspect of the application must be rejected as being manifestly ill-founded within the meaning of Article 27 para. 2 of the Convention.

The applicant also considers that his return to Ghana would constitute a lack of respect for his physical integrity and thereby his private life, as guaranteed by Article 8 of the Convention.

The Government primarily submit that Article 8 (Art. 8) of the Convention is not applicable in the case, given that neither the Convention nor any of its Protocols guarantee any explicit or implicit right to obtain medical care. In the alternative, the Government consider that the interference with the applicant's private life caused by the enforcement of the expulsion order would be in accordance with the law, pursue the legitimate aim of preventing disorder, would be in the interests of the economic well-being of the country and, finally, would be proportionate to those aims and thereby necessary in a democratic society.

In the applicant's view it cannot be argued that every expulsion of an alien would be necessary in pursuance of the legitimate aim of maintaining public order. In his case there is no indication that public order would be jeopardised if he were permitted to remain in Finland until his necessary care has come to an end.

The Commission considers that the refusal to grant the applicant asylum or a residence permit in Finland raises the question whether there has been a lack of respect for his private life. It recalls that the notion of "respect" enshrined in Article 8 (Art. 8) is not clear- cut. This is the case especially where the positive obligations implicit in that concept are concerned. Its requirements will vary considerably from case to case according to the practices followed and the situations obtaining in the Contracting States. In determining whether or not such an obligation exists, regard must be had to the fair balance that has to be struck between the general interest and the interests of the individual, as well as to the margin of appreciation afforded to the Contracting States (Eur. Court H.R., B. v. France judgment of 25 March 1992, Series A no. 232-C, pp. 47 et seq., paras. 44 et seq.). In the field of immigration "Contracting States enjoy a wide margin of appreciation in determining the steps to be taken to ensure compliance with the Convention with due regard to the needs and resources of the community and of individuals" (Eur. Court H.R., Abdulaziz, Cabales and Balkandali judgment of 28 May 1985, Series A no. 94, pp. 33-34, paras. 67 and 68).

In the present case the Commission refers to the factual conclusions it has already drawn when examining the application under Article 3 (Art. 3) of the Convention above. In the light of these conclusions, it also finds no elements indicating that the respondent Government would exceed their margin of appreciation in striking a fair balance between the general interests of the community and the individual interests of the applicant, should he be returned to Ghana. The Commission concludes, therefore, that his return to that country would not in his present state of health amount to a lack of respect for his private life.

It follows that this aspect of the application must also be rejected as being manifestly ill-founded within the meaning of Article 27 para. 2 of the Convention.

The applicant has finally invoked Article 14 of the Convention in support of his application. (...)

The Commission recalls that Article 14 of the Convention prohibits discrimination in the securement of Convention rights and freedoms. Article 14 has no independent existence, since it has effect solely in relation to the "rights and freedoms" safeguarded by those provisions (Eur. Court H.R., Inze judgment of 28 October 1987, Series A no. 126, p. 17, para. 36).

The Commission has found the application to be manifestly ill-founded under both Articles 3 and 8 of the Convention. In the light of the factual circumstances upon which those findings were made, the Commission also finds no elements in the case which might disclose any appearance of discriminatory treatment of the applicant compared to others in a comparable situation to his. Therefore no issue under Article 14 of the Convention arises in the present application.

It follows that this aspect of the case must also be rejected as being manifestly ill-founded within the meaning of Article 27 para. 2 of the Convention.

For these reasons, the Commission, by a majority,
DECLARES THE APPLICATION INADMISSIBLE.

Karara v. Finland

AS TO THE ADMISSIBILITY OF Application No. 40900/98 by John KARARA against Finland
The European Commission of Human Rights sitting in private on 29 May 1998, the following members being present: (...)

Having regard to Article 25 of the Convention for the Protection of Human Rights and Fundamental Freedoms; Having regard to the application introduced on 6 April 1998 by John KARARA against Finland and registered on 24 April 1998 under file No. 40900/98;
Having regard to the reports provided for in Rule 47 of the Rules of Procedure of the Commission;
Having regard to the observations submitted by the respondent Government on 13 and 28 May 1998 and the observations in reply submitted by the applicant on 25, 27 and 28 May 1998;
Having deliberated;
Decides as follows:

THE FACTS
The applicant, a citizen of Uganda born in 1963, is detained facing deportation from Finland. He is represented by Mr Matti Wuori, a lawyer in Helsinki.

The facts of the case, as submitted by the parties, may be summarised as follows.

1. The deportation proceedings
The applicant arrived in Finland in 1991, having married a Finnish citizen, Z. In 1993 and 1995 the applicant's requests for a further residence permit were refused, given his criminal behaviour. He had been convicted on five counts of attempted manslaughter for having raped several women and having had other sexual contacts, knowing that he had contracted an HIV infection. He had been sentenced to over eleven years' imprisonment.

The applicant has been treated against his HIV infection since 1992. In 1995 the applicant and Z divorced. They have no children together. On 23 December 1997 the Ministry of the Interior ordered the applicant's deportation to Uganda and prohibited him from returning to Finland until further notice. The Ministry noted that the applicant no longer held a valid visa or residence permit in Finland; that he had no bonds to the country; and that he had repeatedly infringed Finnish law, thereby demonstrating that he was a danger to the safety of others. Moreover, his return to Uganda would not subject him to inhuman treatment within the meaning of Article 3 of the Convention or to persecution within the meaning of the 1991 Aliens Act (ulkomaalaislaki, utlänningslag 378/1991). Nor would he be sent on to an area where he could face such treatment or persecution.

The applicant appealed to the Supreme Administrative Court (korkein hallinto-oikeus, högsta örvaltningsdomstolen), arguing that his deportation would place him at an immediate risk of dying, given his HIV infection, and subject him to treatment contrary to Article 3 of the Convention. He invoked two medical opinions. In his opinion of 26 November 1997 Dr. M considered that an interruption of the applicant's medication would result in an acceleration of his illness. In his opinion of 21 January 1998 Dr. R noted that the applicant's state of health was good and that his infection was not showing any significant symptoms. Should his medication be interrupted, his illness would progress to the stage which it had reached in February 1997, i.e. to a "symptomatic" stage of HIV infection which was not yet the stage of AIDS. A patient in a comparable situation in February 1997 would run a 40 % risk of reaching the AIDS stage within three years.

In his appeal the applicant also invoked an affidavit by the manager of a support centre for AIDS patients, indicating that as long as he was staying in Finland, the applicant would be provided with the necessary socio-psychological support in order to cope with his illness. The applicant also invoked a certificate of 8 February 1998 issued by Dr. T, a psychotherapist, indicating that as from 1996 the applicant had been seeking treatment against his depression. Before replying to the applicant's appeal on 11 March 1998 the Ministry consulted a further expert. According to Dr. S, the basic AZT treatment against HIV/AIDS would be available in Uganda. Its price had also gone down. The possibility to obtain further medication would depend on the patient's financial circumstances. The patient's position in his or her village and the possible assistance by relatives were also of relevance to the success of the basic treatment. In Finland HIV patients were normally treated with two or three medicines. The need for treatment should be determined before deporting an HIV patient to Uganda. In his rejoinder of 2 April 1998 the applicant also opposed his deportation on the grounds that he was a refugee from Rwanda. Having joined the Rwandan Patriotic Forces in 1990, he had fought against the then Government of the country. He had deserted from the movement after two months of service.

In his rejoinder the applicant also adduced a supplementary opinion by Dr. R. This opinion of 31 March 1998 stated that during 1998 the applicant's basic medication would be replaced by a therapy combining three drugs, this being the medication practice in Finland. The interruption of either the ongoing or the planned medication would result in the loss, probably within a few months, of the care achievements so far.

In his rejoinder the applicant also requested an oral hearing before the Supreme Administrative Court. On 17 April 1998 the Supreme Administrative Court dismissed both the applicant's request for an oral hearing and his appeal as a whole. As regards the medical grounds invoked, the Court noted that the applicant would probably not, in Uganda, receive the same level of treatment against his illness as in Finland. His state of health would therefore possibly deteriorate and his illness could accelerate towards the AIDS stage. Considering, however, the information available on the applicant's current state of health, his deportation would not constitute inhuman or degrading treatment proscribed by Article 3 of the Convention. As regards the applicant's alleged background in Rwanda, the Supreme Administrative Court did not find his submissions credible. His allegation that the deportation would discriminate against him on the basis of his race and colour had not been substantiated and the Supreme Administrative Court found no indication of treatment contrary to Article 14 of the Convention.

2. The disclosure of the Supreme Administrative Court's decision

Following the judgment of the European Court of Human Rights in Z v. Finland (Eur. Court HR, judgment of 25 February 1997, Reports of Judgments and Decisions, 1997-I) the Chancellor of Justice (valtioneuvoston oikeuskansleri, justitiekansler i statsrådet) requested a reopening of the criminal proceedings against the present applicant in so far as the Court of Appeal had ordered that its case-file, including notably Z's medical records, should be kept confidential for a period of ten years. In its decision of 19 March 1998 the Supreme Court (korkein oikeus, högsta domstolen) acceded to this request and ordered that the case-file should be kept confidential for a period of forty years. This conclusion was reached on the grounds that the Act on the Publicity of Court Proceedings (laki oikeudenkäynnin julkisuudesta, lag om offentlighet vid rättegång 945/1984) had been applied in a manifestly incorrect manner, regard being had to the requirements of Article 8 of the Convention. Furthermore, the Supreme Court, apparently ex officio, ordered that during this forty-year period the names and personal identity numbers of the parties to the proceedings should not be revealed to outsiders. Z had not been considered a party to the proceedings.

In its decision of 17 April 1998, dismissing the applicant's appeal against the deportation order, the Supreme Administrative Court referred to the applicant by name and mentioned, inter alia, his HIV infection. Reference was also made to the applicant's conviction of repeated violent offences as well as to his sentence. In the copy of the decision which was made available to the public the information about the applicant's state of health appearing in the medical opinion of 21 January 1998 had been deleted.

According to the applicant, the Supreme Administrative Court's decision was widely reported in media.

3. The detention proceedings

On 3 April 1998 the applicant was released on parole but, in pursuance of section 46 of the Aliens Act, immediately detained by the Helsinki District Court (käräjäoikeus, tingsrätten) with a view to his deportation. In such a matter the District Court may be composed of a single judge and shall review the detention at least every two weeks (sections 48 and 51). On 14 April 1998 the applicant's detention was reviewed by Judge H, who had also been presiding over the criminal trial against him in 1992.

COMPLAINTS

1. The applicant complains that his deportation to Uganda would result in an irrevocable deterioration of his state of health and subject him to inhuman and degrading treatment in violation of Article 3 of the Convention. He is dependent not on the basic AZT medication against HIV/AIDS but on an antiretroviral therapy combining two drugs (and in the future most likely three). Because of the limited availability and the high cost of such medication in Uganda (or Rwanda if he were to be returned by Uganda to that country) he would no longer receive adequate treatment against his illness. Furthermore, he would lack socio-psychological support, as he has no relatives or friends either in Uganda or Rwanda. He also refers to his desertion from the Rwandan Patriotic Forces which would subject him to a risk of punishment and other reprisals.

2. The applicant also complains that his deportation would violate his rights under Article 8 of the Convention, as he would be separated from his friends and acquaintances in Finland.

3. Under Article 8 the applicant also complains that the Supreme Administrative Court's disclosure to the public of his identity and illness, as mentioned in its decision of 17 April 1998, failed to respect his private life within the meaning of Article 8 of the Convention.
4. The applicant furthermore complains that his deportation would also discriminate against him on the basis of his race and thus violate Article 14 of the Convention.
5. The applicant also complains of the denial of an oral hearing before the Supreme Administrative Court. He invokes Article 6 of the Convention and Article 1.C of Protocol No. 7.
6. Finally, the applicant complains that Judge H's review of his detention for deportation purposes was not in accordance with Article 6 of the Convention, as the same judge had presided over the trial against him in 1992.

PROCEEDINGS BEFORE THE COMMISSION

The application was introduced on 6 April 1998 and registered on 24 April 1998. On 20 April 1998 the President of the Commission decided to indicate to the respondent Government, in accordance with Rule 36 of the Rules of Procedure, that it was desirable in the interests of the parties and the proper conduct of the proceedings before the Commission not to deport the applicant to Uganda until the Commission had been able to examine the application no later than 24 April 1998. On 24 April 1998 the Commission decided to communicate to the respondent Government the applicant's complaint under Article 3 of the Convention concerning his forthcoming deportation to Uganda as well as his complaint under Article 8 concerning the disclosure to the public of the Supreme Administrative Court's decision of 17 April 1998. The Commission also prolonged the above-mentioned indication under Rule 36 until 29 May 1998. The Government's written observations were submitted on 13 May 1998. The applicant replied on 25 May 1998. Additional observations were submitted by the applicant on 27 and 28 May 1998 and by the Government on 28 May 1998. On 29 May 1998 the Commission granted the applicant legal aid.

THE LAW

1. The applicant complains that, given his HIV infection, his deportation to Uganda would result in an irrevocable deterioration of his state of health and subject him to inhuman and degrading treatment in violation of Article 3 of the Convention. If removed from Uganda to Rwanda, his desertion from the Rwandan Patriotic Forces would subject him to a risk of punishment and other reprisals. (...)

The Government consider the complaint "ill-founded". In a previous case (No. 2267/1997) the Supreme Administrative Court indeed quashed a deportation order issued in respect of a person in an advanced stage of AIDS. The Government recall, however, that on 21 January 1998 the applicant's state of health was considered good and his infection had not shown any significant symptoms. An interruption of his medication would not yet trigger off the AIDS stage of the infection. In any case, so the Government argue, the progression of the applicant's illness cannot be predicted with certainty, given the individual differences. His medical condition is much better than that of applicant D, who was expected to die of AIDS within a year from the moment his application was examined by the European Court of Human Rights (see Eur. Court HR, judgment of 2 May 1997, Reports of Judgments and Decisions, 1997-III, pp. 784-785, para. 15).

The Government concede that in Uganda the applicant would probably not receive the same level of treatment against his illness as in Finland. This could lead to an acceleration of his illness, if he were to be deported. However, the receiving State has taken measures in order to improve the treatment of HIV patients. To that end it is committed to the extensive campaign by the United Nations (UNAIDS) which requires, inter alia, that medication be provided at a reduced price. Uganda has also reserved hospital beds for HIV patients and the first specialised hospital will be opened in June 1998.

Finally, the Government recall that the applicant never sought asylum with reference to his alleged activities against the Rwandan Government. Up to the appeal proceedings before the Supreme Administrative Court the applicant consistently indicated that he was a citizen of Uganda and did not seek protection against his possible forced return to Rwanda. The Government therefore consider the allegation that he could be returned to the latter country to lack credibility. Even if he were to be returned to Rwanda, the prison sentence which he might face in that country is not in itself sufficient for establishing a real risk that he would be treated contrary to Article 3 of the Convention.

The applicant submits that the situation in respect of care facilities for AIDS patients is notoriously out of control in Uganda. The authorities give priority to preventive measures and treatment of mothers and children. As a social outcast the applicant would have no means of receiving proper care, whether medical or psychological. His return to Uganda would therefore have a decisive negative impact on his chances of survival.

Finally, as for the alleged risk of ill-treatment due to his background in Rwanda, the applicant contends that immediately after requesting a visa to enter Finland he began his involvement with the Rwandan Patriotic Forces which lasted about two months. On account of his desertion from that movement he could face up to ten years in prison as well as reprisals further endangering his life and limb. This risk should also be assessed against his background as a Tutsi.

The Commission recalls at the outset that Contracting States have the right, as a matter of well-established international law and subject to their treaty obligations including the Convention, to control the entry, residence and expulsion of aliens. The Commission recalls that Article 3 (Art. 3) prohibits in absolute terms torture or inhuman or degrading treatment or punishment. Its guarantees therefore apply irrespective of the reprehensible nature of the conduct of the person in question (see the above-mentioned D v. the United Kingdom judgment, pp. 791-792, paras. 46-47).

The Convention organs are not prevented from scrutinising an applicant's claim under Article 3 (Art. 3) where the source of the risk of proscribed treatment in the receiving country stems from factors which cannot engage either directly or indirectly the responsibility of the public authorities of that country, or which, taken alone, do not in themselves infringe the standards of that Article. In any such contexts the Commission must subject all the circumstances surrounding the case to a rigorous scrutiny, especially the applicant's personal situation in the deporting State (ibid., pp. 792-793, paras. 49-50; No. 23634/94, Dec. 19.5.94, D.R. 77-A, p. 133).

(a) Against this background the Commission will first determine whether the applicant's deportation to Uganda would be contrary to Article 3 in view of his present medical condition.

In the case of D v. the United Kingdom the Court found that the applicant's return to St. Kitts would violate Article 3, taking into account his medical condition. The Court noted that the applicant was in the advanced stages of AIDS. An abrupt withdrawal of the care facilities provided in the respondent State together with the predictable lack of adequate facilities as well as of any form of moral or social support in the receiving country would hasten the applicant's death and subject him to acute mental and physical suffering. In view of those very exceptional circumstances, bearing in mind the critical stage which the applicant's fatal illness had reached and given the compelling humanitarian considerations at stake, the implementation of the decision to remove him to St. Kitts would amount to inhuman treatment by the respondent State in violation of Article 3 (Art. 3). The Court nevertheless emphasised that aliens who have served their prison sentences and are subject to expulsion cannot in principle claim any entitlement to remain on the territory of a Contracting State in order to continue to benefit from medical, social or other forms of assistance provided by the expelling State during their stay in prison (see pp. 793-794, paras. 51-54 of the judgment).

In a recent application the Commission has found that the deportation to the Democratic Republic of Congo (formerly Zaire) of a person suffering from a HIV infection would violate Article 3, where the infection had already reached an advanced stage necessitating repeated hospital stays and where the care facilities in the receiving country were precarious (B.B. v. France, Comm. Report 9.3.98, pending before the Court).

In the light of all the material before it the Commission finds that the present applicant's illness has not yet reached such an advanced stage that his deportation would amount to treatment proscribed by Article 3, taking also into account the conditions in Uganda.

(b) The Commission will next determine whether there is a real risk that the applicant's deportation to Uganda would be contrary to Article 3 in view of his alleged activities within the Rwandan Patriotic Forces. (...)

Accordingly, there is no indication that the applicant's deportation to Uganda would violate Article 3 of the Convention on either of the two grounds invoked.
It follows that this complaint must be rejected as being manifestly ill-founded within the meaning of Article 27 para. 2 of the Convention.

2. The applicant also complains that his deportation would violate his rights under Article 8 of the Convention, as he would be separated from his friends and acquaintances in Finland. (...)

The assumed interference with the applicant's right to respect for his private life can therefore be considered justified under Article 8 para. 2 of the Convention. Accordingly, there is no appearance of a violation of that provision on the point in question. It follows that this complaint must also be rejected as being manifestly ill-founded within the meaning of Article 27 para. 2 of the Convention.

3. Under Article 8 the applicant also complains that the Supreme Administrative Court's disclosure to the public of his identity and illness, as mentioned in its decision of 17 April 1998, failed to respect his private life within the meaning of Article 8 of the Convention. (...)

It is true that in a State where the Convention is directly applicable (such as Finland) the domestic courts are competent to examine of their own motion whether the Convention has been complied with. The Commission recalls, however, that this possibility does not absolve an applicant from the obligation of raising the relevant complaint at least in substance before those courts [exhaustion of local remedies] (...).

It follows that this complaint must be rejected pursuant to Article 27 para. 3 of the Convention.

4. The applicant furthermore complains that his deportation would also discriminate against him on the basis of his race and thus violate Article 14 of the Convention.

The Commission finds no indication that the deportation order in respect of the applicant was issued and upheld on discriminatory grounds. Nor is there any indication that the enforcement of the deportation order would contain discriminatory elements. Accordingly, there is no indication of any violation of Article 14, read in conjunction with any of the other provisions invoked in respect of the applicant's deportation.

It follows that this complaint must also be rejected as being manifestly ill-founded within the meaning of Article 27 para. 2 of the Convention.

5. The applicant also complains of the denial of an oral hearing before the Supreme Administrative Court. He invokes Article 6 of the Convention which guarantees, inter alia, the right to a fair and public hearing by an independent and impartial tribunal in the determination of someone's civil rights and obligations. The applicant also invokes Article 1.C of Protocol No. 7 which guarantees that an alien lawfully resident in the territory of a Contracting State shall not be expelled therefrom except in pursuance of a decision reached in accordance with law. He or she shall be allowed, inter alia, to be represented for these purposes before the competent authority (...).

It follows that this complaint must be rejected as beingincompatible ratione materiae with the provisions of the Convention, pursuant to Article 27 para. 2.

6. Finally, the applicant complains that Judge H's review of his detention for deportation purposes was not in accordance with Article 6 of the Convention, as the same judge had presided over the trial against him in 1992.

The Commission finds that Judge H's decision to prolong the applicant's detention for deportation purposes did not involve any determination of his "civil rights or obligations" or of any "criminal charge" against him (...). Accordingly, Article 6 of the Convention is not applicable in respect of this complaint either.

It follows that this complaint must also be rejected as being incompatible ratione materiae with the provisions of the Convention, pursuant to Article 27 para. 2.

For these reasons, the Commission, by a majority, DECLARES THE APPLICATION INADMISSIBLE.

SCC v. Sweden

This case is of particular relevance as it might well have been the first health/return case with the Court (apart from the Tatete one which was friendly settled) since the entry into force of Protocol 11 (November 1998) under which the Commission had been abolished and the Court had been rearranged. Hence the relevance of this 'first section' decision.

FIRST SECTION DECISION AS TO THE ADMISSIBILITY OF Application no. 46553/99 by S.C.C. against Sweden

The European Court of Human Rights (First Section) sitting on 15 February 2000 as a

Chamber composed of
Mr L. Ferrari Bravo, Mr Gaukur Jörundsson, Mr C. Bîrsan, Mrs W. Thomassen, Mr T. Pantîru, *judges*,
and Mr M. O'Boyle, *Section Registrar*;
Having regard to Article 34 of the Convention for the Protection of Human Rights and Fundamental Freedoms;
Having regard to the application introduced on 3 March 1999 by S.C.C. against Sweden and registered on 5 March 1999 under file no. 46553/99;
Having regard to the reports provided for in Rule 49 of the Rules of Court;
Having regard to the observations submitted by the respondent Government on 6 May 1999 and the observations in reply submitted by the applicant on 23 July 1999;
Having deliberated;
Decides as follows:

THE FACTS

The applicant is a Zambian national born in 1962. At present she resides at Spånga, Sweden. She is represented before the Court by Mr Peter Bergquist, a lawyer practising at Tyresö, Sweden.

A. Particular circumstances of the case

The facts of the case, as submitted by the parties, may be summarised as follows.

The applicant entered Sweden on 26 April 1990 with her husband, a first secretary at the Zambian Embassy in Stockholm, and their two children, born in 1988 and 1990. The applicant's two children from a previous marriage, born in 1982 and 1985, remained in Zambia. The applicant was granted a work permit for one year as from November 1992. On 30 December 1993 she applied for an extended work permit. She stated, *inter alia*, that she and her husband did not have a good marriage and that he assaulted her, that she had rented an apartment in Stockholm, and that she could not return to Zambia since she was afraid of her husband's relatives. In December 1993 the applicant's two children who had remained in Zambia were brought to Sweden.

The applicant remained in Sweden until early 1994 when it appears she returned to Zambia in connection with her husband's end of work at the Embassy.

On 17 March 1994 the National Immigration Board (*Statens invandrarverk*) rejected her above application for a work permit. The Board found that she had no connection to Sweden and that she had left the country.

On 8 May 1996 the applicant, having returned to Sweden, applied for a work permit and a residence permit for one year as from August 1996. The investigations made by the National Immigration Board disclosed that she and her husband, together with the four children, had returned to Zambia in 1994 and that they had intended to divorce. However, her husband died before the divorce became final. The applicant stated that she had returned to Sweden in November 1994 in order to pay her debts and because she had been employed at a hotel in Stockholm. She also stated that she stayed in Sweden for economical reasons and that she wanted a residence and work permit limited to one year, after which time she intended to return to Zambia.

On 9 January 1998 the National Immigration Board rejected the application and ordered the applicant's deportation to Zambia. The Board found that neither the applicant's previous stay in Sweden – as the wife of a diplomat – nor the alleged threats against her by her husband's relatives constituted grounds for granting her a residence permit. The Board also took into account that the applicant's children lived in Zambia.

The applicant appealed to the Aliens Appeals Board (*Utlänningsnämnden*). She now stated that she was infected with HIV and that she should be granted a residence permit on humanitarian grounds as the necessary medical care was not available in Zambia. She submitted two medical certificates issued on 2 February and 20 August 1998 according to which the applicant's HIV infection had been detected in 1995. She made regular visits to the hospital. It was planned to commence an anti-HIV treatment during the next year. As such treatment was complicated and required strict adherence it was further indicated that treatment could only commence if the applicant was given a long-term permit to reside in Sweden.

On 10 November 1998 the Appeals Board upheld the Immigration Board's decision. Referring to a decision taken by the Swedish Government on 23 June 1994 (see below), the Appeals Board considered that the applicant's health status did not give reason to grant her a residence permit.

The applicant made a new application for a residence permit. She submitted a medical certificate issued on 25 January 1999, according to which her state of health had deteriorated. As a consequence, the anti-HIV treatment previously envisaged had been initiated. She also submitted a certificate issued on 27 January 1999 maintaining that a deportation of the applicant would result in the termination of her HIV treatment, the consequences of which would be a faster process towards the AIDS stage and her supposed death.

By a decision of 10 February 1999 the Appeals Board rejected the application stating, *inter alia*, that a new application has to be based on circumstances which have not previously been examined in the matter.

The applicant lodged a new application with the Appeals Board on 19 February 1999. In addition to what she had previously stated, she now claimed that she lived with F.R., a Somalian citizen who had been given a permit to reside in Sweden in 1992. He had been suffering from an HIV infection for about ten years. Allegedly, they had met in the summer of 1995 and had been cohabiting since the summer of 1996. The applicant claimed that she had not previously referred to this relationship, since she was afraid that it would be held against her. She further stated that she did not intend to bring her children to Sweden in case she was granted a residence permit. Her brother, who allegedly had taken over the responsibility for her children, planned to send them to school in England.

On 23 February 1999 the Appeals Board rejected the application. The Board noted, *inter alia*, that the applicant had not previously referred to her relationship with F.R. and considered that there were thus reasons to question the seriousness of the relationship. The Board did not find it obvious that the applicant would have been granted a residence permit on the ground of the alleged relationship, had she applied for it according to the main rule laid down in Chapter 2, Section 5 of the Aliens Act (see below). Furthermore, the Board found that it would not be contrary to requirements of humanity to execute the expulsion decision.

On 5 March 1999, following the Court's indication to the Swedish Government that it was desirable that the applicant not be expelled to Zambia before 16 March 1999 (see below), the National Immigration Board stayed the applicant's deportation. The Board's decision is still in force.

B. Relevant domestic law and practice

(...)

As regards serious illness, this may in exceptional cases constitute humanitarian reasons for a residence permit on condition that it is a life-threatening illness for which no treatment can be provided in the alien's home country. Further, care or treatment in Sweden should lead to an improvement in the alien's condition or be life saving. Thus, the alien's condition should be so serious that he or she would be likely to die or his or her health would deteriorate considerably if he or she was to be sent home. These principles have been expressed and applied by the Government in a number of precedent rulings of 17 February 1994 concerning medical humanitarian reasons in general and in rulings of 23 June 1994 and 16 March 1995 concerning HIV infection as a reason for a residence permit. The Government also stated that the mere fact that treatment in Sweden is of a higher quality than in the alien's home country does not constitute grounds for granting a residence permit, nor are financial difficulties in getting the appropriate treatment in the receiving country a reason for granting such a permit.

The National Board of Health and Welfare (*Socialstyrelsen*) stated in an opinion of 25 March 1994, enclosed in the Government's decisions of 23 June 1994 and referred to in the decision of 16 March 1995, that the fact that a person is diagnosed with HIV or AIDS should not alone and generally be decisive of the question of humanitarian grounds. Instead, the assessment should be founded on the alien's general state of health taking serious clinical symptoms into consideration. The Board concluded that it found no reason, in this respect, to make a difference between HIV infection and other diseases with a serious prognosis.

Further, according to the Aliens Act, an alien who is considered to be a refugee or otherwise in need of protection is, with certain exceptions, entitled to residence in Sweden (Chapter 3, Section 4).

An alien who is to be refused entry or expelled in accordance with a decision that has gained legal force may be granted a residence permit if he or she files a so-called new application based on circumstances which have not previously been examined in the case of refusal of entry or expulsion and if (i) the alien is entitled to a residence permit under Chapter 3, Section 4, or (ii) it would be contrary to requirements of humanity to execute the refusal-of-entry or expulsion decision (Chapter 2, Section 5 b).

Also when it comes to enforcing a decision on refusal of entry or expulsion, regard is taken to the risk of torture and other inhuman or degrading treatment or punishment. According to a special provision on impediments to enforcement, an alien must not be sent to a country where there are reasonable grounds for believing that he or she would be in danger of suffering capital or corporal punishment or of being subjected to torture or other inhuman or degrading treatment or punishment (Chapter 8, Section 1).

COMPLAINTS

1. The applicant claims that her state of health will deteriorate if she is expelled to Zambia. The therapeutic regime recently initiated to treat her HIV infection – which enables her to live a practically normal life – requires strict adherence on the part of the applicant. Furthermore, the treatment is not available in Zambia. Thus, her expulsion to that country would impair her health and lower her life expectancy in violation of Articles 2 and 3 of the Convention.

2. The applicant further asserts that the expulsion would violate her right to respect for her family life under Article 8 of the Convention, as she would be separated from F.R.

Allegedly, his state of health prevents him from travelling to Africa.

3. Also under Article 8, the applicant states that her right to enjoy a good reputation has been violated as, allegedly, the Aliens Appeals Board sent one of its decisions concerning her to the wrong address, thus revealing her state of health to other people.

PROCEDURE

The application was introduced on 3 March 1999 and registered on 5 March 1999. On 5 March 1999 the acting President of the First Section decided to indicate to the respondent Government, in accordance with Rule 39 § 1 of the Rules of Court, that it was desirable in the interest of the parties and the proper conduct of the proceedings not to expel the applicant to Zambia until 16 March 1999. On 16 March 1999 the Court (First Section) decided to communicate the applicant's complaints submitted under Articles 2 and 3 of the Convention to the respondent Government under Rule 54 § 3 (b) of the Rules of Court and that the indication under Rule 39 be extended until further notice. The Government's written observations were submitted on 6 May 1999, after an extension of the time-limit fixed for that purpose. The applicant replied on 23 July 1999, also after an extension of the time-limit.

THE LAW

1. The applicant claims that her expulsion to Zambia would impair her health and lower her life expectancy in violation of Articles 2 and 3 of the Convention. (...)

The Government consider that there is nothing to indicate that the expulsion of the applicant would amount to a violation of Article 2 of the Convention. In any event, the Government find it difficult to dissociate the complaint raised under Article 2 from the substance of her complaint under Article 3. They therefore deal with the substance of her complaints under the latter provision.

The Government maintain that there is no evidence that the applicant suffers from any illness related to HIV or that she has reached the stages of AIDS. It is moreover, according to a report submitted on 26 March 1999 by the Swedish Embassy in Zambia, possible for her to receive the same type of treatment in Zambia as in Sweden, however at considerable costs. The Government further assert that the applicant will be able to enjoy the moral and social support of her relatives in Zambia.

The Government conclude that it has not been shown that the applicant's expulsion to Zambia would violate her rights under Articles 2 and 3 of the Convention. In the Government's view, the applicant's complaints are therefore in this regard manifestly ill-founded.

The applicant contends that her state of health is so serious that she is undergoing treatment in order to delay the development of AIDS related symptoms. An interruption of the treatment would be detrimental to her health. The applicant was infected with the HIV virus prior to 1995. The average life expectancy in Africa for a person infected with HIV is 5–7 years from the time of infection, whilst in Sweden HIV is nowadays treated as a chronic disease. If treatment is initiated at an early stage of the infection, the probability of a successful outcome is higher. Modern antiretroviral drugs have the most potent impact on patients who are relatively healthy. For the applicant this means that an expulsion to Zambia would be more deleterious if she is in relatively good health than if she has started to develop AIDS symptoms.

The applicant contests that adequate care can be provided for her in Zambia since modern medicine is not available there. She furthermore lacks the necessary means to disburse for the care at hand in Zambia. Expulsion to Zambia would diminish her quality of life, thus constituting an inhuman treatment contrary to Article 3. It would also shorten her life and affect her career in violation of Article 2. The applicant refers to a medical certificate issued on 20 July 1999, according to which the likelihood that HIV-infected people eventually develop AIDS is close to 100 % and that the applicant over the next few years will most likely develop AIDS and die. However, as a result of the treatment she is presently undergoing the suffering from developing AIDS may well be pushed far into the future. This life-prolonging process has a much better success-rate if the applicant may be given the chance to continue the treatment in Sweden since the standard of care and the monitoring possibilities in Zambia are reduced compared to what can be offered in Sweden.

The Court shares the view of the Government that the complaints raised by the applicant under Article 2 are indissociable from the substance of her complaint under Article 3 in respect of the consequences of a deportation for her life, health and welfare (cf. the D. v. United Kingdom judgment of 2 May 1997, *Reports of Judgments and Decisions* 1997-III, p. 795, § 59). These complaints should therefore be examined in unison.

The Court recalls at the outset that Contracting States have the right, as a matter of well-established international law and subject to their treaty obligations including the Convention, to control the entry, residence and expulsion of aliens. However, in exercising their right to expel such aliens Contracting States must have regard to Article 3 of the Convention, which enshrines one of the fundamental values of democratic societies. The Court has repeatedly stressed in its line of authorities involving extradition, expulsion or deportation of individuals to third countries that Article 3 prohibits in absolute terms torture or inhuman or degrading treatment or punishment (ibid., pp. 791–792, §§ 46–47). The Court is not prevented from scrutinising an applicant's claim under Article 3 where the source of the risk of proscribed treatment in the receiving country stems from factors which cannot engage either directly or indirectly the responsibility of the public authorities of that country, or which, taken alone, do not in themselves infringe the standards of that Article. In any such contexts the Court must subject all the circumstances surrounding the case to a rigorous scrutiny, especially the applicant's personal situation in the deporting State (ibid., pp. 792–793, §§ 49–50; application no. 23634/94, Tanko v. Finland, Commission's decision of 19 May 1994, DR 77-A, p. 133 et seq.).

According to established case-law aliens who are subject to expulsion cannot in principle claim any entitlement to remain in the territory of a Contracting State in order to continue to benefit from medical, social or other forms of assistance provided by the expelling State. However, in exceptional circumstances an implementation of a decision to remove an alien may, owing to compelling humanitarian considerations, result in a violation of Article 3 (see, for example, the above-mentioned D. v. the United Kingdom judgment, p. 794, § 54). In that case the Court found that the applicant's deportation to St. Kitts would violate Article 3, taking into account his medical condition. The Court noted that the applicant was in the advanced stages of AIDS. An abrupt withdrawal of the care facilities provided in the respondent State together with the predictable lack of adequate facilities as well as of any form of moral or social support in the receiving country would hasten the applicant's death and subject him to acute mental and physical suffering. In view of those very exceptional circumstances, bearing in mind the critical stage which the applicant's fatal illness had reached and given the compelling humanitarian considerations at stake, the implementation of the decision to remove him to St. Kitts would amount to inhuman treatment by the respondent State in violation of Article 3 (see pp. 793–794, §§ 51–54 of the judgment).

In a recent application the Commission found that the deportation to the Democratic Republic of Congo (formerly Zaire) of a person suffering from a HIV infection would violate Article 3, where the infection had already reached an advanced stage necessitating repeated hospital stays and where the care facilities in the receiving country were precarious (see application no. 30930/96, B.B. v. France, decision of 9 March 1998; case subsequently struck out by the Court on 7 September 1998).

Against this background the Court will determine whether the applicant's deportation to Zambia would be contrary to Article 3 in view of her present medical condition. In so doing the Court will assess the risk in the light of the material before it at the time of its consideration of the case, including the most recent available information on her state of health (cf. the Ahmed v. Austria judgment of 17 December 1996, *Reports* 1996-VI, p. 2207, § 43).

The Court recalls that the applicant's present medical status was diagnosed in 1995 and that her anti-HIV treatment has just recently commenced. The Court further recalls the conclusion of the Swedish National Board of Health and Welfare that, when assessing the humanitarian aspects of a case like this, an overall evaluation of the HIV infected alien's state of health should be made rather than letting the HIV diagnosis in itself be decisive. The Court finds that the Board's reasoning is still valid.

The Court notes that according to the above-mentioned report from the Swedish Embassy AIDS treatment is available in Zambia. It also notes that the applicant's children as well as other family members live in Zambia. Having regard to the above case-law and in the light of the material before it the Court finds that the applicant's situation is not such that her deportation would amount to treatment proscribed by Article 3.

It follows that this part of the application is manifestly ill-founded within the meaning of Article 35 § 3 of the Convention and must be rejected pursuant to Article 35 § 4 of the Convention.

2. The applicant also complains that her expulsion would violate her right to respect for her family life as she would be separated from F.R. She invokes Article 8 of the Convention. (...)

It is not contested that the decision ordering the applicant's expulsion is based on the relevant provisions of the Aliens Act. The Court further finds that the interference in issue has aims which are compatible with the Convention, namely "the economic well-being of the country". The Court reiterates, furthermore, that it is for the Contracting States to maintain public order, *inter alia*, by exercising their right to control the entry and residence of aliens.

As regards the question whether the expulsion order is "necessary in a democratic society" in pursuit of the above-mentioned aim the Court recalls that the alleged relationship with F.R. commenced at a time when the applicant was illegally residing in Sweden. Consequently, she could not reasonably have expected to be able to continue the cohabitation in Sweden. Moreover, she made no reference to the relationship in her applications to the immigration authorities until early 1999, about three and a half years after it had supposedly started. The Court also notes that the applicant's four children as well as other family members live in Zambia.

In these circumstances, and taking into account the margin of appreciation left to the Contracting States as well as the reasons set out above in respect of Article 3 of the Convention, the Court concludes that the national authorities did strike a fair balance between the applicant's rights on the one hand and the legitimate interests of the Contracting State on the other. Thus, her deportation, if effected, may reasonably be considered "necessary" within the meaning of Article 8 § 2 of the Convention.

It follows that this part of the application is also manifestly ill-founded within the meaning of Article 35 § 3 of the Convention and must be rejected pursuant to Article 35 § 4 of the Convention.

3. Lastly, the applicant claims that her right under Article 8 to enjoy a good reputation has been violated as, allegedly, the Aliens Appeals Board sent one of its decisions concerning her to the wrong address, thus revealing her state of health to other people.

The Court finds that the complaint regarding the postal handling of a decision sent out by the Aliens Appeals Board is unsubstantiated and that it does not disclose any appearance of a violation of Article 8 of the Convention.

It follows that this part of the application is manifestly ill-founded within the meaning of Article 35 § 3 of the Convention and must be rejected pursuant to Article 35 § 4 of the Convention.

For these reasons, the Court, by a majority, **DECLARES THE APPLICATION INADMISSIBLE.**

PRAXIS: THE NEED FOR INFORMATION AND HARMONIZATION

Christopher Baker

INTRODUCTION

Whenever the issue of the legal obligation to provide protection, or rather the need to receive it is raised, an interesting development is witnessed. The right of every person to *seek* and *enjoy* asylum from persecution is explicitly stated in Article 14 of the 1948 Universal Declaration of Human Rights (UDHR), although the obligation of countries to *grant* asylum is absent from the text. While all soft law principles spelled out in the UDHR were codified in the hard law provisions of the two 1966 covenants, the right of asylum was, surprisingly, not transferred. Frequently, it is submitted that the 1951 Geneva Refugee Convention duly expressed the right to seek and enjoy asylum and, thus, it was not necessary that this right be expressed in the covenants. However, the term *asylum* appears only in the preamble to the Refugee Convention, in connection with the need for burden sharing among the signatories, and is found nowhere else in the body of the actual text.[1] Instead, the core article of the Convention deals with the principle of non-refoulement, the prohibition against the expulsion or return of anyone to his or her country of origin if he or she would be subjected to a real threat to life or freedom due to race, religion, political opinion, or membership of a particular social group or nationality (i.e., ethnicity, minority). In practice, this principle has resulted in a negative obligation amounting to de facto asylum. Unfortunately, a number of the countries of the world have been blinded by raw emotion, and in failing to exercise their legal obligations of discretion, have systematically impregnated their own asylum systems with exorbitant and indeed unmanageable numbers.

Strikingly, persons fleeing from war-torn countries (victims of warfare) were not included in the Geneva Convention and still, 50 years later, are excluded

[1] Europe, at last, agreed to include the right to asylum in the EU Charter on Fundamental Rights, Nice, December 2000 (Art. 18).

P.J. van Krieken (Ed.), Health, Migration and Return

from the exclusive refugee status, that is as long as such victims cannot prove that they would be persecuted for reasons of race, religion, political opinion, membership of a social group or nationality. It was hence not only logical but also desirable that a special status for victims of war be established. The 1969 OAU African Refugee Convention was a remarkable turning point in the legal foundation for the recognition of those persons fleeing warfare and was far ahead of most other countries. Europeans did not have such provisions until the year 2000 when the European Commission at last issued a proposal for a Council Directive on temporary protection for victims of war. Before then, however, implicit recognition was derived from Article 3 of the 1950 European Convention on Human Rights (ECHR) and the comparable Article 3 of the 1984 Convention against Torture (CAT). Under these provisions, which are absolute, the type of protection envisioned came to be known as subsidiary protection. Over the years, subsidiary protection has been extended to other groups alleging the need for protection, i.e., humanitarian cases, persons exposed to traumatic experiences, persons with close family ties, and the list goes on. One may indeed conclude from such developments that there has been a level of "inflation" taking place in this field.[2]

In this chapter, the term subsidiary protection is thus meant to cover persons falling outside the 1951 Refugee Convention, the ECHR, and the CAT. A new group of beneficiaries has indeed been created, a main group being those asserting the right to protection based on health and medical related claims. The intended purpose of this contribution is to evaluate the practices in some European countries, including two Baltic states, as well as Canada and the United States, as to how such asylum cases are handled, the rights involved and the provisions extended to such applicants. The main elements are those of legal provisions, international norms and obligations, country of origin practices, and the statistics of applications based on medical claims and those granted relief based on such claims. It should be noted at the outset that most of the countries involved in this study do have national legislation on how to approach asylum

---

[2] In the Netherlands, the new Aliens Act (in force as per 1 April 2001) contains no less than 5 categories, of which only two (+ related family reunification) would appear to be obligatory under international law. Section 27.1 reads: A residence permit for a fixed period as referred to in section 26 may be issued to an alien:(a) who is a refugee under the terms of the Convention; (b) who makes a plausible case that he has good grounds for believing that if he is expelled he will run a real risk of being subjected to torture or to inhuman or degrading treatment or punishment; (c) who cannot, for pressing reasons of a humanitarian nature connected with the reasons for his departure from the country of origin, reasonably be expected, in the opinion of the Minister, to return to his country of origin; (d) for whom return to the country of origin would, in the opinion of Our Minister, constitute an exceptional hardship in connection with the overall situation there; (e) who belongs, as husband, wife or minor child, to the family of an alien as referred to at (a) to (d), has the same nationality as the alien and has either entered the Netherlands at the same time as the alien or has entered it within three months of the date on which the alien referred to at (a) to (d) was granted a residence permit for a fixed period as referred to in section 26.

cases submitted on humanitarian grounds, under which medical cases usually fall. Moreover, there are no real explicit international legal provisions obliging countries to take on the health problems of other states and their nationals, except in the most extreme of situations, such as life or death emergencies. Many countries have admitted applicants citing medical claims under humanitarian and compassionate grounds. A common pattern has emerged in the countries of refuge whereby applicants being denied Convention refugee status have appealed negative decisions, or by submitting new applications allowed under law, and (often for the first time) mention medical conditions, the lack of medical treatment available at home, or if available its inadequacy, as a reason to be allowed entry and residence. Furthermore, it is revealed that once an applicant is admitted into the asylum procedure, exclusive or limited rights of access to health care and other social provisions are enjoyed, varying from country to country. Perhaps the most commonly reported medical condition is psychological disorder, especially PTSS/PTSD. And it should not be surprising that diseases of a psychological nature are not only among the most difficult to diagnose, but also extremely difficult to disprove due to the subjectivity of mental illness or disturbance.

In addition to highlighting the above, this contribution reveals further problems associated with this issue, referred to as "health and return." First of all, international co-operation is lacking among countries, although some have mentioned a desired interest in doing so. It is asserted that such co-operation is practical in order to combat abuse of the asylum system, rejecting unfounded applications, and extending unnecessarily health care rights that should be reserved for a nation's citizens, Convention refugees, and extreme emergency cases.[3] Further, many countries have reported that they lack a database of country of origin health care practices. Some only conduct research on a case-by-case basis and there is an absence of compiling and storing information. It would be useful if information would be systematically collected and stored in a central database; all too often it is assumed that medical treatment is not available when this is not always the case. Moreover, it might be pragmatic to invest in the health care system of countries of origin, preventing future migratory movements, and not merely helping only a few individuals. It has also been found that countries do not keep separate statistics on applications filed by aliens citing (solely) medical claims, either initially or after the initial asylum request was denied. Such practice could be of great assistance to officials of national Immigration Departments. For instance, the Aliens Appeals Board of Sweden, on its own initiative, undertook an investigation recently and found that many new applicants (those who had their request for asylum denied in the first instance but

[3] The utility of proper health care is not herewith dismissed, instead this contribution argues that the focus of problem-solving by the receiving countries is better directed toward the sending countries rather than those few individuals able to cross borders.

were allowed to file new applications), not only claimed to be suffering from some sort of mental disorder but that threats of suicide were reported in 30% of all appeal cases.

Austria[4]

If an application for asylum has been rejected, a decision must then be made as to the order of removal. A stay of removal may be issued on ECHR Article 3 grounds. Although case law is not available, it is probable that if the rejectee has a serious health condition and the health care situation in the country of origin is poor or inadequate to handle the necessary medical treatment, these grounds may also be sufficient to halt the execution of a removal order.

When it is determined that an alien cannot be returned, a temporary residence permit is normally granted and is valid for 1 year and may be extended to the maximum of 3 years after the second extension is granted.

Separate statistics on asylum cases are not kept. The governmental office responsible for such records is the Austrian Federal Asylum Board, established in 1998, and only compiles data relating to appeal decisions.

Belgium

Outside of the Convention refugee status, Belgium has enacted alternative forms of protection. The legal provision is displaced person status for Bosnians and Kosovars and refuge for persons fleeing conflict situations. In such cases, temporary residence permits may be granted and the right to employment may be enjoyed.

Although access to health care and other social provisions are extended to asylum seekers, rejectees, and illegals, the Belgian authorities have undertaken efforts to restrict such access to only the most needed of assistance. There is a right under Belgian law to apply for an extension of stay if the applicant is seriously ill, provided that the applicant can demonstrate the financial means to cover the costs of any necessary medical treatment. Generally, such treatment is limited to emergency cases only and those found to be offering more than humanitarian care to rejectees may be prosecuted. Up until recently, those helping 'rejectees' ran the risk of being penalized, unless the assistance was strictly humanitarian. In November 1998, however, the Committee on Internal Affairs of the Senate approved a Bill aiming at liberalizing the conditions under

---

[4] Unless otherwise indicated, all references and citations are compiled from responses given by officials and others from individual countries to a questionnaire sent out in preparation for the September 2000 expert meeting on the issue of Health and Return as well as Peter van Krieken (2000) *Health Gaps and Migration*, Raoul Wallenberg Institute, Lund, pp. 50-61.

which humanitarian aid may be given to e.g. rejectees. The Bill proposes immunity from prosecution for 'essentially humanitarian' assistance.[5]

As to non-return, it is worth being noted that, in accordance with case law, a stay of the execution of the order of return may be imposed if the applicant, suffering from a serious medical condition, cannot obtain treatment in the country of origin. In a major effort to deal with a massive case-load, a special Committee was set up in late 1999 in order to ensure that cases which had been in process for a couple of years, as well as humanitarian cases, would be granted a residence permit (this one-time regulation was meant to cover 50,000 persons by mid-2000). It was decided to explicitly include all those who suffer from illnesses or are under treatment. This in fact meant that illness per se became a criterion to be granted a residence permit (2000). The new Belgian Aliens Act as proposed by the Government in late 2000 would appear to be far stricter, also where it concerns this specific category.

Canada

When confronted with asylum applications that are based on health issues and requests for non-return, citizenship, and immigration, the procedure Canada uses involves investigating countries of origin in order to determine the health care situation and its availability. Investigations are carried out by appointed field medical officers or medical practitioners. Evidence gathered from these investigations are then taken into consideration in the decision-making process as regards each application where health issues have been cited.

Decisions made on such cases have been conducted generally without extensive media coverage. This issue has not received attention from local NGOs dealing with refugees.

Regarding the legal framework established under Canadian law, paragraph 19 (1)(a) of the Canadian *Immigration Act* deals with medical inadmissibility.

> No person shall be granted admission who is a member of any of the following classes:
> Persons who are suffering from any disease, disorder, disability or other health impairment as a result of the nature, severity or probable duration of which, in the opinion of a medical officer concurred in by at least one other medical officer, they are or are likely to be a danger to public health or to public safety, or their admission would cause or might reasonably be expected to cause excessive demands on health or social services.

In essence, requests for asylum/immigration may be denied on medical grounds. The legal definition for "excessive demand" has been defined as "more than what

[5] MNS, December 1998, p. 19.

is normal or necessary" and is determined with regard to the following: "willingness of family to support the applicant, individual circumstances such as family support and community resources, the availability of health and social services, and the severity of the condition, taking into account the estimated time frames and costs for the applicant's treatment." This provision is subject to several exceptions for applicants in Canada.

Although Canadian law has no provision for refugee status to be granted based on health reasons, those persons whose applications fall under the 1951 Refugee Convention (race, religion, political opinion, nationality, membership in a particular social group) are not refused when applying for permanent resident status based on para.19 (1) of the *Immigration Act.* Those persons not granted refugee status may be granted an evaluation to determine the risk of return to the country of origin. This evaluation is set up under the *Post Determination Refugee Claimants in Canada Class* (PDRCC) and aims to establish an objectively determined risk facing the applicant if he or she were to be returned to the country of origin. Such risk, if there is any, would have to be found to apply in all parts of the country and must be known to apply to the person in question and not to others in or from the country. There must be a risk to the individual's life, excluding deficiencies in adequate health care provisions of the country of origin, a risk of "extreme sanctions" facing the individual, or a risk of inhumane treatment. Those who meet the criteria of the PDRCC may apply for permanent status irrespective of the results of the required medical examination.

Under "Humanitarian and Compassionate" grounds, individuals in Canada may receive authorization to remain in the country while the application for permanent resident status is being evaluated. Health issues may affect the ultimate decisions taken under the humanitarian provisions but will not exclude those who are granted permission to remain in Canada while awaiting the completion of the review of their case:

> These persons, as well as inadmissible spouses of Canadian citizens or permanent residents, or visitors coming for prearranged medical treatment, may ask that admission to Canada be facilitated by the Minister's authority to issue a permit. One consideration in this situation, is whether follow-up treatment is available in the country of origin and, if not, whether this will prevent the person from returning home.

Canada has universal health care offering coverage for hospital, in-patient and out-patient physician services. Health care, including emergency and essential services, is open to all refugees and refugee applicants.

As pertaining to the application of international norms and standards where it concerns country of origin practices, there is an expressed interest within Canada to review information on how other countries deal with such issues and concerns, especially in developing Canadian immigration policies.

Canada conducts research on countries of origin on a case-by-case basis; data gathered are not stored, and such information aids in the decision-making process but does not necessarily play a decisive role. With regard to separate records on asylum applications that are based on medical claims, there is marginal and poorly detailed information on such cases.

In short, as can be seen from the above, the issue of medical claims invoked by applicants in the asylum process is rather complicated from the Canadian perspective. While there are legal provisions and standards that have to be met, at the end of the day, people are allowed, more or less, to stay. Canadian law states that applicants, due to the nature of their medical problems, who would put excessive demands on the health care system of Canada cannot be admitted into the country. However, there are a number of legal avenues open to the rejected applicants, such as the PDRCC and the H&C provisions.

Even after all legal avenues have been exhausted, the asylum application has been rejected, the PDRCC and H&C options have been found not to be appropriate, and a removal order has been issued, the applicant may resort to the Federal Court for relief and request an application to stay the execution of the removal order. In making such a request for relief, medical claims are allowed as part of the record on which the application is based even though in prior proceedings it would have been appropriate to have brought up such medical claims and have had them at that time properly reviewed as part of the evaluation process(es). In applying for a stay of execution, the applicant may argue that there is an imbalance in the medical facilities at home as compared with Canada's or it is also valid if the applicant asserts to be suffering from PTSS. The court has a mixed record in dealing with such cases, having rejected some cases while granting relief in others. It is noted that if an applicant is granted a stay of the execution order, such a stay may be lifted if the applicant's health has improved or the facilities in the country of origin are found to have improved since the time the stay of execution was granted.

Czech Republic

The issue of health related Migration as a topic for discussion has arisen since the new Act of Asylum came into force (1.1.2000). In the framework of the asylum procedure the possibility of granting asylum for humanitarian reasons was established. A particular case is examined from the view of the state of health of the asylum seeker, the global situation in the country of origin (this includes the level of medical care in the country), the particular social situation of the person concerned and special features of the case.

Czech Asylum Law does not contain any special provision concerning the above mentioned problematics. Art. 14 of the Asylum Law is the legal basis for the possibility of granting asylum for humanitarian reasons, even if the reasons for granting asylum based on persecution have not been proved. Art. 14 does not specify any criteria for granting asylum on the ground of humanitarian reasons. An amendment to the Asylum Law is being prepared, but no change regarding "medical cases" has been proposed. The Czech Alien Law provides the possibility of granting a permanent residence permit for humanitarian reasons.

With the increasing number of cases based on medical grounds the need for monitoring the relevant information regarding this problem is also growing.

Denmark

Under Danish law, there is a provision of protection for what is termed as 'de facto refugees', meant to cover "an alien who is not covered by the Convention Relating to the Status of Refugees of 28 July 1951, but where, for reasons similar to those referred to in the Convention or for other serious reasons which give rise to a well-founded fear of persecution or similar injustice, the person concerned should not be forced to return to his country of origin." Special arrangements exist for temporary residence permits to be granted to applicants fleeing the former Yugoslavia and Kosovo, as is found in other Western countries. Applicants may invoke humanitarian grounds to be admitted and residence permits may be authorized if there are other exceptional grounds for doing so, e.g. if it has not been possible to expel the person concerned during a period of at least 18 months. The right of appeal exists if an application is rejected under Convention guidelines to apply under humanitarian considerations. Review of applications is done on a case-by-case basis alongside the relevant background information concerning the country of origin.

Those admitted on humanitarian grounds are granted a temporary residence permit with a possibility of later authorizing a permanent status. Once admitted, one enjoys the right to employment and social rights (social insurance, unemployment benefits, etc.).

It is in section 9(2)(ii) expressly provided that a humanitarian residence permit may be issued only to an alien whose application for a residence permit under section 7, i.e. asylum, has definitively been refused by the Danish Refugee Board (or by the Danish Immigration Service if the asylum application has been considered as manifestly unfounded). The application is to be submitted to the Minister of the Interior. Only aliens staying in Denmark at the time of the submission of the application may apply for a humanitarian residence permit.

An application for a residence permit under section 9(2)(ii) submitted within 10 days after the Danish Refugee Board refused an alien a residence permit under section 7 suspends enforcement of the time-limit for departure.

If an asylum application was considered as manifestly unfounded an application for a residence permit under section 9(2)(ii) will suspend enforcement of the time-limit for departure only if the time-limit for departure has not been exceeded, i.e. application shall be submitted during the asylum procedure.

Taking into account particular circumstances of the individual case the Ministry of the Interior may suspend enforcement of the time-limit for departure.

The applicant shall provide such information as is required for deciding if a permit pursuant to section 9(2)(ii) can be granted. The application is usually accompanied with medical certificates. However, all necessary information is to be collected before the Minister of the Interior makes a decision in the case.

The main practical problems are obtaining reliable and sufficient information concerning the state of health of the applicant and, on the other side, information concerning possible medical treatment in the country of origin.

A health declaration is usually unavoidable when the Ministry of the Interior deals with an application for humanitarian residence permits under section 9(2)(ii). Although the final evaluation is the responsibility of the Ministry of the Interior a health declaration practically constitutes decisive proof of the state of the applicant's health.

A health declaration may be issued either by a public hospital or by a private doctor. There are significantly more applications based on the applicant's psychological rather than physical suffering.

However, case law concerning humanitarian residence permits on health grounds has developed some general criteria for granting this kind of residence permit.

A humanitarian residence permit will be issued to an alien who:

– is suffering from acute, life-threatening or very serious physical or mental diseases,

– if returned to the country of domicile is at risk of suffering a serious handicap or a deteriorating serious handicap which he/she is already suffering.

When making its decision the Ministry of the Interior takes into consideration the access to adequate care in the alien's country of domicile. This means that the Ministry of the Interior in a case where the applicant suffers from very serious physical and/or psychological diseases can refuse the application only if the available information *in concreto* confirms that the alien can receive adequate medical treatment in the country of origin.

The Ministry of the Interior may in this connection request the Danish Ministry of Foreign Affairs to make a statement as to whether it is possible for the alien to receive necessary medical treatment in the country of origin specially taking into account the fact that the alien often belongs to a specific group of persons in that country. According to the Ministry of the Interior's latest practice the fact that the alien's access to adequate care in the country of origin depends on sufficient economic resources may, inter alia, qualify for residence permits on humanitarian grounds.

If treatment is not available in the country of origin the Ministry of the Interior takes into consideration the consequences of the lack of medical treatment in the country of origin.

The burden of proof is balancing between the alien and the Ministry of the Interior. Although there is no strict division of the burden of proof it is usually so that the alien collects information concerning his/her state of health and economic resources while the Ministry of the Interior collects information concerning medical treatment in the country of origin and discounting medical treatment.

The Ministry of the Interior is aware of the fact that Denmark can offer a higher level of medical care than many of the countries where aliens come from. The standard which the Ministry uses in this regard is *appropriate/reasonable* medical treatment. The Ministry of the Interior also has to take into consideration the consequences of a positive decision for the future.

As examples of cases where a humanitarian residence permit could be granted, cases where an alien suffers from AIDS or cancer in the terminal phase could be mentioned. However, it is always an individual assessment which must be made in every single case.

Psychiatric problems are the medical grounds that are most often invoked. Most of the aliens whose asylum applications have been refused have some psychiatric problems. Facing return to the country of origin after a definitively negative answer to the asylum claim, these psychiatric problems usually become worse.

According to practice a humanitarian residence permit may furthermore be issued to an alien suffering from an incurable or very serious mental disease. PTSS/PTSD is the most invoked disease. According to practice, suffering from PTSS/PTSD is however not enough in itself to qualify for a residence permit, except in the case where PTSS/PTSD is equivalent to insanity.

Estonia

Although thus far Estonia has not received any asylum applications based on medical claims, there are legal provisions within Estonian law that deal with the issue of health and asylum related issues. Individuals applying for asylum are entitled to emergency medical care. Treatment of cases outside the Convention context is assisted by generally recognized human rights norms. Asylum applicants do have some rights to medical assistance as asylum reception centres arrange for emergency care and medical examinations as determined by necessity. The law provides for asylum seekers to enjoy these rights until they have been granted asylum or until they have left the country, deported or otherwise.

Finland

Finland has experienced the submission of applications for residence permits based on medical grounds, but, however, no statistics are available. As has been reported as common experience in a number of countries, cases have also arisen in Finland where requests for asylum are denied and applicants subsequently ask to have their cases reconsidered based on health related issues. Nonetheless, Finland does not consider this issue to be a problem as its relative number of asylum applications is small in comparison with other European and North American countries.

The section of the Aliens Act of Finland that deals with medical-related aspects pertaining to applications for asylum can be found in section 20, paragraph 3. A residence permit may be issued to an applicant for medical reasons if medical treatment is unattainable in the country of origin or a third country. A number of qualifying factors are applicable to this section of the Finnish Aliens Act. First of all, a residence permit is only granted in such instances where it is ascertainable that denying a request for a residence permit based on health grounds would be "unreasonable." In ascertaining what is unreasonable, the nature of the illness, the availability of medical care in the country of origin, whether or not the authorities can gather information on the situation of the country of origin, and the necessary means available to the individual to get medical treatment are all taken into consideration in the decision-making process. Following these guidelines, if it is subsequently determined that a refusal to grant a residence permit would be unreasonable, a permit is then issued for one year; however, such a permit is permanent by nature. Temporary fixed-term permits are also issued in cases whereby the applicant suffers from a medical condition that can be treated, for a definitive period only, in Finland but not in the applicant's country of origin or third country. The temporary permit cannot be extended under the same conditions.

Records indicate that in Finland when applicants are granted such residence permits that are of a permanent nature the decisions are not usually appealed, although a small number of cases have been appealed to the Helsinki Administrative Court. However, no separate statistics are available but the Court has denied such appeals on asylum when a temporary permit was granted on health grounds.

There is no new legislation or proposals for regulations concerning medical asylum cases and none exist at this point in time. Applications for asylum based on medical conditions are handled in Finland on a case-by-case basis, whereby officials consider specifically the nature of each individual's illness and his or her chances to obtain treatment. The authorities have reported a lack of access to information on the health care systems of other countries. Health certificates are issued by Finnish doctors in cases where they have decided that an applicant's ability to travel would not be hindered due to his/her medical condition and whether medical treatment can be provided to the applicant in the country of origin. In their certifications, doctors may also make recommendations pertaining to the provision of an escort to accompany the applicant during travel. In the decision-making process and the review of individual cases, medical certificates issued by doctors are taken into consideration.

In deciding on applications based on medical cases where they involve country of origin practices, Finland has not applied international norms or standards.

In gathering information on the health care systems of countries of origin, the country information unit of the Immigration Department in Finland relies on international organizations (e.g. WHO, UN, UNAIDS, World Bank), research institutes and their publications (STAKES, a Finnish-based institute), information made available through organizations in operation in countries of origin, and traditional media sources (e.g. newspapers, periodicals, and nowadays the internet). Currently, attempts are underway to compile gathered information and data in a comprehensive database by the Immigration Department. Most of the information is already publicly available. Those directly involved in the decision-making process, as well as the personnel of the Immigration Department, utilize collected information and data and are transferred on appeal.

There are no separate and specific numbers on asylum applications based upon medical reasons. Finland has no policy to keep such separate statistics.

France

Outside of the Convention refugee status, French law offers "territorial asylum" to individuals who do not meet the criteria for legal refugee status. This provision is designed to offer protection to persons fleeing conflict situations and for compliance with ECHR Article 3. Typically, 1-year temporary residence permits with the right to employment are granted and requests for renewal are subject to review. Also, the possibility exists after 3 years of continual, legal residence and an applicant may apply for a 10-year residence permit.

Regarding health-related issues, authorities are prohibited from enforcing removal orders if the rejectee suffers from an illness and medical treatment is not available in the country of origin. While the person in question has the responsibility to offer the facts of his/her case, a public health official must assess the health care environment of the country of origin. French law, moreover, recognizes a so-called right to health in that an alien may file an application for a temporary residence permit "if indeed his/her state of health requires essential medical services in France."[6]

Germany

It should be noted from the outset that Germany offers protection that goes way beyond the specifications of the 1951 Convention. Outside the category of Convention refugees, there are other options under German law for asylum seekers denied refugee status. Humanitarian relief may be granted and the same rights extended to Convention refugees may be enjoyed (e.g., renewable residence permit for 2 years, permanent after 8 years of legal residence,

[6] Van Krieken, op cit, p. 53.

employment and social rights). A 1993 Law (amended in 1998) describes exactly what kind of services will be provided to asylum seekers.[7] For the category of "others," the same rights as above apply, however, social rights are not as extensive. Those fleeing from war or civil war are entitled to residence for 2 years, employment is subject to conditions and developments within the German labour market, and social subsistence may be available to asylum seekers. The final category is known as Deportation Relief and entails no right of residence, but nonetheless, a one-year renewable permit is granted. Employment may be forbidden or subject to limitations and social rights are the same as for those fleeing from war situations. Officials report that:

Aliens can also claim every imaginable impediment to deportation and have their claims tested in court. However, it has to be said that the status of those merely given limited exceptional leave to remain on these [humanitarian] grounds is rather weak in terms of residence entitlement and barely adequate in social terms to live for an unforeseeable length of time.

The German Aliens Act does thus allow for consideration of applicants not meeting the criteria established by the 1951 Refugee Convention. Execution of an order of return may not be contemplated if there is a risk to the person's life or freedom if the individual were to be returned to the country of origin. For medical considerations to be considered by immigration authorities, a medical certificate must be issued, detailing the diagnosis of the illness, its progression, what treatment is necessary, and what the likely result would be if such treatment was not carried out. The authorities will in the case of a deportation order take into account medical certificates combined with information normally obtained through the Federal Ministry of Foreign Affairs on possibilities for treatment in the country of origin. Under readmission agreements the issue of illnesses – and if need be assistance for and during the actual return journey – can be properly dealt with, both as to the provision of releavnt infromation and as to the treatment.

In this respect it is to be underlined that the Federal Agency concerned ('Bundesamt') focuses on asylum applications, whereas the issue of return is above all dealt with by the Länder (the respective States of which the German Federation, the 'Bundsrepublik', consists). Health aspects are hence a subject of concern both on the Federal level (the decision on the application, Aliens Act arts. 53.4 or 53.6) and the Länder level (decision on (non-)return, e.g. art. 55.2). In general, the number of cases resulting in a (de facto) residence permit ('Duldung') for reasons of health is increasing. This is particularly true for psychologial or psychiatric diseases. The question whether or not to return

[7] Asylbewerderleistungsgesetz (AsylnLG), 30 June 1993, promulgated August 1997, and amended in 1998. See e.g. G. Classen, Krankenhilfe nach dem Asylbewwerberleistungsgesetz, Asylmagazin 11/2000, pp. 11-13. Classen claims that asylum seekers are entitled to many more health services than generally believed.

traumatized erstwhile refugees to the former Yugoslavia raised public awareness. The issue focused on the question whether, and if so where, treatment should or could be provided. In a number of cases a residence permit was granted on the basis of art. 30 of the Aliens Act (whereas art. 32 may in certain cases also be applicable).

Medical certificates in the case of (non-)deportation will generally be checked by Länder authorities. A number of applicants are ultimately entitled to receive medical treatment in Germany and a stay of return is thus executed. As indicated above, in some cases this leads to a de facto residence permit.

The courts involved with refugee and asylum cases are still in the process of setting down specific criteria that should be applied in the decision-making. In 1998, the Federal Administrative Court, the court of last instance for these sorts of cases, decided that the law "covers only those cases in which a lack of treatment would have an essential negative impact on the individual's health or would even threaten that individual's life."[8] However, the courts have ruled since then that return cannot be contemplated if such return would result in "certain death."[9]

As is the case with most of the other countries under study in this chapter, no separate statistics are kept by Immigration Department officials concerning those granted refugee status or who are admitted into the country based on humanitarian grounds, health related or otherwise. However, it would appear that the numbers are rising and that the issue is giving rise to renewed discussions.[10]

---

[8] MNS, April 1999; Au 7K98.31120, with due reference to the BVerwG referred to above. VGH HE B.v. 3 May 1999 – 3 UE 305/98.A with reference to BVerwG 17 October 1995.

[9] Jurisprudence and case-law in Germany is traditionally of great relevance. The following cases may be cited: 1998 Decisions in favour of according possibilities for (continued) treatment in Germany include:

Ethiopia, AIDS, VG (meaning: Administrative Court) Ansbach and BayVHG (meaning regional Higher Court) 16 April 1998; Togo, Cancer, VG Oldenburg 24 February 1998; DR Congo, Diabetes, VG Cologne 5 February 1998; DR Congo, epileptic, VG Cologne 5 February 1998; Moldava, epileptic, VG Ansbach, 4 February 1998; Ethiopia, Diabetes Type 1, VG Ansbach 11 November 1998; Georgia, brain tumour, VG Ansbach 28 January 1998; Georgia, TB, VG Ansbach 12 May 1998; Bosnia PTSS, OVG Saarland 25 March 1998; Afghanistan, epilectic, VG Hamburg 28 August 1998; Iran, serious depression, VG Hamburg 20 August 1998; Ukraïne epileptic and serious depression, VG Hamburg 7 July 1998.

Decisions denying leave of stay: Pakistan, renal dialysis, VG Oldenburg 29 June 1998; DR Congo, AIDS, VG Hanover and OVG NS 5 March 1998; Lebanon, epileptic VG Ansbach 15 January 1998; Yugoslavia, renal disease, VG Oldenburg 30 December 1997; Burkina Fasso, HIV, VG Regensburg 21 July 1998; Congo, diabetes, VG Ansbach 5 August 1998; Ethiopia, diabetes, VG Ansbach 22 September 1998.

[10] See e.g. Angela Birck, Wie krank muss ein Flüchtling sein um von der Abschiebung ausgenommen zu werden, and Van Krieken´s reaction (´Ausreiseverpflichtung und Krankheit) in *Informationsbrief Ausländerrecht* (2000) resp. nr 3 and 12.

Greece

Greek law recognizes two categories of asylum applications that fall outside the Convention refugee guidelines. Firstly, temporary residence permits may be granted to applicants on humanitarian grounds. However, before such a request can even be made, the application for refugee status must have been definitively rejected. Secondly, temporary protection may be extended to applicants who are *force majeur* cases.

The humanitarian cases are granted a 1-year residence permit, which is renewable for one year, and attain the right to employment. Provisions for the *force majeur* cases are decided on a case-by-case basis.

Hungary

The Geneva Convention does not contain the possibility of international protection based solely upon medical reasons. The asylum laws of Hungary provide the possibility to give temporary protection for those persons who do not meet the criteria prescribed in the Geneva Convention, as admitted persons, based upon humanitarian reasons.

The Asylum Act (139th Act of 1997) contains the rights and obligations related to requests for asylum submitted in Hungary, as well as the legal guarantees of the procedure. The Government Decree 24/1998 (02.18.) on the detailed regulations of the asylum procedure, furthermore on the documents of applicants, temporarily protected persons and admitted persons stipulates the details concerning the official procedure.

The Act on the entry, residence and immigration of foreign citizens to Hungary (86th Act of 1993), and the Government Decree 64/1994 (04.30.) issued for its execution, furthermore the Decree of the Ministry of the Interior 9/1994 (04.30.), regulate the conditions for issuing a visa or residence permit based on medical reasons.

Based on the above mentioned asylum laws and regulations, the applicant for asylum is obliged to take part in medical screening, medical treatment, or when the medical authority concerned so orders, based on a potential risk of disease, the necessary vaccination. Due to public health reasons, applicants are accommodated in a separate place in the refugee camps, until a certificate issued by the ÁNTSZ (National Public Health Service) states that the applicant does not suffer from AIDS, leprosy, tuberculosis, acute contagious disease, phthiriasis, and is not virulent or a pathogen-carrier with regard to any of the above mentioned diseases.

Latvia

Latvian law in granting refugee status is based strictly on the 1951 Refugee Convention, thus refugee status is not granted if the claim to such status is based solely on medical grounds. There is an interest, however, among officials in learning how other (European) countries handle the issue of health and return. In practice, a temporary residence permit may be issued on medical grounds if the claimant can offer means to cover all costs related to accommodation and medical treatment (i.e. the individual can pay or has the financial support of relatives, an organization, etc.). At the cost of the state, emergency medical care is offered to asylum seekers as well as to illegal immigrants.

Luxembourg

Only since 18 March 2000 has an alternative form of protection been envisioned under Luxembourg law. The law refers to this alternative form of protection as a "temporary protection scheme." This scheme is designed to offer protection to persons fleeing conflict, war, violence, etc., and the duration of such protection is decided on an individual basis but must not exceed a 3-year limit. No residence permit as such is authorized but rather a certificate to reside is issued. The enjoyment of any other rights is restricted to either social assistance *or* a work permit. Only applicants who are at least 14 years of age are eligible under the temporary protection scheme. Health issues are not specifically mentioned and apparently can only be implicitly derived from ECHR Article 3 provisions.

Netherlands[11]

Asylum seekers in the Netherlands are allowed to include medical conditions in their applications and they have the option to submit a separate application for admission to receive medical care. Those who have their applications rejected because they do not fit the criteria to be granted refugee status may still be granted a residence permit based on humanitarian grounds.

The Netherlands has enacted a so-called trauma policy. This policy stipulates that the individual in question who has applied for a residence permit "must be so traumatized by certain experiences that [he/she] cannot reasonably be expected to return to their country of origin . . . [and that] the incident[s] must be the reason for leaving one's country of origin." Other rules apply, including the evaluation of the credibility of the individual's story and that they must have fled their country within six months of the alleged incident. However, this time period may not be evoked by the authorities as the sole justification for denying an admission

[11] This text is based on a contribution by Renger Visser, IND, The Hague.

request. In some cases, a medical advisor is employed to determine the extent of the psychological suffering the applicant has endured. The final determination of each case is still left to the officials within the Immigration Department. If a permit for residence is granted under the trauma policy it is normally permanent by nature.

A review of asylum applications based on medical reasons reveals that commonly applicants assert to be suffering from psychological disorders. There are some problems associated with these sorts of applications. First of all, the diagnosis of psychological disorders is difficult and the severity of mental illness hard to determine objectively. The most common psychological illness reported is post-traumatic stress syndrome, or PTSS. The problem which PTSS cases pose is that treatment is often better suited if it is attained in the country of origin, in surroundings that are familiar to the individual suffering from PTSS.[12] Furthermore, traumatic stress and other signs of mental disorder can arise due to the insecurity one may feel regarding one's residence status. However, this is not usually sufficient justification to be granted a residence permit in the Netherlands. Financial inability to pay for medical treatment in the country of origin and the standard of care in the country of origin are also insufficient reasons to grant residence permits.

Applications for asylum based on medical grounds are handled on a case-by-case basis. The criteria used for examining such requests are: whether the medical condition a person suffers from can be treated in the country of origin, if withholding medical treatment would result in a medical emergency, and whether the Netherlands is the most appropriate country for treatment. In fact, policy guidelines stipulate that "the only decisive criterion is whether the Netherlands is the most appropriate country from a medical perspective for undergoing medical treatment." Case law has generally respected this principle.

Essentially, then, Dutch policy has created a way in for asylum seekers who fall outside the Convention definition of a refugee but claim to be suffering from one medical ailment or another and the Netherlands happens to offer treatment for such conditions.[13] In fact, during 1998 alone the Netherlands received more

---

[12] In popular culture, post-traumatic stress syndrome ("shell shock") is often discussed in association with soldiers participating in war or war-like situations. Not only is the syndrome difficult to detect among soldiers, but once it is detected, there is often a rush to remove the soldier from the battlefield environment which may actually hinder proper treatment. See, for example, the article in the December 8, 2000 issue of *The Economist* entitled "Trauma and stress: Help that hurts," a review of Ben Shephard's (2000) *A War of Nerves: Soldiers and Psychiatrists 1914-1994* London: Jonathan Cape (pp. 113-114).

[13] In the new Aliens Act, in force as per April 2001, provisions concerning health-related applications have been incorporated. Section 10 states that "An alien who is not lawfully resident may *not* claim entitlement to benefits in kind, facilities and social security benefits issued by decision of an administrative authority. The previous sentence shall apply *mutatis mutandis* to exemptions or licences designated in an Act of Parliament or Order in Council. [This] may be derogated from if the entitlement relates to education, the provision of care that is medically necessary (...). The granting

than 3,500 applications based on medical claims, and the majority of those applications were submitted by rejectees. Further, the generous attitude with which Dutch officials look at such cases often rests on the unfounded assumption that medical treatment is simply not available in the countries of origin.[14] It would be desirable if continuous research on countries of origin and a central database were established in order to deal with such asylum medical cases based on sound reasoning and judgement, and of course out of an awareness of facts on the ground.[15]

Portugal

Asylum applications based on medical claims are extremely rare in Portugal. When they do arise, they are handled on a case-by-case basis. There are no legal

of entitlement does not confer a right to lawful residence." In addition, Section 14.1 (e) contains relevant information, stating that "An application for the issue of a residence permit for a fixed period (...) may be rejected if the alien is not prepared to submit to a medical examination performed in the interests of public health in order to check for the presence of a disease designated by or pursuant to the Infectious Diseases Act or to undergo medical treatment for such a sickness." Section 15.1 (c) states that "An application for the issue of a residence permit for a fixed period (...) may not be rejected on account of the absence of a valid authorisation for temporary stay if it concerns: the alien does not have independent, lasting and sufficient means of subsistence or the person with whom the alien wishes to reside does not have independent, lasting and sufficient means of subsistence." Finally, Section 62 contains the following text which will undoubtedly raise quite some questions, although it would appear to relate to 'travel per se' only: "An alien shall not be expelled as long as his health or that of any of the members of his family would make it inadvisable for him to travel"; in the official comments it can be read: "As long as the health of the alien is such that he cannot travel, he and any members of his family will continue to be lawfully resident on the ground of section 8 (j)(...) Under subsection 1 (a) the rejection of an application means that the alien is no longer lawfully resident in the Netherlands, unless another legal ground for lawful residence as referred to in section 8 exists. Such a ground could be that the alien cannot be required to travel because of his poor health and cannot therefore be expelled."

[14] *Exempli gratiae* court decisions dated 11 March 1999 (Iran), 4 December 1998 (Turkey), 6 November 1998 (Syria), 5 August 1998 (Russian Federation), 9 June 1998 (Bosnia); a most remarkable dictum (Amsterdam District Court, 1996) concerned a Sri Lankan who stuttered: he was allowed to stay as long as the logopaedic treatment was considered necessary. However, the practice both with the Executive and with the Judiciary has over the last two years moved towards what could be labelled a more pragmatic and realistic approach.

[15] Another phenomenon in the Netherlands is the possibility for lawyers to commence what is called a disciplinary procedure against the physician who on behalf of the authorities looked into the case of, for example, a rejectee appealing against his/her return to the country of origin for reasons of ill-health. Under Dutch law, that physician is held responsible for both the individual diagnosis and the information concerning the possibility of treatment in the country of origin. Unlike Canada, where physicians are covered as they act as civil servants and where the procedure can never be directed against the individual physician, and also unlike Germany, where some procedures have been initiated because of a false diagnosis, greatly exaggerating the illness of the applicant, this 'Dutch treat' has resulted in some personalized 'attacks'. Although practice appears to have become more realistic, it is still a special phenomenon worth being studied in detail; see e.g. de Witte-van den Haak, M. and Kernkamp-Maathuis, H., *The Rights and Obligations of the Medical Advisor in Admission Procedures: Some Observations,* (especially prepared for the September 2000 Expert Meeting).

provisions in Portuguese law that deal specifically with the health and asylum issue.

There are recognized alternative provisions to Convention refugee status, designed to extend help to asylum seekers based on humanitarian grounds. Under Portuguese law, subsidiary protection is offered to applicants fleeing from conflict and/or violations of human rights. A residence permit of 1 or 2 years' duration may be granted in such cases, with allowance for renewal up to 5 years. Those granted subsidiary protection are entitled to enjoy the rights of employment, health care, education, and social assistance. Another option is temporary protection, designed to offer refuge to individuals fleeing from conflict situations and displaced persons. Temporary residence permits for a maximum of two years may be granted and the rights to education, health care, and social assistance are extended.

Health care provisions are extended to asylum seekers during the application review process. If an applicant becomes ill during the process, he or she has the right to seek attention at a local health clinic or the emergency room of a local hospital. Special care and follow-up services are also extended to applicants who have been victims of rape, torture, or other abuses. As pertains to the execution of a return order, asylum seekers who have their applications rejected are ordered to return during a set period of time. If there is a failure to comply with a return order and the applicant asserts to be suffering from an illness, the authorities responsible for the execution of the return order are instructed to take into consideration the medical reports submitted and the opinions rendered on the case by the decision-making authority.

Country of origin information is not gathered by Portuguese officials. However, the government has reached medical agreements with its former colonies of Angola, Cape Verde, Guinea-Bissau, Mozambique, and Sao Tome and Principe. These agreements entitle the citizens of those countries to enjoy medical treatment in Portugal. If the medical facilities are not adequate in those countries to treat individuals suffering from certain conditions, temporary visas may be issued, enabling medical treatment to be sought in Portugal at the cost of the Portuguese government.

Romania

Romania has adopted a new law on the status and regime of refugees (Romanian Government Ordinance 102), which came into force in late 2000. In this new law, a proviso has been included which would appear to cover the ill and sick: humanitarian protection may be granted if the applicant can provide conclusive evidence that he/she may be exposed to dangers that threaten their life, bodily integrity or freedom in the country of origin because he/she belongs to a category of 'disadvantaged persons' (Art. 5). It is not yet known in how far the authorities and/or the appeal boards will indeed make use of this proviso for the cases of concern to this Handbook.

Spain

Spanish legislation has established a single asylum system to deal with all asylum requests. If refugee status is not granted, an alternative form of protection may be granted if it is deemed appropriate to do so by the decision-making authorities at the time that the request for the status of refugee is denied. The categories that exist are humanitarian cases and displaced persons (individuals fleeing conflict situations of 'a political, ethnic, or religious character'). Temporary residence permits are granted and the extension of employment and other social rights are generally determined on a case-by-case approach. In-depth information as to granting a (temporary) residence permit or leave of stay is not available.

Sweden

When applications for residence permits based on humanitarian grounds are submitted they often invoke medical conditions as the primary reason as to why the applicant should be granted a Swedish residence permit. Applicants often assert that they cannot travel due to their health and they have no medicine for their particular ailments, as well as the poor conditions that they face in the country of origin such as the lack of safety, poor medical facilities and treatment, and their inability to cover the financial burdens of treatment and medical care. The main problem that decision-makers face in evaluating these cases is the lack of reliable and accurate information regarding the standards and quality of medical facilities and treatment in countries of origin.

Asylum applicants who fall outside the 1951 Convention definition of a refugee, but it is determined by the authorities that they risk, upon return to the country of origin, inhumane or degrading treatment, may be considered to be in need of protection (subsidiary protection) and in this instance can be granted a permanent residence permit. Sweden bases this legal provision on Article 3 from both the Convention Against Torture and the European Convention on Human Rights. Sweden also has another provision in its legislation that covers residence permits for applicants on humanitarian grounds for medical reasons. Applications that fall under this category are handled on a individual basis. The guidelines that the authorities use to evaluate such cases have evolved primarily from case law since 1994. Such guidelines include: whether the medical condition is a life-threatening disease or a disability of an "exceptional kind", the possibility of treatment in the country of origin, whether treatment or care has the chance to aid recovery or is necessary for the person's life. More liberal evaluations of individual cases are generally tolerated if the applicant is a child or if the applicant has contracted a disease or acquired a disability while in Sweden. In short, a permanent residence permit may be issued to an applicant based on humanitarian grounds and a temporary permit to stay may be issued if treatment or an operation of a short and specific period of duration is deemed necessary.

Although Swedish law stipulates that a foreigner should leave the country within two weeks after a final negative decision has been reached, a delay in return may be negotiated with the authorities on a case-by-case basis.

Regarding the execution of return, Swedish law has no clear regulation on the forced return of applicant rejectees to countries of origin based exclusively on medical grounds. Those who have had their applications rejected in a final decision, that is after two prior reviews, may submit a new application for a residence permit. Such an application is then referred to the Aliens Appeals Board. During the review of such new applications, the authorities involved are often confronted with difficulties in the evaluation process. These applications are often accompanied by medical documents stating that the applicant suffers from a mental or psychiatric disorder, such as PTSS. A recent investigation undertaken by the Aliens Appeal Board revealed that a risk of suicide was reported in nearly 30% of all new applications.

The time allotted for the processing of new applications is fairly short, normally lasting for no more than two to three weeks. Medical certificates that are submitted along with the applications are primarily used by the decision-making authorities in giving their final evaluations. Although the Appeals Board has the option to consult with specialized national medical experts for a professional opinion, this option is seldom resorted to as the costs amount to approximately US$3,000 for each consultation. There are reports indicating that officials within the Appeals Board are "seriously concerned" about the medical certificates issued in these cases, especially the PTSS/PTSD cases as doctors within the field use a variety of approaches when handling such psychological cases and issuing medical certificates attesting that an individual actually suffers from the disorder. In response to the prevalence of these cases that the Appeals Board faces, time and financial resources have been invested in order to competently handle the caseload. This task has primarily involved educating staff and inviting psychiatrists to give lectures on PTSS/PTSD and institutional co-operation between the Appeals Board and the National Board for Health and Welfare.

Furthermore, the guidelines followed by the Appeals Board in assessing new applications are essentially identical to those that are applied to the initial cases invoking "humanitarian grounds" for admittance. The Appeals Board has ruled that threats of suicide or other acts of self-destruction (e.g. self-imposed starvation, etc.) made by applicants, and such threats are not in association with medically documented psychological disorders, do not justify granting a residence permit on humanitarian grounds. On the other hand, if such threats of acts of self-destruction are made in connection with a psychological disorder or disease of a serious nature (i.e. regarding compulsory institutional care), the Board is of the opinion that such circumstances may indeed justify the issuing of a residence permit on humanitarian grounds.

Regarding medical care and assistance to rejectees, Swedish law, at the cost of the state, allows for children under 18 years of age to receive all necessary medical treatment. This provision was enacted in order to satisfy compliance with Article 24 of the UN Convention on the Rights of the Child. Adult rejectees are entitled to free emergency medical treatment which Swedish law has defined as follows: general emergency care (including dental care), treatment that cannot wait (including dental care), antenatal and prenatal care, maternity care, contraceptive information, care in association with abortion, and treatment and other measures taken for infectious diseases.

The criteria Sweden has established in its decision-making process regarding asylum applications based on health reasons do not explicitly refer to international norms and standards. Since the mid-1990s, the Swedish government has elaborated on principles to be used by decision-makers in their evaluations of such cases. In essence, only in exceptional cases where the applicant suffers from a fatal illness and care is not provided in the country of origin may a residence permit be issued. Officials report that "the stance of the Government seems to be in line with the conclusion of the European Commission in March 1998 regarding observance of the ECHR, Article 3. Thus it could be stated that Sweden follows internationally accepted norms where it concerns Country of Origin practices, [although] no clear reference is made to these norms."

The collection of information on medical practices in countries of origin is usually conducted during the review of individual cases and is then transferred to a central database, LIFOS, for country of origin information. The information gathered is utilized by decision-makers in their review of individual cases and is intended primarily for use by case officers and the decision-makers within the Migration Board; however, the Appeals Board also has access to the same information. Excluding secret or classified information, individuals may also have limited access to the data. Thus far, information and data collected by the Migration Board have been accepted by the courts. Regarding appeal cases, the Appeals Board is responsible for undertaking its own investigations because applicants largely invoke health related claims after the initial negative decision rendered on their case. With due regard to the Swedish Secrecy Act, collected information on country of origin practices may be shared with other countries.

Separate statistics regarding the acceptance or rejection of asylum applications based on medical claims are not kept. It is reported that few applicants are accepted on medical claims alone, but those who are, are listed in the category of residence permits on humanitarian grounds.

It is worth mentioning that Sweden, unlike several other countries, has developed a quite sensible policy regarding asylum applicants and their alleged medical claims. Before medical treatment can be authorized to begin, Swedish law insists that first a favourable review be granted to the request for a residence permit thereby ensuring that the social and health resources are preserved for those persons lawfully entitled to enjoy such resources. Other countries work from the opposite approach whereby medical treatment is provided even before the application has been reviewed. In consequence, such a policy imposes on other government authorities, those actually responsible for determining if a right of residence exists, the obligation to grant a residence permit.

Switzerland

The issue of health and return has recently been raised by government officials. This has occurred most notably in the Swiss Parliament where MPs have discussed the issue during debates over the new asylum law. Ultimately, the Parliament voted against adopting a proposal that would require the use of an expert opinion by a medical officer for cases under consideration at the Immigration Department. Parliament based its decision on the notion that such medical experts would not be neutral in their evaluations. Swiss law stipulates that asylum applications are to be reviewed on an individual basis. At each instance that a negative decision is rendered, an order for return is subsequently issued. However, before such an order may be carried out, the decision-makers involved must determine whether such an order can be competently executed (i.e. for medical reasons), otherwise a permit for temporary protection in Switzerland is issued, although it should be immediately added that Switzerland is quite unique in returning ill rejectees with either the medicines needed for continued treatment, or with the assurance – which includes active cooperation by the Swiss Embassy sur place – that access to treatment and hence the treatment itself will be secured.

The legal framework within Switzerland for handling asylum applications based upon medical claims is found under Article 14 of the Aliens Act. Orders for the return of individuals who do not qualify as Convention refugees cannot be enforced if inter alia an individual suffers from a serious medical condition, there is a need for medical treatment, and no medical facilities to handle such treatment are available in the country of origin. In these instances, the Swiss authorities have certain options to consider and apply to each case. One alternative is to issue a stay on the order of return, in effect allowing some time to lapse before the order is actually executed. Another possibility is to grant a temporary residence permit. Moreover, different criteria are applied to cases involving minors and elderly people such as foster care, family relationships, etc. While asylum seekers are entitled to medical treatment and assistance, an exemption applies to dental treatment, excluding emergency dental care only. In addition, Swiss practice allows for rejected applicants to be sent home supplied with the necessary medication for treatment and/or access to the Swiss embassy for the express purpose of obtaining medication and/or treatment.

Disputes have arisen between the Immigration Department and the Swiss Physicians Federation (FMH) over the procedures used in handling medical cases. Since the early to mid-1990s agreements between the Immigration

Department and the FMH have been reached, including the appointment of neutral medical examiners and procedures regarding privacy issues and decisions on the return of rejectees with illnesses. What has not been agreed upon is the issue of medical claims based upon psychological disorders. The review of cases in which applicants claim to have developed a psychological disorder due to a return decision and the linkage between such disorders and events that were deemed unlikely in the asylum hearing still prove problematic for decision-makers.

In Switzerland, the development of criteria for the acceptance or denial of applications has not been developed with reference to international norms and standards. Information regarding medical practices in countries of origin is collected by Swiss authorities. Research is conducted with the aid of such sources as the Internet, the media, international organizations, NGOs, fact finding missions, and embassies. Information thus gathered is stored in an electronic database from which reports may be generated on the medical situation in a country of origin. The information is generally accepted by all decision-makers involved, as well as by the Appeals Board and the courts. While access to the information is generally restricted to officials within the Immigration Department and those officials within police departments at the canton level who are responsible for the execution of return orders, there is, however, a project planned for the year 2001 to make access to the central database available as pertaining to information gathered from public sources. Switzerland follows a policy of sharing its information with other countries regarding health practices and the overall medical situation in countries of origin.

The Swiss Immigration Department, seemingly following a recurring pattern found in other countries under focus in this chapter, does not keep separate records or statistics on applicants admitted into the country, temporarily or otherwise, on the basis of medical claims. In essence, however, the Swiss authorities have thought carefully about this issue and have taken some courageous and pragmatic steps to address the situation. The practice of returning individuals who do not meet the legal criteria of refugee status or who are in need of temporary protection outside the country of origin but are nonetheless returned with medication if appropriate is, here at least, highly regarded and worth being considered by other States.

United Kingdom

Although there is no statutory mechanism to grant asylum relief based explicitly on medical claims, UK policy ensures that no person is returned to the country of origin "if there is credible medical evidence that return would reduce (...) life expectancy and subject the returnee to acute physical and mental suffering in circumstances where the UK can be considered to have assumed responsibility for his/her care." Generally, the burden of proof lies largely with the applicant.

For asylum seekers whose applications are rejected, an Exceptional Leave to Remain (ELR) may be granted under ECHR Article 3 grounds[16] or under "exceptional and compassionate" considerations, of which health factors may play a part. An ELR decision entitles the applicant to a 4-year permit and the right to enjoy employment and national health care provisions; where applicable, social security entitlements may also be granted. If medical claims are the main issues at stake, ELR may not always be automatically granted. In practice, the UK has explored the feasibility of making arrangements for health care to be provided in the country of origin when such a decision may be appropriate.

No separate statistics are on file relating to asylum requests or ELR being granted on medical claims.

United States

In the USA, the issue of health and return has not arisen in asylum cases at first instance. The records indicate that only a small number of asylum applications have been filed citing medical issues.[17] "Generally, those cases involve claims of discrimination or claims that the government is failing to provide medical treatment. However, health issues do arise regarding the ability to return a [rejected] asylum seeker or other removable alien to their home country, once the individual [receives] a removal order from [an] immigration court."

The execution of return orders concerning asylum seekers who have had their applications denied confront the officials responsible with several difficulties. The four main problems associated with this issue have been cited as the following:

1. Deportable aliens trying to delay or block their deportation based on health reasons (raising the lack of medical treatment or inferior medical treatment in their home country or other humanitarian concerns);
2. States being unwilling to accept their sick national's return (not issuing travel documents);
3. States which the alien has to transit on route to his/her home country refusing to issue transit visas for deportees with medical conditions; and
4. The person's ability to fly may pose an obstacle to return (e.g., pregnant women may not be able to fly at certain stages of their pregnancy and the US will not attempt to return seriously ill or terminally ill persons).

Under US legislation, medical claims alone are not sufficient to grant residence permits to asylum seekers, at least not in the initial first instance review of their

---

[16] As of October 2, 2000, asylum applications based on ECHR Article 3 provisions are now possible in the first instance.

[17] In a 1996 amendment, the United States broadened its statutory definition of a refugee "to include coercive population control methods as a political opinion. The US Government does not believe that forced abortion or forced sterilization is a health issue, but a human rights issue."

case. While medical issues may be cited in the initial application, the law specifies that the asylum seeker must meet the statutory definition of a refugee in order to receive a positive ruling. Moreover, in the second instance, consisting of a court proceeding, other options become available to the decision-makers involved at this level. Such options, including those of a permanent and a temporary nature, are noted as *Humanitarian or Public Interest Parole*, *Stay of Removal*, or *Cancellation of Removal*. The Humanitarian/Public Interest Parole may be enacted by the Attorney General or the Immigration Department (INS) "on a case-by-case basis for urgent humanitarian reasons or significant public benefit for any alien applying for admission in the US." This option, however, is not an official admittance of the applicant into the country but rather a sort of temporary permit allowing an individual to be "physically present" in the United States. And further, the law stipulates that the alien will be required to depart from the US "when the conditions supporting the parole cease to exist." The second option, known as a stay of removal, is available to district directors and immigration judges. This option allows for the official involved to invoke discretionary authority when reviewing a case and to issue a stay of removal for a period of time and in light of whatever conditions that the official deems to warrant such action; issues of health may be a factor in the ultimate decision taken.

Thirdly, in issuing a cancellation of removal, the relevant authorities may in their decision consider the lack of medical treatment in the applicant's country of origin and its availability in the United States. However, an applicant must meet four other qualifications in order for a cancellation of removal to be granted:

1. [The applicant] has been physically present in the United States for a continuous period of at least 10 years immediately preceding the date of applying for such relief,
2. has been a person of good moral character,
3. establishes that removal would result in exceptional and extremely unusual hardship to the alien's spouse, parent, or child who is a citizen of the United States or an alien lawfully admitted for permanent residence, and
4. does not fall into a disqualifying provision.

US law allows for yet further options to be considered by district directors of the Immigration Department, technically outside the asylum system per se. Such discretionary measures available include granting temporary protected status (TPS) or a deferred enforced departure (DED). TPS is designed to provide temporary protection to applicants who have not been granted the status of refugee, but are nonetheless "fleeing potentially dangerous situations (e.g., civil strife, natural disasters, the foreign state is temporarily unable to handle the return of aliens who are nationals, etc.)." Under guidelines for the DED, the President may authorize the Attorney General to "provide temporary relief from deportation to nationals of designated countries in the United States." These temporary forms of relief may be granted due to medical claims. In general, the

American government does not offer medical care to applicants seeking admission into the United States, exemptions being made for aliens who are "detained."

The Public Health Service provides medical treatment to detained aliens. An individual who is not in detention may be eligible for assistance from the state or local government in his place of residence. There may be some reimbursement to states for this care.

With respect to international norms and standards, no explicit reference is made to their application in the decision-making process or legal framework within the United States. In compiling information on the nature of medical facilities in countries of origin, research is only conducted when health issues arise in specific asylum cases.[18] For the US, this has occurred primarily in cases involving individuals who are diagnosed as HIV+ and/or who have AIDS and "in the context of gender claims based on homosexuality and the availability of health care treatment in the country of origin." Separate statistics on asylum applications which have been filed citing medical claims[19] are not kept nor are records available for applicants who receive some form of temporary relief due to medical reasons.

INFORMATION AND HARMONIZATION

Most of the countries surveyed in this chapter do have legal provisions which in principle should enable them to contemplate the issue of health and return. The one notable exception is Latvia where the law does not foresee a permanent status for individuals who fall outside the Convention definition of a refugee, although protection (i.e. non-refoulement) is granted for those who fall under Art. 3 of the ECHR. International norms and standards, for the most part, are not mentioned explicitly with reference to laws and practices in individual countries in their handling of applicants who have cited solely medical claims. However, at least Canada, Latvia, the Netherlands, and Sweden have expressed a firm interest in how other countries handle such cases, the latter two referring to international and European treaties in their responses.

What is most striking among the countries covered in this survey concerns country of origin practices and the statistics on applicants citing medical claims. First of all, most countries conduct research only as the need arises, on a case-by-

[18] The Division of Immigration Health Services (DIHS) does collect information on country of origin situations and practices and makes recommendations, where appropriate, to the Immigration Department based on information stored in its database. Courts have generally accepted information supplied by the DIHS.

[19] The DIHS reports that it assists the Immigration Department in the review of such applications, on average in 50 cases per year.

case basis. Further, few keep a running central database to store such information. Secondly, the countries concerned do not keep separate statistics on applications citing medical grounds and outcomes reached in the decision-making process. The Netherlands, Sweden, and Switzerland have all mentioned specifically the problems their decision-makers face when handling medical cases where psychological disorders are alleged. Especially with due reference to PTSS, these countries have noted the lack of professional standards within the psychiatric community and the variance in approaches doctors utilize in such cases. It is hereby submitted that countries collaborate with one another in dealing with the issue of non-convention asylum seekers making medical claims, establishing central, ongoing databases that cover country of origin practices to be shared, as necessary, with partner countries. This need becomes particularly clear in the words of one of the participants in the September 2000 Expert Meeting. As GP de Vries stated:

> This expert meeting was unique in that physicians, legal experts and ethicists from different countries discussed the way they are dealing with this very difficult and sensitive subject in a very open manner. Experiences of all the participants and lecturers in all the involved fields were very fruitful. My personal feeling is that this multidisciplinary international knowledge should be shared with a bigger public.
>
> Working as a medical advisor to a national migration/naturalization department, I consider it of the utmost importance to understand and appreciate how other countries – both European and non-European – deal with medical cases which might interfere with asylum procedures and other procedures on residence permits. Furthermore, it is of interest to share information on how in such cases the issue of (non-)availability of medical treatment in countries of origin is being dealt with in the several host-countries.
>
> In regard of the information now available, I conclude that there is a need in Europe and North America for more accurate and internationally accepted information about treatment possibilities in the several countries of origin. The development of an international database on these matters seems to me a rather logical next step. This leads to the question: which information should be included in this database? The information about treatment possibilities in the countries of origin should be accurate and give enough foundation about health issues in *individual* cases. We discussed during the meeting if it is possible to make international accepted norms regarding Country of Origin Practices. It turned out that prima facie there are no absolute standards of health care services which can be used in individual cases. Although the essential drugs list is of great relevance – as e.g. illustrated by the fact that the General Comment on the Rights to Health refers to this list, a database with rather detailed information is in the present context still needed to provide detailed information suitable for such individual cases. Every host country can make his own policy based on this detailed information. A proposition has been made for the content of this database and deserves to be studied.[20]

[20] The database should focus on the availability of PHC and the essential drugs list, and should give indications on the health system in the country concerned, including general access and the

Precise norm-setting in these cases should be done by the state. The state should give the definition of a medical emergency (what are the criteria for medical complaints and illnesses allowing for a continued stay in the host country) and should indicate which information about availability/accessibility in the countries of origin is sufficient for decision-making in individual cases. Medical-ethical-juridical committees could advise the state in defining those norms. Although it will be difficult to agree on internationally accepted norms, the need for harmonized norms is obvious.

It will be a challenge to translate general community approaches and general information into decision-making in individual cases. Together, that is: in a multidisciplinary setting, we have to find an acceptable and workable equilibrium.

It would be helpful if countries began to keep separate statistics and records on the cases they receive involving medical-based asylum applications, with particular emphasis on what information on the country of origin was needed, and which type of information proved to be essential in the decision-making process. Many countries have cited how this issue has arisen in their individual experiences. It is of interest to note the case of the Appeals Board in Sweden, under its own initiative beginning an investigation that revealed 30% of all asylum appeals cases were accompanied by threats of suicide. States have the primary interest of protecting their own lawful citizens and preserving their resources and to offer extension to those individuals who truly need protection, temporarily or otherwise. Offering protection to one who suddenly threatens suicide or is suddenly diagnosed with PTSS may in the long run deny protection to an individual convincingly meeting the definition of a refugee, where a state's true obligations lie.

The right to health is a highly contested issue. One may find reference to such a right in the second generation of human rights but it certainly remains unclear whether a right to health has any cross-border ramifications. Above all, this chapter has revealed that in practice the receiving countries experience asylum cases based upon medical claims rarely in the first instance but rather all too often such claims first appear in the appeal process after a negative decision has been rendered. One may rightly conclude, therefore, that those seeking asylum have recourse to cite health conditions if their application is rejected, a loophole indeed in asylum procedures. It is of the utmost importance, then, that countries eliminate such a loophole and prevent the abuse of their asylum systems. Hence it is urged that governments instruct their respective Immigration Departments to

---

availability of insurance. Listing specialization would help (nephrology, oncology, cardiology etc). Moreover, due attention needs to be paid to psychiatric institutions as well as to traditional healing in the case of PTSD/PTSS. It is of course appreciated that the contents of the databank will differ depending on the needs in the hostcountry: some countries may wish to ensure that care and cure is available up to the standards of the hostcountry, whereas others may wish to focus on PHC, the essential drugs list and other basics, as per the WHO 2000 report and the General Comment on the Right to Health. In any case, the need for harmonization would appear to be obvious.

undertake steps towards the design and implementation of information gathering units in order to gain a true understanding of the health care environments of countries of origin, both the present realities and future potentials. Governments should also emphasize the utility of sharing collected information with partner countries. One way of meeting these goals is to establish a central databank where information (e.g. country of origin practices, case studies, decision-making procedures and outcomes, statistics) can be stored and accessed. It would be interesting to see how much governments spend each year in dealing with medical asylum cases, especially how much is spent on individuals with no legal rights to health care access. Collaboration, not only among countries, but also with international organizations, such as the World Health Organization, in addressing this specific issue, is highly recommended.

Efforts toward harmonization in health and asylum related cases is another important goal. In order to curb abuses and maintain the preservation of the asylum system, harmonizing trends among countries as to how they respond when confronted with medical asylum cases would effectively contribute to the strengthening of Immigration Departments and asylum procedures. Moreover, countries should not hesitate in returning individuals who submit 'manifestly unfounded' applications. As we have seen, frequently medical claims only appear after the first instance review whereupon an individual has been rejected. It goes without saying that a certain amount of critical scepticism is justified. Among the EU countries, there is an even more discernible urgency in working towards harmonization as the Amsterdam deadline of 2004 is quickly approaching. Global harmonization may perhaps speed progress along the EU asylum track, or, conversely, complement one another. Co-operation and agreements with countries of origin would also be valuable in handling medical asylum requests. Western countries are in a position to urge that portions of foreign aid and direct investment funds be assimilated into the health care sectors of countries of origin. It should be stressed, along utilitarian lines, that there is more of an interest in improving the health care of countries as opposed to a few individuals who happen to make it across the border.

It is hoped that the reader, after having studied this Handbook, has gained useful insights regarding the health and residence issue. The problems that governments face and the strain on resources that such cases impose are enormous and underestimated. Countries should now be urged to confront this issue systematically to ensure that the asylum system can handle such cases where appropriate and enforce removal orders where individuals can be or should be treated at home.

In view of the launching by Commissioner Vitorino, in late November 2000, of a broad discussion on asylum and migration, which is supposed to result in policy decisions, in December 2001, it is hoped and expected that the issue of health and responsibilities be included. Yet, it is also appreciated that a difficult issue with so many emotional and sensitive issues may take longer than just one year to yield agreements and results. The present author would herewith like to subscribe to the notion that the debate is just about to start, and will last a couple of years, rather than a couple of months. The above country survey surely shows that only a very few understand the ins and outs of what is really at stake.

BIBLIOGRAPHY

ALFREDSSON, G., MELANDER, G. (1997). *A Compilation of Minority Rights Standards, A Selection of Texts from International and Regional Human Rights Instruments and Other Documents.* Report No. 24. Lund: Raoul Wallenberg Institute.

ALFREDSSON, G., TOMAEVSKI, K. (1998). *A Thematic Guide to Documents on Health and Human Rights.* The Hague, London, Boston: Kluwer.

'ALIENS AND CITIZENS: THE CASE FOR OPEN BORDERS', (1987) In: The Review of Politics, 49(2) Spring.

BANKOWSKI, Z., BRYANT, J.H., GALLAGHER, J. (Eds.) (1997). *Ethics, Equity and Health for All.* Proceedings of the 29th CIOMS Conference, Geneva.

BEAUCHAMP, D.E., STEINBOCK, B. (Eds.) (1999). *New Ethics for the Public's Health.* Oxford: Oxford University Press.

BIRCK, A. (2000). 'Wie krank mub ein Flüchtling sein, um von der Abschiebung ausgenommen zu werden?', In: *Informationsbrief Ausländerrecht*, 4/2000, pp. 209-216.

BLAND, M. (2000). *An Introduction to Medical Statistics,* 3rd edition. Oxford: Oxford University Press.

BOSSUYT, M. (1975). 'La Distinction Juridique entre les Droits Civils et Politiques et les Droits Economiques, Sociaux et Culturelles', In: Human Rights Journal vol. VIII-1, pp. 783-820.

BOSSUYT, M. (1993). 'International Human Rights Systems: Strengths and Weaknesses', In: Mahoney, K.E., Mahoney, P. (Eds.), *Human Rights in the Twenty-first Century: a global challenge*, Dordrecht: Martinus Nijhoff Publishers.

BOVEN, TH.C. VAN, FLINTERMAN, C., WESTENDORP, I. (Eds.) (1998). *The Maastricht Guidelines on Violations of Economic, Social and Cultural Rights.* SIM Special No. 20. Utrecht.

BUCHANAN, D.R. (2000). *An Ethic for Health Promotion, Rethinking the Sources of Human Well-Being.* Oxford: Oxford University Press.

BUQUICCHIO-DE BOER, M. (1998). 'Interim Measures by the European Commission of Human Rights', In: Salvia, M., de Nørgaard, C.A. (Eds.), *The birth of European human rights law: liber amicorum.* Baden-Baden: Nomos.

CARBALLO, M., GROCUTT, M., & HADZIHASANOVIC, A. (1996). 'Women and migration: a public health issue', *World Health Statistics Quarterly*, 49, pp. 158-164.

CARBALLO, M., & SIEM, H. (1996). 'Migration, Migration Policy and AIDS', In: M. Haour-Knipe & R. Rector (Eds.), *Crossing Borders: Migration, Ethnicity and AIDS* pp. 31-49. London: Taylor & Francis.

CARBALLO, M., DIVINO, J.J., ZERIC, D. (1998). 'Migration and Health in The European Union', In: *Tropical Medicine and International Health*, Vol. 3 No. 12 pp. 936-944.

CARENS, J.H. (1992). 'Migration and Morality: A Liberal Equalitarian Perspective', In: *Free Movement.* Barry, B., Goodin, R. (Eds.) London: Harvest Whearsheaf.

CARENS, J.H. (2000). *Culture, Citizenship, and Community, A Contextual Exploration of Justice as Evenhandedness.* Oxford: Oxford University Press.

CORNELIUS, W., MARTIN, P., HOLLIFIELD, J. (Eds.) (1995). *Controlling Immigration: A Global Perspective.* Stanford: Stanford University Ness.

COULTER, A., HAM, C. (Eds.) (2000). *The Global Challenge of Health Care Rationing.* Buckingham: Open University Press.

DANIELI, Y., RODLEY, N.S., WEISÆTH, L. (Eds.) (1996). *International Responses to Traumatic Stress.* New York: Baywood Publishing Company.

DANIELS, N. (1997). 'Limits to Health Care: Fair Procedures, Democratic Deliberation and the Legimitacy Problem for Insurers', In: *Philosophy and Public Affairs*, 26 pp. 303-350.

DANIELS, N., SABIN, J. (1995). 'The Yin and Yang of Health Care System Reform. Professional and Political Strategies for Setting Limits', In: *Archives of Family Medicine*, 4, pp. 67-71.

DANIELS, N., SABIN, J. (1998). 'The Ethics of Accountability in Managed Care Reform', In: *Health Affairs,* 17 (5), pp. 50-64.

DANISH COUNCIL OF ETHICS (1996). *Priority-setting in the Health Service – A Report.* Copenhagen: Danish Council of Ethics.

DEBER, R., NARINA, L., BARANEK, P. et al. (1997). *The Public/Private Mix in Health Care.* Ottawa: National Forum on Health.

DETELS, R., HOLLAND, W., MCEWEN, J., OMENN, G. (1996). *Oxford Textbook of Public Health,* 3rd edition. New York: Oxford University Press.

DIJK, P. VAN, FLINTERMAN, C., JANSSEN, P.E.L. (Eds.) (1998). *International Law, Human Rights.* Lelystad: Koninklijke Vermande.

DUBROW, N. et. al. (1996). 'Helping Child Victims of Violence', In: Danieli, Y., Rodley, N.S., Weisæth, L. (Eds.), *International Responses to Traumatic Stress.* New York: Baywood Publishing Company.

DUMMETT, A., NICOL, A. (1992). *Subjects, Citizens, Aliens and Others: Nationality and Immigration Law.* London: Weidenfeld and Nicolson.

DUNNING, A. (1996). 'Reconciling macro- en micro-concerns: Objectives and Priorities in Health Care', In: OECD, *Health Care Reform: The Will to Change.* Paris: OECD.

DUPUIS, H.M. (1998). *Op het scherp van de snede: goed en kwaad in de geneeskunde.* Amsterdam: Balans.

DUPUY, R.J. (1979). *The Right to Health as a Human Right.* The Hague, London, Boston: Kluwer.

EDDLESTON, M., PIERINI, S. (1999). *Oxford Handbook of Tropical Medicine.* Oxford: Oxford University Press.

EIDE, A. (Ed.) (1994). *Economic, Social and Cultural Rights, a textbook.* The Hague, London, Boston: Kluwer.

EUROPEAN JOURNAL OF HEALTH LAW, 1994- The Hague, London, Boston: Kluwer.

EXTER, A. DEN, HERMANS, H. (Eds.) (1999). *The Right to Health Care in Several European Countries.* The Hague: Kluwer Law International.

FEACHEM, Z., HENSHER, M., ROSE, L. (Eds.) (1999). *Implementing Health Sector Reform in Central Asia, Papers from an EDI Health Policy Seminar held in Ashgabat, Turkmenistan, June 1996.* Washington D.C.: EDI.

FEITSMA, J. (1989). 'Repatriation Law and Refugees', In: *Netherlands Quarterly of Human Rights.* 7(3) pp. 294-307. The Hague: Kluwer Law International.

FIDLER (1999). *International Law and Infectious Diseases.* Oxford.

FIGLEY, C.R. (Ed.) (1985). *Trauma and its wake: The study and treatment of PTSD.* New York.

FINKIELKRAUT, A. (1996). *L'Humanité Perdue: essai sur le XXe siècle.* Paris: Seuil

GREEN, A. (1999). *An Introduction to Health Planning in Developing Countries*, Second Edition. Oxford: Oxford University Press.

GUSHULAK B, MACPHERSON D., PROCHAZKA H, COOPER M., (2000) 'The practice of immigration health in complex emergency situations – a case study of Kosovo from March to July 1999', In: *Refuge* 18(5) pp. 46-51.

GUSHULAK B., MACPHERSON D.W. (2000) 'Population mobility and infectious diseases: the diminishing impact of classical infectious diseases and new approaches for the 21st century', Clin infect dis 31 pp. 776-780.

GUSHULAK B, MACPHERSON D.W. (2000). 'Health issues associated with the smuggling and trafficking of migrants', In: Journal of immigrant health, 2(2) pp. 68-78.

HAM, C. (1997). 'Priority setting in Health Care: Learning from International Experience', In: *Health Policy*, 42 pp. 49-66.

HAM, C. (1998a). *Setting Priorities for Health Care: Why Government Should Take the Lead.* Belfast: Northern Ireland Economic Council.

HEALTH AND HUMAN RIGHTS, An International Quarterly Journal. Cambridge: Harvard School of Public Health.

HEALTH ECONOMICS, Journal 1992- Chichester: Wiley.

HENDRIKS, A. (1994). 'Het Recht op Gezondheidszorg en het IVESCR – Comité', In: *NJCM-Bulletin* Vol. 19 No.2 pp. 171-181.

HERMANS, H.E.G.M., BUIJSEN, M.A.J.M. (2000). *Aanbesteding in de gezondheidszorg.* Maarssen: Elsevier Gezondheidszorg.

HERMANS, H.E.G.M. (2000). *Regulering van de gezondheidszorg.* Maarssen: Elsevier Gezondheidszorg.

HERMANS, H.E.G.M., EXTER A.P. DEN (1999). 'Cross-Border Alliances in Health Care: International Co-operation between Health Insurers and Providers in the 'Euregio Meuse-Rhine', In: *Croatian Medical Journal,* Vol. 40 No. 2 pp. 266-272.

HUISMANN, A., WEILANDT, C., GEIGER, A. (Eds.), *Country Reports on Migration and Health in Europe*. Bonn: Wissenschaftliches Institut der Ärzte Deutschlands e.V.

'IMMIGRATION AND THE WELFARE STATE', (1988). In: Gutmann, A. *Democracy and the Welfare State.* Princeton, NJ: Princeton University Press.

IOM *International Migration*, Quarterly Review. Geneva: IOM.

IOM *Migration and Health,* Newsletter. Geneva: IOM.

IOM (2000). Psychosocial and Trauma Response in Kosovo; achievements and plans 1999-2001. Geneva: IOM.

JONES, C. (2000). *Global Justice, Defending Cosmopolitanism.* Oxford: Oxford University Press.

JONG, J.T.V.M. DE (1994). 'Ambulatory mental health care for migrants in the Netherlands' In: *Curare*, 17(1), pp. 5-34.

JONG, J. DE, & WESENBENK, R., (1997). 'Migration and Health in the Netherlands', In: A. Huismann, C. Weilandt & A. Geiger (Eds.), *Country Reports on Migration and Health in Europe*. Bonn: Wissenschaftliches Institut der Ärzte Deutschlands e.V.

JONG, J. DE (2000). 'Psychiatric Problems Related to Persecution and Refugee Status' In: Helmchen et al. *Contemporary Psychiatry.* Heidelberg.

JOURNAL OF HEALTH ECONOMICS, 1982- Amsterdam: Elsevier Science.

JOURNAL OF HEALTH POLITICS, POLICY AND LAW, 1976- Durham: Duke University Press.

JOURNAL OF IMMIGRANT HEALTH 1999- The Hague, London, Boston: Kluwer.

KASS (1975). 'Regarding the End of Medicine and the Pursuit of Health', In: *The Public Interest* (40).

KING, T. (1983). 'Immigration from Developing Countries: Some Philosophical Issues', In: *Ethics* April.

KRIEKEN, P. J. VAN (2000a). 'Health and Continued Residence, Reason or Pretext', In: *European Journal of Health Law* 7, pp. 29-46.

KRIEKEN, P. J. VAN (2000b). *Health Gaps and Migratory Movements*, Report no. 31. Lund: Raoul Wallenberg Institute.

KRIEKEN, P. J. VAN (2000c). 'Ausreiseverpflichtung und Krankheit' In: *Informationsbrief Ausländerrecht,* December.

LEON, D., WALT, G. (Eds.) (2000). *Poverty, Inequality and Health, An International Perspective.* Oxford: Oxford University Press.

LEVY, J.T. (2000). *The Multiculturalism of Fear.* Oxford: Oxford University Press.

LITTLE, M. (2000). 'Ethonomics, The Ethics of the Unaffordable', In: *Journal of the American Medical Association,* vol. 135 No. 1.

MARMOT, M., WILKINSON, R. (Eds.) (1999). *Social Determinants of Health.* Oxford: Oxford University Press.

MAYNARD, A., KANAVOS, P. (2000). 'Health Economics: An Evolving Paradigm', In: *Health Economics* 9 (3), pp. 183-190.

MERCENIER, P., GRODOS, D. (2000). 'A clearer methodology – Health Systems Research for more effective action', *Studies in Health Service Organisations and Policy,* 15/2000.

MILLER, D. (1992). 'Community and Citizenship', In: Avineri, S., de Shalit, A., (Eds.) *Communitarianism and Individualism.* Oxford: Oxford University Press.

MORAL REALISM VS. MORAL IDEALISM: The Ethics of International Migration. (1987). American Political Science Association.

PANNENBORG, CH.O. (1978). *A new international health order: an inquiry into the international relations of world health and medical care.* Alblasserdam: Davids Decor.

PARKIN, A. (1995). 'Allocating Health Care Resources in an Imperfect World', In: *Modern Law Review,* 58, 867-878.

PLENDER, R. (1997). *Basic Documents on International Migration Law.* The Hague, London, Boston: Kluwer.

POWER, E.J., EISENBERG, J.M. (1998). 'Are we Ready to Use Cost-effectiveness Analysis in Health Care Decision-making? A Health Services Research Challenge for Clinicians, Patients, Health Care Systems, and Public Policy', In: *Medical Care,* 36 (5), pp. 10-17.

RAOUL WALLENBERG INSTITUTE, General Comments or Recommendations adopted by UN Human Rights Treaty Bodies, Vol. I: Human Rights Committee, (2000). *General Comments under article 40, paragraph 4, of the International Covenant on Civil and Poltical Rights,* 3rd edition. *Supplement* (1999). Vol. II: Committee on Economic, Social and Cultural Rights *General Comments under the International Covenant on Economic, Social and Cultural Rights,* 2nd edition. *Supplement* (1999).

RAWLS, J. (1971). A Theory Justice. Cambridge, MA: Harvard University Press.

REICHENBERG, D., FRIEDMAN, S. (1996). *Healing the Invisible Wounds of Children in War: A Rights Approach.* In: Danieli, Y., Rodley, N.S., Weisæth, L. (Eds.) International Responses to Traumatic Stress. New York: Baywood Publishing Company.

ROSCAM ABBING, H.D.C. (1979). *International Organizations in Europe and the Right to Health Care.* Deventer: Kluwer.

ROSCAM ABBING, H.D.C. (1997). 'The Right of the Patient to Quality of Medical Practice and the Position of Migrant Doctors within the EU', In: *European Journal of Health Law,* Vol. 4 No.4.

SALTMAN, R.B., FIGUERAS, J. (Eds.) (1997). *European Health Care Reforms. Analysis of current strategies.* Copenhagen: WHO Regional Office for Europe.

SCHUCK, P.H., SMITH, R.M., (1985). *Citizenship without Consent: Illegal Aliens in the American Polity.* New Haven, CT: Yale University Press.

SOHN, L.B., BUERGENTHAL, T. (Eds.), (1992). *The Movement of Persons Across Borders.* Washington, DC: American Society of International Law.

STEINER, H.J., ALSTON, PH., (1996). *International Human Rights in Context.* Oxford, Clarendon Press.

Swedish Parliamentary Priorities Commission (1995). *Priorities in Health Care – Ethics, Economy, Implementation.* Stockholm: Ministry of Health and Social Affairs.

Taylor, A., George, S. (1998). 'Affordable Health: The way forward', In: *The International Journal of Human Rights,* Vol. 2 No. 2 pp. 1-18.

The World Bank (1997). *A World Bank Country Study: Hashemite Kingdom of Jordan, Health Sector Study.* Washington D.C.: IBRD/The World Bank.

The World Bank (1998). *A World Bank Country Study: West Bank and Gaza, Medium-term Development for the Health Sector.* Washington D.C.: IBRD/The World Bank.

The World Bank Group (1997). *Health, Nutrition & Population.* Washington D.C.: IBRD/ The World Bank.

Tholen, J.H.M.M. (1997). *Vreemdelingenbeleid en Rechtvaardigheid?* Nijmegen.

Toebes, B. (1999). *The Right to Health as a Human Right in International Law.* Antwerp, Groningen, Oxford: Intersentia-Hart.

Velden, K. van der (1995). *Health Matters: Public Health in North-South Perspective.* Amsterdam: Royal Tropical Institute.

Ven, W.P.M.M. van de (1980). *Health as an unobservable: a MIMIC-model of demand for health care*. Leiden.

Ven, W.P.M.M. van de (1984). *Studies in Health Insurance and Econometrics*. Leiden.

Ven, W.P.M.M. van de (1995). 'Choices in Health Care', In: *British Medical Bulletin,* Vol. 51 No. 4 pp. 781-790.

Walzer, M. (1983). *Spheres of Justice: A Defence of Pluralism and Equality*. New York: Basic Books.

Weiner, M. (1995). *The Global Migration Crisis: Challenge to States and to Human Rights*. New York: Harper Collins.

Wilkinson, R. (1996). *Unhealthy Societies.* London.

Wirtz, R. (1999). *De Winst van Ethiek.* Breukelen.

WHO (1997). *World Health Report: Conquering Suffering, Enriching Humanity*. Geneva: WHO.

WHO (1998). *The New Emergency health Kit 1998*. Geneva: WHO.

WHO (1998). *World Health Report: Life in the 21st Century, A Vision for All*. Geneva: WHO.

WHO (1999). *World Health Report: Making a Difference*. Geneva: WHO.

WHO (2000). *World Health Report: Health Systems: Improving Performance*. Geneva: WHO.

Young, I.M. (2000). *Inclusion and Democracy*. Oxford: Oxford University Press.

Zielinski, H.L. (1994). *Health and Humanitarian Concerns: principles and ethics*. Dordrecht: Nijhoff Law.

ABBREVIATIONS

CAT	Convention Against Torture
CEDAW	Convention on the Elimination of All Forms of Discrimination Against Women
CoE	Council of Europe
CRC	Convention on the Rights of the Child
DALE	Disability Adjusted Life Expectancy
DALY	Disability Adjusted Life Years
DG	Director General
ECHR	European Convention on Human Rights
ECOSOC	(UN) Economic and Social Council
ECtHR	European Court of Human Rights
EME	Established market Economies
ESC	European Social Charter
EU	European Union
FDA	Federal Drug Administration
FSE	Former Socialist Economies
GA	General Assembly
GAVI	Global Alliance for Vaccines and Immunization
GC	General Comment
GP	General Practitioner
HC	Health Care
HCS	Health Care Systems
HIPCs	Highly Indebted Poor Countries
HIV/AIDS	Human Immunodeficiency Virus/Acquired Immunodeficiency Syndrome
HRC	Human Rights Committee
HRQ	Human Rights Quarterly
IACHR	Inter-American Commission on Human Rights
IATA	International Air Transport Association
IBRD	International Bank for Reconstruction and Development
ICAO	International Civil Aviation Organisation
ICCPR	International Covenant on Civil and Political Rights
ICESCR	International Covenant on Economic, Social and Cultural Rights
ICJ	International Court of Justice
ICMH	International Centre of Migration and Health
ICMPD	International Centre for Migration Policy Development
IDP	Internally Displaced Person
IFPMA	International Federation of Pharmaceutical Manufacturers Associations
IJRL	International Journal of Refugee Law
ILO	International Labour Organisation
IMF	International Monetary Fund
IMP	The International Migration Policy Program

IND	Immigratie- en Naturalisatiedienst
IOM	International Organisation for Migration
IRO	International Refugee Organisation
MCH	Mother and Child Health
MD	Medical Doctor
MHC	Mental Health Care
NGO	Non Governmental Organisation
NHA	National Health Accounts
NHS	National Health Service
PHC	Primary Health Care
PTSD	Post-traumatic Stress Disorder
PTSS	Post-traumatic Stress Syndrome
QALY	Quality Adjusted Life Years
RWI	Raoul Wallenberg Institute
SID	Society for International Development
STD	Sexually Transmissable Disease
SWAPs	Sector-wide Approaches
TB	Tuberculosis
TEC	Treaty of the European Community
TPO	Transcultural Psychosocial Organisation
TRIPS	Trade Related Intellectual Property Rights
U5MR	Under 5 Mortality Rate
UDHR	Universal Declaration on Human Rights
UN	United Nations
UNDP	United Nations Development Programme
UNFPA	United Nations Population Fund
UNHCR	United Nations High Commissioner for Refugees
UNICEF	United Nations Children Fund
WHO	World Health Organisation
WTO	World Trade Organisation

CONTRIBUTORS / PARTICIPANTS

The following persons contributed to this Handbook and/or participated in the September 2000 Expert Meeting, Noordwijkerhout, the Netherlands.

Philip Backx
Ministry of Justice, The Hague

Christopher Baker
Webster University, Leiden

Willem Beaumont
MD, Municipal Health Centre (GGD), The Hague

Monique Besseling
Webster University, Leiden; Aliens Police, The Hague

Maud de Boer-Buquicchio
Deputy Registrar, European Court of Human Rights, Strasbourg

Frans Bouwen
Co-ordinator for SID Netherlands, Project on the Future of Asylum and Migration; formerly with the World Council of Churches, Geneva

Manuel Carballo
Professor Columbia University NY; Coordinator, the International Committee for Migration and Health, Geneva; formerly WHO

Jeroen Corduwener
Freelance Journalist

Heleen Dupuis
Professor in Medical Ethics, Leiden University; Senator (First Chamber of Parliament), The Hague

André den Exter
Research Fellow in Health Law, Erasmus University, Rotterdam

Johan Feitsma
Retired International Civil Servant

Cees Flinterman
Professor of Human Rights and Director of the Netherlands Institute of Human Rights (SIM) at Utrecht University; Chair, SID Future of Asylum and Migration Project

Ivan Forgács
Professor, Semelweis University, Budapest; former member of the WHO executive board

Kirk Grimmer
Webster University, Leiden

Brian Gushulak
Health Specialist with IOM HQ, Geneva

Herbert Hermans
Associate Professor of Health Law, Erasmus University, Rotterdam

Hans Hogerzeil
Co-ordinator for Policy, Access and Rational Use, Department for Essential Drugs and Medicines Policy, WHO HQ, Geneva

Joop de Jong
Professor of Mental Health and Culture, Free University, Amsterdam; Director of the Transcultural Psychosocial Organization, Amsterdam

Henriëtte Kernkamp-Maathuis and **Monique de Witte-van den Haak**
Lawyers, State's Counsel (Landsadvocaat), The Hague

Peter van Krieken
Special Adviser in International Affairs IND; Professor of International Law and Human Rights at Webster University, Leiden; Chair, Röling Foundation; formerly UNHCR

Pierre Mercenier
Emeritus Professor, Institute for Tropical Diseases, Antwerp

Jacques de Milliano
MD/GP, formerly Chair, Médecins Sans Frontières (MSF), formerly Member of Parliament (Second Chamber), The Hague

Sabrina van Miltenburg
IND, The Hague

Jannes Mulder
MD, Ph.D., Ministry of Health, The Hague

Willibald Pahr
Chair ICMPD; former Minister of Foreign Affairs, Vienna

Erik Palinsky
Webster University, Leiden

Joost van Puijenbroek
IND, The Hague

Kai Träskelin
Judge, Supreme Court, Helsinki

Albert de Vries
Medical Adviser, IND, the Hague

Raoul Wirtz
Research Fellow in Medical Ethics, Leiden University

Hens Wolf
Head, International Department, IND, The Hague

Refugee Law in Context: The Exclusion Clause

Edited by Peter J. van Krieken

Asylum is meant for those who flee injustice. There are asylum seekers, however, who have blood on their hands. They may have been involved in terrorism, they may have committed war crimes or they may be guilty of acts contrary to the purposes and principles of the United Nations. Both the 1951 Refugee Convention and the 1948 Universal Declaration of Human Rights clearly indicate that these persons shall be excluded from refugee status, excluded from asylum. The refugee lawyer, in order to fully appreciate the importance and relevance of this principle, needs to look over the fences of refugee law proper. The insight needed for the decision whether or not to apply the so-called exclusion clause is to be found elsewhere within the realms of international law: international humanitarian law, international criminal law and United Nations law. In this publication experts pay ample attention to developments in these related fields.

Complemented with a wealth of relevant materials, such as informative treaties, conventions and (draft-)resolutions on these very themes, the book is an indipensible guide for all those involved with or concerned about asylum seekers, refugees and the upholding of the principles of refugee law. This collection in fact amounts to a true Article 1F Handbook.

The editor, with almost 20 years experience with UNHCR, is presently lecturing in international law and human rights at Webster University, Leiden, and serves as special advisor for international affairs with the Immigration and Naturalisation Service of the Netherlands Ministry of Justice.

ISBN 90-6704-118-1
price NLG 165.00 / USD 99.00 / GBP 57.75
1999, pages: 344, hardbound

Distributed for T·M·C·Asser press by Kluwer Law International:

For USA, Canada, Central and South America:
Kluwer Law International, Order Department
675 Massachusetts Avenue
Cambridge, MA 02139, USA
Tel (617)354-0140. Fax (617)354-8595
Toll free in USA & Canada. 1-800-577-8118
email: sales@kluwerlaw.com

For Europe and Rest of World:
Kluwer Law International, Order Department
P.O.Box 322
3300 AH Dordrecht, The Netherlands
Tel +31 (0)78-6546454. Fax +31 (0)78-6546474
Freephone in the UK: 0800 963 955
email: sales@kli.wkap.nl